OXFORD MANAGEMENT READERS

ORGANIZATIONAL IDENTITY

ORGANIZATIONAL IDENTITY

A Reader

Edited by

**Mary Jo Hatch and
Majken Schultz**

OXFORD
UNIVERSITY PRESS

OXFORD
UNIVERSITY PRESS

Great Clarendon Street, Oxford OX2 6DP

Oxford University Press is a department of the University of Oxford.
It furthers the University's objective of excellence in research, scholarship,
and education by publishing worldwide in

Oxford New York

Auckland Cape Town Dar es Salaam Hong Kong Karachi
Kuala Lumpur Madrid Melbourne Mexico City Nairobi
New Delhi Shanghai Taipei Toronto
With offices in
Argentina Austria Brazil Chile Czech Republic France Greece
Guatemala Hungary Italy Japan South Korea Poland Portugal
Singapore Switzerland Thailand Turkey Ukraine Vietnam

Oxford is a registered trade mark of Oxford University Press
in the UK and in certain other countries

Published in the United States
by Oxford University Press Inc., New York

ISBN 978-0-19-926947-1

Printed in the United Kingdom by
Lightning Source UK Ltd., Milton Keynes

Acknowledgements

C. H. Cooley, 'Society and the Individual'. Reprinted from *Human Nature and the Social Order* by C. H. Cooley (1902: 42–50, 168–85, 208–10).

G. H. Mead, *The Self*. Reprinted from 'Mind, Self, and Society' by G. H. Mead (1934: 173–9). Copyright 1934 by the University of Chicago Press. Reprinted by permission.

E. Goffman, 'The Arts of Impression Management'. Reprinted from *The Presentation of Self in Everyday Life* by E. Goffman (London 1969, 208–37). Copyright © 1959 Erving Goffman. Reproduced by permission of Penguin Books Limited.

Henri Taijfel and John Turner, 'An Integrative Theory of Intergroup Conflict'. Reprinted from *The Social Psychology of Intergroup Relations* edited by William G. Austin and Stephen Worchel (1979: 38–43). Copyright © 1979 William G. Austin and Stephen Worchel.

Marilynn B. Brewer and Wendi Gardner, 'Who is this 'We'? Levels of Collective Identity and Self Representations', *Journal of Personality and Social Psychology*, vol. 71 (1996), pp. 83–7, 91–3. Copyright © 1996 by the American Psychological Association. Adapted with permission. Reprinted with permission.

Stuart Albert and David A. Whetten, 'Organizational Identity', *Research in Organizational Behavior*, vol. 7 (1985), pp. 263–95. Copyright © 1985 JAI Press Incorporated. Reprinted by permission of Elsevier Science Limited.

Howard S. Schwartz, 'Anti-Social Actions of Committed Organizational Participants: An Existential Psychoanalytic Perspective', *Organization Studies*, vol. 8 (1987), pp. 327–40. Copyright © 1987 EGOS. Reprinted by permission of SAGE Publications Limited.

Blake E. Ashforth and Fred Mael, 'Social Identity Theory and the Organization', *Academy of Management Review*, vol. 14 (1989), pp. 20–39. Copyright © 1989 The Academy of Management. Reprinted with permission.

Mats Alvesson, 'Organization: From Substance to Image?', *Organization Studies*, vol. 11 (1990), pp. 373–94. Copyright © 1990 EGOS. Reprinted by permission of SAGE Publications Limited.

Jane E. Dutton and Janet M. Dukerich, 'Keeping an Eye on the Mirror: Image and Identity in Organizational Adaptation', *Academy of Management Journal*, vol. 34 (1991), pp. 517–54. Copyright © 1991 The Academy of Management. Reprinted with permission.

Linda E. Ginzel, Roderick M. Kramer, and Robert I. Sutton, 'Organizational Impression Management as a Reciprocal Influence Process: The Neglected Role

Acknowledgements

of the Organizational Audience', *Research in Organizational Behavior*, vol. 15 (1993), pp. 227–66. Copyright © 1993 JAI Press Incorporated. Reprinted by permission of Elsevier Science Limited.

Michael G. Pratt and Anat Rafaeli, 'Organizational Dress as a Symbol of Multilayered Social Identities', *Academy of Management Journal*, vol. 40 (1997), pp. 862–98. Copyright © 1997 The Academy of Management. Reprinted with permission.

Karen Golden-Biddle and Hayagreeva Rao, 'Breaches in the Boardroom: Organizational Identity and Conflicts of Commitment in a Nonprofit Organization', *Organization Science*, vol. 8 (1997), pp. 593–611. Copyright © 1997 INFORMS. Reprinted with permission.

Dennis A. Gioia, Majken Schultz, and Kevin G. Corley, 'Organizational Identity, Image, and Adaptive Instability', *Academy of Management Review*, vol. 25 (2000), pp. 63–81. Copyright © 2000 The Academy of Management. Reprinted with permission.

Mary Jo Hatch and Majken Schultz, 'The Dynamics of Organizational Identity', *Human Relations*, vol. 55 (2002), pp. 989–1018. Copyright © 2002 The Tavistock Institute. Reprinted by permission of SAGE Publications Limited.

Mats Alvesson and Hugh Willmott, 'Identity Regulation as Organizational Control Producing the Appropriate Individual', *Journal of Management Studies*, vol. 39 (2002), pp. 619–44. Copyright © 2002 Blackwell Publishers Limited. Reprinted with permission.

Barbara Czarniawska, 'Narratives of Individual and Organizational Identities', *Communication Yearbook 17* (1997: 193–221). Copyright © SAGE Publications Incorporated. Reprinted with permission.

Kimberly D. Elsbach and Roderick M. Kramer, 'Members' Responses to Organizational Identity Threats: Encountering and Countering the Business Week Rankings', *Administrative Science Quarterly*, vol. 41 (1996), pp. 442–76. Copyright © Cornell University, Johnson Graduate School of Management. Reprinted with permission.

George Cheney and Lars Thøger Christensen, 'Organizational Identity: Linkages Between Internal and External Communication' reprinted from the *New Handbook of Organizational Communication* edited by F. M. Jablin and L. L. Putnam (2001: 231–58, 262–9). Copyright © 2001 F. M. Jablin and L. L. Putnam. Reprinted with permission by SAGE Publications.

Contents

Contents

Contents

List of Contributors

Stuart Albert	University of Minnesota, USA
Mats Alvesson	University of Lund, Sweden
Blake E. Ashforth	Arizona State University, USA
Marilynn B. Brewer	Ohio State University, USA
George Cheney	University of Utah, USA
Lars Thøger Christensen	Odense University, Denmark
C. H. Cooley (1864–1929)	American sociologist, active for many years at the University of Michigan, USA
Kevin G. Corley	University of Illinois, USA
Barbara Czarniawska	Gothenburg Research Institute, Gothenburg University, Sweden
Janet M. Dukerich	University of Texas at Austin, USA
Jane E. Dutton	University of Michigan, USA
Kimberly D. Elsbach	University of California, Davis, USA
Wendi Gardner	Northwestern University, USA
Linda E. Ginzela	University of Chicago, USA
Dennis A. Gioia	Pennsylvania State University, USA
E. Goffman (1922–82)	American sociologist, taught anthropology and sociology at the University of Pennsylvania, USA
Karen Golden-Biddle	Faculty of Business, University of Alberta, Edmonton, Alberta, Canada
Mary Jo Hatch	University of Virginia, USA
Roderick M. Kramer	Stanford University, USA
Fred Mael	American Institutes for Research, Washington D.C., USA
G. H. Mead (1863–1931)	American philosopher and psychologist, active for many years at the University of Chicago, USA
Michael G. Pratt	University of Illinois at Urbana-Champaign, USA
Anat Rafaeli	Israel Institute of Technology
Hayagreeva Rao	Northwestern University, USA
Majken Schultz	Copenhagen Business School, Denmark
Howard S. Schwartz	Oakland University, USA
Robert I. Sutton	Stanford University, USA

List of Contributors

Henri Tajfel (1919–82)   Polish psychologist, active at the University of Bristol, UK
John Turner   Australia National University
David A. Whetten   Brigham Young University, USA
Hugh Willmott   University of Cambridge, UK

Introduction

....

Mary Jo Hatch and Majken Schultz

....

Why Study Organizational Identity?

In response to competitive pressures and the desire to be recognized and supported, corporations invest millions every year to strengthen their corporate images and reputations. Led by the best strategic thinking on the matter, business managers select those attributes of their organization that are unique, authentic, and nonimitable, and look for alluring ways to project this image to the outside world as well as into the hearts and minds of their own employees. Research into organizational identity provides a theoretical foundation for these practices and a research base for investigating related questions concerning strategic positioning, organizational differentiation, stakeholder relations, employee involvement, and integrated communication.

However, the study of organizational identity demands a broader focus than that provided by a strictly corporate point of view. Our media-sensitive society exposes organizations and their members more than ever before to influences beyond those under the control of their managers. Opinions and impressions, feelings and fantasies, hopes and expectations expressed by employees, suppliers, customers, shareholders, governments, and their regulatory agents as well as community members, the general public, the media, and political activists—whether positive or negative—all contribute to defining the identity of an organization and sometimes challenge the managerially preferred version. As a result, organizational identity presents an original collage of the experiences and expectations of a wide array of people who view the organization from a multiplicity of perspectives and approach it with a variety of motives.

It could be argued that, in the past, organizations were better able to maintain control of their socialization processes and thus maintain their organizational

1

identity in a desired form. This view suggests that recent interest in studying organizational identity could be due to its increasingly problematic nature. Organizations that harbor greater diversity and reach across larger geographic areas than ever before, stretch the very concept of identity to the breaking point. Thus, although organizational identity has been with us for a long time, it has only become a topic for management researchers in the last 20 years when changes in the environments of most organizations made identity maintenance something of an ongoing worry for the managers and organizations they study.

During the early part of its academic history, organizational identity research was done primarily in marketing and communication, but today its relevance is also recognized by human resource managers, organizational change agents, and strategic planners, as well as by top executives. For example, if a company is to attract the best employees, then potential recruits must hear good things about the company from trusted sources. Glossy corporate recruiting brochures are no longer sufficient to attract talent to a firm. Websites and corporate advertising matter to recruits, as do word of mouth opinions and appearances on high profile lists such as the 100 Best Companies to Work For or the Fortune 500. This means that members of human resource management departments are dependent on the activities of their colleagues in strategy, marketing, and communication whose efforts to influence external testaments to what kind of organization theirs is, bear directly on the organization's ability to recruit the best people.

Another example of the practical importance of organizational identity involves corporate branding. For a corporate brand to be more than an empty promise, employees must follow through on the images that marketers put forward. If the corporate brand rests on images of the superior technical performance of the company's products, then employees had better deliver that superior technical performance. If the image rests on friendly and efficient customer service, then employees had better be friendly and efficient. But it is not enough to insist on employee behavior that fits whatever the marketing department deems to be a desirable image. Setting up systems to control behavior with rewards simply achieves superficial compliance. What companies increasingly need and expect is employees who personally subscribe to the messages they are communicating with their behavior, not just go through the motions. This means that the behavior that supports a corporate brand and builds a strong reputation for the company needs deep roots, it needs to rest in the organization's identity. Otherwise the organization becomes a police state in which employees and the organization pretend to be something they are not.

In general, we believe that it is necessary to consider organizational identity when engaging in any type of organizational change and in management in general. Whether it is in relation to restructuring, rethinking strategy, introducing new technology, grappling with organizational culture, confronting corporate ethics, or acquiring another firm, considering the organization's identity prior to taking action will improve the chances for a successful outcome. *Organizational Identity: A Reader* will present you with these and many other examples and arguments about the importance of organizational identity and give you background for applying research about it to organizations and management practice.

What is Organizational Identity?

The concept of organizational identity was for the most part adapted from sociology and psychology and delivered into the field of organization studies by Stuart Albert and David Whetten in 1985 in their landmark article "Organizational Identity." According to Albert and Whetten, the phenomenon of organizational identity appears whenever members of an organization ask themselves "Who are we?," "What business are we in?," or "What do we want to be?". These authors further specified the definition for scientific study by arguing that organizational identity is that which is central, distinctive, and enduring about an organization. Scholars who followed Albert and Whetten's lead investigated numerous questions: What creates the sense of a collective self or "we-ness" in social relationships such as those found in work groups and organizations? What makes a social group perceive themselves as distinct and different from others? How is the sense of organizational identity influenced by how others perceive the organization? How is it that we are able to recognize an organization across time and place? To what extent do we find continuity through time in the collective life of an organization? Does a firm's organizational identity influence its ethical behavior?

The idea of organizations having identities is problematic for some who believe identity is a strictly individual and particularly human phenomenon. For them, the assertion that identity can belong or be ascribed to an organization is nonsensical because it anthropomorphizes the organization (i.e. treats it as something human when it is not). But many people *do* report feelings of "we-ness" in regard to their organizations, and mostly everyone is willing to make identity-ascribing statements about companies even when they do not personally feel associated with them (IBM is still "Big Blue" to me; or I am impressed by LEGO Company's dedication to children's play). For the most part, all the authors in *Organizational Identity: A Reader*, believe that applying the concept of identity to organizations is a reasonable thing to do, though in a few cases the question of highest concern is not what the organization's identity is, or how it is created and maintained, or even whether it effects organizational performance or individual behavior, but rather how individual's identities are constrained or otherwise influenced by the powerful presence of the organization in their lives.

Some of the authors you will read in *Organizational Identity: A Reader*, present organizational identity strictly as an attribution made by individuals to organizations and thus locate the phenomenon in the minds of individuals. Others regard it as a property of the organization itself, something akin to a distributed consciousness that lies within the group of individuals whose activities comprise the organization. The latter researchers locate organizational identity in the intersubjective space created by group social relations. Although others have focused primarily on its material manifestations in corporate logos and livery (e.g. see, Wally Olins' impressive book *Corporate Identity*), most of the authors whose work appears here consider organizational identity to be socially constructed by the cognitions, emotions, and/or aesthetic appreciations of those who participate in its creation, maintenance, and change.

Where is Organizational Identity Research Headed?

While practical applications of early organizational identity research were underway in marketing, communication, human resource management, and strategic planning, academic scholars extended the reach of organizational identity research into the increasingly radical domains of poststructural and postmodern thought established in literary, critical, and cultural theory. Drawing upon these new ways of thinking, organizational scholars began to question the assumptions made in the first decade of organizational identity research. For instance, one assumption that postmodern and critical scholars have challenged is that people in organizations share the sense of "we" that many early researchers uncritically equated with organizational identity. The most critical among these scholars ask: Is organizational identity simply one more management fad to be used for the exploitation of others? The view that is emerging from this debate is that people can construct themselves as members of an organization without necessarily identifying with it. Critical scholars thus criticize early organizational identity researchers for assuming that high-identifying organizational members are the norm when this is not likely to be the case, and, in their view, should be regarded as an empirical question.

Other researchers who have challenged early scholarship on organizational identity have based their contributions on empirical studies that reveal the complexities and dynamism of organizational identities, and also confront some of the methodological difficulties of operationalizing this concept. Their work, often converging with that of postmodern and critical scholars, presents the notions of flexible identities, multiple identities, and identity narratives. In contrast to early organizational identity research, several of these more recent studies focus on how organizations express their identity differently within different contexts and for different purposes. As a result, instead of defining identity as resting on a stable foundation of the past, these researchers present it as a transitory venue for exercising power, or as a political move to preserve or acquire power now or in the future.

By focusing on the diversity of influences on organizational identity research, the studies of multiple and shifting identities reopen identity theory to the idea of essence (Albert and Whetten's centrality), albeit supplemented by a newfound appreciation of organizational identity's complexity and dynamism. Those who attempt to return to the idea that identity has an essence do so by offering a dynamic concept of identity that is both rooted in the organization's history and heritage *and* in its relationships to other identities and images that swirl around and interpenetrate it at any given moment. Thus, a few studies fuse the early definitions of organizational identity as essence with postmodernist definitions of identity as flux and multiplicity. The result is a return to the paradoxical idea put forward by the sociologists and psychologists who originally theorized individual identity—that identity is both a dynamic process that unfolds over time and a source of stability for those who depend upon it.

Taken as a whole, The Reader presents organizational identity research as a field that is in a state of continuous disintegration and reintegration as it struggles to incorporate ideas from many academic disciplines and numerous empirical cases. While it may seem frustrating at times to see each attempt to render clarity to the subject of organizational identity dashed on the rocks of some new consideration, this is how knowledge grows in interdisciplinary fields like organization studies. By reading the articles presented in The Reader in chronological order, you can watch the field as it diverges, fragments, and converges only to diverge again. If you think about it, this is not unlike the path of development many identities follow, both individual and organizational.

Plan of the Book

This Reader is divided into three sections, each of which will be introduced in more detail in a brief introduction immediately preceding it. But to give you an overview: Part I "The Roots of Organizational Identity" offers a collection of excerpts from some of the original sociological and social psychological sources for the study of organizational identity. Part II "Early Development" follows with six articles written by organizational scholars who are widely regarded as having established organizational identity as a domain of inquiry within the field of organization studies. The Reader concludes in Part III "Recent Developments and Emerging Themes" with eight newer articles that draw on poststructuralist and postmodern philosophy, aesthetic and literary theory, and critical theory and cultural studies to broaden the theoretical foundations of organizational identity research considerably beyond their starting point and indicate future directions this still developing field of inquiry will take. We hope that our selection of readings will provide you with both a sense of the history of the field of organizational identity research, and imagination for its future academic developments and contributions to management practice.

I. THE ROOTS OF ORGANIZATIONAL IDENTITY IN SOCIOLOGY AND SOCIAL PSYCHOLOGY

Introduction to Part I

Tracing the Roots of Organizational Identity Research

....

As a concept that has seen development in philosophy, cultural studies and literary theory as well as psychology, sociology, and anthropology, it is perhaps not surprising to discover that identity has also found a home in organization studies. However, a new field of study does not develop overnight; it takes its point of departure from one, or at most a few, established ideas about which those who want to join the field are expected to know a little something. We therefore selected, for the first section of The Reader, a collection of excerpts from books and articles that provide prominent examples of the original sources for the study of organizational identity.

Please be aware that the need to limit the size of The Reader led us to present a somewhat narrower view of the roots of organizational identity than some organizational identity theorists would advocate. We concentrated on the sources most often referred to by early organizational identity researchers and this led us to select authors from sociology and social psychology, rather than to include the broader range of influences like Sigmund Freud or the post-structuralist philosopher Michel Foucault, either of whom one could argue must be read in order to fully appreciate any application of the identity concept. Our choice for this section was to start where most in the newly forming field began, by referring to Cooley, Mead, and Goffman who were among the first to highlight the social and contextual aspects of identity formation, and thus framed their theories in terms that attracted the attention of researchers investigating social organizations and their identities. We then followed these ideas into social psychology from which early organizational identity theorists borrowed the concept of social identity and adapted it to organizational level thinking.

Charles Horton Cooley: "Society, the Individual and the Social Self" (1902)

(Excerpted from *Human Nature and the Social Order*, 1964, 42–50, 168–85, 208–10)
As a sociologist with a strong social–psychological bent, Charles Horton Cooley was keen to explain society in a way that neither excluded nor privileged the individual. Cooley regarded both individualism and socialism as, at best, partial perspectives and sought their synthesis in an organic view. In *Human Nature and the Social Order*, Cooley (1902/64: 36) stated: "The organic view stresses both the unity of the whole and the peculiar value of the individual, explaining each by the other." Cooley's attempt to explain "each by the other" took its shape from the contrast between distributive ("persons make society") and collective ("society makes persons") aspects of life. His organic synthesis was embodied by the view that: "'society' and 'individuals' do not denote separable phenomena, but are simply collective and distributive aspects of the same thing" (Cooley 1902/64: 37). He went on to explain that "man's psychical outfit is not divisible into the social and the non-social; ... he is all social in the large sense, is all a part of the common human life ... everything human about him has a history in the social past" (Cooley 1902/64: 47–8). Thus Cooley set the stage for defining the self in social terms which many today consider to be his major contribution to the theory of identity.

Cooley (1902/64: 209) foreshadowed interest in organizational identity when he spoke of the group self or "we" as "an 'I' which includes other persons." We also find in Cooley the idea that identity is at least partly shaped by our perceptions of how others see us, which is the definition Jane Dutton and Janet Dukerich gave to organizational image. In their important article "Keeping an Eye on the Mirror" (Part II), these researchers proposed that organizational identity is reflected in the mirror of organizational image. The idea of mirroring was clearly anticipated by Cooley's discussion of the looking-glass self, which you will read about in our selection from his 1902 book *Human Nature and the Social Order*.

Cooley also suggested an idea, heavily promoted recently by postmodernists, that identity is a linguistic construction (Cooley 1902/64: 180–1): "That the 'I' of common speech has a meaning which includes some sort of reference to other persons is involved in the very fact that the word and the ideas it stands for are phenomena of language and the communicative life." Barbara Czarniawska discusses organizational identity as a linguistic phenomenon in her article "Narratives of Individual and Organizational Identities" (Part III).

George Herbert Mead: "The Self" (1934)

(Excerpted from *Mind, Self and Society*, 173–9)

In *Mind, Self and Society*, American sociologist George Herbert Mead presented the self as both dynamic and social. He defined two aspects of the self—the "I" and the "me"—claiming that they are parts of a whole, but that they are separable in behavior and experience. The "I" gives us novel behavior and experience, while the "me," coming from our assumption of the attitudes of others toward us, is more closely aligned with expectations and social responsibility. The two are related by being different phases of a social process in which the "I" is the historical precedent for the "me." Mead (1934: 174–5) explained the dynamic relationship between the two phases as: "The 'I' of this moment is present in the 'me' of the next moment... the 'I' comes in... as a historical figure. It is what you were a second ago that is the 'I' of the 'me'." Mead then claimed that the incorporation of the attitudes of others toward the self (the "me") is the mechanism by which the community becomes part of the individual, and the novelty of the response of which the "I" is capable, is the mechanism by which an individual can alter society.

Albert and Whetten (Part II), along with the organizational identity researchers who followed their lead, emphasized something like the "me" of Mead's formulation of identity and its relationship to the perceptions of the self formed by others. As explained already, the importance of the relationship between organizational identity and others' images of it, was stressed by Dutton and Dukerich (Part II). In his article "Organization: From Substance to Image?" Matts Alvesson (Part II) went so far as to suggest that, in our postmodern times, image is all there is to organizational identity! But in raising the question of the loss of substance, Alvesson pointed back to the (missing) "I" of Mead's formulation. In their article "The Dynamics of Organizational Identity" Mary Jo Hatch and Majken Schultz (Part III) replaced the missing "I" by building a model of organizational identity as a dynamic process that turns continuously around organizational analogs of Mead's "I" and "me".

Erving Goffman: "The Arts of Impression Management" (1959)

(Excerpted from *The Presentation of Self in Everyday Life*, 208–37)

Goffman equated social interaction with dramaturgical performance: Just as theater actors and their audiences conspire to form certain impressions that sustain the show, so everyday "actors" conspire with those who witness their "performances." Goffman's work suggested that identity is a performance and that the actor's skills are relevant to controlling or managing the impressions identity performances leave on others. Thus those referred to as "others" in Cooley and Mead's identity formation process became audiences in Goffman's dramaturgical metaphor. For those interested in organizational identity, the idea of audiences introduced key stakeholders into the debate. This is the insight developed by Kimberly Elsbach and Roderick Kramer in their article "Members' Responses to Organizational Identity Threats: Encountering and Countering the *Business Week* Rankings" and by George Cheney and Lars Christensen in their article "Organizational Identity at Issue: Linkages Between 'Internal' and 'External' Organizational Communication" (Part III).

However, in contrast to Cooley's and Mead's theses that identity derives from the ways in which others regard the self, Goffman suggested that how effectively the self performs for others affects the others' regard for it. In others words, Goffman described, not how others' images are transformed into identity (as was suggested by Cooley and Mead), but how identity can be successfully communicated to others through impression management. Hatch and Schultz (Part III) interpolate this idea into their model of organizational identity dynamics through the process of impressing organizational identity on others.

In his chapter "The Arts of Impression Management", reprinted in The Reader, Goffman not only described how individuals impressed others, but also how those others conspired with the individual to help them maintain successful social interactions. Building on Goffman's work, Linda Ginzel, Rod Kramer, and Robert Sutton developed a theory about the role organizational audiences play in creating and sustaining organizational identity (Part II). Their article's title expresses their thesis: "Organizational Impression Management as a Reciprocal Influence Process: The Neglected Role of the Organizational Audience." Goffman also noted that the context within which exchanges between actors and audiences take place provides shared expectations and guidelines for behavior, thus pointing to the role culture plays in identity formation processes, an idea that was developed further within organizational identity studies by Michael Pratt and Anat Rafaeli in their article "Organizational Dress as a Symbol of Multilayered Social Identities" (Part III). The role of culture is also discussed by Hatch and Schultz (Part III) and Ashforth and Mael (Part II). Goffman's distinction between front stage and back stage is applied by Golden-Biddle and Rao in their chapter "Breeches in the Boardroom: Organizational Identity and Conflicts of Commitment in a Nonprofit Organization" (Part III).

Henri Tajfel and John C. Turner: "An Integrative Theory of Intergroup Conflict" (1979)

(Excerpted from *The Social Psychology of Intergroup Relations*, 38–43)
Reviews of research focused on in-group and out-group identification, competitive ethnocentrism, and negative stereotyping among social groups, led British social psychologists Henry Tajfel and John Turner to propose a theory of social identity/social comparison as a counterpoint to the then dominant idea in social psychology that group morale, cohesiveness, and cooperation are strictly the products of intergroup competition. Tajfel and Turner's view was that identification with an in-group could operate independently of the competition other social psychologists of their day assumed to be the driving force behind group identification. These researchers also noted the power of the "minimal group," that is, simply naming someone a member of a group is enough to create in-group and out-group distinctions, thus suggesting that the construction of organizational identity plays a role in creating the competition that earlier researchers assumed produces group identity.

Tajfel and Turner proposed social categorization as the basis for the definition of a group (1979: 40):

the individuals concerned define themselves and are defined by others as a group ... We can conceptualize a group ... as a collection of individuals who perceive themselves to be members of the same social category, share some emotional involvement in this common definition of themselves, and achieve some degree of social consensus about the evaluation of their group and of their membership of it.

They theorized that social identity is based in the individual's desire to enhance self-esteem using social comparison processes by which individuals differentiate themselves and form positive and negative evaluations of in-groups and out-groups. Differentiation was explained as a need for distinguishing in-group from out-group coupled with the choice of comparison others (based on similarity, proximity, and situational salience) and indicated that this created the foundation for intergroup competition, whereupon they distinguished social competition (motivated by self-evaluation; fed by social comparison processes) from instrumental competition (motivated by self-interest; fed by incompatible goals). Blake Ashforth and Fred Mael were the first organizational researchers to apply Tajfel and Turner's theory to organizations in their article "Social

Identity Theory and the Organization" (Part II), and many organizational identity researchers have since followed their lead.

Marilyn B. Brewer and Wendi Gardner: "Who Is this 'We'?: Levels of Collective Identity and Self-representations" (1996)

(Journal of Personality and Social Psychology, vol. 71, pp. 83–7, 91–3)

In their article "Who Is This 'We'? Levels of Collective Identity and Self Representations", American social psychologists Brewer and Gardner combined the distinction between personal and social identity offered by Cooley and Mead, with Marcus and Kitayama's distinction between independent and interdependent selves. They redefined the interdependent self as relational and placed this category between personal and social identity in Tajfel and Turner's social categorization theory to form their three-level model of identity as personal, relational and collective. According to Brewer and Gardner, personal identity differentiates the self from all others, relational identity reflects the individual's assimilation to particular others, and collective identity reflects assimilation to significant social groups. Thus relational and collective identities involve relatively increasing social extensions of the self beyond personal identity. Brewer and Gardner claimed that these different self-construals coexist within the same individual, but are activated in different contexts and at different times. They also raised the issue of cross-cultural differences in self-construal practices, noting studies that found that Japanese culture tends to activate relational self-construal, whereas US cultures tend to activate personal self-construal.

Brewer and Gardner (1996: 86) claimed that: "within the in-group category, individuals develop a cooperative orientation toward shared problems." They commented that tensions between pressures to differentiate and assimilate exist at all three levels of self-representation: similarity versus uniqueness is the issue at the personal level, intimacy versus separation at the relational level, and inclusion versus distinctiveness at the collective level. They pointed to a dynamic appreciation of the self-concept when they argued that (1996: 91):

At each level of self-representation, these opposing forces of assimilation and differentiation create a dynamic equilibrium that fluctuates with changes in the distance between the self and others. A similar dynamic may account for the shift between levels of self-categorization. When needs for intimacy at the interpersonal level are not being met, collective identities may become more important; prolonged periods of immersion in a depersonalized collective may enhance the importance of recognition of the personal, individuated self, and so forth.

This is similar to the idea Howard Schwartz examined in his article "Anti-social Actions of Committed Organizational Participants: An Existential Psychoanalytic Perspective?" (Part II), although Schwartz relied upon Freudian psychoanalytic theory rather than social psychology to frame his argument.

Brewer and Gardner's work, while much more recent than the other works represented in this part of the book, is important because it provides an empirically grounded, theoretical foundation for the practice in organizational identity studies of generalizing from the individual level of analysis to the organizational.

1 Society and the Individual

C. H. Cooley

Most people not only think of individuals and society as more or less separate and antithetical, but they look upon the former as antecedent to the latter. That persons make society would be generally admitted as a matter of course; but that society makes persons would strike many as a startling notion, though I know of no good reason for looking upon the distributive aspect of life as more primary or causative than the collective aspect. The reason for the common impression appears to be that we think most naturally and easily of the individual phase of life, simply because it is a tangible one, the phase under which men appear to the senses, while the actuality of groups, of nations, of mankind at large, is realized only by the active and instructed imagination. We ordinarily regard society, so far as we conceive it at all, in a vaguely material aspect, as an aggregate of physical bodies, not as the vital whole which it is; and so, of course, we do not see that it may be as original or causative as anything else. Indeed, many look upon "society" and other general terms as somewhat mystical, and are inclined to doubt whether there is any reality back of them.

This naïve individualism of thought—which, however, does not truly see the individual any more than it does society—is reinforced by traditions in which all of us are brought up, and is so hard to shake off that it may be worthwhile to point out a little more definitely some of the prevalent ways of conceiving life which are permeated by it, and which any one who agrees with what has just been said may regard as fallacious. My purpose in doing this is only to make clearer the standpoint from which succeeding chapters are written, and I do not propose any thorough discussion of the views mentioned.

First, then, we have *mere individualism*. In this the distributive aspect is almost exclusively regarded, collective phases being looked upon as quite secondary and incidental. Each person is held to be a separate agent, and all social phenomena are thought of as originating in the action of such agents. The individual is the source, the independent, the only human source, of events. Although this way of looking at things has been much discredited by the evolutionary science and philosophy of recent years, it is by no means abandoned, even in theory, and practically it enters as a premise, in one shape or another, into most of the current thought of the day. It springs naturally from the established way of thinking, congenial, as I have remarked, to the ordinary material view of things and corroborated by theological and other traditions.

Next is *double causation*, or a partition of power between society and the individual, thought of as separate causes. This notion, in one shape or another, is the one ordinarily met with in social and ethical discussion. It is no advance, philosophically, upon the preceding. There is the same premise of the individual as a separate, unrelated agent; but over against him is set a vaguely conceived general or collective interest and force. It seems that people are so accustomed to thinking of themselves as uncaused causes, special creators on a small scale, that when the existence of general phenomena is forced upon their notice they are likely to regard these as something additional, separate, and more or less antithetical. Our two forces contend with varying fortunes, the thinker sometimes sympathizing with one, sometimes with the other, and being an individualist or a socialist accordingly. The doctrines usually understood in connection with these terms differ, as regards their conception of the nature of life, only in taking opposite sides of the same questionable antithesis. The socialist holds it desirable that the general or collective force should win; the individualist has a contrary opinion. Neither offers any change of ground, any reconciling and renewing breadth of view. So far as breadth of view is concerned a man might quite as well be an individualist as a socialist or collectivist, the two being identical in philosophy though antagonistic in programme. If one is inclined to neither party he may take refuge in the expectation that the controversy, resting, as he may hold that it does, on a false conception of life, will presently take its proper place among the forgotten *débris* of speculation.

Thirdly we have *primitive individualism*. This expression has been used to describe the view that sociality follows individuality in time, is a later and additional product of development. This view is a variety of the preceding, and is, perhaps, formed by a mingling of individualistic preconceptions with a somewhat crude evolutionary philosophy. Individuality is usually conceived as lower in moral rank as well as precedent in time. Man *was* a mere individual, mankind a mere aggregation of such, but he had gradually become socialized, he is progressively merging into a social whole. Morally speaking, the individual is the bad, the social the good, and we must push on the work of putting down the former and bringing in the latter.

Of course the view which I regard as sound, is that individuality is neither prior in time nor lower in moral rank than sociality; but that the two have always existed side by side as complementary aspects of the same thing, and that the line of progress is from a lower to a higher type of both, not from the one to the other. If the word social is applied only to the higher forms of mental life it should, as already suggested, be opposed not to individual, but to animal, sensual, or some other word implying mental or moral inferiority. If we go back to a time when the state of our remote ancestors was such that we are not willing to call it social, then it must have been equally undeserving to be described as individual or personal; that is to say, they must have been just as inferior to us when viewed separately as when viewed collectively. To question this is to question the vital unity of human life.

The life of the human species, like that of other species, must always have been both general and particular, must always have had its collective and distributive aspects. The plane of this life has gradually risen, involving, of course, both the aspects mentioned. Now, as ever, they develop as one, and may be observed united in the highest activities of the highest minds. Shakespeare, for instance, is in one point of view a unique and transcendent individual; in another he is a splendid expression of the general life of mankind: the difference is not in him but in the way we choose to look at him.

Finally, there is *the social faculty view*. This expression might be used to indicate those conceptions which regard the social as including only a part, often a rather definite part, of the individual. Human nature is thus divided into individualistic or non-social tendencies or faculties, and those that are social. Thus, certain emotions, as love, are social; others, as fear or anger, are unsocial or individualistic. Some writers have even treated the intelligence as an individualistic faculty, and have found sociality only in some sorts of emotion or sentiment.

This idea of instincts or faculties that are peculiarly social is well enough if we use this word in the sense of pertaining to conversation or immediate fellow feeling. Affection is certainly more social in this sense than fear. But if it is meant that these instincts or faculties are in themselves morally higher than others, or that they alone pertain to the collective life, the view is, I think, very questionable. At any rate the opinion I hold, and expect to explain more fully in the further course of this book, is that man's psychical outfit is not divisible into the social and the non-social; but that he is all social in a large sense, is all a part of the common human life, and that his social or moral progress consists less in the aggrandizement of particular faculties or instincts and the suppression of others, than in the discipline of all with reference to a progressive organization of life which we know in thought as conscience.

Some instincts or tendencies may grow in relative importance, may have an increasing function, while the opposite may be true of others. Such relative growth and diminution of parts seems to be a general feature of evolution, and there is no reason why it should be absent from our mental development. But here as well as elsewhere most parts, if not all, are or have been functional with reference to a life collective as well as distributive; there is no sharp separation of faculties, and progress takes place rather by gradual adaptation of old organs to new functions than by disuse and decay.

To make it quite clear what the organic view involves, so far as regards theory, I will take several questions, such as I have found that people ask when discussing the relation of society and the individual, and will suggest how, as it seems to me, they may be answered.

1. Is not society, after all, made up of individuals, and of nothing else?

I should say, Yes. It is plain, every-day humanity, not a mysterious something else.

2. Is society anything more than the sum of the individuals?

In a sense, Yes. There is an organization, a lifeprocess, in any social whole that you cannot see in the individuals separately. To study them one by one and attempt to understand society by putting them together will lead you astray. It is "individualism" in a bad sense of the word. Whole sciences, like political economy; great institutions, like the church, have gone wrong at this point. You must see your groups, your social processes, as the living wholes that they are.

3. Is the individual a product of society?

Yes, in the sense that everything human about him has a history in the social past. If we consider the two sources from which he draws his life, heredity and communication, we see that what he gets through the germ-plasm has a social history in that it has had to adapt itself to past society in order to survive: the traits we are born with are such as have undergone a social test in the lives of our ancestors. And what he gets from communication—language, education, and the like—comes directly from society. Even physical influences, like food and climate, rarely reach us except as modified and adapted by social conditions.

4. Can we separate the individual from society?

Only in an external sense. If you go off alone into the wilderness you take with you a mind formed in society, and you continue social intercourse in your memory and imagination, or by the aid of books. This, and this only, keeps humanity alive in you, and just in so far as you lose the power of intercourse your mind decays. Long solitude, as in the case of sheepherders on the Western plains, or prisoners in solitary confinement, often produces imbecility. This is especially likely to happen with the uneducated, whose memories are not well stored with material for imaginative intercourse.

At times in the history of Christianity, and of other religions also, hermits have gone to dwell in desert places, but they have usually kept up some communication with one another and with the world outside, certain of them, like St. Jerome, having been famous letter-writers. Each of them, in fact, belonged to a social system from which he drew ideals and moral support. We may suspect that St. Simeon Stylites, who dwelt for years on top of a pillar, was not unaware that his austerity was visible to others.

A castaway who should be unable to retain his imaginative hold upon human society might conceivably live the life of an intelligent animal, exercising his mind upon the natural conditions about him, but his distinctively human faculties would certainly be lost, or in abeyance.

5. Is the individual in any sense free, or is he a mere piece of society?

Yes, he is free, as I conceive the matter, but it is an organic freedom, which he works out in co-operation with others, not a freedom to do things independently of society. It is team-work. He has freedom to function in his own way, like the quarter-back, but, in one way or another, he has to play the game as life brings him into it.

The evolutionary point of view encourages us to believe that life is a creative process, that we are really building up something now and worth while, and that the human will is a part of the creative energy that does this. Every individual has his unique share in the work, which no one but himself can discern and perform. Although his life flows into him from the hereditary and social past, his being as a whole is new, a fresh organization of life. Never any one before had the same powers and opportunities that you have, and you are free to use them in your own way.

It is, after all, only common sense to say that we exercise our freedom through cooperation with others. If you join a social group—let us say a dramatic club—you expect that it will increase your freedom, give your individual powers new stimulus and opportunity for expression. And why should not the same principle apply to society at large? It is through a social development that mankind has emerged from animal bondage into that organic freedom, wonderful though far from complete, that we now enjoy.

It is well to say at the outset that by the word "self" in this discussion is meant simply that which is designated in common speech by the pronouns of the first person singular, "I," "me," "my," "mine," and "myself." "Self" and "ego" are used by metaphysicians and moralists in many other senses, more or less remote from the "I" of daily speech and thought, and with these I wish to have as little to do as possible. What is here discussed is what psychologists call the empirical self, the self that can be apprehended or verified by ordinary observation. I qualify it by the word social not as implying the existence of a self that is not social—for I think that the "I" of common language always has more or less distinct reference to other people as well as the speaker—but because I wish to emphasize and dwell upon the social aspect of it.

Although the topic of the self is regarded as an abstruse one this abstruseness belongs chiefly, perhaps, to the metaphysical discussion of the "pure ego"—whatever that may be—while the empirical self should not be very much more difficult to get hold of than other facts of the mind. At any rate, it may be assumed that the pronouns of the first person have a substantial, important, and not very recondite meaning, otherwise they would not be in constant and intelligible use by simple people and young children the world over. And since they have such a meaning why should it not be observed and reflected upon like any other matter of fact? As to the underlying mystery, it is no doubt real, important, and a very fit subject of discussion by those who are competent, but I do not see that it is a *peculiar* mystery. I mean that it seems to be simply a phase of the general mystery of life, not pertaining to "I" more than to any other personal or social fact; so that here as elsewhere those who are not attempting to penetrate the mystery may simply ignore it. If this is a just view of the matter, "I" is merely a fact like any other.

The distinctive thing in the idea for which the pronouns of the first person are names is apparently a characteristic kind of feeling which may be called the my-feeling or sense of appropriation. Almost any sort of ideas may be associated with this feeling, and so come to be named "I" or "mine," but the feeling, and that alone it would seem, is the determining factor in the matter. As Professor James says in his admirable discussion of the self, the words "me" and "self" designate "all the things which have the power to produce in a stream of consciousness excitement of a certain peculiar sort."[1] This view is very fully set forth by Professor Hiram M. Stanley, whose work, "The Evolutionary Psychology of Feeling," has an extremely suggestive chapter on self-feeling.

I do not mean that the feeling aspect of the self is necessarily more important than any other, but that it is the immediate and decisive sign and proof of what "I" is; there is no appeal from it; if we go behind it it must be to study its history and conditions, not to question its authority. But, of course, this study of history and conditions may be quite as profitable as the direct contemplation of self-feeling. What I would wish to do is to present each aspect in its proper light.

The emotion or feeling of self may be regarded as instinctive, and was doubtless evolved in connection with its important function in stimulating and unifying the special activities of individuals.[2] It is thus very profoundly rooted in the history of the human race and apparently indispensable to any plan of life at all similar to ours. It seems to exist in a vague though vigorous form at the birth of each individual, and, like other instinctive ideas or germs of ideas, to be defined and developed by experience, becoming associated, or rather incorporated, with muscular, visual, and other sensations; with perceptions, apperceptions, and conceptions of every degree of complexity and of infinite variety of content; and, especially, with personal ideas. Meantime the feeling itself does not remain unaltered, but undergoes differentiation and refinement just as does any other sort of crude innate feeling. Thus, while retaining under every phase its characteristic tone or flavor, it breaks up into innumerable self-sentiments. And concrete self-feeling, as it exists in mature persons, is a whole made up of these various sentiments, along with a good deal of primitive emotion not thus broken up. It partakes fully of the general development of the mind, but never loses that peculiar gusto of appropriation that causes us to name a thought with a first-personal pronoun. The other contents of the self-idea are of little use, apparently, in defining it, because they are so extremely various. It would be no more futile, it seems to me, to attempt to define fear by enumerating the things that people are afraid of, than to attempt to define "I" by enumerating the objects with which the word is associated. Very much as fear means primarily a state of feeling, or its expression, and not darkness, fire, lions, snakes, or other things that excite it, so "I" means primarily self-feeling, or its expression, and not body, clothes, treasures, ambition, honors, and the like, with which this feeling may be connected. In either case it is possible and useful to go behind the feeling and inquire what ideas arouse it and why they do so, but this is in a sense a secondary investigation.

Since "I" is known to our experience primarily as a feeling, or as a feeling-ingredient in our ideas, it cannot be described or defined without suggesting that feeling. We are sometimes likely to fall into a formal and empty way of talking regarding questions of emotion, by attempting to define that which is in its nature primary and indefinable. A formal definition of self-feeling, or indeed of any sort of feeling, must be as hollow as a formal definition of the taste of salt, or the color red; we can expect to know what it is only by experiencing it. There can be no final test of the self except the way we feel; it is that toward which we have the "my" attitude. But as this feeling is quite as familiar to us and as easy to recall as the taste of salt or the color red, there should be no difficulty in understanding what is meant by it. One need only imagine some attack on his "me," say ridicule of his dress or an attempt to take away his property or his child, or his good name by slander, and self-feeling immediately appears. Indeed, he need only pronounce, with strong emphasis, one of the self-words, like "I" or "my," and self-feeling will be recalled by association. Another good way is to enter by sympathy into some self-assertive state of mind depicted in literature; as, for instance, into that of Coriolanus when, having been sneered at as a "boy of tears," he cries out:

"Boy! ...
If you have writ your annals true, 'tis there,
That, like an eagle in a dovecote, I
Fluttered your Volscians in Corioli;
Alone I did it.—Boy!"

Here is a self indeed, which no one can fail to feel, though he might be unable to describe it. What a ferocious scream of the outraged ego is that "I" at the end of the second line!

So much is written on this topic that ignores self-feeling and thus deprives "self" of all vivid and palpable meaning, that I feel it permissible to add a few more passages in which this feeling is forcibly expressed. Thus in Lowell's poem, "A Glance Behind the Curtain," Cromwell says:

"I, perchance,
Am one raised up by the Almighty arm
To witness some great truth to all the world."

And his Columbus, on the bow of his vessel, soliloquizes:

"Here am I, with no friend but the sad sea,

The beating heart of this great enterprise,
Which, without me, would stiffen in swift death."

And so the "I am the way" which we read in the New Testament is surely the expression of a sentiment not very different from these. In the following we have a more plaintive sentiment of self:

Philoctetes.—And know'st thou not, O boy, whom thou dost see?
Neoptolemus.—How can I know a man I ne'er beheld?
Philoctetes.—And didst thou never hear my name, nor fame
Of these my ills, in which I pined away?
Neoptolemus.—Know that I nothing know of what thou ask'st.
Philoctetes.—O crushed with many woes, and of the Gods
Hated am I, of whom, in this my woe,
No rumor travelled homeward, nor went forth
Through any clime of Hellas.[3]

We all have thoughts of the same sort as these, and yet it is possible to talk so coldly or mystically about the self that one begins to forget that there is, really, any such thing.

But perhaps the best way to realize the naïve meaning of "I" is to listen to the talk of children playing together, especially if they do not agree very well. They use the first person with none of the conventional self-repression of their elders, but with much emphasis and variety of inflection, so that its emotional animus is unmistakable.

Self-feeling of a reflective and agreeable sort, an appropriative zest of contemplation, is strongly suggested by the word "gloating." To gloat, in this sense, is as much as to think "mine, mine, mine," with a pleasant warmth of feeling. Thus a boy gloats over something he has made with his scroll-saw, over the bird he has brought down with his gun, or over his collection of stamps or eggs; a girl gloats over her new clothes, and over the approving words or looks of others; a farmer over his fields and his stock; a business man over his trade and his bank-account; a mother over her child; the poet over a successful quatrain; the self-righteous man over the state of his soul; and in like manner every one gloats over the prosperity of any cherished idea.

I would not be understood as saying that self-feeling is clearly marked off in experience from other kinds of feeling; but it is, perhaps, as definite in this regard as anger, fear, grief, and the like. To quote Professor James, "The emotions themselves of self-satisfaction and abasement are of a unique sort, each as worthy to be classed as a primitive emotional species as are, for example, rage or pain."[4] It is true here, as wherever mental facts are distinguished, that there are no fences, but that one thing merges by degrees into another. Yet if "I" did not denote an idea much the same in all minds and fairly distinguishable from other ideas, it could not be used freely and universally as a means of communication.

C. H. Cooley

As many people have the impression that the verifiable self, the object that we name with "I," is usually the material body, it may be well to say that this impression is an illusion, easily dispelled by any one who will undertake a simple examination of facts. It is true that when we philosophize a little about "I" and look around for a tangible object to which to attach it, we soon fix upon the material body as the most available *locus*; but when we use the word naïvely, as in ordinary speech, it is not very common to think of the body in connection with it; not nearly so common as it is to think of other things. There is no difficulty in testing this statement, since the word "I" is one of the commonest in conversation and literature, so that nothing is more practicable than to study its meaning at any length that may be desired. One need only listen to ordinary speech until the word has occurred, say, a hundred times, noting its connections, or observe its use in a similar number of cases by the characters in a novel. Ordinarily it will be found that in not more than ten cases in a hundred does "I" have reference to the body of the person speaking. It refers chiefly to opinions, purposes, desires, claims, and the like, concerning matters that involve no thought of the body. *I* think or feel so and so; *I* wish or intend so and so; *I* want this or that; are typical uses, the self-feeling being associated with the view, purpose, or object mentioned. It should also be remembered that "my" and "mine" are as much the names of the self as "I," and these, of course, commonly refer to miscellaneous possessions.

I had the curiosity to attempt a rough classification of the first hundred "I's" and "me's" in Hamlet, with the following results. The pronoun was used in connection with perception, as "I hear," "I see," fourteen times; with thought, sentiment, intention, etc., thirty-two times; with wish, as "I pray you," six times; as speaking—"I'll speak to it"—sixteen times; as spoken to, twelve times; in connection with action, involving perhaps some vague notion of the body, as "I came to Denmark," nine times; vague or doubtful, ten times; as equivalent to bodily appearance—"No more like my father than I to Hercules"—once. Some of the classifications are arbitrary, and another observer would doubtless get a different result; but he could not fail, I think, to conclude that Shakespeare's characters are seldom thinking of their bodies when they say "I" or "me." And in this respect they appear to be representative of mankind in general.

As already suggested, instinctive self-feeling is doubtless connected in evolution with its important function in stimulating and unifying the special activities of individuals. It appears to be associated chiefly with ideas of the exercise of power, of being a cause, ideas that emphasize the antithesis between the mind and the rest of the world. The first definite thoughts that a child associates with self-feeling are probably those of his earliest endeavors to control visible objects—his limbs, his playthings, his bottle, and the like. Then he attempts to control the actions of the persons about him, and so his circle of power and of self-feeling widens without interruption to the most complex objects of mature

24

ambition. Although he does not say "I" or "my" during the first year or two, yet he expresses so clearly by his actions the feeling that adults associate with these words that we cannot deny him a self even in the first weeks.

The correlation of self-feeling with purposeful activity is easily seen by observing the course of any productive enterprise. If a boy sets about making a boat, and has any success, his interest in the matter waxes, he gloats over it, the keel and stem are dear to his heart, and its ribs are more to him than those of his own frame. He is eager to call in his friends and acquaintances, saying to them, "See what I am doing! Is it not remarkable?" feeling elated when it is praised, and resentful or humiliated when fault is found with it. But so soon as he finishes it and turns to something else, his self-feeling begins to fade away from it, and in a few weeks at most he will have become comparatively indifferent. We all know that much the same course of feeling accompanies the achievements of adults. It is impossible to produce a picture, a poem, an essay, a difficult bit of masonry, or any other work of art or craft, without having self-feeling regarding it, amounting usually to considerable excitement and desire for some sort of appreciation; but this rapidly diminishes with the activity itself, and often lapses into indifference after it ceases.

It may perhaps be objected that the sense of self, instead of being limited to times of activity and definite purpose, is often most conspicuous when the mind is unoccupied or undecided, and that the idle and ineffectual are commonly the most sensitive in their self-esteem. This, however, may be regarded as an instance of the principle that all instincts are likely to assume troublesome forms when denied whole-some expression. The need to exert power, when thwarted in the open fields of life, is the more likely to assert itself in trifles.

The social self is simply any idea, or system of ideas, drawn from the communicative life, that the mind cherishes as its own. Self-feeling has its chief scope *within* the general life, not outside of it; the special endeavor or tendency of which it is the emotional aspect finds its principal field of exercise in a world of personal forces, reflected in the mind by a world of personal impressions.

As connected with the thought of other persons the self idea is always a consciousness of the peculiar or differentiated aspect of one's life, because that is the aspect that has to be sustained by purpose and endeavor, and its more aggressive forms tend to attach themselves to whatever one finds to be at once congenial to one's own tendencies and at variance with those of others with whom one is in mental contact. It is here that they are most needed to serve their function of stimulating characteristic activity, of fostering those personal variations, which the general plan of life seems to require. Heaven, says Shakespeare, doth divide

"The state of man in divers functions,
Setting endeavor in continual motion,"

and self-feeling is one of the means by which this diversity is achieved.

Agreeably to this view we find that the aggressive self manifests itself most conspicuously in an appropriativeness of objects of common desire, corresponding to the individual's need of power over such objects to secure his own peculiar development, and to the danger of opposition from others who also need them. And this extends from material objects to lay hold, in the same spirit, of the attentions and affections of other people, of all sorts of plans and ambitions, including the noblest special purposes the mind can entertain, and indeed of any conceivable idea which may come to seem a part of one's life and in need of assertion against some one else. The attempt to limit the word self and its derivatives to the lower aims of personality is quite arbitrary; at variance with common sense as expressed by the emphatic use of "I" in connection with the sense of duty and other high motives, and unphilosophical as ignoring the function of the self as the organ of specialized endeavor of higher as well as lower kinds.

That the "I" of common speech has a meaning which includes some sort of reference to other persons is involved in the very fact that the word and the ideas it stands for are phenomena of language and the communicative life. It is doubtful whether it is possible to use language at all without thinking more or less distinctly of some one else, and certainly the things to which we give names and which have a large place in reflective thought are almost always those which are impressed upon us by our contact with other people. Where there is no communication there can be no nomenclature and no developed thought. What we call "me," "mine," or "myself" is, then, not something separate from the general life, but the most interesting part of it, a part whose interest arises from the very fact that it is both general and individual. That is, we care for it just because it is that phase of the mind that is living and striving in the common life, trying to impress itself upon the minds of others. "I" is a militant social tendency, working to hold and enlarge its place in the general current of tendencies. So far as it can it waxes, as all life does. To think of it as apart from society is a palpable absurdity of which no one could be guilty who really *saw* it as a fact of life.

"Der Mensch erkennt sich nur im Menschen, nur
Das Leben lehret jedem was er sei."[5]

If a thing has no relation to others of which one is conscious he is unlikely to think of it at all, and if he does think of it he cannot, it seems to me, regard it as emphatically *his*. The appropriative sense is always the shadow, as it were, of the common life, and when we have it we have a sense of the latter in connection with it. Thus, if we think of a secluded part of the woods as "ours," it is because we think, also, that others do not go there. As regards the body I doubt if we have a vivid my-feeling about any part of it which is not thought of, however vaguely, as having some actual or possible reference to some one else. Intense self-consciousness regarding it arises along with instincts or experiences which connect it with the thought of others. Internal organs, like the liver, are not thought of as peculiarly ours unless we are trying to communicate something regarding them, as, for instance, when they are giving us trouble and we are trying to get sympathy.

"I," then, is not all of the mind, but a peculiarly central, vigorous, and well-knit portion of it, not separate from the rest but gradually merging into it, and yet having a certain practical distinctness, so that a man generally shows clearly enough by his language and behavior what his "I" is as distinguished from thoughts he does not appropriate. It may be thought of, as already suggested, under the analogy of a central colored area on a lighted wall. It might also, and perhaps more justly, be compared to the nucleus of a living cell, not altogether separate from the surrounding matter, out of which indeed it is formed, but more active and definitely organized.

The reference to other persons involved in the sense of self may be distinct and particular, as when a boy is ashamed to have his mother catch him at something she has forbidden, or it may be vague and general, as when one is ashamed to do something which only his conscience, expressing his sense of social responsibility, detects and disapproves; but it is always there. There is no sense of "I," as in pride or shame, without its correlative sense of you, or he, or they. Even the miser gloating over his hidden gold can feel the "mine" only as he is aware of the world of men over whom he has secret power; and the case is very similar with all kinds of hidden treasure. Many painters, sculptors, and writers have loved to withhold their work from the world, fondling it in seclusion until they were quite done with it; but the delight in this, as in all secrets, depends upon a sense of the value of what is concealed.

I remarked above that we think of the body as "I" when it comes to have social function or significance, as when we say "I am looking well to-day," or "I am taller than you are." We bring it into the social world, for the time being, and for that reason put our self-consciousness into it. Now it is curious, though natural, that in precisely the same way we may call any inanimate object "I" with which we are identifying our will and purpose. This is notable in games, like golf or croquet, where the ball is the embodiment of the player's fortunes. You will hear a man say, "I am in the long grass down by the third tee," or "I am in position for the middle arch." So a boy flying a kite will say "I am higher than you," or one shooting at a mark will declare that he is just below the bullseye.

In a very large and interesting class of cases the social reference takes the form of a somewhat definite imagination of how one's self—that is any idea he appropriates—appears in a particular mind, and the kind of self-feeling one has is determined by the attitude toward this attributed to that other mind. A social self of this sort might be called the reflected or looking-glass self:

"Each to each a looking-glass
Reflects the other that doth pass."

C. H. Cooley

As we see our face, figure, and dress in the glass, and are interested in them because they are ours, and pleased or otherwise with them according as they do or do not answer to what we should like them to be; so in imagination we perceive in another's mind some thought of our appearance, manners, aims, deeds, character, friends, and so on, and are variously affected by it.

A self-idea of this sort seems to have three principal elements: the imagination of our appearance to the other person; the imagination of his judgment of that appearance, and some sort of self-feeling, such as pride or mortification. The comparison with a looking-glass hardly suggests the second element, the imagined judgment, which is quite essential. The thing that moves us to pride or shame is not the mere mechanical reflection of ourselves, but an imputed sentiment, the imagined effect of this reflection upon another's mind. This is evident from the fact that the character and weight of that other, in whose mind we see ourselves, makes all the difference with our feeling. We are ashamed to seem evasive in the presence of a straightforward man, cowardly in the presence of a brave one, gross in the eyes of a refined one, and so on. We always imagine, and in imagining share, the judgments of the other mind. A man will boast to one person of an action—say some sharp transaction in trade—which he would be ashamed to own to another.

Many people of balanced mind and congenial activity scarcely know that they care what others think of them, and will deny, perhaps with indignation, that such care is an important factor in what they are and do. But this is illusion. If failure or disgrace arrives, if one suddenly finds that the faces of men show coldness or contempt instead of the kindliness and deference that he is used to, he will perceive from the shock, the fear, the sense of being outcast and helpless, that he was living in the minds of others without knowing it, just as we daily walk the solid ground without thinking how it bears us up. This fact is so familiar in literature, especially in modern novels, that it ought to be obvious enough. The works of George Eliot are particularly strong in the exposition of it. In most of her novels there is some character like Mr. Bulstrode in "Middlemarch" or Mr. Jermyn in "Felix Holt," whose respectable and long-established social image of himself is shattered by the coming to light of hidden truth.

It is true, however, that the attempt to describe the social self and to analyze the mental processes that enter into it almost unavoidably makes it appear more reflective and "self-conscious" than it usually is. Thus while some readers will be able to discover in themselves a quite definite and deliberate contemplation of the reflected self, others will perhaps find nothing but a sympathetic impulse, so simple that it can hardly be made the object of distinct thought. Many people whose behavior shows that their idea of themselves is largely caught from the persons they are with, are yet quite innocent of any intentional posing; it is a matter of subconscious impulse or mere suggestion. The self of very sensitive but non-reflective minds is of this character.

The group self or "we" is simply an "I" which includes other persons. One identifies himself with a group and speaks of the common will, opinion, service, or the like in terms of "we" and "us." The sense of it is stimulated by cooperation within and opposition without. A family that has had to struggle with economic difficulties usually develops solidarity—"We paid off the mortgage," "We sent the boys to college," and the like. A student identifies himself with his class or his university when it is performing a social function of some kind, especially when it is contending in games with other classes or institutions. "We won the tug of war," he says, or "We beat Wisconsin at football." Those of us who remained at home during the Great War nevertheless tell how "we" entered the war in 1917, how "we" fought decisively in the Argonne, and so on.

It is notable that the national self, indeed any group self, can be felt only in relation to a larger society, just as the individual self is felt only in relation to other individuals. We could have no patriotism unless we were aware of other nations, and the effect of a definitely organized society of nations, in whose activities we all took a generous interest, would be, not to diminish patriotism, as some have unintelligently asserted, but to raise its character, to make it more vivid, continuous, varied, and sympathetic. It would be like the self-consciousness of an intelligent individual in constant and friendly intercourse with others, as contrasted with the brutal self-assertion of one who knows his fellows only as objects of suspicion and hostility. The patriotism of the past has been of the latter kind, and we have hardly considered its higher possibilities. The national "we" can and should be a self of real honor, service, and humane aspiration.

Notes

1. *"The words* ME, *then, and* SELF, *so far as they arouse feeling and connote emotional worth, are* OBJECTIVE *designations meaning* ALL THE THINGS *which have the power to produce in a stream of consciousness excitement of a certain peculiar sort."* Psychology, i., p. 319. A little earlier he says: *"In its widest possible sense,* however, *a man's self is the sum total of all he* CAN *call his,* not only his body and his psychic powers, but his clothes and his house, his wife and children, his ancestors and friends, his reputation and works, his lands and horses and yacht and bank-account. All these things give him the same emotions." *Idem*, p. 291.

   So Wundt says of "Ich": "Es ist ein *Gefühl*, nicht eine Vorstellung, wie es häufig genannt wird." Grundriss der Psychologie, 4 Auflage, S. 265.
2. It is, perhaps, to be thought of as a more general instinct, of which anger, etc., are differentiated forms, rather than as standing by itself.
3. Plumptre's Sophocles, p. 352.
4. Psychology, i, p. 307.
5. "Only in man does man know himself; life alone teaches each one what he is."—Goethe, Tasso, act 2, sc. 3.

2

The Self: The 'I' and the 'Me'

G. H. Mead

We have discussed at length the social foundations of the self, and hinted that the self does not consist simply in the bare organization of social attitudes. We may now explicitly raise the question as to the nature of the "I" which is aware of the social "me." I do not mean to raise the metaphysical question of how a person can be both "I" and "me," but to ask for the significance of this distinction from the point of view of conduct itself. Where in conduct does the "I" come in as over against the "me"? If one determines what his position is in society and feels himself as having a certain function and privilege, these are all defined with reference to an "I," but the "I" is not a "me" and cannot become a "me." We may have a better self and a worse self, but that again is not the "I" as over against the "me," because they are both selves. We approve of one and disapprove of the other, but when we bring up one or the other they are there for such approval as "me's." The "I" does not get into the limelight; we talk to ourselves, but do not see ourselves. The "I" reacts to the self which arises through the taking of the attitudes of others. Through taking those attitudes we have introduced the "me" and we react to it as an "I."

The simplest way of handling the problem would be in terms of memory. I talk to myself, and I remember what I said and perhaps the emotional content that went with it. The "I" of this moment is present in the "me" of the next moment. There again I cannot turn around quick enough to catch myself. I become a "me" in so far as I remember what I said. The "I" can be given, however, this functional relationship. It is because of the "I" that we say that we are never fully aware of what we are, that we surprise ourselves by our own action. It is as we act that we are aware of ourselves. It is in memory that the "I" is constantly present in experience. We can go back directly a few moments in our experience, and then we are dependent upon memory images for the rest. So that the "I" in memory is there as the spokesman of the self of the second, or minute, or day ago. As given, it is a "me," but it is a "me" which was the "I" at the earlier time. If you ask, then, where directly in your own experience the "I" comes in, the answer is that it comes in as a historical figure. It is what you were a second ago that is the "I" of the "me." It is another "me" that has to take that rôle. You cannot get the immediate response of the "I" in the process.[1] The "I" is in a certain sense that with which we do identify ourselves. The getting of it into experience constitutes one of the problems of most of our conscious experience; it is not directly given in experience.

The "I" is the response of the organism to the attitudes of the others; the "me" is the organized set of attitudes of others which one himself assumes. The attitudes of the others constitute the organized "me," and then one reacts toward that as an "I." I now wish to examine these concepts in greater detail.

There is neither "I" nor "me" in the conversation of gestures; the whole act is not yet carried out, but the preparation takes place in this field of gesture. Now, in so far as the individual arouses in himself the attitudes of the others, there arises an organized group of responses. And it is due to the individual's ability to take the attitudes of these others in so far as they can be organized that he gets self-consciousness. The taking of all of those organized sets of attitudes gives him his "me;" that is the self he is aware of. He can throw the ball to some other member because of the demand made upon him from other members of the team. That is the self that immediately exists for him in his consciousness. He has their attitudes, knows what they want and what the consequence of any act of his will be, and he has assumed responsibility for the situation. Now, it is the presence of those organized sets of attitudes that constitutes that "me" to which he as an "I" is responding. But what that response will be he does not know and nobody else knows. Perhaps he will make a brilliant play or an error. The response to that situation as it appears in his immediate experience is uncertain, and it is that which constitutes the "I."

The "I" is his action over against that social situation within his own conduct, and it gets into his experience only after he has carried out the act. Then he is aware of it. He had to do such a thing and he did it. He fulfils his duty and he may look with pride at the throw which he made. The "me" arises to do that duty—that is the way in which it arises in his experience. He had in him all the attitudes of others, calling for a certain response; that was the "me" of that situation, and his response is the "I."

I want to call attention particularly to the fact that this response of the "I" is something that is more or less uncertain. The attitudes of others which one assumes as affecting his own conduct constitute the "me," and that is something that is there, but the response to it is as yet not given. When one sits down to think anything out, he has certain data that are there. Suppose that it is a social situation which he has to straighten out. He sees himself from the point of view of one individual or another in the group. These individuals, related all together, give him a certain self. Well, what is he going to do? He does not know and nobody else knows. He can get the situation into his experience because he can assume the attitudes of the various individuals involved in it. He knows how they feel about it by the assumption of their attitudes. He says, in effect, "I have done certain things that seem to commit me to a certain course of conduct." Perhaps if he does so act it will place him in a false position with another group. The "I" as a response to this situation, in contrast to the "me" which is involved in the attitudes which he takes, is uncertain. And when the response takes place, then it appears in the field of experience largely as a memory image.

Our specious present as such is very short. We do, however, experience passing events; part of the process of the passage of events is directly there in our experience, including some of the past and some of the future. We see a ball falling as it passes, and as it does pass part of the ball is covered and part is being uncovered. We remember where the ball was a moment ago and we anticipate where it will be beyond what is given in our experience. So of our-selves; we are doing something, but to look back and see what we are doing involves getting memory images. So the "I" really appears experientially as a part of a "me." But on the basis of this experience we distinguish that indi-vidual who is doing something from the "me" who puts the problem up to him. The response enters into his experience only when it takes place. If he says he knows what he is going to do, even there he may be mistaken. He starts out to do something and something happens to interfere. The resulting action is always a little different from anything which he could anticipate. This is true even if he is simply carrying out the process of walking. The very taking of his expected steps puts him in a certain situation which has a slightly different aspect from what is expected, which is in a certain sense novel. That movement into the future is the step, so to speak, of the ego, of the "I." It is something that is not given in the "me."

Take the situation of a scientist solving a problem, where he has certain data which call for certain responses. Some of this set of data call for his applying such and such a law, while others call for another law. Data are there with their implications. He knows what such and such coloration means, and when he has these data before him they stand for certain responses on his part; but now they are in conflict with each other. If he makes one response he cannot make another. What he is going to do he does not know, nor does anybody else. The action of the self is in response to these conflicting sets of data in the form of a problem, with conflicting demands upon him as a scientist. He has to look at it in different ways. That action of the "I" is something the nature of which we cannot tell in advance.

The "I," then, in this relation of the "I" and the "me," is something that is, so to speak, responding to a social situation which is within the experience of the individual. It is the answer which the individual makes to the attitude which others take toward him when he assumes an attitude toward them. Now, the attitudes he is taking toward them are present in his own experience, but his response to them will contain a novel element. The "I" gives the sense of freedom, of initiative. The situation is there for us to act in a self-conscious fashion. We are aware of ourselves, and of what the situation is, but exactly how we will act never gets into experience until after the action takes place.

Such is the basis for the fact that the "I" does not appear in the same sense in experience as does the "me." The "me" represents a definite organization of the community there in our own attitudes, and calling for a response, but the response that takes place is something that just happens. There is no certainty in regard to it. There is a moral necessity but no mechanical necessity for the act. When it does take place then we find what has been done. The above account gives us, I think, the relative position of the "I" and "me" in the situation, and the grounds for the separation of the two in behavior. The two are separated in the process but they belong together in the sense of being parts of a whole. They are separated and yet they belong together. The separation of the "I" and the "me" is not fictitious. They are not identical, for, as I have said, the "I" is something that is never entirely calculable. The "me" does call for a certain sort of an "I" in so far as we meet the obligations that are given in conduct itself, but the "I" is always something different from what the situation itself calls for. So there is always that distinction, if you like, between the "I" and the "me." The "I" both calls out the "me" and responds to it. Taken together they constitute a personality as it appears in social experience. The self is essentially a social process going on with these two distinguishable phases. If it did not have these two phases there could not be conscious responsibility, and there would be nothing novel in experience.

The self is not so much a substance as a process in which the conversation of gestures has been internalized within an organic form. This process does not exist for itself, but is simply a phase of the whole social organization of which the individual is a part. The organization of the social act has been imported into the organism and becomes then the mind of the individual. It still includes the attitudes of others, but now highly organized, so that they become what we call social attitudes rather than rôles of separate individuals. This process of relating one's own organism to the others in the interactions that are going on, in so far as it is imported into the conduct of the individual with the conversation of the "I" and the "me," constitutes the self.[2] The value of this importation of the conversation of gestures into the conduct of the individual lies in the superior co-ordination gained for society as a whole, and in the increased efficiency of the individual as a member of the group. It is the difference between the process which can take place in a group of rats or ants or bees, and that which can take place in a human community. The social process with its various implications is actually taken up into the experience of the individual so that that which is going on takes place more effectively, because in a certain sense it has been rehearsed in the individual. He not only plays his part better under those conditions but he also reacts back on the organization of which he is a part.

The very nature of this conversation of gestures requires that the attitude of the other is changed through the attitude of the individual to the other's stimulus. In the conversation of gestures of the lower forms the play back and forth is noticeable, since the individual not only adjusts himself to the attitude of others, but also changes the attitudes of the others. The reaction of the individual in this conversation of gestures is one that in some degree is continually modifying the social process itself. It is this modification of the process which is of greatest interest in the experience of the individual. He takes the attitude of the other toward his own stimulus, and in taking that he finds it modified in that his response becomes a different one, and leads in turn to further change.

....

Notes

1. The sensitivity of the organism brings parts of itself into the environment. It does not, however, bring the life-process itself into the environment, and the complete imaginative presentation of the organism is unable to present the living of the organism. It can conceivably present the conditions under which living takes place but not the unitary life-process. The physical organism in the environment always remains a thing (MS).
2. According to this view, conscious communication develops out of unconscious communication within the social process; conversation in terms of significant gestures out of conversation in terms of non-significant gestures; and the development in such fashion of conscious communication is coincident with the development of minds and selves within the social process.

3

The Arts of Impression Management

E. Goffman

In this chapter I would like to bring together what has been said or implied about the attributes that are required of a performer for the work of successfully staging a character. Brief reference will therefore be made to some of the techniques of impression management in which these attributes are expressed. In preparation it may be well to suggest, in some cases for the second time, some of the principal types of performance disruptions, for it is these disruptions which the techniques of impression management function to avoid.

In the beginning of this report, in considering the general characteristics of performances, it was suggested that the performer must act with expressive responsibility, since many minor, inadvertent acts happen to be well designed to convey impressions inappropriate at the time. These events were called "unmeant gestures." Ponsonby gives an illustration of how a director's attempt to avoid an unmeant gesture led to the occurrence of another.

One of the Attachés from the Legation was to carry the cushion on which the insignia were placed, and in order to prevent their falling off I stuck the pin at the back of the Star through the velvet cushion. The Attaché, however, was not content with this, but secured the end of the pin by the catch to make doubly sure. The result was that when Prince Alexander, having made a suitable speech, tried to get hold of the Star, he found it firmly fixed to the cushion and spent some time in getting it loose. This rather spoilt the most impressive moment of the ceremony.[1]

It should be added that the individual held responsible for contributing an unmeant gesture may chiefly discredit his own performance by this, a teammate's performance, or the performance being staged by his audience.

When an outsider accidentally enters a region in which a performance is being given, or when a member of the audience inadvertently enters the backstage, the intruder is likely to catch those present *flagrante delicto*. Through no one's intention, the persons present in the region may find that they have patently been witnessed in activity that is quite incompatible with the impression that they are, for wider social reasons, under obligation to maintain to the intruder. We deal here with what are sometimes called "inopportune intrusions."

The past life and current round of activity of a given performer typically contain at least a few facts which, if introduced during the performance, would discredit or at least weaken the claims about self that the performer was attempting to project as part of the definition of the situation. These facts may involve well-kept dark secrets or negatively valued characteristics that everyone can see but no one refers to. When such facts are introduced, embarrassment is the usual result. These facts can, of course, be brought to one's attention by unmeant gestures or inopportune intrusions. However, they are more frequently introduced by intentional verbal statements or non-verbal acts whose full significance is not appreciated by the individual who contributes them to the interaction. Following common usage, such disruptions of projections may be called "faux pas." Where a performer unthinkingly makes an intentional contribution which destroys his own team's image we may speak of "gaffes" or "boners." Where a performer jeopardizes the image of self projected by the other team, we may speak of "bricks" or of the performer having "put his foot in it." Etiquette manuals provide classic warnings against such indiscretions:

If there is any one in the company whom you do not know, be careful how you let off any epigrams or pleasant little sarcasms. You might be very witty upon halters to a man whose father had been hanged. The first requisite for successful conversation is to know your company well.[2]

In meeting a friend whom you have not seen for some time, and of the state and history of whose family you have not been recently or particularly informed, you should avoid making enquiries or allusions in respect to particular individuals of his family, until you have possessed yourself of knowledge respecting them. Some may be dead; others may have misbehaved, separated themselves, or fallen under some distressing calamity.[3]

Unmeant gestures, inopportune intrusions, and faux pas are sources of embarrassment and dissonance, which are typically unintended by the person who is responsible for making them and which would be avoided were the individual to know in advance the consequences of his activity. However there are situations, often called "scenes," in which an individual acts in such a way as to destroy or seriously threaten the polite appearance of consensus, and while he may not act simply in order to create such dissonance, he acts with the knowledge that this kind of dissonance is likely to result. The common-sense phrase, "creating a scene," is apt because, in effect, a new scene is created by such disruptions. The previous and expected interplay between the teams is suddenly forced aside and a new drama forcibly takes its place. Significantly, this new scene often involves a sudden reshuffling and reapportioning of the previous team members into two new teams.

Some scenes occur when teammates can no longer countenance each other's inept performance and blurt out immediate public criticism of the very individuals with whom they ought to be in dramaturgical co-operation. Such misconduct is often devastating to the performance which the disputants ought to be presenting; one effect of the quarrel is to provide the audience with a backstage view, and another is to leave them with the feeling that something is surely suspicious about a performance when those who know it best do not agree. Another type of scene occurs when the audience decides it can no longer play the game of polite interaction, or that it no longer wants to do so, and so confronts the performers with facts or expressive acts which each team knows will be unacceptable. This is what happens when an individual screws up his social courage and decides to "have it out" with another or "really tell him off." Criminal trials have institutionalized this kind of open discord, as has the last chapter of murder mysteries, where an individual who has theretofore maintained a convincing pose of innocence is confronted in the presence of others with undeniable expressive evidence that his pose is only a pose. Another kind of scene occurs when the interaction between two persons becomes so loud, heated, or otherwise attention-getting, that nearby persons engaged in their own conversational interaction are forced to become witnesses or even to take sides and enter the fray. A final type of scene may be suggested. When a person acting as a one-man team commits himself in a serious way to a claim or request and leaves himself no way out should this be denied by the audience, he usually makes sure that his claim or request is the kind that is likely to be approved and granted by the audience. If his motivation is strong enough, however, an individual may find himself making a claim or an assumption which he knows the audience may well reject. He knowingly lowers his defenses in their presence, throwing himself, as we say, on their mercy. By such an act the individual makes a plea to the audience to treat themselves as part of his team or to allow him to treat himself as part of their team. This sort of thing is embarrassing enough, but when the unguarded request is refused to the individual's face, he suffers what is called humiliation.

I have considered some major forms of performance disruption—unmeant gestures, inopportune intrusions, faux pas, and scenes. These disruptions, in everyday terms, are often called "incidents." When an incident occurs, the reality sponsored by the performers is threatened. The persons present are likely to react by becoming flustered, ill at ease, embarrassed, nervous, and the like. Quite literally, the participants may find themselves out of countenance. When these flusterings or symptoms of embarrassment become perceived, the reality that is supported by the performance is likely to be further jeopardized and weakened, for these signs of nervousness in most cases are an aspect of the individual who presents a character and not an aspect of the character he projects, thus forcing upon the audience an image of the man behind the mask.

In order to prevent the occurrence of incidents and the embarrassment consequent upon them, it will be necessary for all the participants in the inter- action, as well as those who do not participate, to possess certain attributes and to express these attributes in practices employed for saving the show. These attributes and practices will be reviewed under three headings: the defensive measures used by performers to save their own show; the protective measures used by audience and outsiders to assist the performers in saving the perform- ers' show; and, finally, the measures the performers must take in order to make it possible for the audience and outsiders to employ protective measures on the performers' behalf.

Defensive Attributes and Practices

1. *Dramaturgical Loyalty.* It is apparent that if a team is to sustain the line it has taken, the teammates must act as if they have accepted certain moral obligations. They must not betray the secrets of the team when between performances— whether from self-interest, principle, or lack of discretion. Thus, older members of a family must often exclude a child of the house from their gossip and self- admissions, since one can never be sure to whom one's child will convey one's secrets. Hence it may only be when the child arrives at the age of discretion that the voices of his parents will cease to drop as he enters the room. Eighteenth- century writers on the servant problem cite a similar issue of disloyalty, but here in connection with persons who were old enough to know better:

This lack of devotion [of servants to masters] gave rise to a multitude of petty annoy- ances from which few employers were entirely immune. Not the least harassing of these was the propensity of servants to retail their masters' business. Defoe takes notice of this, admonishing female domestics to "Add to your other Virtues PIETY, which will teach you the Prudence of *Keeping Family-Secrets*; the Want of which is a great Complaint. . . ."[4]

Voices are dropped at the approach of servants too, but in the early eighteenth century another practice was introduced as a means of keeping team secrets from, servants:

The dumb-waiter was a tier table, which, prior to the dinner hour, was stocked with food, drink, and eating utensils by the servants, who then withdrew, leaving the guests to serve themselves.[5]

Upon the introduction of this dramaturgical device in England, Mary Hamilton reported:

"My cousin Charles Cathcart din'd with us at Lady Stormont's; we had dumb-waiters so our conversation was not under any restraint by ye Servants being in ye room."[6]

"At dinner we had ye comfortable *dumb-waiters*, so our conversation was not obliged to be disagreeably *guarded* by ye attendance of Servants."[7]

So, too, members of the team must not exploit their presence in the front region in order to stage their own show, as do, for example, marriageable stenographers who sometimes encumber their office surroundings with a lush undergrowth of high fashion. Nor must they use their performance time as an occasion to denounce their team. They must be willing to accept minor parts with good grace and perform enthusiastically whenever, wherever, and for whomsoever the team as a whole chooses. And they must be taken in by their own performance to the degree that is necessary to prevent them from sounding hollow and false to the audience.

Perhaps the key problem in maintaining the loyalty of team members (and apparently with members of other types of collectivities, too) is to prevent the performers from becoming so sympathetically attached to the audience that the performers disclose to them the consequences for them of the impression they are being given, or in other ways make the team as a whole pay for this attachment. In small communities in Britain, for example, the managers of stores will often be loyal to the establishment and will define the product being sold to a customer in glowing terms linked with false advice, but clerks can frequently be found who not only appear to take the role of the customer in giving buying-advice but actually do so. In Shetland Isle, for example, I heard a clerk say to a customer as the clerk was handing over a bottle of cherry pop: "I do not see how you can drink that stuff." No one present considered this to be surprising frankness, and similar comments could be heard every day in the shops on the island. So, too, filling station managers sometimes disapprove of tipping because it may lead attendants to give undue free service to the chosen few while other customers are left waiting.

One basic technique the team can employ to defend itself against such disloyalty is to develop high in-group solidarity within the team, while creating a backstage image of the audience which makes the audience sufficiently inhuman to allow the performers to cozen them with emotional and moral immunity. To the degree that teammates and their colleagues form a complete social community, which offers each performer a place and a source of moral support regardless of whether or not he is successful in maintaining his front before the audience, to that degree it would seem that performers can protect themselves from doubt and guilt and practice any kind of deception. Perhaps we are to understand the heartless artistry of the Thugs by reference to the religious beliefs and ritual practices into which their depredations were integrated, and perhaps we are to understand the successful callousness of con men by reference to their social solidarity in what they call the "illegit" world and their well-formulated denigrations of the legitimate world. Perhaps this notion allows us to understand in part why groups that are alienated from or not yet incorporated into the community are so able to enter the dirty-work trades and the kind of service occupations which involve routine cheating.

A second technique for counteracting the danger of affective ties between performers and audience is to change audiences periodically. Thus filling station managers used to be shifted periodically from one station to another to prevent the formation of strong personal ties with particular clients. It was found that when such ties were allowed to form, the manager sometimes placed the interests of a friend who needed credit before the interests of the social establishment.[8] Bank managers and ministers have been routinely shifted for similar reasons, as have certain colonial administrators. Some female professionals provide another illustration, as the following reference to organized prostitution suggests:

The Syndicate handles that these days. The girls don't stay in one place long enough to really get on speaking terms with anybody. There's not so much chance of a girl falling in love with some guy—you know, and causing a squawk. Anyway, the hustler who's in Chicago this week is in St. Louis next, or moving around to half a dozen places in town before being sent somewhere else. And they never know where they're going until they're told.[9]

2. *Dramaturgical Discipline.* It is crucial for the maintenance of the team's performance that each member of the team possess dramaturgical discipline and exercise it in presenting his own part. I refer to the fact that while the performer is ostensibly immersed and given over to the activity he is performing, and is apparently engrossed in his actions in a spontaneous, uncalculating way, he must nonetheless be affectively dissociated from his presentation in a way that leaves him free to cope with dramaturgical contingencies as they arise. He must offer a show of intellectual and emotional involvement in the activity he is presenting, but must keep himself from actually being carried away by his own show lest this destroy his involvement in the task of putting on a successful performance.

A performer who is disciplined, dramaturgically speaking, is someone who remembers his part and does not commit unmeant gestures or faux pas in performing it. He is someone with discretion; he does not give the show away by involuntarily disclosing its secrets. He is someone with "presence of mind" who can cover up on the spur of the moment for inappropriate behavior on the part of his teammates, while all the time maintaining the impression that he is merely playing his part. And if a disruption of the performance cannot be avoided or concealed, the disciplined performer will be prepared to offer a plausible reason for discounting the disruptive event, a joking manner to remove its importance, or deep apology and self-abasement to reinstate those held responsible for it. The disciplined performer is also someone with "self-control." He can suppress his emotional response to his private problems, to his team-mates when they make mistakes, and to the audience when they induce unto-ward affection or hostility in him. And he can stop himself from laughing about matters which are defined as serious and stop himself from taking seriously mat-ters defined as humorous. In other words, he can suppress his spontaneous feelings in order to give the appearance of sticking to the affective line, the expressive *status quo*, established by his team's performance, for a display of proscribed affect may not only lead to improper disclosures and offense to the working consensus but may also implicitly extend to the audience the status of team member. And the disciplined performer is someone with sufficient poise to move from private places of informality to public ones of varying degrees of formality, without allowing such changes to confuse him.[10]

Perhaps the focus of dramaturgical discipline is to be found in the manage-ment of one's face and voice. Here is the crucial test of one's ability as a performer. Actual affective response must be concealed and an appropriate affective response must be displayed. Teasing, it often seems, is an informal initiation device employed by a team to train and test the capacity of its new members to "take a joke," that is, to sustain a friendly manner while perhaps not feeling it. When an individual passes such a test of expression-control, whether he receives it from his new teammates in a spirit of jest or from an unexpected necessity of playing in a serious performance, he can thereafter venture forth as a player who can trust himself and be trusted by others. A very nice illustration of this is given in a forthcoming paper by Howard S. Becker on marijuana-smoking. Becker reports that the irregular user of the drug has a great fear of finding himself, while under the influence of the drug, in the immediate presence of parents or work associates who will expect an intimate undrugged performance from him. Apparently the irregular user does not become a confirmed regular user until he learns he can be "high" and yet carry off a performance before non-smokers without betraying himself. The same issue arises, perhaps in a less dramatic form, in ordinary family life, when a decision has to be reached as to the point in their training at which young members of the team can be taken to public and semipublic ceremonies, for only when the child is ready to keep control of his temper will he be a trust-worthy participant on such occasions.

3. *Dramaturgical Circumspection.* Loyalty and discipline, in the dramaturgical sense of these terms, are attributes required of teammates if the show they put on is to be sustained. In addition, it will be useful if the members of the team exercise foresight and design in determining in advance how best to stage

a show. Prudence must be exercised. When there is little chance of being seen, opportunities for relaxation can be taken; when there is little chance of being put to a test, the cold facts can be presented in a glowing light and the performers can play their part for all it is worth, investing it with full dignity. If no care and honesty are exercised, then disruptions are likely to occur; if rigid care and honesty are exercised, then the performers are not likely to be understood "only too well" but they may be misunderstood, insufficiently understood, or greatly limited in what they can build out of the dramaturgical opportunities open to them. In other words, in the interests of the team, performers will be required to exercise prudence and circumspection in staging the show, preparing in advance for likely contingencies and exploiting the opportunities that remain. The exercise or expression of dramaturgical circumspection takes well-known forms; some of these techniques for managing impressions will be considered here.

Obviously, one such technique is for the team to choose members who are loyal and disciplined, and a second one is for the team to acquire a clear idea as to how much loyalty and discipline it can rely on from the membership as a whole, for the degree to which these attributes are possessed will markedly affect the likelihood of carrying off a performance and hence the safety of investing the performance with seriousness, weight, and dignity.

The circumspect performer will also attempt to select the kind of audience that will give a minimum of trouble in terms of the show the performer wants to put on and the show he does not want to have to put on. Thus it is reported that teachers often favor neither lower-class pupils nor upper-class ones, because both groups may make it difficult to maintain in the classroom the kind of definition of the situation which affirms the professional teacher role.[11] Teachers will transfer to middle-class schools for these dramaturgical reasons. So, too, it is reported that some nurses like to work in an operating room rather than on a ward because in the operating room measures are taken to ensure that the audience, whose members number only one, is soon oblivious to the weaknesses of the show, permitting the operating team to relax and devote itself to the technological requirements of actions as opposed to the dramaturgical ones.[12] Once the audience is asleep it is even possible to bring in a "ghost surgeon" to perform the tasks that others who were there will later claim to have done.[13] Similarly, given the fact that husband and wife are required to express marital solidarity by jointly showing regard for those whom they entertain, it is necessary to exclude from their guests those persons about whom they feel differently.[14] So also, if a man of influence and power is to make sure that he can take a friendly role in office interactions, then it will be useful for him to have a private elevator and protective circles of receptionists and secretaries so that no one can get in to see him whom he might have to treat in a heartless or snobbish fashion.

It will be apparent that an automatic way of ensuring that no member of the team or no member of the audience acts improperly is to limit the size of both teams as much as possible. Other things being equal, the fewer the members, the less possibility of mistakes, "difficulties," and treacheries. Thus salesmen like to sell to unaccompanied customers, since it is generally thought that two persons in the audience are much more difficult to "sell" than one. So, too, in some schools there is an informal rule that no teacher is to enter the room of another teacher while the other is holding a class; apparently the assumption is that it will be likely the new performer will do something that the waiting eyes of the student audience will see as inconsistent with the impression fostered by their own teacher.[15] However, there are at least two reasons why this device of limiting the number of persons present has limitations itself. First, some performances cannot be presented without the technical assistance of a sizable number of teammates. Thus, although an army general staff appreciates that the more officers there are who know the plans for the next phase of action, the more likelihood that someone will act in such a way as to disclose strategic secrets, the staff will still have to let enough men in on the secret to plan and arrange the event. Secondly, it appears that individuals, as pieces of expressive equipment, are more effective in some ways than non-human parts of the setting. If, then, an individual is to be given a place of great dramatic prominence, it may be necessary to employ a sizable court-following to achieve an effective impression of adulation around him.

I have suggested that by keeping close to the facts it may be possible for a performer to safeguard his show, but this may prevent him from staging a very elaborate one. If an elaborate show is to be safely staged it may be more useful to remove oneself from the facts rather than stick to them. It is feasible for an official of a religion to conduct a solemn, awesome presentation, because there is no recognized way by which these claims can be discredited. Similarly, the professional takes the stand that the service he performs is not to be judged by the results it achieves but by the degree to which available occupational skills have been proficiently applied; and, of course, the professional claims that only the colleague group can make a judgment of this kind. It is therefore possible for the professional to commit himself fully to his presentation, with all his weight and dignity, knowing that only a very foolish mistake will be capable of destroying the impression created. Thus the effort of tradesmen to obtain a professional mandate can be understood as an effort to gain control over the reality they present to their customers; and in turn we can see that such control makes it unnecessary to be prudently humble in the airs one assumes in performing one's trade.

There would appear to be a relation between the amount of modesty employed and the temporal length of a performance. If the audience is to see only a brief performance, then the likelihood of an embarrassing occurrence will be relatively small, and it will be relatively safe for the performer, especially in anonymous circumstances, to maintain a front that is rather false.[16] In American society there is what is called a "telephone voice," a cultivated form of speech not employed in face-to-face talk because of the danger in doing so. In Britain, in the kinds of contact between strangers that are guaranteed to be very brief—the kinds involving "please," "thank you," "excuse me," and "may I speak to"—one hears many more public-school accents than there are public-school people. So also, in Anglo-American society, the majority of domestic establishments do not possess sufficient staging equipment to maintain a show of polite hospitality for guests who stay more than a few hours; only in the upper-middle and upper classes do we find the institution of the weekend guest, for it is only here that performers feel they have enough sign-equipment to bring off a lengthy show. Thus, on Shetland Isle, some crofters felt they could sustain a middle-class show for the duration of a tea, in some cases a meal, and in one or two cases even a weekend; but many islanders felt it only safe to perform for middle-class audiences on the front porch, or, better still, in the community hall, where the efforts and responsibilities of the show could be shared by many teammates.

The performer who is to be dramaturgically prudent will have to adapt his performance to the information conditions under which it must be staged. Aging prostitutes in nineteenth-century London who restricted their place of work to dark parks in order that their faces would not weaken their audience appeal were practicing a strategy that was even older than their profession.[17] In addition to reckoning with what can be seen, the performer will also have to take into consideration the information the audience already possesses about him. The more information the audience has about the performer, the less likely it is that anything they learn during the interaction will radically influence them. On the other hand, where no prior information is possessed, it may be expected that the information gleaned during the interaction will be relatively crucial. Hence, on the whole, we may expect individuals to relax the strict maintenance of front when they are with those they have known for a long time, and to tighten their front when among persons who are new to them. With those whom one does not know, careful performances are required.

Another condition associated with communication may be cited. The circumspect performer will have to consider the audience's access to information sources external to the interaction. For example, members of the Thug tribe of India are said to have given the following performances during the early nineteenth century:

As a general rule they pretended to be merchants or soldiers, traveling without weapons in order to disarm suspicion, which gave them an excellent excuse for seeking permission to accompany travelers, for there was nothing to excite alarm in their appearance.

Most Thugs were mild looking and peculiarly courteous, for this camouflage formed part of their stock-in-trade, and well-armed travelers felt no fear in allowing these knights of the road to join them. This first step successfully accomplished, the Thugs gradually won the confidence of their intended victims by a demeanor of humility and gratitude, and feigned interest in their affairs until familiar with details of their homes, whether they were likely to be missed if murdered, and if they knew anyone in the vicinity. Sometimes they traveled long distances together before a suitable opportunity for treachery occurred; a case is on record where a gang journeyed with a family of eleven persons for twenty days, covering 200 miles, before they succeeded in murdering the whole party without detection.[18]

Thugs could give these performances in spite of the fact that their audiences were constantly on the watch for such performers (and quickly put to death those identified as Thugs) partly because of the informational conditions of travel; once a party set out for a distant destination, there was no way for them to check the identities claimed by those whom they encountered, and if anything befell the party on the way it would be months before they would be considered overdue, by which time the Thugs who had performed for and then upon them would be out of reach. But in their native villages, the members of the tribe, being known, fixed, and accountable for their sins, behaved in an exemplary fashion. Similarly, circumspect Americans who would ordinarily never chance a misrepresentation of their social status may take such a chance while staying for a short time at a summer resort.

If sources of information external to the interaction constitute one contingency the circumspect performer must take into consideration, sources of information internal to the interaction constitute another. Thus the circumspect performer will adjust his presentation according to the character of the props and tasks out of which he must build his performance. For example, clothing merchants in the United States are required to be relatively circumspect in making exaggerated claims, because customers can test by sight and touch what is shown to them; but furniture salesmen need not be so careful, because few members of the audience can judge what lies behind the front of varnish and veneer that is presented to them.[19] In Shetland Hotel, the staff had great freedom in regard to what was put in soups and puddings, because soups and puddings tend to conceal what is contained in them. Soups, especially, were easy to stage; they tended to be additive—the remains of one, plus everything lying around, served as the beginnings of another. With meats, the true character of which could be more easily seen, less leeway was possible; in fact, here the standards of the staff were stiffer than those of mainland guests, since what smelt "high" to natives could smell "well hung" to outsiders. So, also, there is a tradition on the island which allows aging crofters to retire from the arduous duties of adult life by feigning illness, there being little conception otherwise of a person becoming too old to work. Island doctors—although the current one was not co-operative in this regard—are supposed to recognize the fact that no one can be sure whether or not illness lies hidden within the human body, and are expected tactfully to restrict their unequivocal diagnoses to externally visible complaints. Similarly, if a housewife is concerned with showing that she maintains cleanliness standards, she is likely to focus her attention upon the glass surfaces in her living room, for glass shows dirt all too clearly; she will give less attention to the darker and less revealing rug, which may well have been chosen in the belief that "dark colors do not show the dirt." So, too, an artist need take little care with the décor of his studio—in fact, the artist's studio has become stereotyped as a place where those who work backstage do not care who sees them or the conditions in which they are seen—partly because the full value of the artist's product can, or ought to be, immediately available to the senses; portrait painters, on the other hand, must promise to make the sittings satisfactory and tend to use relatively prepossessing, rich-looking studios as a kind of guarantee for the promises they make. Similarly, we find that confidence men must employ elaborate and meticulous personal fronts and often engineer meticulous social settings, not so much because they lie for a living but because, in order to get away with a lie of that dimension, one must deal with persons who have been and are going to be strangers, and one has to terminate the dealings as quickly as possible. Legitimate businessmen who would promote an honest venture under these circumstances would have to be just as meticulous in expressing themselves, for it is under just such circumstances that potential investors scrutinize the character of those who would sell to them. In short, since a con merchant must swindle his clients under those circumstances where clients appreciate that a confidence game could be employed, the con man must carefully forestall the immediate impression that he might be what in fact he is, just as the legitimate merchant, under the same circumstances, would have to forestall carefully the immediate impression that he might be what he is not.

It is apparent that care will be great in situations where important consequences for the performer will occur as a result of his conduct. The job interview is a clear example. Often the interviewer will have to make decisions of far-reaching importance for the interviewee on the sole basis of information gained from the applicant's interview-performance. The interviewee is likely to feel, and with some justice, that his every action will be taken as highly symbolical, and he will therefore give much preparation and thought to his performance. We expect at such times that the interviewee will pay much attention to his appearance and manner, not merely to create a favorable impression, but also to be on the safe side and forestall any unfavorable impression that might be unwittingly conveyed. Another example may be suggested: those who work in the field of radio broadcasting and, especially, television keenly appreciate that the momentary impression they give will have an effect on the view a massive audience takes of them, and it is in this part of the communication industry that great care is taken to give the right impression and great anxiety is felt that the impression given might not be right. The strength of this concern is seen in the indignities that high-placed performers are willing to suffer in order to come off well: congressmen allow themselves to be made up and to be told what to wear; professional boxers abase themselves by giving a display, in the manner of wrestlers, instead of a bout.[20]

Circumspection on the part of performers will also be expressed in the way they handle relaxation of appearances. When a team is physically distant from its inspectorial audience and a surprise visit is unlikely, then great relaxation becomes feasible. Thus we read that small American Navy installations on Pacific islands during the last war could be run quite informally, whereas a readjustment in the direction of spit and polish was required when the outfit moved to places that members of the audience were more likely to frequent.[21] When inspectors have easy access to the place where a team carries on its work, then the amount of relaxation possible for the team will depend on the efficiency and reliability of its warning system. It is to be noted that thorough-going relaxation requires not only a warning system but also an appreciable time lapse between warning and visit, for the team will be able to relax only to the degree that can be corrected during such a time lapse. Thus, when a school-teacher leaves her classroom for a moment, her charges can relax into slovenly postures and whispered conversations, for these transgressions can be corrected in the few seconds' warning the pupils will have that the teacher is about to re-enter; but it is unlikely that it will be feasible for the pupils to sneak a smoke, for the smell of smoke cannot be got rid of quickly. Interestingly enough, pupils, like other performers, will "test the limits," gleefully moving far enough away from their seats so that when the warning comes they will have to dash madly back to their proper places so as not to be caught off base. Here, of course, the character of the terrain can become important. In Shetland Isle, for example, there were no trees to block one's view and little concentration of dwelling units. Neighbors had a right to drop in upon each other whenever happening to be close by, but it was usually possible to see them coming for a good few minutes before actual arrival. Ever-present croft dogs would usually accentuate this visible warning by, as it were, barking the visitor in. Extensive relaxation was therefore possible because there were always minutes of grace to put the scene in order. Of course, with such a warning, knocking on the door no longer served one of its main functions, and fellow crofters did not extend this courtesy to one another, although some made a practice of scraping their feet a little in entering as an extra, final warning. Apartment hotels, the front door of which opens only when a resident presses a button from the inside, provide a similar guarantee of ample warning and allow a similar depth of relaxation.

I would like to mention one more way in which dramaturgical circumspection is exercised. When teams come into each other's immediate presence, a host of minor events may occur that are accidentally suitable for conveying a general impression that is inconsistent with the fostered one. This expressive treacherousness is a basic characteristic of face-to-face interaction. One way of dealing with this problem is, as previously suggested, to select teammates who are disciplined and will not perform their parts in a clumsy, gauche, or self-conscious fashion. Another method is to prepare in advance for all possible expressive contingencies. One application of this strategy is to settle on a complete agenda before the event, designating who is to do what and who is to do what after that. In this way confusions and lulls can be avoided and hence the impressions that such hitches in the proceedings might convey to the audience can be avoided too. (There is of course a danger here. A completely scripted performance, as found in a staged play, is very effective providing no untoward event breaks the planned sequence of statements and acts; for once this sequence is disrupted, the performers may not be able to find their way back to the cue that will enable them to pick up where the planned sequence had been disrupted. Scripted performers, then, can get themselves into a worse position than is possible for those who perform a less organized show.) Another application of this programming technique is to accept the fact that picayune events (such as who is to enter a room first or who is to sit next to the hostess, etc.) will be taken as expressions of regard and to apportion these favors consciously on the basis of principles of judgment to which no one present will take offense, such as age, gross seniority in rank, sex, temporary ceremonial status, etc. Thus in an important sense protocol is not so much a device for expressing valuations during interaction as a device for "grounding" potentially disruptive expressions in a way that will be acceptable (and uneventful) to all present. A third application is to rehearse the whole routine so that the performers can become practiced in their parts and so that contingencies that were not predicted will occur under circumstances in which they can be safely attended to. A fourth is to outline beforehand for the audience the line of response they are to take to the performance. When this kind of briefing occurs, of course, it becomes difficult to distinguish between performers and audience. This type of collusion is especially found where the performer is of highly sacred status and cannot trust himself to the spontaneous tact of the audience. For example, in Britain, women who are to be presented at court (whom we may think of as an audience for the royal performers) are carefully schooled beforehand as to what to wear, what kind of limousine to arrive in, how to curtsy, and what to say.

Protective Practices

I have suggested three attributes that team members must have if their team is to perform in safety: loyalty, discipline, and circumspection. Each of these capacities is expressed in many standard defensive techniques through which a set of performers can save their own show. Some of these techniques of impression management were reviewed. Others, such as the practice of controlling access to back regions and front regions, were discussed in earlier chapters. In this section I want to stress the fact that most of these defensive techniques of impression management have a counterpart in the tactful tendency of the audience and outsiders to act in a protective way in order to help the performers save their own show. Since the dependence of the performers on the tact of the audience and outsiders tends to be underestimated, I shall bring together here some of the several protective techniques that are commonly employed although, analytically speaking, each protective practice might better be considered in conjunction with the corresponding defensive practice.

First, it should be understood that access to the back and front regions of a performance is controlled not only by the performers but by others. Individuals voluntarily stay away from regions into which they have not been invited. (This kind of tact in regard to place is analogous to "discretion," which has already been described as tact in regard to facts.) And when outsiders find they are about to enter such a region, they often give those already present some warning, in the form of a message, or a knock, or a cough, so that the intrusion can be put off if necessary or the setting hurriedly put in order and proper expressions fixed on the faces of those present.[22] This kind of tact can become nicely elaborated. Thus, in presenting oneself to a stranger by means of a letter of introduction, it is thought proper to convey the letter to the addressee before actually coming into his immediate presence; the addressee then has time to decide what kind of greeting the individual is to receive, and time to assemble the expressive manner appropriate to such a greeting.[23]

We often find that when interaction must proceed in the presence of outsiders, outsiders tactfully act in an uninterested, uninvolved, unperceiving fashion, so that if physical isolation is not obtained by walls or distance, effective isolation can at least be obtained by convention. Thus when two sets of persons find themselves in neighboring booths in a restaurant, it is expected that neither group will avail itself of the opportunities that actually exist for overhearing the other.

Etiquette regarding tactful inattention, and the effective privacy it provides, varies, of course, from one society and subculture to another. In middle-class Anglo-American society, when in a public place, one is supposed to keep one's nose out of other people's activity and go about one's own business. It is only when a woman drops a package, or when a fellow motorist gets stalled in the middle of the road, or when a baby left alone in a carriage begins to scream, that middle-class people feel it is all right to break down momentarily the walls which effectively insulate them. In Shetland Isle different rules obtained. If any man happened to find himself in the presence of others who were engaged in a task, it was expected that he would lend a hand, especially if the task was relatively brief and relatively strenuous. Such casual mutual aid was taken as a matter of course and was an expression of nothing closer than fellow-islander status.

Once the audience has been admitted to a performance, the necessity of being tactful does not cease. We find that there is an elaborate etiquette by which individuals guide themselves in their capacity as members of the audience. This involves: the giving of a proper amount of attention and interest; a willingness to hold in check one's own performance so as not to introduce too many contradictions, interruptions, or demands for attention; the inhibition of all acts or statements that might create a faux pas; the desire, above all else, to avoid a scene. Audience tact is so general a thing that we may expect to find it exercised even by individuals, famous for their misbehavior, who are patients in mental hospitals. Thus one research group reports:

At another time, the staff, without consulting the patients, decided to give them a Valentine party. Many of the patients did not wish to go, but did so anyway as they felt that they should not hurt the feelings of the student nurses who had organized the party. The games introduced by the nurses were on a very childish level; many of the patients felt silly playing them and were glad when the party was over and they could go back to activities of their own choosing.[24]

In another mental hospital it was observed that when ethnic organizations gave hostess dances for patients in the hospital Red Cross house, providing thereby some charity work-experience for a few of their less-favored daughters, the hospital representative would sometimes prevail on a few of the male patients to dance with these girls in order that the impression might be sustained that the visitors were bestowing their company on persons more needful than themselves.[25]

When performers make a slip of some kind, clearly exhibiting a discrepancy between the fostered impression and a disclosed reality, the audience may tactfully "not see" the slip or readily accept the excuse that is offered for it. And at moments of crisis for the performers, the whole audience may come into tacit collusion with them in order to help them out. Thus we learn that in mental hospitals when a patient dies in a manner that reflects upon the impression of useful treatment that the staff is attempting to maintain, the other patients, ordinarily disposed to give the staff trouble, may tactfully ease up their warfare and with much delicacy help sustain the quite false impression that they have not absorbed the meaning of what has happened.[26] Similarly, at times of inspection, whether in school, in barracks, in the hospital, or at home, the audience is likely to behave itself in a model way so that the performers who are being inspected may put on an exemplary show. At such times, team lines are apt to shift slightly and momentarily so that the inspecting superintendent, general, director, or guest will be faced by performers and audience who are in collusion.

A final instance of tact in handling the performer may be cited. When the performer is known to be a beginner, and more subject than otherwise to embarrassing mistakes, the audience frequently shows extra consideration, refraining from causing the difficulties it might otherwise create.

Audiences are motivated to act tactfully because of an immediate identification with the performers, or because of a desire to avoid a scene, or to ingratiate themselves with the performers for purposes of exploitation. Perhaps this latter is the favorite explanation. Some successful women of the street, it seems, are ones who are willing to enact a lively approval of their clients' performance, thus demonstrating the sad dramaturgical fact that sweethearts and wives are not the only members of their sex who must engage in the higher forms of prostitution:

Mary Lee says she does no more for Mr. Blakesee than she does for her other rich customers.

"I do what I know they want, make believe I'm ga-ga over them. Sometimes they act like little boys playing games. Mr. Blakesee always does. He plays the cave man. He comes to my apartment and sweeps me in his arms and holds me till he thinks he's taken my breath away. It's a howl. After he's finished making love to me, I have to tell him, 'Darling, you made me so happy I could just cry.' You wouldn't believe a grown-up man would want to play such games. But he does. Not only him. Most of the rich ones."

Mary Lee is so convinced that her prime stock in trade with her wealthy customers is her ability to act spontaneously that she recently submitted to an operation for prevention of pregnancy. She considered it an investment in her career.[27]

But here again the framework of analysis employed in this report becomes constrictive: for these tactful actions on the part of the audience can become more elaborate than is the performance for which they are a response.

I would like to add a concluding fact about tact. Whenever the audience exercises tact, the possibility will arise that the performers will learn that they are being tactfully protected. When this occurs, the further possibility arises that the audience will learn that the performers know they are being tactfully protected. And then, in turn, it becomes possible for the performers to learn that the audience knows that the performers know they are being protected. Now when such states of information exist, a moment in the performance may come when the separateness of the teams will break down and be momentarily replaced by a communion of glances through which each team openly admits to the other its state of information. At such moments the whole dramaturgical structure of social interaction is suddenly and poignantly laid bare, and the line separating the teams momentarily disappears. Whether this close view of things brings shame or laughter, the teams are likely to draw rapidly back into their appointed characters.

Tact Regarding Tact

It has been argued that the audience contributes in a significant way to the maintenance of a show by exercising tact or protective practices on behalf of the performers. It is apparent that if the audience is to employ tact on the performer's behalf, the performer must act in such a way as to make the rendering of this assistance possible. This will require discipline and circumspection, but of a special order. For example, it was suggested that tactful outsiders in a physical position to overhear an interaction may offer a show of inattention. In order to assist in this tactful withdrawal, the participants who feel it is physically possible for them to be overheard may omit from their conversation and activity anything that would tax this tactful resolve of the outsiders, and at the same time include enough semi-confidential facts to show that they do not distrust the show of withdrawal presented by the outsiders. Similarly, if a secretary is to tell a visitor tactfully that the man he wishes to see is out, it will be wise for the visitor to step back from the interoffice telephone so that he cannot hear what the secretary is being told by the man who is presumably not there to tell her.

I would like to conclude by mentioning two general strategies regarding tact with respect to tact. First, the performer must be sensitive to hints and ready to take them, for it is through hints that the audience can warn the performer that his show is unacceptable and that he had better modify it quickly if the situation is to be saved. Second, if the performer is to misrepresent the facts in any way, he must do so in accordance with the etiquette for misrepresentation; he must not leave himself in a position from which even the lamest excuse and the most co-operative audience cannot extricate him. In telling an untruth, the performer is enjoined to retain a shadow of jest in his voice so that, should he be caught out, he can disavow any claim to seriousness and say that he was only joking. In misrepresenting his physical appearance, the performer is enjoined to use a method which allows of an innocent excuse. Thus balding men who affect a hat indoors and out are more or less excused, since it is possible that they have a cold, that they merely forgot to take their hat off, or that rain can fall in unexpected places; a toupee, however, offers the wearer no excuse and the audience no excuse for excuse. In fact there is a sense in which the category of impostor, previously referred to, can be defined as a person who makes it impossible for his audience to be tactful about observed misrepresentation.

In spite of the fact that performers and audience employ all of these techniques of impression management, and many others as well, we know, of course, that incidents do occur and that audiences are inadvertently given glimpses behind the scenes of a performance. When such an incident occurs, the members of an audience sometimes learn an important lesson, more important to them than the aggressive pleasure they can obtain by discovering someone's dark, entrusted, inside, or strategic secrets. The members of the audience may discover a fundamental democracy that is usually well hidden. Whether the character that is being presented is sober or carefree, of high station or low, the individual who performs the character will be seen for what he largely is, a solitary player involved in a harried concern for his production. Behind many masks and many characters, each performer tends to wear a single look, a naked unsocialized look, a look of concentration, a look of one who is privately engaged in a difficult, treacherous task. De Beauvoir, in her book on women, provides an illustration:

And in spite of all her prudence, accidents will happen: wine is spilled on her dress, a cigarette burns it; this marks the disappearance of the luxurious and festive creature who bore herself with smiling pride in the ballroom, for she now assumes the serious and severe look of the housekeeper; it becomes all at once evident that her toilette was not a set piece like fireworks, a transient burst of splendor, intended for the lavish illumination of a moment. It is rather a rich possession, capital goods, an investment; it has meant sacrifice; its loss is a real disaster. Spots, rents, botched dressmaking, bad hairdo's are catastrophes still more serious than a burnt roast or a broken vase; for not only does the woman of fashion project herself into things, she has chosen to make herself a thing, and she feels directly threatened in the world. Her relations with dressmaker and milliner, her fidgeting, her strict demands—all these manifest her serious attitude and her sense of insecurity.[28]

Knowing that his audiences are capable of forming bad impressions of him, the individual may come to feel ashamed of a well-intentioned honest act merely because the context of its performance provides false impressions that are bad. Feeling this unwarranted shame, he may feel that his feelings can be seen; feeling that he is thus seen, he may feel that his appearance confirms these false conclusions concerning him. He may then add to the precariousness of his position by engaging in just those defensive maneuvers that he would employ were he really guilty. In this way it is possible for all of us to become fleetingly for ourselves the worst person we can imagine that others might imagine us to be.

And to the degree that the individual maintains a show before others that he himself does not believe, he can come to experience a special kind of alienation from self and a special kind of wariness of others. As one American college girl has said:

I sometimes "play dumb" on dates, but it leaves a bad taste. The emotions are complicated. Part of me enjoys "putting something over" on the unsuspecting male. But this sense of superiority over him is mixed with feelings of guilt for my hypocrisy. Toward the "date" I feel some contempt because he is "taken in" by my technique, or if I like the boy, a kind of maternal condescension. At times I resent him! Why isn't he my superior in all ways in which a man should excel so that I could be my natural self? What am I doing here with him, anyhow? Slumming?

And the funny part of it is that the man, I think, is not always so unsuspecting. He may sense the truth and become uneasy in the relation. "Where do I stand? Is she laughing up her sleeve or did she mean this praise? Was she really impressed with that little speech of mine or did she only pretend to know nothing about politics?" And once or twice I felt that the joke was on me; the boy saw through my wiles and felt contempt for me for stooping to such tricks.[29]

Shared staging problems; concern for the way things appear; warranted and unwarranted feelings of shame; ambivalence about oneself and one's audience: these are some of the dramaturgic elements of the human situation.

Notes

1. Sir Frederick Ponsonby, *Recollections of Three Reigns* (New York: Dutton, 1952), p. 351.
2. *The Laws of Etiquette* (Philadelphia: Carey, Lee and Blanchard, 1836), p. 101.
3. *The Canons of Good Breeding*, p. 80.
4. J.J. Hecht, *The Domestic Servant Class in Eighteenth-Century England* (London: Routledge, Kegan Paul, 1956).
5. Hecht, *op. cit.*, p. 208.
6. *Ibid.*, p. 208.
7. *Ibid.*, p. 208.
8. Of course this betrayal is systematically faked in some commercial establishments where the customer is given a "special" cut price by a clerk who claims to be doing this in order to secure the buyer as a steady personal customer.
9. Charles Hamilton, *Men of the Underworld* (New York: Macmillan, 1952), p. 222.
10. Charles Hunt Page, "Bureaucracy's Other Face," *Social Forces*, XXV, pp. 91–2.
11. Howard S. Becker, "Social Class Variations in the Teacher-Pupil Relationship," *Journal of Educational Sociology*, XXV, pp. 461–2.
12. Unpublished research report by Edith Lentz. It may be noted that the policy sometimes followed of piping music by earphones to the patient who is undergoing an operation without a general anesthetic is a means of effectively removing him from the talk of the operating team.
13. David Solomon, "Career Contingencies of Chicago Physicians" (unpublished Ph.D. dissertation, Department of Sociology, University of Chicago, 1952), p. 108.
14. This point has been developed in a short story by Mary McCarthy, "A Friend of the Family," reprinted in Mary McCarthy, *Cast a Cold Eye* (New York: Harcourt Brace, 1950).
15. Howard S. Becker, "The Teacher in the Authority System of the Public School", *Journal of Educational Sociology*, XXVII, p. 139.
16. In brief anonymous service relations, servers become skilled at detecting what they see as affectation. However, since their own position is made clear by their service role they cannot easily return affectation with affectation. At the same time, customers who are what they claim to be often sense that the server may not appreciate this. The

customer may then feel ashamed because he feels as he would feel were he as false as he appears to be.

17. Henry Mayhew, *London Labour and the London Poor* (4 vols.; London: Griffin, Bohn), IV (1862), p. 90.

18. Col. J.L. Sleeman, *Thugs or a Million Murders* (London: Sampson Low, n.d.), pp. 25–6.

19. Louise Conant, "The Borax House," *The American Mercury*, XVII, p. 169, makes this point.

20. See John Lardner's weekly column in *Newsweek*, February 22, 1954, p. 59.

21. Page, *op. cit.*, p. 92.

22. Maids are often trained to enter a room without knocking, or to knock and go right in, presumably on the theory that they are non-persons before whom any pretense or inter-action readiness on the part of those in the room need not be maintained. Friendly housewives will enter each other's kitchens with similar license, as an expression of having nothing to hide from each other.

23. *Esquire Ettiquette* (Philadelphia: Lippincott, 1953), p. 73.

24. William Caudill, Frederick C. Redlich, Helen R. Gilmore and Eugene B. Brody, "Social Structure and Interaction Processes on a Psychiatric Ward," *American Journal of Ortho-psychiatry*, XXII, pp. 321–22.

25. Writer's study, 1953–54.

26. Harold Taxel, "Authority Structure in a Mental Hospital Ward" (unpublished Master's thesis, Department of Sociology, University of Chicago, 1953), p. 118. When two teams know an embarrassing fact, and each team knows the other team knows it, and yet nei-ther team openly admits its knowledge, we get an instance of what Robert Dubin has called "organizational fictions." See Robert Dubin, ed., *Human Relations in Administration* (New York: Prentice-Hall, 1951), pp. 341–5.

27. J.M. Murtagh and Sara Harris, *Cast the First Stone* (New York: Pocket Books, Cardinal Edition, 1958), p. 165.

28. Simone de Beauvoir, *The Second Sex*, trans. H.M. Parshley (New York: Knopf, 1953), p. 536.

29. Mirra Komarovsky, "Cultural Contradictions and Sex Roles," *American Journal of Sociology*, LII, p. 188.

4 An Integrative Theory of Intergroup Conflict

Henri Tajfel and John Turner

Social Categorization and Intergroup Discrimination

The initial stimulus for the theorizing presented here was provided by certain experimental investigations of intergroup behavior. The laboratory analog of real-world ethnocentrism is in-group bias—that is, the tendency to favor the in-group over the out-group in evaluations and behavior. Not only are incompatible group interests not always sufficient to generate conflicts but there is a good deal of experimental evidence that these conditions are not always *necessary* for the development of competition and discrimination between groups (for example, Ferguson & Kelley, 1964; Rabbie & Wilkens, 1971; Doise & Sinclair, 1973; Doise & Weinberger, 1973). This does not mean, of course, that in-group bias is not influenced by the goal relations between the groups (see Harvey, 1956).

All this evidence implies that in-group bias is a remarkably omnipresent feature of intergroup relations. The phenomenon in its extreme form has been investigated by Tajfel and his associates. There have been a number of studies (Tajfel et al., 1971; Billig & Tajfel, 1973; Tajfel & Billig, 1974; Doise, Csepeli, Dann, Gouge, Larsen, & Ostell, 1972; Turner, 1975), all showing that the mere perception of belonging to two distinct groups—that is, social categorization per se—is sufficient to trigger intergroup discrimination favoring the in-group. In other words, the mere awareness of the presence of an out-group is sufficient to provoke intergroup competitive or discriminatory responses on the part of the in-group.

In the initial experimental paradigm (Tajfel, 1970; Tajfel et al., 1971), the subjects (both children and adults have acted as subjects in the various studies) are randomly classified as members of two nonoverlapping groups—ostensibly on the basis of some trivial performance criterion. They then make "decisions," awarding amounts money to pairs of *other* subjects (excluding self) in specially designed booklets. The recipients are anonymous, except for their individual code numbers and their group membership (for example, member number 51 of the X group and member number 33 of the Y group). The subjects, who know their own group membership, award the amounts individually and anonymously. The response format of the booklets does not force the subjects to act in terms of group membership.

In this situation, there is neither a conflict of interests nor previously existing hostility between the "groups." No social interaction takes place between the subjects, nor is there any rational link between economic self-interest and the strategy of in-group favoritism. Thus, these groups are purely cognitive, and can be referred to as *minimal*.

The basic and highly reliable finding is that the trivial, ad hoc intergroup categorization leads to in-group favoritism and discrimination against the out-group. Fairness is also an influential strategy. There is also a good deal of evidence that, within the pattern of responding in terms of in-group favoritism, maximum difference (M.D.) is more important to the subjects than maximum in-group profit (M.I.P.). Thus, they seem to be competing with the out-group, rather than following a strategy of simple economic gain for members of the in-group. Other data from several experiments also show that the subjects' decisions were significantly nearer to the maximum joint payoff (M.J.P.) point when these decisions applied to the division of money between two anonymous members of the in-group than when they applied to two members of the out-group; that is, relatively less was given to the out-group, even when giving more would not have affected the amounts for the in-group. Billig & Tajfel (1973) have found the same results even when the assignment to groups was made explicitly random. This eliminated the similarity on the performance criterion within the in-group as an alternative explanation of the results (see Byrne, 1971). An explicitly random classification into groups proved in this study to be a more potent determinant of discrimination than perceived interpersonal similarities and dissimilarities not associated with categorization into groups.

The question that arises is whether in-group bias in these "minimal" situations is produced by some form of the experimenter effect or of the demand characteristics of the experimental situation—in other words, whether explicit references to group membership communicate to the subjects that they are expected to, or ought to, discriminate. The first point to be made about this interpretation of the results is that explicit reference to group membership are logically necessary for operationalizing in these minimal situations the major independent variable—that is, social categorization per se. This requires not merely that the subjects perceive themselves as similar to or different from others as *individuals*, but that they are members of discrete and discontinuous categories—that is, "groups." Second, a detailed analysis of the subjects' postsession reports (Billig, 1972; Turner, 1975) shows that they do not share any common conception of the "appropriate" or "obvious" way to behave, that only a tiny minority have some idea of the hypothesis, and that this minority does not always conform to it.

The more general theoretical problem has been referred to elsewhere by one of us as follows:

Simply and briefly stated, the argument (e.g., Gerard & Hoyt, 1974) amounts to the following: the subjects acted in terms of the intergroup categorization provided or imposed by the experimenters not necessarily because this has been successful in inducing any genuine awareness of membership in separate and distinct groups, but probably because they felt that this kind of behavior was expected of them by the experimenters, and therefore they conformed to this expectation. The first question to ask is why should the subjects be expecting the experiments to expect of them this kind of behavior? The Gerard and Hoyt answer to this is that the experimental situation was rigged to cause this kind of expectation in the subjects. This answer retains its plausibility only if we assume that what was no more than a hint from the experimenters about the notion of "groups" being relevant to the subjects' behavior had been sufficient to determine, powerfully and consistently, a *particular form* of intergroup behavior. In turn, if we assume this—and the assumption is by no means unreasonable—we must also assume that his particular form of intergroup behavior is one which is capable of being induced by the experimenters much more easily than other forms (such as cooperation between the groups in extorting the maximum total amount of money from the experimenters, or a fair division of the spoils between the groups, or simply random responding). And this last assumption must be backed up in its turn by another presupposition: namely, that for some reasons (whatever they may be) competitive behavior between groups, at least in our culture, is extraordinarily easy to trigger off—at which point we are back where we started from. The problem then must be restated in terms of the need to specify why a certain *kind* of intergroup behavior can be elicited so much more easily than other kinds; and this specification is certainly not made if we rest content with the explanation that the behavior occurred because it was very easy for the experimenters to make it occur [Tajfel, in press].

Two points stand out: first, minimal intergroup discrimination is not based on incompatible group interests; second, the baseline conditions for intergroup competition seem indeed so minimal as to cause the suspicion that we are dealing here with some factor or process inherent in the intergroup situation itself. Our theoretical orientation was developed initially in response to these clues from our earlier experiments. We shall not trace the history of its development, however, but shall describe its present form.

Social Identity and Social Comparison

Many orthodox definitions of "social groups" are unduly restrictive when applied to the context of intergroup relations. For example, when members of two national or ethnic categories interact on the basis of their reciprocal beliefs about their respective categories and of the general relations between them, this is clearly intergroup behavior in the everyday sense of the term. The "groups" to which the interactants belong *need not* depend upon the frequency of inter-member interaction, systems of role relationships, or interdependent goals. From the social–psychological perspective, the essential criteria for group membership, as they apply to large-scale social categories, are that the individuals concerned define themselves and are defined by others as members of a group.

We can conceptualize a group, in this sense, as a collection of individuals who perceive themselves to be members of the same social category, share some emotional involvement in this common definition of themselves, and achieve some degree of social consensus about the evaluation of their group and of their membership of it. Following from this, our definition of intergroup behavior is basically identical to that of Sherif (1966, p. 62): any behavior displayed by one or more actors toward one or more others that is based on the actors' identification of themselves and the others as belonging to different social categories.

Social categorizations are conceived here as cognitive tools that segment, classify, and order the social environment, and thus enable the individual to undertake many forms of social action. But they do not merely systematize the social world; they also provide a system of orientation for *self*-reference: they create and define the individual's place in society. Social groups, understood in this sense, provide their members with an identification of themselves in social terms. These identifications are to a very large extent relational and comparative: they define the individual as similar to or different from, as "better" or "worse" than, members of other groups. (For a more detailed discussion, see Tajfel, 1972b.) It is in a strictly limited sense, arising from these considerations, that we use the term *social identity*. It consists, for the purposes of the present discussion, of those aspects of an individual's self-image that derive from the social categories to which he perceives himself as belonging. With this limited concept of social identity in mind, our argument is based on the following general assumptions:

1. Individuals strive to maintain or enhance their self-esteem: they strive for a positive self-concept.

2. Social groups or categories and the membership of them are associated with positive or negative value connotations. Hence, social identity may be positive or negative according to the evaluations (which tend to be socially

59

consensual, either within or across groups) of those groups that contribute to an individual's social identity.

3. The evaluation of one's own group is determined with reference to specific other groups through social comparisons in terms of value-laden attributes and characteristics. Positively discrepant comparisons between in-group and out-group produce high prestige; negatively discrepant comparisons between in-group and out-group result in low prestige.

From these assumptions, some related theoretical principles can be derived:

1. Individuals strive to achieve or to maintain positive social identity.

2. Positive social identity is based to a large extent on favorable comparisons that can be made between the in-group and some relevant out-groups: the in-group must be perceived as positively differentiated or distinct from the relevant out-groups.

3. When social identity is unsatisfactory, individuals will strive either to leave their existing group and join some more positively distinct group and/or to make their existing group more positively distinct.

The basic hypothesis, then, is that pressures to evaluate one's own group positively through in-group/out-group comparisons lead social groups to attempt to differentiate themselves from each other (see Tajfel, 1974a, 1974b; Turner, 1975). There are at least three classes of variables that should influence intergroup differentiation in concrete social situations. First, individuals must have internalized their group membership as an aspect of their self-concept: they must be subjectively identified with the relevant in-group. It is not enough that the others define them as a group, although consensual definitions by others can become, in the long run, one of the powerful causal factors for a group's self-definition. Second, the social situation must be such as to allow for intergroup comparisons that enable the selection and evaluation of the relevant relational attributes. Not all between-group differences have evaluative significance (Tajfel, 1959), and those that do vary from group to group. Skin color, for instance, is apparently a more salient attribute in the United States than in Hong Kong (Morland, 1969); whereas language seems to be an especially salient dimension of separate identity in French Canada, Wales, and Belgium (see Giles & Powesland, 1976; Fishman & Giles, in press). Third, in-groups do not compare themselves with every cognitively available out-group: the out-group must be perceived as a relevant comparison group. Similarity, proximity, and situational salience are among the variables that determine out-group comparability, and pressures toward in-group distinctiveness should increase as a function of this comparability. It is important to state at this point that, in many social situations, comparability reaches a much wider range than a simply conceived "similarity" between the groups.

The aim of differentiation is to maintain or achieve superiority over an out-group on some dimensions. Any such act, therefore, is essentially competitive.

This competition requires a situation of mutual comparison and differentiation on a shared value dimension. In these conditions, intergroup competition, which may be unrelated to the "objective" goal relations between the groups, can be predicted to occur. Turner (1975) has distinguished between social and instrumental, or "realistic," competition. The former is motivated by self-evaluation and takes place through social comparison, whereas the latter is based on "realistic" self-interest and represents embryonic conflict. Incompatible group goals are necessary for realistic competition, but mutual intergroup comparisons are necessary, and often sufficient, for social competition. The latter point is consistent with the data from "minimal" group experiments that mere awareness of an out-group is sufficient to stimulate in-group favoritism, and the observations (Ferguson & Kelley, 1964; Rabbie & Wilkens, 1971; Doise & Weinberger, 1973) that the possibility of social comparison generates "spontaneous" inter-group competition.

Social and realistic competition also differ in the predictions that can be made about the consequences for subsequent intergroup behavior of winning or losing. After realistic competition, the losing groups should be hostile to the out-group victors, both because they have been deprived of a reward and because their interaction has been exclusively conflictual. However, when winning and losing establish shared group evaluations concerning comparative superiority and inferiority, then, *so* long as the terms of the competition are perceived as legitimate and the competition itself as fair according to these legitimate terms, the losing group *may* acquiesce in the superiority of the winning out-group. This acquiescence by a group considering itself as legitimately "inferior" has been shown in a recent study by Caddick (1974). Several other studies report findings that are in line with this interpretation: losing in-groups do not always derogate, but sometimes upgrade, their evaluations of the winning out-groups (for example, Wilson & Miller, 1961; Bass & Dunteman, 1963).

Retrospectively, at least, the social-identity/social-comparison theory is consistent with many of the studies mentioned in the preceding section of this chapter. In particular, in the paradigm of the "minimal group" experiments (such as Tajfel et al., 1971), the intergroup discrimination can be conceived as being due not to conflict over monetary gains, but to differentiations based on comparisons made in terms of monetary rewards. Money functioned as a dimension of comparison (the only one available within the experimental design), and the data suggest that larger absolute gains that did not establish a difference in favor of the in-group were sacrificed for smaller comparative gains, when the two kinds of gains were made to conflict.

There is further evidence (Turner, in press-a) that the social-competitive pattern of intergroup behavior holds even when it conflicts with obvious self-interest. In this study, the distribution of either monetary rewards or "points" was made, within the "minimal" intergroup paradigm, between self and an anonymous "other," who was either in the in-group or in the out-group. As long as minimal conditions existed for in-group identification, the subjects were prepared to give relatively less to themselves when the award (either in points or in money) was to be divided between self and an anonymous member of the in-group, as compared with dividing with an anonymous member of the out-group. These results seem particularly important, since the category of "self," which is by no means "minimal" or ad hoc, was set here against a truly minimal in-group category, identical to those used in the earlier experiments. Despite this stark asymmetry, the minimal group affiliation affected the responses.

The theoretical predictions were taken outside of the minimal categorization paradigm in a further study by Turner (1978b). He used face-to-face groups working on a discussion task. In each session, two three-person groups discussed an identical issue, supposedly to gain an assessment of their verbal intelligence, and then briefly compared their respective performance. The subjects were 144 male undergraduates. The criterion for intergroup differentiation was the magnitude of in-group bias shown in the ratings of the groups' work. Half the triads, composed of Arts students, believed that verbal intelligence was important for them (High Importance, or H.I.); half, composed of Science students, did not (Low Importance, or L.I.). Half the sessions involved two Arts or two Science groups (Similar Outgroup), and half involved one Arts and one Science group (Dissimilar Outgroup). Finally, in the Stable Difference condition, subjects were instructed that Arts students were definitely superior and Science students definitely inferior in verbal intelligence; in the Unstable Difference condition, there was no explicit statement that one category was better than the other. These variables were manipulated in a 2 X 2 X 2 factorial design.

The results showed that the Arts groups (H.I.) were more biased than the Science groups (L.I.); that similar groups differentiated more than dissimilar groups in the Stable condition, but that they were no more biased (and sometimes even less so) in the Unstable condition; and that, on some of the measures, there was a significant main effect for out-group similarity: in-group bias increased against a similar out-group. Although these data are relatively complex, they do support some of our theoretical expectations and provide an illustration that variations in in-group bias can be systematically predicted from the social-identity/social-comparison theory.

We have argued that social and realistic competition are conceptually distinct, although most often they are empirically associated in "real life." In an experiment by Turner and Brown (1976), an attempt was made to isolate the effects on intergroup behavior of the postulated autonomous processes attributed to a search for positive social identity. Children were used as subjects, and the manipulations involved decisions by the subjects about the distribution of payments for participation in the experiment, to be shared equally by the in-group, between the in-group and out-groups that were made relevant or irrelevant to comparisons with the in-group's performance. Monetary self-interest (of a magnitude previously ascertained to be of genuine significance to the subjects) would have produced no difference in the distribution decisions involving the two kinds of out-group; it would also have led to decisions tending toward maximum in-group profit (M.I.P.) rather than toward maximum difference (M.D.).

M.D. was the most influential strategy in the choices. Furthermore, when the subjects could choose in-group favoritism (M.D. + M.I.P.) and/or a fairness strategy, they were both more discriminatory and less fair toward the relevant than the irrelevant comparison group. Other measures of in-group favoritism produced an interaction between reward level and type of out-group: more discrimination against the relevant than the irrelevant group with high rewards, and less with low rewards. Whatever may be other explanations for this interaction, we can at least conclude that when reward levels are more meaningful, in-group favoritism is enhanced against a more comparable out-group, independently of the group members' economic interests. Indeed, insofar as the subjects used the M.D. strategy, they sacrificed "objective" personal and group gain for the sake of positive in-group distinctiveness.

On the whole, these studies provide some confirmation for the basic social-identity/social-comparison hypotheses.

References

Bass, B. M., & Dunteman, G. Biases in the evaluation of one's own group, its allies and opponents. *Journal of Conflict Resolution*, 1963, 7, 16–20.

Billig, M. *Social categorization in intergroup relations*. Unpublished doctoral dissertation, University of Bristol, 1972.

Billig, M., & Tajfel, H. Social categorization and similarity in intergroup behavior. *European Journal of Social Psychology*, 1973, 3, 27–52.

Byrne, D. *The attraction paradigm*. New York: Academic Press, 1971.

Caddick, B. *Threat to group distinctiveness and intergroup discrimination*. Unpublished manuscript. University of Bristol, 1974.

Doise, W., Csepeli, G., Dann, H. D., Gouge, C., Larsen, K., & Ostell, A. An experimental investigation into the formation of intergroup representations. *European Journal of Social Psychology*, 1972, 2, 202–204.

Doise, W., & Sinclair, A. The categorisation process in intergroup relations. *European Journal of Social Psychology*, 1973, 3, 145–157.

Doise, W., & Weinberger, M. Représentations masculines dans differentes situations de rencontres mixtes. *Bulletin de Psychologie*, 1973, *26*, 649–657.

Ferguson, C. K., & Kelley, H. H. Significant factors in overevaluation of own group's product. *Journal of Abnormal and Social Psychology*, 1964, *69*, 223–228.

Fishman, J., & Giles, H. Language in society. In H. Tajfel & C. Fraser (Eds.), *Introducing social psychology*. Harmondsworth, Middlesex: Penguin Books.

Gerard, H. B., & Hoyt, M. F. Distinctiveness of social categorization and attitude toward ingroup members. *Journal of Personality and Social Psychology*, 1974, *29*, 836–842.

Giles, H., & Powesland, P. F. *Speech style and social evaluation*. London: Academic Press, European Monographs in Social Psychology, 1976.

Harvey, O. J. An experimental investigation of negative and positive relations between small groups through judgmental indices. *Sociometry*, 1956, *14*, 201–209.

Morland, J. K. Race awareness among American and Hong Kong Chinese children. *American Journal of Sociology*, 1969, *75*, 360–374.

Rabbie, J., & Wilkens, C. Intergroup competition and its effect on intra- and intergroup relations. *European Journal of Social Psychology*, 1971, *1*, 215–234.

Sherif, M. *Group conflict and cooperation: Their social psychology*. London: Routledge and Kegan Paul, 1966.

Tajfel, H. Quantitative judgement in social perception. *British Journal of Psychology*, 1959, *10*, 16–29.

Tajfel, H. Experiments in intergroup discrimination. *Scientific American*, 1970, *223*(5), 96–102.

Tajfel, H. La catégorisation sociale. In S. Moscovici (Ed.), *Introduction à la psychologie sociale* (Vol. 1). Paris: Larousse, 1972(b).

Tajfel, H. *Intergroup behaviour, social comparison and social change*. Unpublished Katz-Newcomb Lectures, University of Michigan, Ann Arbor, 1974(a).

Tajfel, H. Social identity and intergroup behaviour. *Social Science Information*, 1974(b), *13*(2). 65–93.

Tajfel, H. The psychological structure of intergroup relations. In H. Tajfel (Ed.), *Differentiation between social groups: Studies in the social psychology of intergroup relations*. London: Academic Press, European Monographs in Social Psychology, 1978.

Tajfel, H., & Billig, M. Familiarity and categorization in intergroup behaviour. *Journal of Experimental Social Psychology*, 1974, *10*, 159–170.

Tajfel, H., Billig, M. G., Bundy, R. P., & Flament, C. Social categorization and intergroup behaviour. *European Journal of Social Psychology*, 1971, *1*, 149–178.

Turner, J. C. Social comparison and social identity: Some prospects for intergroup behaviour. *European Journal of Social Psychology*, 1975, *5*, 5–34.

Turner, J. C. Social categorization and social discrimination in the minimal group paradigm. In H. Tajfel (Ed.), *Differentiation between social groups: Studies in the social psychology of intergroup relations*. European Monographs in Social Psychology. London: Academic Press, 1978(a).

Turner, J. C. Social comparison, similarity and ingroup favouritism. In H. Tajfel (Ed.), *Differentiation between social groups: Studies in the social psychology of intergroup relations*. European Monographs in Social Psychology. London: Academic Press, 1978(b).

Turner, J. C., & Brown, R. J. Social status, cognitive alternatives and intergroup relations. In H. Tajfel (Ed.), *Differentiation between social groups: Studies in the social psychology of intergroup relations*. European Monographs in Social Psychology. London: Academic Press, 1976.

Wilson, W., & Miller, N. Shifts in evaluations of participants following intergroup competition. *Journal of Abnormal and Social Psychology*, 1961, *63*, 428–431.

5

Who is this "We"? Levels of Collective Identity and Self Representations

Marilynn B. Brewer and Wendi Gardner

Until recently, social psychological theories of the self focused on the individuated self-concept—the person's sense of unique identity differentiated from others. Cross-cultural perspectives, however, have brought a renewed interest in the social aspects of the self and the extent to which individuals define themselves in terms of their relationships to others and to social groups (Markus & Kitayama, 1991; Triandis, Bontempo, Villareal, Asai, & Lucca, 1988). Central to this new perspective is the idea that connectedness and belonging are not merely affiliations or alliances between the self and others but entail fundamental differences in the way the self is construed (Brewer, 1991; Markus & Kitayama, 1991; Singelis, 1994; Trafimow, Triandis, & Goto, 1991; Triandis, 1989; Turner, Oakes, Haslam, & McGarty, 1994).

Some of these theories of the social self focus on cross-cultural differences in whether the self is typically construed as individuated or interpersonal. However, all recognize that these different self-construals may also coexist within the same individual, available to be activated at different times or in different contexts. Furthermore, in several theories, achieving an extended sense of self has the status of a fundamental human motivation (Baumeister & Leary, 1995; Brewer, 1991). In other words, individuals seek to define themselves in terms of their immersion in relationships with others and with larger collectives and derive much of their self-evaluation from such social identities (Breckler & Greenwald, 1986; Greenwald & Breckler, 1985). The motivational properties of collective identities are systematically documented in Baumeister and Leary's

(1995) comprehensive review of the evidence in support of a fundamental "need to belong" as an innate feature of human nature.

All of the theories mentioned above draw some kind of distinction between the individuated or *personal* self (those aspects of the self-concept that differentiate the self from all others) and a relational or *social* self (those aspects of the self-concept that reflect assimilation to others or significant social groups). However, implicit in a comparison across these different theories is a further distinction between two levels of social selves—those that derive from interpersonal relationships and interdependence with specific others and those that derive from membership in larger, more impersonal collectives or social categories.

Both interpersonal and collective identities are social extensions of the self but differ in whether the social connections are personalized bonds of attachment or impersonal bonds derived from common identification with some symbolic group or social category. Prototypic interpersonal identities are those derived from intimate dyadic relationships such as parent–child, lovers, and friendships, but they also include identities derived from membership in small, face-to-face groups that are essentially networks of such dyadic relationships. Collective social identities, on the other hand, do not require personal relationships among group members. As Turner, Hogg, Oakes, Reicher, and Wetherell (1987) put it, social identity entails a *depersonalized* sense of self, "a shift towards the perception of self as an interchangeable exemplar of some social category and away from the perception of self as a unique person" (p. 50). Consistent with this view, Prentice, Miller, and Lightdale (1994) distinguished between group identities that are based on *common bonds* (attachment to other group members) and those based on *common identity* (collective identities).

The distinction between interpersonal and collective identities is not simply a matter of the difference between attachments that are based on affect and attachments that are cognitively based. Both levels involve affective and cognitive categorization processes. The difference is a matter of level of inclusiveness. Some social identities can be construed either as interpersonal relationships or as collective identities. Many social roles and professions, for instance, can be experienced in terms of specific role relationships (e.g., parent–child, doctor–patient) or in terms of membership in a general social category (e.g., parents, medical professionals). Consistent with this reasoning, Millward (1995) recently demonstrated a distinction between nurses who construed their career identity in terms of communal–interpersonal relationships with patients and those whose representation of *nurse* was construed in terms of professional intergroup distinctions.

Some other theorists have also made explicit the distinction between interpersonal and collective selves. Triandis (1989) and Greenwald and Breckler (1985; Breckler & Greenwald, 1986), for instance, distinguished among "private," "public," and "collective" facets of the self. The *public self* represents those aspects of the self-concept most sensitive to the evaluation of significant others and consists of cognitions about the self that reflect interactions and relationships with those others. The *collective self*, on the other hand, reflects internalizations of the norms and characteristics of important reference groups and consists of cognitions about the self that are consistent with that group identification.

Recent evolutionary models of human social behavior also call attention to functional distinctions between social attachments at different levels of organization. Caporael (1995; Brewer & Caporael, 1995), for instance, has developed a hierarchical model of group structure as a comprehensive theory of social coordination. According to this model, four fundamental configurations—*dyads* (two-person relationships), *teams* (small face-to-face social and working groups), *bands* (small, interacting communities), and *tribes* (macro-bands characterized by shared identity and communication but without continual face-to-face interaction)—have been "repeatedly assembled" throughout human evolutionary history. Each level represents different forms of functional interdependence and different types of coordination, with associated differences in construals of self and others. These configurations also are represented ontogenetically. Bugental's (1995) review of the literature on social development suggests that the development of attachment relationships and group-oriented relationships represent functionally distinct domains of social competence.

Levels of Self Representation

Table 1 presents one attempt to characterize systematically the differences among the three levels of self-construal that are represented in the current literature on the social self. At the individual level, the *personal self* is the differentiated, individuated self-concept most characteristic of studies of the self in Western psychology (e.g., Pelham, 1993). At the interpersonal level, the *relational self* is the self-concept derived from connections and role relationships with significant others. This corresponds most closely to the interdependent self as defined by Markus and Kitayama (1991) in their analysis of the difference

Table 1. Levels of Representation of the Self

Level of analysis	Self-concept	Basis of self-evaluation	Frame of reference	Basic social motivation
Individual	Personal	Traits	Interpersonal comparison	Self-interest
Interpersonal	Relational	Roles	Reflection	Other's benefit
Group	Collective	Group prototype	Intergroup comparison	Collective welfare

between American and Japanese self-construals. Finally, at the group level is the *collective self*, which corresponds to the concept of social identity as represented in social identity theory and self-categorization theory (Hogg & Abrams, 1988; Turner et al., 1987).

These different aspects of the self refer to different levels of inclusiveness of the conceptualization of the self—the shift from "I" to "we" as the locus of self-definition. This shift in inclusiveness of self-representations is postulated to be associated with corresponding transformations of the bases for content of the self-concept, the frame of reference for evaluations of self-worth, and the nature of social motivation.

The Extended Self-Concept

The idea of the socially extended self goes beyond perceived similarity and other relational connections between self and others. An extended self means that the boundaries of the self are redrawn, and the content of the self-concept is focused on those characteristics that make one a "good" representative of the group or of the relationship. As Brewer (1991) put it, when collective identities are activated, the most salient features of the self-concept become those that are shared with other members of the in-group. The idea that close relationships involve a blurring of the boundaries between the self and a partner also is represented by Aron and Aron's (1986) self-expansion model of motivation and cognition in close relationships. Operationally, this concept is captured in the Inclusion of Other in the Self Scale (Aron, Aron, & Smollan, 1992), which has recently been extended to collective identities (Tropp & Wright, 1995).

Support for the idea that salient interpersonal relationships are incorporated into the self-concept was obtained in a series of studies by Aron, Aron, Tudor, and Nelson (1991) on the parallels between cognitive effects of self-referencing and referencing to close relationship partners. The method and results of Aron et al.'s Experiment 3 are particularly relevant. In this study, married graduate students completed a questionnaire in which they rated themselves and their spouses on a set of 90 diverse traits. The ratings were used to identify aspects of each individual's self-concept for which self-ratings matched ratings of their partner and those for which self-ratings and partner ratings were mismatched. Later, the same individuals made yes–no self-descriptiveness judgments on the same 90 traits on a computer with reaction times recorded. Mean reaction times for matching traits were significantly faster than those for mismatched traits, suggesting that shared characteristics were more salient or accessible aspects of the self-concept.

Smith and Henry (1996) adapted Aron et al.'s (1991) method to assess the influence of salient in-group characteristics on judgments of the self. College student participants were asked to describe themselves and then each of two groups (an in-group based on college major or fraternity, and a corresponding out-group) on the 90 traits used by Aron et al. The researchers having made these group identities salient, then had respondents make yes–no judgments of these same traits on a computer. Analyses of response time data essentially replicated Aron et al.'s earlier findings for spouses. Response times were facilitated for self-descriptive traits that matched those of the relevant in-group and were slower for mismatching traits. For both levels of identity, then, there is evidence that identification with others enhances the accessibility of shared characteristics in the working self-concept.

Self-Concept and Social Comparison

Most theories of personal self-esteem assume that global self-worth at the individual level is derived from self-evaluation of personal traits and characteristics based on interpersonal comparisons to relevant others (Pelham, 1995; Pelham & Swann, 1989; Suls & Wills, 1991). By contrast, the interdependent or relational self-concept is defined in terms of relationships with others in specific contexts, and self-worth is derived from appropriate role behavior (Markus & Kitayama, 1991; Stryker, 1991). (In Table 1, we refer to this process as *reflection*, in the sense that the self is derived from the responses and satisfaction of the other person in the relationship.) Finally, the collective self-concept is determined by assimilation to the prototypic representation of the in-group, with self-worth derived from the status of the in-group in intergroup comparisons (Turner et al., 1987).

Evidence for changes in the bases of self-worth at different levels of self-construal come from efforts to measure global self-esteem separately at the personal and collective levels (Luhtanen & Crocker, 1992). In general, self-esteem at the two levels are positively correlated, but only moderately so (Crocker, Luhtanen, Blaine, & Broadnax, 1994; Luhtanen & Crocker, 1992).

It should be noted here that in-group membership plays different roles in the formation and maintenance of the self-concept at different levels. On the one hand, in-groups provide the frame of reference for self-evaluation at the individual level and for selection of significant others at the interpersonal level. Shared in-group membership is one important basis for determining relevant sources of social comparison. For instance, defining ourselves as social psychologists means that we are more likely to assess our academic qualifications and research abilities in comparison to other social psychologists than to other types of behavioral or social scientists. Furthermore, confirmation of our self-assessment from other in-group members is related to the certainty with which we make trait attributions to ourselves (Pelham & Swann, 1994).

The other role that in-groups play in defining the individual's self-concept derives from comparisons between characteristics shared by in-group members in comparison to relevant out-groups. This is the essence of social identity. When we think of ourselves as social psychologists in this sense, we are most likely to attribute traits and characteristics to ourselves that we share with other social psychologists and that make us distinct from other social and behavioral scientists. The focus on intragroup differences versus intragroup similarities (and intergroup differences) serves as a main indicator of people's relative emphasis on their personal or collective selves (McFarland & Buehler, 1995: Simon, Pantaleo, & Mummendey, 1995).

The distinction between interpersonal comparison and intergroup comparison as determinants of self-evaluations was demonstrated in a recent experiment by Brewer and Weber (1994). In this experiment, participants were randomly assigned to one of two artificial social categories. Social identification with in-group assignment was manipulated indirectly by varying the salience and distinctiveness of the in-group category. After being assigned to a category, participants viewed a videotaped interview with another research participant that provided exposure to an upward or downward social comparison target. In the upward social comparison conditions, the individual on the videotape was exceptionally high in academic achievement and intellectual ability; in the downward social comparison conditions, the same individual played the role of a poor student with relatively low academic accomplishment. Furthermore, the individual on the video was identified either as a member of the viewer's own social category (in-group) or as a member of the contrasting category (out-group).

The predicted outcomes of the experiment were based on the assumption that participants who had been assigned to the nondistinctive social category would be oriented toward intra-group, interpersonal social comparison and would evaluate their own academic abilities in contrast to those of another in-group member but would be unaffected by comparison information about an out-group member. Members of the distinctive social category, on the other hand, were expected to be oriented toward intergroup social comparison and would evaluate their own academic abilities by assimilating to another in-group member but exhibiting contrast to an out-group member.

Participants' self-evaluations of academic aptitude following exposure to the videotapes corresponded exactly to predictions. Participants in the nondistinctive in-group condition had significantly lower self-ratings following exposure to an upward comparison target than to a downward comparison target when the person on the videotape was an in-group member, but self-evaluations were not differentially affected by exposure to upward or downward out-group comparison targets. In contrast, participants in the distinctive in-group condition were more positive in their self-evaluations following exposure to the upward comparison in-group member and more negative following exposure to the downward comparison in-group member. However, exposure to an out-group comparison target had the opposite effect—lowering self-evaluations when the target was high in ability and raising them when the target was low in academic ability. Thus, exposure to the same social comparison information had very different effects on self-evaluations, depending on the individual's relationship to the in-group and focus on personal versus social identity.

Social Motivation

Another important transformation associated with different levels of self-construal is a change in the basic goals of social interaction. There is a fundamental difference between social motives derived from personal self-interest and those derived from concern for the interests of others (McClintock, 1972). As Brewer (1991) postulated, "when the definition of self changes, the meaning of self-interest and self-serving motivations also changes accordingly" (p. 476).

Both Markus and Kitayama (1991) and Baumeister and Leary (1995) stressed that interdependent relationships are characterized by mutual concern for the interests and outcomes of the other. Batson (1994) defined this concern as the basis of altruistic motivation, which he stressed is not to be confused with self-sacrifice (which concerns costs to self) but as the motivation to benefit the other. At the collective level, group welfare becomes an end in itself. Experimental research on social dilemmas has demonstrated the powerful effect of group identification on participants' willingness to restrict individual gain to preserve a collective good (Brewer & Kramer, 1986; Caporael, Dawes, Orbell, & van de Kragt, 1989; Kramer & Brewer, 1984). Identification with in-groups can elicit cooperative behavior even in the absence of interpersonal communication among group members. Within the in-group category, individuals develop a cooperative orientation toward shared problems.

Consequences of Shifts in Levels of Identity

Shift From Personal to Collective Self

The consequences of shifting from personal identity to social identity in levels of self-categorization have been a continuing focus of research derived from social identity theory (Turner, 1982). Although Deaux (1992, 1993) has argued that social identities are integrated into personal identities, there is evidence of discontinuities between self-descriptions and social behavior associated with the two levels of construal (Hogg & Abrams, 1988).

As the results of Smith and Henry's (1996) experiment demonstrate, when a particular social identity is made salient, individuals are likely to think of themselves as having characteristics that are representative of that social category. Social identity, in other words, leads to *self-stereotyping* (Simon & Hamilton, 1994). This effect was demonstrated in an experiment by Hogg and Turner (1987) that involved gender identity. In this study, male and female college students participated in a discussion under one of two conditions. In the personal identity condition, the discussion was between two people of the same sex, and the two discussants held different positions on the issue under consideration. In the social identity condition, the discussion group consisted of four people—two men and two women—and the sexes differed on the issue. The latter arrangement was intended to make categorization by sex particularly salient in the setting and to increase the probability that participants would think of themselves in terms of their gender identity. Following the social interaction, participants in the social identity condition characterized themselves as more typical of their sex and attributed more masculine or feminine traits to themselves than those in the personal identity condition.

Consistent with this perspective, other experimental research has demonstrated that retrieval cues designed to activate the "private" self-representation increase generation of self-cognitions that are quite different from the self-cognitions retrieved when the "collective" self-aspect is activated (Trafimow et al., 1991). These results led Trafimow and colleagues to speculate that private and collective self-concepts are stored in separate locations in memory.

Shift from Personal to Relational Self

Many of the cognitive, emotional, and motivational consequences associated with the cross-cultural differences in self-construal reviewed by Markus and Kitayama (1991) would be expected to hold for shifts in levels of self-representation within the same individual. Indeed, Cheek (1989) argued that personal and social (relational) identities are enduring properties of the self-concept, representing separate sources of individual differences in self-definition. Also, Cousins (1989) demonstrated that both American and Japanese participants produced different types of self-descriptors in response to the Twenty Statements Test (Hartley, 1970) when the instructions were altered from the generic ("I am ...") prompt to prompts situated in specific interpersonal contexts.

Marilynn B. Brewer and Wendi Gardner

Shift from Relational to Collective Self

Less research has been devoted to direct comparisons between interpersonal and collective levels of self-categorization and associated behaviors. One exception is Hogg's (1992, 1993) work on the distinction between interpersonal liking and social identity as sources of attraction to others.

In the research literature on interpersonal attraction, liking between two individuals is strongly related to the similarity between them (Byrne, 1971). People are likely to become friends or lovers to the extent that they perceive that they are similar to each other in preferences, attitudes, and values. At this interpersonal level, attraction seems to be a function of the two individuals' personal traits and the degree of match between their individual identities. On the other hand, research on social categorization and in-group preference suggests that positive evaluations and liking for other individuals can be induced simply by the knowledge that they share a common group identity. In-group members tend to be liked more than out-group members even when we know nothing about their personal characteristics. In general, we tend to assume that fellow in-group members are similar to each other, but in this case liking and similarity seem to be a consequence of group formation rather than its cause (Hogg & Turner, 1985). As a consequence, in-group favoritism can occur in the absence of interpersonal attraction or its antecedents.

To represent the idea that liking is sometimes based on group membership alone, Hogg (1992, 1993; Hogg & Hardie, 1991) has drawn a distinction between idiosyncratic *personal attraction* and depersonalized *social attraction*. Personal attraction is based on personal identities of the individuals involved, and similarity of personal interests, attitudes, and values is the primary basis for this form of liking. Social attraction, on the other hand, is based on preferential liking for in-group over out-group members. To the extent that a particular group member exemplifies the characteristics that are distinctive or important to that group, that individual will be socially attractive to other in-group members, regardless of interpersonal similarity.

Because these two forms of attraction have different origins, it is possible to display preference for an in-grouper we don't like very much and to discriminate against a member of an out-group even if we like that individual personally. Because of this distinction in sources of attraction, it is possible for groups to work together as cohesive units even when members do not like each other interpersonally, a phenomenon that has been demonstrated in laboratory groups (Hogg & Turner, 1985) and in real-life groups such as sports teams (e.g., Lenk, 1969).

Research by Prentice et al. (1994) also has verified the distinction between group identification that is based on direct attachments to the social category and identification based on interpersonal attachments among group members.

In studies of various campus groups, they found that members of groups based on a common identity were more attached to the group than to fellow group members, whereas members of groups based on interpersonal bonds were more attached to members of the group overall and showed a stronger relationship between identification with the group and evaluation of individual group members.

General Discussion

The idea that different levels of inclusiveness define conceptually distinct construals of the self raises a number of interesting questions that are just beginning to be addressed in research on self-representations. One such question is the nature of the interrelationships among these different self systems. Turner and his colleagues (Turner et al., 1987, 1994) have contended that there is a functional antagonism between self-categorizations at different levels of inclusiveness. Taken to the extreme this would imply that social identities at different levels of organization are essentially independent and may include not only different but possibly incompatible representations of the self. At the other extreme, Deaux (1992, 1993) has argued that social identities are integrated into the personal self-concept. In between these two extremes is the idea that the different self systems interact as complementary components of an overall self-concept and self-esteem.

A second important question is what determines which level of self-representation is activated at any particular time. Self-categorization theory (Turner et al., 1994) emphasizes that self-categorizing at different levels is inherently variable and highly dependent on contextual shifts in frames of reference. Other perspectives suggest that one level of self-construal is stable and dominant over others as a function of cultural values and belief systems and socialization (Markus & Kitayama, 1991; Trafimow et al., 1991; Triandis, 1989). Yet a third perspective emphasizes the role of situated goals and motives, including needs for security and self-enhancement (Cialdini et al., 1976; Simon et al., 1995).

The Dynamic Self-Concept

One source of variation in self-representations within individuals is a widely recognized tension or opposition between needs and motives that promote individuation and differentiation of the self from others, and those that promote assimilation and unit formation. These opposing processes appear to play out at each level of self-categorization. At the level of the personal self, individuals seek similarity with significant others but at the same time strive for a sense of uniqueness (Snyder & Fromkin, 1980). The relational self often is characterized in terms of the tension between intimacy and separation from others, particularly in psychoanalytic theories of social development (e.g., Sullivan, 1953). Finally, Brewer's (1991, 1993) theory of optimal distinctiveness holds that collective identities are constrained by the necessity of satisfying simultaneously individual needs for inclusion and distinctiveness.

At each level of self-representation, these opposing forces of assimilation and differentiation create a dynamic equilibrium that fluctuates with changes in the distance between the self and others. A similar dynamic may account for the shift between levels of self-categorization. When needs for intimacy at the interpersonal level are not being met, collective identities may become more important: prolonged periods of immersion in a depersonalized collective may enhance the importance of recognition of the personal, individuated self, and so forth.

Self-Representations and Perception of Others

Shifts in the level of self-categorization also have implications for how other people and groups are perceived. When the personal self is salient, self-schematic traits are chronically accessible as dimensions of evaluation of other individuals (Higgins. King, & Marvin, 1982; Markus, Smith, & Moreland, 1985). Trait dimensions may be less important, however, when others are evaluated from the perspective of the relational self or collective identities.

When collective identities are salient, in-group–out-group categorizations become the most important basis for evaluating others. (Much anecdotal evidence documents the dramatic changes in affect and behavior that occur when an interpersonal relationship is redefined in terms of in-group–out-group distinctions.) Derogation of out-groups is related to collective self-esteem but not to personal self-esteem (Long. Spears, & Manstead, 1994; Luhtanen & Crocker, 1992). A program of research by Jarymowicz (1990, 1991) has demonstrated interesting relationships between activation of the *we* schema and processing of social information. As distinctions between the self and the in-group are diminished, individuals are more likely to respond to others in terms of simplified social categorizations and discriminate more strongly between similar and dissimilar others. These studies complement our own findings that activation of collective identities lowers the threshold for perceived similarity of ambiguous information but suggest that it would also increase reactivity to unambiguously dissimilar information.

The apparent relationship between self-construals and perception of others suggests yet another extension of collective identity theory. Changes in levels of self-categorization reflect not only differences in views of the self but also different *worldviews*. Our programs of research on the social self should be expanded to better understand how changes in self-definition are associated with significant changes in salient values, beliefs, and cognitive representations of the social world. If we acknowledge that different levels of identity represent different perspectives for interpreting social reality, collective identity theory becomes a comprehensive theory for understanding variability within as well as between individuals.

....

References

Aron, A., & Aron, E. (1986). *Love and the expansion of self: Understanding attraction and satisfaction*. New York: Hemisphere.

Aron, A., Aron, E., & Smollan, D. (1992). Inclusion of Other In the Self Scale and the structure of interpersonal closeness. *Journal of Personality and Social Psychology, 63*, 596–612.

Aron, A., Aron, E., Tudor, M., & Nelson, G. (1991). Close relationships as including other in the self. *Journal of Personality and Social Psychology, 60*, 241–253.

Batson, C. D. (1994). Why act for the public good? Four answers. *Personality and Social Psychology Bulletin, 20*, 603–610.

Baumeister, R. F., & Leary, M. R. (1995). The need to belong: Desire for interpersonal attachments as a fundamental human motivation. *Psychological Bulletin, 117*, 497–529.

Breckler, S. J., & Greenwald, A. G. (1986). Motivational facets of the self. In E. T. Higgins & R. Sorrentino (Eds.), *Handbook of motivation and cognition* (Vol. 1, pp. 145–164). New York: Guilford Press.

Brewer, M. B. (1991). The social self: On being the same and different at the same time. *Personality and Social Psychology Bulletin, 17*, 475–482.

Brewer, M. B. (1993). The role of distinctiveness in social identity and group behaviour. In M. Hogg & D. Abrams (Eds.), *Group motivation* (pp. 1–16). London: Harvester Wheatsheaf.

Brewer, M. B., & Caporael, L. R. (1995). Hierarchical evolutionary theory: There *is* an alternative and it's not creationism. *Psychological Inquiry, 6*, 31–34.

Brewer, M. B., & Kramer, R. M. (1986). Choice behavior in social dilemmas: Effects of social identity, group size, and decision framing. *Journal of Personality and Social Psychology, 50*, 543–549.

Brewer, M. B., & Weber, J. G. (1994). Self-evaluation effects of interpersonal versus intergroup social comparison. *Journal of Personality and Social Psychology, 66*, 268–275.

Bugental, D. (1995, June). *Do all social processes follow the same rules? An argument for domain-specificity*. Paper presented at the Personality and Social Psychology preconference, annual meeting of the American Psychological Society, New York.

Byrne, D. (1971). *The attraction paradigm*. New York: Academic Press.

Caporael, L. R. (1995). Sociality: Coordinating bodies, minds, and groups. *Psycologuy*. [on-line serial] 6(1). Available FTP: Hostname: princeton.edu Directory: pub/harnad/ Psycoloquy/1995. volume.6. File: psycoloquy. 95.6.01. group-selection. 1. caporael.

Caporael, L. R., Dawes, R. M., Orbell, J. M., & van de Kragt, A. (1989). Selfishness examined: Cooperation in the absence of egoistic incentives. *Behavioral and Brain Sciences, 12*, 683–739.

Cheek, J. (1989). Identity orientations and self-interpretation. In D. Buss & N. Cantor (Eds.), *Personality psychology: Recent trends and emerging directions* (pp. 275–285). New York: Springer-Verlag.

Cialdini, R., Borden, R., Thorne, A., Walker, M., Freeman, S., & Sloan, L. (1976). Basking in reflected glory: Three (football) field studies. *Journal of Personality and Social Psychology, 34*, 366–375.

Cousins, S. D. (1989). Culture and self-perception in Japan and the United States. *Journal of Personality and Social Psychology, 56*, 124–131.

Crocker, J., Luhtanen, R., Blaine, B., & Broadnax, S. (1994). Collective self-esteem and psychological well-being among White, Black, and Asian college students. *Personality and Social Psychology Bulletin, 20*, 503–513.

Deaux, K. (1992). Personalizing identity and socializing self. In G. Breakwell (Ed.), *Social psychology of identity and the self-concept* (pp. 9–33). London: Academic Press.

Deaux, K. (1993). Reconstructing social identity. *Personality and Social Psychology Bulletin, 19*, 4–12.

Eiser, J. R., & van der Pligt, J. (1984). Accentuation theory, polarization, and the judgment of attitude statements. In J. R. Eiser (Ed.), *Attitudinal judgment* (pp. 43–63). New York: Springer-Verlag.

Fazio, R. H. (1990). A practical guide to the use of response latency in social psychological research. In C. Hendrick & M. Clark (Eds.), *Research methods in personality and social psychology: Review of personality and social psychology* (Vol. 11, pp. 74–97). Newbury Park, CA: Sage.

Greenwald, A. G., & Breckler, S. J. (1985). To whom is the self presented? In B. Schlenker (Ed.), *The self and social life* (pp. 126–145). New York: McGraw-Hill.

Hartley, W. S. (1970). *Manual for the twenty statements problem.* Kansas City, MO: Greater Kansas City Mental Health Foundation.

Higgins, E. T., King, G. A., & Marvin, G. H. (1982). Category accessibility and subjective impressions and recall. *Journal of Personality and Social Psychology, 43*, 35–47.

Hogg, M. A. (1992). *The social psychology of group cohesiveness: From attraction to social identity.* London: Harvester Wheatsheaf.

Hogg, M. A. (1993). Group cohesiveness: A critical review and some new directions. In W. Stroebe & M. Hewstone (Eds.), *European review of social psychology,* (Vol. 4, pp. 85–111). London: Wiley.

Hogg, M. A., & Abrams, D. (1988). *Social identifications: A social psychology of intergroup relations and group process.* London: Routledge.

Hogg, M. A., & Hardie, E. A. (1991). Social attraction, personal attraction, and self-categorization: A field study. *Personality and Social Psychology Bulletin, 17*, 175–180.

Hogg, M., & Turner, J. C. (1985). Interpersonal attraction, social identification and psychological group formation. *European Journal of Social Psychology, 15*, 51–66.

Hogg, M., & Turner, J. C. (1987). Intergroup behaviour, self-stereotyping and the salience of social categories. *British Journal of Social Psychology, 26*, 325–340.

Jarymowicz, M. (1990, February). *Beliefs about self and egocentric versus nonegocentric evaluative standards.* Paper presented at the annual meeting of the European Association of Experimental Social Psychology, Mitzpe Ramon, Israel.

Jarymowicz, M. (1991, September). *The self/we schemata and social categorization effects.* Paper presented at the Conference on Changing Stereotypes, Université René Descartes, Paris.

Kramer, R. M., & Brewer, M. B. (1984). Effects of group identity on resource utilization in a simulated commons dilemma. *Journal of Personality and Social Psychology, 46,* 1044–1057.

Lenk, H. (1969). Top performance despite internal conflict: An antithesis to a functional proposition. In J. Loy & G. Kenyon (Eds.), *Sport, culture and society* (pp. 393–397). New York: Macmillan.

Long, K., Spears, R., & Manstead, A. (1994). The influence of personal and collective self-esteem on strategies of social differentiation. *British Journal of Social Psychology, 33,* 313–329.

Luhtanen, R., & Crocker, J. (1992). A collective self-esteem scale: Self-evaluation of one's social identity. *Personality and Social Psychology Bulletin, 18,* 302–318.

Markus, H., & Kitayama, S. (1991). Culture and the self: Implications for cognition, emotion, and motivation. *Psychological Review, 98,* 224–253.

Markus, H., Smith, J., & Moreland, R. (1985). Role of the self-concept in the perception of others. *Journal of Personality and Social Psychology, 49,* 1494–1512.

McClintock, C. G. (1972). Social motives: A set of propositions. *Behavioral Science, 17,* 438–454.

McFarland, C., & Buehler, R. (1995). Collective self-esteem as a moderator of the frog-pond effect in reactions to performance feedback. *Journal of Personality and Social Psychology, 68,* 1055–1070.

Millward, L. J. (1995). Contextualizing social identity in considerations of what it means to be a nurse. *European Journal of Social Psychology, 25,* 303–324.

Pelham, B. W. (1993). The idiographic nature of human personality: Examples of the idiographic self-concept. *Journal of Personality and Social Psychology, 64,* 665–677.

Pelham, B. W. (1995). Self-investment and self-esteem: Evidence for a Jamesian model of self-worth. *Journal of Personality and Social Psychology, 69,* 1141–1150.

Pelham, B. W., & Swann, W. B., Jr. (1989). From self-conception to self-worth: On the sources and structure of global self-esteem. *Journal of Personality and Social Psychology, 57,* 672–680.

Pelham, B. W., & Swann, W. B. (1994). The juncture of intrapersonal and interpersonal knowledge: Self-certainty and interpersonal congruence. *Personality and Social Psychology Bulletin, 20,* 349–357.

Perdue, C., Dovidio, J., Gurtman, M., & Tyler, R. (1990). Us and them: Social categorization and the process of intergroup bias. *Journal of Personality and Social Psychology, 59,* 475–486.

Prentice, D., Miller, D., & Lightdale, J. (1994). Asymmetries in attachments to groups and to their members: Distinguishing between common-identity and common-bond groups. *Personality and Social Psychology Bulletin, 20,* 484–493.

Simon, B., & Hamilton, D. H. (1994). Self-stereotyping and social context: The effects of relative in-group size and in-group status. *Journal of Personality and Social Psychology, 66,* 699–711.

Simon, B., Pantaleo, G., & Mummendey, A. (1995). Unique individual or interchangeable group member? The accentuation of intragroup differences versus similarities as an indicator of the individual self versus the collective self. *Journal of Personality and Social Psychology, 68,* 106–119.

Singelis, T. M. (1994). The measurement of independent and interdependent self-construals. *Personality and Social Psychology Bulletin, 20,* 580–591.

Smith, E. R., & Henry, S. (1996). An in-group becomes part of the self: Response time evidence. *Personality and Social Psychology Bulletin, 22,* 635–642.

Snyder, C. R., & Fromkin, H. L. (1980). *Uniqueness: The pursuit of difference.* New York: Plenum.

Stryker, S. (1991). Exploring the relevance of social cognition for the relationship of self and society: Linking the cognitive perspective and identity theory. In J. Howard & P. Callero (Eds.), *The self-society dynamic: Cognition, emotion, and action* (pp. 19–41). Cambridge, England: Cambridge University Press.

Sullivan, H. S. (1953). *The interpersonal theory of psychiatry*. New York: W. W. Norton.

Suls, J., & Wills, T. (Eds.). (1991). *Social comparison: Contemporary theory and research*. Hillsdale, NJ: Erlbaum.

Taylor, D. M., & Dube, L. (1986). Two faces of identity: The "I" and the "we." *Journal of Social Issues, 42*(2), 81–98.

Trafimow, D., Triandis, H. C., & Goto, S. G. (1991). Some tests of the distinction between the private and the collective self. *Journal of Personality and Social Psychology, 60*, 649–655.

Triandis, H. C. (1989). The self and social behavior in differing cultural contexts. *Psychological Review, 96*, 506–520.

Triandis, H. C., Bontempo, R., Villareal, M., Asai, M., & Lucca, N. (1988). Individualism and collectivism: Cross-cultural perspectives on self–ingroup relationships. *Journal of Personality and Social Psychology, 54*, 323–338.

Tropp, L. R., & Wright, S. C. (1995, June). *Inclusion of ingroup in the self: Adapting Aron & Aron's IOS Scale*. Paper presented at the annual meeting of the American Psychological Society, New York.

Turner, J. C. (1982). Towards a cognitive redefinition of the social group. In H. Tajfel (Ed.), *Differentiation between social groups* (pp. 15–40). Cambridge, England: Cambridge University Press.

Turner, J. C., Hogg, M., Oakes, P., Reicher, S., & Wetherell, M. (1987). *Rediscovering the social group: A self-categorization theory*, Oxford, England: Basil Blackwell.

Turner, J. C., Oakes, P. J., Haslam, A., & McGarty, C. (1994). Self and collective: Cognition and social context. *Personality and Social Psychology Bulletin, 20*, 454–463.

II. EARLY DEVELOPMENT OF ORGANIZATIONAL IDENTITY THEORY

Introduction to Part II

Early Contributions

....

Albert and Whetten contributed the first formal theoretical statement concerning organizational identity in 1985 and thereby inaugurated this field of study. But their work was soon complemented by others who built upon their ideas and by some, particularly from Europe, whose independent contributions would prove important to this new theme within organization studies. In this section of The Reader we present six of the most influential articles from the first decade of organizational identity research.

....

Stuart Albert and David A. Whetten: "Organizational Identity" (1985)

(*Research in Organizational Behavior*, vol. 7, pp. 263–95)
In their article "Organizational Identity" Albert and Whetten defined organizational identity as that which is central, distinctive, and temporally continuous. However, throughout the article, whenever they discussed temporal continuity, these authors used the term enduring. Thus "central, distinctive, and enduring" became the de facto definition of organizational identity used by those who built upon this landmark study. Today this definition is offered by many researchers in the field without comment, while others make their mark by challenging the validity of one or the other of its components.

You will discover the importance of Albert and Whetten's article in several influential ideas that it presented. In addition to contributing a definition of organizational identity, the article suggests that organizational identity is formed by a process of "ordered inter-organizational comparisons and reflections upon them over time," an idea that has led some scholars to take a process-based, longitudinal approach to theorizing about how organizational

identity is formed, maintained, and changed. Other important ideas contributed by Albert and Whetten include specification of conditions under
which organizational identity will be critically examined (organizational
formation or birth; loss of the founder; spin offs and divestitures; mergers and
acquisitions; rapid growth or decline), and the proposition that a discrepancy
between how insiders and outsiders view the organization can affect organizational health. Finally the article presents the idea that identity in organizations
may be dualistic, or hybrid, in the sense that it contains both utilitarian and
normative aspects.

Howard S. Schwartz: "Anti-Social Actions of Committed Organizational Participants: An Existential Psychoanalytic Perspective" (1987)

(*Organization Studies*, vol. 87, pp. 327–40)
According to Schwartz in "Anti-Social Actions of Committed Organizational
Participants: An Existential Psychoanalytic Perspective", an organization's
ontological function is to provide its members with "a sense of Being, or
identity" (p. 328). Schwartz is interested in cases in which a work organization
forms its own moral community, and argues that such organizations may influence their members' moral orientation to the world at large. Schwartz's thesis
is that a moral community forms on the basis of commitment, commitment
forms on basis of the ontological function of providing identity, and morality
so formed can stand in isolation from or opposition to broader community
norms.

Schwartz's article brought Freud's psychoanalytic theory into the discussion
of organizational identification by defining the concept of an organization
ideal in relation to Freud's ego ideal. In Schwartz's theory, the organization
ideal acts as a substitute for the ego ideal to which the individual aspires in its
search for a return to the infantile narcissistic state of total love and protection.
Schwartz suggested that, at least for those organizational participants whose
personal identities are in question, an organization ideal substitutes for the
ego ideal and thus the organization provides them with a sense of identity.
Schwartz used his theory to explain why some individuals are willing to perform unethical/illegal acts to protect their companies. The famous Silkwood
case provides the primary example through which Schwartz developed his
arguments.

Blake E. Ashforth and Fred Mael: "Social Identity Theory and the Organization" (1989)

(*Academy of Management Review*, vol. 14, pp. 20–39)
In "Social Identity Theory and the Organization", Blake Ashforth and Fred Mael introduced social identity theory (Tajfel and Turner, Part I) to organization studies and contributed a view of organizational identity defined at the subunit level of analysis. This influential article links the individual and organizational levels of analysis, as indicated in this quote: "in crediting a collectivity with a psychological reality beyond its membership, social identification enables the individual to conceive of, and feel loyal to, an organization or corporate culture" (Ashforth and Mael 1989: 26). The article predates Brewer and Gardner's (Part I) more highly specified rendering of the levels of analysis used to conceptualize identity (individual, relational, and collective) by giving a sense of the complexity of organizational identity when all the subunits and individuals that construct it are taken into consideration.

Most importantly, Ashforth and Mael argue that social identification is dependent upon a social construction of organizational or collective identity in the sense that identification processes at the individual level require a referent that takes the form of collective identity. Thus this article defines organizational identity as "a psychological reality [existing] beyond its membership".

Mats Alvesson: "Organization: From Substance to Image?" (1990)

(*Organization Studies*, vol. 11, pp. 373–94)
In his article "Organization: From Substance to Image?" Alvesson investigated the role that external images of organizations play in their internal management practices, paying particular attention to the ways that organizations attempt to manage their images through pseudo-events, pseudo-structures, and pseudo-actions. His thesis is that postindustrial society creates conditions that weaken naturally occurring processes of organizational identity development, which means that managers must concoct corporate substitutes for organizational identity in order to maintain the level of integration required to allow their organizations to continue functioning as economic entities. This concocting, Alvesson claimed, occurs through manipulation of corporate image and, once

managers become invested in managing corporate image, the organization's substance (which he defined as its culture and identity) recedes from view.

An important contribution of this article is a definition of corporate image as: "a holistic and vivid impression held by a particular group towards a corporation, partly as a result of information processing (sense-making) carried out by the group's members...and partly by the aggregated communication of the corporation in question concerning its nature, i.e., the fabricated and projected picture of itself" (1990: 376). Alvesson added this important caveat to his definition: "An image is something we get primarily through coincidental, infrequent, superficial and/or mediated information, through mass media, public appearances, from second-hand sources etc., not through our own direct, lasting experiences and perceptions of the 'core' of the object." By conceptualizing image and identity separately, Alvesson could then theorize about their relationship, which he presented as one of substitutability. That is, in the face of ambiguity or psychological distance from the corporation, management-instilled images replace personal experiences of the corporation in the mental representations of its participants. In short, image replaces substance. As you read this article, be sure to notice how Alvesson's concepts of ambiguity and psychological distance from the corporation parallel Schwartz's specification of members whose personal identity is in question; together these ideas begin to suggest some of the boundary conditions for a theory of organizational identity.

··

Jane Dutton and Janet Dukerich: "Keeping an Eye on the Mirror: Image and Identity in Organizational Adaptation" (1991)

(*Academy of Management Journal*, vol. 34, 517–54)
In the article "Keeping an Eye on the Mirror," Dutton and Dukerich provided a rich case study of an organization faced with an identity threat: namely the homelessness problem in New York City's bus and train terminals. Because the Port Authority was responsible for the terminals, their identity was affected when media pressure to deal with the problem tarnished their image in the public eye. Dutton and Dukerich's analysis of the case presented identity as a process that relates the organization to its environment by allowing it to both adapt to and change that environment. These authors showed how feedback to the organization from the environment (particularly the media) provided a mirror in which the organization saw itself in an undesirable light relative to its normally more positive self-concept. According to these authors, this mirroring

prompted the organization to try to change the undesired external image by taking action on the homelessness problem even though doing this was not in their charter.

Dutton and Dukerich's award winning article is perhaps most highly regarded for having presented the first empirical evidence of the workings of organizational identity and image. In addition to presenting a case that depicted organizational identity in a naturally occurring context, this article defined organizational image as that which the members of an organization perceive that others think or feel about them, a definition they would latter amend by relabeling their organizational image concept *"construed* organizational image" (Dutton, Dukerich, and Harquail 1994). Be sure to notice the differences between Alvesson's definition of organizational image and that offered by Dutton and Dukerich. These differences have resulted in considerable debate and no small amount of confusion in the field of organizational identity studies over how to conceptualize organizational image.

....

Linda E. Ginzel, Roderick M. Kramer, and Robert I. Sutton: "Organizational Impression Management as a Reciprocal Influence Process: The Neglected Role of the Organizational Audience" (1993)

(*Research in Organizational Behavior*, vol. 15, pp. 227–66)
Whereas Alvesson's article addressed organizational image from the perspective of how image might be managed by the organization, "Organizational Impression Management as a Reciprocal Influence Process: The Neglected Role of the Organizational Audience" by Ginzel, Kramer, and Sutton considers the influence of the organizational audience on the impression management process. These authors proposed a model of organizational impression management in which impression management is presented as a reciprocal and interactive influence process that entails cycles of negotiation between top management and segments of the organizational audience.

While it is perhaps the least explicit about the connection between image and organizational identity of any of the articles in The Reader (the connection comes when the authors frame their interest in impression management in terms of the role it plays in managing identity threats presented by an organization's external audiences), it nonetheless extends Goffman's theory of impression management (Part I) to the organizational level of analysis. However, as

87

opposed to Goffman's theory, which was based on a theatrical metaphor and hence on a largely homogeneous rendering of an audience, Ginzel, Kramer, and Sutton argued that organizational audiences are more likely to hold conflicting perceptions, making it much more difficult for top managers to succeed in impression management, which is why these authors focus considerable attention on the reasons why organizational impression management so often fails.

6

Organizational Identity

Stuart Albert and David A. Whetten

The objective of this chapter is to define and develop the concept of identity[1] within an organizational setting, to consider what the term organizational identity might mean that is clear, distinctive, important, useful and measurable. Historically, identity has been treated as a loosely coupled set of ideas, distinctions, puzzles, and concepts that are best considered as a framework or point of view (Erickson, 1980, 1968; James, 1890; Mead, 1934). The empirical questions and hypotheses derived from this framework are not tightly interrelated and clearly bounded as would be the case in a well developed theory (Blumer, 1969). Our task is to build; on this literature, to make the term "organizational identity" scientifically tractable. Specifically, our objective is to define, analyze, and illustrate identity in such a way that multiple empirical questions and hypotheses become visible. So that individual hypotheses and questions can be identified and easily referenced, we use the notation, superscript "Q," to denote statements that are important empirical questions, and "H" to denote statements offered as hypotheses.

Our discussion is organized in two parts. Part I examines a number of issues concerned with conceptualizing and defining organizational identity. Part II illustrates the concept of identity and dual identity in a concrete organization by means of a method that we label *extended metaphor analysis*.

I The Three Criteria Definition of Identity

Organizational identity as a concept has two uses. First, it is employed by scientists to define and characterize certain aspects of organizations—the scientific concept of organizational identity; and secondly, it is a concept that organizations use to characterize aspects of themselves (i.e., identity as a self-reflective question). Our goal in the following discussion is to address both uses, to contribute to the development of identity as a scientific concept, and to examine how organizational members use the concept of self-identity.

With respect to an organization's use of the concept, a prototypical sequence leading to questions regarding identity might be the following: an organization may decide which of several new products to market, which of several companies to acquire, which of several divisions to sell, or how to absorb a 20% budget cut internally. In short, organizations face choices of some consequence. Debate surrounding the alternatives is usually carried out, at least ideally, in terms of some model of rationality in which questions of information, probability, and expected utility dominate the discussion. When these considerations are not sufficient to resolve the question, and the importance of the question is inescapable, questions of information will be abandoned and replaced by questions of goals and values. When discussion of goals and values becomes heated, when there is deep and enduring disagreement or confusion, someone may well ask an identity question: "Who are we?" What kind of business are we in?" or "What do we want to be?"

In this sequence lies a principle of solution; namely, that a problem will be solved in the easiest, most satisfactory way: by obtaining facts if that is easy, by calculation if that is easy, or by discussing values that are easiest to discuss and on which there will most likely be a consensus. Questions of identity will, typically, be raised only when easier, more specific, more quantifiable solutions have failed. When the question of identity is raised, we propose that an organization will form a statement that is minimally sufficient for the purpose at hand. It does so, we speculate, because the issue of identity is a profound and consequential one, and at the same time, so difficult, that it is best avoided. Consequently, under ordinary circumstances, the answer to the identity question is taken for granted.

When the question of identity triggers a search for answers in the organization's culture, philosophy, market position, or membership, we propose, by way of a preliminary definition, that an adequate statement of organizational identity satisfies the following criteria:

1. The answer points to features that are somehow seen as the essence of the organization: *the criterion of claimed central character*.

2. The answer points to features that distinguish the organization from others with which it may be compared: *the criterion of claimed distinctiveness*.

3. The answer points to features that exhibit some degree of sameness or continuity over time: *the criterion of claimed temporal continuity*.

For purposes of defining identity as a scientific concept, we treat the criteria of central character, distinctiveness, and temporal continuity as each necessary, and as a set sufficient. To develop identity as a scientific concept, we bring relevant theory to bear on each of the three criteria of our definition. What we will define as important about an organization will depend on how we characterize the organization as a whole. Consider the notion of organizational culture (Louis, 1981; Pondy, Frost, Morgan, & Dandridge, 1983). Is culture part of organizational identity? The relation of culture or any other aspect of an organization to the concept of identity is both an empirical question (does the organization include it among those things that are central, distinctive and enduring) and a theoretical one (does the theoretical characterization of the organization in question predict that culture will be a central, distinctive, and an enduring aspect of the organization). We will use the three defining criteria of organizational identity as a framework for our discussion. Each criterion, or aspect of a provisional statement of identity, generates a host of empirical questions and poses certain distinctive hypotheses and propositions that together form an emerging research agenda for an identity distinctive framework.

Identity as a Statement of Central Character

What the criterion of central character means is that the concept of organizational identity, whether proposed by a scientist, by another organization, or by the organization itself, must be a statement of identity which distinguishes the organization on the basis of something important and essential. However, no theory at this point is capable of providing a universal list of all aspects of an organization that could be said to be important against those which could be said to be demonstrably unimportant. Often the issues will become important for a purpose. It is therefore not possible to define central character as a definitive set of measurable properties. Instead, for a given organization, a given purpose, and from a given theoretical viewpoint, one must judge what is or is not central.

The central character criterion raises a number of empirical questions about the organization's concept of identity. For example, how do organizations answer the identity question (Q1), and how are their answers affected by the context of the question (Q2)? Just as an individual may supply his fingerprints, name, address or social security number as different forms of identification for different purposes, so an organization may also focus on different essential characteristics depending on the perceived nature and purpose of the inquiry. For example, we expect organizations to provide different answers when they are contemplating acquiring a new subsidiary as opposed to preparing a legal brief supporting a claim for tax exempt status. When making an acquisition, decision makers will likely consider how the alternative business under consideration will affect the culture, product mix, financial status, and strategic goals of the acquiring company. Whereas, in the case of the court battle over a firm's tax classification, the characteristics of its membership, the humanitarian nature of its activities, and the source and use of its revenues will all be scrutinized.

These contrasting statements of identity present an interesting comparison. In the first case, the organization's identity is being discussed between organizational members only and there is no immediate threat to the organization's core identity. In contrast, in the court case the essential characteristics of the organization will be debated openly between adversaries and the outcome will have serious long term ramifications for essential, defining characteristics. A common ingredient in both cases is that the essential characteristics of the respective organizations are the focus of important decision making activities. Organizational leaders are attempting to define the organization's central characteristics as a guide for what they should do and how other institutions should relate to them. Furthermore, the key actors involved are concerned with the impact that future activities will have on the core organizational identity. Thus we see that alternative statements of identity may be compatible, complementary, unrelated, or even contradictory. How organizations elaborate, disambiguate, or defend a given statement of identity in the face of challenge is a fruitful line of research suggested by an identity distinctive framework (Q3).

Identity as a Classification that Identifies: Single, Dual and Multiple Identity

A primary meaning of the term identity in most formulations is that identity is a classification of the self that identifies the individual as recognizably different from others (and similar to members of the same class). This is the sense of identity that Erickson refers to as *individual* identity (Erickson, 1980, p. 109). In this usage, identity is linked with the term identification. Identity serves the function of identification and is in part acquired by identification.

While it is likely that there will be some empirical overlap between the essential and unique criteria of identity (in those cases where an essential element of an organization also makes it unique from others), these criteria are nonetheless logically independent, since all essential characteristics need not be unique and vice versa. For example, in the quest for brand loyalty it is not sufficient for a company to point out to consumers the essential ingredients in a product that justify its purchase. Marketing campaigns go beyond this and emphasize how a product differs from all other competing products, which may share most or even all of the same ingredients.

Organizations define who they are by creating or invoking classification schemes and locating themselves within them. From a scientific point of view

(McKelvey, 1983; McKelvey & Aldrich, 1983; Scott, 1981), the classification schemes implied by statements of identity are likely to be highly imperfect. The schemes may not be completely elaborated or defined, their dimensions may be assembled without a consistent plan and without care to their independence. The organization may only be ambiguously or vaguely located within each scheme, and different schemes may be employed on different occasions with self-interest the only principle of selection.

The dimensions selected to define an organization's distinctive identity may be quite eclectic, embracing statements of ideology, management philosophy, culture, ritual, etc. Relevant dimensions may include habitual strategic predispositions; for example, a known willingness to take high risks, as might be the case for a company that is distinctively defined by its entrepreneurial activities. Indeed, in those cases in which a distinctive identity is prized, one might expect organizations to select uncommon dimensions of interorganizational comparison as well as uncommon locations along more widely employed dimensions. In addition, which classification scheme is invoked may well depend on the perceived purpose to which the resulting statement of identity will be put. In this sense there is no one best statement of identity, but rather, multiple equally valid statements relative to different audiences for different purposes.

From our point of view, the formulation of a statement of identity is more a political–strategic act than an intentional construction of a scientific taxonomy. We treat the problem of imprecise, possibly redundant, or even inconsistent multiple classifications at different levels of analysis not as a methodological problem to be solved, nor as a deficiency of the concept of identity, but as a description of the facts of self-classification to be examined and explained. What is of interest is studying the ways in which the organizational self-classification implied and articulated by a statement of identity departs from the requirements of a scientific taxonomy (McKelvey, 1983). It is important to entertain the possibility that precise self-classification may be both impossible and, more importantly, undesirable for a number of reasons (Q4):

1. Ambiguous classification may prevent the organization from being typecast and thereby rendered more predictable than desired.

2. The complexity of the organization may make a simple statement of identity impossible.

3. Since organizations change over time, an overly precise or microclassification might quickly become outdated.

4. Since identity is usually assumed and only critically examined under certain conditions and then resolved with a minimal answer, we would not expect the formulation of identity to be honed to great precision.

For these, as well as other reasons, our view of organizational identity refers to a process of classification that is typically at variance with the cannons of constructing scientific taxonomies (for example, that the same organization must be classified into the same categories by multiple independent observers or judges). Indeed, what we find fascinating about this concept are the dynamics behind cases where agreement is unlikely. This leads us to wonder, "Under what circumstances and on what bases will there be disputes about the issue of identity change, and under what conditions and in what ways will these disputes be resolved?" (Q5).

The identity examination process can be conducted both internally and externally with varying degrees of specificity (Meyer & Rowan, 1977). Externally, the question, "What kind of organization is this?" is asked by scientists to establish boundaries of generalizability, by laymen to facilitate social interaction and commerce, and by public officials to establish responsibility and eligibility. In general, this question can be answered adequately utilizing a fairly gross categorization scheme (e.g., age, business/nonbusiness, approximate number of members, scope of activities, and location). In contrast, the more piercing question, "Who are we?" tends to focus on more specific, sensitive, and central characteristics (e.g., ethical, entrepreneurial, employee-oriented, stagnating, and predatory).

However it is conducted, the search is always for that formulation that will distinguish the organization from others. For the individual, the search for identity has historically sought to distinguish man from machine (what is alive from what is not) and man from other "lower" forms of animals. A traditional answer to what makes man distinctive and therefore provides his identity is that he has a self; whereas, machines and animals do not. The important point is that how distinctiveness is defined depends critically on what other objects of comparison are deemed relevant.

Two issues are closely associated with the notion of identity as a classification that identifies: the issue of distinguishing between public and private identity, and the issue of conveying identity to others.

One of the traditional distinctions within the identity literature is between the presentation of self to outsiders (public identity or personal) and the private perception of self (private identity). This distinction suggests two propositions at the organizational level: First, the greater the discrepancy between the way an organization views itself and the way outsiders view it (keeping "intentional ambiguity" within reason), the more the "health" of the organization will be impaired (i.e., lowered effectiveness [H1]). When organizational members possess a view of the organization's goals, mission, and values, that differs radically from views held by outsiders such as customers, regulatory bodies, financial institutions and competitors, the organization will have difficulty generating the political and resource support necessary to guarantee its survival (Cameron & Whetten, 1983a; Goodman & Pennings, 1977; Pfeffer & Salancik, 1978). Second, publically presented identity will typically be both more positive (H2) and more monolithic (H3) than the internally perceived identity. For example, universities typically present themselves as the realization of different but harmonious purposes, such as teaching, research and service, rather than as organizations torn between conflicting objectives. The university does not make its claim for public resources on the desirability of creatively managing the tension derived from inherently incompatible goals. It prefers to see itself as an umbrella for the synergistic combination of diverse and valued ends.

While information about organizational identity is often disseminated via official documents such as annual reports and press releases, public identity is also often conveyed through signs and symbols. An identity distinctive framework highlights questions surrounding the choice and modification of these symbols, such as logos and sales slogans, product packaging, and the location and appearance of the corporate headquarters. This does not mean that the study of signs and symbols is the exclusive province of an identity framework. However, the study of signs and symbols does naturally arise out of a conception of identity as identification (as in "identification with").

Many credit the miraculous recovery of the Chrysler corporation to the public's (congress, bankers, customers, unions) identification with Lee Iacocca as a dedicated, energetic, innovative leader whose company deserved another chance. He successfully portrayed Chrysler as an under-dog who was fighting for survival against great odds. By aligning his company's cause with core societal values, he was able to weld together a diverse coalition of supporters.

Mono and Dual Identity Organizations
In both everyday language as well as in more formal scientific discourse, we tend to treat most organizations as if they were either one type or another, for example, church or state, profit or nonprofit. This taxonomic tradition assumes that most organizations have a single and sovereign identity. The alternative assumption is that many, if not most, organizations are hybrids composed of multiple types (H4).

By a hybrid we mean an organization whose identity is composed of two or more types that would not normally be expected to go together. Of such an organization we would say that it is part X and part Y, the simplest case of which is a hybrid of two types, a dual identity organization. Thus, it is not simply an organization with multiple components, but it considers itself (and others consider it) alternatively, or even simultaneously, to be two different types of organizations.

We take as indirect evidence for the existence of hybrids the difficulty of applying any taxonomic scheme to any set of existing organizations, which almost always results in a number of cases that are difficult to classify (Scott, 1981, p. 45). Rather than attribute the difficulty of achieving precise classification solely to deficiencies of the taxonomic scheme itself (e.g., imprecise rules of classification, insufficient information about the organization), we prefer to point to the probable existence of genuine hybrids.

We distinguish two forms of duality, one in which each unit within the organization exhibits both identities of the organization and one in which each internal unit exhibits only one identity—the multiple identities of the organization being represented by different units. The former, in which each internal unit exhibits the properties of the organization as a whole, we label the *holographic* form. The latter, in which each internal unit exhibits only one identity, is the *ideographic* or *specialized* form. These two forms of internal structure give rise to very different kinds of organizations.

The ideographic form of dual identity is analogous to Thompson's (1967) concept of buffering an organization's core technology with support systems in that the central mission of the organization is sheltered from external demands by a cadre of specialists who are only marginally involved in the core activities and ideology of the organization. Often, their primary commitment is to their professional role in the organization, rather than the central institutional values of the organization. An example of this structural arrangement might be a bank that is operated by a religious organization. The central decision makers are also church officials committed to advancing the interests of the church through the bank, as well as insuring that the bank operates according to the moral code of the church. But the peripheral functions of the banking operation (e.g., accountants and computer operators) are performed by personnel hired primarily on the basis of their technical expertise. Within this structural arrangement the organization's pluralism is evident across units but not within units. Each unit is staffed with pure-types and interaction between units is limited by the normal structural impediments of couple bureaucratic institutions.

In contrast, the holographic form of dualism is more similar to the Theory Z approach to management proposed by Ouchi (1981) in which different, and to some extent conflicting, management styles are blended together and diffused evenly throughout the entire organization. In the case of the bank operated by a religious order, the holographic form would require that all members of the organization be members of the sponsoring church and that their performance would be evaluated using the joint criteria of technical proficiency and religiosity.

It is interesting to speculate about the relative adaptive advantage of the holographic and ideographic organizations. On the one hand the ideographic organization is likely to possess greater variety, since it contains greater specialization and more pure types. (Relaxing the condition that all elements must subscribe to a common value system in a normative organization allows for greater variability.) Hence, following Ashby's law of requisite variety (1962) members of ideographic organizations should be better prepared to monitor diverse environmental conditions and formulate appropriate recommendations for adaptive organizational modifications (H5).

On the other hand, the obvious disadvantage of the ideodentic organization is the relative difficulty it has gaining commitment from its members for a given course of action. While it has become almost axiomatic to state that organizations are composed of political interest groups vying for control over the collective resources (Pfeffer & Salancik, 1978), the conflict in an ideographic organization is more fundamental. It is a struggle, not simply over alternative budget proposals, but over the very soul of the institution. In the case of the religiously owned bank this type of struggle will be signaled by the accountants referring to the controlling administrators as impractical religious fanatics and the accountants being labeled as valueless mercenaries. As the relative power of the various ideological groups builds and diminishes, the identity of the organization as a whole will be altered in complexion, leading outsiders to complain that the organization cannot decide what it wants to be or who it wants to serve. Hence, while the holographic organization has less diversity to draw upon in formulating a "correct" plan of action, once a plan has been proposed leaders will be able to draw upon common characteristics across all units as the basis for establishing consensus (H6).

Identity Over Time

The temporal aspect of the concept of identity is essential. A central proposition in the identity literature is that loss of identity (in the sense of continuity over time) threatens an individual's health. In fact, it was Erickson's original observations that the disturbances of army personnel after World War II might be derived from their loss of continuity with their previous life that led him to originate the concept of ego identity as a sense of sameness over time which was necessary for psychological health (Erickson, 1968).

Is this the same as saying that change is difficult? In a certain sense, yes, since change may involve loss. But what an identity framework adds that is distinctive is a concern with the characteristic ways human beings deal with loss through mourning, grief, and ritual. Therefore, by applying an identity framework to the study of organizations we are naturally led to ask questions about mourning and grief during changes involving loss, and about the existence, desirability, and feasibility of identity-related rituals [e.g., "organizational funerals" conducted for plants that are closing or subsidiaries that are being sold, (Albert, 1984)].

At the individual level, an identity distinctive inquiry is one that examines the interplay between what an individual may potentially become, what is available to him at a given time, and how those sets of roles and identities are themselves changing over time (Lifton, 1970). Specifically, it addresses three issues: (1) the potential of the individual assuming different identities or roles; (2) the kinds of roles or identities currently available; and (3) how the relationship of (1) to (2) is affected by the historical forces operating at the time.

At the organizational level it is interesting to speculate about the analogues of gaining and losing identity-related roles, such as parent and child, friend and enemy, policeman and outlaw, leader and follower, teacher and pupil. Certainly the frequent reference to terms like industry leader, maverick, predator, and entrepreneur in the business literature suggests that organizational roles exist. An identity distinctive framework underscores the need to examine how new roles come into existence, how organizations choose (or back into) one role rather than another, and how that action affects the organization's internal and external identity. The identity interaction model (Cooley, 1922; Goffman, 1959; Mead, 1934) states that individual identity is formed and maintained through interaction with others. At the organizational level this poses the question of whether an organization can be said to undergo socialization into a particular role through interaction with other organizations (Q6). If so, are the general laws that describe the socialization of an organization similar to those that describe the socialization of an individual into an organization?

The identity literature suggests that similar processes indeed occur at both levels. In discussing individual identity formation, Erickson (1968) analyzes the problem of identity formation in terms of a series of comparisons: (1) outsiders compare the target individual with themselves; (2) information regarding this evaluation is conveyed through conversations between the parties ("polite boy," "messy boy") and the individual takes this feedback into account by making personal comparisons with outsiders, which then; (3) affects how they define themselves. It follows from this logic that organizational identity is formed by a process of ordered inter-organizational comparisons and reflections upon them over time (Albert, 1977).

When identity becomes a salient issue: some time-dependent hypotheses. Perhaps the most useful contribution of the individual identity literature to the temporal aspect of identity is in the form of a question: Can we predict when organizational identity will emerge as an issue for an organization as a function of time-dependent processes that affect many if not all organizations (Q7)? While we acknowledge that life cycle development/concepts are controversial, especially at the organizational level (Cameron & Whetten, 1983b), we propose that the concept of identity suggests by analogy a number of intriguing testable hypotheses at the organizational level. Specifically, we suggest that the question of organizational identity will be particularly salient or important during the following life cycle events (H7–12):

1. *The formation of the organization (H7).* When the organization is forming and defining exactly what its niche will be, questions of goals, means, technology (all of which are components of defining who and what the organization is) will be salient.

2. *The loss of an identity sustaining element (H8)*. If, for example, the founder of a young organization prematurely leaves, a period of soul-searching about organizational identity will occur in the process of searching for a suitable successor.

3. *The accomplishment of an organization's raison d'etre (H9)*. The March of Dimes has become the classic example of an organization that worked itself out of a reason for existing. In that case, the organization maintained its central mission of raising money for health research and shifted its focus from polio to birth defects. But a wide range of alternatives were examined at the time, including some which would have significantly altered the central focus of the organization.

4. *Extremely rapid growth (H10)*. When the ratio of choices faced by an organization is very high relative to its perceived constraints, a condition that might occur when profits or other resources greatly exceed their habitual use, then we can expect the organization to consider issues of identity. In a sense this is a condition analogous to adolescence when excess capacity is in search of use and direction.

5. *A change in "collective status" (H11)*. Marriage, birth, and divorce have been noted as marker events likely to trigger the reevaluation of a person's self definition. In organizations, the threat of a hostile takeover, the consummation of a carefully planned merger, the divestiture of a previously central subsidiary, or the acquisition of a firm outside the parent company's industry will likely precipitate sharp debates regarding institutional mission, values, and identity.

6. *Retrenchment (H12)*. Retrenchment necessarily involves the definition of organizational identity because it requires the use of budgeting priorities which in turn require an answer to the question of who and what an organization is and what it wants to be (i.e., its descriptive and prescriptive identity) (Whetten, 1980). We hypothesize that the issue of organizational identity may be most acute during retrenchment following a period of slow rather than rapid growth. When organizations grow slowly, they acquire additional goals, missions, and objectives (and the different definitions of identity which these tend to imply). The incompatibility of the differing definitions remains latent until retrenchment forces their discovery.

We can further develop the issue of identity change over time by means of the following diagram utilizing four common life cycle events (Birth, Growth, Maturity, Retrenchment) as markers for the temporal dimension. For purposes of illustration the two poles of the Y axis are labeled U for utilitarian identity, and N for normative identity. These two orientations will be described more extensively in the second half of the paper. For our discussion of Figure 1, it will be sufficient to think of a normative organization as a church, and a utilitarian organization as a business. Five paths are illustrated in Figure 1 representing several hypothetical paths of identity change (or lack of change)

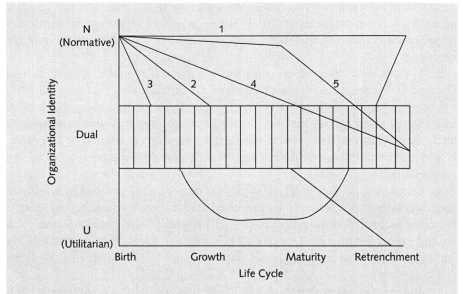

Fig. 1. Alternative paths of identity change over the organizational life cycle.

that may take place over the organizational life cycle. To simplify the diagram we have shown these paths for only the normative organizations. A complete diagram would also include the mirror image of these five paths for utilitarian organizations. Before we comment on each path we would like to propose a general tendency for the entire set of monotonic curves, specifically the tendency for monoidentity organizations to assume dual identities.

The drift from mono to dual identities. A common proposition in the life cycle literature is that the identity of organizations frequently shifts from A to B at critical transition points (Kimberly, 1980; Lodahl & Mitchell, 1980). This generally occurs very gradually, and hence has been referred to as identity drift. Our proposal is related but different in an important way. We, too, are convinced that a key to understanding the evolution of an organization is tracking shifts in its identity over time, but we are primarily interested in the drift from A, or B, to AB. While the shift in an organization's identity by a process of *substitution* is obviously an important aspect of the life cycle model, it is the shift resulting from the process of *addition* that we feel has been overlooked in the literature thus far. The arrows in Figure 1 illustrate our belief that over time there is a general tendency for mono-identity organizations to acquire a dual identity (H13). With increasing size churches may become more like businesses and businesses may adopt more of the normative structure and values of churches.

There are a number of reasons for postulating a drift towards dualism—reasons which are, in effect, a statement of the advantages and disadvantages of mono vs. dual identity at different points in the life cycle. Without attempting a comprehensive discussion in advance of the empirical documentation of the dualistic shift in a given case, the following reasons for expecting a dualistic shift seem plausible.

1. *Environmental complexity.* If the environment within which the organization is embedded grows more complex over time, presenting both a mix of opportunities and constraints, then a dual identity organization should have adaptive advantages over a mono-identity organization (H14). Again, following Ashby's principle of requisite variety, organizational effectiveness depends in part on the match between organizational complexity and environmental complexity. We propose that over time organizations acquire dual identities both to exploit the opportunities of an increasingly complex and changing environment, as well as to cope with increases in environmentally imposed constraints and regulations. The rapid increase in administrative ratio in institutions of higher education during the past two decades in response to a potential expansion in governmental regulation and intervention illustrates this purpose.

2. *Duality by default.* There is a tendency for some organizations, particularly those in the public sector, to acquire multiple identities simply because they become the repository of all things that other organizations will not undertake (H15). For organizations with relatively little control over the scope of their mandate we expect this will be a common path to duality.

3. *The problem of identity divestiture.* It is generally easier to acquire a new identity during growth than to divest an identity during a time of retrenchment (Albert, 1984). Organizations tend to become committed to what they have been and seldom substitute new identifying characteristics for old ones (H16). If this proposition is true, then a drift towards duality would seem to be the necessary result of a process of identity accretion.

4. *Organizational success.* Very often organizations that are eminently successful in pursuing a single identity enter a second domain of activity because of their success in the first (H17). For example, the highly profitable and visible business firms in major metropolitan cities are often invited to assume a major role in supporting the arts. Similarly, a highly successful church may find itself overwhelmed with the administrative and economic detail necessary to meet the needs of its burgeoning congregations. In both cases, the highly successful mono-identity organization tends to acquire a dual identity by virtue of its success.

Path specific hypotheses. Path 1 of Figure 1 illustrates an organization that retains its identity throughout its life cycle. Paths 2 and 3 portray an organization changing its identity over the course of its life cycle, but consistently retaining a single identity (normative followed by utilitarian). In Path 2 this change is permanent, whereas in Path 3 the organization reverses back to its earlier ideological roots after a brief period of trying a new identity. While these shifts may be deliberate, for example, to exploit new opportunities, they are more likely to occur as a result of identity drift, especially for young organizations (H18) (Lodahl & Mitchell, 1980). As noted earlier, the identity of an organization during the growth phase of its life cycle exists often only in a latent form. It is taken for granted and lies submerged under the press of the day-to-day problems of managing growth. Under these conditions organizations often begin to play roles and take on orientations different from those originally envisioned by its founders. But this transformation process often occurs so unobtrusively and at such a slow pace that it is not fully recognized until an organizational crisis forces members to explicitly examine their collective identity. In some cases when the shift is recognized it is welcomed and pursued with great intensity (Path 2), while in others organizational members are shocked by the extent of the drift and take deliberate actions to return to their ideological roots (Path 3).

Fundamentalist churches and medical clinics provide interesting examples of these two paths. Many fundamental Christian denominations have undergone a radical shift in identity with the advent of the "electronic church." Several religious groups sponsor programs on television, including "wholesome family entertainment," Sunday morning services, revivals, talk shows, and fund raising campaigns for Christian colleges. This dramatic change in the form of worship has created considerable debate in the sponsoring church organizations. Advocates point to expanded impact, while detractors lament the loss of intimacy and the apparent intrusion of commercialism into their religious experience. The question, "Are we a church or a broadcasting service?" has led some churches to drop or at least modify their support of religious programming on television.

In a similar fashion when a group of independent physicians join together to form a medical clinic, debates over the identity of the emerging organization are quite predictable. The doctors hire professional managers to handle the business aspects of the clinic, but because they are part owners in the operation they insist on making recommendations for how the clinic could be operated more effectively. However, when the business managers respond to pressures to increase profitability with such measures as cost cutting, the doctors invariably complain about a loss of concern for the welfare of their patients. Discussions between the physicians bearing on the question, "Are we a business or a humanitarian organization?" influence the clinic's movement along Paths 2 and 3.

In general, we hypothesize that with increasing size and over time, a church will begin to look more like a business (H19), than a growing business will look like a church (H20). This occurs for the reasons outlined by Weber (1968) in his discussion of the routinization of charisma. Young, normative organizations are generally founded upon the ideological vision of a charismatic leader. Over time, the success of the movement creates administrative challenges that can be met adequately only by the establishment of formal organizational structures, rules, procedures, etc. Empirical support for this proposition comes from Pettigrew's (1979) study of English public (our private) schools. He found that public schools which were the most successful through their initial growth and maturity phases replaced their entrepreneurial founder with a "steady state manager" capable of routinizing what initially began as an ideologically driven educational program.

However, it is also interesting to examine the case of utilitarian organizations that acquire a normative identity. To some extent this is the path described by Selznick (1957) in his discussion of the process of institutionalization in which the technical activities of an organization become infused with value beyond that associated with their technical function. As part of this process, businesses begin to define their value in terms of their contribution to the broad normative purposes of the society, instead of the more narrow economic marketplace. Selznick argues that institutionalization involves and requires that administrators become statesmen. The assumption of this new role is associated with a new set of incentives to maintain society's values and culture whether through philanthropy, assuming an active role in a private sector sponsored employment and training program (like the National Alliance of Businessmen), or by encouraging executives to take leaves of absence to serve in full time government or ambassadorial positions, teach in universities, and so forth.

A particularly interesting case of the acquisition of dual identity is an economic organization that acquires a normative identity by establishing relations with normative organizations. For example, a business may donate time and money to a charitable organization such as the United Way or the local arts council. If such activities are undertaken over a long enough time period and with enough commitment and emphasis, they may become part of the business' identity as a civic minded organization, a commitment which then becomes part of its fundamental character and which distinguishes it from other businesses. The advantage of a normative identity that is assumed by means of an interorganizational relationship rather than by a transformation of the organization itself is the ease with which such relationships can be modified or terminated when required. On the other hand, it can be argued that establishing an inter-organizational link to a normative organization, rather than signaling movement towards the acquisition of a dual identity, is precisely the mechanism for avoiding it. The organization is in the position to claim a normative identity without the internal modification that the acquisition of such identity requires.

If Path 4 illustrates an incremental and long term tendency towards dual identity, Path 5 illustrates the hypothesis that scarcity motivates the acquisition of dual identity (H17). At such times, dual identity can occur for both internal and external reasons. Faced with retrenchment, a church, for example, may hire financial experts who may become so important that the financial criteria they espouse, such as cost effectiveness, may come to directly challenge other principles of decision making and the identity of the organization in the process. In its struggle for economic survival the normative organization may rightly fear the ironic truth of the slogan that it may be necessary to destroy the organization in order to save it. With respect to its external environment the organization may point to the economic benefits of its continued existence. The church in this example may point to its role in providing services to the poor which otherwise would have to be provided by others. Thus, a normative organization under attack can be expected to prepare a utilitarian defense, just as a threatened utilitarian organization will also seek to defend itself on normative grounds (H22). Economic-utilitarian organizations will claim not only that they provide jobs and earn a profit for their stockholders, but that they contribute to the community at large. Who, after all, contributed to the museum when it was in need or gave jobs to the poor and absorbed the cost of training them, etc.

Summarizing our discussion of the pressures supporting the adoption of multiple identities, we hypothesize that Path 1 occurs infrequently (H23) and that Paths 2 and 3 occur less frequently than Paths 4 and 5 (H24).

II An Illustration of Dual Identity

A Strategy for Discovering the Dimensions of Identity

As a scientific concept, identity can be conceived of as a multidimensional construct where the problem is to identify, define, and then measure the dimensions of interest. There is, of course, no mechanical discovery procedure for what dimensions should be considered in a given case, just as, at the level of individuals, there is no agreed upon list of identities or roles that an individual might assume in the world. Our discussion thus far has considered the normative utilitarian dimensions. There are a large number of others that may be of interest but whatever dimensions are selected, the challenging scientific project is always how to define and measure them.

There are two broad, well-established approaches to the problem of definition and measurement (Pondy & Olson, 1977). The approaches differ in the extent that one begins with precisely defined dimensions. One may begin with no dimensions in mind at all. This approach, associated with an anthropological tradition, is purely inductive. A given organization is examined in detail without an explicit preconceived theoretical viewpoint, and those dimensions that define what is core, distinctive, and enduring are arrived at by inductive generalization from the organization's peculiar characteristics. At the other extreme, one may work deductively from a theoretical viewpoint that suggests or supplies relatively well defined identity-relevant dimensions. For example, the dimension of profit and nonprofit is likely to be considered important in all economic treatments of the organization, and this dimension has achieved some definitional precision based on a body of theory and accepted practice, namely, the law.

A third alternative that we illustrate here adopts a middle course. If there is no comprehensive theory to predict how many identities an organization has, or how the dimensions of each are to be defined, then another alternative is to *characterize* rather than to define each provisional identity and then carry out what we call *extended metaphor analysis* (EMA) as a way of retrospectively sharpening the definition of each identity and the dimensions that underlie or compose it.

Extended metaphor analysis can be viewed as a method for defining and characterizing one organization in terms of another. With respect to the normative–utilitarian dimension, EMA is a way of asking in what ways a given organization is like a church (representing a normative organization), or a business (representing a utilitarian organization). The ability to sustain two altern-ative metaphoric descriptions of the organization is the primary test of duality. To establish duality it must be shown that each metaphor can be applied to events of fundamental character that distinguish the organization from others, over time. The hypothesis of duality also assumes power to the extent that the metaphor is capable of being applied to a wide variety of organizational events, in short, to the extent that the "fit" between the target organization and its metaphoric analogue is both close and extensive.

The target organization we have selected for demonstrating this method is the modern research university. Our hypothesis is that this organization has a dual identity, that of a church (normative identity) and a business (utilitarian identity). Further, we postulate that the identity of the modern research university has shifted from its normative, largely religious origins towards an increasingly utilitarian posture. This shift from a single to a dual identity illustrates Path 4 in Figure 1.

The discovery that an organization has a dual identity can be an important key in understanding its behavior under any circumstances, but particularly when issues of identity are assumed to be pivotal. One such time, according to our previous analysis, is retrenchment. For this reason we will follow our brief description of the university as a dual identity organization with a description of some of the implications of dual identity for understanding how this type of organization responds to retrenchment. As noted earlier, a dual identity organization facing retrenchment would be expected to encounter a host of difficulties in formulating policy and strategy and coping with internal conflict.

A Characterization of the Normative–Utilitarian Dimensions

We will preface our analysis of the comprehensive research university with a more extensive discussion of the normative and utilitarian constructs, drawing on the works of Parsons (1960), Etzioni (1975), and Cummings (1981).

A utilitarian organization is defined as one that is oriented towards economic production (Parsons, 1960). The principal case is the business firm, which will be the subject of our illustration. The business firm is an organization governed by values of economic rationality, the maximization of profit, and the minimization of cost, and for which financial return is both a condition of continuing operation and a central symbol of success. "Products are marketed on a full payment-of-cost basis involving prices governed by marginal utility, not by 'need.' Loyalties and obligations to the organization are defined in terms of 'self-interest.' Remuneration is the major means of control over lower participants and calculative involvement characterizes the orientation of the large majority of participants" (Etzioni, 1975, p. 31, and 47).

The business firm is expected to "pay its way" on a utility-marginal productivity basis. In the long range it is expected to meet its costs through the monetary proceeds of its operations, with profit the symbol of its success and effective operation. An employee is expected to be paid what his services are worth as determined by a competitive market and will not be blamed for quitting if he can do better.

The business firm is a relatively centralized organization. Its procedures are removed from "democratic" norms. This centralization is legitimized by the expectation that management will be competent and that the interests of management and of the employees will be similar.

The concept of normative identity is typified by Parsons' pattern maintenance organization, the principal examples of which center on organizations with primarily "cultural," "educational," and "expressive" functions (Parsons, 1960, p. 40). Examples of organizations with clear normative patterns are: religious organizations, including churches, orders, and monasteries; a subcategory of political organizations that have a strong ideological program; general hospitals, universities, and voluntary associations. Normative power is the major source of control over most lower participants, whose orientation to the organization is characterized by high commitment. Compliance rests principally on the internalization of organizational directives that are accepted as legitimate. Leadership rituals, manipulation of social and prestige symbols, and resocialization are among the more important techniques of control (Etzioni, 1961).

Utilitarian organizations are largely managed by information, normative organizations by ideology, a distinction between two logical systems of management that was the subject of Cummings' presidential address (Cummings, 1981). As Cummings states:

Management by information places major emphasis upon the instrumental function of managerial action and of organizational roles in society.... This logic of management is most expressly seen in the technical functions of organizations and in the development of technologies and structures that are appropriate for processing and implementing nonstrategic decisions. Management-by-ideology...aims to design...organizational systems to serve the expressive functions of organizations in a society. The roles of leaders and followers are quite different in this management system. The purposes of organizations are assumed to be posterior, they are assumed to be basically rationalizations for organizational action. In addition, the cohesiveness of organizations is provided not by information, logic, and rationale, but by the acceptance of shared values, shared beliefs, and intensive socializational experience (Cummings, 1981, p. 2).

With these preliminary comments regarding the underlying constructs, we turn now to a description of the university as a dual identity organization.

The University's Dual Identity as Church and as Business
The university emerged from the cloistered environment of the monastery as the Age of Enlightenment created a demand for and legitimized the public pursuit of knowledge and understanding (Taylor, 1980). Consequently, it is quite natural to expect that the university of today should contain vestiges of its religious origins (Nisbet, 1979). This can be seen in the fact that both the church and the university have assumed the role of "living in the world, but not of the world." This means that they both assume that they have been given the role of leading the world rather than being led by external secular forces. Members of both organizations view outsiders as heathens to be converted/educated. It is believed that this transformation will make vulgar men virtuous. The value of this metamorphosis is supported in both institutions by an elaborate set of beliefs about the blessings of being righteous/knowledgeable. These include: being released from the bondage of sin/ignorance; enjoying the benefits of inspiration/wisdom; and earning a sense of personal pride as a result of disciplining base instincts to achieve a higher, more righteous/refined level of development. Personal sacrifices (including financial contributions to the agent of transformation) are justified in terms of enhanced long term rewards (blessings in heaven/enhanced life time earnings).

Neither institution is expected to compete for members (parishioners/students) in the same way that businesses compete for clients or customers. Indeed, that would be viewed by our society as undignified. (Only recently, as both institutions have suffered significant drops in membership, have they resorted to extensive advertising for support.) In general, society expects both institutions to be slow to change because they both serve as significant repositories of tradition. Universities and churches provide relief from the fast-paced, often meaningless and haphazard, day-to-day activities. Religious and educational traditions, symbols, and rituals provide members a much needed representation of stability and security in their otherwise chaotic, anomic life. They enable individuals to periodically reaffirm what they feel are society's core values (Kamens, 1977).

For example, churches and universities have constructed elaborate rites-of-passage to commemorate the transitions from youth to adulthood (Bar Mitzvah), single life to married life (marriage), uneducated to learned (graduation). In these ceremonies participants and spectators alike renew their commitment to the underlying value system of their society. Recognizing the importance of these key transitions occurring under the aegis of these ideological institutions, civil marriages and "voc-tech" educational degrees are viewed with contempt by the true believers. They are viewed as instrumental transactions, rather than rites-of-passage. Because they don't recognize that part of the reason for going to college is to become socialized into a culture, and that part of the reason for getting married is to reaffirm support for essential moral values, the legitimacy of these secular imitations of sacred events is discredited by the faithful.

The university is like an ecumenical council. Each department has its own faith (discipline) and the university basically represents a "federation of faiths." The university derives its status from the quality of the federation members (colleges). Its function is to adjudicate disputes between the various denominations (departments) and to facilitate collaboration on issues of common concern. This arrangement accounts for the reluctance of university administrators to allocate resources disproportionately across departments. To say that Department A should have part of its funds withdrawn so that they can be given to Department B is tantamount to saying that the beliefs, values, and claims of one faith are more valid than those of another.

A common problem in all ideological organizations is assessing effectiveness. How can you measure the effectiveness of a teacher in fostering inquisitiveness, or the effectiveness of a minister in increasing faith? Because it is impossible to arrive at a consensus about how to measure ideological goal fulfillment, there is a tendency in churches and universities to substitute measures of efficiency for measures of effectiveness (Whetten, 1981). Since performance measures have a powerful effect on members' allocation of time and effort across activities, the natural consequence is that the organization inevitably becomes means instead of ends oriented.

For example, because we can't determine what percentage of a minister's congregation are admitted into heaven when they die, the quality of a minister's performance is instead judged by the average attendance at his meetings and the size of this congregation's weekly contributions. Similarly, since we can't quantify the long term impact of a teacher on a student we make some assumptions about the maximum number of students a teacher can effectively instruct and then treat faculty/student ratios as indicators of the quality of education.

There are many similarities between the ideology of the professor and the priest. Both universities and churches extoll the virtues of poverty. Somehow, being poor is supposed to be enobling. Being rich, on the other hand, is viewed as debilitating because it interferes with one's single minded pursuit of religious/scholarly objectives. This view is of course consistent with the finding that under certain conditions the provision of external incentives for a task can undermine its perceived intrinsic worth (Deci, 1977).

The similarity between the ideology of the professor and the priest is also reflected in the explanation given for either individual forsaking his/her "calling" and joining a secular organization. In both cases, they basically conclude that the personal sacrifices they are required to make as members of the clergy or faculty are not worth the benefits. (These include low salary, restricted choice of places to live, pressures of the job, and in some cases the opportunity to marry and have a family.) In both cases defectors generally do not leave until they are personally convinced that leaving the university or church is not tantamount to ending up in purgatory, i.e., it is still possible to be intelligent, cultured, idealistic, religious, single-mindedly committed to a life of service or learning after leaving the university or church.

Churches and universities have similar socialization practices and reward status hierarchies. Both require a long apprenticeship, or novice period, during which a person is formally scrutinized by senior members of the organization. This period of proving oneself does not simply focus on technical skill proficiency. The commitment of the novice to the ideology of the organization is also critical. Once novices are ordained/given tenure, they have considerable autonomy in the organization. Consequently, the organization is very vulnerable to claims of both malpractice (failure of technical skills) and malfeasance (failure to fulfill normative expectations). Hence the need for very long socialization periods in both organizations (graduate school, post doc, assistant professor/divinity school, internship, assistant minister).

That a university also has an identity as a utilitarian organization is evident from the claim that its training will be of use to the individual and to society. The concept of utility is at the heart of the notion of service which is part of the trinity of missions (teaching, research, and service) by which the organization justifies its support. The demonstrated utility of applied science and technology during World War II encouraged the view that science and technology were not to be valued for their own sake, but because they were necessary for both an enhanced quality of life and national defense. Federal research support for scientists, for which the university served as a conduit, helped change the identity of the university from a religious institution to a utilitarian one (Moynihan, 1980).

Since that time the university has had considerable difficulty satisfying its normative goal of living in the world but not of the world. As the amount of resources required to support research grew substantially in recent decades, universities found themselves increasingly competing with secular institutions for external support (Coleman, 1973). The requirements for competing successfully in the secular marketplace have resulted in a significant transformation of the academy. Normatively it still clings to its medieval roots as a religious institution, but its reward structure has become increasingly outcome-oriented. For example, faculty are rewarded less for how much wisdom they instill in the next generation, than for the number of publications they produce. The logic underlying this reward structure is that publications are a more fungible commodity than wisdom. The university can take publications and Nobel prizes into the marketplace and use them to barter for resources to buy the newest model of electron microscopes, etc.

The dysfunctional outcome of this trend is that the university is increasingly viewed by its members and external support groups as more instrumental (Jencks & Riesman, 1968; Kerr, 1963). Consequently, the organization is less able to use normative devices for securing commitment to the institution's goals. When faculty members perceive that they are being evaluated on the basis of the volume and quality of the commodities they are producing for the organization to sell in the marketplace, rather than on the basis of their contribution to the organization's missions of spreading the gospel of enlightenment, they respond in kind. One highly visible sign of this shift in commitment is the rapid growth of faculty unions in higher education (Cameron, 1982).

When we state that the university has begun to assume a utilitarian identity as well as a normative one, we mean more than that it has utilitarian goals as part of its mission statement. The internal organizing rules, norms, and attitudes increasingly reflect a utilitarian point of view. Our hypothesis is that the transformation of the university from a normative to a hybrid organization has occurred so slowly that its impact on internal work activities has largely gone unnoticed by participants. The lack of tension between these conflicting personas in the past can also be attributed to the combination of its peculiar organizational structure and relatively abundant resource support. The loosely coupled (Weick, 1976) ideographic structure of the university has acted as a set of boundaries, keeping apart what might be conflicting points of view, philosophies of education, rules of procedure, and priorities. Because it is a loosely coupled system, not only have departments that might be expected to champion normative vs. utilitarian identities been kept separate, but faculty (who as a body represent a normative identity) and administration (who represent a utilitarian orientation) rarely tend to cross the boundary between them. Professors of humanities rarely become accountants and vice versa.

During retrenchment, however, the conflict between normative and utilitarian identities, previously latent during growth and stability, becomes manifest in a series of issues:

Selective vs. across-the-board cuts. Small cuts, perhaps out of a sense of fairness and a desire to avoid the maximum pain caused any one unit will generally be distributed across the board. We hypothesize that a normative organization should be better able to sustain a deep across-the-board cut than a utilitarian one because normative organizations typically require a period of long socialization which generates a feeling of cohesiveness and common faith (H25).

The argument for across-the-board cuts is either that all elements of the organization are equally important to its survival and/or that it is impossible to tell which element is more important than any other. In our previous discussion of the university as an ecumenical council we pointed out that it is difficult to argue that one faith is more important than another on grounds that both faiths can accept. For this reason, university members will prefer that even deep cuts be administered across-the-board (Whetten, 1981).

Normative and utilitarian components within a dual identity organization may be expected to argue that *its* strategic focus is the one that the organization as a whole should adopt. Business and professional schools, and to some extent the sciences, particularly the applied sciences such as engineering, would be expected to propose some version of utilitarianism; namely, the doctrine that things ought to be valued according to their utility as determined in the market-place. Non-applied disciplines might well be expected to champion an alternative theory, such as the value of knowledge as an intrinsic good.

What is retained in a normative organization is likely to be different than what is retained in a utilitarian organization if only because the principles on which such decisions are made are quite different (H26). In a normative organization, the principle for determining what ought to be retained is tradition. In a utilitarian organization, the principle is cost-effectiveness (i.e., the instrumental claim that to delete something and retain something else maximizes some overall utility). In the case of the university, we could expect the university's normative components to respond to retrenchment by deleting all forms of knowledge other than those that existed in the medieval university. What is new is suspect. On the other hand, the utilitarian elements of the university should press to retain all that has value in the market place regardless of its date of origin. In parallel with this preference, we can expect normative elements of the university to utilize qualitative criteria in making decisions whereas utilitarian elements should prefer quantitative criteria.

Attitudes toward leadership. There is some reason to believe that normative and utilitarian organizations have different patterns of leadership (H27).

Stinchcombe states, "Utilitarian organizations tend to have a multi-level, highly differentiated rank structure....Normative organizations tend not only to be comparatively egalitarian, but also to stress the distinction between members and nonmembers, insiders ("believers") vs. outsiders ("heretics"), as the central status criterion, over any internal differentiations" (Etzioni, 1975, p. 278). If this characterization of the difference between normative and utilitarian organizations is true (and we can think of some major exceptions), then members of utilitarian organizations should expect the problem of retrenchment to be solved at the top, while members of normative organizations will demand greater participation and consultation.

Effective leaders of dual identity organizations should personify and support both identities. University presidents who were never professors (ordained members of the priesthood) will always be considered managers, not leaders. This deficiency should impair their effectiveness during retrenchment when they must be perceived as the champion of the normative as well as the utilitarian values of the institution.

Impact of retrenchment on organizational members. In utilitarian organizations, it is expected that members will stay or leave the organization depending primarily on the presence or absence of economic incentives (Hirschman, 1970). A threat to the economic health of the organization will cause members to leave. In normative organizations, however, it is assumed that members will leave only if they suffer a loss of faith. A leader of a normative organization will therefore expect disclosure of an outside threat to bind members more closely to the organization and to mobilize them in its defense. We hypothesize that the reverse will be true for utilitarian organizations (H28). In addition, normative organizations may have a greater tendency to regard themselves as unique than utilitarian organizations. If this is true, then individuals should be especially reluctant to leave since they will feel that they have nowhere else to go.

Organizational learning. Utilitarian organizations can be expected to seek management advice from outsiders more readily than normative organizations, who are probably inclined to believe that only an insider, a true member of the faith, can understand the workings of the organization (H29). For example, when the university has management problems, it is unlikely to hire outside management consultants for fear that they will not understand the culture of the organization or that they will make recommendations alien to it. The university is more likely to form a blue ribbon committee of Nobel prize winners (high priests) to solve internal management problems despite the fact that these individuals have little management expertise.

Planning for scarcity. Normative organizations are often prevented by law, and most certainly by ideology, from storing purely economic wealth against the contingency of future scarcity. Economic wealth not pressed into the service of the normative ideology of the organization would be considered misused. As a consequence, normative organizations will always be economically vulnerable, unless they are able to hide their wealth (from themselves and others) and/or unless they are able to redefine its meaning (H30).

The problems experienced by Boystown, a well known home for orphans located near Omaha, Nebraska, in the early 1970's reflect this point. A newspaper article in the *Omaha Sun* in 1972, reported that Boystown had an endowment of over $209 million, or $300,000 for every resident—making it one of the richest incorporated villages in the United States. Since fund raising campaigns are based primarily on a perception of extreme need, this revelation was embarrassing to administrators at Boystown and made soliciting extremely difficult for several years. In an effort to justify their wealth, the trustees of Boystown announced an ambitious campaign to fund research on problems of youth.

Merger and divestiture. One common solution to retrenchment is merger since savings can often be achieved by eliminating duplication. Merger, however, is much more difficult if what is being brought together constitutes different faiths (H31). While there are always difficulties associated with merging two units, merger between utilitarian units can claim justification that both can accept, namely the bottom line. Mergers between normative components or units does not have recourse to this common justification. In extreme cases, the argument is often made that merger is the only means to survival, but the critic is always present who will say that merger entails the loss of the organization, not its survival. Hence, just as it is extremely difficult, if not impossible, to merge faiths, so also is it impossible to divest a faith without a sense of irreparable loss.

Attitudes toward marketing the mission of the organizations. Utilitarian organizations engage in advertising and marketing, while normative/religious organizations engage in missionary work. In both cases, the organization seeks the benefits of increased size and support. Normative organizations, however, sometimes object to advertising on the grounds that selling something of intrinsic worth is demeaning or undignified. The argument seems to be based on the claim that if something of intrinsic worth can be demonstrated to have instrumental value, its intrinsic worth is diminished (i.e., to sell is to diminish the value of what is sold, see Deci, 1977). For this reason, we can expect the normative core of the university to be ambivalent about "selling" the university to outside constituents (H32).

The discovery of priorities. Not only would normative vs. utilitarian organizations be expected to arrive at different priorities in response to scarcity, but perhaps even more importantly, they will differ in the means by which those judgments are formulated (H33). As we have pointed out, normative and utilitarian organizations have different attitudes toward leadership, authority, participation, etc., all of which are involved in formulating priorities. The task of leadership in dual identity organizations undergoing retrenchment is to invent a mechanism for the discovery of organizational priorities that does not a priori value one organizational identity as more important than another; to do otherwise is to prejudge the issue which is at stake.

This example of the university as a church and as a business is intended to demonstrate the face validity of the concept of dual identity and to point to its potential theoretical and practical utility. We have not attempted a full and complete description of a business or a church, nor have we sought to identify all those features within the university to which they might be applied. Both of these tasks form the subject matter for future research along with the consideration of other metaphors and the possibility that a given organization may have more than two identities. The necessary first step however was to demonstrate that at least some aspects of the university could be viewed in terms of those two metaphors. Ultimately, the case for duality should be grounded not merely in the *type and importance* of organizational events that fit within another kind of organization, but by the *extent and distribution* of metaphorically interpretable events throughout the organization. An isolated instance is unlikely to be decisive (although it may be instructive). This was in part the reason that it was important to demonstrate that many aspects of the university could be viewed as churchlike or businesslike. Of course, EMA does not address the question of whether the university in our example *is* a church or *is like* a church (in some ways). If a university's identity as a school (neither church nor business) shrinks, there is a point where one may want to say *it is* a church and/or a business, not that it acts like them. Exactly when this point is reached is not something we can comment on here, but bears further thought.

Further Description of Extended Metaphor Analysis
Since the ability to sustain two alternative metaphoric interpretations of those organizational events that are somehow central, endure over time, and differentiate the organization from others is a major test of the hypothesis of dual identity, it is appropriate to comment about EMA in greater detail. EMA is in part a technique of sense making (Weick, 1969). One way in which an individual or organization makes sense of an event is by locating it as an instance of a more general law or framework. This is the hallmark of one form of scientific explanation, that Hempel and Oppenheim call the covering law model (1965). EMA can be conceived of as a method for constructing and elaborating a framework, i.e., an alternative organizational identity, within which events can be located and in terms of which they can be seen as sensible and intelligible. In concrete terms, the method consists of the evocation and testing of comparative and metaphoric statements of the following kind. With respect to some puzzling organizational event, (e), is the organization more like an X organization or a Y organization? Is (e) more likely to occur in X or Y? (frequency criterion). Is (e) better understood or made sense of if we think of

it as occurring in organization X rather than Y (sense making criterion). Can we predict some new fact if we assume that the organization is like an X rather than a Y (predictive criterion). If for a given organization we proceed in this manner asking in what ways it is like a large number of different organizations and we consistently come up with only the same two organizations in which a large class of events make sense, than we tentatively entertain the hypothesis of dual identity.

Of course, it is important to point out that metaphors distort and mislead as well as inform and make sense of aspects of organizational life. Hence, as part of the method, it is important also to include the question, in what ways is it misleading or inappropriate to consider a given organization to be like another.

We summarize this discussion of EMA in the following five steps.

1. Assemble a group of puzzles, difficulties, dilemmas, problems, features, characteristics, etc. for a target organization. For example, in our previous illustration take the puzzle that universities tend not to hire management consultants.

2. Characterize and broadly define a set of alternative organizations, institutions, etc. This is a critical step. If the candidates for multiple identity are narrowly chosen; for example, if it is proposed that an organization is both a high tech and a chemical company, it is not clear that this multiple classification will clarify anything of interest. Therefore, it is impossible to determine in the abstract whether an identity candidate will be of practical use.

3. Carry out EMA, as in our example of the university, asking in what ways the target is like each of the metaphor candidates.

4. Determine whether the target organization faces any of the six conditions predicted to be times when the issue of identity is likely to be salient (Figure 1). This suggests the extent to which conflicts over deep seated identity issues are likely to be visible for investigation (and by inference, the extent to which organizational difficulties and conflicts will likely be attributable to conflicts between identities).

5. Using each metaphoric identity predict a new set of difficulties that were not included in the original set obtained in step 1, and/or a new set of difficulties that could arise under another set of conditions, for example, merger rather than or in addition to retrenchment. In this step we treat organizational identity as a Gestalt of properties. If a candidate identity is that of a church, for example, then we know that rituals will tend to be present along with certain kinds of goal preferences, etc. A description of a church, therefore, provides a domain to be searched for possible analogies. Does the target organization have rituals? In what way are they similar and in what way different to those of the church, etc.? Each metaphoric identity can be searched for areas of similarity and difference to the target organization.

Summary and Conclusions

Conceptually, this chapter focused on the meaning, significance, and definition of the term identity as it is applied to organizations. We have presented identity as:

1. A particular kind of question. The question, "What kind of organization is this?" refers to features that are arguably core, distinctive, and enduring. These features reveal the identity of the organization. We have pointed out that identity literature is largely silent on which features an organization will select or claim. What is clear, however, is that organizations are capable of supplying multiple answers for multiple purposes and that to recognize that fact and study the conditions that provokes different answers and the relationship of those answers to each other is an identity distinctive inquiry.

2. A distinctive framework for investigation. One value of the term identity and its conceptual surround is that it invites us to consider certain issues, ask certain questions, examine certain phenomena in a particular way that, if not exclusive, is at least distinctive. For example, the entire set of propositions examining the life cycle represents an identity instinctive point of view. New questions arise, such as whether organizations are socialized into their societal roles by rules and procedures isomorphic to those that describe and explain how individuals are socialized into organizations.

3. A critique of the mono identity assumption. A major objective of this chapter has been to introduce and illustrate the concept of dual identity and to explore its implications for the management of organizations.

In general, this chapter should be read as a beginning formulation of the identity of organizational identity in which we have proposed a set of ideas, empirical questions, and hypotheses that together might be considered core, distinctive, and enduring. What the identity literature offers is not a single concept or theory but a diverse set of ideas, modes of analysis, questions and propositions. It is this richness that may be of use to organizational theory.

Notes

1. While we will use the terms of organizational identity, organizational culture, and organizational character, we do no intend this usage to imply a principle of reductionism or its opposite. Identity and character usually apply to individuals, culture applies to societies. An organization is neither. Thus, while we use the terms organizational identity and organizational character, we do not wish to treat the organization as an individual, which

is to claim that the whole is like one of its parts; nor, while we retain the term organizational culture, do we wish to treat an organization as identical to the society in which it is embedded, which is to claim that the part is the same as the whole.

....

References

Albert, S. A delete design model for successful transitions. In J. Kimberly and R. Quinn, (Eds.), *Managing transitions*. New York: W. W. Norton & Co., 1983 (forthcoming).

Albert, S. Temporal comparison theory. *Psychological Review*, 1977, 84, No. 6, 485–503.

Ashby, W. R. Principles of the self-organizating system. In H. Von Forester and G. W. Zopf (Eds.), *Principles of self-organization*. New York: Pergamon Press, 1962.

Blumer, H. What is wrong with social theory? In H. Blumer (Ed.), *Symbolic interactionism: Perspective and method*. Englewood Cliffs: Prentice Hall, 1969.

Calder, B. J. An attributional theory of leadership. In B. M. Staw & G. R. Salancik, (Eds.), *New directions in organizational behavior*. Chicago: St. Clair Press, 1977.

Cameron, K. S. The relationship between faculty unionism and organizational effectiveness. *Academy of Management Journal*, 1982, 25, 6–24.

Cameron, K. S. & Whetten, D. A. *Organizational effectiveness: A comparison of multiple models*. New York: Academic Press, 1983a.

Cameron, K. S. & Whetten, D. A. Models of the organizational life cycle: applications to higher education. *Review of Higher Education*, 1983b, 6, 269–300.

Coleman, J. S. The university and society's new demands upon it. *Content and Context: Essays on College Education*, Carl Kaysen (Ed.), New York: McGraw-Hill, 1973.

Cooley, C. H. *Human nature and the social order*. New York: Scribner, 1922.

Cummings, L. L. The logics of management. *Academy of Management Review*, October, 1983, Vol 8, No 4, pp 532–538.

Deci, E. L. Effects of externally mediated rewards on intrinsic motivation. *Journal of Personality & Social Psychology*, 1977, 18, 105–118.

Erickson, E. H. *Identity and the life cycle*. New York: Norton, 1980.

Erickson, E. H. *Identity, youth, and crises*. New York: Norton, 1968.

Etzioni, A. *A comparative analysis of complex organizations*. New York: Free Press, 1961.

Goffman, E. *The presentation of self in everyday life*. New York: Doubleday, 1959.

Goodman, P. S. & Pennings, J. M. *New perspectives on organizational effectiveness*. San Francisco: Jossey-Bass, 1977.

Hempel, C. G. & Oppenheim, P. Studies in the logic of explanation. In C. G. Hempel (Ed.), *Aspects of scientific explanation*. New York: Free Press, 1965.

Hirschman, A. O. *Exit, voice and loyalty*. Cambridge, Mass.: Harvard University Press, 1970.

James, W. *The principles of psychology*, Vol. 1. New York: Holt, 1890.

Jencks, C. & Riesman, D. *The academic revolution*. Garden City, N.J.: Doubleday, 1968.

Kamens, D. H. Legitimate myths and educational organization: The relationship between organizational ideology and formal structure. *American Sociological Review*, 1977, 42, 208–219.

Kerr, C. *The uses of the university*. Cambridge, Mass.: Harvard University Press, 1963.

Kimberly, J. Initiation, innovation, and institutionalization in the creation process. In J. Kimberly and R. Miles (Eds.), *The organizational life cycle.* San Francisco: Jossey-Bass, 1980.

Lifton, R. *Boundaries.* Random House, 1970.

Lodahl, T. M. & Mitchell, S. M. Drift in the development of innovative organizations. In John Kimberly and Robert Miles (Eds.), *The organizational life cycle.* San Francisco: Jossey-Bass, 1980.

Louis, M. R. A cultural perspective on organizations: the need for and consequences of viewing organizations as culture-bearing milieux. *Human Systems Management,* 1981, *2,* 246–258.

McKelvey, B. *Organizational systematics.* University of California Press, 1983.

McKelvey, B. & Aldrich, H. Populations, natural selection, and applied organizational science. *Administrative Science Quarterly,* 1983, *28,* 101–128.

Mead, G. H. *Mind, self and society,* Chicago: University of Chicago Press, 1934.

Meyer, J. W. & Rowan, B. Institutionalized organizations: formal structure as myth and ceremony. *American Journal of Psychology,* 1977, *83,* 340–363.

Moynihan, D. P. State vs academe. *Harpers,* Dec. 1980, 31–40.

Nisbet, R. The future of the university. In S. M. Lipset (Ed.), *The Third Century: America as a Post Industrial Society.* Stanford University: Hoover Institute Press, 1979.

Ouchi, W. *Theory Z: How American business can meet the Japanese challenge.* Reading, MA: Addison-Wesley, 1981.

Parsons, T. *Structure and process in modern societies.* Glencoe, Ill.: Free Press, 1960.

Pettigrew, A. On studying organizational cultures. *Administrative Science Quarterly,* 1979, *24,* 570–81.

Pfeffer, J. & Salancik, G. *The external control of organizations: A resource dependence perspective.* New York: Harper and Row, 1978.

Pondy, L. R., Frost, P. J., Morgan, G., & Dandridge, T. C. *Organizational symbolism.* Greenwich, Conn.: JAI Press, Inc., 1983.

Pondy, L. R. & Olson, M. L. Theory of extreme cases. (Working paper no. 878). Urbans: University of Illinois College of Commerce and Business Administration, 1977.

Robbins, R. Identity, culture and behavior. In J. Honigmann (Ed.), *Handbook of Social and Cultural Anthropology.* Chicago: Rand McNally, 1973.

Scott, W. R. *Organizations: Rational, natural, and open systems.* Englewood Cliffs, N.J., Prentice Hall, 1981.

Selznick, P. *Leadership in administration.* New York: Harper and Row, 1957.

Taylor, W. Leadership in higher education. Paper presented at Innovative Approaches to Higher Education Administration. Champaign, Ill., 1980.

Thompson, J. D. *Organization in action.* New York: McGraw-Hill, 1967.

Weber, M. *On charisma and institution building.* Chicago: University of Chicago Press, 1968.

Weick, K. E. Educational organizations as loosely coupled systems. *Administrative Science Quarterly,* 1976, *21,* 1–19.

Weick, K. E. *The social psychology of organizing.* Reading, Mass.: Addison-Wesley, 1969.

Whetten, D. A. Organizational responses to scarcity: exploring the obstacles to innovation in education. *Educational Administrative Quarterly,* 1981, *3,* 80–97.

Whetten, D. A. Sources, responses and effects of organizational decline. In R. Kimberly, R. H. Miles & Associates (Eds.), *The organization life cycle.* San Francisco: Jossey-Bass, 1980.

7

Anti-social Actions of Committed Organizational Participants: An Existential Psychoanalytic Perspective*

Howard S. Schwartz

Introduction

In the movie *Silkwood*, a managerial employee of a nuclear chemical corporation is observed by Karen Silkwood as he retouches the photographs of welds in fuel rods intended for nuclear reactors. The man is evidently a committed organizational participant, concerned about the effects on the company, and its employees, of late delivery on a contract. He does not appear to be a loathsome, evil creature, and yet, the activity he is engaged in is not only illegal, it is potentially destructive in an order of magnitude that is sickening to contemplate. The question that I wish to address in this paper is how this man, and others like him— loyal, moral and dedicated within the context of their organizational lives—can engage in actions, in the context of their work, that are morally reprehensible.

The answer that I will propose goes to the very root of the connection between the individual and the organization, in the sense that it concerns the way in which the organization influences the individual's moral orientation toward the world, and hence the individual's voluntary social action. What we shall see is that a work organization can form its own moral community, that it can form that community on the basis of commitment, that commitment is itself to be explained on the basis of a function that participants require organizations to serve, and that the morality of a community so formed can easily stand in isolation from, and even opposition to, the broader community in which it exists and with whom it interacts.

When the individual's moral community becomes limited to the work organization, the psychological significance of work can change. From an exchange relationship between workers who produce a product or service and consumers who use it and pay for it, work can come to be experienced as an internal process within the organization—an exchange between the organization and its employees. Understood in terms of this internal process, transactions between producers and consumers can take on an indifferent, and even a hostile affective colloration. Under these psychological conditions, the relations of an organization with its environment, including the work that it does, can become exploitative, manipulative, and often even aggressive.

The function that I will use to explain the concept of organizational commitment will be called the 'ontological function', by which I shall mean the function of providing a sense of Being, or identity, to the participants. The idea that organizations can provide their participants with a sense of identity is certainly not a new one in organizational thought. What I wish to offer in this paper is a sense of why that function is required, what its psychology is, and what it means; for in understanding these features of the process we will be able to understand how this apparently beneficial phenomenon, and the organizational commitment which results from it, can turn sour and malignant and can lead to the most terrible consequences.

Why the Ontological Function is Required

The crucial step in the analysis of the ontological function is to ask the question why is it required? The answer has to be that, in many cases, as Lichtenstein (1977) has pointed out, people's sense of identity is tenuous in the extreme.

This seems absurd. How can a person's sense of identity be tenuous? Are not people what they are? Is that not their identity? The answer is that, for the most part, people are not what they are, or, what is the same thing, cannot permit themselves to be what they are.

Thus, it makes sense to us to say: 'He has made something of himself', or 'She has become somebody'. What we have to notice about these expressions is the implication that, if the persons in question had allowed themselves to be what they were before they became something or somebody, they would not have been anything or anybody. They would not, that is to say, have had an identity. This is to say that having an identity, at least in our culture, is something of an achievement. Again, we have the notion of the 'has been'. The 'has been' is somebody who once was somebody, but is no longer anybody.

Taking these things together, what we find is that having an identity is not something that we can take for granted, that it is something which we must achieve if we are to have it at all, and that we must continue to achieve if we are to maintain it. In other words, having an identity is a status that is always in question.

Moreover, there is clearly a judgemental element in these assertions. Making something of oneself is good, not making something of oneself is bad. Being somebody is good, being a 'has been' is bad. Thus, the question of identity reflects acceptance or rejection, affirmation or denial. Finally, it seems at least plausible that if these sorts of judgements are common when we judge others, something similar probably goes on when we assess and consider ourselves. We not only have the possibility of denying identity to others, but of denying it to ourselves. Indeed, the question of our own identity would, like the question of the identity of others, be continually in question at all times. Never, apparently, can we simply permit ourselves to be simply what we are.

Now, not allowing ourselves to be what we are just because that is what we are, means that we cannot take ourselves as the measure of what we are supposed to be. We look outside ourselves to find out who we are supposed to be, if we are going to be anything at all—if we are going to have an identity. I shall submit that we fashion social institutions largely to provide an answer to this question. In this way, I shall argue, social institutions, and specifically work organizations, develop an ontological function. In the meantime, though, the question becomes, why is it that people are not what they are, or cannot permit themselves to be what they are?

The Existential Psychoanalytic Psychology of the Ontological Function

To understand that people cannot permit themselves to be what they are is to recognize that at our psychological base lies self-rejection. In order to understand this self-rejection we must come to an understanding of where and when it originates as a stable part of the psychological structure.

In psychoanalytic theory, self-rejection is not a component of our original psychological configuration. On the contrary, to begin with the infant experiences itself without any self-critical sense whatever. Its experience is that of being the centre of a loving world.

Freud (1957/1914) referred to the attendant sense of cosmic significance and self-love as *narcissism*. The response of others who are oriented toward the child gives the child its sense of importance. Moreover, the child's love of these 'mirroring' others, its opening itself to them, allows it to bask in their love for it, and to experience that love as love for itself (Lichtenstein, 1977).

But while love for others permits self-love, it is also the lever by which self-rejection enters into the child's mental configuration. For as time goes on, and as the child comes to enter into more complex relations with its parents and with the world, certain spontaneous actions on the part of the child become unacceptable to the parents and to others generally, and the child's love for them, its openness to them, and its need for their love, leads to its experiencing their rejection as self-caused rejection, and therefore as self-rejection, or guilt.

In the course of coming to live with others, bringing them into our minds as the 'internal objects' (Klein, 1948) with whom the meaning of our lives is transacted, their rejection of us becomes internalized as our rejection of ourselves to form a stable part of our psychological configuration. It is thus that a permanent wound to our narcissism is created, thus that we cannot permit ourselves to be what we are, thus that the locus of our identity shifts from who we are to who others will permit us to be, and thus that the need for the ontological function is developed.

The ontological function refers to the projection of the possibility of a return to narcissism, to being the centre of a loving world, to regaining a stable, self-contained identity and a sense of Being without self-rejection as its core. It refers to a specification of that person who will be able to be exactly who he or she is and will not be required, under penalty of rejection, to be someone else.

Freud (1957/1914, 1955/1921; Chasseguet-Smirgel, 1985) refers to the specification of the person one must become in order to return to narcissism as the *ego ideal*. Recognizing that the ego ideal is defined in terms of social interaction, it becomes possible to regard the pattern of ideal social interaction in which the ego ideal is embedded, and by which it is defined, as itself a discernible ideal entity. We can see this ideal entity taking various forms, as defined by ideology (Chasseguet-Smirgel, 1985): the community of saved souls, the community of post-revolutionary society, etc. For our purposes, we may limit discussion to the case in which the ego ideal takes the form of an organiza-tion. Giving this ideal pattern of organization a name, we shall refer to it as the *organization ideal* (Schwartz, 1987b).

Thus, the organization ideal is an idea (in Freud's terms a 'leading idea') of organizational life characterized by an integration of spontaneity, on the one hand, and conformance with the requirements of loved others on the other hand. It represents a synthetic unity of subject and object, self and other, freedom and necessity, activity and passivity. We may now observe that the ontological function of the organization consists in specifying an organization ideal to serve as an ego ideal for organizational participants. Up to this point, we may also observe, there is no problem. All that we have described is benign.

There is no way yet to understand why a person would commit criminal and anti-social acts because of concern for the corporation.

In order to understand how that can happen we need to go more fully into the psychology of the ego ideal and organization ideal. The problem is that the ego ideal, whether considered individually or as the organization ideal, is never attained. In order to see why this is so, it is necessary to return to the discussion of the roots of the self-rejection which makes the ontological function necessary.

We saw before that self-rejection arises from the internalization of the rejection of loved others. But if this were all that it amounted to, then we could imagine that the return to narcissism could be a real possibility. If one pleases the loved others, they will love one in return and one will again be the centre of a loving world.

There are two problems here. The first is that orienting oneself toward pleasing others in order to gain their love means, already, that one is not the centre of their world. Rather, those whose love one organizes one's life around are the centre of one's own. For the fact is that by orienting my life around their love I am conceding my dependence on them, and conceding the fact that they do not, and I cannot make them, love me for myself alone. Rather, if they are to love me, they will love me out of motives arising from within themselves. Accepting that one cannot have ontological hegemony over the world, that in order to have the love of others one must limit one's claims and one's sense of self-importance, amounts to self-rejection. Thus, if the organization ideal is to succeed in offering a return to narcissism, it must be based upon a redefinition of the self and of others in a way which denies the differences among us—which defines us as being essentially the same and having the same motives and the same centre. The problem is that, as individuals, we all remain different from the abstract self so defined, and therefore stand in perpetual contrast to it.

The second problem is that, even if I give up centrality in an attempt to gain love, the outcome must ultimately be disillusioning. For ultimately, it is the facts of biology that determine that the world is not a loving place, and the love of loved others, early in life, served only to conceal this fact. The point is that the threat of loss of love on the part of the apparently omnipotent parents is experienced so powerfully because it *reveals* to the infant how vulnerable, finite and, ultimately, mortal it is; and vulnerability, finitude and mortality remain facts. In other words, what the loss of love establishes for the infant is that its narcissism was an illusion. This revelation may be repressed, but it can never be eliminated as a basic element of the psychological configuration. I think we can see from this where another part of our internalized self-rejection comes from. It consists in the rejection of the vulnerability, finitude and mortality that go along with one's organic identity. Thus, the ego ideal and the organization ideal ultimately symbolize immortality. Again we can see why the ego ideal, and the organization ideal along with it, can never be achieved. Immortality is, of course, out of the question.

Thus, the ontological function, which consists in the specification of an organization ideal as a project of the return to narcissism, essentially requires the creation of illusion. We may now add the obvious fact that this illusion, if it is going to serve its purpose, must be taken as a fact. Accordingly, the ontological function of the organization must also involve the shielding of the illusion from reality, the maintenance of the illusion as an apparent fact in the face of its illusory character. It is this dual process—the creation of illusion and the preservation of the apparent facticity of the illusion—that leads to the malignant consequences we wish to explain.

Organizational Aspects of the Ontological Function

We may now define the term 'organizational commitment', in a way that is consistent with its usage in traditional organizational psychology (e.g. Schein 1983/1968; Mowday et al. 1982) as the situation in which a person's identity is specified by the organization's ontological function. It describes a person, in other words, whose ego ideal is the organization ideal. Our question then becomes, how is it possible to explain morally reprehensible actions on the part of organizationally committed individuals, in the course of their organizational activity?

Three features of the ontological function interact to permit this explanation. They are (1) the content of the organization ideal, (2) the relationship of the individual to the organization ideal, and (3) defense of the identity through defense of the organization ideal.

Content of the Organization Ideal

In the case of the work organization, we may observe that the content of the organization ideal must (a) be social—that is to say it must be an image of social interaction among individual ego ideals, relating to each other in frictionless, mutually supportive, job-specific interaction. This amounts to the requirement, mentioned earlier, that the members of the organization have redefined themselves in terms of the organization and therefore as essentially identical. It must (b) be powerful—in the sense that the individuals, as organized, are rational, know what they are doing, and are competent to do what they are doing and in control of the situation. This would be a presupposition of the possibility of the organization being immortal and therefore providing immortality for those individuals redefined in terms of it. And (c), it must be free of anxiety at the level of identity. That is to say, the individuals involved would have to be conceived as performing their organizational roles, not out of a feeling of obligation or compulsion, so as to avoid internal or external rejection, but out of desire or self-expression—not out of lack, but out of plenitude. This would be the equivalent of specifying that the two mentioned causes of anxiety, individuality and mortality, have been overcome.

Various elements of these contents of the organization ideal have been promulgated by normative organization theorists such as the human relations school (e.g. Mayo, 1933), the industrial humanists (e.g. Argyris, 1964), and students of bureaucracy (e.g. Weber, 1947).

Relationship of the Individual to the Organization Ideal

As we saw before, humans never reach the ego ideal. That would imply immortality. This is so for the organization ideal as well. Organizations *never* reach the organization ideal. That would imply frictionless interaction among totally competent, perfectly rational individuals acting purely out of desire. It would imply an organization not only in perfect coexistence with its environment, but assured of the permanent continuity of this coexistence. This would imply that the organization would be in total permanent control of its environment. This is so unlikely that we can only believe it to be possible because we need to believe it.

Committed organizational participants, who require that the organization specify an identity for them, are precisely those who have the need to believe this. They are thus likely to feel that deviations from the organization ideal are the result of the fact that it is they who do not fulfil the conditions of their identity. The resultant feeling therefore must be one of personal responsibility for failure—the anxiety experienced as personal shortcoming, or shame.

Baum (1983) has pointed out the pervasiveness of the feeling of shame among organizational participants. He has observed that superiors can invoke shame among their subordinates simply by doing their job. This brings us to another point regarding the relationship of individuals to the organization ideal. It is related to the necessity of defending the illusion of the organization ideal from being revealed as an illusion, in order to maintain the ontological function. This implies that while committed organizational participants believe that their lapse from the organization ideal is a failure on their own part, they may believe that others fulfill the organization ideal.

An important feature of organizational phenomenology in this connection is the experience of hierarchy (Schwartz, 1983, 1987a, 1987b). It is possible to reconcile individual failure, and even the failure of one's associates to measure up to the organization ideal, with the maintenance of belief in the organization ideal through the belief that, at higher levels of the organization, people do approach the organization ideal. Indeed, one may go so far as to say that a large part of organizational dramaturgy is devoted to the enactment of the presumed competence and goodness of organizational superiors (Klein and Ritti, 1984). This point obviously relates as well to the motivation to proceed 'up the organizational ladder', as the organizationally defined path to the ego ideal.

Defense of Identity through Defense of the Organization Ideal

To the extent that the individual is committed, derives his/her identity from the ontological process, that identity is put into question by threats to the organization's existence. Indeed, one can go even farther than this and say that, *to the extent that the individual's identity is an organizational identity, threats to the organization are experienced as threats to the individual.* Thus, defense of the organization becomes self-defense. Moreover, since the organization ideal is an ideal, threats to the organization are perceived as having a hostile colloration, as aggression, as bad. Defense of the organization may be experienced as a righteous and virtuous action, therefore, regardless of the light in which such action may be seen by the organization's environment—which is seen, after all, as the source of the aggression. Finally, recalling that the organization is seen as the organization ideal, we may note that it is not only real threats to the organization that are seen as reprehensible acts of aggression. It can even be mere threats to the image of the organization as perfect. Thus, in a similar fashion, 'slander against the State' is considered a crime in the Soviet Union.

Explaining Anti-social Actions of Committed Participants

Putting these three elements together gives us an adequate theoretical base for understanding how committed organizational participants can engage in illegal and anti-social acts.

First, and most obvious, we may observe how the interaction of belief in the ideal character of the organization with feelings of shame over one's own failure to fulfil the organization ideal, can lead to the sort of malignant obedience to authority investigated by Milgram (1963). Feelings of shame over failing to meet the ego ideal lead to a moral delegitimation of the self and its natural responses. One is, after all, not what one is supposed to be, and therefore one's spontaneous responses should not be taken as the determinants of one's action. On top of that, higher authority is what it is supposed to be, and therefore its directives are experienced as morally enhanced, and more credible as moral directives, than the individual's own moral feelings. But while this process surely explains some anti-social activity on the part of committed participants, it does not explain all of it. Specifically, it does not explain the actions of those who gave the orders and, generally, it does not explain self-directed anti-social action, a class which probably includes the retouching of photographs described in the first paragraph.

The key to the understanding of self-directed anti-social actions lies in the phenomenology of the individual who experiences threat to the organization as threat to his/her own identity. The point here is that, since individuals never reach the ego ideal, identity is always in question; and since the organization itself falls short of the organization ideal, in the sense of being less in control of its circumstances than its own mythology requires, the precarious conditions that all organizations face all the time may be interpreted as the result of unfair, hostile and aggressive acts on the part of outside forces—who must be playing unfairly, after all, since the organization is the organization ideal and is therefore doing everything properly and correctly. Under the circumstances the committed individual may feel that the moral response is one of hostility and aggression.

In order to get a more rounded perspective on what this anti-social action amounts to, it may be useful to consider the relationship between the organization and its environment. The organization serves, through the committed individual's belief in the organization ideal, an immortality function for the individual (Schwartz, 1985). It is, in effect, an instrument for the denial of the individual's finitude. But in order to fulfil this function, it must itself be considered to be immortal. As we have seen, the individual denies his or her mortality by defining him or herself as part of an organization that is conceived to be in perfect, permanent control of its environment. But organizations are subject to the same question of their identity as individuals are. They are never perfectly in control of their environments. Nor, it is important to note, should they be.

The point is, that from a systems perspective, the environment *should* be in control of the organization. The environment is, after all, where everyone who is not a committed organizational participant exists and has such identity as they can manage to have. From the point of view of the environment, the organization is a source of goods and/or services. It is in exchange for the supply of these goods and/or services that the environment provides resources, its own resources, that permit the organization to continue. When the organization fails to provide such goods and/or services as the environment deems sufficient to balance its investment of resources, the environment responds by withholding resources *and thereby threatens the survival of the organization.* What's wrong with that?

When work is viewed as one side of an exchange relationship between producer and consumer, it always makes sense to ask, in evaluating an organization,

'What is it good for?' What does the organization do *for its environment* that makes it worthwhile for the environment to keep it in existence at a cost to itself? But this is not a question that is asked by committed organizational participants. For them, the criterion of worth is not defined by the environment but by the organization. Indeed, the criterion of worth is the organization ideal.

Thus, what appear from an extra-organizational perspective to be legitimate demands that the environment places on the organization, appear from the standpoint of the committed participant to be illegitimate, hostile and aggressive challenges to the organization's and the individual's existence.

When we referred before to the need of the committed participant to believe that the organization controls its environment we were putting the matter too mildly. What we can see now is that the committed participants cannot tolerate the organization having an independent environment at all. From this individual's standpoint, the environment is ontologically linked to the organization, in that its meaning is a function of the organization's needs and agenda. Thus, rather than the organization existing and justifying itself by fulfilling needs of the environment, the environment is thought to exist in order to admire and attend to the organization.

Earlier, we saw that the ego ideal symbolizes the return to narcissism. Now we can see how the organization ideal does so as well. Only now it is the organization that is narcissistic, and just as the narcissistic child expects the world to revolve around it, so the organizationally committed individual expects the world to revolve around the organization, conceived as the organization ideal. Moreover, just as the infant responds with rage when the world does not respond to its whims, so the committed participant may respond with self-righteous, hostile, aggressive, and even criminal activity when the world does not respond to the whims of the organization.

Thus, what we see is that anti-social actions, from the standpoint of the broader social world, are by no means to be regarded as an aberration from normal organizational activity on the part of organizationally committed participants. On the contrary, they appear to be a natural concomitant of organizational commitment itself. 'Evil', Hobbes said, 'is a robust child' (cited in Becker, 1975). We might add, and for the very same reason, that it can also be a robust organization.

Organizational Commitment and Anti-social Socialization

The observation that anti-social organizational behaviour is a natural concomitant of organizational commitment, which itself would be expected to be related to organizational effectiveness and perhaps social usefulness makes it important for us to consider the question of the circumstances under which such behaviour might take place. While this is properly a question for further research, it does seem possible to use previous work on organizational commitment and socialization as providing a basis for informed speculation and for establishing possible directions for research.

For present purposes I shall restrict myself to a previously mentioned work by Schein (1983/1968) which I think provides some very interesting clues. Schein says:

One mechanism [for building commitment] is to invest much effort and time in the new member and thereby build up expectations of being repaid by loyalty, hard work, and rapid learning. Another mechanism is to get the new member to make a series of small behavioural commitments which can only be justified by him through the acceptance and incorporation of company values. He then becomes the agent of his own socialization. Both mechanisms involve the subtle manipulation of guilt. (Schein, 1983/1968: 195).

Going beyond the case of the new recruit to the general case of the organization participant who has been selected for special treatment, and putting this matter in terms of the ego ideal, it seems to me this passage is suggesting that selected participants will most strongly take the organization ideal as their ego ideal when (1) the organization succeeds in presenting itself as an organization ideal, (2) progress toward this organization ideal seems probable for the individual in question, and (3) other possibilities for the ego ideal have been eliminated. It further suggests that guilt is involved both in the attraction toward the organization ideal and in the elimination of alternatives. The influence of guilt (or shame, as we shall see) may provide a key to the whole process.

Take the guilt involved in the presentation and accessibility of the organization ideal. The organization lavishes resources on the participant, indicating to the participant that if he or she takes the organization as an organization ideal, the hierarchical route to that ideal is open to him or her. The participant, if he or she is to think him or herself worthy of these resources and of the promise of more to come, 'must repay the company with loyalty and hard work. He would feel guilty if he did not'.

The crucial question to ask at this point is, where do these resources really come from? The answer can only be that they come from the environment. Proximal control over them may rest with the organization, to be sure. But ultimately, of course, they must originate outside the organization. The organization can be no more than a steward for these resources. Accordingly, such a relationship of guilt as may exist would have to be caused by an unbalanced exchange relationship between the participant and the environment, the producer and the consumer. Thus, it appears that the first step in the process through which organizational commitment comes to develop anti-social potentialities is through an obscuring, on the part of the organization, of the source of the resources it employs.

We can see this obscuration in Schein's observation that the organization builds up 'expectations of being repaid by loyalty, hard work, and rapid learning'. We can see where hard work and rapid learning go into balancing the exchange relationship between participant and environment, but loyalty to the organization? The point to be noted here is that, in the most fundamental sense, with regard to the exchange relationship of work, the organization is not a party in the transaction. The organization, strictly speaking, is simply a patterning of this very complex relationship. This is at least one meaning that can be given to Karl Weick's (1969) observation that the organization does not exist, but only the process of organizing. Thus, bringing the organization in as the main party in the transaction is already an act of obscuration.

How is this obscuration possible? I suggest that it becomes possible through the same process in which the organization comes to present itself as an organization ideal. The organization, as a process, once had a positive effect on its environment; and the environment, eager to have the relationship continue, bestowed upon the process an attribution of identity, of causal centrality, and entrusted the constructed entity with the resources which it now commands. Thus, the environment relinquished proximal control over these resources out of the very admiration and idealization of the organization which make it attractive to the individual rising in its ranks.

But there is more involved than this. By asserting its control over the participant's guilt, the organization asserts its right to end it and asserts that it, itself, is free of it; and along with that, is free of the limitation and finitude that the phenomenology of guilt contains. In other words, it presents itself as being beyond, as transcendence of, guilt, finitude and limitation—as the solution to the problem of identity, the return to narcissism, the ego ideal in organized form, the organization ideal.

Moreover, by offering to absolve the participant of guilt in exchange for loyalty, the organization creates a self-fulfilling proposition. For loyalty, after all, is the acceptance of the organization as one's ego ideal, by which act one does, after all, believe that one is getting away from one's finitude, limitation and guilt—in the terms used earlier, one creates for oneself an identity. Thus, the commission of the psychic act of organizational loyalty is the very self-deception, the obscuration, which, from one's own point of view, gives oneself identity, gives the organization life, and motivates one to entice others, both within the organization and outside it, to do the same.

Now take the technique of getting behavioural commitments. One example Schein uses is the Communist brainwashing practice of forcing a public confession from a prisoner. Another is the act of enticing a rebellious individual to accept a promotion. In both cases, what we see is a behaviour that invokes shame among the individual's prior reference group, as a violation of its own ego ideal—a shame which can only be avoided by rejecting the previous reference group as a source of potential admiration, restricting oneself to the organization ideal, and limiting the circle of one's identifications to those who also have taken the organization ideal as their ego ideal. Then, what would otherwise be seen as shameful actions come to be viewed as signs of commitment and highly valued. This has the effect of refreezing the participant's identity into the organization's meaning system and, effectively, of isolating that meaning system from its environment.

Given that actions, no matter how shameful they look to the environment, may be looked upon as worthwhile within the organization; and given that by presenting itself as an organization ideal the organization obscures the moral relationship that exists between participant and environment, it is clear that anything has become possible. When we repeat the point made earlier, that identity so defined is threatened by the very existence of an independent environment, it appears that it is only circumstances that prevent the possible from becoming probable.

Conclusion

These last considerations show how the potentiality for anti-social actions is built right into the process of the socialization for organizational commitment. They also show how it is precisely those organizations which had, at one time, a favourable response from their environments that are most likely to build up the sort of commitment that may lead to anti-social actions when the favour with which the organization is held begins to slip. This second point has to be a cause for pessimism, since it implies both that (1) nothing is stable about the kind of identity which commitment to an 'excellent' (Peters and Waterman, 1982) organization offers, and that (2) there is no way of dealing with this problem in a programmatic, institutional fashion, since any institution which was successful in dealing with it would itself be subject to the process of degeneration which has been suggested.

Moreover, there is no cause for optimism in the idea that the solitary individual may be able to withstand the organization's blandishments and maintain a strong moral sense. For while some rare individuals will do so, many will not. It is, of course, the organization that selects those individuals upon whom it will shower resources and raise to positions of power, expecting commitment in return. Then the solitary individual becomes a deviate, and there is no necessity in this work to repeat what we know about how groups deal with deviates. Look at what happened to Karen Silkwood.

All in all, there is not much cause for optimism in any of the considerations adduced in this paper. But, then, it is the demand that all of our stories have the happy endings that lead to these dynamics in the first place.

··

Note

* Earlier versions of this paper were presented at the American Academy of Management meeting, Chicago, Illinois, August, 1986; and at the meeting of the American Society for Public Administration, Anaheim, California, April, 1986. The author wishes to thank Walter Nord for helpful comments on an earlier draft of this paper.

··

References

Argyris, Chris. (1964). *Integrating the individual and the organization*. New York: Wiley.

Becker, Ernest. (1975). *Escape from evil*, New York: Free Press.

Baum, Howell S. (1983). 'Autonomy, shame and doubt: Power in the bureaucratic lives of planners'. *Administration and Society* 15(2): 147–184.

Chasseguet-Smirgel, Janine. (1985). *The ego ideal: A psychoanalytic essay on the malady of the ideal*. New York: Norton.

Freud, Sigmund. (1955). *Group psychology and the analysis of the ego*. Standard edition, Volume 18, London: Hogarth. (Originally published, 1921.)

Freud, Sigmund. (1957). *On narcissism: An introduction*. Standard edition, Volume 14. London: Hogarth. (Originally published, 1914.)

Katz, Daniel, and Robert L. Kahn. (1966). *The Social Psychology of Organizations*. New York: Wiley.

Klein, Stuart M., and R. Richard Ritti. (1984). *Understanding organizational behavior* (Second edition). Boston: Kent.

Lichtenstein, Heinz. (1977). *The dilemma of human identity*. New York: Aronson.

Mayo, George Elton. (1933). *The human problems of an industrial civilization*. New York: Macmillan.

Milgram, Stanley. (1963). 'Behavioural study of obedience'. *Journal of Abnormal and Social Psychology* 67: 371–378.

Mowday, Richard T., Lyman W. Porter, and Richard M. Steers. (1982). *Employee–organization linkages*. New York: Academic Press.

Peters, Thomas J., and Robert H. Waterman. (1982). *In search of excellence: Lessons from America's best-run companies*. New York: Harper and Row.

Schein, Edgar H. (1983). 'Organizational socialization and the profession of management' in *Psychological foundations of organizational behavior* (Second edition). Barry M. Staw (ed.), 191–201. Glenview, Ill.: Scott, Foresman. (Originally published, 1968.)

Schwartz, Howard S. (1983). 'Maslow and the hierarchical enactment of organizational reality'. *Human Relations* 36(10): 933–956.

Schwartz, Howard S. (1985). 'The usefulness of myth and the myth of usefulness: A dilemma for the applied organizational scientist'. *Journal of Management* 11(1): 31–42.

Schwartz, Howard S. (1987a). 'Rousseau's *Discourse on Inequality* revisited: psychology of work at the public-esteem stage of Maslow's hierarchy'. *International Journal of Management* (forthcoming).

Schwartz, Howard S. (1987b). 'On the psychodynamics of organizational totalitarianism'. *Journal of Management* (forthcoming).

Weber, Max (1947). *The theory of social and economic organization* (edited by Talcott Parsons). New York: Free Press.

Weick, Karl E. (1969). *The social psychology of organizing*. Reading, Mass.: Addison-Wesley.

8

Social Identity Theory and the Organization

Blake E. Ashforth and Fred Mael

Organizational identification has long been recognized as a critical construct in the literature on organizational behavior, affecting both the satisfaction of the individual and the effectiveness of the organization (Brown, 1969; Hall, Schneider, & Nygren, 1970; Lee, 1971; O'Reilly & Chatman, 1986; Patchen, 1970; Rotondi, 1975). However, as discussed below, theoretical and empirical work has often confused organizational identification with related constructs such as organizational commitment and internalization and with affect and behaviors, which are more appropriately seen as antecedents and/or consequences of identification.

Social identity theory (SIT) can restore some coherence to organizational identification, and it can suggest fruitful applications to organizational behavior. SIT offers a social–psychological perspective, developed principally by Henri Tajfel (1978, 1981; Tajfel & Turner, 1985) and John Turner (1975, 1982, 1984, 1985). Following a review of the literature on SIT, the antecedents and consequences of social identification in organizations are discussed. This perspective is then applied to three domains of organizational behavior: socialization, role conflict, and intergroup relations.

Social Identity Theory

According to SIT, people tend to classify themselves and others into various social categories, such as organizational membership, religious affiliation, gender, and age cohort (Tajfel & Turner, 1985). As these examples suggest, people may be classified in various categories, and different individuals may utilize different categorization schemas. Categories are defined by prototypical characteristics abstracted from the members (Turner, 1985). Social classification serves two functions. First, it cognitively segments and orders the social environment, providing the individual with a systematic means of defining others. A person is assigned the prototypical characteristics of the category to which he or she is classified. As suggested by the literature on stereotypes, however, such assignments are not necessarily reliable (e.g., Hamilton, 1981).

Second, social classification enables the individual to locate or define *him- or herself* in the social environment. According to SIT, the self-concept is comprised of a *personal* identity encompassing idiosyncratic characteristics (e.g. bodily attributes, abilities, psychological traits, interests) and a *social* identity encompassing salient group classifications. Social *identification*, therefore, is the perception of oneness with or belongingness to some human aggregate. For example, a woman may define herself in terms of the group(s) with which she classifies herself (I am a Canadian; I am a woman). She perceives herself as an actual or symbolic member of the group(s), and she perceives the fate of the group(s) as her own. As such, social identification provides a partial answer to the question, Who am I? (Stryker & Serpe, 1982; Turner, 1982).

Note that the definition of others and the self are largely "relational and comparative" (Tajfel & Turner, 1985, p. 16); they define oneself relative to individuals in other categories. The category of *young* is meaningful only in relation to the category of *old*. It should be noted, however, that social identification is *not* an all-or-none phenomenon. Although many social categories are indeed categorical (e.g., Canadian, female, a member of XYZ Co.), the extent to which the individual identifies with each category is clearly a matter of degree. Further, such identities tend to be viewed positively inasmuch as the individual vests more of his or her self-conceptions in valued personas (Adler & Adler, 1987; Schneider, Hall, & Nygren, 1971). Thus, Jackall (1978) found that people working at menial jobs in a bank often distanced themselves from their implied identity (e.g., This is only a stopgap job; I'm trying to save enough to start my own business).

The major focus of both SIT and the present paper is to understand the implications of the second function of classification, that of social identification.

Social Identification and Group Identification

Social identification appears to derive from the venerable concept of *group identification* (Tolman, 1943). (Indeed, we will use social and group identification interchangeably.) The literature on group identification suggests four principles that are relevant to our discussion. First, identification is viewed as a perceptual cognitive construct that is not necessarily associated with any specific behaviors or affective states. To identify, an individual need not expend effort toward the group's goals; rather, an individual need only perceive him- or herself as psychologically intertwined with the fate of the group. Behavior and affect are viewed only as potential antecedents or consequences (Foote, 1951; Gould, 1975). As noted below, this conceptualization distinguishes identification from related concepts such as effort on behalf of the group (behavior) and loyalty (affect). However, our view does contrast with some literature on SIT, which includes affective and evaluative dimensions in the conceptualization of identity (e.g., Tajfel, 1978).

Second, social/group identification is seen as personally experiencing the successes *and* failures of the group (Foote, 1951; Tolman, 1943). Often, identification is maintained in situations involving great loss or suffering (Brown, 1986), missed potential benefits (Tajfel, 1982), task failure (Turner, 1981), and even *expected* failure (Gammons, 1986).

Third, although not clearly addressed in the literature, social identification is distinguishable from internalization (Hogg & Turner, 1987) (cf. Kelman, 1961; O'Reilly & Chatman, 1986). Whereas identification refers to self in terms of social categories (I am), internalization refers to the incorporation of values, attitudes, and so forth within the self as guiding principles (I believe). Although certain values and attitudes typically are associated with members of a given social category, acceptance of the category as a definition of self does not necessarily mean acceptance of those values and attitudes. An individual may define herself in terms of the organization she works for, yet she can disagree with the prevailing values, strategy, system of authority, and so on (cf. "young Turks," Mintzberg, 1983, p. 210; "counterculture," Martin & Siehl, 1983, p. 52).

Finally, identification with a group is similar to identification with a person (e.g., one's father, football hero) or a reciprocal role relationship (e.g., husband-wife, doctor-patient) inasmuch as one partly defines oneself in terms of a social referent. To be sure, the various literatures reach this conclusion from different directions. Whereas identification with a group is argued to be predicated on the desire for self-definition, identification with an individual—referred to as "classical identification" (Kelman, 1961, p. 63)—is argued to be predicated on the desire to appease, emulate, or vicariously gain the qualities of the other (e.g., Bandura & Walters, 1963; Kets de Vries & Miller, 1984). Kelman (1961), for example, argued that in classical identification the individual "attempts to be like or actually to be the other person" (p. 63). Nevertheless, the element of self-definition suggests that these forms of identification are *complementary*. Indeed, we will suggest that organizations often seek to generalize identification with an individual to identification with the organization through the routinization of charisma.

Social Identification and the Organization

The individual's organization may provide one answer to the question, Who am I? Hence, we argue that organizational identification is a specific form of social identification. This search for identity calls to mind a family of existential motives often alluded to in the literature on organizational behavior, including searches for meaning, connectedness, empowerment, and immortality (e.g., Denhardt, 1987; Fox, 1980; Katz & Kahn, 1978). To the extent the organization, as a social category, is seen to embody or even reify characteristics perceived to be prototypical of its members, it may well fulfill such motives for the individual. At the very least, SIT maintains that the individual identifies with social categories partly to enhance self-esteem (Hogg & Turner, 1985; Tajfel, 1978). This is understandable in view of the relational and comparative nature of social identities. Through social identification and comparison, the individual is argued to vicariously partake in the successes and status of the group: Indeed, positive and negative intergroup comparisons have been found to affect a member's self-esteem accordingly (Oakes & Turner, 1980; Wagner, Lampen, & Syllwasschy, 1986).

The individual's social identity may be derived not only from the organization, but also from his or her work group, department, union, lunch group, age cohort, fast-track group, and so on. Albert and Whetten (1985) distinguished between holographic organizations in which individuals across subunits share a common identity (or identities) and ideographic organizations in which individuals display subunit-specific identities. General examples of the former include Ouchi's (1981) Theory Z organization in which "management styles are blended together and diffused evenly throughout the entire organization" (Albert & Whetten, 1985, p. 271) and Mintzberg's (1983) missionary organization in which members strongly subscribe to a common set of values and beliefs. Given the comparative rarity of such organizations, however, the notion of a single or blended organizational identification is problematic in most complex organizations. Thus, as discussed below, the organizationally situated social identity may, in fact, be comprised of more or less disparate and loosely coupled identities. This parallels work in various social domains, which indicates that individuals often retain multiple identities (Allen, Wilder, & Atkinson, 1983; Hoetler, 1985; Thoits, 1983).

Unfortunately, despite the longevity of the social/group identification construct, little research has been conducted on identification with organizations, as defined here. Conventional research on organizational identification has not distinguished identification from internalization or cognition from behavior and affect. For example, Hall et al. (1970) defined organizational identification as "the process by which the goals of the organization and those of the individual become increasingly integrated and congruent" (pp. 176–7), and Patchen (1970) defined it as shared characteristics, loyalty, and solidarity. The lone exception is a study by O'Reilly and Chatman (1986) that distinguished among compliance, identification, and internalization. However, following Kelman's (1961) lead, they defined identification as "involvement based on a desire for affiliation" (p. 493), rather than as perceived oneness with the organization.

A particular problem in this area is the frequent confusion between *organizational identification* and *organizational commitment*. Some theorists equate identification with commitment, while others view the former as a component of the latter (see Wiener, 1982). The authors of the Organizational Commitment Questionnaire (OCQ) (Mowday, Steers, & Porter, 1979, p. 226)—the most frequently used measure of commitment during the last decade (Reichers, 1985)—defined organizational commitment as "the relative strength of an individual's identification with and involvement in a particular organization." In their view, commitment is characterized by a person's (a) belief in and acceptance of the organization's goals and values, (b) willingness to exert effort on behalf of the organization, and (c) desire to maintain membership. This formulation includes internalization, behavioral intentions, and affect, but *not* identification as presently defined. Further, although identification is defined as organization-specific, internalization and commitment may not be. An organization's goals and values may be shared by other organizations. Commitment scales consistently feature generalized usage of the terms *goals* and *values*, as in the OCQ item, "I find that my values and the organization's values are similar" (Mowday et al., 1979, p. 228). Respondents are not asked to limit responses to values that are specific to their organization, if indeed they could. Thus, an individual can score high on commitment not because he or she perceives a shared destiny with the organization but because the organization is a convenient vehicle for personal career goals. If another organization proved more convenient, such an individual could transfer to it without sacrificing his or her goals. For the individual who identified with the organization, however, leaving the organization necessarily involves some psychic loss (e.g., Levinson, 1970).

This argument is supported by Mael's (1988) study of employed business and psychology students. He constructed a 6-item measure of organizational identification based on the present formulation (e.g., "This organization's successes are my successes," p. 52), and subjected it and the 15-item OCQ to confirmatory factor analysis. The two-factor model produced a χ^2/df ratio of 2.03 : 1 (i.e., 328.13/188) and an adjusted goodness-of-fit index of 0.825; the single-factor model produced a ratio of 2.46 : 1 (i.e., 465.14/189) and an index of 0.780. The superior fit of the two-factor model suggests that the identification and commitment constructs are indeed differentiable.

In summary, the SIT conception of organizational identification as shared identity is new to the organizational behavior literature. To date, the perception of identification has been confused with internalization of organizational goals and values, and with behavior and affect. This is most clearly evident in research on organizational commitment. Unfortunately, this confusion has impeded application of the rich findings of SIT to organizations.

Antecedents and Consequences of Social Identification in Organizations

Antecedents

Social Identity Theory is contradictory to conventional views of group relations because according to it *in-group favoritism tends to occur even in the absence of strong leadership or member interdependence, interaction, or cohesion.* Laboratory studies utilizing SIT's minimal group paradigm have demonstrated that simply assigning an individual to a group is sufficient to generate in-group favoritism (Brewer, 1979; Tajfel, 1982). Favoritism is not dependent on prior perceptions of interpersonal similarity or liking, and it occurs even when there is no interaction within or between groups, when group membership is anonymous, and when there is no link between self-interest and group responses (Turner, 1984). Even explicitly *random* assignment of individuals to groups has led to discrimination against out-groups and increased intragroup cooperation and cohesion (e.g., Billig & Tajfel, 1973; Locksley, Ortiz, & Hepburn, 1980).

This led Turner (1984, p. 530) to propose the existence of a "psychological group," which he defined as "a collection of people who share the same social identification or define themselves in terms of the same social category membership." A member of a psychological group does not need to interact with or like other members, or be liked and accepted by them. It is his or her perception of being, say, a loyal patriot or sports fan that is the basis for incorporation of that status into his or her social identity. The individual seems to reify or credit the group with a psychological reality apart from his or her relationships with its members (Turner, 1984).

The SIT literature suggests several factors of direct relevance to organizations, which most likely increase the tendency to identify with groups. The first is the *distinctiveness* of the group's values and practices in relation to those of comparable groups (Oakes & Turner, 1986; Tolman, 1943). Distinctiveness serves to separate "figure from ground," differentiating the group from others and providing a unique identity. Mael (1988) sampled the alumni of a religious college and found a positive association between the perceived distinctiveness of the college's values and practices and identification with the college.

Distinctiveness partly explains the missionary zeal often displayed by members of organizations that are new and innovative (e.g., Perkins, Nieva, & Lawler, 1983) or organizations that pursue unique goals (e.g., Hall et al.'s 1970 study of the U.S. Forest Service).

Within the organization, distinctiveness in group values and practices needs to be qualified by the clarity and impermeability of group domains or boundaries. For example, although it is likely that the values and practices of two functionally based subunits are more differentiated than those of two market-based subunits, suggesting distinctiveness, the former are more likely to be sequentially or reciprocally interdependent and physically contiguous, suggesting a blurring of distinctiveness. This indeterminate distinctiveness may account for the mixed support for SIT in several field studies (Brown, Condor, Mathews, Wade, & Williams, 1986; Brown & Williams, 1984; Oaker & Brown, 1986; Skevington, 1981).

Interestingly, even *negatively* valued distinctions have been associated with identification. Negatively regarded groups often utilize such defense mechanisms as recasting a negative distinction into a positive one (Black is beautiful), minimizing or bolstering a negative distinction (We're not popular because we avoid playing politics), or changing the out-group with which the in-group is compared (Lemaine, Kastersztein, & Personnaz, 1978; Skevington, 1981; Wagner et al., 1986) (cf. *social creativity*, Tajfel & Turner, 1985). And the stronger the threat to the group, the stronger the defensive bias (van Knippenberg, 1984). Such machinations might partly explain a person's often fierce identification with countercultures (e.g., Martin & Siehl, 1983) or disaffected groups in organizations (e.g., Jackall, 1978).

A second and related factor that increases identification is the *prestige* of the group (Chatman, Bell, & Staw, 1986; March & Simon, 1958). This is based on the earlier argument that, through intergroup comparison, social identification affects self-esteem. Mael (1988) found that perceived organizational prestige was related to organizational identification among samples of working university students and religious college alumni. Individuals often cognitively (if not publicly) identify themselves with a winner. This accounts in part for the bandwagon effect often witnessed in organizations, where popular support for an individual or idea suddenly gains momentum and escalates, thus creating a rising star. Desires for positive identifications effectively *create* champions, converting "the slightest sign of plurality into an overwhelming majority" (Schelling, 1957, p. 32).

Third, identification is likely to be associated with the *salience of the out-group(s)* (Allen et al., 1983; Turner, 1981). Awareness of out-groups reinforces awareness of one's in-group. Wilder (cited in Wilder, 1981) categorized one set of subjects into two groups (in-group/out-group condition), allegedly on the basis of preference for certain paintings, and a second set into one group (in-group—only condition). Subjects assumed greater homogeneity in the in-group when an out-group was present (in-group/out-group condition) than when no specific out-group was salient (in-group—only condition). Awareness of the out-group underscored the existence of a boundary and caused subjects to assume in-group homogeneity. Similarly, Kanter (1977) found that the presence of females in a male-dominated sales force induced the males to exaggerate perceived masculine traits and differences between the sexes.

The well-known effects of intergroup *competition* on in-group identification (e.g., Friedkin & Simpson, 1985) are a special case of this principle. During competition, group lines are drawn more sharply, values and norms are underscored, and we/they differences are accentuated (Brown & Ross, 1982; van Knippenberg, 1984) (cf. *cognitive differentiation hypothesis*, Dion, 1979). Skevington (1980), for example, found that when high-status nurses (where status was based on training) were led to believe they would be merged with low-status nurses, they increased their in-group favoritism, emphasizing their distinctiveness and superiority over the low-status group.

Finally, the set of factors traditionally associated with group formation (interpersonal interaction, similarity, liking, proximity, shared goals or threat, common history, and so forth) may affect the extent to which individuals identify with a group, although SIT suggests that they are *not necessary* for identification to occur. It should be noted, however, that although these factors facilitate group formation, they also may *directly* cue the psychological grouping of individuals since they can be used as bases for categorization (Hogg & Turner, 1985; Turner, 1984).

In complex organizations, the pervasiveness of this set of antecedents—the categorization of individuals, group distinctiveness and prestige, out-group salience, and group formation factors—suggests that group identification is likely to be prevalent. Also, although the SIT literature indicates that categorization is sufficient for identification to occur, the pervasiveness of formal and informal groups in organizations suggests that categorization is seldom the only factor in identification. Thus, the consequences of identification suggested by SIT, discussed below, may well be *intensified* in organizations.

Consequences

The SIT literature suggests three general consequences of relevance to organizations. First, individuals tend to choose activities congruent with salient aspects of their identities, and they support the institutions embodying those identities. Stryker and Serpe (1982) found that individuals for whom a religious role was salient reported spending more time in that role and deriving satisfaction from it, and Mael (1988) found that the identification of alumni with their alma mater predicted their donating to that institution, their recruiting of offspring and others, their attendance at functions, and their satisfaction with the alma mater. Thus, it is likely that identification with an organization enhances support for and commitment to it.

A second and related consequence is that social identification affects the outcomes conventionally associated with group formation, including intra-group cohesion, cooperation, and altruism, and positive evaluations of the group (Turner, 1982, 1984). It is also reasonable to expect that identification would be associated with loyalty to, and pride in, the group and its activities. However, it should be noted that, given our discussion of psychological groups, this affinity need not be interpersonal or based on interaction. Dion (1973) demonstrated that one may like other group members, despite their negative personal attributes, simply by virtue of the common membership (cf. *personal vs. social attraction*, Hogg & Turner, 1985). In short, "one may like people as group members at the same time as one dislikes them as individual persons" (Turner, 1984, p. 525).

Identification also may engender internalization of, and adherence to, group values and norms and homogeneity in attitudes and behavior. Just as the social classification of others engenders stereotypical perceptions of them, so too does the classification of oneself and subsequent identification engender the attribution of prototypical characteristics to oneself (Turner, 1984, 1985). This self-stereotyping amounts to depersonalization of the self (i.e., the individual is seen to *exemplify* the group), and it increases the perceived similarity with other group members and the likelihood of conformity to group norms.

Finally, it is likely that social identification will reinforce the very antecedents of identification, including the distinctiveness of the group's values and practices, group prestige, salience of and competition with out-groups, and the traditional causes of group formation. As the individual comes to identify with the group, the values and practices of the in-group become more salient and perceived as unique and distinctive (e.g., Tajfel, 1969).

Perhaps the greatest contribution that SIT makes to the literature on organizational behavior is the recognition that a psychological group is far more than an extension of interpersonal relationships (Turner, 1985): Identification with a collectivity can arise even in the absence of interpersonal cohesion, similarity, or interaction and yet have a powerful impact on affect and behavior. As discussed below, in crediting a collectivity with a psychological reality beyond its membership, social identification enables the individual to conceive of, and feel loyal to, an organization or corporate culture. Indeed, Turner (1982) claimed that "social identity is the cognitive mechanism which makes group behaviour possible" (p. 21).

Applying Social Identity Theory to Organizations

The explanatory utility of SIT to organizations can be illustrated by applications to organizational socialization, role conflict, and intergroup relations.

Organizational Socialization

According to the literature on organizational socialization, organizational newcomers are highly concerned with building a *situational definition* (Katz, 1980). Newcomers, it is argued, are unsure of their roles and apprehensive about their status. Consequently, in order to understand the organization and act within it, they must learn its policies and logistics, the general role expectations and behavioral norms, the power and status structures, and so forth (Ashforth, 1985).

However, organizational newcomers also are often concerned with building a *self-definition*, of which the social identity (or identities) is likely to comprise a large part. For many years, writers in the personological tradition of personality theory have noted the link between socialization and the self-concept, suggesting that the emergence of situational and self-definitions are intertwined (see Hogan, 1976). A developing sense of *who* one is complements a sense of *where* one is and what is expected. In complex organizations, the prevalence of social categories suggests that social identities are likely to represent a significant component of individuals' organizationally situated self-definitions, and, indeed, many studies document this idea (see, for example, Fisher, 1986; Mortimer & Simmons, 1978; and Van Maanen, 1976).

Developing Social Identifications

Although the SIT literature is relatively mute about *how* social identification occurs, the literature on organizational socialization suggests that situational definitions and self-definitions both emerge through *symbolic interactions* (Ashforth, 1985; Coe, 1965; Reichers, 1987). Symbolic interactionism holds that meaning is not a given but evolves from the verbal and nonverbal interactions of individuals. For our purposes, *interaction* is defined broadly to include any symbolic transmission, from product advertisements to orientation sessions. (As the SIT literature reviewed above makes clear, interaction need not be interpersonal—though in organizations, of course, it often is.) Through symbolic interactions the newcomer begins to resolve ambiguity, to impose an informational framework or schema on organizational experience.

With regard to self-definitions in particular, Van Maanen (1979) argued that conceptions of the self are learned by interpreting the responses of others in

143

situated social interactions. Drawing on the works of Charles Horton Cooley, George Herbert Mead, and Herbert Blumer, among others, he maintained that through interactions individuals learned to ascribe socially constructed labels such as ambitious, engineer, and upwardly mobile to themselves and others. An example was provided by Becker and Carper (1956). They interviewed graduate students in physiology, most of whom initially viewed physiology as a stopgap pending acceptance into medical school. Becker and Carper found, however, that through immersion in the social milieu many students gradually assumed the identity of physiologists. Frequent interaction and social comparison with fellow students, observation of professors, and tutelage and reinforcement by professors slowly shaped students' interests, skills, self-conceptions, and their understanding of the paradigms, values, norms, and occupational choices in the field.

This perspective on social identification in organizations suggests at least three implications. First, consistent with our earlier discussion, it suggests that the often-noted effect of organizational socialization on the internalization of organizational values and beliefs is comprised in part of an *indirect* effect via identification; that is, socialization affects identification, which in turn affects internalization. As noted, through self-stereotyping the individual typically adopts those characteristics perceived as prototypical of the groups with which he or she identifies. Albert and Whetten (1985) argued that an organization has an identity to the extent there is a shared understanding of the central, distinctive, and enduring character or essence of the organization among its members. This identity may be reflected in shared values and beliefs, a mission, the structures and processes, organizational climate, and so on. The more salient, stable, and internally consistent the character of an organization (or in organizational terms, the stronger the culture), the greater this internalization (Ashforth, 1985).

However, socialization also has a *direct* effect on internalization, as suggested by the argument that one may internalize an organization's culture without necessarily identifying with the organization, and vice versa. The relative importance of the direct (socialization → internalization) and indirect (socialization → identification → internalization) effects most likely vary across organizations, subunits, and roles. Van Maanen (1978) distinguished between investiture processes that ratify the newcomer's incoming identity and divestiture processes that supplant the incoming identity with a new organizationally situated identity. Total and quasi-total institutions such as prisons, military and religious organizations, professional schools, and organizational clans provide prime examples of divestiture. In order to reconstruct the newcomer's social identity, such organizations often remove symbols of newcomer's previous identities; restrict or isolate newcomers from external contact; disparage newcomer's status, knowledge, and ability; impose new identification symbols; rigidly prescribe and proscribe behavior and punish infractions; and reward assumption of the new identity (Fisher, 1986; Goffman, 1961; Van Maanen, 1976, 1978). In such cases internalization of organizational values depends largely on the extent of identification with the organization, subunit, or role. Indeed, the more the organization's identity, goals, values, and individual role requirements deviate from the societal mainstream, the greater the need for organizationally situated identification.

A second implication of the social identification perspective stems from the notion of *reification*. The existing organizational behavior literature does not adequately explain how an individual can identify with, or feel loyal and committed to, an organization per se. The implicit assumption is that regard for individuals simply generalizes to the group, that interpersonal relationships somehow are cognitively aggregated to create an individual–organization relationship (Turner, 1984). We reverse this logic and argue that identification with a group can arise quite separately from interpersonal interaction and cohesion. In perceiving the social category as psychologically real—as embodying characteristics thought prototypical of its members—the individual can identify with the category per se (I am a Marine). Thus, identification provides a mechanism whereby an individual can continue to believe in the integrity of his or her organization despite wrongdoing by senior management or can feel loyal to his or her department despite a complete changeover of personnel.

Third, the social identification perspective also helps to explain the growing interest in symbolic management (Pfeffer, 1981) and charismatic or transformational leadership (Bass, 1985). To the extent that social identification is recognized by managers to relate to such critical variables as organizational commitment and satisfaction, managers have a vested interest in managing symbolic interactions. Although the coherence of a group's or organization's identity is problematic, we believe that symbolic management is designed to impart this identity, or at least management's representation of it. Through the manipulation of symbols such as traditions, myths, metaphors, rituals, sagas, heroes, and physical setting, management can make the individual's membership salient and can provide compelling images of what the group or organization represents (Pondy, Frost, Morgan, & Dandridge, 1983).

Interestingly, Martin, Feldman, Hatch, and Sitkin (1983) noted that organizational cultures "carry a claim to uniqueness—that one institution is unlike any other" (p. 438). We contend that it is precisely because identification is *group-specific* that organizations make such claims. It is tacitly understood by managers that a positive and distinctive organizational identity attracts the recognition, support, and loyalty of not only organizational members but other key constituents (e.g. shareholders, customers, job seekers), and it is this search for a distinctive identity that induces organizations to focus so intensely on advertising, names and logos, jargon, leaders and mascots, and so forth.

This link between symbolism and identification sheds light on the widespread interest in charismatic leaders. Because charismatic leaders are particularly adept at manipulating symbols (Bass, 1985), they are likely to engender social and/or classical identification, that is, identification with the organization, the leader, or both. Where the identification is classical, it may be generalized to the organization through the routinization of charisma (Gerth & Mills, 1946). Trice and Beyer (1986) contrasted the development of two social movement organizations founded by charismatic individuals: Alcoholics Anonymous (AA) and the National Council on Alcoholism (NCA). The charisma of the AA's founder was routinized through an administrative structure, rites and ceremonies, oral and written tradition, and so forth, whereas the charisma of the NCA's founder was poorly routinized. The result, concluded Trice and Beyer, is that the NCA has experienced greater difficulty maintaining the support of its members and donors.

Identification and the Subunit
It should be noted, however, that the newcomer's emerging situational definitions and self-definitions are apt to be largely *subunit-specific*. First, task interdependencies and interpersonal proximity are greater in the individual's immediate work group, suggesting a greater need for, and ease of, interaction. Second, given that people prefer to compare their emerging beliefs with similar others (cf. social comparison theory, Festinger, 1954) and that interpersonal and task differentiation are greater between, than within, subunits (Lawrence & Lorsch, 1967), it is likely that the newcomer will look first to his or her workgroup peers. Third, given interdependence, proximity, and similarity, the subunit may be viewed by members as a psychological group, thus facilitating social influence. According to Turner (1985; Hogg & Turner, 1987), the self-stereotyping occasioned by psychological grouping causes one to *expect* attitudinal and perceptual agreement with group members, such that disagreement triggers doubt and, in turn, attitudinal/perceptual change. Thus, the newcomer's perceptions gravitate toward those of the group. Finally, given the importance of the situational definition to job performance and the centrality of the social identity to the self-concept, it is likely that a normative structure will emerge to regulate and maintain these conceptions. This is consistent with Sampson's (1978) proposition that people attempt to manage their lives in order to establish a sense of continuity in their identity (identity mastery). The upshot is that immediate groups often are more salient "than a more abstract, complex, secondary organization" (Brown, 1969, p. 353).

Organizational socialization, then, can be seen under the SIT perspective as an attempt to symbolically manage newcomers' self-, if not situational, definitions by defining the organization or subunit in terms of distinctive and enduring central properties. Identification with the organization provides (a) a mechanism whereby the individual can reify the organization and feel loyal and committed to it per se (i.e., apart from its members) and (b) an indirect path through which socialization may increase the internalization of organizational values and beliefs.

Role Conflict

Given the number of groups to which an individual might belong, his or her social identity is likely to consist of an amalgam of identities, identities that could impose inconsistent demands upon that person. Further, these demands also may conflict with those of the individual's *personal* identity (Cheek & Briggs, 1982; Leary, Wheeler, & Jenkins, 1986). Note that it is not the identities per se that conflict, but the values, beliefs, norms, and demands inherent in the identities.

In organizations, conflicts between work-group, departmental, divisional, and organizational roles are somewhat constrained by the *nested* character of these roles; that is, each hierarchical level encompasses the former such that the roles are connected in a means-end chain (March & Simon, 1958). Accordingly, the values and behavioral prescriptions inherent in the organizational role tend to be a more abstract and generalized version of those inherent in the work-group role. Nevertheless, even nested identities can be somewhat at odds with one another (Rotondi, 1975; Turner, 1985; Van Maanen, 1976). In the course of assuming a given identity (e.g., department), the group becomes more salient and both intragroup differences and intergroup similarities are cognitively minimized, thus rendering both lower order (e.g., workgroup) and higher order (e.g., organization) identifications less likely. Also, given the association between identification and internalization, a lack of congruence between the goals or expectations of nested groups may impede joint identification. Not surprisingly, then, Brown (1969) found that task interdependencies and the cohesion of the individual's functional unit were negatively related to organizational identification or internalization.

We speculate that the inherent conflict between organizationally situated identities typically is *not* resolved by integrating the disparate identities. First, given the breadth of possible identities, integration would most likely prove cognitively taxing. Second, given the often unique and context-specific demands of an identity, integration would be likely to compromise the utility of each identity to its particular setting. Instead, it is maintained that conflict between identities tends to be cognitively resolved by ordering, separating, or buffering the identities. Suggestions of such processes abound. First, the individual might define him- or herself in terms of his or her most salient social identity (I am a salesman) or personal attribute (I want to get ahead); he or she also might develop a hierarchy of prepotency so that conflicts are resolved by deferring to the most subjectively important or valued identity (Stryker & Serpe, 1982;

Thoits, 1983). Adler and Adler (1987) described how varsity basketball players resolved the conflict between their athletic and academic roles by defining themselves as athletes first and students second and by reducing their involvement in academics accordingly. Second, the individual might defer to the identity that experiences the greatest environmental press and might minimize, deny, or rationalize the conflict (If I hadn't bribed the official, I would have lost the contract). This is akin to Janis and Mann's (1977) notion of *defensive avoidance*. Third, the individual might cognitively decouple the identities so that conflicts simply are not perceived (cf. *value separation*, Steinbruner, 1974). Laurent (1978) discussed how managers often are reluctant to inform subordinates about critical matters, yet as subordinates, they complain about the failure of their own managers to inform them. Finally, the individual might comply *sequentially* with conflicting identities so that the inconsistencies need not be resolved for any given action (cf. *sequential attention*, Cyert & March, 1963). An example is provided by Morton Thiokol, the manufacturer of the faulty solid rocket booster that led to the 1986 crash of the space shuttle *Challenger*. A senior engineer of the company helped reverse a decision not to launch the *Challenger* when he was asked to "take off his engineering hat and put on his management hat" (Presidential Commission, cited in Vaughan, 1986, p. 23).

Related to this idea, Thoits (1983) suggested that the benefits of holding multiple roles (role accumulation), including resource accumulation, justification for failure to meet certain role expectations, and support against role failure or loss, are more likely to accrue if identities remain segregated: "The actor's resources will be valuable to others who do not share those resources themselves, the legitimacy of excuses cannot be checked, and the consequences of role failure or loss can be contained more within one sphere of activities" (p. 184).

To the extent this argument is valid, it suggests that one's identity is an amalgam of loosely coupled identities and that "the popular notion of the self-concept as a unified, consistent, or perceptually 'whole' psychological structure is possibly ill-conceived" (Gergen, 1968, p. 306). This is consistent with evidence from SIT that particular social identities are cued or activated by relevant settings (Turner, 1982, 1985) (cf. *situational identity*, Goffman, 1959; *subidentity*, Hall, 1971; *hard* vs. *soft* identity, Van Maanen, 1976). Most individuals slide fairly easily from one identity to another. Conflict is perceived only when the disparities are *made salient* (Greene, 1978). Thus, in SIT role conflict is endemic to social functioning, but for the most part remains latent: Only when individuals are forced to simultaneously don different hats does their facility for cognitively managing conflict break down.

The argument also suggests that when an individual compartmentalizes identities, he or she may fail to integrate the values, attitudes, norms, and lessons inherent in the various identities. This in turn suggests the likelihood of (a) double-standards and apparent hypocrisy (illustrated by Laurent's, 1978, observation) and (b) selective forgetting. For example, in assuming the identity of foreman, one may eventually forget the values that were appropriate to the prior identity of worker that now *contradict* the demands of the new identity (e.g., Lieberman, 1956); that is, one unlearns tendencies that interfere with the ability to embrace the new, valued identity. Perhaps, then, wisdom is little more than the ability to *remember* the lessons of previous identities, and integrity is the ability to *integrate* and *abide by* them.

Intergroup Relations

For pedagogical purposes, we assume an ideographic organization, that is, one comprised of subunits in which members of each share a social identity specific to their subunit. This assumption allows us to speak of a shared subunit or group identity, even though in complex organizations the degree and foci of consensus remains problematic.

Given this assumption, SIT suggests that *much intergroup conflict stems from the very fact that groups exist*, thus providing a fairly pessimistic view of intergroup harmony (Tajfel, 1982). More specifically, in SIT it is argued that (a) given the relational and comparative nature of social identifications, social identities are maintained primarily by intergroup comparisons and (b) given the desire to enhance self-esteem, groups *seek* positive differences between themselves and reference groups (Tajfel, 1978, 1981; Smith, 1983). Experimental and field research do suggest that groups are willing to sacrifice large monetary gains that do not establish a positive difference between groups for smaller gains that do (Brewer & Silver, 1978; Brown, 1978; Turner, Brown, & Tajfel, 1979), that in-group members adopt more extreme positions after comparison with an out-group than with fellow in-group members (Reid, 1983), and that members prefer and selectively recall information that suggests intergroup differences rather than similarities (Wilder, cited in Wilder, 1981; Wilder & Allen, 1978). This suggests that groups have a vested interest in perceiving or even provoking greater differentiation than exists and disparaging the reference group on this basis (cf. *social vs. instrumental competition*, Turner, 1975). Further, this tendency is exacerbated by contingencies that make the in-group per se salient (Turner, 1981; Wilder, 1981), such as a threat to the group's domain or resources (Brown & Ross, 1982; Brown et al., 1986) or, in Tajfel's (1978) terms, where the group's identity is *insecure*.

The tendency toward subunit identification in organizations, discussed above, suggests that subunits tend to be the primary locus of intergroup conflict. This tendency is exacerbated by competition between subunits for scarce resources and by reward and communication systems that typically focus on subunit functioning and performance (Friedkin & Simpson, 1985; March & Simon, 1958).

As noted, however, field research regarding the relationship between subunit differentiation and identification has been inconclusive because it has confounded the basis of subunit formation (functional vs. market) and extent of interdependence (pooled, sequential, reciprocal). Further, Brown and Williams (1984) suggested that individuals who regard their group identity as synonymous with their organizational identity are unlikely to view other groups negatively. Just as a strong group identity unifies group members, so too should a strong organizational identity unify organizational members. This is consistent with experimental research (Kramer & Brewer, 1984) and the earlier discussion of holographic organizations.

However, where the organizational identity is *not* strong and groups *are* clearly differentiated and bounded, the tendency toward biased intergroup comparisons suggests several effects.

Effects of Biased Intergroup Comparisons
First, the in-group may develop negative stereotypes of the out-group and deindividuate and depersonalize its members (Horwitz & Rabbie, 1982; Wilder, 1981). Hewstone, Jaspars, and Lalljee (1982) studied British schoolboys from private and state secondary schools because of the history of conflict between the two systems. They found that the groups differed in their perceptions of themselves and each other, and that out-group perceptions were generally negative. What's more, these perceptions included self-serving (or group-serving) implicit theories of why the groups differed and attribution biases that rationalized the successes and failures of each group (cf. *social attribution*, Deschamps, 1983).

This suggests a second effect of in-group bias: It *justifies* maintaining social distance and subordinating the out-group (Smith, 1983; Sunar, 1978). The in-group is seen as deserving its successes and not its failures, while the opposite obtains for the out-group. Thus, Perrow (1970) found that members of functional subunits across 12 industrial firms were less likely to criticize the performance of their own unit and more likely to advocate that their unit receive additional power than were members from any other subunit in their particular organization. Similarly, Bates and White (1961) sampled board members, administrators, doctors, and nurses from 13 hospitals and found that each group believed it should have more authority than the other groups were willing to allow, and Brown et al. (1986) found that members of five departments in an industrial organization tended to rate their own department as contributing the most to the company.

Third, given symbolic interactionism, the desire for positive group differentiation, and the stereotyping of self, in-group, and out-group, emerging biases may soon become a contagion (Turner, 1984) that can be easily mobilized against the out-group. In-group members often come to share pejorative perceptions of the out-group and experience the real or imagined slights against other members as their own. Thus, major conflicts often cause an organization to polarize into rival camps, where, if an individual is not on one side, he or she is believed to be on the other side (Mintzberg, 1983). In the above study of hospitals, Bates and White (1961) found that where two groups disagreed on which should have greater authority over a particular issue, respondents from each group rated the amount of authority their own group should have higher than for issues which were *not* in dispute, and gave the *lowest* rating to the group with which they disagreed. The initial disagreement had polarized each group's perception of the situation.

Finally, such competition exacerbates the above tendencies because it threatens the group and its identity. Thus, as Horwitz and Rabbie (1982) noted, "Both experimental and naturalistic observations suggest that hostility erupts more readily between [groups] than between individuals" (p. 269). In-group and out-group relations may be marked by competition and hostility *even in the absence of "objective" sources of conflict* (e.g., scarce resources). Indeed, Turner (1978) found the more comparable the out-group, the *greater* the in-group bias. Hence, organizational subunits may claim to be positively differentiated precisely because they are not. This contrasts sharply with the conventional view that group conflict reflects competition over rewards external to the intergroup situation (cf. *realistic group conflict theory*, Campbell, 1965; Tajfel & Turner, 1985).

Qualifications to Intergroup Comparisons
The dynamics of intergroup comparison, however, need to be qualified by the relative status of the groups. The identity of a low-status group is implicitly threatened by a high-status group, hence the defensive biases in differentiation noted earlier. A high-status group, however, is less likely to feel threatened and, thus, less in need of positive affirmation (Tajfel, 1982; van Knippenberg, 1984). Accordingly, while a low-status group (such as a noncritical staff function or cadre of middle managers) may go to great lengths to differentiate itself from a high-status comparison group (such as a critical line function or senior management), the latter may be relatively unconcerned about such comparisons and form no strong impression about the low-status group. This indifference of the high-status group is, perhaps, the greatest threat to the identity of the low-status group because the latter's identity remains socially unvalidated.

Although the previous discussion suggests that subunits engage endlessly in invidious comparisons, three streams of research on SIT suggest otherwise. First, just as individuals select similar others for social comparison, groups also restrict their comparisons to similar, proximal, or salient out-groups (Tajfel & Turner, 1985). Thus, the purchasing department may be relatively unconcerned with the machinations of, say, the shipping or human resources departments.

Second, van Knippenberg (1984) maintained that individuals are capable of making social comparisons on *multiple* dimensions, and that mutual appreciation is possible where individuals are superior on complementary or different dimensions. The individuals validate each other's relative superiority. Analogously, a field experiment by Mummendey and Schreiber (1984) involving political parties found that in-group favoritism was strong on dimensions regarded as important to the in-group, but that *out-group* favoritism existed on dimensions regarded as *unimportant* to the in-group but important to the out-group. It is quite conceivable that differentiated subunits would acknowledge one another's differential expertise *without* necessarily compromising positive differentiation.

Finally, research on experimental and ethnic groups indicates that groups are less likely to evidence ethnocentrism and defensive biases if differences in the distribution of scarce resources or the outcomes of social comparisons are viewed by the subordinate group as *legitimate or institutionalized* (Caddick, 1982; Tajfel & Turner, 1985). Indeed, in such cases the group may internalize the wider social evaluation of themselves as inferior and less deserving. By accident or design, systems of authority and expertise in organizations (Mintzberg, 1983) often serve precisely this legitimating function, suggesting some stability in intergroup relations.

In summary, SIT argues that in the absence of a strong organizational identity, the desire for favorable intergroup comparisons generates much conflict between differentiated and clearly bounded subunits. This is especially so if a group's status is low or insecure. However, this conflict may be mitigated to the extent that groups compare themselves on different dimensions or view the outcomes of comparisons as legitimate or institutionalized.

....

Implications for Research

Given the paucity of research on SIT in organizations, a research agenda might focus on three objectives. First, in view of the frequent confusion of organizational identification with such related constructs as commitment, loyalty, and internalization, the discriminability of identification should be established. Mael's (1988) confirmatory factor analysis of the Organizational Commitment Questionnaire and his new measure of organizational identification offer a promising start. However, given the argument that individuals often have *multiple* (and conflicting) identities within the organization, research should focus on salient subgroups as well as the organization per se. Indeed, insofar as identification facilitates commitment and the like, researchers should consider investigating commitment itself at the subgroup level. Recent work on *dual* and *multiple* commitments is instructive in this regard (e.g., Reichers, 1986).

A second focus of research might be the proposed antecedents and consequences of social identification. Although experimental and cross-sectional field research have substantiated the social–psychological premises of SIT, the dynamics of identification have not been established. Accordingly, longitudinal field research that focuses on a variety of newly created subunits or organizations or on organizational newcomers is strongly recommended. Such a design would help to explore (a) how the antecedents interact to influence identification, (b) what antecedents (if any) are necessary or sufficient, (c) the sequencing and timing of effects, and (d) if threshold conditions exist.

Finally, although the applications of SIT to organizational behavior were not intended to be exhaustive, they do suggest several specific avenues for field research. For one, the role of organizational socialization can be assessed by structured observation of the interplay among symbolic interactions, symbolic management, and the emergence of social identities. Of particular interest are the posited effects that identification has on a person's internalization of organizational values and on his or her reification of the organization. Also important are the mechanisms by which identification with leaders becomes generalized to the organization. For another, the disjointed resolution of role conflicts can be evaluated by verbal protocol analysis of conflict-laden decisions made over time. Of interest here are the factors associated with selecting a means of resolution, the possibility of stable styles of resolution, the effects of different means, and, more generally, the degree to which various identities are cognitively integrated, the relative salience and priority of various identities across organizations, subunits, hierarchical levels, and individuals, and the interaction among role change, identity change, and selective forgetting. Finally, the roles that social identification and comparison processes have in intergroup conflict can be gauged by analyzing relevant within- and between-group interactions. Research is particularly scarce on the factors that affect the perception of group insecurity (and, hence, the desire for positive differentiation), the selection of reference groups, the dimensions for intergroup comparison, and the perceived legitimacy and institutionalization of the organizational status quo. From an organizational development perspective, research should focus on the fairly unique means, suggested by SIT, of reducing dysfunctional intergroup conflict, such as enhancing the salience and value of the organizational identity, increasing group security or at least legitimating necessary intergroup differences, and individuating out-group members.

Conclusion

According to SIT, the individual defines him- or herself partly in terms of salient group memberships. Identification is the perception of oneness with or belongingness to a group, involving direct or vicarious experience of its successes and failures. Group identification and favoritism tend to occur even in the absence of strong leadership or member interdependency, interaction, or cohesion. Identification is associated with groups that are distinctive, prestigious, and in competition with, or at least aware of, other groups, although it can be fostered by even random assignment to a group. Identification can persist tenaciously even when group affiliation is personally painful, other members are personally disliked, and group failure is likely. The concept of identification, however, describes only the cognition of oneness, *not* the behaviors and affect that may serve as antecedents or consequences of the cognition. Identification induces the individual to engage in, and derive satisfaction from, activities congruent with the identity, to view him- or herself as an exemplar of the group, and to reinforce factors conventionally associated with group formation (e.g., cohesion, interaction). This perspective, applied to several domains of organizational behavior, suggests that:

1. Organizational socialization can be understood in part as an attempt to symbolically manage the newcomer's desire for an identity by defining the organization or subunit in terms of distinctive and enduring central characteristics. Identification enables the newcomer to reify the organization and feel loyal and committed to it per se, and facilitates the internalization of organizational values and beliefs.

2. Individuals have multiple, loosely coupled identities, and inherent conflicts between their demands are typically not resolved by cognitively integrating the identities, but by ordering, separating, or buffering them. This compartmentalization of identities suggests the possibility of double standards, apparent hypocrisy, and selective forgetting.

3. In ideographic organizations, the desire for a salutary social identity predisposes organizational subunits to intergroup conflict on characteristics that are mutually compared. Thus, intergroup conflict may arise even in the absence of such objective causes as scarce resources.

In summary, the concept of identification has been neglected in organizational research. The reformulated conception of identification as perceived oneness with a group, suggested by social identity theory, offers a fresh perspective on a number of critical organizational issues, only a few of which have been explored here.

References

Adler, P., & Adler, P. A. (1987) Role conflict and identity salience: College athletics and the academic role. *Social Science Journal*, 24, 443–455.

Albert, S., & Whetten, D. A. (1985) Organizational identity. In L. L. Cummings & B. M. Staw (Eds.), *Research in organizational behavior* (Vol. 7, pp. 263–295). Greenwich, CT: JAI Press.

Allen, V. L., Wilder, D. A., & Atkinson, M. L. (1983) Multiple group membership and social identity. In T. R. Sarbin & K. E. Scheibe (Eds.), *Studies in social identity* (pp. 92–115). New York: Praeger.

Ashforth, B. E. (1985) Climate formation: Issues and extensions. *Academy of Management Review*, 10, 837–847.

Bandura, A., & Walters, R. H. (1963) *Social learning and personality development*. New York: Holt, Rinehart & Winston.

Bass, B. M. (1985) *Leadership and performance beyond expectations*. New York: Free Press.

Bates, F. L., & White, R. F. (1961) Differential perceptions of authority in hospitals. *Journal of Health and Human Behavior*, 2, 262–267.

Becker, H. S., & Carper, J. W. (1956) The development of identification with an occupation. *American Journal of Sociology*, 61, 289–298.

Billig, M., & Tajfel, H. (1973) Social categorization and similarity in intergroup behavior. *European Journal of Social Psychology*, 3, 27–52.

Brewer, M. B. (1979) In-group bias in the minimal intergroup situation: A cognitive-motivational analysis. *Psychological Bulletin*, 86, 307–324.

Brewer, M. B., & Silver, M. (1978) In-group bias as a function of task characteristics. *European Journal of Social Psychology*, 8, 393–400.

Brown, M. E. (1969) Identification and some conditions of organizational involvement. *Administrative Science Quarterly*, 14, 346–355.

Brown, R. (1978) Divided we fall: An analysis of relations between sections of a factory workforce. In H. Tajfel (Ed.), *Differentiation between social groups: Studies in the social psychology of intergroup relations* (pp. 395–429). London: Academic Press.

Brown, R., Condor, S., Mathews, A., Wade, G., & Williams, J. (1986) Explaining intergroup differentiation in an industrial organization. *Journal of Occupational Psychology*, 59, 273–286.

Brown, R. J., & Ross, G. F. (1982) The battle for acceptance: An investigation into the dynamics of intergroup behavior. In H. Tajfel (Ed.), *Social identity and intergroup relations* (pp. 155–178). Cambridge, England: Cambridge University Press.

Brown, R., & Williams, J. (1984) Group identification: The same thing to all people? *Human Relations*, 37, 547–564.

Brown, R. W. (1986) *Social psychology, the second edition*. New York: Free Press.

Caddick, B. (1982) Perceived illegitimacy and intergroup relations. In H. Tajfel (Ed.), *Social identity and intergroup relations* (pp. 137–154). Cambridge, England: Cambridge University Press.

Campbell, D. T. (1965) Ethnocentric and other altruistic motives. In D. Levine (Ed.), *Nebraska symposium on motivation* (Vol. 13, pp. 283–311). Lincoln: University of Nebraska Press.

Chatman, J. A., Bell, N. E., & Staw, B. M. (1986) The managed thought: The role of self-justification and impression management in organizational settings. In H. P. Sims, Jr., D. A. Gioia & Associates (Eds.), *The thinking organization: Dynamics of organizational social cognition* (pp. 191–214). San Francisco: Jossey-Bass.

Cheek, J. M., & Briggs, S. R. (1982) Self-consciousness and aspects of identity. *Journal of Research in Personality*, 16, 401–408.

Coe, R. M. (1965) Self-conception and professional training. *Nursing Research*, 14, 49–52.

Cyert, R. M., & March, J. G. (1963) *A behavioral theory of the firm*. Englewood Cliffs, NJ: Prentice-Hall.

Denhardt, R. B. (1987) Images of death and slavery in organizational life. *Journal of Management*, 13, 529–541.

Deschamps, J. C. (1983) Social attribution. In J. Jaspars, F. D. Fincham, & M. Hewstone (Eds.), *Attribution theory and research: Conceptual, developmental and social dimensions* (pp. 223–240). London: Academic Press.

Dion, K. L. (1973) Cohesiveness as a determinant of ingroup-outgroup bias. *Journal of Personality and Social Psychology*, 28, 163–171.

Dion, K. L. (1979) Intergroup conflict and intra-group cohesiveness. In W. G. Austin & S. Worchel (Eds.), *The social psychology of intergroup relations* (pp. 211–224). Monterey, CA: Brooks/Cole.

Festinger, L. (1954) A theory of social comparison processes. *Human Relations*, 7, 117–140.

Fisher, C. D. (1986) Organizational socialization: An integrative review. In K. M. Rowland & G. K. Ferris (Eds.), *Research in personnel and human resources management* (Vol. 4, pp. 101–145). Greenwich, CT: JAI Press.

Foote, N. N. (1951) Identification as the basis for a theory of motivation. *American Sociological Review*, 16, 14–21.

Fox, A. (1980) The meaning of work. In G. Esland & G. Salaman (Eds.), *The politics of work and occupations* (pp. 139–191). Toronto: University of Toronto Press.

Friedkin, N. E., & Simpson, M. J. (1985) Effects of competition on members' identification with their subunits. *Administrative Science Quarterly*, 30, 377–394.

Gammons, P. (1986, November 3) Living and dying with the Woe Sox. *Sports Illustrated*, pp. 22–23.

Gergen, K. J. (1968) Personal consistency and the presentation of self. In C. Gordon & K. J. Gergen (Eds.), *The self in social interaction* (Vol. 1, pp. 299–308). New York: Wiley.

Gerth, H. H., & Mills, C. W. (Eds.) (1946) *From Max Weber: Essays in sociology*. New York: Oxford University Press.

Goffman, E. (1959) *The presentation of self in everyday life*. Garden City, NY: Doubleday.

Goffman, E. (1961) *Asylums: Essays on the social situation of mental patients and other inmates*. Garden City, NY: Doubleday.

Gould, S. B. (1975) *Organizational identification and commitment in two environments*. Unpublished doctoral dissertation, Michigan State University, Lansing.

Greene, C. N. (1978) Identification modes of professionals: Relationship with formalization, role strain, and alienation. *Academy of Management Journal*, 21, 486–492.

Hall, D. T. (1971) A theoretical model of career subidentity development in organizational settings. *Organizational Behavior and Human Performance*, 6, 50–76.

Hall, D. T., Schneider, B., & Nygren, H. T. (1970) Personal factors in organizational identification. *Administrative Science Quarterly*, 15, 176–190.

Hamilton, D. L. (Ed.) (1981) *Cognitive processes in stereotyping and intergroup behavior*. Hillsdale, NJ: Erlbaum.

Hewstone, M., Jaspars, J., & Lalljee, M. (1982) Social representations, social attribution and social identity: The intergroup images of 'public' and 'comprehensive' schoolboys. *European Journal of Social Psychology*, 12, 241–269.

Hoetler, J. W. (1985) A structural theory of personal consistency. *Social Psychology Quarterly*, 48, 118–129.

Hogan, R. (1976) *Personality theory: The personological tradition*. Englewood Cliffs, NJ: Prentice-Hall.

Hogg, M. A., & Turner, J. C. (1985) Interpersonal attraction, social identification and psychological group formation. *European Journal of Social Psychology*, 15, 51–66.

Hogg, M. A., & Turner, J. C. (1987) Social identity and conformity: A theory of referent informational influence. In W. Doise & S. Moscovici (Eds.), *Current issues in European social psychology* (Vol. 2, pp. 139–182). Cambridge, England: Cambridge University Press.

Horwitz, M., & Rabbie, J. M. (1982) Individuality and membership in the intergroup system. In H. Tajfel (Ed.), *Social identity and intergroup relations* (pp. 241–274). Cambridge, England: Cambridge University Press.

Jackall, R. (1978) *Workers in a labyrinth: Jobs and survival in a bank bureaucracy*. Montclair, NJ: Allanheld, Osmun.

Janis, I. L., & Mann, L. (1977) *Decision making: A psychological analysis of conflict, choice, and commitment*. New York: Free Press.

Kanter, R. M. (1977) Some effects of proportions on group life: Skewed sex ratios and responses to token women. *American Journal of Sociology*, 82, 965–990.

Katz, D., & Kahn, R. L. (1978) *The social psychology of organizations* (2nd ed.). New York: Wiley.

Katz, R. (1980) Time and work: Toward an integrative perspective. In B. M. Staw & L. L. Cummings (Eds.), *Research in organizational behavior* (Vol. 2, pp. 81–127). Greenwich, CT: JAI Press.

Kelman, H. C. (1961) Processes of opinion change. *Public Opinion Quarterly*, 25, 57–78.

Kets de Vries, M. F. R., & Miller, D. (1984) *The neurotic organization: Diagnosing and changing counterproductive styles of management*. San Francisco: Jossey-Bass.

Kramer, R. M., & Brewer, M. B. (1984) Effects of group identity on resource use in a simulated commons dilemma. *Journal of Personality and Social Psychology*, 46, 1044–1057.

Laurent, A. (1978) Managerial subordinacy: A neglected aspect of organizational hierarchies. *Academy of Management Review*, 3, 220–230.

Lawrence, P. R., & Lorsch, J. W. (1967) *Organization and environment: Managing differentiation and integration*. Boston: Harvard University Press.

Leary, M. R., Wheeler, D. S., & Jenkins, T. B. (1986) Aspects of identity and behavioral preference: Studies of occupational and recreational choice. *Social Psychology Quarterly*, 49, 11–18.

Lee, S. M. (1971) An empirical analysis of organizational identification. *Academy of Management Journal*, 14, 213–226.

Lemaine, G., Kastersztein, J., & Personnaz, B. (1978) Social differentiation. In H. Tajfel (Ed.), *Differentiation between social groups: Studies in the social psychology of inter-group relations* (pp. 269–300). London: Academic Press.

Levinson, H. (1970) A psychologist diagnoses merger failures. *Harvard Business Review*, 48(2), 139–147.

Lieberman, S. (1956) The effects of changes in roles on the attitudes of role occupants. *Human Relations*, 9, 385–402.

Locksley, A., Oritz, V., & Hepburn, C. (1980) Social categorization and discriminatory behavior: Extinguishing the minimal intergroup discrimination effect. *Journal of Personality and Social Psychology*, 39, 773–783.

Mael, F. (1988) *Organizational identification: Construct redefinition and a field application with organizational alumni*. Unpublished doctoral dissertation, Wayne State University, Detroit.

March, J. G., & Simon, H. A. (1958) *Organizations*. New York: Wiley.

Martin, J., Feldman, M. S., Hatch, M. J., & Sitkin, S. B. (1983) The uniqueness paradox in organizational stories. *Administrative Science Quarterly*, 28, 438–453.

Martin, J., & Siehl, C. (1983) Organizational culture and counterculture: An uneasy symbiosis. *Organizational Dynamics*, 12(2), 52–64.

Mintzberg, H. (1983) *Power in and around organizations.* Englewood Cliffs, NJ: Prentice-Hall.

Mortimer, J. T., & Simmons, R. G. (1978) Adult socialization. In R. H. Turner, J. Coleman, & R. C. Fox (Eds.), *Annual review of sociology* (Vol. 4, pp. 421–454). Palo Alto, CA: Annual Reviews.

Mowday, R. T., Steers, R. M., & Porter, L. W. (1979) The measurement of organizational commitment. *Journal of Vocational Behavior*, 4, 224–247.

Mummendey, A., & Schreiber, H. J. (1984) "Different" just means "better": Some obvious and some hidden pathways to in-group favouritism. *British Journal of Social Psychology*, 23, 363–368.

Oaker, G., & Brown, R. (1986) Intergroup relations in a hospital setting: A further test of social identity theory. *Human Relations*, 39, 767–778.

Oakes, P. J., & Turner, J. C. (1980) Social categorization and intergroup behavior: Does minimal intergroup discrimination make social identity more positive? *European Journal of Social Psychology*, 10, 295–301.

Oakes, P., & Turner, J. C. (1986) Distinctiveness and the salience of social category memberships: Is there an automatic perceptual bias towards novelty? *European Journal of Social Psychology*, 16, 325–344.

O'Reilly, C., III, & Chatman, J. (1986) Organizational commitment and psychological attachment: The effects of compliance, identification, and internalization on prosocial behavior. *Journal of Applied Psychology*, 71, 492–499.

Ouchi, W. G. (1981) *Theory Z: How American business can meet the Japanese challenge.* New York: Avon.

Patchen, M. (1970) *Participation, achievement and involvement on the job.* Englewood Cliffs, NJ: Prentice-Hall.

Perkins, D. N. T., Nieva, V. F., & Lawler, E. E., III. (1983) *Managing creation: The challenge of building a new organization.* New York: Wiley.

Perrow, C. (1970) Departmental power and perspectives in industrial firms. In M. N. Zald (Ed.), *Power in organizations: Proceedings of the first annual Vanderbilt Sociology Conference* (pp. 59–89). Nashville, TN: Vanderbilt University Press.

Pfeffer, J. (1981) Management as symbolic action: The creation and maintenance of organizational paradigms. In L. L. Cummings & B. M. Staw (Eds.), *Research in organizational behavior* (Vol. 3, pp. 1–52). Greenwich, CT: JAI Press.

Pondy, L. R., Frost, P. J., Morgan, G., & Dandridge, T. C. (Eds.) (1983) *Organizational symbolism.* Greenwich, CT: JAI Press.

Reichers, A. E. (1985) A review and reconceptualization of organizational commitment. *Academy of Management Review*, 10, 465–476.

Reichers, A. E. (1986) Conflict and organizational commitments. *Journal of Applied Psychology*, 71, 508–514.

Reichers, A. E. (1987) An interactionist perspective on newcomer socialization rates. *Academy of Management Review*, 12, 278–287.

Reid, F. J. M. (1983) Polarizing effects of intergroup comparisons. *European Journal of Social Psychology*, 13, 103–106.

Rotondi, T., Jr. (1975) Organizational identification: Issues and implications. *Organizational Behavior and Human Performance*, 13, 95–109.

Sampson, E. E. (1978) Personality and the location of identity. *Journal of Personality*, 46, 552–568.

Schelling, T. C. (1957) Bargaining, communication, and limited war. *Journal of Conflict Resolution*, 1, 19–36.

Schneider, B., Hall, D. T., & Nygren, H. T. (1971) Self-image and job characteristics as correlates of changing organizational identification. *Human Relations*, 24, 397–416.

Skevington, S. M. (1980) Intergroup relations and social change within a nursing context. *British Journal of Social and Clinical Psychology*, 19, 201–213.

Skevington, S. M. (1981) Intergroup relations and nursing. *European Journal of Social Psychology*, 11, 43–59.

Smith, K. K. (1983) Social comparison processes and dynamic conservatism in intergroup relations. In L. L. Cummings & B. M. Staw (Eds.), *Research in organizational behavior* (Vol. 5, pp. 199–233). Greenwich, CT: JAI Press.

Steinbruner, J. D. (1974) *The cybernetic theory of decision: New dimensions of political analysis.* Princeton, NJ: Princeton University Press.

Stryker, S., & Serpe, R. T. (1982) Commitment, identity salience, and role behavior: Theory and research example. In W. Ickes & E. S. Knowles (Eds.), *Personality, roles, and social behavior* (pp. 199–218). New York: Springer-Verlag.

Sunar, D. G. (1978) Stereotypes of the powerless: A social psychological analysis. *Psychological Reports*, 43, 511–528.

Tajfel, H. (1969) Cognitive aspects of prejudice. *Journal of Social Issues*, 25(4), 79–97.

Tajfel, H. (1978) The achievement of group differentiation. In H. Tajfel (Ed.), *Differentiation between social groups: Studies in the social psychology of intergroup relations* (pp. 77–98). London: Academic Press.

Tajfel, H. (1981) *Human groups and social categories: Studies in social psychology.* Cambridge, England: Cambridge University Press.

Tajfel, H. (1982) Instrumentality, identity and social comparisons. In H. Tajfel (Ed.), *Social identity and intergroup relations* (pp. 483–507). Cambridge, England: Cambridge University Press.

Tajfel, H., & Turner, J. C. (1985) The social identity theory of intergroup behavior. In S. Worchel & W. G. Austin (Eds.), *Psychology of intergroup relations* (2nd ed., pp. 7–24). Chicago: Nelson-Hall.

Thoits, P. A. (1983) Multiple identities and psychological well-being: A reformulation and test of the social isolation hypothesis. *American Sociological Review*, 48, 174–187.

Tolman, E. C. (1943) Identification and the post-war world. *Journal of Abnormal and Social Psychology*, 38, 141–148.

Trice, H. M., & Beyer, J. M. (1986) Charisma and its routinization in two social movement organizations. In B. M. Staw & L. L. Cummings (Eds.), *Research in organizational behavior* (Vol. 8, pp. 113–164). Greenwich, CT: JAI Press.

Turner, J. C. (1975) Social comparison and social identity: Some prospects for intergroup behaviour. *European Journal of Social Psychology*, 5, 5–34.

Turner, J. C. (1978) Social comparison, similarity and in-group favouritism. In H. Tajfel (Ed.), *Differentiation between social groups: Studies in the social psychology of intergroup relations* (pp. 235–250). London: Academic Press.

Turner, J. C. (1981) The experimental social psychology of intergroup behavior. In J. C. Turner & H. Giles (Eds.), *Intergroup behaviour* (pp. 66–101). Chicago: University of Chicago Press.

Turner, J. C. (1982) Towards a cognitive redefinition of the social group. In H. Tajfel (Ed.), *Social identity and intergroup relations* (pp. 15–40). Cambridge, England: Cambridge University Press.

Turner, J. C. (1984) Social identification and psychological group formation. In H. Tajfel (Ed.), *The social dimension: European developments in social psychology* (Vol. 2, pp. 518–538). Cambridge, England: Cambridge University Press.

Turner, J. C. (1985) Social categorization and the self-concept: A social cognitive theory of group behavior. In E. J. Lawler (Ed.), *Advances in group processes* (Vol. 2, pp. 77–122). Greenwich, CT: JAI Press.

Turner, J. C., Brown, R. J., & Tajfel, H. (1979) Social comparison and group interest in ingroup favouritism. *European Journal of Social Psychology*, 9, 187–204.

van Knippenberg, A. F. M. (1984) Intergroup differences in group perceptions. In H. Tajfel (Ed.), *The social dimension: European developments in social psychology* (Vol. 2, pp. 560–578). Cambridge, England: Cambridge University Press.

Van Maanen, J. (1976) Breaking in: Socialization to work. In R. Dubin (Ed.), *Handbook of work, organization, and society* (pp. 67–130). Chicago: Rand McNally.

Van Maanen, J. (1978) People processing: Strategies of organizational socialization. *Organizational Dynamics*, 7(1), 19–36.

Van Maanen, J. (1979) The self, the situation, and the rules of interpersonal relations. In W. Bennis, J. Van Maanen, E. H. Schein, & F. I. Steele (Eds.), *Essays in interpersonal dynamics* (pp. 43–101). Homewood, IL: Dorsey Press.

Vaughan, D. (1986) *Structural secrecy and organizational misconduct: NASA and the space shuttle Challenger*. Paper presented at the meeting of the Academy of Management, Chicago.

Wagner, U., Lampen, L., & Syllwasschy, J. (1986) In-group inferiority, social identity and out-group devaluation in a modified minimal group study. *British Journal of Social Psychology*, 25, 15–23.

Wiener, Y. (1982) Commitment in organizations: A normative view. *Academy of Management Review*, 7, 418–428.

Wilder, D. A. (1981) Perceiving persons as a group: Categorization and ingroup relations. In D. L. Hamilton (Ed.), *Cognitive processes in stereotyping and intergroup behavior* (pp. 213–257). Hillsdale, NJ: Erlbaum.

Wilder, D. A., & Allen, V. L. (1978) Group membership and preference for information about others. *Personality and Social Psychology Bulletin*, 4, 106–110.

9

Organization: From Substance to Image?

Mats Alvesson

Introduction

During the last ten years the ideational dimensions of organizations and management have been heavily emphasized both in corporate practice and in organization theory. The interest in organizational culture and symbolism, corporate identity, images, visions, etc. is, however, often understood in an a-historical and a-sociological way. The broader lines of development in society and organizations that make these dimensions salient and more significant than before have hardly been investigated.

This chapter looks at the current interest in images in corporations. For a considerable time, there has been a focus on the images of products, brands and—later—corporations in the practice of and writings on marketing. Especially in service marketing, corporate images are seen as important. The present chapter concentrates on the role and significance of corporate images from an organizational perspective, emphasizing the management of images as a crucial skill and field of activity in a particular kind of socio-cultural context and in specific organizational conditions. Even though it can be argued that images are always present in social life and/or in the minds of people, it will be stressed in this chapter that to a greater or lesser degree they are salient and recognized as significant in managerial work and corporate life. Images are being singled out as crucial factors and suitable objects (targets) for managerial action only under specific conditions. One way of formulating the purpose of the chapter is to say that it aims to formulate a historically and sociologically conscious 'contingency theory' of corporate images: to account for some external and internal organizational conditions that trigger off attention from top management to corporate images in relation not only to external groups, but also to organizational personnel.

Even though this chapter concentrates on images, related topics like organizational and other forms of cultures and corporate identity will also be treated, both as aspects of significance for understanding the topic of image and as expressions of an overall general trend which makes the ideational dimensions of greater significance for organizational functioning and performance.

I will start by saying something about the relationship between corporate identity and images; argue that identity problems of many modern professions and organizations call for a focus on corporate images; then point to some trends which underlie this and, finally, characterize the modern corporation as one which draws upon, and partly also provides, the material and socio-cultural base for high discretion for top management in terms of anchoring (favourable) images among internal and external stakeholders. A brief empirical illustration in the form of a case study of a computer consultancy firm will also be provided.

Corporate Identity and Image

The general economic and socio-cultural development and situation provides the background for the present preoccupation with issues like culture, identity, profile and image in organizational analysis. The elaboration of these concepts is grounded in a rapidly changing and increasingly problematic social order— and potential disorder—, which heightens the importance of identity, culture and image. An example of this is the conceptualization of structures in organizations such as the 'corporate identity' (e.g. Alvesson 1989b; Berg 1986; Margulies 1977). The analogy suggests that by strengthening the organization's identity—its experienced distinctiveness, consistency and stability—it can be assumed that individuals' identities and identifications will be strengthened with what they are supposed to be doing at their workplace, which thus facilitates the integration of the whole organization. These identifications seem to be more and more problematic due to rapid changes, increased social mobilization, decline of the traditional work ethic, etc.

In a society or an organization where the identity of individuals is clearly based in the substantive activities of the collective, the need to focus on the 'identity' of the corporation as a specific topic would hardly be necessary. It is the identity problems in our general culture (including the parts of it that exist in corporations) that accounts for the preoccupation with corporate identities. Seen from a psychological point of view, which includes meaning, motivation, involvement, and identification with one's work, many modern jobs and organizations do not seem automatically to confirm and strengthen the work identity of the employees. Similarly, other traditional sources of social identity such as the local community and class appear to have decreased in importance as a result of spatial changes and restructuring of industry and business in modern, capitalistic societies during the last decades (Lash and Urry 1987). Of particular significance for our argument is that the linkage between employee and work, or between employee and the organizational context in which she/he is located, is often weak. At the corporate level, the core activities are increasingly not distinct enough or forceful in themselves to produce an identity. In a society characterized by rapid changes, mass communication, and production processes where the relationship between what is being produced and social needs are increasingly hard to detect, corporate identity becomes an issue of specific attention and social engineering efforts. Corporate identity as something which is developed naturally and spontaneously as an undifferentiable part of the basic activities of the corporation seems only rarely to characterize the modern sectors of the economy.

In the same way, it is real problems with the meaning of work that account for the latest innovation in leadership theory, stressing its role as 'the management of meaning' (e.g. Berg 1986; Pondy 1978; Smircich and Morgan 1982). It is the loss of meaning (or at least a lack of clarity in the meaning of tasks and organizational work) that emphasizes this dimension of managerial work. Similarly, it can be argued that the absence of meaning in work accounts for the great interest in 'motivation' during recent decades—'motivation as a surrogate for meaning' (Sievers 1986). In a society and in organizations where tasks correspond to a whole and the utility (social significance) of the products were self-evident, the need for a particular actor communicating the meaning would be less significant. Something similar can be said of the image of the organization. It is when the content of work and the organization do not speak for themselves, that images are given systematic attention.

Before going into further detail, a brief discussion of the meaning of image is called for. The concept is tricky to define and its ontological status is not easy to establish. It is sometimes used to refer to somebody's inner picture of a particular object, and at other times it refers to the communicated attributes of an object. In the former sense, an image is primarily created by an agent for his or her own sake. Image can be defined as '... the subjective record of sense-experience (which) is not a direct copy of actual experience, but has been "projected", in the process of copying, into a new dimension, the more or less stabile form we call a *picture*' (Langer 1957: 144). In the second sense, the image bears the imprints of a *sender* trying to project a certain impression to an audience. It can of course also be argued that the image exists somewhere 'in between' the communicator and the audience. An image is then a result of projection from two directions. Especially concerning corporations, products, brands, etc., the images of interest from top management's point of view, are not those emerging in the absence of particular efforts to produce an impression, or as Bernstein (1984) puts it, image '... means a fabrication of public impression created to appeal to the audience rather than to reproduce reality...' (p. 13).

The two dimensions of image—inner picture (sense image) and fabrication (communicated image)—might create some confusion. It can be argued that images, in the sense of an inner, holistic impression of an object always exist. So do perceptions, views, opinions, attitudes, and meanings, etc. This means that there cannot be more or less image. Images cannot be more or less salient or significant. Langer (1957: 145), for example, suggests that

'Images are our readiest instruments for abstracting concepts from the tumbling stream of actual impressions. They make our primitive abstractions for us, they are our spontaneous embodiments of general ideas.'

According to this view, there might be differences between images. They might be more or less true (false) or (in)accurate, but images are an unavoidable part of social and psychological reality and thus do not vary throughout history in terms of significance. I do not disagree with this view on image as a psychological concept, but in the present Chapter, as in large areas of the whole field of research and managerial practice concerning images in relation to corporations, a different, more sociological view on image is used. The intentions behind the image are thus an important aspect. A corporate image thus refers to a holistic and vivid impression held by a particular group towards a corporation, partly as a result of information processing (sense-making) carried out by the group's members (as indicated by Langer above) and partly by the aggregated communication of the corporation in question concerning its nature, i.e. the fabricated and projected picture of itself. Image as a phenomenological fact, in the sense that the image as a specific idea, instrumentally exploited, becomes salient in a particular social context as a non-trivial part of management and organizational functioning is experienced by local actors to capture something meaningful, and thus is not a historical constant, but rather is contingent upon social, cultural and material factors. In certain societies, times and organizations, the idea of an 'image' does not make sense, at least not as something significant for the successful carrying out of economic activity.

In this Chapter, image refers to something affected by the intentions of particular actors (a company), for whom the image is singled out as a particular concept and target for instrumental action. The image is not a tightly integrated part of the reality (the referent) it is supposed to say something about, but is loosely coupled to this and can be affected in itself, without directly affecting what the image refers to. This view is in harmony with that of most authors concerned with corporate images (e.g. Berg and Gagliardi 1986; Bernstein 1984; Dichter 1985; Normann 1984, etc.).

This view of image makes it possible to identify conditions when it becomes meaningful and important to pay attention to images. Two such conditions might be the significance of people's impressions and attitudes for the organization's activity and the degree of ambiguity. If the attitudes of a particular group have no significance for an organization, then there is not much point in talking about the latter's 'image' in the group, at least not in the sense mentioned here. The more sensitive a person or a corporation is towards the subtlety of opinions and attitudes among the target group, the stronger are the reasons for paying attention to 'image'. The more ambiguity characterizing the nature of the business and products of a corporation, the greater is the significance of its image.

However, the 'management of image' (to use business language) rests upon the notion of distance. An image is primarily a picture of something developed or at least affected by a person or a public about an object in the absence of frequent interaction with, a deep relation with, good knowledge and overview of or close contact with the object. If we have a lot of information about an object and are not too biased (positively or negatively) to it, then the picture of it is too complex and multifaceted to be captured by the concept of an image. An image is something we get primarily through coincidental, infrequent, superficial and/or mediated information, through mass media, public appearances, from second-hand sources etc., not through our own direct, lasting experiences and perceptions of the 'core' of the object. To create favourable attitudes among employees through corporate advertising (as in mass-media, but with the employees as a target group) focusing on the president as a symbol is rather pointless if it is a small corporation where everybody has a daily contact with the president. The experiences based on personal contact carry more weight in forming opinions and beliefs than the message in the advertisement. Richness of information makes the image concept inappropriate, at least as a central concept in the field of management.

It is of course problematic to talk about 'objective reality' in social science and normally I do not, but, a few comments on objectivity may be helpful at this point. An image differs somewhat from the 'objective reality' it is assumed to illuminate. It is a representation of an object. The relationship between an image and the reality it is supposed to cover is, at best, ambiguous. Berg and Gagliardi (1986) even suggest that there is a 'need for falsification, i.e. to show the company other than it is'. The difference, however, does not necessarily have to be a matter of the image being false, but is more a question of selectivity, inadequacy, or an uncritical attitude. As Boorstin (1961) says, an image is created to present and make a certain kind of believable impression. It must not be perceived as untrue and the manufacturers must avoid producing images which might too easily be proven false. Boorstin stresses that: 'An image is ambiguous. It floats somewhere between the imagination and the senses, between expectation and reality.' (p. 193).

Too large a difference might be problematic for a corporation, but no management is interested in image management which presents a broad and nuanced picture stressing aspects which would illuminate not only (what many people would perceive as) the positive but also the negative (weak) sides of the business. As suggested above, a corporate image does not allow too much complexity. The objective of image management is to produce an appealing picture of the company for various publics (employees, customers, shareholders, government, etc.) and to position it in a beneficial way.

This might be achieved in various ways and a range of strategies in image management is possible, from highlighting good points to covering up or drawing attention away from bad or weak aspects of the company. Another option is simply to communicate the company's 'true' features in the most creative and positive way imaginable. Complex phenomena such as organizations can be portrayed in an endless number of ways, without violating 'truth' (which for all practical purposes is socially constructed). Normally, the formulations and messages chosen are those which have positive connotations. Beyond viewing images in terms of black and white, they often can be seen as being located in a grey zone between the true (honest) and false (dishonest), even though 'white' and 'black' images also exist.

An interesting and significant issue is that not only external groups, usually with far from perfect knowledge of the corporation in question, but also employees have come to be viewed as an important audience for the image issue. This might be interpreted as a consequence of increased ambiguity—from the perspective of employees—characterizing many organizations. While the identity of the corporation does not 'take care of itself' there is a call for—and a space for—specific actions aiming at fabricating images. To the degree that employees are holding these, it means that the feeling of identity is created through mental structures rather than through objective reality. Image management and internal marketing, targeted on employees, are hot topics in today's management practice (Berg 1986) and theory, especially in the service sector (Grönroos 1984; Normann 1984). Again, I believe we can understand this better if we consider changes in the historical–societal context. I shall describe these changes as a development from 'substance' to 'image'. This means, among other things, that corporate identity emerges to a lesser degree from the (service) production processes and to an increasing degree from systematic efforts to anchor certain images of the corporation in the consciousnesses of the personnel.

From Substance to Image

This formulation of development in modern society tries to capture some important, interrelated, tendencies. These concern the very nature of society and culture, its socio-structural and socio-material characteristics, which have changed from having formed a unity, in which social relations, the material aspects of existence and the cultural patterns were relatively stable, well integrated and easily understandable to becoming more and more fragmented and 'artificial' (for example automation, information technology, professional people employed to take care of human services, etc.). In a certain sense, we can say that society's 'substantive' nature has been reduced. This is illustrated in the writings of many of the cultural sociologists of today, for example (Baudrillard 1985; Lasch 1984; Ziehe and Stubenrauch 1982). Lasch (1984: 19) describes the developments as '...the replacement of a reliable world of durable objects by a world of flickering images...' The 'imaginary' of today's society includes the impressions and pictures we get of political and organizational leaders, people with whom we interact (on an often short-time and superficial basis), the objects (like commodities) we are dealing with (in and outside work) and the general view of the total world as it appears to us.

I think that we can point to four distinct elements in these inter-related tendencies, from a social order characterized by 'substance' to one whose trademark is 'image'.

Cultural Changes

The first concerns the cultural changes resulting in new socialization forms and a psychology of today's people which differs from the one prevalent half a century ago. A survey of the research during the last decade on the relationship between cultural change—which is in essence a product of economic changes of a basic character—and changed forms of socialization indicates rather far-reaching changes in the social psychology of man in the most advanced societies. Ziehe and Stubenrauch (1982) talk about a fragmentation of social totality, on an economic-material, a socio-cultural and an individual level.

They suggest that the cultural changes bring about a character with, in relation to the earlier common character, an identity that is in a sense weaker, more vulnerable but also more flexible and less prone to discipline under repressive social conditions (as in the case of boring and harshly controlled work). A 'heightening' of the need for 'subjectivity', for feeling involved, for meaning and gratification as a condition for psychic well-being, characterize most people of today to a much higher degree than was the case 20–30 years ago. This point is also emphasized by Sennett (1977). He suggests that in people's consciousness, 'objective' factors and forces have become less important over recent decades, while the significance of personal and subjective dimensions are seen to be more and more crucial for the understanding of all types of social phenomena. The barriers between the person and his environment, which formerly were strong enough to protect the individual, have been continuously weakened over the course of a century and have been replaced by a narcissistic involvement of the self in all areas of life.

Other social psychologists, sociologists and historians account for cultural development and the present situation in a similar way. Lasch (1978) talks about 'the narcissistic culture' and sketches a picture of a fragmented society and fragmented individuals, with weak moral ethics and super-egos where the sense of a coherent self is achieved through compensatory acts in consumption, of people and relations as well as products and therapy, in a vainless hunt for gratification and grandiosity. According to many authors, identity problems and a distorted sense of the self have become increasingly prevalent (Kohut 1977; Lasch 1978, 1984). As Lasch (1984: 32) remarks, identity has lost its solidity, definiteness and continuity. It has become uncertain and problematic. Weak and flexible identities, a strong need for feeling involved and confirmed, a refusal to be 'disciplined' or subordinated to authority and bureaucracy etc. lead to an increased pressure on top managers to use more persuasive methods of leadership and organization (Alvesson 1989a). Earlier capitalists and managers could be 'free riders' on the social psychology created by traditional culture, the Protestant work ethic etc., even though it seems that at least some of these are invested in the maintenance of that traditional culture. The cultural support for leadership—which for so long has been taken for granted—has started to fade away, calling for compensatory actions. At the same time, the prestructuring of people's world-view by the traditions and culture passed on by one generation to next has been weakened, which means that people are more 'open minded' about various meanings, values, images, etc. They are more 'culturally flexible' than former generations and have a less rigid commitment to social class. This, of course, creates a receptiveness for images and an increased probability that management will succeed in '...developing a social consensus and social definition around the activities being undertaken' at work places (Pfeffer 1981: 21).

Increased Complexity and Turbulence

A second aspect concerns the increased complexity and turbulence of the modern world. We live in a complex world, characterized by interaction with a lot of different people, organizations (of whom most are barely known) and production processes where the relationship between the single employee's efforts and tasks and the final product is often very hard to recognize, and where most people and situations known to us are heavily mediated by the mass-media, PR and so on. In short, we receive a large number of pictures and ideas of phenomena, people and institutions of which we have little first-hand and extensive experience in a more or less accurate and more or less comprising form. As Salancik and Pfeffer (1978) argue, information processing is always affected by social groups. The tendency is for not only the primary social groups, but also for an increasing number of social groups and institutions to be involved in that process. Related to this point is an increased distance between people and the institutions which have an impact on their lives. Earlier, it was basically the local community and local business. Today's consumption in advanced society presents another picture:

'In an age when the average consumer has only the vaguest notion of the actual activities of a vast, complex corporation, the public image of the corporation substitutes for more specific or more circumstantial notions of what is going on.' (Boorstin 1961: 191)

The complexity aspect might be connected to some insights produced by proponents of postmodernism. One important feature of modern development emphasized by this orientation, is an ongoing reduction of integration and wholeness in society, decreasing the possibilities to get a meaningful understanding of the whole. Baudrillard (1985), drawing on an analogy with physics, suggests that the rapid change in present society brings about a lack of meaning, integration and an ability to distance oneself from the rapid changes taking place.

'... we experience, in all our societies ... an acceleration of all bodies, all messages and all processes in every direction ... Every fact, every political, historical and cultural characteristic gets in power of its extention through the medias a kinetical force, that for ever takes it away from its own space and forces it to a hyper space, where it totally loses direction while it never will return from there.' (Baudrillard 1985: 24)

Baudrillard's position is representative of the so-called postmodernism orientation, which is currently in vogue within some circles of sociology, social philosophy and the arts (Foster 1983) as well as in organization theory (Calás and Smircich 1987; Cooper and Burrell 1988). Perhaps the most well-known figure in this field, Lyotard (1979), argues against the 'meta-narratives' in social science and philosophy, i.e. intellectual systems and theories which try to produce an understanding of the totality. As Power (1986) comments, 'postmodernism is an assault on unity'.

My point here concerns not so much the accuracy and merits of postmodernism *per se*, but rather the fact that this type of thinking becomes popular. It parallels the current debates on changes in culture / socialization / psychology both in time and content. Both reflect the current social situation in advanced late-capitalistic society.

The general societal fragmentation, the loss of integrated cultural patterns, the 'anomic' character of social life and the loss of the traditionally internalized work ideology, 'motivation crises' toward traditional work conditions, and the rapid changes in these conditions during recent years might be seen as a general cultural background of the greatest significance for a number of intellectual streams, not only organizational culture / symbolism research, but also the narcissism debate, postmodernism and poststructuralism, etc. A common theme here is socio-cultural fragmentation as a consequence of increased complexity, turbulence and the technocratization of the life-world.

The Expansion of the Service Sector

A third aspect of the development from 'substance' to 'image' has to do with basic changes in the economy. Crucial is the expansion of the service and information sectors and the recent decrease in the production sector. These changes might also be related to the current interest in images. The material base of economic activity has weakened considerably as a consequence of a diminishing part of the economy in late-capitalistic/post-industrial society being occupied with the transformation of raw material to goods. Service activities are normally intangible. Travel, freight forwarding, repair, consulting, haircut, education, health care etc., are hard to try out, inspect or test before they are bought. Surrogates for the stuff then play an important role. Tangible products, which, to a much larger extent, are part of a production economy differ in that they can actually be experienced, touched or even tested in advance (Levitt 1981). The intangible products (services) have become more common and more corporations and personnel are nowadays working with typically intangible products. (Of course, almost all products/services contain at least some elements of both tangibility and intangibility, but here there is no need to be precise on that point.)

As noted by Offe (1985) service work is very often defined negatively, through the attributes that are *not* part of that work. That service labour produces non-material outcomes, which cannot be stored or transported, is a common definition. Service activity is also considered to be hard to measure and rationalize. All these aspects point to the less tangible and immaterial character of corporations working in that field. This means that the opinions and evaluations of service work and corporations will be dependent on surrogates for the concrete core of the activity, at least as much as on the product (i.e. service);

'The product will be judged in part by who offers it—not just who the vendor corporation is but also who the corporation's representative is. The vendor and the vendor's representative are both inextricably and inevitably part of the 'product' that prospects must judge before they buy. The less tangible the generic product, the more powerfully and persistently the judgment about it gets shaped by the packaging—how it's presented, who presents it, and what's implied by metaphor, simile, symbol, and other surrogates for reality.' (Levitt 1981: 97)

A reasonable hypothesis is that the expansion of the service sector in the economy has brought the issue of the image of the corporations to the fore. Corporate image is considered to be of great importance for the perceived service quality in this kind of business (Alvesson 1989b; Grönroos 1984; Normann 1984, etc.).

Two other types of company, or organizational activity are similar to many service companies in having the attributes of high-level uncertainty from the viewpoint of customers. One concerns the producers of technically complex, expensive products such as personal computers, where the 'normal' consumer (a layman) is not likely to be able to make a qualified evaluation of the product and its priceworthiness. Here, brand and corporate image matter a great deal. The other concerns complex transactions in industrial marketing, where the buyer might be dependent on the goodwill and/or competence of the producer in ways that are difficult to predict and formally regulate at the time when the purchase is made (the contract is written). This type of transaction normally leads to a much closer relationship between the producer and the purchasing organization than in the market relationship, where there is competition and the actors are exchangeable (Håkansson and Johansson 1982, etc.). When such a close relationship has been established, the image of the producer ceases to be relevant—experience and knowledge achieved by the customer in the course of time have replaced it. But at the point when a complex transaction is to be made for the first time, the corporate images of companies selling products involving this type of transaction are likely to be significant. (In some cases, the image of the purchaser might also be significant, if there is a high level of uncertainty involved in the situation and the producer must make transaction-specific investments.)

The expansion of industries producing technically complex products—such as the electronics industries—and the increased complexities in transactions, partly following from this, has probably also put corporate images more into focus during recent decades.

The Role of Mass Media

A fourth aspect, touched upon as a part of the complexity problem but one that can be differentiated from this, concerns the expansion of mass media. Since the Graphical revolution, events of all kinds have been turned into 'news', but more important than the 'real' events, according to Boorstin (1961), are the 'pseudo-events'. A pseudo-event is a happening which is not spontaneous, but has been planted for the immediate purpose of being reported or reproduced. Pseudo-events are incited in order to attain publicity. They are activities which take place as part of image management. Interviews, press conferences, portraits in the mass media of persons or corporations, anniversaries, campaigns etc. are examples. Pseudo-events have gradually come to overshadow spontaneous events as sources of impressions and attitudes. To a large extent, this is due to the expansion of mass media. The elites in society, in politics, business etc. spend a lot of resources trying to use the possibilities of the mass medias.

The attention paid in the mass media to business and the importance of good publicity also brings about a restraint for managers. The fact that corporations have to survive in an increasingly complex and politicized environment means that managers must consider the legitimacy aspects of the society's perception of corporations to a greater degree. Obeying laws and producing profits are not enough. Various demands concerning ecology, (equal treatment of) gender and minorities, employment, etc., must also be met. Besides engaging in 'real' practices which avoid frustrating interest groups, the achievement of legitimacy is partly a matter of symbolic activity aimed at producing the right kind of impressions (Meyer and Rowan 1977; Richardson and Dowling 1986).

An interesting aspect of the role of mass media is its heavy focus on what is new at the expense of history and tradition. Jamison (1983: 125) writes that

'... the very function of the news media is to relegate ... recent historical experiences as rapidly as possible into the past. The informational function of the media would thus be to help us forget to serve as the very agents and mechanism for our historical amnesia.'

Mass media thus weakens the impact of traditions, history and culture and reinforces the cultural 'freisetzung' discussed above. People become less 'rigid' and more 'open-minded' about impressions. The images thereby can more easily be constructed through mass media, which simultaneously removes obstacles and carries new images.

The Imaginary Character of Modern Organizations

Of course, the developments outlined here, are closely interrelated. Locally based, small-scale service work does not call for so much attention to images. The local community probably develops its opinion irrespective of the face-lifting operations of the service person or company in question. It is the combination of increased service business and other types of 'image-sensitive' organizations and increased complexity, scale and distance between company and customers (employee and 'the core' of the company) that make the image an important topic for management's attention and action. The development of mass media also contributes to that complexity: the accelerating streams of news, pseudo-events, messages, images, pre-manufactured ideals and values (i.e. fashion) etc. reduce the simplicity of life. The increased interest in producing images creates competition between companies such that '... the contexts of western societies are overcrowded with symbolic representations, forcing organizations to create stronger and maybe falser images to make an imprint on the context' (Berg and Gagliardi 1986: 20). The general expansion of mass media also contributes to the destruction of traditional cultural patterns and, as explained above, affects socialization and the psychology of the younger generation.

This can be reformulated in terms of identity problems. While the material, as well as symbolic, conditions previously assisted individuals to more easily sustain an unproblematic sense of self, the world-openness (existential uncertainty) of today's social and organizational life leads to a precariousness of social and personal identity. In such a situation:

'Life then becomes dominated by a self-defeating preoccupation with effecting social closure upon world-openness through the control of nature, self and social relations.' (Knights and Willmott 1985: 26)

To this we can add a readiness and receptiveness for the messages which facilitate projecting into significant objects and situations a picture which is appealing, familiar and reduces uncertainty. Communicated corporate images thus reduce an identity-threatening anxiety and help to attain a closure upon the precariousness of meaning created by fragmented cultural patterns, increased complexity and ambiguity, the noise level of modern mass-media and labour processes aiming at creating favourable impressions rather than transforming material.

The effects on organizations of these developments are summarized in Table 1, which portrays substance and image as concepts characterizing ideal types of social order (e.g. a society, a community or an organization). This means that image signifies an 'outer reality'. The substance and image exist in between the facade of the corporation and the impression held by the significant groups being addressed. If we modify our focus somewhat and also talk about images in the sense of a person's inner picture of an object (a sense-image), we might say that this is primarily determined by the substance or 'essence' of the object in the first case (the 'substance' order) and primarily by communicated images (including pseudo-events) in the second case (the 'image' order). (In addition, culture, tradition and subjectivity also matter, of course.) In the 'substance' case, impressions and inner pictures emerge spontaneously. They are governed by traditions, material reality and social practices. They are basically non-intentional. In the 'image' case, systematic efforts to affect impressions are made. The intentional production of images are an important determinant behind the impressions of corporations.

In an 'image order', communicated images have a major influence on people's image (inner pictures) of the object. The difference between organizations characterized primarily by 'substance' and those of a more 'imaginary' type, can be identified by the amount of time, resources and skills invested in activities and conditions whose primary and explicit targets are the impressions of the (internal and/or external) groups the company wants to affect. The significance of 'placebo effects' (i.e. the effects accomplished through actions,

Table 1. Organizational Patterns of 'Substance' and 'Image' Types

	Social Orders/Organizations Characterized by:	
	Substance	Image
Interaction patterns with institutions of relevance in work	Long-term, stable close interaction, often with a small-scale institution, limited number of institutions involved	High social mobility of members, large-scale organizations, a large number of geographically dispersed institutions involved
Meaning patterns in relation to work	Relatively fixed definitions of the situation and the activities at work	Ambiguous situation
Employee's source of knowledge about the whole organization and his top management	Direct, first-hand experience. Some personal contact with leaders	Direct experience covers only a minor part of the organization Systematically mediated information is important. No first-hand knowledge of top managers
Reality test	Reasonable ability to make judgements about organizational life in terms of overview and nature of material reality. (Distortions/selective, biased perception are caused by traditional frames of meaning and other historically developed cultural factors)	Large parts of organizational reality exist beyond true and false categorization (from the perspective of an individual) Distortions/selective, biased perception in reality view are likely to occur
Basis for perception of reality	The real, concrete world (plus of course, traditions, ideologies, etc.)	The reality is understood through systematically mediated as well as 'spontaneously' appearing images of the world
Dominating competence	Technical skills, content orientation	Social manipulation, personality orientation[1]
(Typical) organizational basis for success	Concrete economic and technical activity, material output	Symbolic management, the production of favourable images, attainment of legitimacy[2]
Principle for control	Task-orientation, direct control (through orders and formalization)	Manipulation of beliefs (indirect impact)

[1] The ongoing development from an emphasis on technical skills to social skills during the last fifty years or so has been stressed by many social psychologists (for example Riesman 1969). The importance of 'personality orientation' for 'service organizations' is discussed by, for example, Normann (1984).

[2] Some aspects on the increasing need for organizations to get legitimacy are mentioned by Meyer and Rowan (1977) and Alvesson (1987).

campaigns etc. with no substantive outcomes, but entirely dependent upon whether people believe in them or not) is another indicator of the strength of the 'substance' and 'image'-dependency of corporations (cf. Dichter 1985). The more substance, the more 'objectively' measurable dimensions, like material and technical quality etc., matter, the less significant are the beliefs loosely coupled to the core activities. The more the image, the stronger the effect on corporate performance produced by skilfully orchestrated activities leaving the product/services untouched, but aiming at their perception.

Of course, outer images are often confused with the 'real nature' of the objects these are supposed to portray, for example when people believe that the appearance of a P.R.-minded politician or top executive in the mass media gives a 'true' picture of him or her. In a certain sense, the images are as 'real' as the reality they are referring to. The images affect people's beliefs and behaviour and the whole social world, partly through the element of a self-fulfilling prophecy, which is inherent in an image held by a significant group.

In a typical 'image' order, many activities, events and structures which are loosely coupled to the carrying out of productive activity and the achievement of efficiency, in a strict sense, are of crucial importance. Management is, to a large degree, a matter of 'window-dressing' and communicating messages which lead to the anchoring of favourable images in the minds of various target groups—internally and externally. The concepts of pseudo-events, pseudo-actions and pseudo-structures capture various aspects of this type of management. Pseudo-events have been discussed already (Boorstin 1961). Pseudo-actions are activities carried out only for the sake of affecting the perceptions of an audience, without being recognized as having that intention. This is what Pfeffer (1981) terms management as symbolic action. It does not have a substantive (physical) outcome, but influences attitudes and sentiments through the perception of an ambiguous situation. Pseudo-structures are organizational structures which do not have an impact on the efficiency producing activities of the corporation, but have a legitimizing potential. The structures signal the right kind of values and create a favourable impression (cf. Meyer and Rowan 1977). We can even talk about pseudo-cultures or, as Louis (1985: 79) formulates it, '. . . a "for-public-consumption" culture at the top, one deliberately designed by the ruling elite to be passed down through the organization'. This is not a 'real' culture, but something that might be perceived as such, internally or externally.

Of course, these (pseudo-) events, actions and structures, might be extremely difficult to separate clearly from those events, actions and structures which aim for and succeed in achieving more substantive outcomes and do not have as their major target the impressions of people. Difficulties in empirically separating the 'pseudo' from the 'non-pseudo' (substantive) dimensions from each other and the recognition that the elements are often intertwined do not prevent us from stressing the heuristic value of this distinction.

Most organizations are, of course, both of a 'substance' and 'image' nature. Concrete activities aim to achieve some more or less visible and measurable results. Dependence of the attitudes and impressions of various stake-holders are important, and energy and resources are directed to an explicit treatment of how optimal images can be developed, maintained and strengthened. The relative importance of the substance and image parts varies, however, and we can imagine typical cases of organizations functioning on the substance or the image side of a continuum between two extremes.

Historically, I believe we can talk about a trend from the former to the latter. Today, more organizations and more people than ever in organizations could be characterized as being closer to the second type of social order, that is, in historical perspective, extremely 'imaginary' in terms of how the organization in which a person works, its top management, the purpose and other important aspects of the organization and its environment appear and become visible (or perhaps how the visibility becomes very ambiguous) for the person. The successes of many corporations are, to an increasing degree, affected by how they manage their images. Doing a good job in a narrow technical and functional sense is not enough. Many corporations also demand the right image anchored in the group of customers in order to ensure their collaboration in the carrying out of services in which the customer is engaged in the production process by making decisions on how this is to be carried out precisely (as in haircutting or consultancy work). It is in this context that we can understand the preoccupation with the image of an organization, preoccupation that not only includes external groups but also the employees in the organization. The 'image' in that case is beyond what is directly possible to affect. It is when an organization becomes difficult to perceive by its members and when its nature and purpose, style, ideals, ambitions and quality of its management become too unclear and ambiguous, that the image of the corporation becomes a topic of interest and significance.

An Empirical Illustration: A Professional Service Organization

Many of the points made above can be illustrated through the case study of a computer consultancy corporation conducted by this author and reported at length elsewhere (Alvesson 1989b, 1989c).

The organization is a middle sized, Swedish based, international corporation, employing around 500 people, the majority being computer experts with relatively high education levels and advanced experience. The company's business is the development of information systems for middle-sized and large client organizations. This is typical for today's economy, in the sense that it hardly existed only three or four decades ago. It might be seen as a representative of today's service and information society, although here I am using the case solely to illustrate some of the ideas in the chapter.

Crucial for the success of this company is the management of images. Of course, 'substantive' issues like technical competence and the ability to carry out consultancy projects are basic, but beyond that, images appear as important targets for managerial action. This is the case both externally and internally.

The espoused business concept of the company is to combine computer and management knowledge in order to improve the corporate strategy of the client. The client's information problems are said to be treated from an overall management and business perspective and not only in a narrow, technical way. In the annual account of 1986 it says, for example, that the business concept of the company is to '...combine management knowledge with computer technical knowledge in order to make the clients more competitive and effective'. This combination is considered to be more prestigious than 'ordinary' computer consultancy work.

Management take great pains to communicate this view, both to employees and to customers. What the company is really doing, however, is not entirely clear in this regard. The variety of consultancy projects is enormous. Many of these contain little or no top management aspects; others do. One informant expressed the following view on the business concept:

'It says that we are computer consultants, combined with management consultants, *but the parts of consultancy dealing with management issues, the founders (which has left the daily operations of the company) stood for.* They did not recruit people who had that orientation, but only computer consultants.' (Senior consultant)

To a significant degree, however, the leaders have managed to anchor the view that the combination of computer knowledge and the use of a business perspective on the client's problem characterizes the company. Of a number of equally (in)accurate interpretations of what the company is actually doing, the one most favourable in terms of impressing the client's evaluations and producing a feeling of corporate pride among the employees has been chosen and is relatively successfully communicated. Some employees are sceptical of this view of the corporation, but the majority accept it. Even though this part of the corporate image is sometimes contradicted by reality, the latter is too ambiguous to be allowed to be captured in a clear-cut manner. The nature of this business opens up the possibilities of fabricating this image. The image is of course also governing reality in the sense that its very existence affects how both the consultants and the client define and act in the projects. On the whole, however, the image is rather loosely connected to what people are really doing in the company (Alvesson 1989a: ch. 10).

The formal structure of the company might also be related to the concept of image. While the company is organized as an adhocracy, its structure is rather complicated. In certain respects it changes all the time depending on the projects going on. It also differs heavily from a bureaucracy in the sense that it is much more ambiguous. The number of hierarchical levels can be counted in several ways and this does not reveal much anyway. The point of interest here is that 'officially' the company is said to be a very flat one, with a minimum degree of hierarchy including only two hierarchical levels: consultants and subsidiary managing directors. This version is communicated very strongly. It certainly contains elements of truth, but in reality, the situation is much more complex. It could, for example, also be stressed that there are project managers, assistant managers, a president for the Swedish part of the corporation and a president for the whole company (Alvesson 1989a: ch. 6). On the whole, however, the management succeeds in affecting the employees' image of the nature of the company in this regard. The important point here is that the employees are not left to themselves to understand the formal organizational structure. Instead, the interpretation of structure is the target of managerial action. The rather weak impact on actual behaviour of the formal structure and the efforts of management to draw attention to and affect people's impressions of the anti-hierarchical nature of it means that the concept 'pseudo-structure' captures important aspects of it.

The business concept and the formal organizational structure are just examples of how images put their imprints on this organization. Several circumstances account for their central role in this case. The services produced are very hard to evaluate. What the company is heading for is to maximize 'the customer's experienced quality.' (The 'perceived service quality' is a crucial concept in service marketing [Grönroos 1984].) The technical and functional quality of what is accomplished is clearly subordinated to this. The corporate image is of importance to produce the experience. The creation of favourable impressions is consequently of importance for this type of company. Internally, many organizational conditions are hard to evaluate from the employee's point of view. Material conditions (raw material, machinery, etc.) are non-significant in this type of business. Hundreds of diverse consultancy projects are taking place, many of these geographically dispersed and the individual employee has a limited overview. The rapid changes and dynamic character of this branch in general and the company concerned in particular increases the difficulties to attain and maintain such an overview. Sources mediating knowledge— especially top managers—are significant, while the personal experiences and direct observations of the employee are insufficient. Organizational reality is ambiguous in this case and various substitutes for the direct observations are important. Images, at least partly fabricated by top management, then play important roles. These images can hardly be said to be false in this case, but produce rather an exaggerated and slightly misleading picture of some of the (positive) features of the company.

Conclusion

This Chapter tries to capture some important tendencies in contemporary business and working life. This has partly been done through an investigation of the preconditions for the singling out of images as a specific feature of corporations, and a significant target for managerial action and systematic control. I have argued that at least three conditions must be present for 'the rise of the corporate image'. The first is a loosening up of traditional culture, lessening the grip over emerging meaning patterns and interpretative schemes that have been transferred from older generations to younger ones. Such a cultural change, a fragmentation of well-integrated, holistic western culture and subcultures increases the space for various agents to exercise successful cultural influence on a local level. Good possibilities for the fabrication of images, loosely coupled to traditional and stable meaning patterns come out of this opening up of the ideational space.

The second has to do with material changes mainly resulting from the decline of industrialism, the increasing importance of the service sector and the general trend towards more and more complexity in an organizational society. When the production of physical goods becomes less important and the intangible products (services, information, etc.) increasingly dominate the economy, the chances of making safe judgements, and anchoring evaluations in material reality are reduced. Together with increased complexity, ambiguity increases. The more the ambiguity, the greater the material and perceptual space for images.

The third important aspect concerns the means of production of images. The greater the significance of mass media in a society, the more significant mass communication becomes for corporations. In mass-media society the competition for souls is hard. As Boorstin (1961) says, real life events, of importance in themselves, without being orchestrated for a certain audience, have lesser impact than pseudo-events, which are more mass-medial. The communication of images then becomes possible and also crucial. The latter holds true particularly for 'image-sensitive' companies, such as the computer consultancy company described above. But when a substantial number of all corporations try to project their images to the market, the less 'image-sensitive' organizations must follow in order not to be 'forgotten' as a result of the overcrowding of images in the society.

The interest behind corporate images and similar ideational phenomena as corporate culture, identity etc., and the management of these, can be defined in negative or positive terms. (The words here are not to be seen as value statements.) The negative aspect concerns the evolving problems of getting a clear picture of the context of one's work situation, of understanding the organization, its character and its product. Formulated like this, explicit efforts in communicating an image of the corporation to the employees might be viewed as acts which try to counteract some problematic features of modern enterprises. Images, if they don't violate the object they are supposed to cover, might fulfil a perfectly socially legitimate role in order to increase understanding.

The current preoccupations in organization theory and management practice with images, culture and identity is then seen as a defensive operation in order to compensate for the increasing complexity and ambiguity in and surrounding organizational life, the lack of (self-evident) meaning and clear identity and purpose in organizations and the gradual fading away of the traditional cultural patterns, which used to assure organizations and leaders of a workforce with a suitable work ethic and a psychological disposition for subordination under management and, thus, social integration at the workplace.

In a positive sense, the evolving situation might be seen as an opportunity for management. Focus on image is then viewed as pro-action rather than re-action. The chances to define reality for larger groups—to control other people's definition of reality—have been improved. Culture, traditions, social and material circumstances and the activities people are carrying out in organizations, do not (any longer) have a definitive impact on their definitions of the situation, leaving increased space for purposive–rational acts aiming to control these definitions. The scope of management has increased and the reality-defining part of management is now seen, not as a subordinate aspect of traditional leadership—comprising instrumental, supportive, participative and controlling elements—but as an important topic in itself. This might be formulated as material reality in itself and/or historically developed and deeply ingrained collective definitions of reality which nowadays provide, to a lesser degree than before, an obstacle for top management's and other social elite's possibilities in the social engineering of people's impressions and beliefs of reality.

A critical way of formulating the issue is to say that the increased difficulty that many people in organizations have of obtaining a clear picture of the social order in which they exist is the basis for the present campaigns of managers, supported by researchers and consultants, to anchor favourable views of the organizational reality in the minds of the employees. It is the ambiguity of this order, from the perspective of the employees, that forms the need and subsequent basis for the potential success of managers in using public mass media (for example press advertising where the target group includes the employees) as well as internal means (like top managers making themselves visible and saying/doing the 'right' things on a video or directly in front of an audience of employees) to produce 'appropriate' definitions of reality for the employees of the corporation. It might, of course, be argued that reality in itself is ambiguous and it is always perceived not in itself, but from the subjectively loaded positions of various people. True: and images—in one form or another—will always appear. To direct specific attention to the topic from an instrumental (managerial) perspective and to exploit rationally the ambiguity or reality does not, however, leave it undisturbed. The ambiguity of reality is often distorted rather than reflected, thus increasing the difficulties in getting a reasonably accurate overview of the world which, in itself, is complicated and difficult enough to understand without corporations and mass media making things worse, trying to transform organizational activity into a plethora of images, pseudo-events, management of minds and face-lifting operations.

Note

* I wish to acknowledge the helpful comments of Harry Abravanel, Bob Cooper, Bengt Sandkull and Linda Smircich as well as of David Hickson and the three reviewers of O.S. for helpful comments on earlier versions of this chapter.

References

Alvesson, M. 1987 *Organization theory and technocratic consciousness*. Berlin, New York: de Gruyter.

Alvesson, M. 1990a 'On the popularity of organizational culture'. *Acta Sociologica* 33(1): 31–49.

Alvesson, M. 1989b *Ledning av kunskapsföretag* (Management of knowledge-based companies). Stockholm: Norstedts.

Alvesson, M. 1989c 'Cultural-ideological means of management control'. Paper, Department of Business Administration, University of Stockholm.

Baudrillard, J. 1985 'År 2000 kommer inte att äga rum'. (The year 2000 will never occur). *Res. Publica*: 23–37.

Berg, P. O. 1986 'Symbolic management of human resources'. *Human Resource Management Journal* 25: 557–579.

Berg, P. O., and P. Gagliardi 1986 'Corporate images: A symbolic perspective of the organization–environment interface'. Working paper, University of Lund, Sweden.

Bernstein, D. 1984 *Company image and reality. A critique of corporate communications*. Eastbourne: Holt, Rhinehardt and Winston.

Boorstin, D. 1961 *The image. A guide to pseudo-events in America*. Atheneum: New York.

Calás, M., and L. Smircich 1987 'Is the organizational culture literature dominant but dead?' Paper presented at S.C.O.S. International Conference on the Symbolics of Corporate Artifacts, Milan, June 1987.

Cooper, R., and G. Burrell 1988 'Modernism, postmodernism and organizational analysis'. *Organizational Studies* 9/1: 91–112.

Mats Alvesson

Dichter, E. 1985 'What's in an image?' *The Journal of Consumer Marketing* 2/1: 75–81.

Foster, H., *editor* 1983 *Postmodern culture*. London: Pluto Press.

Grönroos, C. 1984 *Strategic management and marketing in the service sector*. Lund: Studentlitteratur.

Håkansson, H., and J. Johansson 1982 *Analys av industriella affärsförbindelser*. (Analysis of industrial business relations). Stockholm: MTC.

Jamison, F. 1983 'Postmodernism and consumer society' in *Postmodern culture*. H. Foster (ed.). London: Pluto Press.

Knights, D., and H. Willmott 1985 'Power and identity in theory and practice'. *The Sociological Review* 33: 22–46.

Kohut, H. 1977 *The restoration of the self*. New York: International University Press.

Langer, S. 1957 *Philosophy in a new key*. Cambridge, Mass.: Harvard University Press.

Lasch, C. 1978 *The culture of narcissism*. New York: Norton.

Lasch, C. 1984 *The minimal self. Psychic survival in troubled times*. London: Picador.

Lash, S., and J. Urry 1987 *Disorganized capitalism*. Cambridge: Polity Press.

Levitt, H. 1981 'Marketing intangible products and product intangibles'. *Harvard Business Review* (May–June): 94–102.

Louis, M. R. 1985 'An investigator's guide to work-place culture' in *Organizational culture*. P. J. Frost et al. (eds). Beverly Hills: Sage.

Lyotard, J. F. 1979 *The postmodern condition. A report on knowledge*. Minneapolis: University of Minnesota Press.

Margulies, W. P. 1977 'Make the most of your corporate identity'. *Harvard Business Review* (July–August): 66–74.

Meyer, J., and B. Rowan 1977 'Institutionalized organizations: Formal structures as myth and ceremony'. *American Journal of Sociology* 83: 340–363.

Normann, R. 1984 *Service management*. Chichester: Wiley.

Offe, C. 1985 *Disorganized capitalism*. Cambridge: Polity Press.

Pfeffer, J. 1981 'Management as symbolic action: The creation and maintenance of organizational paradigms' in *Research in organizational behaviour, Vol. 3. ed.* Greenwich, Conn: JAI Press.

Pondy, L. R. 1978 'Leadership as a language game' in *Leadership: where else can we go?* M. W. McCall and M. M. Lombardo (eds). Durham: Duke University Press.

Power, M. 1986 'Modernism, postmodernism and organisation'. Paper presented at International Workshop on Aspects on Organisation, University of Lancaster, January 1986.

Richardson, A. J., and J. B. Dowling 1986 'An integrative theory of organizational legitimation'. *Scandinavian Journal of Management Studies* 3: 91–109.

Riesman, D. 1969 *The lonely crowd*. New Haven: Yale University Press.

Salancik, G. R., and J. Pfeffer 1978 'A social information processing approach to job attitudes and task design'. *Administrative Science Quarterly* 23: 224–253.

Sennett, R. 1977 *The fall of public man*. New York: Vintage.

Sievers, B. 1986 'Beyond the surrogate of motivation'. *Organization Studies* 7/3: 335–351.

Smircich, L., and G. Morgan 1982 'Leadership: The management of meaning'. *Journal of Applied Behavioral Science* 18: 257–273.

Ziehe, T., and H. Stubenrauch 1982 *Pladoyer für ungewohnliches Lernen. Ideen zur Jugendsituation*. Reinbek bei Hamburg: Rowohlt Taschenbuch Verlag.

10 Keeping an Eye on the Mirror: Image and Identity in Organizational Adaptation*

Jane E. Dutton and Janet M. Dukerich

The homelessness problem is perhaps a blight on that professionalism that we like to display, and that we are so proud of, and I think this is of great concern there. Again, there may be some conflicting issues on spending money to help solve the problem, but I think that's a value. We build beautiful facilities, we take pride in that, and the homelessness issue is something that obviously affects the perceptions of us.

(facility staff member, Port Authority of New York and New Jersey, 1989).

Theoretical Perspective

Models of how environments and organizations relate over time have typically assigned causal primacy to either environmental or organizational forces. Advocates of institutional theory, resource dependence, and population ecology have highlighted the environmental, and strategic choice theorists have emphasized the organizational. Still other theorists have assigned primacy to some combination of the two forces (e.g., Hambrick & Finkelstein, 1987; Hannan & Freeman, 1984; Singh, Tucker, & House, 1986; Tushman & Romanelli, 1985). None of these theories treat in depth the processes by which environments and organizations are related over time. Although the language theorists have used implies that a process determines how environments and organizations are

---

* This chapter was originally published as an article in 1991, i.e. before the events of September 11, 2001.

connected—organizations chose strategies in response to environmental changes, or environmental selection mechanisms favor one structural form more than others—views of the process through which these relationships are accomplished are currently limited (Sandelands & Drazin, 1989).

In this research, we developed a framework for conceptualizing the process through which organizations adapt to and change their environments. Conceptually and empirically, we took seriously the assertion that organizations respond to their environments by interpreting and acting on issues (e.g., Daft & Weick, 1984; Dutton, 1988b; Dutton & Duncan, 1987; Milliken, 1990). Patterns of actions in response to issues over time create patterns of organizational action that in turn modify an organization's environment. Our claims were built from a case study of how the Port Authority of New York and New Jersey[1] has defined and responded to the issue of the rising number of homeless people present in the facilities it operates.

The case study was used to generate a framework for understanding how organizations and their environments interrelate over time. We employed the idea that organizations have identities (Albert & Whetten, 1985; Ashforth & Mael, 1989) that influence how individuals interpret issues as well as how they behave toward them. The assertion that organizational identity affects issue interpretations and actions has received some support from other studies of organizational adaptation (Meyer, 1982; Miles & Cameron, 1982). The present study also built on ideas from impression management (e.g., Tedeschi, 1981), suggesting that individuals seek to influence how others see and evaluate their organization. The article crosses between macro and micro organizational theory to explain how the Port Authority has dealt with the homelessness issue.

Issues as a Starting Point

Our perspective is that some organizational actions are tied to sets of concerns that we call issues. Issues are events, developments, and trends that an organization's members collectively recognize as having some consequence to the organization. Issues can arise from changes inside the organization, such as employees threatening to stage a strike or a new technology transforming a product or service, or changes originating externally, such as a demographic trend, a regulatory act, or a supply shortage.

The definition of an issue by a collectivity is a "social construction" (Hilgartner & Bosk, 1988). Issue definitions often emerge and evolve over time, and they can be contested (Dutton, 1988a; El Sawy & Pauchant, 1988; Feldman, 1989; Isabella, 1990; Weiss, 1989). Which issues gain attention and how they are interpreted are important concerns, as issues represent focal points that galvanize interest and direct attention in organizations because of the consequences associated with action or inaction. In some cases, issues activate decisions; in other cases, issues incite neglect or intentional inaction (Bachrach & Baratz, 1972).

A focus on issues as a starting point for interpretation and action in organizations charts a different course for seeing patterns of organizational action than a traditional decision-making view. Researchers who look at decisions as creators of patterns in organizational actions (e.g., Mintzberg, Raisinghini, & Thèorêt, 1976; Nutt, 1984) have used the end point of a process—a choice or an absence of choice—as the defining referent and described who and what were involved in producing a certain pattern of action. Typically, researchers define a decision and trace backward from that point to find interpretations for it and actions relevant to it. In contrast, a focus on issues begins with an issue or a collective construction that some datum, fact, or event is of concern for an organization and then proceeds forward from this recognition point to find relevant actions and interpretations. Like the "garbage can model" of decision making (Cohen, March, & Olsen, 1972), an issue focus underlines the importance of attention allocation and sensitivity to context. Unlike the garbage can model, an issue focus is open to changes in issue interpretations over time. The present research adds to research on the temporal dimensions of interpretations (e.g., Dutton, 1988a; Isabella, 1990) by describing how organizational context contributes to how and when issue interpretive changes occur.

For organizations, some issues are routine and expected, and organizational members can easily classify them. The issues fit existing categories and, once classified, elicit a well-learned response (Starbuck, 1983; Starbuck & Milliken, 1988; Weick, 1988). The well-learned responses are types of organizational "recipes," or patterns of routinized behaviors that are easily available and rewarded in an organization (Weick, 1979). Other issues are not as easily interpreted or processed, however. Issues may be problematic because they are nontraditional: they have not been encountered in the past and thus do not easily fit well-used categorization schemes. Alternatively, issues may be problematic because of the feelings they evoke. Current models of issue diagnosis and organizational adaptation reveal very little about how the level of emotion an issue evokes affects individual and collective processes. Issues that are hot—those that evoke strong emotions—represent different types of stimuli and activate different responses from individuals and organizations than cooler, less affectively charged issues.

The Purpose of the Present Study

Our interest in how individuals and organizations make sense of and act on nontraditional and emotional strategic issues drew us to the case of the Port Authority of New York and New Jersey and its dealings with the issue of

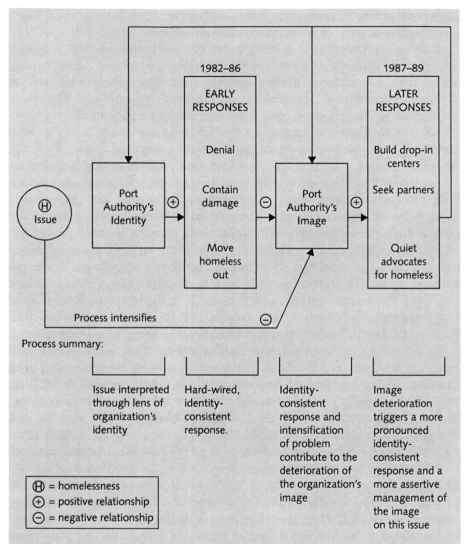

Fig. 1. Simplified depiction of the role of organizational identity and image in the Port Authority's response to homelessness.

homelessness. The study was designed to generate new theory on how individual interpretations and organizational action on an issue are related over time.

In brief, our analysis revealed that an organization's identity and image are critical constructs for understanding the relationship between actions on and interpretations of an issue over time. Both constructs emerged clearly from a theme analysis of the data. An organization's *identity*, or what organizational members believe to be its central, enduring, and distinctive character (Albert & Whetten, 1985), filters and molds an organization's interpretation of and action on an issue. Organization members monitor and evaluate actions taken on issues because others outside the organization use these actions to make character judgments about it (Alvesson, 1990) and, by implication, its members. Organization members use an organization's image, which is the way they believe others see the organization, to gauge how outsiders are judging them. Deterioration of an organization's image is an important trigger to action as each individual's sense of self is tied in part to that image. Thus, individuals are motivated to take actions on issues that damage their organization's image (Ashforth & Mael, 1989; Cheney, 1983). At the same time, the organization's identity limits and directs issue interpretations and actions. These actions in turn may gradually modify the organization's future identity or make certain features of the identity more or less salient. Figure 1 presents a brief summary of the role of organizational identity and image in the Port Authority's response to homelessness.

Methods

A case study methodology was well suited to our goal of generating and building theory in an area where little data or theory existed (Yin, 1984), where we could study a process as it unfolded over time, and where we could use "controlled opportunism" to respond flexibly to new discoveries made collecting new data (Eisenhardt, 1989: 539).

We selected the case of how the Port Authority of New York and New Jersey has responded to the issue of homelessness because of the issue's social relevance and its visibility to both organization members and outside constituencies. In this sense, the case meets the criteria for an "extreme case," one in which the process of theoretical interest is more transparent than it would be in other cases (Eisenhardt, 1989).

Data Sources

The story of how the Port Authority and the issue of homelessness are related was built from five sources: (1) open-ended interviews with 25 employees of the Port Authority conducted from September 1988 to May 1989, (2) all reports, memos, and speeches prepared within the Port Authority on homelessness from November 1982 until March 1989, (3) articles from regional newspapers and magazines published from March 1986 through November 1988 that mentioned both the Port Authority and homelessness, (4) regular conversations with the head of the Homeless Project Team, a temporary task force of Port Authority employees charged with examining the corporation's response to the issue of homelessness, and (5) notes from an all-day training session with Port Authority facility staff members sponsored by the Homeless Project Team in May 1989. All informants were full-time employees of the Port Authority.

Informants

Individuals from four groups with different types of contact with and responsibility for the homelessness issue were informants. We interviewed the Port Authority's executive director and three top-level managers who were involved with the issue; all six members of the Homeless Project Team, line managers with responsibility for the facilities that were actively trying to deal with the issue; five staff members from the public affairs, corporate planning, and budget offices with responsibility for developing and analyzing ideas for a Port Authority response to the issue; and finally four people who dealt hands-on with the homeless in various Port Authority locations, including police officers and customer service managers.

Our initial research objective was to explore differences in how groups in the organization interpreted and responded to the issue. The objective was consistent with research on organizational culture (e.g., Martin & Meyerson, 1988) and the creation of meaning in organizations (e.g., Donnellon, Gray, & Bougon, 1986), which led us to expect a high degree of inconsistency, disagreement, and ambiguity in how organization members interpret strategic issues. However, the data generated by the informants indicated a surprisingly consistent pattern of issue interpretations. Thus, the pattern of interpretations revealed in this study emphasizes the dominant logic (Prahalad & Bettis, 1986), collective beliefs (Walsh, Henderson, & Deighton, 1988), and consensual elements (Gioia & Sims, 1986) in how the homelessness issue was interpreted over time.

Interview Questions

The interview guide targeted data on five clusters of variables, which Table 1 describes. The average interview lasted two hours, with one researcher asking questions while the other took notes. More than half of the interviews were tape-recorded and transcribed verbatim.

Data Analysis

"Analyzing data is at the heart of building theory from case studies" (Eisenhardt, 1989: 11). Two analyses were critical for the purposes of this chapter: construction of the issue's history as depicted in interpretations,

Table 1. Interview Guide

Variable Clusters	Illustrative Questions
Issue interpretation	
Emotionality	As you think about the homelessness issue, what adjectives would you use to describe the issue?
Distinctiveness and similarity to other strategic issues	How do you see this issue as different from other strategic issues facing the Port Authority?
Perceived hotness	Imagine there was a thermometer for gauging how hot the homelessness issue was. Please indicate how hot you believe this issue is on a 7-point scale and explain the basis for your rating.
Interrelationships with other issues	What other issues inside or outside of the Port Authority is the homelessness issue related to?
Personal involvement in the issue	
Time spent on it	Describe your involvement in the issue. When did you
Amount of direct contact with homeless people	first get involved? How much of your time do you spend dealing with the issue? How has your involvement
Change in involvement	changed over time?
Organizational processing and actions on the issue	
When first noticed	Describe how and when the homelessness issue first became an issue at the Port Authority.
Major milestones	What have been the major milestones in the processing of the issue?
Major setbacks	What have been the major setbacks in the process?
Major successes	What have been the major points of success?
Perceived effectiveness of issue processing	
Costs and benefits of the Port Authority's involvement	What do you believe will be the major benefits and costs of the Port Authority's involvement in the homelessness issue?
Evaluation of the Homeless Project Team's handling of the issue	How has the Homeless Project Team affected you and how will you know if it's been a success?
Organizational context for the issue	
Shared values at the Port Authority	If you were to describe the values that people share at the Port Authority, what would they be?
Institutional mission	How would you describe the overall mission of the Port Authority?

actions, and events from 1982 into 1989 and use of theme analysis to explain the pattern of interpretations and actions over time. Both analyses emerged from an identifiable set of steps.

Step 1: Devising and coding using a contact summary form. Following the procedures Miles and Huberman (1984) recommended, we used a contact summary form for recording the main themes, issues, problems, and questions in each interview; one researcher originated each form and the other coded it. We defined themes as recurrent topics of discussion, action, or both on the part of the actors being studied (Bjorkegren, 1989). Like a recurring melody in music, a theme captures the central ideas or relationships in an interview (Bjorkegren, 1989).

189

Step 2: Developing a complete theme list. The contact summary forms for the 25 interviews generated 84 themes, which we collapsed into seven major groupings based on a very general classification of theme substance. For example, "organizational reactions to homelessness" and "the identity of the Port Authority" were broad theme categories. The first broad category included 14 different themes, each addressing unique ways that the Port Authority responded to the homelessness issue, such as denying being in the social service business or reacting negatively to other agencies' failures to take responsibility for the issue. We used the themes for two distinct purposes: to isolate commonalities in how Port Authority members interpreted homelessness and to suggest an explanation for the issue's history in terms of our dominant theme categories—the importance of organizational image and identity. Next, each theme was assigned a separate sheet on a coding form in preparation for step 3.

Step 3: Coding the interview data onto the themes. Each interview was coded sentence by sentence onto a theme list in order to document and evaluate the degree and breadth of support for particular themes across informants. After completing the theme-based coding process, we were able to evaluate the degree of support for each theme indicated by the number of theme-related points mentioned both within and across interviews.

Step 4: Constructing an issue history. We used questions on the meaning of the issue and on milestones in its processing to construct a history of how the Port Authority interpreted and responded to the issue over the period studied. Informants consistently identified 1982 as the year in which homelessness became an issue for the organization. Thus, we did not set the starting date but saw it emerge from informants' accounts of milestones in the issue's processing. Information from memos, speeches, and meeting minutes served as important supplements to interview data in constructing the issue history. We consulted members of the Homeless Project Team to validate the issue history once it was completed.

The Issue

The presence of homeless people has always been part of the scene at transportation facilities. Several informants noted the qualitative shift that took place in the early 1980s, when people previously referred to in the transportation trade as "bums, winos, and bag ladies" were transformed into "the homeless." During the last several years, the number of homeless people living and spending time at transportation facilities has dramatically increased. For the Port Authority, an agency that runs many diverse transportation-related facilities, the rising number of homeless people at its facilities caused increasing problems with the delivery of quality transportation service. One of our informants described the change this way:

Well, a lot of it had to do with the change in the type of people. . . . And the bus terminal always had its share of down-and-out people, but you were able to move them along and get some kind of arrangement with them. But as the numbers increased, you couldn't do that. And the nature of the people began to change, and they began to get younger, and in some respects the people [the Port Authority's patrons] became more afraid of them because they were rowdier, they were more imposing.

In addition to the trend of rising numbers and change in type, three other issue characteristics were mentioned by more than ten informants as distinguishing homelessness from other strategic issues of importance to their organization. First, informants consistently mentioned the issue's broad scope and its linkages to other regional issues such as decreasing housing availability and changes in the skills represented in the region's labor market. Second, they emphasized the links between homelessness and other negative issues such as drugs and crime—links that magnified the fear and aversiveness that individuals expressed about the issue. Finally, close to two-thirds of the Port Authority informants mentioned the lack of control that they felt the organization had over the issue and possible solutions. One facility manager's description of his frustration with the issue captures that assessment well:

I think with all of the building and fixing and all of those good, concrete, reassuring things that we did and still do, and the feeling, the good feeling that we got from being in control, I think this has been undermined in a way by the homeless problem. I think that it said to us, "Look, here is something that you really can't control, and you can't fix it, and you can't caulk it, you can't waterproof it, you can't dig it, and you can't make it go away."

This lack of control and other themes revealed in our analysis can be better understood in light of the distinctive features of the organizational context in which members of the Port Authority struggled to make sense of and respond to the homelessness issue. We describe the organizational context in two sections. First, we describe general features of the Port Authority. Next, we discuss aspects of the organization's identity as perceived by its members. Those perceptions proved crucial for explaining the evolution of interpretations of the issue and actions on it over time. Although we did not originally intend to make the organization's identity so central to the explanation of how the organization adapted to this issue, individuals' senses of the organization's identity and image were metathemes that emerged from our data analysis, and we believe they organize the evolutionary story in a compelling way. Following descriptions of five phases into which we divided the history of the issue, we return to the substance of the Port Authority's identity and image to analyze how they give coherence to the evolution of interpretations, emotions, and actions and also to draw general inferences about the usefulness of these constructs for models of organizational adaptation.

The Site

General Features

The Port Authority of New York and New Jersey was established on April 30, 1921, the first interstate agency ever created under a clause of the Constitution permitting compacts between states with congressional consent. Its area of jurisdiction, the "port district," is a 17-county bistate region encompassing all points within a 25-mile radius of the Statue of Liberty. The mandate of the agency was to promote and protect the commerce of the bistate port and to undertake port and regional improvements that it was not likely private enterprise would invest in or that either state would attempt alone. The Port Authority provides wharfage for the harbor that the two states share, improves tunnel and bridge connections between the states, and, in general, undertakes trade and transportation projects to improve the region.

Most public authorities in the United States were established to develop and operate a single public improvement project like a bridge or an airport; the Port Authority was the first multipurpose public authority (Caro, 1974). Today it owns and operates 35 facilities, including the World Trade Center; the Port Authority Bus Terminal at 42nd Street; Journal Square Path Center; Kennedy, LaGuardia, and Newark airports; PATH train service,[2] and many tunnels, bridges, and marine facilities. The mission of the Port Authority remains very broad—to protect the economic vitality of the New York—New Jersey Port District. The organization defines itself as being in the business of transportation.

The Port Authority is the largest public authority in the United States, employing 10,000 people and having total assets of approximately $5 billion and an annual budget of $1 billion. It supports itself through issuing bonds and collecting user fees and leasing revenues. An executive director and a board of commissioners selected by the governors of the two states run the organization.

The Identity of the Port Authority

Six attributes summarize the informants' views of the characteristics that distinguished their organization (Albert & Whetten, 1985). First, 100 percent of our informants called the Port Authority a professional organization with a uniquely technical expertise, ill-suited to social service activities. Second, informants (44%) referred to their organization as ethical, scandal-free, and altruistic. Third, 36 percent described it as a first-class, high-quality organization and a provider of superior service. Fourth, 36 percent of informants said the agency prided itself on its high commitment to the welfare of the region. Part of this dimension of the Port Authority's identity was a sense that the organization "spoke for the region" and symbolized its successes and short-comings. Fifth, informants (32%) mentioned the loyalty of employees and their sense of the Port Authority as family. Finally, a fourth of our informants expressed a view of their organization as distinctive in terms of being a fixer, a "can-do" organization. As the story will reveal, the organization's identity was an important element of members' interpretations of the issue, acting both to prompt and constrain issue-related action and resulting in issue-related emotions.

Interpretations of and Actions on Homelessness

The Port Authority's struggle with the homelessness issue can be mapped onto five phases, each distinctive in terms of the interpretation of the issue current in the organization and its actions. Figure 2 presents a synopsis of the five issue phases as a timeline. The arrows indicate that once the actions so-designated were implemented, they continued over time. The arrows also show that the Port Authority's action repertoire expanded over the issue's history.

Although we present the five phases as though clear, identifiable signs separated one from another, they in fact shaded into each other. The path of understanding and responding to this issue can be thought of as an evolving history of interpretations, emotions, and actions. This history offers important insights into the organizational processes at work in creating patterns of action.

The five phases are described in terms of three components: key events, major interpretations, and major actions. The key events of each phase are the major developments and changes that informants identified as significant during a given phase of the issue's evolution. The events are crucial for comprehending how organization members interpreted the issue at each point in time and how and why the organization took certain actions. Although certain events appeared to have caused a certain action or interpretation, we refrain from making such causal inferences. Our purpose is to provide a relatively complete description of how interpretations and actions coevolved in the context of a series of unfolding events against the backdrop of this particular organization.

Phase 1: Homelessness is a Police-Security Issue (1982–84)

Homeless people have always been part of the landscape for transportation services. The features that are important for the delivery of effective service to

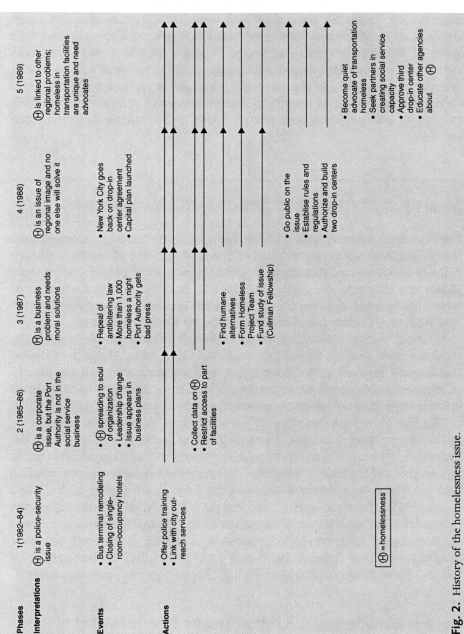

Phases	1 (1982–84)	2 (1985–86)	3 (1987)	4 (1988)	5 (1989)
Interpretations	Ⓗ is a police-security issue	Ⓗ is a corporate issue, but the Port Authority is not in the social service business	Ⓗ is a business problem and needs moral solutions	Ⓗ is an issue of regional image and no one else will solve it	Ⓗ is linked to other regional problems; homeless in transportation facilities are unique and need advocates
Events	• Bus terminal remodeling • Closing of single-room-occupancy hotels	• Ⓗ spreading to soul of organization • Leadership change • Issue appears in business plans	• Repeal of antiloitering law • More than 1,000 homeless a night • Port Authority gets bad press	• New York City goes back on drop-in center agreement • Capital plan launched	
Actions	• Offer police training • Link with city out-reach services	• Collect data on Ⓗ • Restrict access to part of facilities	• Find humane alternatives • Form Homeless Project Team • Fund study of issue (Cullman Fellowship)	• Go public on the issue • Establise rules and regulations • Authorize and build two drop-in centers	• Become quiet advocate of transportation homeless • Seek partners in creating social service capacity • Approve third drop-in center • Educate other agencies about Ⓗ

Ⓗ = homelessness

Fig. 2. History of the homelessness issue.

transportation agency clients also attract the homeless. The facilities are warm in the winter and cool in the summer. They are clean, have toilets and running water, and guarantee people some degree of personal safety through the constant presence of police. Thus, for most transportation agencies and the police who patrol them, dealing with a certain number of homeless people has long been a normal part of business.

Key Events

In 1982, several factors converged to make homelessness a more prominent issue for the Port Authority, particularly at the bus terminal. First, organization members noted a marked rise in the number of homeless people present in their facilities. Second, a $226 million renovation that had just been completed at the bus terminal accentuated the visibility of the homeless. The renovation, which increased the building's square footage by about 40 percent, opened up new space for use by passengers and homeless people alike. At the same time, a large number of single-room-occupancy hotels in New York City closed. As one informant told us, "As the Manhattan real estate market picked up, these hotels were closed, and we had an increase in the number of homeless people, without many skills, without abilities, and without much money, all ending up out on the streets. A fair number of them ended up in the Port Authority bus terminal." The bus terminal's renovation accentuated the problem of the homeless by creating a strong contrast between the beautification of the facility, accomplished by adding space and expensive works of art, and the presence of homeless people who "smelled and looked dirty." To patrons and workers, homeless people marred the Port Authority's attempt to spruce up the bus terminal. For an organization that prided itself on being "the builder of beautiful structures," homeless people were a stain on its identity.

Major Interpretations

During 1982, organization members defined homelessness as a police or security issue: the presence of homeless people was problematic for Port Authority customers, and something had to be done. As one informant said, "The issue was 'How do we keep these people out of our facility?' Plain and simple, because they were interfering with our patrons in the sense that they felt that they were not safe because of their presence." The police were, and continue to be, a major source of organizational contact with the homeless at the bus terminal; police officers were also the organization members who carried out action on the issue. Customers confronted the police when they wanted someone from the Port Authority to "do something about this problem!" The organization employs 1,500 fulltime officers, constituting the 26th largest police department in the United States, and 130 of them were assigned to the bus terminal. At this time, the police at the bus terminal and the facility's managers dealt with the issue; there was no coordinated corporate response.

Major Actions
The existence of an antiloitering law in New York City gave Port Authority police the option of insisting that homeless people leave the bus terminal. In 1982, bus terminal managers took two additional issue related actions. First, they hired a consultant to train police officers on how to move people out of the facility in a manner that "acknowledged the difficult nature of the problem." Second, they established a relationship with the city's Human Resources Administration and the Manhattan Bowery Corporation[3] to develop an outreach program to "give the police some place to send these people." The officers helped workers from the Manhattan Bowery Corporation transport homeless persons from the Port Authority's facilities to shelters run by the Human Resources Administration.

Summary
Early Port Authority actions on homelessness were facility-based, limited in scope, and focused on the bus terminal. The organization framed the issue as primarily a police and security matter, an interpretation that, given the city's antiloitering law, helped contain the problem. Actions to engage the assistance of New York City's social service support system were also part of the facility-based solution at this time.

Phase 2: Homelessness is a Corporate Issue, but the Port Authority is Not in the Social Service Business (1985–86)

Demarcations between phases in the relationship between the homelessness issue and the Port Authority are not clear-cut. However, in the 1985–86 period, Port Authority members changed the way they talked about the issue. This change could be attributed to a number of different events and to the recognition that the problem extended beyond the bus terminal.

Key Events
Informants described having a growing awareness in 1985–86 that the homelessness issue was no longer confined to the bus terminal, where it was well understood and routines had been developed to deal with it. Now, the homeless were present in several Port Authority facilities. The appearance of homeless people at the World Trade Center and the airports—the organization's flagships—was the key to making the issue visible at the senior management level. Organization

members did not expect to see the homeless in these facilities, and their presence conflicted with central components of the Port Authority's identity:

It wasn't until homeless people started to show up at the World Trade Center ... and the image of the World Trade Center as being a place where homeless people were began to raise its head, that people started to say, "Wait, geez, this is a problem. . . ." It [homelessness] started to show up finally in corporate documents as an issue. It never did before, because everybody knows the bus terminal is an aberration, but when it started to show up at the World Trade Center, and then ultimately, one or two people at the international arrivals building at Kennedy Airport and at LaGuardia Airport, then it began to touch upon the heart and soul of the organization.

The departure of the Port Authority's executive director and the appointment of a new director was another key event during this period. The leadership change was significant on several counts. First, facility managers and staff members assigned to work on homelessness argued that the momentum to recognize and deal with the issue at the bus terminal had come from the former director. That momentum dissolved with his departure, and advocates for the issue felt that they had to start over from the beginning. Second, the new executive director's vision for the organization was "returning to its basic businesses." The new director wanted to "[show others that] the Port Authority could run like a business." One implication of this change in vision was an emphasis on using business practices and business justifications as a basis for drawing attention to issues.

In 1986, for the first time the issue of homelessness appeared in business plans for several line departments. Simultaneously, the public affairs department became increasingly concerned about the issue as the rate and intensity of customer complaints increased. The new director openly expressed a strong personal aversion to straying from the main businesses of the Port Authority and "getting into the social service business."

Major Interpretations
In 1985–86, the interpretation of the issue shifted to a recognition that the problem was corporate-wide, not just a bus terminal police issue. The definition of homelessness as a corporate issue came about because Port Authority departments began to include the costs of dealing with the problem in their budgets. As one informant noted, "Corporate issues are identified theoretically through the business-planning process, which is both a strategic planning and a budgeting process." However, 85 percent of the informants mentioned that although they recognized at this time that homelessness was a corporate issue, they asserted they were not in the social service business. During this time, employees at all levels focused on how to minimize negative fallout from the issue by removing and restricting the problem as it presented itself at various facilities.

Major Actions

Three major actions distinguished the issue phase. First, the board and the executive director asked a group of staff members to collect data, analyze it, and make recommendations for a corporate policy on homelessness. Police and facility staff viewed this action as a sign that corporate attention was being directed at the issue. As one upper-level manager stated, the results from this analysis represented "the first time that it [homelessness] was explicitly recognized as a problem and put in writing." Second, actions at the facility level intensified: bus terminal managers (1) sought and obtained more extensive outreach services, with daytime as well as nighttime assistance, through a contract with the Volunteers of America, a not-for-profit social service provider that sent volunteers to Port Authority facilities to assist homeless people and encourage them to go to shelters, and (2) closed or restricted access to areas of the bus terminal and removed patron benches from the waiting areas. The purpose of these actions was to make the bus terminal an undesirable place to be by "making it as unattractive and uncomfortable to the homeless as possible." As one informant told us, "I think some of it was motivated by aesthetics, that you didn't have the people sitting around and maybe they would find someplace else to go." The organization implemented similar types of outreach services and actions to make the facilities unattractive to the homeless at the two other Port Authority locations where the issue was visible, the World Trade Center and Journal Square Transportation Center.

The third action was an attempt by the bus terminal staff to manage patrons' understandings of and reactions to homeless people by issuing and posting a lengthy description of the types of homeless that patrons were observing at the bus terminal. This action was the first of many attempts to improve the image of the Port Authority using a well-learned recipe: "educating others or helping them get smart on the issue."

Summary

During this second issue phase, Port Authority members did not significantly change how they interpreted or acted in response to the issue. In fact, this phase can best be characterized as involving doing the same, but doing it harder. Although informants recognized a shift in corporate understanding of the issue, the organization maintained its fragmented, facility-based response with an overarching goal of "get[ting] the homeless out of here." Denial that the Port Authority was a social service agency accompanied the intense localized response. At the time, the staff at the bus terminal began to try to manage others' understanding of the issue of homelessness, an attempt that was to become more prominent as the staff became more involved with the issue and as the image of the bus terminal—and of the Port Authority through its affiliation with the bus terminal—deteriorated. This phase also marked the beginning of some serious soul-searching by employees and upper management focused in particular on what the role of the Port Authority should be with respect to this issue. As one informant put it, "And then we were saying to ourselves . . ., Can we get them out of there? Should we get them out of here? What are we supposed to do with them? Whose responsibility is this?" This type of concern ushered in the third issue phase.

Phase 3: Homelessness is a Business Problem and a Moral Issue (1987)

In 1987, several events contributed to changing the way the issue was framed and the level and type of the Port Authority's response to it.

Key Events
In late 1986, several events shifted the Port Authority's view of its responsibility for homelessness. First, informants indicated the nature of the homeless people spending time at transportation facilities abruptly changed, primarily because of the influx of crack, a derivative of cocaine that is easily obtained, relatively inexpensive, and very addicting. Links between homelessness, drugs, and crime accentuated the original problem. The increase in drug use and an associated increase in crime served to highlight the importance of police actions. However, at this same time the city's antiloitering law was repealed, significantly restricting the ability of facilities in the city to move the homeless out. For the police, the repeal of the antiloitering law "tied their hands," resulting in a real "blow to police morale." As one informant told us, "It's not that we ever arrested people for loitering. But the antiloitering law's existence allowed us, without as much hoopla, to ask people to move on or to leave."

The absence of a contract between the police officers' union and Port Authority management, dating from spring 1985, exacerbated the issue. There were tensions between the union and management, with the officers caught in the middle. "The individual police officers, in the middle of that issue, wondered who to take their direction from, management on the one hand reminding them of their oath to uphold the laws of the states of New York and New Jersey and the rules and regulations of the Port Authority. And on the other hand, the union advising them that they may end up losing their homes if they violate someone's civil rights."

The police union put pressure on the Port Authority to grant certain concessions by generating unfavorable press coverage about the organization. The union hired a public relations agency "to float stories about the Port Authority." The stories were intended to put pressure on the Port Authority to hire more police. "They [the public relations firm] generate publicity all the time, and the publicity is aimed at embarrassing the Port Authority and creating this climate of fear and stuff around its facilities to promote the police position, you know ... that they need more cops and that sort of stuff." The bad press about the Port Authority peaked in late 1987 and early 1988, when 65 percent of the articles in the New York and New Jersey newspapers we reviewed were negative in tone. The Port Authority received negative press for its attempts to control homelessness through tightening regulations. A sample excerpt follows: "In its last board meeting before Christmas, the Port Authority of New York and New Jersey played Scrooge to Jersey City's poor by outlawing begging and sleeping at the Journal Square PATH Transportation Center" (*Jersey Journal*, December 11, 1987).

At the same time, in 1987 the number of homeless people congregating at Port Authority facilities surpassed 1,000 on some nights. This number represented an important threshold that, in the minds of organization members, made the issue no longer deniable for the organization.

Major Interpretations
The most significant change in the way the issue was defined during this period involved upper-level management's acceptance of some organizational responsibility for dealing with the issue and an acknowledgment that it was much more than a police problem. This interpretive shift represented an expanded concern for humane solutions and a heightened awareness of the issue's severity. An excerpt from an important internal memo from January 1987 illustrates this shift: "It is important to recognize that the agency is not in a position to solve the problems of the homeless. ... The Port Authority's homeless policy is to encourage individuals to leave our facilities and find more appropriate shelter and services, and to minimize their return. ... We seek to do this in a humane manner, through the assistance of social service agencies. ..." The shift in the way that the issue was now being defined was subtle. There was still extensive denial of responsibility for solving the problem in any way beyond alleviating the burden on facility staffs, but there was new concern with choosing moral or humane solutions. Thirty-six percent of the informants noted the importance at this time of the Port Authority's acting and looking humane. In addition, there was a recognition that some of the social service mechanisms that were in place were having a positive effect and diminishing the burden on facility staffs.

Major Actions
The repeal of the antiloitering law provided a major impetus to the development (technically, an updating) of facility rules and regulations. The rules and regulations first appeared at the bus terminal, but the procedure spread rapidly

to the other Port Authority locations. Police and facility staff viewed the regulations as important because they "gave us a mechanism to deal with certain types of personal conduct for anyone in our facilities." Nevertheless, the facility police viewed their options for dealing with the homeless as highly constrained, leaving many of them feeling "as if you're pumping out the ocean."

Informants at all levels acknowledged that space restrictions and closing off parts of the building were ineffective in minimizing the visibility of the homeless. Port Authority actions during this period indicated resignation to two facts: the problem could not be solved through outreach or restrictions alone, and the organization needed to take a stand.

And then we kind of gave up, you know, we gave up some space.... They just sort of took over the waiting room. That was it. You know, we just didn't know what to do, you know, when you get 15 degree temperatures at night, and there's absolutely no place for them to go. And so, we said, well, how are we in good conscience going to throw them out of this facility?.... And this was the first time that people really began to look at it and say, 'Wait a minute, you know, this is a real moral issue.' And this was when we decided to make the commitment. And while Grand Central and every place else was throwing them out, we weren't.

In 1987, top management reluctantly admitted the need to develop a coordinated corporate response to the issue. It was during late 1987 that the executive director decided to form a centralized project team, the Homeless Project Team, whose major responsibilities would include developing a Port Authority policy on homelessness, shifting the burden from the facility staffs, and reducing the amount of top management time spent on the issue. In 'many of our informants' minds, the formation of this team signaled that the Port Authority was ready to do something about this issue.

Another key symbol of top-level management's commitment to the issue was granting a one-year fellowship, the Cullman Fellowship, to a public affairs employee to study how the transportation industry was addressing the homelessness issue. The Port Authority established the Cullman Fellowship in 1962 to allow a staff member to undertake a one-year special project that was advantageous to both the individual's career and the agency. One informant described the significance of funding a fellowship that focused on this type of issue as follows: "It was a very risky thing for the Port Authority to do, because it is not typical of the transportation kind of issue or business or economic development issue that this kind of a conservative organization would generally grant."

Summary

In 1987, the level and type of attention being paid to the issue changed. Two important symbolic actions signaled internal and external constituencies that top management was now interested in the issue: the formation of the

Homeless Project Team and the granting of the Cullman Fellowship. Early in 1987, the "batten down the hatches" response dominated, evidenced by the increase use of rules and regulations, restrictions on access to facilities and closing of parts of facilities. Although there was evidence that assistance from social service agencies and the use of rules and regulations were providing some relief, the problem worsened in terms of the numbers of homeless people. Several events transformed this early response into acceptance that the Port Authority needed to do something different and to do it in a way that did not violate the moral standards embedded in the organization's way of doing things. At this time, a rise in negative press coverage about the Port Authority severely damaged the organization's image. With the hands of facility police tied by the antiloitering law change, police-based solutions proved unsuccessful. In addition, the image of the authority as inhumane really bothered some of our informants and reaffirmed the importance of taking a more "humane stance" on the issue. Since the hotness of the homelessness issue increases with the coldness of the weather, a humane stance meant not endangering anyone "by throwing them out into the cold temperatures."

Phase 4: Homelessness is an Issue of Regional Image, and No One Else Will Deal with it (1988)

The year 1988 represents a period of significant action on homelessness for the Port Authority.

Key Events

Three events are important for understanding the unfolding of the interpretations, emotions, and actions concerning homelessness during this period. First, there was the launching of a $5.8 billion capital plan for the organization, aimed at updating facilities and improving the image of regional services to enhance the area's international competitiveness. This campaign introduced resource constraints and created expectations for positive press coverage and a corresponding positive image. As one informant said,

We had embarked on this capital campaign at the airports and all of our facilities. We needed the resources to handle the program. It gave us the impetus ... so we need to control other priorities as much as possible, particularly at the airports. From an organizational standpoint, we are focused on the major initiatives. We expected all of this positive press about the capital plan, and instead, all we have gotten is negative press about homelessness. It overshadows the positive.

The other two events were reactions to Port Authority actions on the issue during this phase. In order to do something "different," the organization decided to commit capital funds to establishing drop-in centers designed to provide social services to the homeless at two locations near its facilities. The two events related to this action were: (1) New York City informally agreed to take over the operation of the first center to be built but subsequently resisted doing so, and (2) there was organized opposition to the opening of a second drop-in center.

Major Interpretations

A speech given by the Port Authority's executive director in January to the Partnership for the Homeless in New York City publicized and structured the dominant interpretation of the homelessness issue and the organization's relationship to it for the first half of 1988. Many informants saw the speech as clear evidence that the Port Authority was publicly committed and was going to "do something" about the issue. This speech contained several critical points for understanding the actions and future interpretations of the Port Authority on this issue.

First, there was continued denial that the organization was "in the social service business." Second, the director described the homelessness problem as a regional responsibility, noting that the failure to solve it would have devastating consequences for the region. The speech symbolically associated homelessness with the fiscal crisis of New York City during the 1970s, an association that effectively communicated the seriousness of the issue for the entire region. The speech indicated that the issue's scope had broadened considerably and represented an attempt to involve others in the Port Authority's efforts to deal with the issue.

In the minds of organization members, positive actions could not overcome the damage to the Port Authority's image, and the stain from homelessness had spread to the entire region. As one top-level manager said, "The quality of life of the region is severely impacted by having as a kind of visible ornament, a large number of people who are described as homeless. . . . It creates an environment of extraordinary depression in a transportation mix which is already congested, difficult, and harassed. In some ways, like the graffiti on the subways, it is both a fact and a symbol that the environment is out of control." Some members believed that the Port Authority as an organization and the New York–New Jersey area as a region were unable to compete effectively in the international transportation market because of the image damage to the Port Authority.

At this time, the organization's leadership acknowledged that no one else would solve the issue, leaving them no choice but to get significantly involved:

And so, once it became clear that we were really going to have to become more aggressive, I think at that point there was a kind of watershed which said, "We are going to have to do some things which clearly stretch our mandate, which commit both dollars and cents beyond what is appropriate, and what is probably on some level defensible, because the agencies that have this responsibility are just not prepared to act."

Informants were distinctly emotional when they described the realization that "the Port Authority was forced to get involved because no one else would." Anger, frustration, and disappointment that other organizations had shirked their responsibilities by not solving the problem were expressed by 56 percent of our informants.

Informants' descriptions of the Port Authority board's discomfort with the financial commitments to homelessness also revealed the negative emotions that accompanied heightened issue investment. One top-level manager expressed this feeling bluntly: "The board is very unhappy, and I think rightly so. They feel that we're spending money, which we are, which is money that is desperately needed for other things in terms of our mandate."

Emotional reactions, however, involved more than unease and anger at the organization's new role. Some informants described hurt and frustration brought on by accusations about their personal characters based, they believed, on outsiders' judgments of Port Authority actions on this issue. Many of the organization members felt good about what it was doing with the homeless but thought that others believed that the Port Authority was acting inhumanely. This discrepancy was distressing and hurtful for individuals. As one facility manager said,

You know, the guy that's running the Lincoln Tunnel doesn't have a full perception of how the bus terminal or the homeless impact what he does on a day-to-day basis. But the minute he leaves and he goes to the cookout in his neighborhood and he meets somebody and this person says, "What do you do for a living?" "Oh, I work for the Port Authority." They say, "How can you stand that bus terminal, what can you do?" That's the name. That's the symbol of the Port Authority. It's the standard bearer. And you know, so personally everybody that's involved in any aspect of working for the Port Authority is identified with that place and with that issue.

Another facility manager described a case in which the press had "bashed" the Port Authority and made derogatory comments about the manager's personal character because of the Port Authority's refusal to set up tables in its facilities during Thanksgiving to serve the homeless. In fact, although the press did not report it, the Port Authority had paid for 400–500 Thanksgiving meals served at a local soup kitchen. The manager was deeply troubled because of the inaccuracy (in his mind) of the external portrait of the Port Authority and the misinterpretation of his actions: "When you see your name in print and they call you callous and you know that in your heart you are probably one of the more compassionate people about this issue, it's hard not to get angry."

During phases 3 and 4, the Port Authority's image suffered acutely from the association with homelessness. There was remarkable consensus from informants about the image's substance. Their view was that outsiders saw the Port Authority as dirty (65 percent of informants used this term), dangerous (56%), ineffective (52%), and inhumane (24%) because of its association with homelessness.

At this time, the issue was clearly emotionally charged both individually and organizationally, and Port Authority actions heated up accordingly.

Major Actions

The most dramatic actions during this period involved financing and renovating facilities for two drop-in centers. In early 1988, the board approved expenditures for building and operating centers to service the bus terminal and the World Trade Center and was committed to opening them within a year. The total cost (initial operating and capital expenses) for these facilities was close to $2.5 million.

All our informants viewed the May 1988 completion and opening of the Open Door Drop-in Center, adjacent to the bus terminal, as a significant accomplishment, symbolizing the Port Authority's commitment to the issue. The center's opening reaffirmed members' views of the organization as able to "get things done." As an upper-level manager said, "There have been more major achievements than anybody would ever imagine because of the circumstances and the speed with which we have put this thing together."

In October 1988, New York City's Human Resources Administration went back on its informal agreement to take over the financing of the operation of the Open Door Drop-in Center, and the Port Authority altered its stance on the issue. First, some members of the Homeless Project Team and upper management expressed hesitancy about getting into building and managing drop-in centers. In their minds, the incident with the center taught them that they should not try to solve the problem of homelessness at that level because "we just get burned." As one informant told us, "Next time we will live with the problem much longer." Members of the task force and top management sensed that the process that had been used to get the center up and running created "expectations that the Port Authority would fund and operate facilities or created the impression that somehow the homeless at the bus terminal were the Port Authority's problem." Organization members became committed to eliminating this impression. Actions in the next issue phase were partly attempts to alter this false set of expectations.

Organization members also saw the financing and building of the second drop-in center as a significant milestone in processing the issue. This second drop-in center, the John Heuse House, officially opened in December to serve the homeless in lower Manhattan, near the World Trade Center. But the organized opposition of downtown business interests had made getting city approval for the facility a rocky process.

Jane E. Dutton and Janet M. Dukerich

Summary

The year 1988 was a critical phase in the Port Authority's relationship to the homelessness issue. It marked a turning point in the sense that the organization now viewed the issue and justified action with a sense of resigned heroism—a sense that no one else would solve the problem, so the Port Authority would step in, in its usual, excellent way. The attachment of homelessness to concerns such as New York City's fiscal crisis and regional problems reframed the issue and broadened its boundaries (Feldman, 1989). The resigned admission that the organization had to take action on the issue was accompanied by a great deal of emotion about the unfavorable image the Port Authority had in the press, a sense of outrage that those responsible were not doing their job, and a sense of embarrassment and anger generated by negative press coverage of Port Authority actions on homelessness. The formation of the Homeless Project Team helped to congeal a set of initiatives that had already begun in earlier phases. Its members were important catalysts for establishing the two drop-in centers. Instrumental involvement in the issue significantly escalated during this period, evidenced by the expenditure of $2.5 million to fund the renovation for and initial operation of the Open Door Drop-in Center and the renovation for the John Heuse House.

Phase 5: Homelessness is an Issue of Regional Competitiveness, and the Port Authority is a Quiet Advocate (late 1988–early 1989)

Although the Port Authority's relationship to the issue of homelessness is still evolving, data collection for this study ended in May 1989.

Key Events

When active data collection was nearing an end, one event stood out in the minds of informants. In its February 27, 1989, issue, *Newsweek* published a particularly damaging article entitled "The Nightmare of 42nd Street." The article portrayed the bus terminal as a dangerous place for both commuters and the homeless, "a vortex of hopelessness, crime and despair." One day after this article was published, the Port Authority's board convened an emergency group to "try to do something dramatic to turn around the Port Authority image." The formation of this group signaled heightened frustration with the tarnishing of the organization's image through the equation of the Port Authority with the bus terminal and the strong association of the bus terminal and homelessness. The *Newsweek* article and information the organization collected during this period also led to the acknowledgment and articulation that the problem with the bus terminal was far broader than homelessness—it also involved the issues of loitering and drug abuse.

Major Interpretations

During the spring, informants indicated an increasing awareness that although there had been some significant victories, the homelessness problem was not going away. The press was still bashing the Port Authority although with less intensity than during the previous two years. Informants acknowledged that the previous winter had been mild, making the visibility of homeless people in Port Authority facilities unusually low. At the same time, several of the organization's initiatives, such as revising the rules and regulations and providing social service assistance, were producing some positive results. Top management claimed that the number of complaint letters received weekly was significantly lower than it had been the previous year, going from an average of seven letters a week at the bus terminal to an average of one letter a week.

Completion of the Port Authority—funded drop-in centers for the homeless signaled an increasing acknowledgment that the organization was getting more and more into the business of homelessness. As one informant put it, "Yeah, we're two feet deep into the business of homelessness, and we don't want to be." Another informant displayed the ambivalence that accompanied this change in level of involvement: "We may be throwing a lot of resources at this, but our heart just isn't in it."

A shift occurred in the Port Authority's definitions of its role in the homelessness issue. Members of the Homeless Project Team said that role was helping others "create capacity" for single men, the typical homeless people at transportation facilities. So, although management still adamantly denied that the organization was in the housing or social service business, they sought to accomplish some social service objectives "by increasing the capacity of other agencies that are better equipped to substantively address this issue."

Major Actions

The Port Authority continued to implement the formulas for dealing with the issue that it had developed over the previous six years. It established outreach services at the airports. It also financially backed a deal with Jersey City to set up a drop-in center and a single-room-occupancy hotel to be run by Let's Celebrate, originally a soup kitchen and pantry operator, near Port Authority facilities at Journal Square. The drop-in center concept was consciously modeled after the John Heuse House arrangement, which management viewed as a more successful and appropriate model than the Open Door Drop-in Center because it minimized the visibility of Port Authority involvement through turning operations over to a service group. The Port Authority encountered delays and resistance to these facility solutions but treated the resistance as "normal" and "part of the process." The sense of urgency and outrage that had accompanied previous setbacks with the first two drop-in centers were notably absent.

As one informant told us, "You learn that those people who fight you the hardest, may turn around and be your biggest advocate."

Awareness of rising Port Authority involvement in the issue (spending more money, adding services at more facilities) coexisted with a conscious attempt to minimize the organization's public association with the issue. Management explicitly designed its policy to favor the role of "quiet advocate for the single homeless male." Consistent with this thrust was a desire to *not* take the credit for any action on or solutions to the problem. For example, one staff member who remarked that a local paper's coverage of an incident had been "balanced" and "good" explained that this meant the paper had not mentioned that the Port Authority had played any role in bringing about the successful solutions the article described. As a top manager explained, "I don't want any credit. Let them take the credit. Let the bastards who fought us six months earlier take the credit. It's easy to give the credit. I prefer to work behind the scenes."

Part of the quiet advocate role involved educating others about the special needs of homeless people at transportation facilities. The Port Authority began to actively seek connections with other transportation agencies on the issue. For example, members of the Homeless Project Team began to meet with their counterparts at the Metropolitan Transportation Authority. As one Homeless Project Team member explained, "We are trying to broaden the circle of people who participate, working with the business community as a team." The form of these partnerships and the sorts of solutions implied were not made explicit. However, the Homeless Project Team stated that the agency would offer its "special expertise and viewpoint on the issue to New York City and to businesses who needed it."

Publicity on the Cullman Fellowship and other efforts to manage outsiders' impressions of the Port Authority's stand on homelessness had an unintentional consequence. Increasingly, people both within and outside the organization viewed it as a leader on the issue. Informants described the Port Authority as "on the cutting edge of what a transportation agency can do on this issue" and as offering "the most creative solutions to this problem." However, some managers were quick to see that this reputation was a double-edged sword: "I think there is another temptation, which is a peculiar Port Authority temptation. There's a tendency in a lot of places around this organization that wants people to get involved in something, and they want to be leaders in it. I just want to deal with this problem, not become a leader on it."

Summary

The relationship of the Port Authority homelessness took a new turn in 1989. Although the organization's position was still not solidified (one informant said, "We are still like an amoeba with this issue"), its actions were increasingly deliberate and intentionally highlighted or downplayed. During the part of 1989 in which we collected data, the Port Authority managed the context in which the issue was affecting it more actively than before. These efforts included searching for partners with whom to design new collective solutions to this regional crisis. Efforts involved presenting information about the issue and information about the Port Authority's actions on the issue in a way that would minimize image damage by disassociating the organization from the issue. The efforts took place within the constraints of taking actions consistent with the Port Authority's identity, actions that complemented its perceived expertise. At the same time, the organization was increasingly recognized as a leader on how to deal with homelessness in the transportation industry. Port Authority members expressed tremendous pride in the organization's method for dealing with the homeless. In their eyes, it was the "most humane approach" used by any transportation agency in the region.

The Role of Organizational Identity and Image

The story of the Port Authority's relationship to the issue of homelessness is still unfolding today. Despite the story's complexity, the evolution of interpretations, actions, and emotions is sufficiently suggestive to allow us to extract, examine, and build on several important themes.

Two central themes that emerged from our analysis of interviews, media coverage, and internal memos focus on the role that the organization's identity and image played in creating the pattern of how individuals in the organization interpreted and responded to the homelessness issue. Specifically, we found that the Port Authority's identity, or how organization members saw it, played a key role in constraining issue interpretations, emotions, and actions. At the same time, the organization's image—how organization members thought others saw it—served as a gauge against which they evaluated and justified action on the issue. In addition, the organization's image was an important mirror for interpretations that triggered and judged issue action because of a close link between insiders' views of the organization and insiders' and outsiders' inferences about the characters of organizational members.

Over time, actions taken on issues reposition an organization in its environment by modifying tasks, allocation of resources, and assignments of personnel. The pattern of action on issues can therefore reinforce or, potentially, transform the organization's identity and image through individuals' sense-making efforts, and the process of adaptation continues.

Jane E. Dutton and Janet M. Dukerich

The Importance of Organizational Identity

The Port Authority's identity is a critical construct for understanding the evolution of issue interpretations, emotions, and actions over time. We discussed the consensual attributes of that identity earlier and present them again in Table 2, which also summarizes the relationship between the Port Authority's identity and issue interpretations, emotions, and actions by using examples from the phases described in the issue history. The elements in this table provide important material for the beginning of a theory of how organizational identity affects adaptation processes through its effect on issue interpretations, emotions, and actions.

Identity and Issue Interpretations

The Port Authority's identity shaped its members' interpretations of homelessness in at least three different ways. First, the organization's identity served as an important reference point that members used for assessing the importance of the issue. Perceptions of issue importance are in turn important predictors of willingness to invest in an issue (Dutton, Stumpf, & Wagner, 1990). The issue was important because it threatened key elements of identity. In particular, informants' sense of the Port Authority as a high-quality, first-class institution made the presence of homeless people problematic. The expanding scope of the issue over time can be seen as an indication that the issue was being seen as more important and urgent as it threatened central identity components. Although Port Authority members were uncomfortable with the stain on the organization's identity when the problem worsened at the bus terminal, they interpreted it as even more threatening when the presence of homeless people affected the quality of flagship facilities such as the World Trade Center and the airports. Further, the intractability of the issue and members' sense of not being able to control it were anathema in an organization that considered itself to be a "fixer" and "doer." Additionally, Port Authority members not only emphasized the importance of "looking humane" in their actions, but also focused on "being humane." Thus, the organization's identity defined what aspects of the issue were seen as a threat and helped to locate solutions that could transform the issue into an opportunity (Jackson & Dutton, 1988). For example, some informants described the use of partnering strategies in phase 5 as representing an opportunity for the Port Authority "to show its stuff" to other transportation agencies. As Meyer (1982) found in his study of hospital employees' interpretations of a doctors' strike, ideology—in this case, beliefs about identity—shaped the meanings given to the event and the set of legitimate solutions.

Port Authority members' sense of the issue's importance was also related to the occurrence of identity-inconsistent responses. When the organization took

Table 2. Organization's Identity and Issue-Related Behaviors

Characteristics of Port Authority's Identity	Percentage of Informants Who Mentioned Characteristic	Examples of Relationship to Issue Behaviors		
		Interpretations	Emotions	Actions
Professionalism, technical expertise, no social service expertise	100	Constraints what are considered legitimate versus illegitimate issues: Not in social service business (phase 2)	Evokes strong negative emotion if identity compromised: Engineers holding AIDS babies (phase 4)	Provides recipes for issue action: Getting selves and others "smart" on the issue (phase 2)
Ethicality, altruism, public service ethic	44	Activates salient issue categories: Moral and business issues (phase 3)	Negative emotion evoked if negative image assumed to be the identity: Anger at bad press (phase 3)	Sets parameters for acceptable and unacceptable action: No moving the homeless out into the cold (phase 3)
Commitment to quality	36	Reference point for assessing importance of the issue: Homeless spoil attempt at beautifying bus terminal (phase 1) and stain image of Port Authority flagships (phase 2)	Negative emotion evoked when not able to resolve the issue: Frustration in not being able to fix the problem (phase 2)	Provides guidelines for evaluating issue success: Speed of completion of drop-in centers (phase 4)
Commitment to region's welfare	36			
Employee loyalty and employees as family	32	Identity-inconsistent behaviors signal heightened issue commitment: Granting fellowship for study of nontraditional issues seen as risky (phase 3)		
Can-do mentality	25		Strong emotions expressed when identity reinforced in unusual situation: Port Authority—funded drop-in centers provide better service than New York City social services (phase 4)	

actions that members saw as inconsistent with its identity, they judged the issue as more important and the organization as more committed to it than they had previously. Informants' interpretations of the significance of the Port Authority's granting the fellowship to study homeless people at transportation facilities illustrates this connection. The grant was seen as risky and unconventional, and several informants viewed the nontraditional character of this action as a sign that top management saw the issue as serious and worthy of action commitments.

The Port Authority's identity also constrained what members saw as legitimate interpretations. In the early issue phases, the organization's identity was a critical force in defining homelessness as an issue to which the Port Authority should not respond. Organization members justified nonaction using the rationale that the Port Authority excelled in its technical skills but lacked the social service skills necessary to deal with homelessness.

The organization's identity affected the meanings members gave the issue. Two terms frequently applied were "moral issue" and "business issue." Each issue category had associated with it a set of routines and solutions for dealing with the issue (Dutton & Jackson, 1987). However, more important for the argument developed here, different aspects of the Port Authority's identity were associated with each category: homelessness as a business issue with the high-quality-organization identity component, and homelessness as a moral issue with the ethical and altruistic identity component. Thus, these two aspects drove the application of different categories to the issue, which engaged different interpretations of the issue's significance and activated different recipes for solving the problem over time.

Identity and Issue Emotions

The organization's identity was also significant in explaining the direction and level of emotional expression about the issue. This connection was most vivid in phase 4. Informants expressed negative emotion when inappropriate involvement of individuals or the organization in certain activities compromised the Port Authority's identity. For example, informants told us stories about architects holding babies with AIDS, engineers changing diapers, and sanitation engineers cleaning filthy bathrooms—all related to the issue of homelessness. Whether the substance of the stories was accurate is less important than the values that the stories conveyed, a great disdain about the inappropriate diversion of technical skills for the delivery of social services. This disdain was a strong defense for not responding to the homelessness issue, particularly in the 1982–86 period. The sense of not being able to control homelessness further delayed Port Authority involvement. However, these defenses were no longer sustainable when the problem worsened and the issue's visible appearance in Port Authority facilities other than the bus terminal severely damaged the organization's image.

At the same time, the Port Authority's identity also produced positive emotions when organizational actions were identity-consistent, especially when those actions were in arenas in which organization members did not expect action. For example, opening the two drop-in centers in the Port Authority's record-breaking style was a source of pride and a sense of accomplishment for informants at all levels of the organization.

Identity and Issue Actions
The Port Authority's identity also affected the pattern of issue-related actions. First, the identity affected action through the link to issue interpretations and emotions discussed above. However, it also affected action directly by providing guidelines for evaluating success, recipes for solutions, and parameters for acceptable ways of resolving the issue. An argument could be made that objective characteristics of the situation—the increase in the number of homeless people in Port Authority facilities and increased constraints on feasible actions as a result of the repeal of the antiloitering law—created the push for action. The present emphasis on organizational identity doesn't negate the influence of such other forces; rather, it is meant to enrich understanding of the particular responses this organization made. Thus, although a resource dependency perspective (Pfeffer & Salancik, 1978) could be used to explain the increase in the number of actions the Port Authority took, particularly after phase 3, the concept of identity is helpful in understanding how those actions were shaped.

The Port Authority's identity offered implicit guidelines for evaluating the effectiveness of its actions on the issue. Using the speed with which the two drop-in centers were completed as a criterion for the success of the Homeless Project Team and overall success in dealing with the issue typified this connection. Organization members used efficiency in task completion as an important barometer of the Port Authority's success with the issue even though they admitted that the actual problem, in terms of the number of homeless at facilities, had not changed.

Individuals' senses of the Port Authority's identity were associated with a set of routines, or standard procedures for dealing with the issue, whose activation engaged ways of doing things members identified as "typical of the Port Authority." In this sense, an organization's identity is closely tied to its culture because identity provides a set of skills and a way of using and evaluating those skills that produce characteristic ways of doing things (Nelson & Winter, 1982; Swidler, 1986). As Child and Smith (1987) pointed out, "cognitive maps" like identity are closely aligned with organizational traditions. An organization's identity is one of the vehicles through which "preconceptions determine appropriate action" (Weick, 1988: 306). For example, when the homelessness issue was no longer deniable, the Port Authority went to work to "get smart on the issue." The phrase describes the organization's ideal approach to a problem—investigating and analyzing it from all angles. Members learned a great deal about the unique attributes of homeless people at transportation facilities. Some informants saw this engagement of learning routines as typical of the Port Authority and indicative of its professionalism. Members also saw searching for partners for dealing with the issue and framing the issue as related to the region's future as actions that "typified the Port Authority's approach to things."

Finally, individuals' senses of the organization's identity did more than activate a set of familiar routines for dealing with the issue. That identity also constrained what were considered acceptable or legitimate solutions (Meyer, 1982). The frequent claims that throwing homeless people out in the cold was not the Port Authority's way of dealing with the issue well illustrate that link. Several informants directly compared the Port Authority's response to that of Grand Central Station, where police were moving homeless people out "into the cold," to illustrate the limits of what they saw as legitimate action for coping with the issue.

The Port Authority's upper-level managers were also concerned about doing too much on the issue, such as providing direct outreach or other social services to the homeless. Three considerations fueled this concern. First, these managers were adamant about not straying from their main business of transportation. Providing social services was perceived as a "deviation from our basic area of business" because it would have required hiring people trained in social services. Second, upper-level managers did not want to appear to be leaders on the issue, for they felt that taking such a role would "blur accountability" for the homeless, relieving city agencies of their responsibilities. Third, there was a continual concern over attracting more homeless to Port Authority facilities if services were provided. Thus, upper management sought to maintain a policy of moderation, focusing on actions consistent with the organization's identity.

In sum, a knowledge of individuals' beliefs about an organization's identity is crucial for discerning the importance of an issue, its meanings, and its emotionality. These interpretations, shaped by the organization's identity, move individuals' commitment, involvement, indifference, and resistance in particular directions and thereby direct and shape organizational actions.

The Importance of Organizational Image

An organization's identity describes what its members believe to be its character; an organization's image describes attributes members believe people outside the organization use to distinguish it. Organizational image is different from reputation: reputation describes the actual attributes outsiders ascribe to an organization (Fombrun & Shanley, 1990; Weigelt & Camerer, 1988), but image describes insiders' assessments of what outsiders think. Both organizational image and identity are constructs held in organization members' minds. They capture two of the key ways that an organization becomes meaningful to individuals and motivate individuals to action in particular ways and at particular times. In the case of the Port Authority and its dealings with homelessness, image changes triggered the organization's later, more substantive response to the issue, particularly in 1987. Active attempts to manage the organization's image on this issue also explain the changing issue-related actions.

Organizational Image and Individuals' Motivation
An organization's image matters greatly to its members because it represents members' best guesses at what characteristics others are likely to ascribe to them because of their organizational affiliation. An organization's image is directly related to the level of collective self-esteem derivable from organizational membership (Crocker & Luhtanen, 1990; Pierce, Gardner, Cummings, & Dunham, 1989). Individuals' self-concepts and personal identities are formed and modified in part by how they believe others view the organization for which they work.

Impetus to take action to improve the damaged image resulting from the Port Authority's association with homelessness was more than organizationally based. As the story revealed, the damage to the organization's image hurt individuals personally. Spoiled organizational images transfer to organization members (Sutton & Callahan, 1987), and this link tightens when actions that affect the organization's image are public and irrevocable. As Weick noted, in such situations actions "become harder to undo" and "harder to disown" (1988: 310). As a result, individuals are strongly motivated and committed to take actions that will restore their organization's image.

The close link between an individual's character and an organization's image implies that individuals are personally motivated to preserve a positive organizational image and repair a negative one through association and disassociation with actions on issues. This explanation complements Sutton and Callahan's (1987) description of how companies' bankruptcy filings caused their managers' efforts to restore their own self-images in the eyes of critical organizational audiences. Similarly, in the Port Authority's struggle with the issue of homelessness we observed defensive tactics designed to actively manage outsiders' impressions of the organization; however, the Port Authority's actions were subject to the constraint of doing things that were consistent with the organization's identity.

Organizational Image and Impression Management
Individuals in organizations actively monitor organizational actions on social issues because such actions can be especially character-enhancing or damning.

215

Port Authority members became aware of their organization's image through personally distant media, like the press, and through close ones, like conversations with friends. Informants' accounts documented the triggers to personal and organizational action the negative press coverage set off. As the story suggested, press coverage of the Port Authority on this issue was particularly vivid and disturbing during phase 4. Most staff members working on this issue also mentioned friends and family as active sources of feedback on the organization's image and the pride or shame that this close feedback provided. The connection between individuals' senses of self and the Port Authority's image created incentives to manage the impression others had of the organization's actions.

As our history ended in 1989, the Port Authority members were continuing to try a variety of impression and image management tactics to see if they could transform the organization's image without violating attributes that defined its core identity. The evolution of actions was a continuous experimentation and learning process that became more deliberate over time. Although organization members denied responsibility for the problem throughout, when they saw no alternative, they took identity-consistent action in deliberate and significant ways. However, as the significance of actions on the issue increased—that is, as the human and monetary resources invested increased—the Port Authority began to plan which actions it wanted to highlight and which it wanted to conceal. When we stopped collecting data in mid-1989, the organization was acting as an advocate for the homeless, educating and sharing information with other transportation agencies on what could be done, but it was intentionally maintaining a low profile in the development of programs and services. In the minds of the members of the Homeless Project Team and most of upper management, the costs of being associated with taking responsibility for homelessness far outweighed any gains from being seen as a builder of superior drop-in centers.

The evolution of actions that we observed over time was partially trial-and-error image management that became more assertive (designed to create a positive image) and less defensive (designed to mend a negative image) over time (Tedeschi & Melburg, 1984). The facility-based solutions were largely reactive, based on attempts to conceal, contain, and eliminate the problem. However, as the problem became more severe and image deterioration amplified emotional reactions to the issue, the organization went into high gear on homelessness in an instrumental sense and low gear in a public sense. In a way that was consistent with its technically expert, high-quality, ethical, and fixer-doer identity, the organization proposed and funded major outreach facilities for the homeless near three of its affected facilities.

In sum, deterioration in the Port Authority's image was an important trigger for and accelerator of issue-related action. Changes in the organization's image fueled investment in and motivation to work on the issue in two distinct ways. First, it prompted personal investment because of members' concerns about how the organization's image was affecting others' views of themselves. Second, it provided important political ammunition for justifying and legitimating further issue commitment (Pettigrew, 1987). The Port Authority's image became a direct target for action as management became more aggressive and deliberate in its actions on the issue.

Discussion and Implications

The ideas of image and identity and their links to patterns of issue interpretation, action, and emotion reinforce some well-known ideas about organizational adaptation and suggest important new directions for theory and research.

The story of the Port Authority and the role of identity and image in it suggest that organizational context matters in explaining patterns of change. Treatments of organizational adaptation and strategic change have argued and documented that claim well (e.g., Bartunek, 1984; Miles & Cameron, 1982; Pettigrew, 1987; Tushman & Romanelli, 1985). The Port Authority's struggle with the homelessness issue also supports adaptation researchers' assertions that organizational context affects patterns of change through its effect on how issues are interpreted (e.g., Dutton & Duncan, 1987; Milliken, 1990; Meyer, 1982; Normann, 1977). However, two persistent themes—that what people see as their organizations' distinctive attributes (its identity) and what they believe others see as distinctive about the organization (its image) constrain, mold, and fuel interpretations—help link individual cognitions and behaviors to organizational actions. Because image and identity are constructs that organization members hold in their minds, they actively screen and interpret issues like the Port Authority's homelessness problem and actions like building drop-in centers using these organizational reference points. In this way, organizational image and identity and their consistency or inconsistency help to explain when, where, and how individuals become motivated to push for or against organizational initiatives. As other change researchers have noted (Child & Smith, 1987; Hinings & Greenwood, 1988), it is inconsistency between various conditions in an organization and its context that precipitates action.

The relationship between individuals' senses of their organizational identity and image and their own sense of who they are and what they stand for suggests a very personal connection between organizational action and individual motivation. It suggests that individuals have a stake in directing organizational action in ways that are consistent with what they believe is the essence of their organization. Actions are also directed in ways that actively try to manage outsiders' impressions of the organizations' character (its image) to capture a positive reflection. This connection between organization, employees' self-concepts, and their motivation to invest in and act on issues in particular ways uncovers a new way of thinking about the organizational adaptation process, a perspective in which organizational impression management is an important driving force in adaptation.

Thinking about organizational adaptation processes as attempts at impression management raises several intriguing theoretical and research questions. First, what is the link between managing impressions of organizations and what and how issues are interpreted? Because an organization's association or disassociation with certain issues defined in particular ways has consequences for individuals' careers (Chatman, Bell, & Staw, 1986), impression management concerns are important in determining when and how issues are interpreted. Previous research has assumed these interpretations are important elements in the adaptation process (e.g., Dutton & Duncan, 1987); if that is so, impression management processes hold important clues for discovering how environments and organizations correlate over time. Second, how do impression management processes direct organizational actions? In the Port Authority's struggle with homelessness, we saw impression management concerns become more prominent over time as informants' senses of the organization's image deteriorated. Organization members cared how others judged Port Authority actions on this issue. They pushed for types of actions that reflected positively on the Port Authority and, by association, on themselves as well. Serious consideration of these questions reveals the role that impression management processes play in the adaptation process. By linking individual motivation to organizational action, we begin to see new links between microprocesses (individual motivations) and macro behaviors (patterns of organizational change).

Issue interpretations and actions by Port Authority members reflected changes in public awareness and attention to homelessness in the media and "other arenas of public discourse" (Hilgartner & Bosk, 1988: 53). The waxing and waning of the national attention given to this issue eased or accentuated internal difficulties in legitimating mobilization and investment in the issue. For adaptation researchers, this connection suggests that the rise and fall of issues in broad institutional environments affects issue interpretation and action within an organization. This viewpoint is consistent with population ecologists' and institutional theorists' claims that external context constrains organizational change patterns (e.g., Hannan & Freeman, 1984; Zucker, 1988). Other organizational theorists have linked external context to organizational change through the idea of industry recipes (e.g., Huff, 1982; Spender, 1989). The idea presented here is similar; we suggest that meanings in use and legitimated in a broad external context constrain what issues or ideas have currency in organizations.

Such a view urges adaptation researchers to consider how changes occurring in a public issues arena mold and modify issue interpretations.

In conclusion, the story of the Port Authority's struggle with the homelessness issue provides fertile ground for unearthing new considerations for students of organizations. Consistent with the spirit of Glaser and Strauss (1967), the story reveals new ideas for theory building, particularly for the domain of organizational adaptation. The idea that an organization's identity and image are central to understanding how issues are interpreted, how reactions are generated, how and what types of emotions are evoked, and how these behaviors are related to one another in an organizational context is very simple. It suggests that individuals in organizations keep one eye on the organizational mirror when they interpret, react, and commit to organizational actions. Researchers in strategy, organization theory, and management might better understand how organizations behave by asking where individuals look, what they see, and whether or not they like the reflection in the mirror.

....

Notes

Daphne Futter was an important research assistant on this project. We thank Susan Ashford, Daj Bjorkegren, Arthur Brief, Thomas D'Aunno, Daniel Denison, Martha Feldman, William Foraker, Ari Ginsberg, Stuart Hart, Susan Jackson, Debra Meyerson, Michael Moch, Douglas Orton, Anat Rafaeli, Lance Sandelands, Zur Shapira, David Skidd, Pringle Smith, Karl Weick, and Janet Weiss for their suggestions and comments. We also thank our informants at the Port Authority of New York and New Jersey who gave so generously of their time.

1. We may subsequently refer to the agency as the Port Authority.
2. PATH stands for Port Authority Trans-Hudson commuter line.
3. The Manhattan Bowery Corporation is a "community corporation," a neighborhood-based agency that administers social services where needed.

....

References

Albert, S., & Whetten, D. 1985. Organizational identity. In L. L. Cummings & B. M. Staw (eds.), *Research in organizational behavior*, vol. 7: 263–95. Greenwich, CT: JAI Press.

Alvesson, M. 1990. Organization: From substance to image? *Organization Studies*, 11: 373–94.

Ashforth, B., & Mael, F. 1989. Social identity theory and the organization. *Academy of Management Review*, 14: 20–39.

Bachrach, P., & Baratz, B. 1962. The two faces of power. *American Political Science Review*, 56: 947–52.

Bartunek, J. 1984. Changing interpretive schemes and organizational restructuring. *Administrative Science Quarterly*, 29: 355–72.

Bjorkegren, D. 1989. *It doesn't have to be that way.* Paper presented at the Organizational Behavior Teaching Conference, Columbia, MO.

Caro, R. 1974. *The power broker: Robert Moses and the fall of New York.* New York: Vintage Books.

Chatman, J., Bell, N., & Staw, B. M. 1986. The managed thought. In H. P. Sims & D. A. Gioia (Eds.), *The thinking organization*: 191–214. San Francisco: Jossey-Bass.

Cheney, G. 1983. The rhetoric of identification and the study of organizational communication. *Quarterly Journal of Speech*, 69(2): 143–58.

Child, T., & Smith, C. 1987. The context and process of organizational transformation. *Journal of Management Studies*, 24: 565–93.

Cohen, M. D., March, J. G., & Olsen, J. P. 1972. A garbage can model of organizational choice. *Administrative Science Quarterly*, 17:1–15.

Crocker, J., & Luhtanen, S. R. 1990. Collective self-esteem and ingroup bias. *Journal of Personality and Social Psychology*, 58: 60–7.

Daft, R., & Weick, K. 1984. Toward a model of organizations and interpretation systems. *Academy of Management Review*, 9: 284–96.

Donnellon, A., Gray, B., & Bougon, M. 1986. Communication, meaning and organized action. *Administrative Science Quarterly*, 31: 43–55.

Dutton, J. E. 1988a. Perspectives on strategic issue processing: Insights from a case study. In P. Shrivastava & R. Lamb (Eds.), *Advances in strategic management*, vol. 5: 223–44. Greenwich, CT: JAI Press.

Dutton, J. E. 1988b. Understanding strategic agenda building in organizations and its implications for managing change. In L. R. Pondy, R. J. Boland, & H. Thomas (Eds.), *Managing ambiguity and change*: 127–44. Chichester, England: John Wiley & Sons.

Dutton, J. E., & Duncan, R. B. 1987. Creation of momentum for change through the process of strategic issue diagnosis. *Strategic Management Journal*, 8: 279–95.

Dutton, J. E., & Jackson, S. B. 1987. Categorizing strategic issues: Links to organizational action. *Academy of Management Review*, 12: 76–90.

Dutton, J. E., Stumpf, S., & Wagner, D. 1990. Diagnosing strategic issues and managerial investment of resources. In P. Shrivastava & R. Lamb (Eds.), *Advances in strategic management*: 143–67. Greenwich, CT: JAI Press.

Eisenhardt, K. M. 1989. Building theory from case study research. *Academy of Management Review*, 14: 532–50.

El Sawy, O. A., & Pauchant, T. C. 1988. Triggers, templates and twitches in the tracking of emerging strategic issues. *Strategic Management Journal*, 9: 455–73.

Feldman, M. 1989. *Order without design.* Stanford, CA: Stanford University Press.

Fombrun, C., & Shanley, M. 1990. What's in a name? Reputation building and corporate strategy. *Academy of Management Journal*, 33: 233–58.

Gioia, D. A., & Sims, H. P. 1986. Introduction: Social cognition in organizations. In H. E. Sims & D. A. Gioia (Eds.), *The thinking organization*: 1–19. San Francisco: Jossey-Bass.

Glaser, B., & Strauss, A. 1967. *The discovery of grounded theory: Strategies for qualitative research.* London: Weidenfeld.

Hambrick, D., & Finkelstein, S. 1987. Managerial discretion: A bridge between polar views of organizational outcomes. In L. L. Cummings & B. M. Staw (Eds.), *New directions in organizational behavior*: 369–406. Greenwich, CT: JAI Press.

Hannan, M., & Freeman, J. 1984. Structural inertia and organizational change. *American Sociological Review*, 49: 149–64.

Hilgartner, S., & Bosk, C. L. 1988. The rise and fall of social problems: A public arenas model. *American Journal of Sociology*, 94: 53–78.

Hinings, C. R., & Greenwood, R. 1988. *The dynamics of strategic change*. New York: Basil Blackwell.

Huff, A. 1982. Industry influences on strategy reformulation: *Strategic Management Journal*, 3: 119–31.

Isabella, L. 1990. Evolving interpretations as a change unfolds: How managers construe key organizational events. *Academy of Management Journal*, 33: 17–41.

Jackson, S., & Dutton, J. 1988. Discerning threats and opportunities. *Administrative Science Quarterly*, 33: 370–87.

Martin, J., & Meyerson, D. 1988. Organizational culture and the denial, channeling, and acknowledgement of ambiguity. In L. R. Pondy, R. J. Boland, & H. Thomas (Eds.), *Managing ambiguity and change*: 93–126. Chichester, England: John Wiley & Sons.

Meyer, A. 1982. Adapting to environmental jolts. *Administrative Science Quarterly*, 27: 515–83.

Miles, M. B., & Huberman, A. M. 1984. *Qualitative data analysis*. Beverly Hills, CA: Sage Publications.

Miles, R. H., & Cameron, K. 1982. *Coffin nails and corporate strategies*. Englewood Cliffs, NJ: Prentice-Hall.

Milliken, F. 1990. Perceiving and interpreting environmental change: An examination of college administrators' interpretation of changing demographics. *Academy of Management Journal*, 33: 42–63.

Mintzberg, H., Raisinghini, A., & Théorêt, L. 1976. The structure of unstructured decision processes. *Administrative Science Quarterly*, 21: 246–75.

Nelson, R., & Winter, S. G. 1982. *An evolutionary theory of economic change*. Cambridge, MA: Harvard University Press.

Normann, R. 1977. *Management for growth*. London: Wiley.

Nutt, P. 1984. Types of organizational decisions. *Administrative Science Quarterly*, 29: 414–50.

Pettigrew, A. 1987. Context and action in the transformation of the firm. *Journal of Management Studies*, 24: 649–70.

Pfeffer, J., & Salancik, G. R. 1978. *The external control of organizations*. New York: Harper & Row.

Pierce, J., Gardner, D., Cummings, L. L., & Dunham, R. B. 1989. Organization-based self-esteem: Construct definition measurement and validation. *Academy of Management Journal*, 32: 622–48.

Prahalad, C. K., & Bettis, R. 1986. The dominant logic: A new linkage between diversity and performance. *Strategic Management Journal*, 7: 485–501.

Sandelands, L. E., & Drazin, R. 1989. On the language of organization theory. *Organization Studies*, 10: 457–78.

Singh, H., Tucker, D., & House, R. 1986. Organizational legitimacy and the liability of newness. *Administrative Science Quarterly*, 31: 171–93.

Spender, J. C. 1989. *Industry recipes*. Cambridge, MA: Basil Blackwell.

Starbuck, W. H. 1983. Organizations as action generators. *American Sociological Review*, 48: 91–102.

Starbuck, W. H., & Milliken, F. 1988. Executives' perceptual filters: What they notice and how they make sense. In D. Hambrick (Ed.), *The executive effect: Concepts and methods of studying top managers*: 35–65. Greenwich, CT: JAI Press.

Sutton, R., & Callahan, A. L. 1987. The stigma of bankruptcy: Spoiled organizational image and its management. *Academy of Management Journal*, 30: 405–36.

Swidler, A. 1986. Culture in action: Symbols and strategies. *American Sociological Review*, 51: 273–86.

Tedeschi, J. T. (Ed.). 1981. *Impression management theory and social psychological research*. New York: Academic Press.

Tedeschi, J. T., & Melburg, V. 1984. Impression management and influence in the organization. In S. D. Bacharach & E. J. Lawler (Eds.), *Research in the sociology of organizations*, vol. 3: 31–58. Greenwich, CT: JAI Press.

Tushman, M., & Romanelli, E. 1985. Organizational evolutions: A metamorphosis model of convergence and reorientation. In L. L. Cummings & B. M. Staw (Eds.), *Research in organizational behavior*, vol. 7: 171–222. Greenwich, CT: JAI Press.

Walsh, J. P., Henderson, C. M., & Deighton, T. 1988. Negotiated belief structures and decision performance: An empirical investigation. *Organizational Behavior and Human Decision Processes*, 42: 194–216.

Weick, K. E. 1979. *The social psychology of organizing*. Reading, MA: Addison-Wesley.

Weick, K. E. 1988. Enacted sensemaking in crisis situations. *Journal of Management Studies*, 24: 305–17.

Weigelt, K., & Camerer, C. 1988. Reputation and corporate strategy: A review of recent theory and applications. *Strategic Management Journal*, 9: 443–54.

Weiss, J. A. 1989. The powers of problem definition: The case of government paperwork. *Policy Sciences*, 22(2): 97–121.

Yin, R. 1984. *Case study research*. Beverly Hills, CA: Sage Publications.

Zucker, L. (Ed.). 1988. *Institutional patterns and organizations*. Cambridge, MA: Ballinger Publishing Co.

Organizational Impression Management as a Reciprocal Influence Process: The Neglected Role of the Organizational Audience

Linda E. Ginzel, Roderick M. Kramer, and
Robert I. Sutton

> The job of management is to interpret, not to get the work of the organization done
>
> Weick and Daft (1983, pp. 90–91).

"Every organization," as Pfeffer observed (1981), "has an interest in seeing its definition of reality accepted...for such acceptance is an integral part of the legitimation of the organization and the development of assured resources" (p. 26). Consequently, when events occur that challenge or call into question an organization's definitions or interpretations of reality, organizational leaders often feel compelled to engage in efforts to protect, repair, and enhance the images of the organization and its leadership (Ashforth & Gibbs, 1990; Dutton & Dukerich, 1991; Sutton & Kramer, 1990). For example, when identity-threatening or stigmatizing events befall an organization, leaders typically provide explanations for those events that are intended to minimize damage to the organization's image and their own reputations. Thus, after the Exxon Valdez spilled millions of gallons of oil into Alaskan waters, Exxon's top management offered numerous interpretations intended to shape the perceptions of employees, stockholders, suppliers, the press, the American public, owners of Exxon service stations, the Alaskan Government, and the Federal Government. Similarly, after the space shuttle Challenger exploded, NASA administrators took great pains early on to point out that the decision-making process had been as careful is possible.

The notion that organizational leaders are expected not only to manage an organization's performance, but also *perceptions* of its performance is a central assumption of the symbolic management (Pfeffer, 1981) and impression management (Meindl, 1990; Sutton & Kramer, 1990) perspectives. According to such perspectives, organizational leaders are held responsible for making sense of an organization's actions and promoting its image to individuals both within and outside the organization. If, as these perspectives suggest, organizations are socially constructed systems of shared meanings, then one of top management's primary tasks is to provide "explanations, rationalizations, and legitimation for the activities undertaken in the organization" (Pfeffer, 1981, p. 4).

Prior research on organizational impression management has focused largely on the interpretations or explanations provided by top management. For example, researchers have examined the use of self-serving attributions to reduce the negative impact of poor or mediocre financial performance on firms' reputations (e.g., Salancik & Meindl, 1984; Staw, McKechnie, & Puffer, 1983) and to reduce the stigma of corporate bankruptcy (Sutton & Callahan, 1987). As a result, this literature has conceptualized impression management largely as a unidirectional influence process. Explanations and interpretations are viewed as emanating from an organization's top management and directed at various individuals, groups, and institutions that compose the organization's audience. Relatively little attention has been given to the role that these various organizational audiences play in shaping the impression management process.[1] With respect to the Alaskan oil spill, for example, existing theory on organizational impression management has much to say about the explanations or impression management strategies that Exxon's top management might use to influence the interpretations held by audiences including employees, stockholders, and the press. Yet this work says little about how or why top management's initial perceptions of these audiences affected the particular impression management strategies they selected. Moreover, this work offers few insights about how the negative reactions of these audience members to initial interpretations affected subsequent modifications in the explanations provided by Exxon's leaders. This gap parallels research on organizational leadership, which has concentrated on leaders, while devoting little attention to the actions and attributes of followers (Meindl, 1990).

Shifting attention to the impact of the audience on the impression management process raises a variety of interesting and largely unanswered questions. For example, what happens when members of the organization's audience call into question, challenge, or reject the interpretations offered by top management? What happens when conflicts arise between the interpretations offered by top management and the organizational audience? What factors contribute to such "interpretive" conflicts? How does the organization's top management respond to such conflicts? How do top managers' perceptions of organizational audiences affect the accounts they generate? How does the presence of a particular audience that is perceived to be hostile or antagonistic to the organization affect the interpretations top management offers? What happens when members of various audiences challenge the adequacy of top management's accounts, or regard those accounts as banal, incomplete, incoherent, or incredible?

These questions suggest that impression management is a process of reciprocal influence in which the presence of the organizational audience affects both the initial attempts to explain an organization's actions or performance, as well as ongoing attempts to resolve interpretive conflicts. In conceptualizing impression management as an interactive process involving organizational actors (top management) and the targets of their influence attempts (the members of the organizational audience), this essay develops the idea that organizational impression management resembles a process of "reciprocal sensemaking." A key feature of this reciprocal process is that while the accounts offered by top management are sometimes consistent with the interpretations generated by members of their organizational audiences, at other times, these interpretations conflict. We contend that, to resolve such interpretive conflict, top management and organizational audiences engage in a negotiation-like process. We next introduce a framework that explicates and weaves together the elements of this interactive process.

Impression Management as a Process of Negotiation

This section first describes the basic elements of our framework and then explains how these elements interact to affect the dynamics of impression management. We use Dow Corning Wright's recent efforts to manage the controversy over the safety of its breast implants to illustrate the framework, particularly to illustrate the complexity of impression management when both sympathetic and antagonistic audiences respond to organizational interpretations.

Elements of the Framework

The four basic elements in the framework are: (1) precipitating events; (2) the organization's top management; (3) members of the various organizational audiences; and (4) top management's accounts (see Figure 1).

Precipitating Events
The initial impetus for top management to engage in impression management is a precipitating event that is sufficiently vivid to prompt top managers,

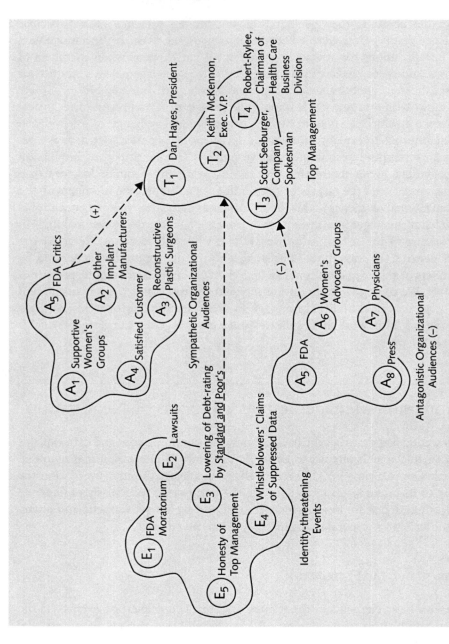

Fig. 1. Elements of organizational impression management: Dow Corning and the implant controversy.

organizational audience members, or members of both groups to try to make sense of that event. Precipitating events take two primary forms (Schlenker, 1980; Tedeschi & Riess, 1981). First, identity-enhancing events provide opportunities for the organization to enhance its image and the reputations of its top managers. Second, identity-threatening events create predicaments that call into question or undermine the organization's preferred image and threaten to tarnish the reputation of its top managers.

Identity-enhancing events are sometimes strongly linked to visible organizational actions and outcomes, such as exceptionally good economic performance, sponsoring a major sporting event, or making an important donation to medical research. In other instances identity-enhancing events may have weak links to organizational actions. For example, the Persian Gulf War provided many U.S. organizations with an opportunity to enhance their own images by associating with the victory. Department stores placed advertisements in local newspapers that listed employees who had served in the conflict. These announcements were ostensibly intended to express appreciation to patriotic store employees. But such announcements also provided an opportunity for these organizations to bask in the reflected glory of the military success, or to engage in positive impression management via association (Cialdini et al., 1976).

Identity-threatening predicaments often center around what appear to be either faulty decisions, inattention to emerging problems, or neglect of ethical or social responsibilities. The spectacular explosion of the space shuttle created an immediate, and as it turned out, enduring, legacy of doubt for NASA administrators who had always up to that point enjoyed a reputation for flawless decision making and judgment.

These examples suggest that precipitating events may be anticipated or unanticipated. The issuance of corporate reports, scheduled press conferences, and shareholder meetings provide organizations and their top managers with predictable opportunities for impression management. In such cases, top managers typically have well-developed routines, fine-tuned through years of trial and error learning, that can be used to put a positive spin on events. In contrast, unexpected events are especially difficult for top managers to cope with when they immediately place the organization's image or reputation in doubt. In addition, top management may not have readily available explanations to offer to explain the predicament. The Alaskan oil spill, the arrest of the Watergate burglars, the explosion of the space shuttle Challenger, the Iran-Contra scandal, the accident at Three Mile Island, the Tylenol tampering episode, and Union Carbide's Bhopal disaster are only a few of the many examples of unanticipated identity-threatening predicaments that have received wide public attention and have been discussed by organizational theorists.

In the case of Dow Corning Wright, the nation's leading manufacturer of silicone gel breast implants, the precipitating event was the following warning issued by FDA Commissioner David Kessler on December 24, 1991: "Women need to be urged strongly to consider the risks of these implants" and "the implants have been on the market a long time and women have been lulled into thinking they are risk free. They are not" (*Los Angeles Times*, p. 1). A few weeks later, the FDA placed a moratorium on the sale of implants, asserting, "Physicians should cease using [implants] and manufacturers should stop distributing them," adding that the FDA "cannot assure women of their safety at this time" (*Los Angeles Times*, January 7, 1992, p. 1).

In some instances, an organization's top management can anticipate that an upcoming event is likely to harm their organization's image. Under these circumstances, they often make efforts to prevent or minimize the potential stigma. Such actions are designed to preempt or deter criticism or blame. When members of the Reagan administration became concerned that expectations about the then-forthcoming arms control talks with Gorbachev in Iceland were far too high, they took deliberate steps to dampen expectations. For example, they informed the press that they should be only "cautiously optimistic" about the outcome of the talks. Moreover, they urged the public to avoid "heightened expectations," stressing the talks were intended to be both informal and preliminary (Sutton & Kramer, 1990). In other instances, top management may itself take the initiative in providing interpretations of an event after it occurs because they believe that such accounts will protect or enhance the organization's reputation. For example, as soon as they discovered that tainted Tylenol tablets had likely caused deaths, Johnson and Johnson's management began an aggressive campaign to salvage the reputation of their corporation and the product (Snyder & Foster, 1983). Such actions convey the impression of being on top of the crisis and being responsible and reactive, rather than prodded into action.

Sometimes an organization's management provides interpretations only after an individual or group initiates discussion of the forthcoming or past event. For example, bankruptcy lawyers sometimes advise the top managements of firms that have filed for protection from creditors under Chapter 11 of the Federal Bankruptcy code to avoid mentioning the filing to customers and suppliers and to only provide accounts about the bankruptcy if customers or suppliers mention it first (Sutton & Callahan, 1987). And Dow Corning Wright chose to ignore early indications of potential health risks associated with implant use until the FDA brought the issue to the attention of the press and public.

In many cases, little or no ambiguity exists about whether an event is identity-threatening or identity-enhancing. For Raytheon, the American company making the Patriot missiles that were so effective against the Iranian SCUDs, the Persian Gulf War provided what appeared to be a unique and unexpected opportunity for identity-enhancement (ironically, later accounts would call into question their accuracy and reliability, creating an equally sudden and unexpected predicament).[2] For NASA and Morton Thiokol, in contrast, the explosion of the space shuttle Challenger constituted a serious and unambiguous identity-threatening predicament. Often, however, there may be considerable uncertainty in the minds of top management or members of the organizational audience as to whether a particular event constitutes a success or failure. Changes in financial performance, for example, can have ambiguous implications for an organization's image. In the early 1980s, CEO Lee Iaccoca claimed that Chrysler's quarterly losses were a success because they were far lower than had occurred in prior quarters, suggesting a turnaround was in the making. Yet some critics asserted that Iaccoca was excessively optimistic given that his company was still losing money. Thus, it may be unclear whether an event threatens the organization's image.

Even if clearly threatening, there may be doubt about who is responsible for the predicament and how much blame they deserve. It was unclear for many months how much the terrorist bombing of Pan Am Flight 107 over Lockerbie posed an identity-threatening predicament for Pan Am (which had insufficient airport security), the State Department (which had failed to warn Pan Am about threats to U.S. airlines), or the Central Intelligence Agency (which had at least two of its agents on board carrying sensitive documents about the release of U.S. hostages) (Emerson & Duffy, 1990).

There may be significant asymmetries in the perceived ambiguity of events for top management and members of the organizational audience. Top management may have access to inside information which clarifies events and helps them sort through the various accounts available for an event. They also know whether they are being sincere, honest, fully disclosing, and so forth. In contrast, organizational audience members may be dependent on sketchy, incomplete, and contradictory accounts; they may have significant doubts about the honesty of top management or the completeness of its disclosures.

Top Management
For the purposes of the present analysis, top management is defined as the individual or individuals that the organizational audience turns to for interpretations when predicaments arise. Top management constitutes the organization's symbolic figureheads who are the guardians and promoters of the organization's image. The composition of the organization's top management varies across organizations. In a small organization, it may be a single individual, such as the organization's founder. In other cases, it may be a board of directors or a management team.

There are often other individuals in an organization who are also in a position to provide official explanations and interpretations. For example, public relations personnel and information officers are typically given formal authority to interpret events associated with the organization and provide explanations that reflect top management's views. In our framework, they are an important and legitimate extension of top management. Other individuals within the organization may offer views on their own initiative that are not endorsed by the organization's top managers. Whistleblowers, for example, are antagonistic audience members who just happen to be observing events from within the organization. In the case of Dow Corning Wright, Thomas D. Talcott, a former Dow materials engineer, served as an expert witness against the company, stating he had opposed development of fluid silicone gel devices because he thought they were too dangerous.

Organizational Audiences

For most organizations, the audience that routinely observes its actions (or that may become observers during a predicament) is large and complex. Organizational audiences include exchange partners who provide resources to the organization or who themselves depend upon the organization's resources. Organizational audiences also include groups that confer or detract legitimacy. These audiences can reside within the organization, as in the case of employees, associates, shareholders, and directors, or may reside outside of the organization, as in the case of customers or clients, competitors, suppliers, special interest groups, and governmental agencies. All of these audience members can potentially accept, challenge, or reject the accounts that are offered by top management or by their official spokespersons. Dow Corning's organizational audience included past and potential future customers, regulatory bodies such as the FDA and the National Cancer Institute, physicians' groups (including both sympathetic doctors such as plastic surgeons and critics such as surgeons who felt the risk of reconstruction outweighed the benefits), and women's groups (both those who favored the use of implants as a critical component of reconstructive surgery and adapting to breast cancer surgery; as well as those opposed the use of implants on health grounds).

Organizational audiences can differ along a number of dimensions. They may differ in terms of their power and access to information; they can differ in terms of the nature of their relationship with the organization, ranging from high dependence to low dependence. For our purposes, the most important distinction is the orientation or predisposition of a given audience toward top management. We draw a distinction between *antagonistic* audience members and *sympathetic* audience members. Sympathetic audiences are as those whose preferred interpretation of that event is consistent with top management's public account. In contrast, antagonistic audiences are those whose preferred interpretation of an event clashes with the top management's account. We focus on this dimension because our framework emphasizes forces that affect top managers' construal of an event, the initial accounts provided for an event, and subsequent modifications in account. We contend that top managers will try to develop initial accounts that provoke as much sympathy and as little antagonism as possible, that top managers often make errors in judgment about which accounts will provoke the most widespread sympathetic response, and that when initial accounts provoke more antagonism than anticipated, antagonistic audience members may pressure top managers to change their accounts over time.

Rather than a static feature of relationships between audience members and the organization or its top management, a given audience member's orientation as sympathetic or antagonistic is determined by the perceived costs and benefits associated with top management's account of the event. For example, Elsbach and Sutton's (1992) study of radical social movement organizations indicates that official spokespersons for the Sierra Club, a liberal environmental activist organization, are routinely antagonistic toward the radical environmental activist organization, Earth First! when its members take actions that violate societal norms (e.g., driving metal spikes into old redwood trees to prevent them from being cut). But spokespersons for the Sierra Club are consistently sympathetic when members of Earth First! make statements about the importance of protecting ancient redwood trees from the logging industry.

Similarly, the perceived costs or benefits of a given interpretation may lead some audience members who are usually antagonistic to the organization to become sympathetic with regard to a specific event. For example, both PepsiCo and Adolph Coors, who were testing new sparkling waters, decided against running ads that would remind consumers of Perrier's benzene contamination problem and thus threaten the reputation of similar products. Because these firms were all involved in the fast-growing sparkling water industry, as Craig Wealtherup, president of Pepsi-Cola Co., remarked: "Why should we slow the leader and rock the entire category?" (Sellers, 1990, p. 278). Even competitors can emerge as sympathetic audiences for one another if they face shared incentives.

Top Management's Accounts

A central assumption of symbolic management and impression management perspectives is that the meaning of organizational events is provided in large part by top management. One of the primary ways top management accomplishes this task is through the use of accounts (Scott & Lyman, 1968). Accounts have been defined as "verbal remedial strategies" that provide "explanations for problematic behaviors designed to rectify a predicament" (Gonzales, Pederson, Manning, & Wetter, 1990, p. 610). Accounts can assume many forms, including press releases, interviews, memos, statements in annual reports, statements during press conferences, off the record remarks, and revelations in autobiographical memoirs. Accounts represent top management's construal of an event.

Top managers use accounts both to bolster the positive image of the organization when identity-enhancing opportunities arise, and to minimize blame or stigma when identity-threatening events befall it.[3] When confronted with a potentially negative event, top management may offer (1) *excuses* that concede negative interpretations of the event, but deny or externalize responsibility for it (Scott & Lyman, 1968); (2) *refusals* by which top management denies guilt, claims that the event was misrepresented, attributes blame to others or attempts to evade the questionable event (Schonbach, 1980); (3) *justifications* where top management accepts responsibility for the event, but denies any pejorative interpretations (Scott & Lyman, 1968); (4) *concessions or apologies* with top management admitting partial or total guilt, expressing regret, and perhaps offering restitution (Schonbach, 1980).

When confronted with a positive event, in contrast, top management will most likely attempt to increase the desirable implications of the event through the use of acclaiming tactics, including "enhancements" intended to boost the apparent desirability of the event and "entitlings" intended to heighten top management's perceived responsibility for the event (Schlenker, 1980).

Even the statement "No comment" is a form of account that can be used by top management. Although it may be regarded as inadequate or defensive by some audience members, it nonetheless provides top management with the time needed to formulate a more detailed response. Moreover, it may be used to convey the impression that the problem is under serious review and will be dealt with confidentially. Or it may be used by top management in an attempt to characterize a problem as trivial and not meriting further discussion. For example, during the Gerber baby food tampering scare in 1986, there were no recalls and no Gerber executives appeared on television to explain the firm's position. "The Gerber reaction stood in marked—and some say unfavorable— contrast to the high-profile recall of Tylenol capsules by Johnson and Johnson just weeks earlier . . . In this news-intensive age, the public expects to see a furrow-browed CEO out in front and apologetic whenever hints of malfeasance crop up. Perhaps the long-standing Gerber approach to problems—conservative and low-profile—is not tailored to the times" (Pick, 1986, p. 9).

Phases in the Impression Management Process

Having introduced the basic elements in our framework, we now turn to describing the dynamic interactions among these elements. These are broken down into three distinct phases: (1) an initial phase in which top management generates an account intended to either enhance or protect its image; (2) a second phase in which members of the organizational audience react to the account; and (3) a third phase characterized by attempts to negotiate resolution of the conflict, in which top management attempts to resolve the discrepancies between its account and the interpretations provided by members of the organizational audience.

Phase I: The Account Generation Process
The first phase in the impression management process involves recognition that an event has occurred (or is expected to occur) that has the potential either to detract from or contribute to the desired image of the organization. According to our framework, top management's construal of an event is shaped both by characteristics of the event itself and the various organizational audiences, sympathetic and antagonistic, to whom top management feels accountable (see Figure 2).

Top management usually recognizes that it cannot impose its own interpretations on organizational audiences unless that interpretation is perceived to be acceptable by those audiences. Knowing this, top management may engage in actions that attempt to predict how different audiences will react to their account. As Weick (1979) noted, much of organizational thinking involves "implicit conversations with phantom others. The audience 'present' at most episodes of thinking is potentially influential on the way in which that thinking unfolds and the conclusions that come from it" (p. 69).

To anticipate the reactions of the organizational audience, top management may rely on mental simulations, trying to imagine how different scenarios will

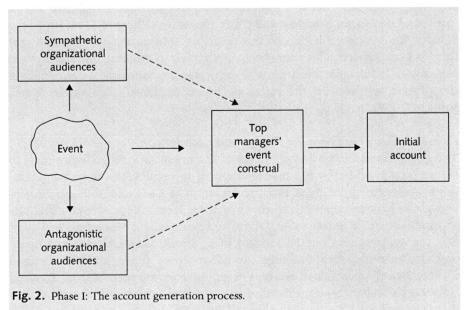

Fig. 2. Phase I: The account generation process.

unfold. Kahneman and Tversky (1982) termed this the simulation heuristic and suggested it is likely to be used to construct possible scenarios when developing predictions and plans when uncertainty exists. Research on the simulation heuristic has shown that visualizing and rehearsing possible outcomes causes decision makers to judge those outcomes as more likely to occur (Carroll, 1978; Hoch, 1984; Sherman, Cialdini, Schwartzman, & Reynolds, 1985).

How might top management's expectations about audience reactions affect their mental simulations? In a recent experimental investigation of the effects of simulation thinking on decision making in conflict situations, Kramer, Meyerson, and Davis (1990) showed that imagining worst case scenarios about an adversary's behavior led decision makers to have more negative expectations about interaction compared to those who had been asked to imagine best case scenarios, even though all of the information available was identical in both situations. If top managers imagine only hostile responses, they may generate worst case scenarios that are unduly pessimistic. If, in contrast, they focus on positive reactions to a given predicament, they may tend to generate best case scenarios, and overestimate the probability that their accounts will be accepted.[4] Top management's attempts to mentally rehearse or anticipate audience reactions illustrates the interactive and reciprocal nature of the influence process that occurs during impression management. It may also influence their strategic choices as to how best to respond to an emerging predicament.

In the case of Dow Coming Wright, top management's initial account was directed towards challenging the credibility of the claims of the antagonistic audience. After the FDA had announced its moratorium on silicone breast implants, Dan Hayes, President and Chief Executive Officer of Dow, urged the FDA to "bring science back into this decision." Moreover, he requested that they "rely on experts with appropriate credentials to evaluate immune system response . . . If this review is done with experts in immunology, we're confident the process will support the safety of breast implants" (*Los Angeles Times*, January 7, 1992, p. 1).

Phase II: Audience Reaction to Top Management's Account
The next phase occurs when segments of the organizational audience react to the account provided by top management. If top management and organizational audiences agree about the interpretation of the event, then no discrepancy exists between their perceptions and there is no interpretive conflict: The account is accepted at face value. Often, however, audience members will question top management's initial account of an event. Skeptical audience members, for example, may challenge the adequacy of the account or demand clarification of unexplained issues. For example, some members of Stanford University's audience—both internal and external—rejected the explanations that were provided for the alleged misallocation of federal funds.

In the course of questioning or rejecting accounts, audiences may put forth competing interpretations. These interpretations often place top management and the organization in a less flattering light than did management's initial public account. For example, Charles Keating, founder and head of Lincoln Savings, contended that his organization's failure was hastened by false accusations of fraud and abuse. Federal prosecutors and business writers rejected this interpretation and asserted that Mr. Keating was the driving force behind an array of unethical and unlawful actions associated with Lincoln Savings, including manufacturing false earnings, taking excessive salaries and fees, and buying-off U.S. Senators to fend-off the Federal Home Loan Bank Board's investigation (Rudnitsky, 1989; Smart, 1990).

The net result of these actions is that top management becomes aware that its account conflicts with that of some or all of the organizational audiences, leading to a state of interpretive conflict (see Figure 3).

Interpretive conflict can take many forms. For example, new evidence may suggest that the original account offered by top management was incomplete or inaccurate. Changes over time such as new developments and unforeseen consequences that contradict the initial account provided by top management may be another reason for them to provide a revised account of an event. Warren Anderson, Union Carbide's chairman during the 1984 chemical disaster that killed more than 2,000 people in Bhopal, India, contended that the massive gas release at Bhopal was due to sabotage. He stated that, "The technology employed at Bhopal was sound, and the plant was well-designed—facts that I expect we'll have no trouble showing in court if that's necessary." Anderson

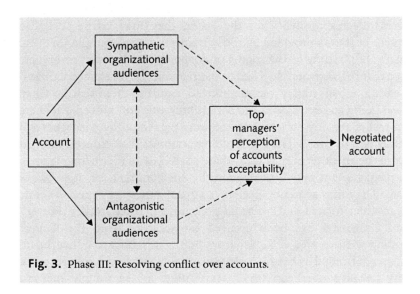

Fig. 3. Phase III: Resolving conflict over accounts.

continued to be haunted, however, by an earlier statement he made, that under conditions existing at the Bhopal plant, it "shouldn't have been operating" (Nelson-Horchler, 1986, p. 20).

Alternatively, audiences may challenge the truthfulness of the account that has been offered because top managers have presented inconsistent explanations. The consistency of an account may become especially problematic when multiple organizational spokespersons offer conflicting accounts. For example, some observers argued that Perrier's failure to come forward candidly as soon as the tainted product was discovered may have damaged the company's credibility: "People will remember that the company re-arranged the truth to serve its public relations needs . . . They grabbed for anything that might help explain the contamination . . . Everyday I saw another article that disclosed new facts and refuted what had been said before . . . Perrier ought to tell what the real story is" (Crumley, 1990, pp. 52–53).

In the case of identity-enhancing predicaments, interpretive conflicts may surround issues of credit and entitlement. Top management may claim credit for an event to which the audience feels it is not entitled. When Gorbachev received credit in the international press for arranging a pre-summit meeting with President Reagan, the Reagan administration quickly responded by noting that while Mr. Gorbachev may have set up the summit, they deserved credit as well because they had arranged the date (Sutton & Kramer, 1990).

The accounts offered by top management can sometimes become predicaments in their own right, exacerbating the difficulties of developing accounts that are acceptable to organizational audiences. When audience members perceive that they have been mislead by managers' statements about whether an identity threatening event will occur, about the severity of the event, or about management's responsibility for the event, they may refuse to believe any subsequent accounts provided by those managers. For example, in Sutton and Callahan's (1987) study of the stigma of corporate bankruptcy, several creditors reported that management had lied to them about the financial condition of the firm before the bankruptcy was announced, assuring them that no Chapter 11 filing was going to occur. After the bankruptcy was announced, these creditors refused to believe any subsequent accounts presented by managers who had apparently lied to them. Thus, misleading accounts that reduced interpretative conflict in the short term may exacerbate such clashes in the long term.

Top management may actively scan the environment for signs of audience reactions. They may send out "feelers" to groups they are especially concerned about, conduct formal and informal polls, and market studies. For example, Stanford University has been accused by auditors from the Government Accounting Office and U.S. Senators with misallocating overhead costs from research funded by the federal government. Stanford has suffered negative publicity because overhead funds were used for seemingly inappropriate purposes including buying a yacht and supporting a wedding reception for Stanford's president. Top university administrators, with the help of a public relations firm, have responded that most of the charges were legitimate and that the few that were inappropriate occurred because of accounting errors rather than intentional abuse. The administration attempted to assess the success of these early efforts at "spin control" by asking some groups of staff members if they accepted or rejected the initial accounts provided by university officials.

The diverse set of audience responses to Dow Corning's efforts to reassure the public about the safety of its implants illustrates the complexity of the impression management process once the role of the audience is made salient. Critics of the devices emerged within the medical community almost immediately, even though breast implants had been on the market for thirty years, and had been used by an estimated two million women. When FDA Commissioner David A. Kessler requested a voluntary moratorium on the use of the devices, he cited a "considerable number of case reports from rheumatologists saying that they are seeing an increasing number of autoimmune disorders among breast implant patients" (*Los Angeles Times*, January 7, 1992, p. 1).

As noted earlier, whistle-blower Thomas D. Talcott emerged as a vocal critic of Dow. But consumer advocacy groups also followed suit. Public Citizen, a Washington-based watchdog group critical of breast implants reported that "about 155,000 of 2.3 million women who had implants suffer serious complications, including infections, and leaks or ruptures of the silicone implant material into their bodies" (*Los Angeles Times*, November 17, 1991, p. 5). Similarly, National Women's Health Network, an advocacy group, filed a claim with the Federal Trade Commission against plastic surgeons' groups using implant, accusing them of "'false and misleading' advertising in their lobbying efforts to seduce women to the operating table" (*Los Angeles Times*, November 17, 1991, p. 5).

Dissatisfied implant recipients and breast cancer support groups became quite vocal. Marie Walsh, President of the Breast Implant Information Foundation of Southern California, lobbied the FDA to have the silicone breast implants removed. She said 300 women in Orange County with complications from the implants are on her organization's mailing list. (*Los Angeles Times*, January 7, 1992, p. 14). Walsh's group is linked to the Command Trust Network which was also founded by women who had a history of implant related problems and the desire to reach out to others (*Los Angeles Times*, December 10, 1990, p. 1).

All of the audiences were not antagonistic to Dow's cause or its claims, however. Sympathetic audiences included satisfied implant users. "I don't believe I would have gone through with the mastectomy if reconstruction hadn't been available," stated Vicki Schomburg, a cancer patient who received a breast implant after a mastectomy (*Los Angeles Times*, January 7, 1992, p. 14). "It has given me back my life . . . I could not have gotten through the trauma of losing a breast without the reconstruction," stated Sheila Berkman, who replaced the breast she lost to cancer with a silicone gel implant (*Los Angeles Times*, November 15, 1991, p. 1).

As Pam DeLuca, President of "Why Me?," a national breast cancer patient support organization, noted, "This is a major issue to breast cancer support groups around the country who believe that reconstruction via implant is the only way most women have of feeling whole again after breast cancer surgery.... With all the scare stories about implants, these women have been overlooked" (*Los Angeles Times*, September 26, 1991, p. 22).

Members of the medical community in favor of implant use concurred with these sentiments. Dr. Lawrence N. Seifert, a spokesman for the American Society for Aesthetic Plastic Surgery said today's implants are safer and the techniques are better then ever before (*Los Angeles Times*, December 24, 1991, p. 1). Dow Corning's competitors also rallied to argue against implant critics. Gary Mistlin, Chief Financial Officer of Mentor Corporation, one of the smaller implant makers, said, "Our company's philosophy is that the product is perfectly safe" (*Los Angeles Times*, November 15, 1991, p. 1).

Even as Dow Corning attempted to respond to these claims as to the safety and efficacy of its product, they were confronted with new and equally serious predicaments. The media added yet another complicating wrinkle to Dow's impression management predicament, suggesting that, "Outsiders warned Dow Corning that it was worsening its problems and flunking the crisis management test by appearing inadequately concerned about the women and uncooperative with the U.S. Food and Drug Administration's investigation" (*Los Angeles Times*, February 12, 1992, p. 4). Thus, in addition to charges of defending an unsafe product, top management now had to contend with the claim that it was incompetent at doing its job of reassurance and "spin control."

In addition, Dow Corning's honesty and integrity were called into question. It was revealed that since the FDA's call for a moratorium on the sale and use of the devices (in part due to confidential information from internal Dow documents), Dow Corning fought government efforts to obtain those internal documents which they finally made public on February 10, 1992, the media reported that "The memos depict the manufacturer as eager to market a new line of implants and reluctant to conduct studies on the health consequences of silicone gel leakage" (*Los Angeles Times*, February 11, 1992, p. 1). The very same day Dow Corning released these internal documents, Keith R. McKennon was named as their new chairman and chief executive.

Dow Corning's experience illustrates the major role the organizational audiences play in the impression management process. The diverse claims of both sympathetic and antagonistic audiences highlights how difficult it is to produce a single coherent account that will satisfy all of the claims of all of the audiences. It also illustrates the emergence of new predicaments, increasing the level of conflict between top management and its audience.

Phase III: Resolving Conflict Over Accounts

Interpretive conflict indicates a gap between what the top management of an organization are expected to do, and what they have done. Leaders are expected to be in control of their organizations (Salancik & Meindl, 1984); such control includes providing rational interpretations or explanations of events that are persuasive to organizational audiences. Interpretive conflict thus indicates a failure that potentially calls leader's competence into question. Moreover, such failures are especially aversive to leaders because they have made a public commitment to an interpretation that has been openly questioned or rejected. In Goffman's (1959) terms, aversive embarrassment can occur because managers have presented a public "face" that falls short of the expectations others hold for those occupying leadership roles.

Interpretive conflict is also aversive to organizational audience members because it threatens their presumptions about the rationality and consistency of organizational decision making. The failure of the organization to provide a convincing or coherent account of its actions undermines their confidence in its leadership. Because the audience typically consists of people who depend on the organization for resources, the perception that top management is not really in control of events may threaten their security. Thus, we assume that, when interpretive conflicts arise, both top management and audience members are motivated to make their interpretations more congruent.

When the interpretations offered by top management conflict with those generated by audiences, we propose that top management and the audience frequently engage in a process that resembles a "negotiation" regarding the appropriate interpretation or "spin" to put on the event. This negotiation process can be characterized as a series of interlocked cycles of behavior (Weick, 1979) during which organizational leaders propose different accounts, and organizational audiences either accept those accounts, propose modifications, or reject them.

As noted earlier, there are many different kinds of accounts that top management can use to resolve conflict and the associated opposition of important audiences to its interpretations. The selection of a given strategy is likely to depend on top management's perceptions of the most effective options available to it given the potential audience reactions it anticipates. Such factors highlight that impression management and symbolic management activities are embedded within complex political environments. Thus, to understand the strategic nature of the account generation process, it is important to consider such factors as the relative power of the various audiences, their relationship with top management, and their history of previous interaction. In selecting one strategy over another, top management presumably engages in calculations regarding the political costs and efficacy of different approaches to resolving interpretive conflict.

To the extent that top management's accounts fail to satisfy ongoing concerns of the organizational audiences, numerous cycles of negotiation and account iteration may be necessary before top management and the audience reach agreement about the meaning of the event. We argue that the cycle of interlocked behavior continues until organizational actors and their audiences have reduced, or eliminated, perceived equivocality regarding the event. As audience members become satisfied, the salience of the predicament decreases, and the cycle is complete insofar as ambiguity or lack of consensus regarding the event's interpretation has been resolved. In such cases, top management and their organizational audiences have achieved a "settlement" regarding the final interpretation to be placed on the event.

The 1986 Iceland Arms Control Talks between the United States and the Soviet Union initially appeared to be an identity-threatening event for the Reagan administration because no agreement was reached between the two parties (Sutton & Kramer, 1990). The press widely regarded the talks as a missed opportunity for Reagan. Moreover, both American and Soviet officials appeared dejected when they announced that the talks had failed. Yet subsequent efforts at "spin control" by administration officials emphasized that, despite first appearances, the talks were a great success because, as Secretary of State George Schultz put it, "for the first time the two sides agree to dramatic reductions in nuclear and strategic arms" (Sutton & Kramer, 1990, p. 240). The press began to describe the outcome of these talks more positively, until attention was diverted by other events.

The case of Dow Corning illustrates how these negotiation cycles unfold, as the organization's top management tries to deal with emerging information that invalidates or undermines its initial accounts. Recall that, rather than trying to counter the FDA's claims of implant risks with data of its own, Dow Corning initially decided to attempt to discredit its critics, calling into question their status as experts familiar with the medical consequences of implant use. Sympathetic audiences were quick to rally to Dow's support. For example, Dr. Norman Cole, President of the American Society of Plastic and Reconstructive Surgeons, called for the resignation of the FDA Commissioner Kessler. He asserted that Kessler's call for a moratorium on implants had "created hysteria, anxiety and panic" (New York Times, January 16, 1992, p. A15).

In response to claims that its implants were unsafe, Dow announced that research data from hundreds of scientific studies, many internally conducted, showed that the implants were safe. The company made selective memos and documents available to the press. At a news conference, Robert Rylee, Chief of Dow's health care businesses, stated that the "cumulative body of credible scientific evidence shows that the implants are safe and effective" (New York Times, January 14, 1992, p. A1).

At the same time that Dow was trying to reassure the public that the scientific data supported its claims of safety, other leaked internal documents revealed that considerable dissension within the company had existed for years regarding the lack of systematic testing of the implants. According to informed sources and internal memorandum, scientists within Dow had repeatedly urged more thorough evaluation of the implants (*New York Times*, January 13, 1992, p. A1). In response to these claims, Dow officials responded, "Internal memos are not science... they are a printed record of one side of a two-way conversation" (*New York Times*, January 14, 1992, p. A13).

On January 16, as Dow tried to deal with the growing criticism of both the safety of its product as well as the honesty and responsiveness of its top management, a new predicament emerged. Standard and Poor's Corporation, a previously silent member of the organizational audience, announced that it was lowering the debt rating for Dow because it expected large numbers of law suits to be initiated against the company. On the same day, Mentor, the second largest implant manufacturer in the United States, announced that, although it considered the silicone gel implants safe, it was switching to another design that used a saline solution instead.

As the FDA continued to release more and more data from independent studies showing that implant use posed a variety of health risks, Dow's top management found it increasingly difficult to claim they were safe. In addition, a month later, internal memos were leaked showing that Dow management had been informed they were potentially hazardous. In response, Dow initiated a series of bold new accounts. First, it announced it would replace its chief executive officer on February 11, 1992. In addition, it announced that it would no longer criticize the FDA's statements about safety. Finally, it warned doctors that some of the commonly used practices associated with implant use, such as telling patients to massage them to avoid build up of scar tissue, were potentially dangerous because they might increase the likelihood of rupture.

The new chief executive officer announced he would turn his attention to the issue of implant safety and that Dow would implement a variety of new programs, including starting a registry to follow implant users, and providing financial help for women who wanted their implants removed but could not afford it. Dow officials said that they expected the new CEO to bring a "sympathetic image with him" (*New York Times*, February 11, 1992, p. A1).

Dow received considerable positive press associated with these bold steps. For example, a business consultant who had been one of Dow's most visible critics, stated, "[these changes] look good... They had identified the crisis manager at the highest level and told everyone else to go back and run the business" (*New York Times*, February 11, 1992, p. A12).

When subsequent hearings continued to raise concerns about the use of implants, however, Dow announced it would conduct additional safety tests and, while claiming the implants were still safe, declared that it would give women a $600.00 warranty and free replacement if they agreed never to sue the company (*San Francisco Examiner*, February 21, 1992, p. A1). On the same day, it announced it may discontinue manufacturing implants. Kermit Campbell, a Dow vice president, announced that, "We expect the market to be smaller... It is not large enough for four manufacturers" (*San Francisco Examiner*, February 21, 1992, p. A1).

The example of Dow Corning's experience in trying to negotiate a favorable image of both its product and management illustrates the complex interactive nature of the process of organizational impression management. Much as Figure 1 suggested, top management's attempt to achieve a positive resolution of its predicament was hampered by the emergence of new and unexpected antagonistic audiences, as well as new and unexpected predicaments. What initially began as a straightforward conflict over the question of product safety enlarged to include questions of the responsibility of the company's management, its honesty, and its financial soundness.

We have argued that the organizational audience plays an active role in shaping the impression management process. In the next section, we elaborate on this theme by drawing out some of the implications of our framework. In particular, we suggest some of the reasons why top management's efforts at impression management fail. These reasons include psychological and organizational factors that lead top management and members of the organizational audience to view events differently, as well as strategic complexities associated with trying to formulate accounts that can simultaneously please multiple, diverse audience members.

Why Impression Management Fails

The need for top management to resort to negotiating the proper interpretation of an event underscores several important aspects of organizational impression management. It illustrates that an organization's image is not created or sustained solely by top management. In addition, it illustrates the power that organizational audiences often have to shape such accounts. Because of their power, organizational audiences often do not passively accept the various accounts offered by top management. Instead, they claim the right to participate in the process of managing the organization's image. Thus, an organization's image represents a collaborative social construction between an organization's top management and the multiple actors who comprise the organizational audiences. A particular interpretation of an organization's image may be proposed by top management, but that interpretation must in turn be endorsed, or at the very least not rejected, by their various audiences if it is to persist.

We assume that, given top managers' incentives for maintaining positive organizational and personal images, they will provide accounts that they anticipate audience members will regard as acceptable. For example, the press releases and interviews given by corporate officials at Exxon regarding the Alaskan oil spill were presumably not intended to create the impression that Exxon was incompetent, callously indifferent to the environment, or manipulative. Yet these interpretations were held by many audience members. Numerous articles in newspapers and magazines asserted that Exxon's Chairman and his top management team repeatedly underestimated public reaction to the Valdez spill and offered accounts suggesting that the public had little to lose from the spill (Lukaszewski, 1989). These miscalculations are thought to explain much of Exxon's fall from 6 to 110 on *Fortune* magazine's list of America's most admired companies following the Valdez spill (Nulty, 1990). These articles also contended that top management's insensitive and sometimes conflicting accounts dampened the loyalty of Exxon employees.

Similarly, Audi of America's top management certainly did not expect their initial account of a mechanical problem in its cars to ultimately harm the reputation of their organization or its product. Yet one report indicated that "In 1986–87, Audi's response to nearly 230 reported injuries and four reported deaths attributed to sudden and unexpected acceleration was to insist that the upscale drivers it had identified as its demographic market didn't know how to drive a car . . . Audi stonewalled in its contention that the acceleration problems stemmed from owners shifting gears without stepping on the brake, and who then compounded the error by plopping their foot on the gas instead of the brake" (Garcia, 1990, p. 166). Negative reports in national publications eventually pushed Audi to recall all 1978–86 automatic shift 5000S cars. Audi New car sales fell sharply and so did Audi resale values (Garcia, 1990).

These examples are not unusual. Recent journalistic accounts document how frequently top managers and their advisors make poor judgments about the consequences of their efforts to impart positive spin, especially given the costs of such failures. These poor judgments raise the question: Why do accounts fail? More specifically, what contributes to the difficulties that top managers have in generating acceptable accounts? And why might top managers' accounts differ from the interpretations of the same events held by various members of the organization's audience?

The incentives for top managers may, in some cases, simply differ from some or all audience members. For example, top management has incentives to take credit for identity-enhancing events and deflect blame for identity-threatening events. In contrast, members of their audiences such as competitors outside the organization or rivals for the throne within the organization may have incentives to attenuate the credit and accentuate the blame received by top management. As Pfeffer (1981) noted, symbolic management activity occurs in the context of political environments in which actors are competing for valuable but scarce resources. As a result, there are often incentives for others to topple or undermine top management's accounts.

Nonetheless, even when there are incentives for top management and for their organizational audiences to hold congruent interpretations of an event, top managers often fail to present accounts that are acceptable to these audiences. The accounts generated by audiences often differ substantially from those generated by top management. In this section, we propose a variety of psychological and organizational processes that contribute to the divergence in their interpretations. Moreover, when top managers and audience members do have incentives to advance conflicting interpretations of an event, cognitive biases can widen the gap between accounts presented by top management and various audience interpretations of the event.

Psychological Factors

A variety of psychological processes may lead top managers and organizational audiences to explain events in systematically different ways. For example, perceptual and informational differences such as the divergence between the perspectives of actors and observers (Jones & Nisbett, 1972) may lead top management (as actors) and organizational audiences (as observers) to apportion credit and blame differently for a given event. This section considers several cognitive biases that have important consequences because they may cause top managers to overestimate the probability that their attempts at impression management will be successful, and thus miscalculate their ability to control their organization's image.

Egocentric Biases
Top managers may misperceive audience reactions because they overestimate the congruence between their views and those held by the audience. Research on egocentric biases has shown that parties to a conflict often assume that the other side will perceive a situation in much the same terms that they do. This tendency has been observed in both laboratory simulations and historical cases studies (Jervis, 1976). Similarly, research on the false consensus effect has shown that people tend to overestimate the prevalence of their own viewpoint (Ross, Greene, & House, 1977). Ross (1977) has proposed that decision makers' own viewpoints are likely to be more familiar and thus more cognitively available to them. Availability and ease of recall may determine frequency estimates (Tversky & Kahneman, 1973).

If top managers assume that their reactions to an event are representative of those held across organizational audiences, then they are likely to overestimate the probability that their account will be accepted. For example, when economics professor Michael E. Levine became dean of Yale's School of Organization & Management in 1988, he eliminated most organizational behavior professors and classes in an effort to bring the school closer to mainstream business schools. His initial justifications for this decision suggest that he overestimated how widely this viewpoint was held by key organizational audiences including students, alumni, recruiters, administrators at other management schools, and the business press. *Business Week* reported that this decision led some graduates and alumni to be deeply dissatisfied with their school. As Byrne (1990) reported:

At graduation, many students refused to shake the dean's hand and accept a diploma from him. Some took the opportunity to hand him a letter of protest. Reflecting the resentment of the dean as an outsider who violated the so-called traditions of the school, alums paid for an airplane to fly overhead, towing a banner with this message: "Boesky. Milken. Lorenzo. Levine. All raiders will fall." (p. 58)

If top managers are isolated or working in private, then they may be especially prone to egocentric views that have been subjected to insufficient "reality testing" (Janis, 1983; Sick, 1985). For example, before implementing 600 layoffs in February 1983, the top managers of Atari seemed to be avoiding contact with most other members of the company for several months. They were also physically isolated from other employees and engaged in little written or oral communication with employees. Apparently, during this time, top managers had convinced themselves that they were dismissing the poor performers in the company. But when they provided this justification to employees who survived this round of layoffs, those employees viewed this account as evidence that top managers were arrogant and detached from the other members of corporation. As one middle manager put it:

Top management went around and spoke to everybody. What they said was, "Now we've gotten rid of all the rummies and the company's strong and all the good people are left." And they never should have said that. They should have said, "Because of business problems we have to let people go." But they said, "We've gotten rid of all the scum," and that wasn't the case at all. And everybody knew it and everybody resented it. So it just got worse and worse. (Sutton, Eisenhardt, & Jucker, 1986, p. 23)

Positive Illusions

Recent research on positive illusions suggests another set of reasons top management may generate accounts that diverge from those produced by audience members. We will consider the effects of three kinds of positive illusions: overly positive self-evaluation, illusions of control, and unrealistic optimism.

Individuals often maintain unrealistically rosy views about themselves (Brown, 1986; Taylor, 1989; Taylor & Brown, 1988). Most people perceive themselves as better than others. They perceive themselves, for example, as more rational, more intelligent, more trustworthy, more honest, and more cooperative than others (Goethals, 1986; Kramer, Newton, & Pommerenke, 1991; Messick, Bloom, Boldizer, & Samuelson, 1985; Messick & Sentis, 1979). These patterns suggest individuals' judgments tend to be self-enhancing across a wide variety of contexts. Because of overly positive self-evaluation, top management may overestimate the positivity of its reputation or image in the eyes of the organizational audience. Consequently, they may underestimate audience disenchantment or readiness to criticize their public accounts.

Illusions of control reflect a tendency for individuals to overestimate their own instrumentality (Crocker, 1982; Langer, 1975). Because of the illusion of control, top management may be overly confident of their ability to direct the course of events. High-level decision makers in organizations often assume uncritically that they can manage events successfully as they arise (Janis, 1983, 1989; Jervis, 1976). Ironically, organizational audiences may contribute to top management's illusions of control. To the extent that they attribute responsibility for organizational outcomes to top management, the illusion of control may be reinforced (Meindl, 1990).

Unrealistic optimism reflects a tendency for individuals to be unrealistically optimistic about future outcomes (Weinstein, 1980). Individuals tend, for example, to perceive their futures as better than average and to predict that more positive than negative events will happen to them. Because of unrealistic optimism, top managers may be overly optimistic that their attempts at impression management will be accepted or well-received, especially if past efforts have been successful. As a result of unrealistic optimism, they may adopt riskier strategies (Tyler & Hastie, 1991). For example, following a previous spectacular success, they might try to take too much credit for a subsequent opportunity for identity-enhancement (Seligman, 1975).

These illusions are not restricted to top managers. The organizational audience may suffer from positive illusions of its own that can serve to undermine top management's accounts. They may assume that they would not have made the same mistakes given the same information, claiming, "We would have seen the predicament coming. I would not have made that error and neither should they have."

Stereotypes
Stereotypes of various organizational audiences held by top management can affect the impression management process in several ways. First, they can lead to unrealistically negative, worst case expectancies about interaction with antagonistic audience members (Brewer, 1979; Hamilton, Sherman, & Ruvolo, 1990; Kramer, 1989). Top management may underestimate the intelligence of antagonistic audiences, their support in the community, or their capabilities and resources. Negative stereotypes of the press and other administration

critics led members of the Nixon administration to underestimate the intelligence, tenacity and motivation of the press and the public during the investigations of the Watergate burglary (Janis, 1983).

Similarly, negative stereotypes of antagonistic organizational audiences may lead top management to underestimate the potential for a positive resolution of interpretive conflict. Because decision makers tend to see outgroup members as less cooperative, less friendly, less rational, and less changeable (Brewer, 1979), top management may be overly pessimistic when generating an account that they believe these audiences will accept.

Second, stereotypes may lead top managers to overestimate the homogeneity of their organizational audiences. Group members tend to perceive members of other groups as having greater homogeneity than actually exists (Linville & Jones, 1980; Brewer, Dull, & Lui, 1981). Thus, when trying to formulate accounts that organizational audiences are likely to accept, top management may underestimate the diversity of opinions and expectations that exist.

Stereotyping can have comparable effects on audience's perceptions of managers. Audience members often expect their leaders to be consistent, rational, and action-oriented (Meindl, 1990). Accordingly, when leaders appear to deviate from those expectations, or their accounts display an absence of those qualities, they may be judged particularly harshly.

Organizational Factors

We have discussed several cognitive and motivational biases that might lead top management to misjudge the potential audience reactions and to over-assume consensus regarding their interpretation of a given predicament. In addition to such psychological factors, organizational factors may also contribute to divergence in the accounts produced by top management and organizational audiences.

Role Constraints

Impression managers and their audiences obviously occupy different roles (CEO, shareholder, government regulator, special prosecutor). The roles individuals occupy can affect the accounts they produce in several ways. First, roles can influence attitudes and values (Kahn & Wolfe, 1964; Lieberman, 1956). Accordingly, the way in which top management describes an event may be influenced by the particular attitudes and values associated with the organization and/or their role as top management.

Roles may also affect the salience, availability and accessibility of information. Top management, for example, may have had to sort through a great deal of information, much of it conflicting and ambiguous, about the factors leading up to an event. In trying to explain why the O-ring problem was not solved when it was first discovered, NASA officials pointed out that the space shuttle was plagued by literally hundreds of potentially equally serious design problems. Organizational audiences, in contrast, may only have limited, yet perhaps vivid information about the consequences of the event.

Organizational Routines

Organizations often interpret and respond to events in terms of well-learned routines and procedures (March & Simon, 1958). Management can invoke such preexisting routines for handling predicaments that have been anticipated. Many organizations, aware of the possibility that predicaments can erupt at any time, have set up contingency plans and even created special departments for handling such predicaments (Nelson-Horchler, 1986). They often establish procedures designed to minimize blame once a predicament does arise.

Organizational routines can lead to interpretive conflict in two ways. First, the mere existence of such routines may, ironically, foster overconfidence on the part of top management that they can manage a predicament should one arise. Because the organization has a procedure for managing crises, it may expend less effort trying to prevent them. By categorizing a predicament as one that falls within the normal range of crises it expects to encounter, top management may generate accounts that, from the audiences' perspective, seem to minimize the severity of the event.

Top management may have difficulty deciding whether an event is simply a "normal" predicament that can be handled by existing routines and procedures, or a unique case requiring special attention. When the space shuttle Challenger first exploded, NASA tried to present this as a regrettable but nonetheless not unanticipated event. Accidents, according to NASA, are normal risks associated with a complex technology. This account implied that the shuttle explosion fell in the same category as the fire that killed three Apollo astronauts earlier. Only after its long inattention to the O-ring design was uncovered did NASA have to treat the event differently and invoke new routines for responding to governmental, press, and public demands for clarification.

This example highlights another problem associated with routines. Public attitudes and mood may have shifted since the routines were originally created. New norms and expectations about corporate responsibility may be in place that existing routines do not encompass. Accordingly, top management may fail to make adequate allowances for the uniqueness of a particular predicament. What would have worked or was an acceptable response when the routines were conceived may no longer work. Thus, when NASA provided only a cursory and incomplete account of the fire that killed the three Apollo astronauts, the press more or less accepted its version. The press investigating the shuttle explosion was far less amiable and compliant.

Multiple Audience Effects

We suggested earlier that one of the difficulties top management faces when trying to generate acceptable or convincing accounts is that there are multiple audiences to whom they feel accountable and must satisfy. In this section, we elaborate on some of the ways in which the presence of multiple audiences exacerbates the complexity of the impression management process and contributes to the potential for interpretive conflict. These complexities assume two primary forms, which we term *informational complexity* and *strategic complexity*.

Informational Complexity

As the number of audiences increases, there is likely to be an increase in the number of issues that are perceived by top management to be at stake. The more diverse the audience and the more heterogeneous its expectations and motives, the more complex becomes the task facing top management in trying to process, interpret, and aggregate information and generate an account. As Midgaard and Underdal (1977) observed, one of the important consequences of increasing the number of parties to a bargaining process is that it tends to become "less lucid, more complex, and therefore, in some respects, more demanding. As [the number of parties] increases, there will be more values, interests, and perceptions to be integrated or accommodated" (p. 332).

As a consequence, the amount of information that top management must process is substantial. In addition, the perceived ambiguity of the situation may increase: it becomes less obvious to top management what crucial issues need to be addressed in their accounts and who the primary targets of the account should be. Thus, the proliferation of parties and issues makes the symbolic management tasks more complex because, as the number of interested parties increases, so does the difficulty in constructing a single, coherent account that will satisfy all members of the audience. Even the task of finding a common mutually acceptable language or vocabulary of discourse may become impossible or difficult.

Informational complexity can also lead to higher levels of ambiguity regarding other parties' positions or interests (Midgaard & Underdal, 1977; Walton & McKersie, 1965; Winham, 1977). Because of the volume of information that has to be processed, there is less opportunity for top management to probe and validate alternative hypotheses regarding the interests or needs of the other parties. As Winham (1977) noted, complexity "increases the ambiguity of information available to them and makes that information subject to more varying interpretations" (p. 351).

As the amount of information that must be processed increases, top management may experience *information overload* (Morley, 1982; Winham, 1977), leading to stress, and so forth (Janis, 1989). Increases in the amount of information that must be processed can also affect *how* that information is processed. Gilbert and his colleagues (Gilbert, 1989; Gilbert & Krull, 1988; Gilbert & Osborne, 1989) have demonstrated how "cognitive busyness" reduces people's ability to engage in complex inferential reasoning. Similarly, when processing demands are high, negotiators may have a greater tendency to rely on judgmental heuristics (Tversky & Kahneman, 1974) which facilitate rapid processing and evaluation of information. Although the use of such heuristics reduces the "cognitive" burden on top management, it can also diminish the quality of their decision making process. For example, information that happens to be more available in memory (Tversky & Kahneman, 1974) or more salient (Neale, 1984) may be overweighted during decision making.

Strategic Complexity
Increasing the number of audience members whose perspectives and interests must be accommodated also increases the strategic complexity associated with the symbolic management process. All of the processes characteristic of an effective bargaining process—the exchange of information about interests and needs, attempts to find integrative proposals that are mutually satisfying, and so forth—become more difficult as the number of parties to the process increases (Kramer, 1991).

The problem of account generation becomes considerably more complicated in multi-audience contexts because accounts directed at one party and aimed at producing one effect may produce quite different consequences for another audience. For example, top management might prefer to offer a particularly nonresponsive or hostile account to an audience perceived to be antagonistic. However, to the extent that this account will also be evaluated by sympathetic or friendly audiences, top management must be careful that its accounts are not misconstrued or alienating.

On the other hand, offering an account that is too conciliatory or revealing might open top management up to attacks by unsympathetic audiences. In the case of a highly threatening identity-predicament, top management may engage in particularly punitive strategies. Thus, even though they might prefer cooperating with a given audience, they may avoid doing so in order to establish a reputation for toughness that may prove beneficial later. This logic is similar to what game theorists have called the "demonstration effect" (Wilson, 1989) and what Smith (1988) referred to more colloquially as "porcupine power."

As these examples illustrate, top management needs to worry not only about the direct effects of their behavior on the particular audience with whom they happen to be interacting at the moment, but also the *collateral* affects of that behavior on others with whom they might have to deal with subsequently or concurrently.

The emergent difficulties attendant with multi-audience settings are illustrated also by considering other strategies that symbolic managers might use. Fiske and Taylor (1991) identified a number of strategies that such actors can use to try to create positive impressions on an audience. *Behavioral matching* entails tailoring one's own behavior to that of the target. For example, if the target is a modest, self-effacing person, then top management may try to strategically display self-effacing behaviors themselves. Behavioral matching presumably exploits the similarity-attraction relationship. Symbolic managers might try account matching—tailoring their language, images, metaphors, and so forth to a given audience.

Another technique is conforming to situational norms. Situations invoke notions of "situated identity" (Alexander & Knight, 1971). Thus, when an oil spill occurs, the public might expect apologies, contrition, and energetic interventions. Bhopal was one of the worst industrial disasters in history. "But Union Carbide stirred public respect in the days immediately after the tragedy by kicking in a crisis communication plan that portrayed the company as being genuinely concerned for the victims." Union Carbide's chairman, Warren Anderson flew to India within hours of the accident. He served as the company's chief spokesman, fielded questions from reporters from around the world and called the disaster Union Carbide's 'highest priority.' If only Exxon's chairman Rawl had responded so quickly and compassionately to defuse the oil spill crisis..." (*Communication World*, May–June, 1990).

The execution of such strategies becomes more problematic as the number of target audiences increases. A successful match between top management and one audience member may increase mismatch with another. Similarly, because different audiences may invoke different norms and expect different behaviors, it may be hard to find a behavior that is judged to be appropriate and consistent to all. Finally, Fiske and Taylor emphasize the importance of the appearance of consistency in beliefs and behavior. Staw (1981) also emphasized that observers expect organizational leaders to be consistent. It is more difficult to be consistent when multiple audiences are present.

Top management may experience increasingly severe *role conflict* or *role strain* (Kahn & Wolfe, 1964; Kressel, 1981). In the context of influence situations, role conflict and role strain in negotiations has most often been discussed with respect to the effects of constituents on a negotiator's behavior. For example, Kressel (1981) observed that, "[n]egotiators may be pressured by their constituents into presenting the constituents' demands vehemently and without backing down, while their opposite numbers across the bargaining table may expect these same negotiators to adhere to norms of moderation and compromise" (p. 227). Similar role strain may be associated with trying to interact with multiple negotiation parties. There may be no single, consistent set of behaviors that a negotiator can use that will be effective with all of the parties with whom he or she must interact.

Directions for Future Research

We noted at the outset of this chapter that much of the literature on impression management has focused only on the impression manager, with relatively little attention given to how an organization's audience can influence the impression management process. Our analysis suggests that future research may benefit from investigating how various audience characteristics shape the impression management process. For example, Dutton and Dukerich (1990) present a case study of the Port Authority of New York and New Jersey and its dealings with the issue of homelessness. Examining how groups in the organization interpreted the issue differently enabled them to explore the relationship between audience responses and organizational action across time. Just as Chen and Meindl (1991) have shown how leadership researchers can learn key lessons by studying followers rather than leaders, turning attention from organizational impression managers to their audiences may open up new lines of inquiry and provide new insights.

Previous studies have examined the attributions in annual reports and subsequent changes in stock prices (Staw, McKechnie, & Puffer, 1984; Salancik & Meindl, 1984). But researchers have not examined how the ongoing process of negotiation between top managers and shareholders unfolds and modifies their separate and shared interpretations in the process. Our perspective suggests that researchers might examine these cycles of interlocked behavior in more detail. The give and take between these parties might be examined, for example, through an examination of videotapes and transcripts of exchanges.

According to our framework, top management engages in a process of negotiation with organizational audiences to resolve interpretive conflict. Our analysis has said little about this negotiation process. This is clearly an important direction for future research. We propose that the negotiation process varies depending on the relationship between top management and the audience. When the relationship is sympathetic, top management and the audience might be expected to have a supportive and cooperative orientation toward each other. As a consequence, they may use integrative strategies that further their joint interests and goals. For example, they might more readily exchange information that will help top management to generate a mutually agreeable account. When the relationship is antagonistic, top management may adopt more distributive (zero-sum) or contentious strategies. For example, they may be more likely to misrepresent or conceal information and use threats and other coercive tactics.

Along related lines, our analysis has not described the dynamics of this conflict resolution process in any detail. When does interpretive conflict fail to get resolved or escalate? Our discussion implied that the negotiation cycles continue until interpretive conflict is resolved. But what happens when top management reaches an impasse or stalemate with the organizational audience? Research on escalation and de-escalation dynamics (Kahn & Kramer, 1990; Pruitt & Rubin, 1986) suggests that, as a conflict escalates, dissatisfaction between the parties spreads to other issues, generating new predicaments for top management. In addition, the intensity of the conflict and the rigidity of the parties may also increase. We would predict that more cycles will be needed to resolve conflict under these conditions.

The perspective developed here also suggests that additional theory building and research is needed about the differences between managing impressions of organizations and those of individuals. Much research has examined specific impression management strategies used by individuals, but little attention has focused on how effective such strategies are for organizational impression management. The range of impression management strategies available to top management may be more constrained than those available to individuals acting alone because organizational actors are influenced by organizational norms and practices. For example, although individuals may use apologies for their transgressions, the culture of the organization or the political realities of the environment within which it is embedded may require members never to accept blame or apologize for past actions that are associated with the organization.

There may also be actions available to people who are trying to protect the image of an organization that are not tenable for individuals acting alone. In particular, in order to protect the image of an organization, strategies can be used to create the impression that past organizational transgressions were due to people who have been removed from the organization. Top management can and does engage in instrumental scapegoating (Bonazzi, 1983) where expendable actors are sacrificed for the "good of the company." For example, one month after the FDA announced its moratorium on silicone breast implants, Dow Corning Corp. announced a shift in its top officers. Keith McKennon replaced Lawrence Reed as chief executive and John Ludington as board chairman (Los Angeles Times, February 11, 1992, p. 1). Studies in organizational succession suggest that this is one effective way to cope with a crisis because it serves the function of suggesting that the organization itself is sound, only the incumbent leaders were inept (Pfeffer & Salancik, 1978). An analogous argument at the individual level sounds less plausible.

In a similar vein, because individuals are only partially included in the organizational roles (Katz & Kahn, 1978), when individual members commit transgressions that the audience construes as an organizational action, impression managers can claim that these individuals acted alone and that their behavior was not endorsed by the organization. For example, Elsbach and Sutton's (1992) study of radical social movement organizations found that when members

253

committed illegitimate actions (e.g., placing a metal spike in an old redwood tree) official organizational spokespersons routinely asserted that although individual members may have taken such actions they were acting alone rather than as a member of the organization. Because the human components of these organizations are partially included and all members occupy other roles in society (Katz & Kahn, 1978) official spokesperson roles in these organizations could be decoupled from the illegitimate actions of individual members. As a result, spokespersons could reasonably claim that the organization could not be blamed for the transgressions of individuals acting outside their roles.

Sometimes impression managers read their audiences quite well. We would argue that President Bush was quite adept at managing impressions of the Persian Gulf conflict, especially with respect to quieting any concerns regarding the similarity between this conflict and Viet Nam. Jesse Jackson provides another example of an individual who has learned to skillfully match not only the content of his rhetoric, but even its form and timing to the requirements of the audience. When asked by the press why he consistently utilized short, memorable but rather sloganistic phrases, Jackson highlighted the necessity of speaking in terms of "epigrams, in quotable phrases, *as a way of protecting yourself against the media.* . . . You can protect the integrity of what you're saying. And, of course, *this is a sound-bite generation*" (Simon, 1991, p. 238, emphases added). Jackson's response acknowledges that an important organizational audience—the press (and, by implication, the public who will ultimately consume the media's message) prefers short, concise statements that fit the six or so seconds available each evening on the nightly news.

Our framework also suggests that future research should examine which kinds of impression management strategies are most effective for responding to different kinds of audiences, especially to sympathetic versus antagonistic audiences. In the case of antagonistic audiences, for example, top management may benefit from engaging in attempts to discredit or undermine the legitimacy of critical organizational audiences. Although an unsavory practice, derogation of organizational critics can be an effective strategy, especially if the credibility of those critics is somewhat suspect. As noted earlier, Dow Corning elected to call into question the FDA's claims by implying they were relying on the wrong kinds of medical experts. Similarly, when Ralph Nader first exposed safety problems with the Corvair, GM engaged in a plan to discredit him, and the Nixon administration tried to discredit Daniel Ellsberg by getting hold of his psychiatrist's records. When Robert Kennedy became a highly vocal critic of the Johnson administration's handling of the Viet Nam War, Lyndon Johnson questioned Kennedy's manhood by suggesting to the press and the public that such critics were "nervous nellies."

Another way of discrediting an antagonistic audience is through "feather ruffling." Feather ruffling entails the use of strategies that are designed to provoke an emotional outburst from an opponent, thereby making them look foolish or out of control (Pruitt & Rubin, 1986).

Such strategies presume that the antagonistic audience is itself vulnerable or weak in one or more respects. In situations where top management is less powerful or more dependent, other strategies such as ingratiation may be tried. When dealing with sympathetic audiences, top management may resort to more cooperative or conciliatory strategies in generating accounts. For example, top management may wine and dine critical audiences. Members of the Reagan administration, following what appeared to be the collapse of the Iceland talks, actively courted members of the press, giving them unprecedented access to administration officials (Sutton & Kramer, 1990).

Many of these strategies may entail substantial risks that should also be considered in future research. The use of coercive strategies such as threats may backfire, leading to an escalation of conflict between top management and its critics. They may also alienate previously neutral or sympathetic audiences and/or lead others to emerge to support the critics. And conciliatory accounts that acknowledge the legitimacy of critical audiences may legitimate critics and thus increase their power over the organization.

Finally, although we believe that conceptualizing impression management as a negotiation-like process involving top management and the organizational audiences contributes to our understanding of the dynamic nature of the impression management process, it also is limited in some regards. It may not apply when top management sometimes chooses not to negotiate with the organizational audience. Negotiation may be perceived as too costly, risky, and runs the risk of elevating the status of organizational critics, as well as adding attention and weight to the legitimacy of their claims. Also, it may not apply when top management assume, correctly or falsely, that no possibility exists for a negotiated resolution of interpretive conflict. As Neale and Bazerman (1991) have shown, negotiators often believe that their interests are inherently incompatible, leading them to fail to discover existing opportunities for conflict resolution.

....

Summary and Conclusions

The conceptual framework presented in this chapter makes several contributions to our understanding of the process of symbolic management and impression management in organizations. Previous research in this tradition has provided fairly comprehensive discussions of the range of strategies that organizational actors can use to manage meaning. It has not, however, specified when or why particular accounts or strategies succeed or fail. The framework we have offered identified several reasons why impression management efforts fail. Organizational leaders may set the wrong expectations. Attempts to set optimistic expectations that serve short-term goals might lead to long-term disenchantment, loss of credibility, and even stronger attributions of incompetence or failure when reality fails to live up to the high expectations set earlier. NASA, in search of Congressional support and to stimulate waning public interest in space, pushed the image of the space shuttle as a reliable and safe technology—one that politicians and school teachers could ride. When the Challenger exploded, this myth exploded as well, creating a variety of stigmas: the public had been misled, management was wrong to think it was safe. Moreover, because of the biases we have identified, top management may be slow to recognize an emerging predicament and may even deny an event is a predicament.

In closing, we feel it is important to emphasize that there is much to organizational life that is more important than successful impression management or "spin control." Full and honest disclosures can have important benefits—especially in terms of long-term relationships among organizations and their constituencies. The goal of our analysis is not to suggest, therefore, that top management is better off misrepresenting an organization's accomplishments, avoiding responsibility for its problems, or concealing organizational blemishes. While any theory that addresses the efficacy of the symbolic and impression management processes may have implications for such strategic ends, we regard such aims to be outside the spirit of our work. Instead, we regard the conceptual framework presented here as useful in a more positive sense. As Pfeffer (1981, 1991) has argued, to be truly effective, managers must be adept at motivating, building commitment, maintaining morale, creating excitement about organizational goals, and creating visions of what the future can be. Thus, managers need to understand how to present favorable images through competent and acceptable accounts for their actions. Incompetence at doing so, we would add, can drain energy and resources, claiming top management's attention, detracting it from more important agendas and diverting its attention from important organizational goals.

Acknowledgments

We wish to thank Susan Ashford, Larry Cummings, Jane Dutton, Kimberly D. Elshach, D. Charles Galunic, Lisa Helich, Edward E. Jones, Boaz Keysar, Jeffery Pfeffer, and Barry Staw for their contributions to this essay. Preparation of this paper was supported by grants from the Dispute Resolution Research Center, Kellogg Graduate School of Management, Northwestern University, and the General Electric Foundation.

Notes

1. A notable exception is Weick (1979), who notes that top management's actions are often formulated in anticipation of the reaction of key organizational audiences. Along related lines, Biggart (1981) argues that management style is not unidirectional because subordinates actively respond to and may undermine a given style. And Ginzel (in press) makes a similar point regarding the reciprocal nature of feedback processes in social interactions.

2. Critics of the patriot missile, evaluating data released after the conclusion of the Persian Gulf conflict, asserted that in fact the missile had not been very effective at all. For example, Dr. Theodore Postel, a physicist and former Pentagon science advisor, published an article in *International Security*, a leading political science journal, that questioned the efficacy of the missiles. He claimed that the poorly designed Iranian SCUDS actually disintegrated in the dense atmosphere of their own accord. The Patriot missiles would rush upward toward this debris, firing their rockets and creating a huge fireball that in fact had little impact (*New York Times*, January 1, 1992, p. A8).

3. The use of the term accounts refers to *public* accounts provided by top management. Such accounts may differ from internal or private accounts made to trusted organizational insiders.

4. Most likely, simulating worst case scenarios would lead top management to engage in protective impression management strategies that derive from concerns over engendering disapproval and serve to forestall challenges from others (Arkin, 1981).

References

Alexander, C.N., Jr., & Knight, G.W. (1971). Situated identities and social psychological experimentation. *Sociometry, 34*, 65–82.

Arkin, R.M. (1981). Self-presentation styles. In J. T. Tedeschi (Ed.), *Impression management theory and social psychological research* (pp. 311–333). New York: Academic Press.

Ashforth, B.E., & Gibbs, B.W. (1990). The double-edge of organizational legitimation. *Organization Science, 1*, 177–194.

Bies, R.J. (1987). The predicament of injustice: The management of moral outrage. In L.L. Cummings & B.M. Staw (Eds.), *Research in organizational behavior* (Vol. 9, pp. 289–320). Greenwich, CT: JAI Press.

Biggart, N.W. (1981). Management style as strategic interaction: The case of Governor Ronald Reagan. *The Journal of Applied Behavioral Science, 17*, 291–308.

Bonazzi, G. (1983). Scapegoating in complex organizations: The results of a comparative study of symbolic blame-giving in Italian and French public administration. *Organization Studies, 4*, 1–18.

Brewer, M.B. (1979). In-group bias in the minimal intergroup situation: A cognitive-motivational analysis. *Psychological Bulletin, 86*, 307–324.

Brewer, M.B., Dull, V., & Lui, L. (1981). Perceptions of the elderly: Stereotypes as prototypes. *Journal of Personality and Social Psychology, 41,* 656–670.

Brown, J.D. (1986). Evaluations of self and others: Self-enhancement biases in social judgment. *Social Cognition, 4,* 353–376.

Byrne, J.A. (1990, October 29). The best B schools. *Business Week,* pp. 52–58.

Carroll, J.S. (1978). The effect of imagining an event on expectations for the event: An interpretation in terms of the availability heuristic. *Journal of Experimental Psychology: Human Learning and Memory, 14,* 88–96.

Chatman, J.A., Staw, B.M., & Bell, N.E. (1986). The managed thought: The role of self-justification and impression management in organizational settings. In H.P. Sims, D.A. Gioia, & Associates (Eds.), *The thinking organization: Dynamics of social cognition.* San Francisco, CA: Jossey-Bass.

Chen, C.C., & Meindl, J.R. (1991). The construction of leadership images in the popular press: The case of Donald Burr and People Express. *Administrative Science Quarterly, 36,* 521–551.

Cialdini, R.B., Borden, R.J., Thorne, A., Walker, M.R., Freeman, S., & Sloan, L.R. (1976). Basking in reflected glory: Three (football) field studies. *Journal of Personality and Social Psychology, 34,* 366–375.

Crocker, J. (1982). Biased questions in judgment of covariation studies. *Personality and Social Psychology Bulletin, 8,* 214–220.

Crumley, B. (1990, April). Fizzz went the crisis. *International Management, 45*(3), 52–53.

Dutton, J.E., & Dukerich, J.M. (1991). Keeping an eye on the mirror: The role of image and identity in organizational adaptation. *Academy of Management Journal, 34,* 517–554.

Dowling, J., & Pfeffer, J. (1975). Organizational legitimacy: Social values and organizational behavior. *Pacific Sociological Review, 18,* 122–136.

Elsbach, K.D., & Sutton, R.I. (1992). Enhancing organizational legitimacy through illegitimate actions: A marriage of institutional and impression management theory. *Academy of Management Journal, 35,* 699–738.

Emerson, S., & Duffy, B. (1990). *The fall of Pan Am 103: Inside the Lockerbie investigation.* New York: Putnam.

Fiske, S.T., & Taylor, S.E. (1991). *Social cognition* (2nd ed.). New York: McGraw-Hill.

Ford, J.D., & Bacus, D.A. (1987). Organizational adaptation to performance downturns: An interpretation-based perspective. *Academy of Management Review, 12,* 366–380.

Garcia, A. (1990, May/June). PR bloopers. *Communication World, 7*(6), 164–168.

Ginzel, L.E. (in press). The impact of biased inquiry strategies on performance judgments. *Organizational Behavior and Human Decision Processes.*

Goethals, G.R. (1986). Fabrication and ignoring social reality: Self-serving estimates of consensus. In J. Olsen, C.P. Herman, & M. Zanna (Eds.), *Relative deprivation in social comparison: The Ontario Symposium* (Vol. 4). Hillsdale, NJ: Erlbaum.

Goffman, E. (1959). *The presentation of self in everyday life.* Garden City, NY: Doubleday.

Gonzales, M.H., Pederson, J.H., Manning, D.J., & Wetter, D.W. (1990). Pardon my gaffe: Effects of sex, status, and consequence severity on accounts. *Journal of Personality and Social Psychology, 58,* 610–621.

Hamilton, D.L., Sherman, S.J., & Ruvolo, C.M. (1990). Stereotype-based expectancies: Effects on information processing and social behavior. *Journal of Social Issues, 46,* 35–60.

Hoch, S.J. (1984). Availability and interference in predictive judgment. *Journal of Experimental Psychology: Learning, Memory, and Cognition, 10,* 649–662.

Janis, I.L. (1983). *Groupthink* (2nd ed.). Boston, MA: Houghton Mifflin.

Janis, I.L. (1989). *Crucial decisions: Leadership in policymaking and crisis management.* New York: Free Press.

Jervis, R. (1976). *Perception and misperception in international politics.* Princeton, NJ: Princeton University Press.

Jones, E.E. (1964). *Ingratiation.* New York: Appleton-Century-Crofts.

Jones, E.E., & Nisbett, R.E. (1972). The actor and the observer: Divergent perceptions of the causes of behavior. In E.E. Jones, D. Kanouse, H.H. Kelley, R.E. Nisbett, S. Valins, & B. Weiner (Eds.), *Attribution: Perceiving the causes of behavior* (pp. 79–94). Morristown, NJ: General Learning Press.

Jones, E.E., & Wortman, C. (1973). *Ingratiation: An attributional approach.* Morristown, NJ: General Learning Press.

Kahn R.L., & Kramer, R.M. (1990). Untying the knot: Dynamics of deescalation of international conflicts. In R.L. Kahn & M. Zald (Eds.), *Nation-states and organizations.* San Francisco, CA: Jossey-Bass.

Kahn, R.L., & Wolfe, D. (1964). Role conflict in organizations. In R.L. Kahn & E. Boulding (Eds.), *Power and conflict in organizations.* New York: Basic Books.

Kahneman, D., & Tversky, A. (1982). The simulation heuristic. In D. Kahneman, P. Slovic, & A. Tversky (Eds.), *Judgment under uncertainty: Heuristics and biases.* Cambridge: Cambridge University Press.

Katz, D., & Kahn, R.L. (1978). *The social psychology of organizations* (2nd ed.). New York: Wiley.

Kramer, R.M. (1989). Windows of vulnerability or cognitive illusions? Cognitive processes and the nuclear arms race. *Journal of Experimental Social Psychology, 25,* 79–100.

Kramer, R.M., Meyerson, D., & Davis, G. (1991). How much is enough? Psychological components of "guns versus butter" decisions in a security dilemma. *Journal of Personality and Social Psychology, 58,* 984–993.

Kramer, R.M., Newton, E., & Pommerenke, P. (1991). Self-enhancement biases and negotiator judgment: Effects of self-esteem and mood. *Organizational Behavior and Human Decision Making.*

Langer, E.J. (1975). The illusion of control. *Journal of Personality and Social Psychology, 32,* 311–328.

Leary, M.R., & Kowalski, R.M. (1990). Impression management: A literature review and two-component model. *Psychological Bulletin, 107,* 34–47.

Lieberman, S. (1956). The effects of changes in roles on the attitudes of role occupants. *Human Relations, 2,* 385–402.

Linville, P., & Jones, E.E. (1980). Polarized appraisals of out-group members. *Journal of Personality and Social Psychology, 38,* 689–703.

Lukaszewski, J.E. (1989, Fall). How vulnerable are you? Lessons from Valdez. *Public Relations Quarterly, 34*(3), 5–6.

March, J.G., & Simon, H.A. (1958). *Organizations.* New York: Wiley.

Meindl, J.R. (1990). On leadership: An alternative to conventional wisdom. In B.M. Staw & L.L. Cummings (Eds.), *Research in organizational behavior* (Vol. 12, pp. 159–204). Greenwich, CT: JAI Press.

259

Messick, D.M., Bloom, S., Boldizer, J.P., & Samuelson, C.D. (1985). Why we are fairer than others? *Journal of Experimental Social Psychology, 21*, 480–500.

Messick, D.M., & Sentis, K.P. (1979). Fairness and preference. *Journal of Experimental Social Psychology, 15*, 418–434.

Meyer, J.W., & Rowan, B. (1977). Institutionalized organizations: Formal structure as myth and ceremony. *American Journal of Sociology, 83*, 340–363.

Nelson-Horchler, J. (1986, October 13). Advent of crisis teams. *Industry Week, 231*, 20–21.

Nulty, P. (1990, April 23). Exxon's problems: Not what you think. *Fortune, 121*(9), 202–224.

Pfeffer, J. (1981). Management as symbolic action. In L.L. Cummings & B.M. Staw (Eds.), *Research in organizational behavior* (Vol. 3, pp. 1–52). Greenwich, CT: JAI Press.

Pfeffer, J., & Salancik, G.R. (1978). *The external control of organizations: A resource dependence perspective.* New York: Harper & Row.

Pick, G. (1986, July/August). Gerber's baby under stress. *Across the Board, 23*(7/8), 9–13.

Pruitt, D.G., & Rubin, J.Z. (1986). *Social conflict.* New York: Random House.

Ross, L. (1977). The intuitive psychologist and his shortcomings: Distortions in the attribution process. In L. Berkowitz (Ed.), *Advances in experimental social psychology* (Vol. 10). New York: Academic Press.

Ross, L., Greene, D., & House, P. (1977). The "false consensus effect": An egocentric bias in social-perception and attribution processes. *Journal of Experimental Social Psychology, 13*, 279–301.

Rudnitsky, H. (1989, November 27). Good timing, Charlie. *Forbes, 144*(12), 140–144.

Salancik, G.R., & Meindl, J.R. (1984). Corporate attributions as strategic illusions of management control. *Administrative Science Quarterly, 29*, 238–254.

Schlenker, B.R. (1980). *Impression management.* Monterey, CA: Books/Cole.

Schonbach, P. (1980). A category system for account phases. *European Journal of Social Psychology, 10*, 195–200.

Scott, M.B., & Lyman, S.M. (1968). Accounts. *American Sociological Review, 23*, 46–62.

Seligman, M.G.P. (1975). *Helplessness: On depression, development and death.* San Francisco, CA: W.H. Freeman.

Sherman, S.J., Cialdini, R., Schwartzman, S., & Reynolds, P. (1985). Imagining can heighten or lower the perceived likelihood of contracting a disease: The mediating effect of ease of imagery. *Personality and Social Psychology Bulletin, 11*, 118–127.

Sick, G. (1985). *All fall down: America's tragic encounter with Iran.* New York: Penguin.

Simon, R. (1991). *Roadshow.* Beverly Hills, CA: Morrow.

Smart, T. (1990, September 10). Nabbing the S&L crooks. *Business Week*, pp. 84–86.

Snyder, L., & Foster, L. G. (1983). An anniversary review and critique: The Tylenol crisis. *Public Relations Review, 2*(3), 24–34.

Staw, B.M., McKechnie, P.I., & Puffer, S.M. (1983). The justification of organizational performance. *American Science Quarterly, 28*, 582–600.

Sutton, R.I., & Callahan, A.L. (1987). The stigma of bankruptcy: Spoiled organizational image and its management. *Academy of Management Journal, 30*, 405–436.

Sutton, R.I., & Kramer, R.M. (1990). Transforming failure into success: Impression management, the Reagan administration, and the Iceland arms control talks. In R.L. Kahn & M. Zald (Eds.), *Nation-states and organizations.* San Francisco, CA: Jossey-Bass.

Sutton, R.I., Eisenhardt, K.M., & Jucker, J.V. (1986). Managing organizational decline: Lessons from Atari. *Organizational Dynamics, 14*, 17–29.

Taylor, S.E. (1989). *Positive illusions: Creative self-deception and the healthy mind.* New York: Basic Books.

Taylor, S.E., & Brown, J.D. (1988). Illusion and well-being: A social psychological perspective on mental health. *Psychological Bulletin, 103*, 193–210.

Tedeschi, J.T., & Riess, M. (1981). Identities, the phenomenal self, and laboratory research. In J.T. Tedeschi (Ed.), *Impression management theory and social psychological research* (pp. 3–22). New York: Academic Press.

Tversky, A., & Kahneman, D. (1973). Availability: A heuristic for judging frequency and probability. *Cognitive Psychology, 5*, 207–232.

Tyler, T., & Hastie, R. (1991). The social consequences of positive illusions. In R. Lewicki, M. Bazerman, & B. Sheppard (Eds.), *Research on negotiations in organizations* (Vol. 3). Greenwich, CT: JAI Press.

Weick, K.E. (1979). Cognitive processes in organizations. In B.M. Staw (Ed.), *Research in organizational behavior* (Vol. 1, pp. 41–74). Greenwich, CT: JAI Press.

Weick, K.E., & Daft, R.L. (1983). The effectiveness of interpretation systems. In K.S. Cameron & D.A. Whetten (Eds.), *Organizational effectiveness: A comparison of multiple models* (pp. 71–93). New York: Academic Press.

Weinstein, N.D. (1980). Unrealistic optimism about future life events. *Journal of Personality and Social Psychology, 39*, 806–820.

III. RECENT DEVELOPMENTS IN ORGANIZATIONAL IDENTITY THEORY

Introduction to Part III

Recent Developments and Emerging Themes

....

We have organized the articles in Part III according to four central themes that have emerged in recent academic research on organizational identity: multiple identities, stability and change in organizational identity, managing and controlling identity, and communicating identity. These themes give some sense of the diversity that has grown within the organizational identity field since its inception, mostly as the result of importing influential ideas from the fields of literary, critical and cultural studies, and drawing more generally from post-structural and postmodern philosophy. Although this diversity makes the articles in Part III more challenging to read, in our minds it is important to include them because they considerably expand the theoretical underpinnings of organizational identity research and promise a rich future for the field. In the following subsections we introduce you to each of the themes and to articles that contributed to defining them.

....

Theme 1: Multiple Identities

One aspect of the early conceptualization of organizational identity that was subsequently challenged is the notion that identity is shared among all organizational members. The articles by Pratt and Rafaeli and by Rao and Golden Biddle offer insight into how identity unfolds through the manifestation of multiple layers or dimensions in the definitions members of the same organization give when they define who they are. Although each article refers to a different organizational issue (dress codes versus corporate governance) and relies upon different theoretical frameworks (symbolism versus impression management), both are based in rich qualitative studies that show the multiplicity of identity in its sense-making and self-categorizing processes.

Michael G. Pratt and Anat Rafaeli: "Organizational Dress as a Symbol of Multilayered Social Identities" (1997)

(*Academy of Management Journal*, vol. 40, pp. 862–98)

Pratt and Rafaeli studied a hospital rehabilitation unit where a debate on what kind of dress to wear (street wear or scrubs) revealed the multiplicity of interpretations various subgroups in the hospital associated with these alternative dress codes. Their article provided empirical evidence of multiple identities in organizations, and explained how organizational identity is connected to organizational culture through its expression in organizational symbols (in this case, dress). Following Tajfel and Turner, and Ashford and Mael, these researchers defined social identity as "self-categorizations that individuals use to denote their sense of belonging," but emphasized how such self-categorizations are embedded in cultural assumptions and values using the self-defining symbol of organizational dress to reveal the multiple layers of meaning they claimed are inherent in social identity. Building on Albert and Whetten's notion of hybrid identities, Pratt and Rafaeli exposed the tension between the local hospital subunit and more universal professional identities that lay behind the debate over which dress code to follow in the hospital rehabilitation unit.

Karen Golden-Biddle and Hayagreeva Rao: "Breaches in the Boardroom: Organizational Identity and Conflicts of Commitment in a Nonprofit Organization" (1997)

(*Organization Science*, vol. 8, pp. 593–609)

This article offered another empirical study of how identity construction processes influence organizational action, thus be sure to compare it to the other case studies in this reader by Dutton and Dukerich (Part II) and Pratt and Rafaeli (Part III.i). In this study Golden-Biddle and Rao offered a description of how organizational identity was threatened, repaired, and preserved in a series of organizational actions that involved top management and the board of directors of a large nonprofit organization, thus this article addressed how organizational identity is related to corporate governance. In their depiction of the organizational process by which identity was threatened, the authors drew on Goffman's theatrical distinction between frontstage and backstage. Similar to

Pratt and Rafaeli, the authors addressed conflicting and multiple constructions of identity within an organizational setting. Using the concept of holographic hybrid identities, originally suggested by Albert and Whetten, Golden-Biddle and Rao analyzed the tensions between a volunteer-driven board identity and an identity of family and friends working together in a nonprofit organization. The case further shows how individual and organizational identities are interconnected through processes of identification.

Theme 2: Stability and Change in Organizational Identity

The two articles on stability and change present the case for seeing identity as a dynamic process rather than a static construct. The first article explicitly challenges Albert and Whetten's definition of identity as enduring by linking identity to organizational change. The second describes organizational identity as a set of interrelated processes (expressing, impressing, mirroring, and reflecting) through which both organizational culture and images influence organizational identity, and vice versa. The processes presented in this second paper depict organizational identity as dynamic, yet capable of offering an organization and its audiences a sense of stability. Although both articles are theoretical, they present a number of implications for future empirical research and for managerial practice.

Dennis A. Gioia, Majken Schultz, and Kevin Corley: "Organizational Identity, Image and Adaptive Instability" (2000)

(*Academy of Management Review*, vol. 25, pp. 63–82)
Gioia, Schultz, and Corley presented a challenge to Albert and Whetten's (Part I) definition of identity as enduring, arguing instead that identity is instable and adaptive. These authors argued that, because organizations often use the same labels to describe who they are for decades, their identities may not always appear to be changing. However, organizational identity does change due to the fact that the meanings and interpretations of the labels used to describe identity shift over time (e.g. what it means to be a "technology company" today may mean something different than it did in the past or what it will mean in the future). The authors claimed that these shifts in interpretations allow organizations to adapt to ever-shifting environments, while still

preserving a stable sense of self; a state that these authors refer to as "adaptive instability." They also claimed that organizational images are becoming increasingly fluid in postindustrial society, which creates a much more unstable condition for the construction of identity by forcing organizations to adapt their identities to always fluctuating external perceptions and expectations. Based in an elaboration of the many different applications of the image concept (such as those proposed by Dutton and Dukerich and Alvesson, Part II), the authors showed how the interdependencies between identity and image trigger comparison processes (as suggested by Tajfel and Turner, Part I) between variations of "who we think we are" and "who they think we are," leaving the organization with different ways of responding, such as seeking to change organizational identity based on transient impressions. The authors discussed the limitations of identity adaptation, arguing that although the construction processes of both identity and image become increasingly interdependent, they each maintain a core of independence.

Mary Jo Hatch and Majken Schultz: "The Dynamics of Organizational Identity" (2002)

(*Human Relations*, vol. 55, pp. 989–1019)
In "The dynamics of organizational identity" Hatch and Schultz followed Cooley and Mead (both in Part I), each of whom argued that self identity emerges from a process involving (1) how others see you (Mead called this the "me") and (2) who you know yourself to be (Mead called this the "I"). Hatch and Schultz proposed organizational analogies to Mead's "I" (organizational culture) and "me" (organizational images). Thus this article offers a model of organizational identity as emerging from processes in which organizational culture and stakeholder images play influential roles. Hatch and Schultz defined the processes linking identity to image as mirroring (based on Dutton and Dukerich, Part II) and impressing (based on Goffman's impression management, Part I), and those linking identity to culture as reflecting and expressing. Because these processes are mutually influential and ongoing, the Hatch and Schultz model can account for both stability and change. They then demonstrated the application of their model by diagnosing two dysfunctional identity dynamics—organizational narcissism and hyper-adaptation—in terms of disjunctions among the four processes. Be sure to notice the similarities between organization narcissism and Schwartz's notion of the organization ideal (Part II) and Cheney and Christensen's organizational self-seduction (Part III.iv). Their discussion of hyper-adaptation offers an explanation for Alveson's image over substance view of identity (Part II).

Theme 3: Identity as Narrative and Discourse

Both articles in this part draw upon literary theory and poststructuralist philosophy to argue that identity, whether individual or collective, is constructed through narrative or discourse. The narrative character of identities is rooted in the extent to which language is used to construct meaning, both for the self and for others. Over time, the use of language to construct identities forges discourses (think of continuing conversations in which people float in and out of the ongoing discussion) and the discourses can take on a life of their own that feeds back on the identities that are thereby constructed. Thus, both articles also draw upon a key idea from critical theory—that, rather than defining their own identity, organizational members are defined by the identities that management or organizational audiences construct for them.

Barbara Czarniawska: "Narratives of Individual and Organizational Identities" (1997)

(*Communication Yearbook*, vol. 17, pp. 193–221)
In the 1990's, public sector organizations throughout the Western world were suffering a loss of legitimacy in the face of growing concerns over inefficiencies and ineffectiveness in their managerial practices. Sweden suffered more than most due to the iconic stature of the Swedish model of welfare. In her article "Narratives of Individual and Organizational Identity" Czarniawska analyzed the responses of Sweden's public sector organizations to pressure to emulate the efficiencies of business management practices (the much lauded "enterprise culture" hoisted upon the public sector by well-meaning European governments), which she interpreted as threats to their organizational identity. Based on longitudinal studies conducted in several public sector organizations in Sweden, Czarniawska showed how identity unfolds through narrative processes "emerging from interactions between actors." According to Czarniawska, identity is a "continuous process of narration where both the narrator and audience formulate, edit, applaud and refuse various elements of the ever-produced narrative." Using empirical examples, she showed how identity is constituted and challenged through the uses of stories in an environment in which public organizations, consultants, media, and citizens interacted in the search for a new identity for the Swedish public sector. In presenting a case of organizational responses to external identity threats, her study parallels those of Dutton and Dukerich (Part II) and Elsbach and Kramer (Part III.iv), however she extended their conclusions when she presented the dynamics of modern identity in the definitions

and redefinitions that openness, differentiation, reflexivity, and individuality bring, a view complemented by Hatch and Schultz's model of organizational identity dynamics (Part III.ii).

Organizational Control Producing the "Appropriate Individual" (2002)

(*Journal of Management Studies*, vol. 39, pp. 619–44)
In their article, Alvesson and Wilmott revealed the ways that managers use culture to form and transform identity in organizations through "identity regulation," that is, acts that define the person, their morals and values, knowledge and skills; group categorizations; rules of the game; and the social construction of the organizational context. According to these authors, managerial attempts to regulate identity are accomplished through discursive practices. They emphasized the sophistication of managers who use these discursive practices to influence worker's sense of self through the "identity work" that all employees engage in when they use organizationally influenced narratives to form, repair, maintain, strengthen, or revise their sense of self. But the authors also argued that the concept of identity could be used to encourage an emancipatory use of the same social control processes. Although Alvesson and Wilmott's primary target was how identity regulation serves oppressive ends in organizations, they also considered how the regulation process could be used to liberate individuals who work in new flat, flexible, and decentralized organizations. They claimed that these new organizational forms provide "a space for micro-emancipation" by allowing employees to redefine work, skills, and organizational values for their own purposes.

Theme 4: Audiences for Identity

The concept of organizational identity has often been conjoined with issues of communication management by students of impression management and researchers interested in the effects of the media on organizations. The first of these two articles considers the effects of ranking systems on the organizations that are subject to these comparisons and how threats from being ranked poorly or well effect organizational member's perceptions of their organization's identity. The second examines the effects of organizational attempts to influence the attitudes of others and how these efforts simultaneously influence organizational members.

Kimberly D. Elsbach and Roderick M. Kramer: "Members' Responses to Organizational Identity Threats: Encountering and Countering the Business Week Rankings" (1996)

Elsbach and Kramer studied responses by members of eight US business schools to perceived identity threats presented by *Business Week* magazine's rankings of top 20 US business schools. As such, their study presented empirical evidence concerning the effects of organizational audiences (in their case, the media and the publics it is presumed to influence) have on how organizational members perceive the identity of their organizations and represent it to others in order to manage their impressions. Their study is an empirical application of the ideas about organizational identity threats presented by Ginzel, Kramer, and Sutton and about social identity theory presented by Ashforth and Mael (both from Part II). These researchers found that members of all the business schools they sampled perceived the rankings as threatening and defined two dimensions of the perceived threat. The first was the threat to how members defined their organization's core, distinctive, and enduring qualities—*Business Week's* reliance on student and recruiter opinions challenged traditional definitions of identity rooted in the schools' reputations for research. The second was the threat posed by pinpointing a school's position in a presumed status hierarchy (*Business Week* gave each school an explicit positional ranking vis-à-vis other top 20 schools that violated many of their previous claims about their relative position in the hierarchy of top schools). Elsbach and Kramer found that the members of ranked schools tended to respond to the perceived threat of being ranked either by emphasizing aspects of their identity that were not measured by *Business Week,* magazine's ranking system (e.g. research excellence, diverse student body) or by selective categorization within the *Business Week* system (e.g. we did well for a public school amidst so many better-funded private schools). This article reveals the cognitive dynamics that occur between organizational members and organizational audiences in the shaping of organizational identity.

George Cheney and Lars T. Christensen: "Organizational Identity: Linkages Between Internal and External Communication" (2001)

(*New Handbook of Organizational Communication,* 231–58, 262–9)
In their article, Cheney and Christensen argued that the distinction between identity and image is disappearing due to the overlapping practices of internal and external communication, such as using media-based advertising to influence

271

employees via internal marketing. These authors contend that, although organizations that adopt these practices continue to claim they are communicating to their external constituencies, they are more likely to be communicating largely to themselves, a practice communication scholars refer to as auto-communication. The theory these authors proposed is that auto-communication reconfirms organizational self-definitions (identity) and thus reproduces internally the images of how managers would like their organizations to be perceived by outsiders without any real dialogue with those outside the organization. The authors claimed that the problem of auto-communication further challenges managers who are expected to communicate their organization's identity within an increasingly crowded communication environment in which fewer and fewer people are listening. Cheney and Christensen argued that organizations are concerned with the preservation of their sense of self and that the discursive and rhetorical definitions of "outsiders" and their perceptions of the organization are inscribed within the organization's own universe of meaning and thus become extensions of the self rather than feeding into external adaptation processes. In their view, what is "out there" only reflects what is "in here," which is what makes identity construction a self-referential (auto-communicative) process.

III.i. MULTIPLE IDENTITIES

12 Organizational Dress as a Symbol of Multilayered Social Identities

Michael G. Pratt and Anat Rafaeli

Patients who wear pajamas, and see hospital garb around them think of themselves as sick. If *they and their caretakers wear street clothes*, patients will think of themselves as moving out of the sick role, and into rehabilitation. They will be ready for life outside the hospital. This is the rehab philosophy, and this is what makes this unit unique.

> Head nurse of a rehabilitation unit; emphasis ours

We are medical and health professionals. We do professional work. We take care of sick patients, we deal with their bodily fluids, and get their slime all over us. So we should all look like medical professionals, *we should be dressed in scrubs*.

> Nurse on the evening shift of the same unit; emphasis ours

These two women both work on the same hospital rehabilitation (rehab) unit. Yet their portrayals of who they are and whom they care for are as dramatically different as the dress each proposes to wear. In this article, we focus on the role that dress served for members of this organization. We argue that these descriptions of "appropriate" attire were not incidental; rather, our analysis suggests that dress served as a symbol that facilitated the organization and discussion of multiple issues relating to a central question: Who are we as nurses on this unit? That is, dress served as a convenient and useful window allowing members of the organization to look at the multiple and competing *social identities* inherent to their organization (Albert & Whetten, 1985; Dutton & Dukerich, 1991; Tajfel & Turner, 1985). Social identities, broadly defined, refer to those self-categorizations that individuals use to denote their sense of belonging (i.e., identification) with particular human aggregates, or groups (Ashforth & Mael, 1989; Tajfel & Turner, 1985). Social identities help individuals answer the question, Who am I?, by delineating the social groups in which they are members.

Building on an in-depth case study of a debate about organizational dress, in this article we develop the thesis that the symbol of dress, in itself vivid, visible, yet seemingly simple, offers a useful and accessible medium for disclosing conflicting organizational issues that are less easily grasped or discussed. Specifically, dress will be shown to serve as a convenient medium for representing competing perceptions of two social identities. Conversations about the differences regarding these identities, we argue, were avoided because they were stressful and arduous to sort through. A focus on dress, however, made the process of negotiating and navigating these multifaceted, or "hybrid" (Albert & Whetten, 1985), identities more manageable. The debate about the appropriateness of each form of dress therefore facilitated the conversation about issues innate to the social identity of the nurses on the unit. These issues included why the nurses were there (their mission), whom they served (their clients), what services they provided (their roles), how they were to be seen in the medical hierarchy (their status), and who should be making key decisions regarding the organization (decision making).

These findings are explained and elaborated in the latter part of this article. We begin, however, by briefly outlining the theoretical edifice upon which our analysis is built. Specifically, we provide an overview of current theory and research on symbols in organizations, especially as they relate to organizational dress, and we review what is known about the relationship between symbols and the concepts of culture and social identity. The report of our methods and findings in the latter part of the article then illustrates and supports the thesis *that conflicts over dress can symbolize and help negotiate a complex set of issues that represent multiple and conflicting social identities.*

Theoretical Background

Organizational Symbolism, Organizational Identity, and Organizational Dress

Scholars in a variety of disciplines, including anthropology, sociology, psychology, and the humanities, have contributed to the long intellectual history of the study of symbols (Geertz, 1973; Goffman, 1959; Linstead & Grafton-Small, 1992; Manning, 1987). In this body of literature, the term "symbol" has included any "thing" (an event, object, relationship, etc.) that conveys meaning. A more recent stream of research has adopted a narrower focus on the role of symbols in creating and maintaining meanings in organizations (cf. Dandridge, 1983; Dandridge, Mitroff, & Joyce, 1980; Ornstein, 1986; Pfeffer, 1981a; Pondy,

Frost, Morgan, & Dandridge, 1983; Rosen, 1985; Trice & Beyer, 1984, 1993). This stream of research, known as the study of organizational symbolism, encompasses examinations of artifacts, language, metaphors, dramaturgy, rites and rituals, stories, and myths (cf. Abravanel, 1983; Clark, 1972; Martin, Feldman, Hatch, & Sitkin, 1983; Mitroff & Kilmann, 1976; Pondy, 1983; Smircich, 1983; Trice & Beyer, 1984, 1993).

Trice and Beyer (1993: 86) attempted to disentangle the various meanings of the term and suggested that organizational symbols are specific "cultural forms" that are distinct from organizational language, narratives, and practices. They further proposed that there are three distinct types of symbols: objects, settings, and performers. Using this typology, we focus in this article on *object symbols*. Trice and Beyer specifically emphasized that object symbols are context specific, which implies that the meaning of a symbol depends on the context in which it appears. The meaning of a symbol within one organization, therefore, may differ from its meaning in a different organization or at a different place or time in the same organization.

Researchers have proposed that organizational culture is often the context in which the meaning of a symbol is "enacted," because culture defines the shared frame of reference that typifies organizations and guides members' perceptions and behavior (Bate, 1990; D'Andrade, 1984; Louis, 1983; Schein, 1985; Trice & Beyer, 1993). The literature on organizational culture suggests two dynamics that relate organizational symbols and culture. To begin, symbols have been argued to be cultural forms, or vehicles, for the enactment of an organizational culture. At the same time, cultures are argued to be the assumptions, or the frames, that determine the meaning of symbols (cf. Dandridge et al., 1980; Ornstein, 1986; Pfeffer, 1981a; Pondy et al., 1983; Rosen, 1985). Schein (1990), for example, referred to tangible object symbols, or "artifacts," as the first "level" of culture (cf. Hatch, 1993).

Past researchers addressing the symbol of organizational dress have viewed dress as a symbol of a concept related to an organization's culture: organizational identity[1] (e.g., Rafaeli & Pratt, 1993). According to Hatch (1993), organizational identity beliefs are grounded in cultural assumptions and values, but they specifically involve only those characteristics that are seen as self-defining. That is, dress as a symbol can be expected to reflect those organizational characteristics that refer to the question, Who am I?, or those characteristics that are believed to be central, enduring, and distinct (Albert & Whetten, 1985; Ashforth & Mael, 1996; Dutton & Dukerich, 1991; Dutton, Dukerich, & Harquail, 1994). However, others have argued that dress and other symbols symbolize different social identities, such as professional or gender identities (Davis, 1992; Pratt & Dutton, 1996). What is therefore unclear is how multiple identities play out in the context of one symbol in one organizational setting.

Michael G. Pratt and Anat Rafaeli

Dress and Its Organizational Functions: A Brief Review

Although recent treatments of organizational dress have often been relegated to discussions about "dressing for success" (cf. Cho & Grover, 1978; Levitt, 1981; Molloy, 1975, 1977; Solomon, 1986, 1987; Solomon & Douglas, 1983), the study of dress and its role in corporate and other social organizations has a long and distinguished history (cf. Becker, Greer, Hughes, & Strauss, 1961; Goffman, 1959; Simmel, 1971; Singer, Brush, & Lublin, 1965; Stone, 1962; Veblen, 1899). Organizational dress comprises the clothing (e.g., jacket, skirt, pants) and artifacts (e.g., name tag, smock, jewelry) that employees of an organization wear while at work (Rafaeli & Pratt, 1993). As Rafaeli and Pratt (1993) noted in their review of the meaning and impact of this symbol, organizational dress serves two key functions: it asserts control, and it conveys identity (cf. Davis, 1992; de Marley, 1986; Forsythe, 1990; Forsythe, Drake, & Cox, 1985; Fussell, 1983; Joseph, 1986; Joseph & Alex, 1972; Lurie, 1981; Ribeiro, 1986; Roach-Higgins & Eicher, 1992; Solomon & Douglas, 1987; Squire, 1974).

First, organizational dress is a *mechanism* for asserting organizational control (Joseph, 1986; Lurie, 1981). Thus, issues of organizational versus individual control often underlie issues of dress. As Lurie stated, individual control is usurped any time an organization dictates an individual's dress: "No matter what sort of uniform it is—military, civil, or religious... to put on such livery is to give up one's right to act as an individual.... What one does, as well as what one wears, will be determined by external authorities" (1981: 18).

Hochschild's (1983) work on flight attendants, Kanter's (1972) work on communes, and Joseph's (1986) work on uniforms additionally indicate a connection between strong organizational control over dress codes (e.g., through uniforms) and members' increased compliance with a wide range of organizational rules. Rafaeli and Pratt (1993) attempted to explain the link between control over dress and member compliance by drawing upon theories of "deindividuation," role theory, and cognitive dissonance. They concluded that compliance can be obtained by making all members dress similarly or conspicuously, in a way that is markedly different from how non-members dress. To illustrate, the conspicuous dress of medical professionals has long been used to reveal hierarchical distinctions and to enforce control. Becker and colleagues vividly described this process: "On their very first day medical students put on white, the color symbolic of modern medicine. For the rest of their lives they will spend a good many hours of every day among people who wear uniforms, more often white than not, which tell the place of each in the complicated division of work and the ranking system of the medical world" (1961: 4). These associations between attire and control are taught to medical professionals through formal and informal means at very early stages of their medical socialization (Becker et al., 1961; Janowski, 1984).

Our study continues this research on dress and control by illustrating how a debate about what to wear revealed a power struggle on the unit that was this study's setting. However, instead of taking a solely managerial perspective and focusing on how managers manipulate dress to increase compliance, we examined how both managers and employees attempted to assert control in an organization by advocating a particular dress code. We also illustrate how acceptance of a particular dress code conveyed more than simple adherence to organizational rules, by showing how a debate about dress symbolized a conflict over social identities.

Second, and perhaps better documented, dress is a powerful symbol of the core and distinctive values and beliefs of an organization (Becker et al., 1961; Cialdini, Borden, Thorne, Walker, Freeman, & Sloan, 1976; Davis, 1992; Fussell, 1983; Goffman, 1959; Hall, Lamb, & Perlmutter, 1982; Joseph, 1986; Lurie, 1981; Solomon & Douglas, 1983, 1987). This assertion has been supported both in the popular press and in theory and research on organizational culture and symbolism (cf. Trice & Beyer, 1993).

There are also strong connections between dress and core aspects of various professions (cf. Abbott, 1988; Campbell-Heider & Hart, 1993), especially medical professions. Becker, Greer, Hughes, and Strauss (1961) and others have noted that medical professionals adopt and endorse white uniforms because white represents cleanliness and sterility. Similarly, Bishop suggested that medical professionals have donned distinctive dress for centuries: "There is abundant evidence to show that the costume of the physician in the past has been, generally speaking, of such a distinctive character as to proclaim its wearer as a follower of the healing art. This peculiarity of costume dates back to the time when the roles of the magician, of the priest, and of the physician were united" (1934: 193).

The attire of nurses has been a particularly powerful symbol of their professional identity. As Siegel noted: "The uniformed appearance of the nurse has become so interwoven with her identity that it is probably difficult, if not impossible, for anyone to conceptualize 'nurse' without automatically including her symbolic attire" (1968: 314).

The attire traditionally associated with nurses is a white uniform with a white cap, an outfit reminiscent of the "Nightingale era" (Siegel, 1968). The most distinctive part of nurses' uniforms has been their color: white. According to Siegel, this color symbolizes many meanings, including "purity, meticulousness, crispness, glamour, serenity, efficiency, sterility, fear, coldness, comfort, confidence, science, laboratory, health, illness, emergency, surgery, isolation, and so forth" (1968: 315). The styles of these uniforms have tended to be conservative and functional (for instance, they have large pockets for carrying supplies and well-tailored sleeves that will not dip into patients' food), and they are made of durable fabrics that withstand several washings (cf. Nerone, 1986; Siegel, 1968).

Traditional nursing uniforms have also tended to be both homogeneous and conspicuous. In other words, all nurses wore similar attire, and they wore attire that clearly distinguished them from those who were not nurses (cf. Rafaeli & Pratt, 1993). Today, however, nursing attire is neither homogeneous nor conspicuous. Although many nurses continue to wear white uniforms, there has been, since the beginning of the 1960s, a trend against the exclusive use of traditional whites. Nurses may now be found wearing a variety of medical and other attire while at work, including surgical scrubs, lab coats, colored smocks and tunics, and even street clothes (cf. Gardner & Simkins, 1976; Janowski, 1984; Pisker & Vigiano, 1988; Siegel, 1968; Stubbs, Buckle, Hudson, Butler, & Rivers, 1985). Street clothes, in particular, are often worn in pediatric, psychiatric, and rehabilitation units (Gardner & Simkins, 1976; Goodstein, 1981; Lavender, 1987; Petrovich, Bennet, & Jackson, 1968; Pisker & Vigiano, 1988; Trauer & Moss, 1960).[2]

As the quotes that open this article suggest, different participants in the present study saw dress as symbolizing different and sometimes conflicting social identities. Our data suggest that such disagreements were inherent to the organization we studied. In light of such data, we view this study as extending previous work that implies a connection between dress and core organizational values in three ways. First, we explicitly argue that dress serves as a key symbol not only of core values, but also of the more fundamental notion of organizational identity. In the emerging stream of research on the topic of organizational identity (Albert & Whetten, 1985; Ashforth & Mael, 1996; Dutton & Dukerich, 1991), there is little work on how identity is represented through organizational symbols such as dress. Our focus on object symbols can be contrasted with the focus in other explorations of identity on *substantive management* (Ashforth & Mael, 1996). The latter examine the interplay between identity and strategic managerial action, such as the adoption of new technologies, routines, or public policies (cf. Dutton & Dukerich, 1991).

Second, we offer *empirical* insights about identity theorists' claims that organizations can consist of multiple and sometimes competing identities (Albert & Whetten, 1985; Ashforth & Mael, 1996). There are recent claims in the organizational culture literature that cultures can be viewed as differentiated or fragmented (Martin, 1992; Meyerson & Martin, 1987); similarly, there is growing recognition among identity researchers that organizations and their members can have differentiated[3] (Albert & Whetten, 1985), nested (Feldman, 1979), or fragmented identities (Pratt, 1994). However, despite theoretical claims about multiple identities, empirical research on organizational identity still tends to treat it as a unified phenomenon (see, for instance, Martin's [1992] integration perspective on culture). That is, researchers have advocated a monolithic view of organizational identity (Albert & Whetten, 1985).

Similarly, there is scant theoretical or empirical research on the impact of the existence of conflicting identities within organizations. Some researchers have suggested that members may react to such contradictions with ambivalence (Ashforth & Mael, 1996; Pratt, 1993), but the present study examined more broadly the "identity negotiation" process (cf. Swann, 1987). By studying discussions and debates about dress, we gained unique insights into how members recognize and cope with competing identities.

Third, our article broadens discussions of identity in organizations to include professional identities (Abbott, 1988, 1993; O'Connor & Lanning, 1992; Pratt & Dutton, 1996; Trice, 1996; Van Maanen & Barley, 1984). In the study described below, we showed how discussions about competing forms of dress made manifest the multiple and conflicting professional and organizational identities that coexisted in the organization we studied. Our findings suggest that dress can be a useful vehicle for representing and negotiating a complex web of identity-related issues that together identify a member of an organization.

Methods

We were invited to conduct this study by a manager who was trying to decide what her employees should wear. Our collection of data was motivated by our interest in organizational dress. Yet what we found ourselves talking about was various facets of identity. To facilitate our understanding of the dynamics of dress and identity in the context we were studying, in our data collection we sought information about both the context and the perspectives of multiple constituents within this context on dress in the organization.

The Context: Rehabilitation Medical Care

The study took place in the rehabilitation unit of a large midwestern university hospital. The unit has 24 beds, all of which were occupied throughout the study. It employs 35 registered nurses (RNs) and 6 physicians full-time. Approximately 60 other professionals also come in contact with the patients and staff of the unit, including physical therapists, social workers, and administrative clerks. The same head nurse has been the unit's formal manager for 17 years. During the 8 years preceding the study, this head nurse had performed only managerial duties and had not worked directly with patients. The management staff of the unit includes an assistant head nurse and an education specialist, who also perform little or no actual patient care. Decision making on the unit is highly centralized.

Technically, rehabilitation begins when other forms of medical care have ended: its goal is to help patients adapt to independent life *after* having completed medical treatments. Thus, all patients in the unit had received medical treatments in another part of the hospital, had been pronounced medically stable, and were assumed ready for rehabilitation care. Rehabilitation is considered the responsibility of groups of professionals known as "rehab teams" (Stavros & Lyden, 1988). Each patient on the rehabilitation unit we observed is assigned such a team, which can include a doctor, a nurse, a psychologist, a social worker, an occupational therapist, a physical therapist, a dietitian, and the patient and his or her immediate family. The professionals in a particular patient's team are determined according to his or her medical problem and condition.

Patients' time on the unit is spent in one of two modes: interaction with various members of the rehabilitation team, which typically occurs in the mornings, and rehabilitation education and routine health care procedures such as baths and bowel programs, which typically occur in the evening. Nurses on the unit work in three shifts known as the day, evening, and night shifts. Each shift has 5–6 nurses with degrees, 2–3 practical nurses,[4] and a charge nurse who directs the operations of the shift. Nurses tend to work fixed shifts, moving infrequently. To illustrate, the charge nurse of the evening shift had been working evenings for 13 years prior to the study. Nurses on the unit play multiple roles. They act as teachers and consultants when they help patients implement the various rehabilitation strategies prescribed by the rehabilitation teams. But they also act as providers of medical care, like other nurses, when they give patients medication or help with bowel programs. Thus, like clinical social workers, rehabilitation nurses perform both a medical role and a social work role (Meyerson, 1994).

At the time of our study, the unit was experiencing various tensions emanating from both internal and external sources. A long, heated, hospital-wide strike by nurses had strained relations between nurses and hospital management. The strike had caused many nurses to leave the organization, so staffing was low. In addition, the unit was faced with an increase in the number of patients who required traditional acute medical care.[5] Thus, a relatively small number of licensed staff members had to treat a large number of acutely ill patients. Consequently, the unit had hired a large number of nonlicensed and temporary nurses.

Latent and more permanent tensions also accompanied the work of nurses on the unit. Specifically, nurses had to subordinate themselves to physicians, although the latter were sometimes less experienced than the nurses were and often met with patients less frequently.[6] A social worker described these frustrations:

Our nurses, in many cases, are in a position to know better what should go on with a patient than some of the young doctors. I saw that happens just recently. Two young women, one was a doctor and one was a nurse, disagreed at rounds about medications for the patients. The nurse in question had many years of experience and she has great confidence in her ability and so do we. The doctor has no experience on the services and lots and lots of education. The determination went to the doctor. Nobody was surprised. It's got to be really frustrating for the nurses... nurses often get squeezed out.

Nurses on the unit wore street clothes before and during this study, in accordance with a dress code established by the head nurse 14 years earlier (in 1975). Our study followed the course of a debate in the unit about changing this dress code. The debate was triggered by a sign that appeared in the nurses' lounge one evening. This sign asked each nurse to indicate her attitude about changing the dress code to scrubs. This sign disappeared three or four days after it was posted.[7] However, its mere appearance sparked a debate about changing nurses' dress. In trying to manage this debate, the head nurse took two steps: (1) she asked us to explore what impact a change in nurses' dress might have on the patients, and (2) she established a special "dress task force."

Our Two Roles: Researchers and "Dress Experts"

Our interaction with the organization could be construed as conducting "action research" (Barker & Barker, 1994; Bartunek, 1993; Yunker, 1994) since we took two overlapping but conceptually distinct roles. For the head nurse and members of the unit, we were experts on organizational dress who could help the unit address the question of nurses' dress. As researchers, we were trying to unravel the meanings and implications of employees' request for a change in an organizational dress code. We were particularly intrigued by the fact that employees requested a change from a permissive and heterogeneous dress code (wearing street clothes) to a restrictive and homogeneous dress code (wearing scrubs). We were puzzled that members of the unit were willingly considering a more restrictive dress code that would demolish their autonomy over their dress. This request contradicted prevalent arguments in the organizational literature that employees seek greater autonomy (e.g., Pfeffer, 1981b). In our role as dress experts, we assisted members of the organization in their search for the best dress code for unit nurses. During the course of the study, we occasionally provided the members of the dress task force with what they labeled "technical assistance in doing research on the dress question." For example, we provided them with articles about nurses' attire, helped them organize a guest lecture about the history of and current trends in nurses' dress, and designed ballots that would assess modal preferences regarding dress among nurses. We also provided members of the task force with descriptive statistics that represented nurses' and patients' preferences. Toward the end of the study, we presented what we had learned to all the members of the unit. We were *not* paid by the organization for any of this work. Throughout the study, all members of the organization knew that our involvement with the unit was motivated primarily by our research interest.

Data Collection

Pursuing our role as researchers, we engaged in five distinct means of data collection:

1. Participation in the dress code task force. We participated in the ad hoc task force that was formed to find a resolution to the petition to change the dress code. All members of the task force were aware of our research interest in organizational dress and of our university affiliation with a department of organizational psychology. We recorded and transcribed all the meetings of the task force, which was chaired by the clinical nurse specialist of the unit and composed of two staff nurses, the educational specialist of the unit, the assistant to the unit's head nurse, and us. We were told that all the members of the task force had volunteered their participation. More than six weeks passed between the group's official formation and its first meeting. However, after the first meeting, the task force met more or less regularly every two to three weeks over a period of approximately four months.

2. Unstructured observations. Throughout the duration of the study, we observed the staff, the patients, and the operations of the unit. These observations helped us comprehend the nature of the work involved, as well as the interpersonal dynamics that accompanied this work. Occasionally, these observations also provided opportunities for talking to members of the unit about the dress issue. Nine such visits (three in each shift) were conducted at predetermined times to ensure observations during the early, middle, and late stages of each shift. Additional visits were conducted on a random basis. We conducted observations in a nonobtrusive manner and did not coordinate them in advance with anyone on the unit. Each observation session lasted between one and two hours.

Our presence during these observations was explained to the members of the unit in a sign posted in the nurses' lounge that announced that we might be seen around the unit because we were researchers helping the unit with the dress question. The sign invited members of the unit to approach and talk to us about the dress issue if they were so inclined. Detailed notes about each observation were typed up after it had occurred.

3. Semistructured interviews. In order to collect more focused data, we interviewed a sample of 38 members of the unit selected through a process of stratified, proportional, random sampling. First, four groups of people who played important roles in the unit were identified. The four groups were nurses, physicians, patients, and other professionals. Then, a subsample of people from each of these groups was selected. The size of each subsample was proportional to the total number of people in each group. We randomly selected the subsamples from the unit's employment and patient rosters. Thus, the sample of interviewees comprised 19 full-time nurses, 6 from the day shift, 6 from the night shift, and 7 from the evening shift; 4 physicians; 4 other professionals (e.g., psychologists, social workers, and occupational therapists); and 11 patients or members of patients' families. We designed a semistructured interview schedule that focused on the question of the nurses' dress code. Four separate but similar interview schedules were prepared for interviews with members of the various subsamples. (Appendix A gives a sample schedule.) Interviews lasted between 40 and 90 minutes and were recorded and transcribed verbatim. We interviewed unit members during their work time and interviewed others during the day or during visiting hours. Everyone we approached agreed to be interviewed and signed an informed consent form.

4. **Free associations.** We also asked nurses to provide their free associations with eight terms. We determined which terms to use from the initial interview with the head nurse and our review of the available literature on dress, rehabilitation treatment, and nursing. Specifically, nurses were asked to note the first five words that came to mind in response to the following terms: uniform, rehabilitation, hospital, scrubs, doctor, dress code, nurse, and street clothes.

5. **Formal documents.** We collected and scanned documents and training materials relevant for or used in the unit. These documents included hospital and unit policy manuals (e.g., "Rehabilitation Nursing Specialty Practice," a hospital document), training manuals of the hospital and the unit, various forms used in the unit and the hospital, and newspaper and other archival data about the hospital and the unit.

Data Analysis

These multiple sources yielded a large amount of qualitative, narrative data and a smaller amount of quantitative data. We conducted an initial set of quantitative analyses about two specific questions: (1) What are patients' feelings and preferences about nurses' dress? and (2) What are nurses' preferences regarding the dress code? To advance our theoretical understanding of the dynamics that surrounded organizational dress, we then conducted an inductive analysis of the qualitative data. Following the iterative process recommended by Strauss and Corbin (1990) and Miles and Huberman (1984), we traveled back and forth between the data and an emerging structure of theoretical arguments. The recurrent visits to the data helped us build and refine an increasingly coherent conceptual framework that captures and explains the richness evident in the data and also makes a sound theoretical contribution.

Initially, we scanned the data in search of dominant themes. Examples of themes that we identified at this stage are "street clothes represent the uniqueness of rehabilitation patients," "nurses want the autonomy to decide on their dress," and "rehab isn't what it used to be." We identified more than 50 such themes. We also noticed that on only a few occasions (less than 10 percent) did the *same* informant advocate *one* dress form to represent *one* theme or issue (e.g., street clothes and status). In other cases (more than 60 percent), the *same* informant appeared to use the *same* dress form to signal his or her stance on *different* issues. For example, the head nurse wanted to retain street clothes both because of their link to the rehabilitation philosophy and because of their implications for patients. In yet a third pattern of responses (approximately 25 percent), the *same* informant used *different* dress forms to signal his or her stance on *different* issues. For example, one nurse noted that she appreciated street clothes because of their link to the rehabilitation philosophy but was for scrubs because she wanted to be able to decide to wear them.[8]

We then brainstormed alternative conceptual structures that would describe the manner in which these themes could be related to each other. For example, at this point we noted that dress was often representing issues having to do with what it meant to be a nurse on this unit. We then sought theory or research in organizational behavior that might help us comprehend the role of dress in this unit and to which we felt this study of dress might contribute. We had started the study because of an interest in organizational dress, but the initial stages of the data analysis suggested to us that dress was, in this context, part of a larger organizational process. We decided that the most appropriate theoretical framework was that of organizational identity and organizational symbolism. Once we had agreed on this broad conceptual structure, we reviewed all the data and discovered ten dominant identity meanings of dress that appeared in most or all of our data sources.

Next, we sought to discover how and when these meanings of dress appeared in the various sources of data we had collected; Appendix B summarizes the results of this analysis. At this stage, we also tried to identify whether clusters, or subgroupings, could be identified in the data. In other words, we tried to answer questions such as these: Are certain themes more predominant among staff members with higher tenure?... among those on certain shifts?... within a certain role? We found the biggest differences arose between the responses of nurses on different shifts (day versus evening and night) *and* between nurses in different hierarchical positions (managerial versus floor nurses).

This wave of analysis helped crystallize how each piece of data fit with previous work on identity and symbolism and how the pattern of our findings could enhance available theoretical knowledge on these notions. At the end of this phase, we were able to articulate the thesis advanced in this article: that dress was used to symbolize and negotiate a complex and contradictory set of issues that represented the social identities of the nurses on this unit. The remainder of this article explains, illustrates, and elaborates this thesis.

....

Findings

Our findings suggest that nurses attempted to answer the abstract and complex question, Who are we as nurses of this unit?, through discussing the question, What should we wear? Nurses' conversations about dress, however, did not reveal a simple or unitary notion of identity; rather, multiple forms of dress were used to represent multiple and conflicting perspectives on multiple identities. In brief, a debate over dress revealed the complexity of the social identities that existed on the unit.

Organizing Multiple Perspectives on Dress: A Web of Identity Issues

Our analysis of the data suggests that informants used particular forms of dress (e.g., street clothes or scrubs) to represent a variety of issues related to their social identities. The data further revealed that these patterns of individual responses were not random; rather, choices of particular dress forms reflected distinct subgroups. Two important characteristics that defined subgroups were shift membership (day versus evening shift) and hierarchical membership (management versus staff nurses). Each of these subgroups preferred a particular dress option because of the social identity issues it represented. To illustrate, day shift nurses typically preferred street clothes because they preferred the rehabilitation unit identity, while evening and night shift nurses preferred scrubs because they represented the acute care unit identity. In contrast, issues surrounding professional identity divided floor nurses from managerial nurses. Thus, our analysis revealed that managers tended to prefer street clothes, which represented a patientcentered identity, and floor nurses preferred scrubs, which symbolized an autonomous professional identity. Figure 1 illustrates this complex web of identities and issues.[9]

Dress and Hybrid Unit Identities

To begin, the dress debate revealed that the organization was characterized by a hybrid identity. According to Albert and Whetten, a hybrid identity "is composed of two or more types that would not normally be expected to go

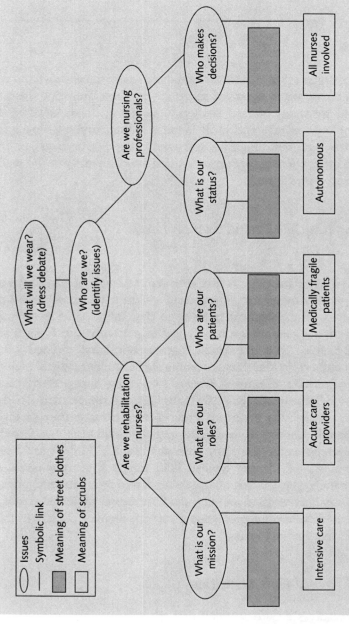

Fig. 1. Web of identity issues evoked by dress debate.

together" (1985: 270). Members' views of this unit's organizational identity included two opposing identities: rehabilitation unit and acute or intensive care unit. Table 1 illustrates the differences between the two identities. As is noted in Table 1, providing rehabilitation differs from providing traditional hospital acute care because rehabilitation involves wearing street clothes rather than traditional nursing attire, is performed along with a team of other professionals rather than by one nurse alone, and consists of helping and teaching patients, in addition to providing routine medical attention. Furthermore, the focus of rehabilitation on teaching patients to care for themselves is different from acute care's focus, which is on helping patients regain medical health or stability.

Our data suggest, however, that the competing identities summarized in Table 1 existed simultaneously on the unit. Table 2 illustrates how data from various informants included references to both the rehabilitation and the acute care identities. As is evident in Table 2, everyone associated with the unit, including physicians, social workers, managers, nurses, and patients, recognized both identities: that of a unit providing rehabilitation, and that of a unit providing acute medical care.[10]

In other words, as Table 2 suggests, the unit was seen as one that provided both education (rehabilitation) and traditional nursing (acute care). Nurses were expected to serve both as educators and as caregivers. Patients, moreover, varied considerably in their medical conditions: some were medically stable (rehabilitation), while others were more fragile (acute care). Each dress form (street clothes and scrubs) represented one identity (rehabilitation and acute

Table 1. Key Indicators of Rehabilitation and Acute Care Identities

Rehabilitation identity	Acute care identity
Nurses wear street clothes	*Nurses wear scrubs*
Patients wear street clothes	Patients wear pajamas
Patients walk around	Patients stay in bed
Patients are disabled, but able to care for themselves	Patients are sick, dependent on medical staff
Patients stay on the unit one to four months	Patients stay on the unit less than one month
Patients learn to function in regular, nonhospital environment	Patients require special hospital equipment such as IVs and ventilators
Nurses teach patients	Nurses take care of patients
A team of professionals develops a treatment plan for each patient	Individual professionals apply expertise individually to patients
Families participate in the care of patients	Families visit patients, but medical treatment is left to professionals

Table 2. Multiple Unit Identities: Data from Multiple Informants

Informant	Rehabilitation identity	Acute care identity
Physicians	[In rehab we] teach patients how to do things at home, particularly the medical routines with bowel, bladder, skin care, medications, etc., and to a significant degree with the functional activities, dressing, eating, getting yourself out of the wheelchair and in and out of bed.	[This unit has a] traditional nursing role, which is providing nursing care which includes the usual kinds of things like keeping a person clean with a bath, and giving them food, and dealing with their nutritional needs. Many times that's artificial, tubes, that sort of things— dealing with intravenous medications, and oral medications, and wound care.
Other medical professionals (rehab team)	We are talking about bringing a person back to function. The function is actually defined by the person involved. Nurses are responsible for teaching the families, which is a real important part of rehab. The families actually take over where we leave off.	The growing problem that is very real is that we are taking patients sooner. Patients are much sicker than they have been historically. Patients still have tubes. Our people still have problems, the bowel and bladder issues of the sick. They're still very sick.
Management	Acute care is caring for a sick person and the nurse is the care giver, nurturer, the person who takes care of them. We wanted that perception to be different in our unit, that the nurse's role was to help them learn to take care of themselves.	We now have patients who are sicker than they have ever been in the past. Over the last few years that's been a pattern. They come to us sicker now and there is a true part of our population at any one time who is sick and needs to be treated as if they are sick.
Nurses	We are trying to get them ready for being discharged from the hospital, and to quit thinking of themselves as being patients in a hospital, but just as people who have a long-term disability and are getting ready to go home.	There was a very high acuity, patients were very sick, and there were few nurses, so the unit was very stressful. So we're going home with green slime and yellow slime and every kind of slime all over your clothes. These patients need constant attention, they have the kinds of problems that other surgical units have.
Patients	When you go to rehab you have so much progress to make, you are going to be here for so long, you have to start doing things on your own and start doing what you want to do. The psychological aspect of rehab is 90 percent of the progress you are going to make, is having the right attitude, and they try to treat me like I can do that.	My husband had aspirated pneumonia, and the stroke affected his swallowing. He can't swallow. He's now on the G-tube. He has to be suctioned right now about every hour or hour and a half. They also found that he has an aneurysm in his stem of his brain the size of a pea. They did an MRI and that's where they found it. He also had clogging of his arteries leading to the heart, so they chose not to do the surgery because of the aneurysm. Other than that, everything's been good.

care, respectively). That the data in Table 2 were collected in response to our questions about dress on the unit reinforces our assertion that, for members of this organization, the dispute about dress was actually a dispute about the issues that dress represented.

Our data further revealed that the general question of unit identity consisted of a set of subquestions or issues. Specifically, the question, Who are we as a unit?, comprised these subparts: Why are we here? Whom do we serve? and What do we do? Put another way, questions about dress were interpreted in these terms: What is our mission? Who are our patients? and What are our roles?

Rehabilitation Unit Identity: Its Issues and Dress Code

As Figure 1 suggests, the rehabilitation unit identity encompassed a variety of issues: unit mission, unit patients, and nurses' tasks. The first issue, the unit's mission (which was also known as the "rehab philosophy"), comprised the core set of beliefs that historically defined rehabilitation nursing. For as long as nurses could recall, the rehabilitation philosophy had been what made the unit unique because it set a goal of helping patients (also called "clients") make a transition from being patients to being independent individuals outside the hospital. That street clothes served as a central symbol of this mission was evident in all types of data that we collected (see Appendix B). To illustrate, one nurse described the unit mission as follows:

We are creating an environment in which [clients] can become rehabilitated by giving them the information, knowledge and expertise. Our focus is helping them identify a new state of health.... [this is why we should wear street clothes].

Another day shift nurse explained in an interview:

The philosophy behind [street clothes] is based on the fact that we want patients to see a distinct difference between the acute care unit and the rehabilitation unit.

The transition these informants made from talking about the mission of the unit to talking about the unique dress code of the unit illustrates how the two notions were tied in their minds. This sentiment was also expressed in a pamphlet that was distributed to new patients on the unit, which stated this:

We believe that patients who wear pajamas will think of themselves as "sick," and by wearing street clothes, patients think of themselves as moving out of the "sick" role and into rehabilitation.

Nurses similarly linked "street clothes" with "rehabilitation" in their free association responses in that both sets of associations centered around notions of healthy and personal situations. Recurring associations to both terms were "personal," "friendly," and "normal."

A second issue associated with the rehabilitation identity was the nature of the unit's patients. Specifically, the debate about dress seemed to represent arguments regarding the extent to which patients on the unit were acutely ill or medically stable. This debate was critical because the condition of patients directly impacted the demands on the unit and its employees. Moreover, the medical stability of patients was an element that historically had differentiated rehabilitation from other forms of medical care. In this context, street clothes symbolically represented the assumption that patients on the unit were well enough to receive rehabilitation treatment and to function independently. According to the perceptions of day shift nurses, the majority of the unit's clients were medically stable. As one nurse explained,

[they] are really much more like clients than patients. They are in [the process of] getting better in that transition period.

These perceptions of patients as medically stable were related to day shift nurses' choice of dress code. To illustrate, a nurse noted:

If we are going to be their teachers, and they are going to act as if they are healthy, we shouldn't be wearing scrubs.

A third identity issue concerned roles. Day shift nurses saw their dominant role requirements as ones that reflected a rehabilitation identity. Obviously, the level of patient acuity indicated what tasks team members performed. What appeared in our data, however, was that there were drastic differences between the day and evening shift nurses in the perceptions of dominant tasks. These differences existed even though *all* nurses treated the *same* patients. Day shift nurses saw their role as comprising predominantly rehabilitation tasks. This statement by one day shift nurse summarizes that view:

On the day shift, the main focus of our patients is getting them up into their wheel-chairs and then dressed for their appointments to leave. For most of the day, they are gone. And then I attend a lot of [rehab team] meetings and do a lot of paperwork and that kind of thing.

Our observations of nurses working different shifts confirmed that day shift nurses did indeed have tasks that fit better with the rehabilitation identity. For example, day shift nurses often attended meetings with other rehabilitation team members and developed patient programs. They also engaged in "acute care tasks," such as lifting patients into and out of wheelchairs and dressing them for their various therapy sessions. But rehabilitation roles were most often indicated as dominant role behaviors for day shift nurses, while acute care roles were viewed as dominating the later shifts.

These perceived differences in dominant role behaviors were associated with different types of dress. Street clothes were seen as appropriate for the tasks of day shift nurses, and scrubs were deemed appropriate for the tasks of evening shift nurses. As one day shift nurse explained:

When you are seen by a lot more of the administrators and the rest of the rehab team . . . and you have a lot of meetings, you feel comfortable in your own [street] clothes.

In short, day shift nurses viewed street clothes as representing various issues associated with a rehabilitation unit identity. Specifically, they saw the unit's rehabilitation mission, its medically stable patients, and its dominant roles to be tightly bound to street clothes—and ultimately to the notion of rehabilitation.

Acute Care Unit Identity: Its Issues and Dress Code

The second quote in the opening of this article is from an evening shift nurse who saw the unit as providing acute rather than rehabilitation care. Like the day shift nurses, evening and night shift nurses[11] associated dress with the unit's mission, its patients, and its roles. However, the perceptions of each of these were almost diametrically opposite, in spite of the fact that all the nurses worked on the same unit and with the same patients.

To begin, the evening and night shift nurses saw the mission of the unit as acute care, and not rehabilitation. Members of the evening and night shift were aware of the rehabilitation philosophy and its historical importance, but they believed that this identity was no longer appropriate. The evening shift nurses' request for scrubs, in particular, signaled a challenge to this mission. Scrubs are medical attire typically associated with surgery and acute care nursing.

The request for scrubs was seen as a challenge to the rehabilitation identity in that its focus was on individual medical professionals providing medical care to sick patients. As one evening shift nurse complained: "This doesn't feel like rehab to me. It feels like I'm working in ICU."[12] Nurses associated this new unit mission with a new dress code: scrubs. To illustrate, one nurse noted that this unit had "the kinds of problems that other surgical units have. . . . So people started saying, 'I'm tired of going home in green slime. Why can't we wear scrubs?'"

The link between scrubs and more traditional forms of nursing (e.g., acute care) was also evident in the free association responses. The term "scrubs" elicited associations similar to those generated by the terms "hospital" and "uniforms." Associations with both of these terms centered around illnesses, medical treatments, and physical ailments or handicaps.

Night and evening shift nurses' perception of patients also differed from those of their day shift counterparts. The request for scrubs was an attempt to signal a perception that the patient population had become more fragile. To illustrate:

Most of our patients on the unit now aren't "rehab-able"—I mean they aren't rehab patients when they first get to us. They are coming to us right from ICUs so they are really sick.

This association between scrubs and patient acuity was salient when conversations about dress shifted to conversations about patient acuity, and vice versa. Thus, in the minds of organization members, patient acuity was intimately tied to dress code:

We are getting patients that have more secretions—they are a lot sicker. They are not really the rehab persons that I started with—having been here six years ago it was different...I was one of the people who signed to wear the scrubs.

Not only was the change in patient population associated with a new dress code for nurses (scrubs), it also called for a new dress code for the patients themselves, as the following quotes illustrate:

They know they're sick and you're not going to fool them by saying "you're wearing street clothes and we're going to tell you you're not sick." I mean people are smarter than that...

and

We used to require every single patient to put street clothes on. We don't do that anymore. Some patients don't get out of bed. They don't get dressed because they're too sick.

Finally, evening and night shift nurses advocated scrubs because they felt that their dominant role behaviors were acute care tasks. Like day shift nurses, evening and night shift nurses performed tasks related to both rehabilitation and acute care. For example, evening shift nurses spent time educating patients and their families, a role related to the unit's rehabilitation identity. However, they felt that acute care activities monopolized their time, as one nurse described:

On the evening shift, we do a large majority of the work: showers, baths, [and] bowel programs. Not like the day shift.

All members of the evening shift described acute care tasks as salient. Once again, these dominant role behaviors were associated with dress, as the following quote illustrates:

We do a lot more as far as the bowel program. You are suctioning patients and doing a lot of things like that. For such things, I personally would not like to wear my street clothes. I'd like to wear my scrubs.

In short, evening and night shift nurses viewed scrubs as representing various issues associated with an acute care unit identity. Specifically, they saw the unit's mission, its medically fragile patients, and its dominant roles to be tightly bound to scrubs because the unit's identity was really based in acute care.

Dress and Hybrid Professional Identities

The debate about the unit's dress code also served to surface divisions in nurses' perceptions of professional identity that coexisted on the unit and were apparent to most members of the unit. Table 3 reveals that floor nurses, nurse managers, physicians, patients, and other rehabilitation team specialists had two views on the professional identity of nurses. The first view we call patient-centered. Central to this identity, referred to by previous authors as the "Florence Nightingale identity" (cf. Jones, 1988; Siegel, 1968) or "ministering angels identity" (Jones, 1988; Summers, 1984, 1989), is the idea that nurses should act first and foremost in accordance with the wishes, needs, and dictates of their patients (cf. Chacko & Wong, 1984; Davis, 1974; Watts et al., 1990).

The second view we call the autonomous or nurse-centered professional identity. This identity evokes the professional model of physicians more than the traditional model of nursing and suggests that nurses should make their own decisions regarding their behavior and that those decisions should be trusted. This distinction is similar to that found by Milward (1995) in her studies of nurses in Britain. She referred to two professional identities: the "patient centered" one, a communal-interpersonal identity that is associated with low status, and the "professional distinctiveness" one, an instrumental-intergroup identity that is associated with higher status.

The debate about professional identity comprised two issues: What is our status?[13] and Who makes decisions? Moreover, as with the hybrid unit identity, evocation of certain issues tended to polarize subgroups within the organization. Differences regarding issues of professional identity, however, did not follow differences in shifts. Rather, professional issues became clear when we compared what the dress code meant to managerial and floor nurses. Managers tended to adopt the patient-centered professional identity, while floor nurses advocated the autonomous one. These differences were embodied in their choices of dress codes.

Patient-Centered Professional Identity: Its Issues and Dress Code

As Table 3 suggests, management felt that nurses should wear street clothes "for the patients." This logic became clear when the head nurse first reacted to

Table 3. Multiple Professional Identities: Data from Multiple Informants

Informant	Nurses as servants to others: patient-centered	Nurses as autonomous: nurse-centered
Physicians	Nurses not only are going to be taking care of people who are quite sick even though they are on a rehabilitation unit, I would say that nurses now have patients that even more need the effect that the unit does reinforce. I think it would be really poor [to wear scrubs].... They [patients] are the very people who need every subtle cue you can come up with to counteract that self-image [of the sick role].	Nurses are going through an evolution. Nurses are a part of the tradition of being a servicing group of women... or service in the need of others. They've taken more authority, responsibility now... they make nice salaries and they are less willing to be treated as second-rate people.
Other medical professionals [rehab team]	Interviewer: [With regard to dress] If it came down to patients wanting one thing and nurses wanting another thing, which would you vote for? Informant: I guess I would vote for the patients.	[Dress is], at least, expressing a change in her self-concept of herself. If nurses are struggling for anything, they are struggling for recognition for their professional preparation or competence. May be a change in dress would accomplish that.
Management	I think it was about 17 years ago that we went to street clothes... That was the statement and the philosophy our dress code expressed—that the reason we do it for the patients... I said it can't be a majority rule—we have to find out, "Does it [street clothes] indeed make a difference [to patients]?"	I think nurses want to have the ability to wear anything they want to. I think that they want to say "If I feel real really grungy and I know tomorrow who I'm going to have and they need suctioning and tube feeding and bowel accidents, I want to have the option of wearing uniforms."
Nurses	My primary purpose here is to serve that patient, and work. When I interviewed here—it was an observation that I made when I was here that day—people were not wearing uniforms. That immediately felt right to me, because the clients are really much more clients than patients. They are to be getting better in that transition period. The process, I do believe, is affected by what we wear.	I was one of the people who signed up to wear scrubs. I don't know that I would wear them every day, but I was signing up for the freedom to do that.
Patients	No. I don't think that they should be allowed to wear scrubs, actually. It's just because it's been really good for me to see nurses wear whatever they want—wearing street clothes.	If I were a female nurse, those things [scrubs] are anything but flattering... I would still leave it up to them— whatever they would like to wear.

296

the dress ballot. According to the head nurse, she warned the floor nurses that they needed to subordinate their desire for a new dress code to the needs of the patients. She explicitly explained:

I said it can't be a majority rule. We have to find out, "Does it [street clothes] indeed make a difference [to the patients]?" and this is what will make the decision.

She similarly said of the ballot incident:

Some nurses seemed to think at the beginning, when the ballot was signed, that it would be just a majority rule—that if the staff wanted to change the dress code, and more than 50% agreed, then they could. I made it real clear that that was not the case.

By framing her reactions to the dress code in this way, the head nurse asserted her position that the needs and wishes of the nurses were secondary to those of the patients. Her stance, similar to that taken by many other professionals and patients on the unit (see Table 3), was that nurses' professional identity should be patient centered. Stated differently, the status of nurses was sub-servient to that of patients. Patients' needs, not nurses', were of paramount importance. As a result, nurses were supposed to wear street clothes.

The head nurse's reaction to the dress ballot and subsequent declaration that nurses should wear street clothes also implied assumptions about how and by whom decisions were made on the unit. These discussions about how to make the decision about dress came to symbolize how unit decisions were made. Following the head nurse's logic, as articulated below, the street clothes option came to symbolize one decision-making process: that all key decisions on the unit were to be made by the head nurse or other unit managers:

I'm responsible for the budget for the personnel and for all the commodities on the unit and for the integrity of the structure of the operations of the unit. I'm also responsible for maintaining collaborative relationships with the other departments ... and for prob-lem solving with other departments in the institution that relate to our unit ... Certainly, [I'm] primarily responsible for the nursing care that all the patients receive and I am responsible 24 hours a day, seven days a week ... And since it is my responsibility to maintain [the unit] as a rehabilitation unit, since I believe that is an important role, I said it can't be a majority rule.

The unit's management, in turn, supported both the head nurse's stance on the dress code and her stance on how the decision about the dress code should be made. That is, they viewed her top-down decision making as legitimate and backed keeping the street clothes dress code, which in turn strengthened the association between street clothes and centralized decision making on the unit. This association was further strengthened by the fact that it was common knowledge that the head nurse had had a central role in instituting the street clothes dress code several years back. As one floor nurse lamented:

[The head nurse] does not want nurses to wear scrubs on this unit. She has said so very clearly . . . that unless there is a clear mandate, like we are all going to rebel here, that it'll stay street clothes. I mean, that is what I really think will happen—and in some ways, that's a shame.

Keeping the street clothes dress code, therefore, symbolized how decisions were made on the unit and who made them. Ironically, the street clothes dress code, which allowed floor nurses considerable autonomy in choosing what to wear to work, came to symbolize a lack of professional autonomy and centralized managerial decision making on the unit.

Autonomous Professional Identity: Issues and Dress Code

Although floor nurses understood the traditional identity of nursing as one based on service and "servitude," they perceived an alternative that would support a professional identity and their autonomy. Ironically, their symbol for autonomy was a dress code that limited options for work clothes to scrubs. At first, we were puzzled that nurses would choose to limit their dress options. In previous work (Rafaeli & Pratt, 1993), we predicted that organization members would be likely to gravitate toward greater choice in organizational dress. This seemingly paradoxical behavior became clear, however, when the link between scrubs and professional autonomy became apparent.

Scrubs represented two aspects of professional autonomy, as summarized in Figure 1: status and decision making. First, scrubs symbolized high status because they were associated with prestigious health care professionals and prestigious health care responsibilities. For example, one doctor thought that rehabilitation nurses wanted to wear scrubs in order to associate with the prestigious intensive care unit (ICU) nurses, who typically wore scrubs. An association with the ICU, the physician noted, meant "a certain level of respect that rehabilitation nursing currently does not have." Similarly, a floor nurse explained how scrubs represented the highest degree of professional autonomy found in the health care system:

[Scrubs] are associated with the highest technical areas in the health care system. The closer you get to a medical task, the more valued you tend to be . . . [scrubs] mean you have a special skill. That you are almost as smart as a doctor.

More broadly, in the context of all the participants in the unit, the demand for scrubs represented a struggle for greater professional recognition: nurses were *not* to be treated "just like some visitor" to the unit.[14] Rather, nurses should be clearly identifiable as professionals and should look the part. A social worker suggested:

[Dress is], at least, expressing a change in her concept of herself. If nurses are struggling for anything, they are struggling for recognition of their professional preparation or competence. Maybe a change in dress would accomplish that.

The evening shift nurses' call for a scrubs dress code, therefore, signaled that nurses deserved higher status. It did so by re-creating the medical hierarchy and then placing rehabilitation nurses higher in that hierarchy (cf. Becker et al., 1961).

Floor nurses also used scrubs to signal a need for greater participation in unit decision making. As autonomous professionals, floor nurses noted, they should be allowed to decide what to wear. Thus, scrubs was seen as a symbol of the challenge to the centralized decision making on the unit. As two nurses explained:

We need to create the environment we are working in . . . I think everybody has to have input. If most of us would be happier in scrubs, I think we need to do that.

and

I'm sure we'll continue to have the current [street clothes] dress code. And that's too bad. Because we're adults and we should be allowed to decide what we wear.

The link between scrubs and participative decision making was also noted by the chair and other members of the dress code task force. When describing the dress conflict, the clinical nurse specialist commented to us that the demand for scrubs represented members' "first step toward self-governance." Similarly, a member of the task force told us, "nurses are fighting about scrubs . . . what they want is the opportunity to assert their opinion."

In sum, dress on this unit represented multilayered social identities. Interwoven into what it meant to be a rehab nurse in this hospital were multiple and competing issues regarding the identity of the unit and the profession. When we communicated these findings to the nurses on the unit, they responded by adopting a new dress code—one that allowed nurses to wear either street clothes *or* scrubs. This solution suggests that they embraced and accepted the complexity that our analysis unraveled. This analysis and the findings that sparked it have the potential to increase understanding of the role of dress and other symbols in organizations that contain complex unit, professional, or other social identities.

Discussion and Implications

This chapter documents the transition from our original interest in the study of dress to an interest that included complex notions of multilayered social identities. We believe that the transition we experienced offers support for our thesis that dress served as a vehicle for representing and negotiating a web of multiple and contradictory identity-related issues. Our study, therefore, illustrates how an examination of organizational symbolism can offer a view into organizational identity and ambivalence, as well as identity conflict and management.

The complex relationship we documented between the symbol of dress and an organizational reality poses a challenge to the prevailing (though often unstated) assumption in the organizational literature that belief systems and the symbols that represent them are stable and resistant to change (cf. Schein, 1985, 1991; Sproull, 1981). Our study unravels how organization members used dress to reflect multiple perspectives on multiple issues. Consistent with the differentiation and the fragmentation perspectives on organizational cultures and the hybrid view of organizational identities, it appears that the saliency of issues, perspectives on these issues, and associated identity beliefs may vary in different parts of the same organization (cf. Albert & Whetten, 1985; Barley, 1991; Feldman, 1979; Martin, 1992; Meyerson, 1990; Pratt, 1994; Smircich, 1983; Weick, 1991). This variation is projected onto the meanings that members of the organization confer upon symbols. Our study documented this process with respect to the symbol of organizational dress, but we believe our thesis can be generalized to other symbols. By implication, our findings therefore challenge the assumption of an "integration perspective" or a "monolithic identity" that suggests that a symbol represents one core set of organizational values.

One hypothesis that our data suggest but that we could not explore in this study is that the lack of integration of belief systems and symbol interpretation will be particularly striking when organizations experience rapid and powerful changes. There is reason to believe that rapid and extreme changes will give rise to multiple issues and multiple symbolic meanings (cf. Ashforth & Mael, 1996). The organization we studied was in a state of turmoil when the debate about the dress code emerged: a strike had just ended, and there was acute understaffing along with an increase in patient acuity. This turmoil may have impacted upon the issues that arose in the unit and consequently, upon the meaning of dress. To illustrate, it may be that scrubs came to symbolize "fragile patients" because of the increase in patient acuity on the unit.

This hypothesis suggests a link between organizational events and the meaning of organizational symbols (cf. Welcomer, Gioia, & Kildruff, 1993). Subsequent research should more closely examine the relationship between the multiplicity of issues and opinions that a symbol can represent and organizational changes. Such research is inherently important, given the exponential rate of change in modern organizations (cf. Sasseen, Neff, & Sansoni, 1994; Weigert & Franks, 1989) and the possible increase in symbolic activity that may accompany this change. Health care organizations, in particular, might be excellent contexts for examining the relationship between change and symbolic activity, as recent developments in managed care threaten to throw these organizations into a state of chaos. Moreover, managers of health care organizations need to be sensitive to a change or an increase in symbolic activity and conflict. Such increases may indicate confusion and upheaval as various groups attempt to define what it means to be a provider of health care, given new organizational mandates.

The interdependencies among symbols, current issues, and core belief systems might also shed some light on how cultures, identities, and symbols can change within organizations. Our findings suggest that symbols not only represent *core values and beliefs* but may also come to represent a variety of *event-driven issues* within an organization (e.g., dress represented the change in the patient population). As symbols are reinterpreted in the context of different issues, they take on multiple meanings. As such meanings are shared, they may become part of the organization's identity and culture (Hatch, 1993). Hence, in this study, organizational dress represented more than just the unit's rehabilitation identity. As members considered their alternatives for a dress code, the meaning of each dress option came to signify the complex set of issues that the notion of rehabilitation represented, including the unit's mission, patients, and employee roles. Therefore, the discussions of dress ultimately led to both a new dress code and a broader understanding of what it meant to be a rehabilitation nurse in this hospital.

In a related vein, our data extend previous work on organizational and social identities and how they are expressed and negotiated within organizations (Albert & Whetten, 1985; Ashforth & Mael, 1989; Dutton & Dukerich, 1991; Dutton et al., 1994; Tajfel & Turner, 1985; Turner, 1987). We assert that social identities in organizations can be multilayered. To answer the question, Who am I?, in this unit meant considering an amalgam of unit and professional identities, which in themselves were multilayered because they comprised opposing values and beliefs.

Thus, organizational scholars studying organizational identity need to keep in mind a number of factors. First, there are multiple identities that a given employee may be drawing upon. Second, these multiple social identities may in themselves be hybrids (e.g., dualistic or fragmented). Third, particular conditions might make particular layers of identity more salient than others (cf. Feldman, 1979). On this unit, for example, external pressures may have driven the increased awareness of the acute care identity. Fourth, particular sources of self-definition may influence embraced layers of social identity. In this unit, group membership seemed to play a key role in identity salience. This link complicated the solution of the dress debate because a nurse could advocate street clothes when thinking of herself as a member of the day shift, but then advocate scrubs when reminded of her status as a floor nurse (cf. Tajfel & Turner, 1985).

Viewing social identities in organizations as being multilayered not only impacts how researchers think about organizational identity, but also how the construct of identity can or should be measured. Our thesis suggests that identity scholars should be sensitive to the fact that "where you sit" may determine "what you see" regarding organizational identities and their symbols (cf. Bazerman, 1991; Dutton & Jackson, 1987; Feldman, 1979; Tversky & Kahneman, 1974). Instruments that are sensitive to multiple perspectives—and consequently, multiple identities—may help scholars understand more richly the dynamics of identity and even identity conflict within organizations. Symbols (and debates about them) may be among such instruments.

Our findings specifically suggest that the management of symbols may be one vehicle for discussing ideological contradictions, dualities in organizational belief systems, and other sources of "sociological ambivalence" (Merton, 1976). Previous authors have argued that such normative contradictions are often ignored (Coser, 1979; Merton, 1976; Parsons, 1951) or are resolved through the adoption of mediating myths (cf. Abravanel, 1983; Scheid-Cook, 1988). Our study suggests that internal organizational contradictions may be acknowledged and embraced through symbols. Symbols such as dress may therefore become the focus of communication among members not because they themselves are important; rather, they become important because they offer a concrete representation and an accessible communication medium about otherwise abstract and threatening contradictions.

Debating symbolic representation of conflicting identities and identity issues may further help organizational *subgroups* manage internal inconsistencies. In this unit, the advocacy of two dress styles may have helped manage conflict by legitimizing both sides of the debate. The rehabilitation nurses we studied eventually resolved the dress debate by adopting a policy that allowed nurses the choice of wearing street clothes or scrubs to work. This solution symbolically maintained that this unit had elements of *both* rehabilitation and acute care and that the profession was *both* patient-centered and autonomous. That is, it symbolized the unit's plurality. The solution also acknowledged the ambivalence that may be unavoidable in this unit, given its unique care-giving charter (cf. Meyerson & Martin, 1987; Pratt, 1993). In this manner, dress served to bring together opposing sides without creating "one big happy family." It provided integration without consensus, which may be essential, given that ambivalence and ambiguity are inherent to social life (cf. Feldman, 1991; Linstead & Grafton-Small, 1992).

Furthermore, conversations about a symbol may help *individuals* manage their own conflicting beliefs. The symbol of dress in our study did more than just facilitate the management of identity conflicts between and among subgroups. Our data suggest that individuals in this unit used organizational dress to mark for themselves their stances on a variety of identity-related issues.

Yet the dress style preferred when one issue was considered was not always consistent with that preferred when a different issue became salient. Interestingly, members did not feel a need to reconcile conflicting feelings about dress. Thus, a nurse could maintain that she would vote for scrubs because they gave her control over decision making, while a bit earlier she had maintained that she endorsed street clothes because she saw herself as a teacher, not an acute care provider. In other words, symbols allow members to deal with contradiction by compartmentalizing[15] potentially difficult identity conflicts (cf. Pratt, 1994; Smith, 1968; Swann, 1987).

More generally, organizational dress may be particularly useful for examining the dynamics of identity conflicts within organizations (cf. Geertz, 1971; Van de Ven, 1985). Dress is similar to other symbols in that its meaning can be multivocal (Martin, 1992). However, dress has characteristics that are not shared by other object symbols and that extend its usefulness as a symbol of identity conflicts: it is highly visible and highly malleable. Dress behaviors such as attaching personal pins or buttons to uniforms, for example, may offer non-verbal indicators of multiple identities in that they signal tension between the need to individuate and the need to belong, or tension among conflicting desires to belong to different social groups (cf. Davis, 1992; Simmel, 1971). Thus, dress can not only take on a variety of meanings in organizations but can also be relatively easily shaped and adapted to outwardly reflect competing demands imposed by multiple identities (Davis, 1992; cf. Rafaeli, Dutton, Harquail, & Mackie-Lewis, 1997).

It is, of course, important to recognize this study's obvious limitations. First, this was a qualitative, inductive study, and it cannot provide grounds for hypothesis testing. Rather, what has been offered here is a conceptual framework. This framework and the hypotheses that it suggests regarding the roles of various symbols, including organizational dress, in sorting out issues of social identity need to be tested in future, quantitative studies. Second, the nature of our study suggests that we should be cautious in applying our findings to other organizational contexts and populations. To begin, this study could be argued to be a single case study, in that we observed one unit of one organization. Moreover, our induction builds on a study of a university hospital, which can be argued to be a unique organizational form. Also, because of the traditions surrounding medical attire, dress may be a more salient issue in hospital settings than in other settings (cf. Bishop, 1934; Gjerdingen, Simpson, & Titus, 1987), and this salience may have led to the rich attributions to the symbol that we observed and reported.

Similarly, our study focused on a somewhat unique group of employees, health care professionals engaged in medical rehabilitation. We particularly focused on nurses, most of whom are women. It may be that women are more sensitive than men to dress and appearance issues (cf. Rafaeli et al., 1997). Such sensitivity on the part of our participants might also have served to magnify the importance of the dress symbol in the context we studied. In other words, it may be that the dynamics we describe cannot be generalized to other hospitals, to other groups of employees, or to other settings in which symbols do not have the history and cultivation that dress has in medical settings. We believe, however, that available theory and research about organizational symbolism (cf. Dandridge, 1983; Dandridge et al., 1980; Ornstein, 1986) and social identity (cf. Ashforth & Mael, 1996; Pratt & Dutton, 1996) support our assertion that similar dynamics can be observed in other types of organizations and with other symbols. Additional research is necessary to empirically validate this assertion.

In sum, we believe that our study offers new insight for emerging theory and research on the meaning and impact of the symbol of organizational dress. Our data suggest that requests for a change in dress code should not be dismissed as trivial or unimportant. Rather, such requests should be embraced as opportunities for unraveling what this symbol represents for members and constituents of organizations. It appears that, as Geertz noted, "man is an animal suspended in webs of significance he himself has spun" (1973: 5). We add here that employees are animals who use *symbols* such as dress to spin webs of organizational significance that suspend, surround, and perhaps even clothe them.

....

Notes

Portions of this article were written while the authors were at the University of Michigan. We wish to thank the Interdisciplinary Committee on Organizational Studies (I.C.O.S.) at the University of Michigan for financial and intellectual support for the study. We are especially indebted to Shankar Nair, James Wade, and three anonymous reviewers for their assistance with the final version of our manuscript and to Stephen Barley, Jane Dutton, Debra Meyerson, and Lance Sandelands for comments on earlier drafts of this work. We also appreciate the input of faculty and students at the University of Notre Dame, the University of Illinois at Urbana-Champaign, the University of Texas at Austin, and Yale University.

1. We adopt the perspective taken by Hatch (1993) and others that organizational identity is narrower than organizational culture and specifically refers to self-defining values and beliefs. We recognize that this assertion is still somewhat controversial. The debate between identity and culture, however, is outside of the scope of this work.

2. This trend toward more and varied types of dress has met with considerable debate. Some nurses view the movement away from the traditional white uniform, which they see as symbolic of servitude, as a sign of newfound professional autonomy and

confidence (cf. Janowski, 1984; Levine, 1988; Siegel, 1968). Other nurses assert that only by reassuming the traditional white uniform can they attain the professional self-esteem, respect, and appreciation they—as members of a profession—deserve (Goodstein, 1981; Smith & Nerone, 1986).

3. See Albert and Whetten's (1985) discussion of ideographic and holographic hybrid identities.

4. These are nurses who have not completed a formal nursing degree.

5. Members of the unit disagreed about the reasons for this increase in patient acuity and about the extent to which it was a permanent rather than a temporary change. Some attributed it to seasonal changes and hence assumed the number of acutely ill patients would go down after the summer. Others argued that the situation was a result of changes in medical and insurance policies and hence assumed it was a permanent change that would not disappear.

6. Such tensions are not unique to this unit (cf. Chacko & Wong, 1984; Davis, 1974; Watts, McCaulley & Priefer, 1990).

7. We actually never got to see this sign, and no one admitted to knowing what had happened to it.

8. Initially, the result of these multiple representations of dress was confusion. The unit was like the mythical Tower of Babel—but in reverse. Instead of people trying to say the same thing using different languages, members were using the same "language" (object symbol) to say very different things. Our intervention helped resolve these confusions not because we could find "the right meaning of dress" but rather because we helped members express and recognize many meanings and issues inherent in the dress conflict.

9. The web illustrated in Figure 1 did not exist in the mind of any single organization member. Rather, each member used a particular dress form or forms to represent his or her stance on particular issues. The web of meanings depicted in Figure 1 became apparent to us only when we, as outsiders, tried to comprehend the meaning and implications of the dispute about dress on the unit.

10. One reason for the salience of the hybrid identity may have been a transition in the unit. Informants made recurrent references to rehabilitation as the "old" identity and to "acute care" as the "current" or "new" identity.

11. Although less vocal than their evening shift counterparts, the night shift nurses' stances on unit identity issues were identical to those of the evening shift nurses. For this reason, evening and night shift nurses are mentioned together throughout this section.

12. ICU is a common acronym for intensive care unit, which is a prototypical acute care unit.

13. The issue of status could also be seen as being linked to unit identity, in that status is often a function of the team or organization in which one is a member. We chose to discuss this issue primarily as a professional identity issue because the data suggested that nurses were primarily worried about their status as professionals rather than the status of their organization.

14. Our data revealed that because rehabilitation nurses wore street clothes, it was often difficult to distinguish nurses from patients and their families.

15. The nurses may have experienced little dissonance because each dress form reflected a different personal frame of reference. Perceptions of reality that are shaped by a specific

frame of reference may endow symbols with specific meanings that are different from those occurring when another frame of reference is adopted. Thus, moving from the frame of staff nurse to the frame of day shift nurse could have led to different interpretations of the concept of street clothes without causing internal conflict.

References

Abbott, A. 1988. *The system of professions*. Chicago: University of Chicago Press.

Abbott, A. 1993. The sociology of work and occupations. In J. Blake & J. Hagen (Eds.), *Annual review of sociology*, vol. 19: 187–209. Palo Alto, CA: Annual Reviews.

Abravanel, H. 1983. Mediatory myths in the service of organizational ideology. In L. R. Pondy, P. Frost, G. Morgan, & T. Dandridge (Eds.), *Organizational symbolism*: 273–293. Greenwich, CT: JAI Press.

Albert, S., & Whetten, D. 1985. Organizational identity. In L. L. Cummings & B. M. Staw (Eds.), *Research in organizational behavior*, vol. 7: 263–295. Greenwich, CT: JAI Press.

Ashforth, B., & Mael, F. 1989. Social identity theory and the organization. *Academy of Management Review*, 14: 20–39.

Ashforth, B., & Mael, F. 1996. Organizational identity and strategy as a context for the individual. In J. Baum & J. Dutton (Eds.), *Advances in strategic management*, vol. 13: 17–62. Greenwich, CT: JAI Press.

Barker, S., & Barker, R. T. 1994. Managing change in an interdisciplinary inpatient unit: An action research approach. *Journal of Mental Health Administration*, 21(1): 80–91.

Barley, S. R. 1991. Contextualizing conflict: Notes on the anthropology of disputes and negotiations. In M. H. Bazerman, R. J. Lewicki, & B. Sheppard (Eds.), *Research on negotiation in organizations*: 165–199. Greenwich, CT: JAI Press.

Bartunek, J. M. 1993. Scholarly dialogues and participatory action research. *Human Relations*, 46: 1221–1233.

Bate, P. 1990. Using the culture concept in an organizational development setting. *Journal of Applied Behavioral Science*, 26: 83–106.

Bazerman, M. 1991. Foundations of decision processes. In B. M. Staw (Ed.), *Psychological dimensions of organizational behavior*: 453–479. New York: Macmillan.

Becker, H., Greer, B., Hughes, E. C., & Strauss, A. 1961. *Boys in white: Student culture in medical school*. Chicago: University of Chicago Press.

Bishop, W. J. 1934. Notes on the history of the medical costume. *Annals of medical history, new series*, 6(May): 193–218.

Campbell-Heider, N., & Hart, C. A. 1993. Updating the nurse's bedside manner. *Image: Journal of Nursing Scholarship*, 25(2): 133–139.

Chacko, T., & Wong, J. K. 1984. Correlates of role conflict between physicians and nurse practitioners. *Psychological Reports*, 54: 783–789.

Cho, E., & Grover, L., 1978. *Looking terrific: Express yourself through the language of clothing*. New York: G. P. Putnam's Sons.

Cialdini, R. B., Borden, R. J., Thorne, A., Walker, M. R., Freeman, S., & Sloan, L. R. 1976. Basking in reflected glory: Three (football) field studies. *Journal of Personality and Social Psychology*, 34: 366–375.

Clark, B. R. 1972. The organizational saga in higher education. *Administrative Science Quarterly*, 17: 178–184.

Coser, R. L. 1979. *Training in ambivalence: Learning through doing in a mental hospital*. New York: Free Press.

D'Andrade, R. G. 1984. Cultural meaning systems. In R. A. Shweder & R. A. LeVine (Eds.), *Culture theory: Essays on mind, self, and emotion*: 88–119. Cambridge: Cambridge University Press.

Dandridge, T. C. 1983. Symbol's function and use. In L. R. Pondy, P. Frost, G. Morgan, & T. Dandridge (Eds.), *Organizational symbolism*: 69–79. Greenwich, CT: JAI Press.

Dandridge, T. C., Mitroff, I., & Joyce, W. F. 1980. Organizational symbolism: A topic to expand organizational analysis. *Academy of Management Review*, 5: 77–82.

Davis, F. 1992. *Fashion, culture and identity*. Chicago: University of Chicago Press.

Davis, M. 1974. Intrarole conflict and job satisfaction on psychiatric units. *Nursing Research*, 23: 482–488.

de Marley, D. 1986. *Working dress*. London: B. T. Batsford.

Dutton, J. E., & Dukerich, J. M. 1991. Keeping an eye on the mirror: Image and identity in organizational adaptation. *Academy of Management Review*, 34: 517–554.

Dutton, J. E., Dukerich, J. M., & Harquail, C. V. 1994. Organizational images and member identification. *Administrative Science Quarterly*, 39: 239–263.

Dutton, J. E., & Jackson, S. E. 1987. Categorizing strategic issues: Links to organizational action. *Academy of Management Review*, 12: 76–90.

Feldman, M. 1991. The meaning of ambiguity. Learning from stories and metaphors. In P. Frost, L. F. Moore, M. R. Louis, C. C. Lundberg, & J. Martin (Eds.), *Reframing organizational culture*: 145–156. Newbury Park, CA: Sage.

Feldman, S. 1979. Nested identities. *Studies in Symbolic Interaction*, 2: 399–418.

Forsythe, S. M. 1990. Effect of applicant's clothing on interviewer's decision to hire. *Journal of Applied Social Psychology*, 20: 1579–1595.

Forsythe, S., Drake, M. F., & Cox, C. E. 1985. Influence of applicant's dress on interviewer's selection decisions. *Journal of Applied Psychology*, 70: 374–378.

Fussell, P. 1983. *Class*. New York: Ballantine Books.

Gardner, G., & Simkins, R. 1976. Does it really matter what nurses wear in the intensive care unit? *Maternal Child Nursing*, July/August: 239.

Geertz, C. 1971. *Myth, symbol, and culture*. New York: Norton.

Geertz, C. 1973. *The interpretation of culture: Selected essays*. New York: Basic Books.

Gjerdingen, D. K., Simpson, D. E., & Titus, S. L. 1987. Patients' and physicians' attitudes regarding physicians' professional appearance. *Archives of Internal Medicine*, 147: 1209–1212.

Goffman, E. 1959. *The presentation of self in everyday life*. Garden City, NY: Doubleday.

Goodstein, F. 1981. The woman in white: It's time to put the nurse back into that image. *Journal of Practical Nursing*, February: 29.

Hall, E., Lamb, M. E., & Perlmutter, M. 1982. *Child psychology today*. New York: Random House.

Hatch, M. J. 1993. The dynamics of organizational culture. *Academy of Management Review*, 18: 657–693.

Hochschild, A. 1983. *The managed heart*. Los Angeles: University of California Press.

Janowski, M. J. 1984. My love affair with uniforms. *American Journal of Nursing*, August: 1241–1244.

Jones, A. 1988. The white angel (1936): Hollywood's image of Florence Nightingale. In A. H. Jones (Ed.), *Images of nurses*: 221–242. Philadelphia: University of Pennsylvania Press.

Joseph, N. 1986. *Uniforms and nonuniforms: Communication through clothing*. New York. Greenwood Press.

Joseph, N., & Alex, N. 1972. The uniform: A sociological perspective. *American Journal of Sociology*, 77: 719–730.

Kanter, R. M. 1972. *Commitment and community: Communes and utopias in sociological perspective*. Cambridge, MA: Harvard University Press.

Lavender, A. 1987. The effects of nurses changing from uniforms to everyday clothes on a psychiatric rehabilitation ward. *British Journal of Medical Psychology*, 60: 189–199.

Levine, D. 1988. Dressing for success: Nursing style. *Imprint*, 35(5): 50–54.

Levitt, M. 1981. *The executive look: How to get it—How to keep it*. New York: Atheneum.

Linstead, S., & Grafton-Small, R. 1992. On reading organizational culture. *Organization Studies*, 13: 331–355.

Louis, M. R. 1983. Organizations as culture-bearing milieux. In L. R. Pondy, P. Frost, G. Morgan, & T. Dandridge (Eds.), *Organizational symbolism*: 39–54. Greenwich, CT: JAI Press.

Lurie, A. 1981. *The language of clothes*. New York: Random House.

Manning, P. 1987. *Semiotics and fieldwork*. Newbury Park, CA: Sage.

Martin, J. 1992. *Cultures in organizations: Three perspectives*. New York: Oxford University Press.

Martin, J., Feldman, M. S., Hatch, M. J., & Sitkin, S. B. 1983. The uniqueness paradox in organizational studies. *Administrative Science Quarterly*, 28: 438–453.

Merton, R. K. 1976. *Sociological ambivalence and other essays*. New York: Free Press.

Meyerson, D. 1990. Uncovering socially undesirable emotions: Experiences of ambiguity in organizations. *American Behavioral Scientist*, 33: 296–307.

Meyerson, D. 1994. Interpretation of stress in institutions: The cultural production of ambiguity and burnout. *Administrative Science Quarterly*, 39: 628–653.

Meyerson, D., & Martin, J. 1987. Cultural change: An integration of three different views. *Journal of Management Studies*, 24: 623–647.

Miles, M. B., & Huberman, A. M. 1984. *Qualitative data analysis*. Beverly Hills, CA: Sage.

Milward, L. 1995. Contextualizing social identity in consideration of what it means to be a nurse. *European Journal of Social Psychology*, 25: 303–324.

Mitroff, I., & Kilmann, R. H. 1976. On organization stories: An approach to the design and analysis of organizations through myths and stories. In R. H. Kilmann, L. R. Pondy, & D. P. Slevin (Eds.), *The management of organization design*, vol. 1: 189–207. New York: North-Holland.

Molloy, J. T. 1975. *Dress for success*. New York: Warner Books.

Molloy, J. T. 1977. *The woman's dress for success*. Chicago: Follett.

Nerone, B. J. 1986. Nursing style: Is your image showing? *Imprint*, 33(1): 34–37.

O'Connor, S., & Lanning, J. 1992. The end of autonomy? Reflections on the postprofessional physician. *Health Care Management Review*, 17(1): 63–72.

Ornstein, S. 1986. Organizational symbols: A study of their meanings and influences on perceived organizational climate. *Organizational Behavior and Human Decision Process*, 38: 207–229.

Parsons, T. 1951. *The social system*. New York: Free Press.

Petrovich, D. V., Bennett, J. R., & Jackson, J. 1968. Nursing apparel and psychiatric patients: A comparison of uniforms and street clothes. *JPN and Mental Health Services*, 6(6): 344–348.

Pfeffer, J. 1981a. Management as symbolic action. In L. L. Cummings & B. M. Staw (Eds.), *Research in organizational behavior*, vol. 3: 1–52. Greenwich, CT: JAI Press.

Pfeffer, J. 1981b. *Power in organizations*. Boston, MA: Pitman.

Pisker, H., & Vigiano, W. 1988. A study of whether uniforms help patients recognize nurses. *Hospital and Community Psychiatry*, 39(1): 78–79.

Pondy, L. R. 1983. The role of metaphors and myths in organization and in the facilitation of change. In L. R. Pondy, P. Frost, G. Morgan, & T. Dandridge (Eds.), *Organizational symbolism*: 157–166. Greenwich, CT: JAI Press.

Pondy, L. R., Frost, P. J., Morgan, G., & Dandridge, T. C. (Eds.) 1983. *Organizational symbolism*. Greenwich, CT: JAI Press.

Pratt, M. G. 1993. *When actions speak louder than words: The behavioral enactment of ideological conflict among caregivers*. Working paper, University of Illinois at Urbana-Champaign.

Pratt, M. G. 1994. *The happiest, most dissatisfied people on earth: Ambivalence and commitment among Amway distributors*. Unpublished dissertation, University of Michigan, Ann Arbor.

Pratt, M. G., & Dutton, J. E. 1996. *Owning up or opting out: On ambivalence, identity extension, and collective action*. Working paper, University of Illinois at Urbana-Champaign.

Rafaeli, A., Dutton, J., Harquail, C. V., & Mackie-Lewis, S. 1997. Navigating by attire: The use of dress by female administrative employees. *Academy of Management Journal*, 40: 9–45.

Rafaeli, A., & Pratt, M. G. 1993. Tailored meanings: On the meaning and impact of organizational dress. *Academy of Management Review*, 18: 32–55.

Ribeiro, A. 1986. *Dress and morality*. London: B. T. Batsford.

Roach-Higgins, M. E., & Eicher, J. 1992. Dress and identity. *Clothing and Textiles Research Journal*, 10(4): 1–8.

Rosen, M. 1985. Breakfast at Spiro's: Dramaturgy and dominance. *Journal of Management*, 11: 31–48.

Sasseen, J., Neff, R., & Sansoni, S. 1994. The winds of change blow everywhere. *Business Week*, October 17: 92–93.

Scheid-Cook, T. 1988. Mitigating organizational contradictions: The role of mediatory myths. *Journal of Applied Behavioral Science*, 24: 161–171.

Schein, E. 1985. *Organizational culture and leadership*. San Francisco: Jossey-Bass.

Schein, E. 1990. Organizational culture. *American Psychologist*, 45: 109–119.

Schein, E. 1991. What is culture? In P. Frost, L. F. Moore, M. R. Louis, C. C. Lundberg, & J. Martin (Eds.), *Reframing organizational culture*: 243–253. Newbury Park, CA: Sage.

Siegel, H. 1968. The nurse's uniform: Symbolic or sacrosanct? *Nursing Forum*, 7: 315–323.

Simmel, G. 1971. *On individuality and social forms: Selected writings*. Chicago: University of Chicago Press.

Singer, J. E., Brush, C. A., & Lublin, S. C. 1965. Some aspects of deindividuation: Identification and conformity. *Journal of Experimental Social Psychology*, 1: 356–378.

Smircich, L. 1983. Organizations as shared meanings. In L. R. Pondy, P. Frost, G. Morgan, & T. Dandridge (Eds.), *Organizational symbolism*: 55–65. Greenwich, CT: JAI Press.

Smith, D. 1968. Dogmatism, cognitive consistency, and knowledge of conflicting facts. *Sociometry*, 31: 259–277.

Smith, B., & Nerone, B. J. 1986. Marketing a profitable nursing image: Recognizing that image is power. *Imprint*, 33(1): 26–30.

Solomon, M. 1986. Dress for effect. *Psychology Today*, 20(4): 20–28.

Solomon, M. 1987. Standard issue. *Psychology Today*, 21(12): 30–31.

Solomon, M. R., & Douglas, S. P. 1983. The power of pinstripes. *Savvy*, March: 59–62.

Solomon, M., & Douglas, S. 1987. Diversity in product symbolism: The case of female executive clothing. *Psychology and Marketing*, 4: 184–212.

Sproull, L. 1981. Beliefs in organizations. In P. C. Nystrom & W. H. Starbuck (Eds.), *Handbook of organizational design*, vol. 2: 203–224. London: Oxford University Press.

Squire, G. 1974. *Dress and society 1560–1970*. New York: Viking.

Stavros, M. K., & Lyden, D. 1988. Working together: The health care team. In A. J. Punwar (Ed.), *Occupational therapy: Principles and practices*: 71–81. Los Angeles: Williams & Wilkins.

Stone, G. P. 1962. Appearance and the self. In R. A. Marshall (Ed.), *Human behavior and social processes: An interactionist approach*: 86–118. Boston: Houghton-Mifflin.

Strauss, A. L., & Corbin, J. 1990. *Basics of qualitative research: Grounded theory procedures and techniques*. Newbury Park, CA: Sage.

Stubbs, D. A., Buckle, P. W., Hudson, M. P., Butler, P. E., & Rivers, P. M. 1985. Nurses' uniforms: An investigation of mobility. *Journal of Nursing Studies*, 22(3): 217–229.

Summers, A. 1984. Images of the nineteenth century nurse. *History Today*, 34 (December): 40–42.

Summers, A. 1989. Ministering angels. *History Today*, 39 (February): 31–37.

Swann, W. B. 1987. Identity negotiation: Where two roads meet. *Journal of Personality and Social Psychology*, 53: 1038–1051.

Tajfel, H., & Turner, J. C. 1985. The social identity theory of intergroup behavior. In S. Worchel & W. G. Austin (Eds.), *Psychology of intergroup behavior*: 7–24. Chicago: Nelson-Hall.

Thomas, J., & Gioia, D. 1991. *Sensemaking in top management teams: Image and identity in strategic issue interpretation*. Working paper, Pennsylvania State University, University Park.

Trauer, T., & Moss, A. V. 1980. Psychiatric patients' opinions of nurses ceasing to wear uniforms. *Journal of Advanced Nursing*, 5: 47–53.

Trice, H. 1996. *Occupational subcultures in the workplace*. Ithaca, NY: ILR Press.

Trice, H., & Beyer, J. 1984. Studying organizational cultures through rites and ceremonials. *Academy of Management Review*, 9: 653–669.

Trice, H., & Beyer, J. 1993. *The cultures of work organizations*. Englewood Cliffs, NJ: Prentice-Hall.

Turner, J. C. 1987. *Rediscovering the social group: A self-categorization theory*. New York: Basil Blackwell.

Tversky, A., & Kahneman, D. 1974. Judgement under uncertainty: Heuristics and biases. *Science*, 185: 1124–1131.

Van de Ven, A. 1985. Spinning on symbolism: The problem of ambivalence. *Journal of Management*, 11: 101–102.

Van Maanen, J., & Barley, S. R. 1984. Occupational communities: Culture and control in organizations. In B. M. Staw & L. L. Cummings (Eds.), *Research in organizational behavior*, vol. 6: 287–365. Greenwich, CT: JAI Press.

Veblen, T. 1899. *The theory of the leisure class: An economic study of institutions*. New York: MacMillan.

Watts, D. T., McCaulley, B. L., & Priefer, B. A. 1990. Physician-nurse conflict: Lessons from clinical experience. *Journal of the American Geriatrics Society*, 38: 1151–1152.

Weick, K. 1991. The vulnerable system: An analysis of the Tenerife air disaster. In P. Frost, L. F. Moore, M. R. Louis, C. C. Lundberg, & J. Martin (Eds.), *Reframing organizational culture*: 117–130. Newbury Park, CA: Sage.

Weigert, A., & Franks, D. 1989. Ambivalence: A touchstone of the modern temper. In D. D. Franks & E. D. McCarthy (Eds.), *The sociology of emotions: Original essays and research papers*: 205–227. Greenwich, CT: JAI Press.

Welcomer, S. A., Gioia, D. A., & Kildruff, M. 1993. *Seizing the moral high ground: The symbolic construction of a crusade*. Paper presented at the annual meeting of the Academy of Management, Atlanta.

Yunker, G. W. 1994. Action research and organizational development. *Personnel Psychology*, 47: 187–189.

Appendix A Interview Schedule

1. Can you tell me about the staff on the unit?
   Total number of nurses (full- and part-time)
   Breakdown by type (RNs, LPNs, NRPs, aides, assistants, etc.)
   What other people work on the unit other than nurses?
2. Can you tell me about the patients?
   How many?
   We understand there are different types of patients?
   Is there anything we should know about the families?
3. Anything else we should know about the unit?
4. Can you tell me about your job on the unit?
   What is your job title? What does your job entail?
   How long have you worked in this position? On this unit?
   How long have you worked in nursing?
5. Can you tell me how the issue of dress on the unit started?
   When was the issue first brought to your attention?
   How did you learn about it?
   Can you think of key events that preceded it?

Was there anything unusual about the unit at the time?
How/where was the issue raised? By all the nurses? Only a few?
Why do you think it was raised?

6. How do you think nurses on the unit should be dressed? Why?
7. How do you feel about the dress issue? Why?
8. How do you think the nurses on the unit feel? Why?
9. How do you think your management feels about it?
10. How do you think this issue will be resolved? Why?
11. How would you like to see this issue resolved?
12. Is there anything else you would like to add?

Thank you very much for your time and cooperation!

Appendix B Identity Themes and Data Sources

| Identity theme | Dress code task force | Unobtrusive observations | Semistructured interviews | | | Free associations | Formal documents |
			Nurses	Unit professionals	Patients		
Street clothes and rehabilitation mission	Yes	Yes	Yes	Yes	Yes	Yes	Yes
Scrubs and acute care mission	Yes	Yes	Yes	Yes	Yes	Yes	No
Street clothes and rehabilitation instructor roles	Yes	Yes	Yes	Yes	Yes	Yes	Yes
Scrubs and acute care roles	Yes	Yes	Yes	Yes	No	Yes	No
Street clothes and well patients	Yes	Yes	Yes	Yes	Yes	Yes	Yes
Scrubs and sick patients	Yes	Yes	Yes	Yes	Yes	Yes	Yes
Street clothes and low status	Yes	No	Yes	Yes	Yes	No	No
Scrubs and high status	Yes	No	Yes	Yes	Yes	Yes	No
Street clothes and centralized decision making	Yes	No	Yes	Yes	No	No	Yes
Scrubs and participative decision making	Yes	No	Yes	Yes	Yes	No	No

Breaches in the Boardroom: Organizational Identity and Conflicts of Commitment in a Nonprofit Organization

Karen Golden-Biddle and Hayagreeva Rao

Since the publication of Berle and Means's (1932) classic thesis on the separation of ownership from management in large organizations, students of corporate governance have grappled with the problem of how to reduce potential conflicts of interest between shareholders and managers (Fligstein and Freeland 1995; Useem 1996). Agency theory, the dominant approach to research on corporate governance, holds that the separation of ownership from management constitutes an efficient division of labor. However, it also recognizes that self-interested top managers, by virtue of their expertise and superior access to information, can misrepresent performance, misallocate resources, and engage in self-dealing at the expense of shareholders (Jensen and Meckling 1976). In the agency framework, the establishment of an independent board of directors consisting of legal outsiders is one of three major mechanisms (along with incentive schemes and the external takeover market) that exist to ensure alignment between the interests of managers and owners (Fama and Jensen 1983). The board of directors serves as a watchdog that seeks to minimize conflicts of interest between managers and shareholders; it designs incentive schemes for the managers, and approves proposals initiated by managers. In turn, board members have a powerful incentive to be vigilant monitors because the organization's human capital is diminished when there is a breakdown of internal control and an activation of the costly takeover market (Fama and Jensen 1983, p. 315).

Organizational sociologists have critiqued the agency theory model of boards as limited, because it overlooks how boards are embedded in structural, political, cognitive, and cultural contexts (Granovetter 1985; Hirsch et al. 1987; Zukin and DiMaggio 1991, pp. 14–20). Structural embeddedness means that the functioning of a board is contingent on its ties to other boards; director interlocks situate organizations in an intercorporate network (Pfeffer and Salancik 1978) and serve as a conduit for the transmission of practices inimical to the interests of the shareholder, such as poison pills (Davis 1991). Indeed, recent research findings cast doubt on the independence of "outside" directors who are recruited on the basis of their social connections rather than expertise (Davis 1993). Political embeddedness means that political struggles between business and nonbusiness organizations shape the role of boards. For example, Roe (1991) argued that the initial separation of ownership from management was not an inevitable consequence of large organizations, but arose due to legal and regulatory constraints stemming from populist pressures and the efforts of influential managers. Cognitive embeddedness means that actions of the board are affected by structured regularities of mental processes. Retrospective rationality, for example, can enable directors to escalate commitment to a losing course of action even in the face of contrary evidence (Staw and Ross 1987). Finally, cultural embeddedness implies that beliefs and understandings shared by organization members guide the behaviors of directors; for example, the central, distinctive, and enduring belief that 3M is an innovative organization may shape how directors construct their roles in the organization.

Although there is an expanding body of work about how the functioning of boards is shaped by structural connections to other boards (Davis 1993), the rise of political activism by investor groups (Roe 1991, Romano 1993), and the cognitive biases of boards (Zajac and Westphal 1996), there is no empirical work on how the functioning of boards is shaped by the cultural context. In this paper, we seek to illuminate the cultural embeddedness of boards by examining how organizational identity influences the construction and enactment of the director's role and shapes interactions among board members and managers.

Drawing on the social constructionist perspective (cf. Berger and Luckman 1966, Knorr-Cetina 1981, Rabinow and Sullivan 1979), we conceptualize the board role differently than the one developed in agency theory. In contrast to viewing the board role as an objective entity comprised primarily of fiduciary and legal considerations, we see this role as constitutive of, and inseparable from, the shared meanings held by organizational members, e.g., employees, donors, and activists elected to the board. That is, the board role is construed, enacted, and interpreted during everyday, face-to-face interactions among members (Berger and Luckman 1966, Geertz 1983, Schutz 1976) within particular organizational arenas. Thus, the members' constructions of the board role may include, but are not necessarily limited to, fiduciary and legal attributes.

Organizational identity—the shared beliefs of members about the central, enduring and distinctive characteristics of the organization—constitutes part of the shared meanings held by members. In a social constructionist perspective, identity becomes an important and collectively-held frame invoked by members to both interpret and to take action; that is, to make sense of their world (Gephart 1993, Weick 1995). Indeed, several researchers have suggested that organizational identity influences not only how members define themselves, but also their interpretation of issues and roles, responses to problems, and feelings about outcomes (Albert and Whetten 1985, Ashforth and Mael 1989, Dutton and Dukerich 1991, Dutton et al. 1994). Further, this research suggests that members do not solely construct mono-lithic organizational identities; hybrid identities can be developed in which members incorporate two or more different and potentially conflicting dimensions that are not normally expected to go together (Albert and Whetten 1985). These dimensions can be separately maintained by different segments of the organization, and generate an ideographic identity, or diffused throughout the organization, and produce a holographic identity (Albert and Whetten 1985, Louis 1990). In the present study, we are concerned with the latter case of hybrid identity.

One consequence of the holographic construction of hybrid identity is that it can generate significant intra-role conflict for role incumbents. A central premise of role theory is that intra-role conflict is generated when different stakeholders hold different views of an incumbent's role (Gross et al. 1958, Kahn et al. 1964, Roos and Starke 1980). In their classic study, Gross et al. (1958) identified a number of typical situations in which incumbents of the school superintendent position experienced incompatible expectations placed on them by different groups such as teachers, board members, and parents, and were forced to choose among them. A theoretical extension of this line of thinking introduced in the present study, is that role incumbents in an organization with a holographic form of hybrid identity could experience intra-role conflict even in the absence of multiple stakeholders with rival expectations. In this case, latent contradictions embedded in perceived organizational identity could be precipitated and become visible during breaches in the ongoing social order, manifesting themselves as, what we term, "conflicts of commitment" for role incumbents. That is, these organizational members would experience incompatible expectations placed on them by their own desire to uphold the different dimensions of the hybrid identity.

Research suggests that when faced with contradictions such as the ones arising from either type of intra-role conflict, social actors experience "role strain," (Goode 1960) which they seek to alleviate by engaging in "face-work" (Goffman 1959, 1967, p. 12). In this case, face-work assumes a defensive orientation; actors invoke "face-saving" strategies. These strategies are comprised of oral accounts and/or actions directed toward mitigating negative impressions and repairing the image and reputation of themselves and their organizations (Sutton and Callahan 1987, Tedeschi and Melburg 1984). Further, as suggested by Goffman (1959), members develop and rehearse these accounts backstage in the less public and more informal area of action, and perform them frontstage, in the public, more official area of action.

Some interesting research questions arise when the previous discussion on identity and impression management is placed in the context of boards and corporate governance. How does a hybrid organizational identity shape the way board members define themselves, and construct and enact their role? What do board members do when a breach in the prevailing expectations of the board role renders hitherto latent contradictions in organizational identity visible?

We explored these two questions in a nonprofit organization called Medlay (a pseudonym), through a qualitative, field-based study. This type of study was particularly suited to our overall goal of examining corporate governance and organizational identity, because it enabled us to study how board members construed and enacted their role over time (Dutton and Dukerich 1991; Pettigrew 1979), and to discern how the board and managers made sense of a breach in their expected role. Furthermore, we chose to study a nonprofit organization because, in contrast to for-profits, which must distribute their profits, nonprofits can put income into fund balances or reserves. We reasoned, therefore, that the expectation of board members to be vigilant monitors of management is even more important in nonprofit organizations.

Briefly, our analyses disclose how both organizational and individual members' identities shape the construction and enactment of the board role through the processes of identification and action. When public actions breach the prevailing expectations of the board role, contradictions in the organizational identity surface, creating "conflicts of commitment" for board members, and threatening governance in Medlay. An influential subset of directors and top managers resolve the breach and preserve Medlay's identity by using different "face-saving" strategies to bridge the contradiction of being vigilant monitors and friendly colleagues.

Research Methodology

Research Setting

Medlay is an example of a mutual type of nonprofit organization, in which, as Hansmann (1986) points out, formal control rests with patrons because directors are systematically elected by members, volunteers, or donors following defined procedures and policies. Some organizational economists assert that mutual nonprofits are analogous to for-profit boards dominated by "outside" members, such as institutional investors or venture capitalists. Ben-Ner (1986) contends that the mutual nonprofit makes donors or customers into *de facto* owners by making them members of the organization and by giving them the right to elect their representatives to the board of directors. Elections enable donors or customers to exercise "voice" in the affairs of the organization by choosing activists to be board members. In turn, because activists are motivated by self-interest to provide wealth or time to further the social cause in question, they are bound to take their task seriously (Fama and Jensen 1983).

Medlay was founded in the early part of this century by a few medical professionals who saw their mission as communicating what little knowledge existed about particular diseases to both the public and physicians. Today, Medlay is a national organization comprised of both medical and nonmedical members whose continuing mission is to eliminate particular diseases through research, education, and service. Structurally, Medlay consists of a national office and numerous affiliates throughout the United States, each managed by paid staff and governed by an independent board. Medlay's organizational chart is depicted in Figure 1.

Medlay's board of directors has several formal functions within its general charter of "constructing the broad policy framework within which the entire organization operates." Specifically, the board's major duties are to:

review and determine broad program objectives and activities, determine plans and establish procedures in accordance with the Bylaws, elect the volunteer officers of Medlay, receive and act on all reports of officers and committees, and determine policies and practices that relate to national headquarters operations, e.g., approve the National headquarters budget, and appoint staff officers of the organization, as defined in the Bylaws.

The national-level board consists of activist volunteers, usually those who have volunteered in Medlay's affiliates, who are elected systematically by current volunteers following procedures and policies outlined in the bylaws. At the time of our research, the national board was meeting twice a year and was

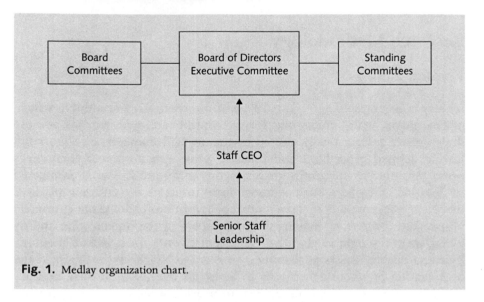

Fig. 1. Medlay organization chart.

composed of more than 100 voting members. In addition to the voting members, prior board members "of eminence" designated as honorary life volunteers, as well as past board officers, would attend the meetings as nonvoting participants, but with full privileges during discussions.

Staff managers recognize that the board is large, but explain that its size assures adequate representation of the grassroots communities that comprise Medlay. When describing the board, a few managers referred to it as a "representative assembly." Representation is an issue which the board takes seriously. As specified in board policy, exactly one-half of the board members represent the medical profession, and the other half represent non-medical professions.

The executive committee, which meets at least three times a year, is the smaller governing leadership unit of the board of directors to which other working committees report. The board chair-elect is designated chair of this committee. The executive committee reviews all committee recommendations and financial information, i.e., the budget, before going to the full board of directors for review and approval.

Since the mid-1980s, Medlay has faced increased competition in its fundraising efforts. The board chair called attention to this by noting that, "As we enter the 1990s . . . we need a renaissance in fundraising . . . we must change with the time . . ." This pressure increased during the fieldwork when Medlay's fundraising efforts fell short of goals for the first time in the memory of current organizational members.

Data Collection

The research is based on both authors' involvement with top management (staff) and volunteer leaders (board members) in Medlay during the period of June 1990 to December 1993 and is based on two avenues of data collection: (1) formal executive development sessions with the organization conducted by both authors during 1992 and 1993, and (2) fieldwork conducted by the first author primarily at the national office of Medlay during 1990 and 1991. The executive development sessions provided a quasi-informal setting for the authors to observe top managers (staff), to understand how they described their actions and the behavior of volunteers, and to conduct "casual interviews," (Lofland and Lofland 1984) which involved asking questions to the participants. The access to Medlay for fieldwork originated when two Medlay executives attended a university-based development program in April 1990, where the first author presented a session on organizational culture. Afterward, they asked her to study the organization's culture. These executives paved the way for her to enter Medlay as a known researcher and unpaid ethnographer whose role was to conduct a cultural analysis of the organization. One executive provided an office area and access to senior-level meetings. The fieldwork lasted 10 months, with an average of three days per week in Medlay.

Initially, the first author sought to understand how managers and board members interpreted their experiences in Medlay. Early in the research, senior managers of Medlay identified the "board's questioning of the budget" as one such experience that had occurred just prior to the commencement of the fieldwork, and which was still ongoing. As a result, the researcher sought to become included in the meetings being held to address the situation, and elicited information about the actors involved, what specifically had happened, and how different groups of actors construed the event. The board leadership, top management, and board members emerged as the "conceptually meaningful groups" (Gephart 1993) for the examination of the budget questioning. At the same time, data were being collected that helped to place the budget questioning into the larger Medlay context. Detailed data were collected from three sources: participant observation, semi-structured interviews, and archives.

1. Participant Observation. Participant observation involves watching members' everyday actions and listening to how they describe and interpret both their own and others' actions (Diesing 1972; Van Maanen 1982). Data was collected from "casual interviews" with informants during everyday contacts (such as while walking to a meeting), formal volunteer and staff meetings during which the members expected the researcher to take notes (thus, verbatim accounts could be collected), and informal encounters, such as lunches, dinners, or hallway discussions. Participant observation data were recorded in extensive and typewritten field notes, approximating 700 pages.

319

2. Semi-Structured Interviews. Additionally, thirty semi-structured interviews, each lasting an average of one and one-half to two hours, were conducted by the first author with key staff and volunteer leaders at various sub-units within Medlay. Given identification of the "conceptually meaningful groups," particular attention was paid to interviewing the key national-level volunteers, including the current board officers and past board chair, as well as every member of the senior management staff (e.g., the CEO and his direct reports) and other relevant managers and board members.

3. Archival Sources. Archival documentation consisted of meeting minutes, publications, and internal memos. These documents were collected and analyzed in order to both further contextualize and refine observations developed from participant observation and interviews, and to validate the generated themes.

Data Analysis

As is typical with other research based on qualitative data (cf. Diesing 1971; Eisenhardt 1989), we used an iterative approach to circle back and forth between data and concepts. First, in the field, we generated and refined experience-near (Geertz 1983) or first-order (Gioia and Chittipeddi 1991) themes disclosed in the field data. Here, for example, we identified top management's view of the board-top manager relationship, the prevalence of talk about being volunteer-driven, and the extent of hugging and kissing as greeting in Medlay. After identifying a theme, we sought additional data for comparison, a practice known as theoretical sampling (Agar 1980; Gephart 1993; Glaser and Strauss 1967), to determine the extent of agreement and disagreement, as well as plausible interpretations of the meaning of the emerging themes. For example, we sought to determine which managers held the disclosed view of the board-management relationship, whether board members held similar views, and whether actors disclosed different views in different settings, e.g., whether managers conveyed one view in front of directors and another in their absence.

Throughout the research, our goal was to increase the dependability of the data (Diesing 1971), the type of contextual validity that is concerned with understanding the human system in its particularity to the extent possible from the members' perspectives. Dependability enables the researcher to assert that a certain uniformity exists in the data collected (a theme), and that the resulting interpretations authentically and plausibly, though not with absolute certainty or accuracy (Golden-Biddle and Locke 1993), explain what was researched. To this end, we compared particular sources of data (e.g., an interview with one person) with other collected data (e.g., observation and interview data from different people) to disclose any systematic bias present in data sources. And we used multiple sources of data to balance the weaknesses of any one source with the strengths of another source.

Once out of the field, we generated experience-distant (Geertz 1983), or second-order (Gioia and Chittipeddi 1991) themes through conversations that linked first-order themes with our experiences of Medlay leadership, the field data, and the extant literature on boards. It was at this stage that we sought to explicitly depict the cultural complexity in the board-top manager relationship that we had observed, but which had not been well-developed in the literature. We selected the questioning of the budget as the focal point of our analyses for the following reasons. It was the most compelling and dramatic example of that complexity, it was a highly significant event for Medlay members, and it rendered manifest the latent contradictions that board members experienced. Additionally, it provided the empirical setting in which all of the "conceptually meaningful groups" (identified above) interacted on a face-to-face basis. Through draft versions, and then through revisions based on reviewers' comments, we have refined that complexity to mean how identity shapes the board role and the conflicts of commitment that board incumbents face in an organization characterized by a hybrid identity.

In the next two major sections, we integrate the empirical data with our analyses to portray first, the construction and importance of the hybrid organizational identity in Medlay and how it shapes the board role, and second, what happens when an action occurs that breaches expectations of that role. In both sections, actual data are indented or placed in quotations, whereas our analyses remain outside the quotes.

....

Medlay's Organizational Identity and the Role of the Board

Medlay as a Volunteer-driven Organization

Reflecting the broader American culture within which it exists, Medlay prides itself in encouraging broad volunteer participation and strong volunteer governance. . . . One of the most often stated, least understood parts of our culture is that Medlay is a volunteer-driven organization. Ultimately, the only truly unique part of our culture is that volunteers govern our destiny. This concept and principle is sacrosanct, and must be preserved for us to be fully accountable to the public and to our mission statement. Obviously, since we are a large organization, it is essential that we employ and retain highly skilled professional staff. However, it is critical that the volunteers not relinquish their responsibility.

This excerpt, delivered to board members and management by the board chair (who has since become staff CEO), portrays a central, distinctive, and enduring belief in Medlay as a *volunteer-driven organization*. The middle portion of the board chair's statement most clearly delineates the importance of this belief:

Ultimately, the only truly unique part . . . is that volunteers govern our destiny. This . . . is sacrosanct, and must be preserved. . . .

In public meetings and interviews, board members and managers alike affirmed both the volunteer-driven identity and their commitment to that attribute of Medlay. Some typical comments include:

You would never (as a staff person) make hardly any kind of organizational change without volunteers buying in. . . . [Senior executive, national headquarters.]

This is an organization in which volunteers run and make decisions. There's a tremendous commitment on the part of volunteers . . . Volunteers are unpaid staff. . . . [Current national board member and previous board chair.]

The top manager implements the policies of Medlay which are the creation of the volunteers. . . . The volunteers, they have the responsibility for making the judgments. [Retired Medlay staff CEO and former Medlay volunteer.]

. . . (Medlay) is a volunteer organization. I don't know how many employees there are. The staff, they are the glue that holds it together, but decisions are basically made by volunteers and implemented by volunteers with staff support. So it is a volunteer organization. [Former national board member and honorary life volunteer.]

Medlay's identity as volunteer-driven, and leadership's desire to uphold this identity creates an expectation that directors will participate actively in running the organization. This expectation is supported, for example, in board policy, which prevents staff from voting on board matters. During the fieldwork, staff members followed this policy in all but one committee meeting, where they tried to vote along with the volunteers. However, one astute volunteer questioned the total vote as too large for the number of volunteers present, and reminded those present of the policy forbidding staff from voting. They took another vote, this time without staff participating. Later, after a lunch break when the chair reconvened the committee, he noted,

I am reminded that the votes for items brought before this committee are restricted to volunteer members of the committee. We use staff for input. Volunteers are the ones who make the decisions.

In addition, staff provide input into discussions only when asked to do so by the volunteers, or when they are scheduled ahead of time to present relevant information. Even the staff CEO adhered to this expected behavior. Early in the fieldwork, the first author noticed that the staff CEO had not said much during a board leadership long-range planning meeting. Asked during a break why he hadn't said much, he replied, "the role of staff is to be quiet." Finally, staff are socialized from the beginning of their employment about the importance of working as an *"advisor"* to volunteers. For example, in employee orientation sessions, senior managers personally take part in conveying the advisory role to organizational newcomers, noting that staff should,

counsel volunteers on the effect of policy on programs..., provide information, provide tools and techniques, administer the nominations process...

support the volunteers in their decision-making, evaluation and policy-making efforts.

And the manual provided to all new staff also affirms the construction of the staff role as advisor.

...you will notice that volunteer activities tend to be task-oriented while staff activities tend to be people-oriented. In other words, volunteers tend to perform the active tasks while staff provide support, counsel, resources, guidance, continuity and encouragement. Moreover, volunteers are public figures while staff tend to avoid the limelight. In this way, we continue to emphasize the volunteer-intensive nature of our mission.

Medlay as a Family of Friends

Upon entering Medlay, newcomers notice immediately that when board members, other volunteers, and staff greet, they hug and kiss one another, interacting in a way that is normally reserved in American culture for family or good friends.[1] As Goffman (1967, p. 41) notes, greetings are important ceremonial interactions in which actors demonstrate both that the relationship is the same as what it was since their last farewell, and that they will commit to continuing it during the present encounter. That commitment in Medlay is to continuing relationships based on friendliness and conflict avoidance.

The enactment of these relations is especially prominent among national board members who have cultivated strong friendships with each other over the 20 to 30 years that they have worked together on various projects and committees. Because the organization pays volunteer expenses associated with attending meetings and working on Medlay projects, senior-level volunteers have a number of opportunities to see each other during the year. The board chair and president, for example, annually travel anywhere from 50,000 to more than 300,000 miles for meetings and conferences throughout the world. During their time together at Medlay meetings, these volunteers indicate that they go to dinner "with old friends to catch up" on their personal lives, conveying a reunion-like atmosphere associated with the board meetings.

As two different volunteers, each with more than 30 years of association with Medlay, remarked,

We (my wife and I) have many old friends and we frequently refer to it (our relationship with Medlay) as a family because of all of the friendships that we have developed all over the country and literally all over the world.

I have been deeply committed (to Medlay)... My wife is also a great volunteer and has worked side by side... So we have been in it together, which reinforces both of our commitments.

These comments highlight the board members' perceptions of Medlay as a family, as well as their desire to view themselves as members of this family.

As part of being a family member and relating in a friendly manner, Medlay board members very rarely expressed disagreement during meetings. Board leadership periodically emphasized the need to avoid public disagreement. One comment expressed by the board chair to executive committee members is illustrative:

We must pull together to face some of today's challenges to Medlay... hash out our differences but always do so in a collegial sense... with other groups (in society) nipping at our heels, there has never been a time more important for us to work together and be the best we can be.

Additionally, during the fieldwork, on the few occasions when board members raised difficult or troublesome questions during meetings, leaders sought quickly to reinstate agreement. And later, often during lunch or break conversations, board leaders *always* and *informally* oriented the new, more junior members to the norms by explaining that such disagreement was "unfortunate."

Similarly, management is taught to avoid conflict with each other and volunteers. Specifically, managers learn to handle disagreements with volunteers by first seeking out other staff in order to get guidance, and then bringing in "friendly" volunteers to settle the problem with the other volunteer. Thus, staff avoid direct disagreement by using other volunteers to help ease the situation. This solution is a common one in Medlay, as typified in the staff saying, "put a volunteer between yourself and trouble." Indeed, whenever the authors invoked this saying in front of Medlay managers, they always laughed and shook their heads in agreement.

One of the major ways in which the context of friendly, conflict-free relations is maintained is through the selection and promotion of national-level board members who "do not make waves." Though framed differently by board and management leaders, the end result of the selection processes is to elect directors who will help to maintain the current construction of the board role and board–top management interactions, especially concerning the avoidance of conflict. As one long-time board member explained:

One factor that is very helpful, I think, is a movement through the chairs to give a very good depth of experience in all areas for those who are going to be either chairman or president . . . There is a long period of indoctrination for those who are willing to go that route, so you have very highly and widely experienced volunteers who are ready for those positions.

And managers explained:

I (and others) work hard to have only the safest volunteer selected to the national board, and especially to the executive committee . . . we try to get our candidates elected as senior volunteer leadership.

Commonly [explained another top manager] if the volunteer makes waves, they won't be put on other committees . . . That's the end of their career as a national volunteer.

The pervasiveness of conflict avoidance in Medlay is illustrated in part by the diversity of data sources pointing to this theme. Managers, for example, typically commented, "We go out of our way not to offend somebody." This principle also influenced the research. When bringing the researcher into new areas of the organization, informants separately told her that they had to make certain that people knew this ahead of time so that they wouldn't be "offended." Additionally, a major consulting firm's report noted that "Medlay's nonconfrontational culture makes change difficult and slow."

As a result of this conflict avoidance, the few disagreements that did emerge in Medlay were usually contained to the less public, backstage areas of informal conversation. The frontstage areas of committee and full board meetings were characterized by tact and a concerted effort to avoid conflict. Indeed, Medlay managers often referred to meetings in Medlay as "ceremony," meaning that meetings only confirmed what everyone already expected to happen. This was true even for the budgeting process, a clearly fiduciary responsibility of the board.[2] Consequently, Medlay's identity as a family, and leadership's desire to uphold this identity through conflict avoidance, created an expectation that directors will be friendly and avoid conflict.

How Identity Shapes the Board Role

The preceding portrait highlights Medlay's hybrid organizational identity, which consists of the two potentially incompatible dimensions of being volunteer-driven and a family of friends. Table 1 depicts each of these dimensions, along with the implied board role and the three different sources of data from which they were developed (members' views, practices, and formal documents). The volunteer-driven dimension of Medlay's identity suggests a board role as vigilant monitor, whereas the family of friends dimension suggests the role of friendly colleague; directors are simultaneously expected to vigilantly monitor management and to maintain friendly ties with each other and top managers.

The preceding portrait also suggests that directors feel a personal desire to uphold Medlay's organizational identity and the associated board role. Through often more than 20 years of association with Medlay, directors fulfill personal needs and enhance their individual identities, or views of themselves. Being a volunteer in Medlay, for example, creates a continuous social network of people, or "family," who share similar interests and passions, and relate to and care about each other. Further, by volunteering, Medlay directors fulfill their needs for altruism. As two board members noted:

We are volunteers and we want to give because that is why you are a volunteer. And I go back to what my father said, something for which you expect no money and no praise, just the satisfaction you get because you know that you have done the right thing. [Former board president and honorary life member.]

Table 1. Organizational Identity and the Implied Board Role in Medlay

	Identity dimension	
	Volunteer-driven	Family of friends
Implied board role	Vigilant monitor	Friendly, supportive colleague
Members' views		
Board chair	"Ultimately, the only truly unique part . . . is that volunteers govern our destiny. This . . . is sacrosanct, and must be preserved. . . ."	"We must pull together to face some of today's challenges . . . but always do so in a collegial sense."
Top managers	"You would never make hardly any kind of organizational change without volunteers buying in. . . ."	". . . if volunteers make waves, they won't be put on other committees . . . That's the end of their career as a national volunteer."
	"The volunteers, they have the responsibility for making the judgments."	
Other board members	"This is an organization in which volunteers run and make decisions."	"We (my wife and I) have many old friends and we frequently refer to [Medlay] as a family. . . ."
Practices	Only volunteers can vote No paid person can be on the board Staff are quiet during board meetings	Volunteer as media spokesperson Greetings of hugs and kisses Conflict avoidance in meetings Selection/promotion of "safe" directors
Formal documents	Staff manual: ". . . volunteers . . . perform the active tasks while staff provide support, counsel, resources, guidance, continuity and encouragement. . . ."	Consulting firm report: "Medlay's non-confrontational culture makes change difficult and slow."

What I have found about Medlay is that it is a reflection of the best parts of the American people themselves. What I mean by that is, first of all, people do not volunteer for Medlay unless they want to help other people. That is the nature of joining. [Current board member, former board president.]

Finally, being a Medlay volunteer enhances board members' sense of professional esteem and competency. Medlay volunteers are treated with high regard, both by Medlay staff and by the medical profession. For example, for a physician to serve as Medlay's board president is an honor in the medical field. And only volunteers in Medlay are interviewed by the media. Congruent with a volunteer-driven identity, staff consider it an error in judgment for them to seek or receive media exposure.

Following from this discussion, in Figure 2 we posit a model of four mutually interdependent elements that shape the board role through the joint processes of identification (Dutton et al. 1994) and action. The cognitive process of identification connects individuals' and organizational identities, denoting that overlapping attributes exist between them (Dutton et al. 1994). Identification is strongest when members believe that preserving the organization's identity also fulfills their own needs (Erez and Earley 1993, cited in Weick 1995). In Medlay, directors' desires for esteem, altruism, and social affiliation are highly congruent with the organization's identity of being volunteer-driven and a family of

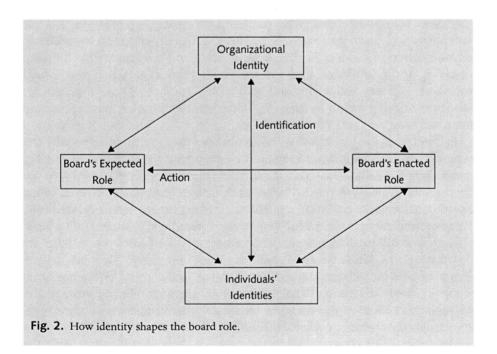

Fig. 2. How identity shapes the board role.

friends. Identification is further strengthened by members' positive associations with the organization (Dutton et al. 1994). Medlay board members are proud that their efforts have resulted in the organization's funding of Nobel laureate research, and more generally, are proud to be members of the organization.

I think it is the greatest volunteer organization in the world that I am aware of . . . the organization is something that generates the best of the people who are volunteers. [Former board member and honorary life member.]

I was privileged to have served as Medlay's president. And in that period of time I came to see the enormous and very powerful and talented network of volunteers that has sustained the entire cause. . . . [Former board president, current member.]

I don't think there is any doubt that Medlay is *the* outstanding volunteer health agency in not only the United States but in the world. And that's fairly generally recognized. [Current medical board member.]

Action, the second process depicted in our model, is a behavioral process consisting of the actions taken by board members as they seek to fulfill their role. The board's expected role is a preconceived notion with regard to what will take place (Weick 1995), in this case, how board members should act. When board members act in a manner consistent with the expected board role, they create congruence between the expected and enacted board role. Furthermore, these board members' actions maintain individuals' and organizational identities, and reaffirm the overlap between them. For Medlay board members, being volunteer-driven and altruistic creates expectations that the volunteers will participate actively in running the organization by selflessly devoting hours of service. Further, being a family of friends as well as fulfilling needs of social affiliation and esteem creates the expectation that board members will act collegially and will avoid conflict. Thus, expectations structure ongoing action by affecting what members notice, remember, and infer, and how they act (Weick 1995).

In Medlay, as long as board members believe that everyone, especially the senior board leadership and top managers, are acting for the good of Medlay, and as long as conflict is avoided, departures from the expected board role can be overlooked and incumbents experience little role strain. However, when board members take actions in a public setting that breach their expected role, latent contradictions in the hybrid identity are surfaced which hinders individuals' abilities to fulfill particular needs. This creates a type of intra-role conflict for board members which we call "conflicts of commitment." They are neither able to uphold the different dimensions of the organization's identity nor fulfill some of their key needs. The existence of these conflicts threatens the organization's identity and weakens members' identification with the organization. Further, when people face conflicts of commitment, they experience strain, which they try to alleviate by reducing their identification with the organization, acting to transform the hybrid identity into a monolithic identity, or engaging in facework directed toward mitigating the situation.

In the next section, we examine what occurred in Medlay when some board members engaged in conflict. In this case, during a full board meeting, some directors questioned board leadership about the budget, including "lavish" travel expenditures. We analyze how these budget questions breached the ongoing governance process in Medlay, and thereby threatened organizational identity, and created conflicts of commitment for the board members. In addition, we detail the actions of board members and leadership when faced with these conflicts of commitment.

The Breach and Conflicts of Commitment in the Boardroom

Creating the Breach: Questions About the Budget

In the months preceding the annual June board meeting, some board members informally expressed concern about the growing administrative expenditures, especially the travel expenditures incurred by senior board leaders and top managers, and increasing numbers of staff. Their concerns reached the formal arena during the June 1990 national board of directors meeting when, according to Medlay senior managers, "for the first time in the history of the organization, the board of directors questioned the proposed budget."

A few board members questioned board and staff leadership about the increasing number of employees at the headquarters, the overall proposed 10 percent increase in the budget, surging travel expenditures, including what they described as "lavish" travel expenditures incurred by some board members and top managers, and the amount of savings, if any, generated from the recent purchase of a building. They expressed their concerns about these rising expenditures in light of Medlay's decline in revenues. In particular, some members questioned whether money dedicated to funding research in accordance with board policy was instead being used to offset rising administrative costs.

Both staff and board leadership reported that the most vocal questioner was a female board member (Jane) who asked specific questions about staffing levels and travel. Jane represented a large west coast division long regarded as a maverick division of Medlay. Leadership indicated that Jane had "nothing to lose by asking the controversial questions" because she was not going any higher in the volunteer career ranks at Medlay. A few years earlier, they explained, Jane had launched an attempt to become the first female chair of the

329

board, but was overlooked by the nominating committee because she had been "sort of a renegade." Instead, the committee nominated a woman with a much less controversial style who was subsequently elected as the first (and only, to date) female chair of Medlay's national board of directors.

Immediately after the questioning, the board chair responded by proposing that he would set up a budget review committee to examine the budget figures more closely and to examine the feasibility of a budget reduction. He proposed further to hold an open forum on the budget at the November meeting solely to address these questions and take further questions from board members about the budget. As a result, the board voted to pass the proposed budget. However, the board stipulated that their approval be subject to the implementation of the chair's proposal, as shown in the following excerpt from the meeting minutes.

Amendment #1: That all questions raised during the budget discussions at the June meeting will be responded to in a studious way, directly in writing to the Board; moreover, there will be an opportunity at the next time the Board meets for open discussion of the budget; and

Amendment #2: That concurrent with the report of the Budget Committee to the Board; there be a report on the impact of reducing the budget levels.

Questioning the budget in a public forum constituted a breach, or interruption (Weick 1995), in the expectation that Medlay board members would avoid conflict. In turn, this unexpected event surfaced the latent contradiction in hybrid identity between being volunteer-driven and a family of friends, and confronted members with a conflict of commitment. Directors could no longer uphold both identity dimensions; they faced a choice between exercising vigilance and maintaining volunteer control, or avoiding further conflict and safeguarding the principle of friendship.

In his response to the questioning, the board chair invoked organizationally-sanctioned and identity-consistent "face-saving" strategies to shut down, or at least contain, the breach. By appointing a special committee and scheduling an open forum on the budget, the Board Chair used the face-saving strategy of *restitution* (Tedeschi and Melburg 1984); action designed to signal responsiveness to board members' concerns and adherence to the Medlay identity. Table 2 describes this face-saving strategy, as well as others used by leadership to handle the breach, and which will be developed below.

Repairing the Breach: Backstage Activity

Subsequent to the June meeting, the board chair (Jim) formed the budget review committee, which was composed of five volunteers, all of whom were

Table 2. "Face-Saving" Strategies Used by Medlay Leadership to Repair Identity

Type of strategy and definition	Examples
Restitution: action designed to respond to expressed concerns and make good on damages or perceived problems.	Board Chair appointed a special committee of volunteers to examine the budget; also scheduled an open forum of the budget at the next board meeting. In open forum, Board Chair lets audience know that leadership has spent "considerable time and effort addressing the questions and that he sees "need for even more volunteer involvement in the budgeting process."
Account: a construction of the perceived breach designed to minimize its severity or negative repercussions.	During the Executive Committee's review of the written responses to the board's questions, the Board Chair suggests that leadership "speak positively" and "be positive and upbeat" ... and that the current budget numbers are "good" and "real." During the open forum, a number of those who presented stated that they support the budget.
Justification: a specific type of account designed to convince others of the worthiness of their efforts and minimize the undesirable nature of the situation.	During the open budget forum, presenters noted that they have cut the budget by 10% by reducing those areas with the "least adverse affect" yet with substantial savings; One member specifically notes that "I am satisfied with the substantial savings ... I'm not sure it's productive to rehash the issues any further. ... " Some committee members seeking to explain the travel expenditures during the open forum as travel to "non-luxurious" locations.
Props: a device used to support an actor's role performance.	The bull's-eye target used by the Board Chair during the open forum. A committee member's use of the only overhead transparency during the open forum with, "Let's get on with business with our lean budget."

long-tenured, senior members of board leadership. None of the original budget questioners were appointed to the committee. The charge to the committee was to:

... gain an in-depth understanding of the budget in order to acquire a sound basis for evaluating the impact of a decrease in the proposed budget. Inherent in that charge will be to respond to the budget questions that were raised at the June meeting.

Noting that the questioning of the budget initiated a lot of activity on the part of staff leadership, one top manager proclaimed that he had "never seen so much time spent on the budget as we have done since the June board meeting." Staff prepared all of the responses to the board questions and themselves met to reduce the budget by 10 percent. When the special board committee met in August, the staff presented their recommendations. According to the minutes of that meeting, those present included the members of the committee, the board chair, relevant top managers, and "Jane, who attended at the invitation of the board chair." After line-by-line review of the budget and the proposed reductions, the committee recommended that the Finance and Executive committees accept "management's plan to reduce the budget," and that the board initiate a process to include "more volunteer involvement in the budgeting process."

At the regular executive committee meeting held in September 1990, the finance committee chair (Harry), reported on the budget review committee's progress. Top managers were also present in this meeting, but conformed to their advisory role and stayed in the background. The following is an excerpt from this discussion concerning the prepared responses to the board questions.

HARRY (Finance Chair): "We appointed a special review committee for the budget as a result of the questions raised relative to the budget at the June meeting." He distributes the preliminary responses to each of the questions posed, including justification for the headquarters' move, plans to cut headquarters staff through attrition, and evidence that the amount of money dedicated to research is increasing. He explains that the responses were prepared by the staff finance department and reviewed by the budget committee.

DAVE (Executive Committee Member): "I am having trouble with the prepared responses. Reading the prepared answers, I see an adversarial frame of mind in them.... That's what we'll be hit with at the board meeting...if the questions are not answered directly, the responses will be interpreted as a smoke screen.... We need to tell them that we saved money...currently what exists is almost an over-explanation to justify what we've done...these responses affect the credibility of this group, the board and the finance committee."

JOHN (Executive Committee Member): "This is a perception issue that's very important."

JIM (Board Chair): "I appreciate that we should look at the adversarial position of this and also point out that we brief ourselves and be prepared to speak very positively and with very succinct statements regarding the efforts and the budgeting process. There is an attitude that we need to go into the annual meeting with. More than in the entire history of Medlay organization, we have numbers that are good, numbers that are real in the budgeting process.... We ought to be positive and up-beat.... It's very clear that we have answers for the questions that were asked.... We need to leave here with strong confidence in leadership and the budget."

STAN (Executive Committee Chair/Board Chair Elect): "Thank you. That's exactly the attitude that I would like to see conveyed."

After further discussion, the executive committee voted to approve the budget review committee's recommendations and take them to the meeting of the full board.

In their remarks, the committee members express concern about how the full board will receive the budget review committee's responses. Jim, in particular, suggests that all members "speak positively," and "be positive and upbeat" in their attitude going into the meeting. Further, Jim suggests that the budget numbers used "now more than in the entire history of Medlay" (where "now" refers to the period after the work by the special committee) are "good" and "real." Here, Jim begins to articulate the development of an *account*, a construction of the situation designed to minimize the severity or negative repercussions of the predicament (Schlenker 1980, Scott and Lyman 1968). If the board members accept the account, Jim will have minimized the disruption (Schlenker and Weigold 1992), and helped to heal the breach.

A significant amount of the repair activity has occurred backstage. Leadership took very specific action to redress the conflict by including "Jane," one of the original budget questioners, in at least part of the backstage action, and by explicitly developing their "account": the way they would frame the events when they conducted the open budget forum frontstage, face-to-face with the entire board.

Bridging Contradictions: Frontstage Activity

The "Open Forum on the Budget" was held during the national board meeting in November at a large, national-chain hotel. The forum was held in a large salon, in which chairs and a long table were placed at the front for the five members of the budget review committee, the board chair and chair-elect, and two top managers: the senior vice president of finance, and the CEO. The audience consisted of approximately 250 people who were current board members, top managers, and honorary life members of the board. No media representatives or outsiders were present, other than the first author. The audience members were seated in folding chairs arranged in three sections facing the front table. In between each section of chairs were standing microphones for audience members to use during the forum. Upon entering the room, each audience member received a $6'' \times 8''$ index card and was instructed to write down questions for the presenters which would later be collected.

The meeting began a few minutes after 3:00 PM and was scheduled to end at 4:30 PM.

JIM (Board Chair): Welcomes those present, outlines the "ground rules" and explains there will be short presentations on the budget with time for questions and answers at the end. He says that "the spirit is to present the budget to the best of our ability and to allow for discussion to the limits of our abilities. . . . At the June Board meeting, a committee was appointed to address the questions on the budget which came up from the members. I can assure you that significant time and effort has been put into addressing these questions by the staff and volunteers. We hope today to have clear communication with the budget. . . . I'd like to make three points. First, the budget presented in June was balanced. Second, the June operating budget did not call for a 10 percent increase in expenditures over the prior year. Third, the headquarters operating budget is now less than the previous year. . . . I am convinced that the revised budget developed by the CEO is lean and deserves your support. . . . However, . . . we have found the need for even more volunteer involvement than we have had in the past....I have made a recommendation to the finance committee to address this issue." At this point, the chair turns the meeting over to Stan.

STAN (Board Chair-Elect/Executive Committee Chair): Introduces the members of the budget review committee. "The charge of the committee was to attain in-depth knowledge of the budget and to assure...a sound basis...for a...decrease.... Through this process, we realize that it is not possible or practical for any one board member to become sufficiently familiar with all parts of the budget. Thus, the committee was very helpful in getting an idea of the key reductions and ways to reduce costs." Then, he indicates that committee members will now respond to the questions posed in June by the board members. He ends by stating, "I recommend adoption of the budget revision."

HARRY (Finance Chair/Budget Review Committee Member): Reviews the budget components for the audience in great detail.

TOM (Budget Review Committee Member): "This committee has cut the budget presented in June by 10 percent. The reductions that have been made are those with the least adverse affect. These include staff costs, operating costs and capital expenditures.... Through attrition, staff salary and benefit expenses have been cut....Operating expenses have been reduced...by postponing programs and reducing general administrative costs. Finally, capital expenditures have been reduced...by primarily deferring planned purchases."

STAN (Board Chair Elect/Executive Committee Member): Discusses savings associated with the purchase of a new building which "have been spent to enlarge the various programs of Medlay."

BOB (Budget Review Committee Member): Reports on the move to the current headquarters, concluding with, "as a result of the thoroughness and openness through the work of this committee, I am satisfied that substantial savings have resulted from the move. Plus, we have equity in a building now....I'm not sure it's productive to rehash the issues any further...."

After Bob finished, a few of the committee members added their comments on the budget reductions. At this point, it is 4:20 and there has been no interaction with the audience.

In his opening statement, Jim upholds the volunteer-driven identity of Medlay by letting the audience know that volunteers have spent "significant time and effort" addressing the board members' questions, and that he sees the "need for even more volunteer involvement." Additionally, in their statements, the committee members present a *defense* of the revised operating budget and the savings resulting from the purchase of a new building.

JIM (Board Chair): "It is time for you to raise any questions indeed that you might have....I will moderate. You may go to the microphone or ask questions on the cards."

As Jim says it is time for questions from the audience, he reaches down under the table and reveals a large bull's-eye target that consists of professionally drawn black concentric circles against a white background. Jim places it across his front and pretends that he is the target. Everyone laughs.

Jim's display of the bull's-eye target associated with opening up the meeting to questions from the full board was clearly planned, though unexpected by the audience. Used in sports, a target enables a person to take aim and to give his/her best shot to hit the bull's-eye. At one level, the target points to Jim as the focal point of criticism; he is willing to bear the tough questions, even those which hit the bull's-eye. As the board's senior leader, the members take direct aim at him when they criticize the budget. However, at another level, the target becomes a shield that protects Jim from criticism by diffusing the situation with humor. Thus, the bull's-eye target as symbol illuminates the double image of board members as vigilant monitors who have the opportunity to ask tough questions, and also as friends who share laughter and avoid asking tough questions.

Jim begins to share the questions on the cards, and asks particular committee members to address them. There is no verbal interaction with the audience as the committee answers the questions.

At this point, an audience member rises and goes to the microphone. This woman's name is Jane, and as she rises, a few managers indicate to the first author that "she is the one we told you about" who raised the "difficult questions at the June board meeting."

JANE: Jane indicates that she would like to "clarify the question" that someone else had asked. Then, she proceeds to answer the question herself. "While I have the microphone, let me say that I have never been in a forum that is so informational...that sensitizes all of us to what is going on. For example, the difference between the use of unrestricted legacy funds and the general operating program year to year." Then she asks, "If you want more money to go to research, where does that money come from?"

The committee members respond to her question.

JIM: Adds that "in order to raise the money going to research, we have to take from either operating or medical awards.... Traditionally, we have spent interest income for increases in operating expenses and unrestricted legacy funds for increases in research, with some exceptions."

JANE: Then suggests that the "two policy issues for the Board are: 1. How much money do you want to go to research? and 2. Where do you want to take the money from?" At this point, she thanks the committee again for "providing such detailed information." She then steps away from the microphone and returns to her seat.

At this point, Jim thanks Jane for her comments.

On one hand, Jane upholds Medlay's identity of being volunteer-driven by acting like a vigilant monitor and involved director. She asks about increasing money for research, an issue which feeds directly into board members' concerns about conveying a positive image to the public at large, and she frames the policy questions that members should consider in future discussions.

On the other hand, Jane also safeguards the friendly nature of Medlay's identity by avoiding direct confrontation. Specifically, she twice compliments leadership for conveying the detailed information and asks her questions in a moderate, somewhat neutral tone of voice. Rather than further widening the breach, Jane has assisted leadership in healing the breach and restoring their credibility.

JIM: Returns to taking questions from the cards, indicating that there are some questions about the number of staff and volunteers representing Medlay at international meetings. "There's a perception that travelers need the finest of hotels." He turns to the committee and says, "Who hasn't had a chance to respond yet?"

The audience as well as the committee laugh.

TOM: "When looking at the travel budget, you must consider that this is a worldwide fight. . . . there is nothing luxurious about Liberia!"

STAN: Indicates that because volunteers traveling for Medlay give up their own time at their offices which reduces their income, "they should travel and be housed properly."

The sensitivity of travel expenditures is illustrated by the chair's question, "Who hasn't had a chance to respond yet?" and the accompanying audience nervous laughter. Both Tom and Stan respond to the question with *justifications* for the travel expenditures, a face-saving strategy that seeks to minimize the undesirable nature of the situation. Here, Tom and Stan invoke a sense of fulfilling Medlay's mission, and the notion of volunteer sacrifice to travel to "non-luxurious" locations as specific justifications.

The board chair closes discussion on this question by indicating that international support for other organizations (and the resultant travel expenditures for Medlay) will be a future policy issue for board members to address.

At this point, another person rises and goes to the microphone. This woman's name is Clara, and she is a significant donor to Medlay in addition to being a board member.

CLARA: "I want to thank the committee in response to what I have heard here today. Regarding travel, though, I would hope that the committee would continue to look at the travel expenditures." Then she asks whether there is still a cap on increases in salaries, to which the committee responds yes. Then she adds, "The reduction in unrestricted legacy funds bothers me. Why does the trend keep declining?"

The committee responds to her that these present times are unusual.

CLARA: "Then if that is the case, don't tell us to go out and raise more money, for you'll just spend it on administration."

At this point, the audience laughs.

JIM: As Clara leaves the microphone, he notes the board will continue to examine the trend in unrestricted moneys. And he says the committee will continue to look further into the issue of whether Medlay is "trimming all of the costs that we should be trimming."

While Jim is talking to the audience, Harry approaches Clara and discusses her questions with her more fully.

Clara, an influential board member due to her donor status, continues the discussion of travel expenditures through her comments. In a manner similar to Jane's, Clara, too, upholds the expectation that board members are friendly, by first complimenting the special committee, and then using a regular tone of voice to convey her concern about increasing expenditures. However, not being satisfied with the committee's response, she briefly departs from that expectation (as indicated by the audience laughter) by warning that board members will not be as willing to raise funds if leadership does not address the problem of increasing expenditures. Signifying Clara's importance and status, Harry approaches Clara as she leaves the microphone, to talk further about her concerns.[3]

CARL (Special Committee Member): Declares it is 5:00, and moves to close the meeting by noting, "We can even handle conflicts and challenges in our ranks...a real benefit for all of us to clear the air....Now, let's get on with business with our lean revised budget...." As he says this, he shows the only transparency used during the forum, on which is written: "Let's get on with business with our lean budget."

The next day, the board approved the budget overwhelmingly. They also approved two resolutions to affirm the need for board involvement and to create a board "budget committee." At the conclusion of the voting, Jim, the Board Chair, noted that,

"There was a great deal of participation by volunteers in the budget this year, and even the chair can learn the budget! All of you as the board passed a very sound budget."

Together, the actions taken by board and staff leadership and other board members at the open budget forum reinforced the attribution that everyone was trying their very best to maintain the identity of Medlay as a volunteer-driven and friendly organization, and to fulfill the board role as vigilant monitor and friendly colleague. Board members who asked questions felt that they had done their best as vigilant, yet collegial directors. Similarly, board leaders and top managers felt that they were not only responsive to the idea of greater volunteer involvement in the budgeting process, but that the budget issue had been redressed without a heated confrontation. Thus, by bridging the contradictions between vigilance and friendship, the conflicts of commitment receded and Medlay's identity was preserved.

How Crises Threaten Organizational Identity and Create Conflicts of Commitment

Based on the preceding portrait of governance in Medlay, we develop in Table 3 a process model of how crises threaten organizational identity and create conflicts of commitment for board members. Whereas Table 1 shows the

Table 3. A Process Model of How Departures from Expected Board Governance Threaten Organizational Identity and Create Conflicts of Commitment for Board Members

Phase	1	2	3
Process	Creating the breach	Repairing the breach	Bridging contradictions identified by breach
Timeframe	June board meeting	August–October	November board meeting
Site of action	Frontstage	Backstage	Frontstage
Actions by board members	"First ever" questioning of budget in meeting by some directors about increasing administrative costs and "lavish" travel expenses.	Jane attends special budget committee meeting in August.	Jane asks questions and compliments leadership on "Informative" session. Clara asks questions in a collegial manner; does suggest that expenses need to decline or volunteers will stop donating their time.
Actions by leadership	Board chair forms special committee to review budget; schedules "open forum" on budget at next board meeting Restitution	Top managers reduce budget by 10% and develop written responses to board budget questions; chair convenes special budget committee meeting and invites Jane; executive committee meets and reviews budget committee's recommendations Account	Leadership/budget committee address board questions from June meeting in open forum meeting, and take questions in writing and from the floor Restitution Account Justification Props
Conflicts of commitment	Board faces conflict: vigilant monitor vs. friendly colleague.	Leadership tries to resolve conflict.	Leadership bridges contradiction in identity; conflict of commitment recedes.
Organizational identity	Threatened	Under repair	Preserved

creation and ongoing maintenance of identity and its influence on the board role, Table 3 depicts what occurs when departures from expected role performance trigger a breach. There is a three-phased process associated with the Medlay budget situation: (1) creating the breach, (2) repairing the breach, and (3) bridging the contradictions surfaced by the breach. Each phase is described in terms of major process, timeframe, site of action, actions taken by board members, actions taken by board and staff leadership, and the effect on organizational identity and conflicts of commitment.

In phase 1, questioning the budget created the breach because it departed from the expectation that board members avoided conflict. In turn, this departure surfaced the latent contradictions in identity and confronted board members with a conflict of commitment: Which dimension of the identity do they uphold? The Board Chair immediately invoked the face-saving strategy of restitution in the effort to shut down the breach. In phase 2, leadership worked backstage to repair the breach by informally including Jane, one of the original budget questioners, in the meeting of the Budget Review Committee, and by developing an "account" of their responses to the board questions in preparation for the upcoming forum on the budget. In phase 3, frontstage was once again the site of both board and leadership action, as all worked together in a friendly and collegial manner to bridge the contradictions in identity rendered visible by the breach. Although leadership enacted face-saving strategies in all three phases, these strategies assumed the greatest prominence in phase 3, as leadership publicly sought to bring closure to the breach.

Discussion

Our study of the unfolding and ongoing processes of governance in Medlay extends the literature on corporate governance in two respects. First, by showing how the functioning of the board is shaped by the identity of the organization, it addresses a central limitation of the agency theory conception of the board as shaped by fiduciary and legalistic pressures. Although some organizational scholars have begun to address this limitation by analyzing how board functioning is shaped by structural (Davis 1993), political (Romano 1993), and cognitive (Zajac and Westphal 1996) contexts, to date there has been no empirical work on how the functioning of boards is shaped by the cultural context. This paper illuminates the cultural embeddedness of boards by showing how organizational identity, in combination with the processes of identification and action, influences the construction and enactment of the director's role. In particular, our analyses show that the board role in Medlay was not only encoded in formal documents, but also was embedded in its Janus-like organizational identity as a volunteer-driven organization and a family of friends.

This study also extends the literature on corporate governance by introducing the idea of *conflicts of commitment*, which highlights a greater complexity in board members' actions and decisions. A prevailing agency-based explanation for the failure of outsider-dominated boards to assert vigilance is that board members experience *conflicts of interest*, a form of inter-role conflict that stems from occupying multiple roles with potentially incompatible expectations. For example, an outside director may also be an executive of a key supplier, customer, or a bank. By contrast, this study suggests that another testable explanation for ineffective vigilance of boards is *conflicts of commitment*, a form of intra-role conflict that stems from the incumbent's own commitment to a hybrid organizational identity. Whereas role theory research has conceptualized intra-role conflict as occurring when multiple stakeholders place conflicting demands on role incumbents, this type of intra-role conflict occurs in the absence of multiple stakeholders; it is based on the members' own strain in adhering to conflicting aspects of the organization's identity. Thus, when actions occur that breach expected role performance, latent contradictions in organizational identity emerge, and members are faced with the conflict of upholding one dimension of identity while undermining the other.

A related implication stemming from our study of boards is that the "outsider-insider" dichotomy in board research can be misleading because outsiders become members, to varying degrees, through their identification with the organization's identity. This process does not just occur in Medlay (Dutton et al. 1994). For example, alumni who serve as trustees of a university, or arts enthusiasts who serve as on the board of a museum may be outsiders in the sense of being nonemployees, but may nevertheless feel a strong sense of membership and identification. Similarly, in the for-profit world, it is also possible that venture capitalists who own a chunk of equity and serve on the board (like A.C. Markkula of Apple) may also feel identified with the organization. Likewise, directors on the board of a firm belonging to a Japanese keiretsu or a South Korean chaebol feel themselves to be part of a larger organizational network.

Taken together, these preceding observations suggest that models of corporate governance, and in particular those based on agency theory, need to incorporate into their studies nonfiduciary dimensions of organizational life, e.g., cultural embeddedness. Absent an understanding of social, structural, cultural, political and cognitive contexts, prevailing models of governance are neither realistic nor generalizable. Moreover, students of boards and other governance structures need to be sensitive to when directors' embeddedness in the organizational context is a source of strength and when it is a source of constraint (Granovetter 1985). Thus, ties that bind can also blind. For example, "outside" directors may work closely with management because they share similar beliefs, but that cultural embeddedness can also inhibit them from providing criticism and expressing dissatisfaction.

This study also contributes to research on organizational identity and points to some propositions that can be examined in future research. Although several studies have shown how organizational identity shapes individual-level outcomes such as involvement and commitment (see Whetten et al. 1992 for a review), and management responses to social concerns (Dutton and Dukerich 1991), there has been little discussion about how organizational identity shapes the social construction of key roles. The present study suggests a model for how organizational identity shapes the role of the board of directors. In particular, we posit that organizational and individual identities shape the expected and enacted board role through the processes of identification and action. The first process, identification, denotes the overlap in the attributes of organizational and individual identity. The Medlay study provides support for the proposition posed by Dutton et al. (1994) that a strong identification results from consistency in those attributes. Additionally, the board's expected role is derived from organizational and individual identities. Given the strong identification in Medlay, both identities place consistent expectations on the board role and frame the construction of this role as vigilant monitor and friendly colleague. Action is the second process, and it denotes that when board members act consistent with role expectations, the prevailing construction of that role, and identification with organizational identity will be maintained.

Although some writers have suggested that organizational identity may be composed of contradictory elements (Albert and Whetten 1985, Louis 1990), there has been little study of the effects of hybrid identity on organizational phenomena. This study proposes that the holographic form of hybrid identity (in which conflicting dimensions of identity are diffused throughout the organization) generates the potential for conflicts of commitment for board role incumbents. Indeed, it suggests that the greater the divergence of dimensions incorporated into holographic hybrid identity, the greater the potential for this type of intra-role conflict to occur. Finally, the study suggests that the existence of either form of intra-role conflict may further induce and complicate leadership's repair work; leadership must both recreate a sense of internal balance and identification for individual board members, and restore the organization's identity.

Studies to date concerning identity-threatening events and leadership's responses to them (Dutton and Dukerich 1991; Elsbach 1994; Elsbach and Sutton 1992; Sutton and Callahan 1987) have focused primarily on members' responses to identity-threats that have involved audiences external to the organization. In contrast, the present study shows how a breach in expected role performance exposed latent contradictions in identity that necessitated leadership's response. No external audience was involved, and there was no evidence from the study that any member wanted to have outside audiences become aware of the breach. Our study demonstrates that when the organization's identity is threatened by internal members, an elite team, consisting of members of the board's executive committee and top managers, worked in concert to restore order and repair identity. This suggests that, when faced with internally-generated identity threats, coalitions seeking to redress the threat can consist of members whose interests might otherwise seem incompatible.

Furthermore, in their repair work, Medlay leadership worked frontstage to institute restitution immediately upon breach creation and also to bring the breach to closure; they utilized the backstage primarily to develop their accounts. Moreover, leadership employed predominantly those face-saving strategies that drew upon and sought to reaffirm the volunteer-driven dimension of Medlay's identity. And all were presented in a collegial, friendly style. In contrast to prior studies involving external audiences, Medlay leadership did not use the face-saving strategies of denial or acknowledgment. This suggests, then, that identity-threatening events involving internal audiences may induce one repertoire of responses, while those involving external audiences may induce a different repertoire.

The limitations of this study also deserve elaboration, and point to directions for future research on boards and organizational identity. This study examined contradictions between vigilance and friendship that surfaced due to questioning of the budget. Contradictions in hybrid organizational identity also need to be examined in different situations. For example, contradictions can become prominent for directors when firms enter new markets and meet resistance. Similarly, contradictions in organizational identity may besiege boards of directors when organizations embark on diversification—thus, the goal of maximizing shareholder value may conflict with the goal of growth. Another limitation is that this study examined a situation in which both directors and top managers cooperated to restore identity. Clearly, there is a need to study what happens in permanently failing organizations (Meyer and Zucker 1989), where there is hostility among stakeholders, especially stockholders and employees, and presumably less motivation for cooperation.

Finally, this study suggests that examining issues of board governance requires qualitative, field-based studies of ongoing relationships between directors and top managers *in* organizations. Large-scale quantitative studies that examine the effect of board composition and structure on compensation or the fates of C.E.O.s are useful to the extent that they provide a bird's eye view of corporate governance. However, field-based, qualitative studies of interactions between board members and top managers are necessary to provide a complementary worm's eye view of the ongoing corporate governance process in for-profit and nonprofit organizations.

Acknowledgments

The authors thank Rikki Abzug, Jean Bartunek, Pranab Chatterjee, Mary Ann Glynn, Consuelo Kertz, Karen Locke, Denise Rousseau, and Dennis Young for their helpful comments on an earlier version of this manuscript. In particular, we want to express our appreciation to the editor and anonymous reviewers at *Organization Science* who provided thoughtful comments that greatly assisted the development of this paper. We would also like to extend a special thank you to the leadership of Medlay, who generously opened their organization for research purposes.

The research was done while Karen Golden-Biddle was at Emory University.

Notes

1. During the field research, the first author noted in field notes that she first began to be hugged and/or kissed upon greeting at two months, coinciding in time with informants telling her that she had "survived the test" of not betraying confidences. In Medlay, they noted, this is quite a feat since the gossip network is extremely efficient.

2. Both board and staff leadership explained that the budget is typically approved by the full board with little discussion. The normal procedure is for management, with some input by senior volunteers, such as the board chair and the board treasurer, to develop the budget. Any differences are worked out informally before the board's finance committee meets to review these budget figures. After the finance committee adopts the budget, its chair (also the board treasurer) presents the budget for review to the executive committee. Finally, the board and finance committee chairs jointly present the budget to the full board of directors for their review and approval at the June meeting each year. Without much discussion, board members ratify the budget.

3. We do not have the longitudinal data necessary to discern whether or not there is significance to the fact that the only two public questioners of the budget in this forum are female. Both Jane, as a renegade individual with nothing to lose, and Clara, as a key donor, act as a "moral conscience" to the board, reminding them of their obligations as monitors. Perhaps gender is a factor here, to the extent that it indicates marginal status in a predominantly white male culture, such as Medlay, and is accompanied by a greater propensity to vigilantly monitor leadership.

References

Agar, M. H. (1980), *The Professional Stranger*, Orlando: Academic Press.

Albert, S. and D. Whetten (1985), "Organizational Identity," In L. L. Cummings and B. M. Staw (Eds.), *Research in Organizational Behavior*, Volume 7, Greenwich, CT: JAI Press, 263–295.

Ashforth, B. E. and F. Mael (1989), "Social Identity Theory and the Organization," *Academy of Management Review*, 14, 20–39.

Ben-Ner, A. (1986), "Nonprofit Organizations: Why Do They Exist in Market Economics?" in S. Rose-Ackerman (Ed.), *The Economics of Nonprofit Institutions*. Oxford, UK: Oxford University Press, 94–113.

Berger, P. and T. Luckmann (1966), *The Social Construction of Reality*, New York: Doubleday.

Berle, A. and G. C. Means (1932), *The Modern Corporation and Private Property*, New York: Macmillan.

Davis, G. M. (1991), "Agents Without Principles? The Spread of the Poison Pill through the Intercorporate Network," *Administrative Science Quarterly*, 36, 583–613.

—— (1993), "Who Gets Ahead in the Market for Corporate Control: The Political Economy of Multiple Board Memberships," *Academy of Management Best Paper Proceedings*, 202–206.

Diesing, P. (1971), *Patterns of Discovery in the Social Sciences*, New York: Aldine Publishing.

Dutton, J. E. and J. M. Dukerich (1991), "Keeping an Eye on the Mirror: The Role of Image and Identity in Organizational Adaptation," *Academy of Management Journal*, 34, 517–554.

——, ——, and C. V. Harquail (1994), "Organizational Images and Member Identification," *Administrative Science Quarterly*, 39, 239–263.

Eisenhardt, K. M. (1989), "Building Theories from Case Study Research," *Academy of Management Review*, 14, 4, 532–550.

Elsbach, K. D. (1994), "Managing Organizational Legitimacy in the California Cattle Industry: The Construction and Effectiveness of Verbal Accounts," *Administrative Science Quarterly*, 39, 57–88.

—— and R. I. Sutton (1992), "Acquiring Organizational Legitimacy through Illegitimate Actions: A Marriage of Institutional and Impression Management Theories," *Academy of Management Journal*, 35, 4, 699–738.

Fama, E. F. and M. C. Jensen (1983), "Separation of Ownership and Control," *Journal of Law and Economics*, 26, June, 327–349.

Fligstein, N. and R. Freeland (1995), "Theoretical and Comparative Perspectives on Corporate Governance," *Annual Review of Sociology*, 21, 21–43.

Geertz, C. (1983), *Local Knowledge*, New York: Basic Books.

Gephart, R. P. (1993), "The Textual Approach: Risk and Blame in Disaster Sensemaking," *Academy of Management Journal*, 36, 6, 1465–1514.

Gioia, D. and K. Chittipeddi (1991), "Sensemaking and Sensegiving in Strategic Change Initiation," *Strategic Management Journal*, 12, 433–448.

Glaser, B. G. and A. L. Strauss (1967), *The Discovery of Grounded Theory: Strategies for Qualitative Research*, New York: Aldine Publishing Co.

Goffman, E. (1959), *The Presentation of Self in Everyday Life*, New York: Doubleday Anchor Books.

—— (1967), *Interaction Ritual: Essays on Face-To-Face Behavior*, New York: Pantheon Books.

Golden-Biddle, K. and K. Locke (1993), "Appealing Work: An Investigation of How Ethnographic Works Convince," *Organization Science*, 4, 4, 595–616.

Goode, W. J. (1960), "A Theory of Role Strain," *American Sociological Review*, 25, 483–496.

Granovetter, M. (1985), "Economic Action and Social Structure: The Problem of Embeddedness," *American Journal of Sociology*, 91, 481–510.

Gross, N., W. S. Mason, and A. W. McEachern (1958), *Explorations in Role Analysis: Studies of the School Superintendency Role*, New York: John Wiley and Sons, Inc.

Hansmann, H. B. (1986), "The Role of Nonprofit Enterprise," in S. Rose-Ackerman (Ed.), *The Economics of Nonprofit Institutions*, Oxford, UK: Oxford University Press, 57–84.

Hirsch, P. M., S. Michaels, and R. Friedman (1987), " 'Dirty Hands' versus 'Clean Models': Is Sociology in Danger of Being Seduced by Economics?" *Theory and Society*, 16, 317–336.

Jensen, M. C. and W. H. Meckling (1976), "The Theory of the Firm: Managerial Behavior, Agency Costs and Ownership Structure," *Journal of Financial Economics*, 3, 305–360.

Kahn, R. L., D. M. Wolfe, R. P. Quinn, J. P. Snoek, and R. A. Rosenthal (1964), *Organizational Stress: Studies in Role Conflict and Ambiguity*, New York: Wiley.

Knorr-Cetina, K. (1981), *The Manufacture of Knowledge: An Essay on the Constructivist and Contextual Nature of Science*, New York: Pergamon Press.

Lofland, J. and L. Lofland (1984), *Analyzing Social Settings*, Belmont, CA: Wadsworth Publishing Company.

Louis, M. R. (1990), "Acculturation in the Workplace: Newcomers as Lay Ethnographers," in B. Schneider (Ed.), *Organizational Climate and Culture*, San Francisco, CA: Jossey Bass, 85–129.

Meyer, M. and L. Zucker (1989), *Permanently Failing Organizations*, Newbury Park, CA: Sage Publications.

Pettigrew, A. (1979), "On Studying Organizational Cultures," *Administrative Science Quarterly*, 570–581.

Pfeffer, J. and G. Salancik (1978), *The External Control of Organizations*, New York: Harper and Row.

Rabinow, P. and W. M. Sullivan (1979), *Interpretive Social Science: A Reader*, Berkeley, CA: University of California Press.

Roe, M. (1991), "A Political Theory of American Corporate Finance," *Columbia Law Review*, 91, 10–67.

Romano, R. (1993), "Public Pension Fund Activism in Corporate Governance Reconsidered," *Columbia Law Review*, 93, 795–853.

Roos, L. and F. A. Starke (1980), "Roles in Organizations," in W. Starbuck and P. Nystrom (Eds.), *Handbook of Organization Design*, Oxford, England: Oxford University Press, 290–308.

Schlenker, B. R. (1980), *Impression Management*, Monterey, CA: Brooks-Cole.

—— and M. F. Weigold (1992), "Interpersonal Processes Involving Impression Regulation and Management," *Annual Review of Psychology*, 43, 133–168.

Schutz, A. (1976), "The Social World and the Theory of Social Action," in A. Broderson (Ed.), *Collected Papers II: Studies in Social Theory*, Netherlands: Nijhoff, 91–105.

Scott, W. R. and Lyman, S. (1968), "Accounts," *American Sociological Review*, 33, 46–62.

Staw, B. and J. Ross (1987), "Behavior in Escalation Situations: Antecedents, Prototypes and Solutions," in L. L. Cummings and B. M. Staw (Eds.), *Research in Organizational Behavior*, 9, 39–78.

Sutton, R. I. and A. L. Callahan (1987), "The Stigma of Bankruptcy: Spoiled Organizational Image and Its Management," *Academy of Management Journal*, 30, 405–436.

Tedeschi, J. T. and V. Melburg (1984), "Impression Management and Influence in the Organization," *Sociology of Organizations*, 3, 31–58.

Useem, M. (1996), *Investor Capitalism*, New York: Basic Books.

Van Maanen, J. (1982), "Fieldwork on the Beat," in Van Maanen, Dabbs and Faulkner (Eds.), *Varieties of Qualitative Research*, Beverly Hills, CA: Sage Publications, 103–151.

Weick, K. E. (1995), *Sensemaking in Organizations*, Thousand Oaks, CA: Sage Publications.

Whetten, D. A., L. Lewis and L. J. Mischel (1992), "Towards an Integrated Model of Organizational Identity and Member Commitment," Working Paper (available from the authors).

Zajac, E. and J. Westphal (1996), "Who Shall Succeed: How CEO/Board Preferences and Power Affect the Choice of New CEO's," *Academy of Management Journal*, 39, 64–90.

Zukin, S. and DiMaggio, P. J. (1990), "Introduction," in S. Zukin and P. J. DiMaggio (Eds.), *Structures of Capital*, Cambridge, UK: Cambridge University Press, 1–36.

III.ii. STABILITY AND CHANGE IN ORGANIZATIONAL IDENTITY

14 Organizational Identity, Image, and Adaptive Instability

Dennis A. Gioia, Majken Schultz, and Kevin G. Corley

In recent years identity and image have become the subjects of rather intensive organizational study, perhaps because both concepts are multilevel notions dealing with individual and organizational issues and because both can lend insight into the character and behavior of organizations and their members. Whether those insights concern personal versus organizational identity (Ashforth & Mael, 1989), threats to identity (Elsbach & Kramer, 1996), organizational image and identification (Dutton, Dukerich, & Harquail, 1994), organizational image as an end state (Alvesson, 1990), adaptation (Dutton & Dukerich, 1991), issue interpretation (Gioia & Thomas, 1996), or member commitment (Whetten, Lewis, & Mischel, 1992), identity and image have acquired the status of key concepts employed to describe and explain individual and organizational behavior (see Whetten & Godfrey, 1998). In this article we focus attention primarily on the concepts of *organizational* identity and image.

Essential to most theoretical and empirical treatments of organizational identity is a view, specified by Albert and Whetten (1985), defining identity as that which is central, enduring, and distinctive about an organization's character. Scholars have predicated virtually all later treatments of organizational identity on these definitional pillars. In contrast, scholars have seen organizational image as a broader concept, which includes notions involving the ways organization members believe others see the organization (Dutton & Dukerich, 1991); fabricated, projected pictures aimed at various constituencies (Bernstein, 1984); and the public's perception of a given organization (Berg, 1985).

In this chapter we argue that there is a close reciprocal relationship between organizational identity and various forms of image—a relationship that augurs for some reconsideration of the bases for the normally accepted conception of

349

identity. We argue further that this reconsideration is important, because the consequences of adhering to the now taken-for-granted conception have implications not only for our ways of thinking about organizations and their members but especially for the ways in which we think about how organizations change. This is particularly the case as organizations deal with increasingly complex and turbulent environments and as the role of the media in organizational life becomes more pronounced.

Our main contention is that organizational identity, contrary to most treatments of it in the literature, is actually relatively dynamic and that the apparent durability of identity is somewhat illusory. We argue that the seeming durability of identity is actually contained in the stability of the *labels* used by organization members to express who or what they believe the organization to be, but that the meaning associated with these labels changes so that identity actually is mutable. Therefore, we reconceptualize organizational identity as a potentially precarious and unstable notion, frequently up for redefinition and revision by organization members. We argue that the instability of identity arises mainly from its ongoing interrelationships with organizational image, which are clearly characterized by a notable degree of fluidity. Perhaps most important, we argue further that the instability of identity is actually adaptive in facilitating organizational change in response to environmental demands.

Although in recent theory and research on organizational identity one finds acknowledgment of its potentially changeable character (see the conversations in Whetten & Godfrey, 1998), scholars continue to downplay, underplay, or inadequately develop the implications of reconceptualizing identity as dynamic. Certainly, the presumption of stability has allowed researchers to more easily develop measures of an organization's identity, but we have come to a point in the theoretical development of the concept at which we need to account for its dynamism.

We first offer a brief exploration of the nature of organizational identity by weaving together multiple views from the literature; we then offer an overview of multiple forms of organizational image, followed by a description of the interrelationships between identity and image. We develop a depiction of the processes by which identity becomes unstable and mutable because of its complex interrelationships with image. Our initial approach to this depiction has its roots in realist ontological assumptions (i.e., it presumes some substantive basis for identity), suggesting a view of identity as changing incrementally. We then invoke several alternative views that not only help to produce an enhanced, multiperspective understanding of the nature of identity (Gioia & Pitre, 1990; Schultz & Hatch, 1996) but also serve to clarify and dramatize the degree to which identity can become malleable. These two alternative perspectives (a revisionist history view and a postmodern view) are predicated on nominalist ontological assumptions (i.e., they presume that identity is a subjective, socially constructed phenomenon).

Taken together, these three perspectives lead to some provocative implications for our conceptualization of identity—implications that motivate a constructive attempt to reconcile a seeming paradox concerning the relationship of organizations and their environments. On the one hand, the creation and maintenance of an apparently enduring identity are essential to long-term success (Albert & Whetten, 1985; Collins & Porras, 1994); on the other hand, organizations must possess the ability to adapt quickly to increasingly turbulent environments as an essential condition for well-being and even survival (Brown & Eisenhardt, 1997; D'Aveni, 1994; Eisenhardt, 1989; Gustafson & Reger, 1995). Given the preference for order and stability in light of the need for change, one might thus reason that organizations must learn to change and yet somehow stay the same (cf. Gagliardi, 1986). Through the concept of "adaptive instability," we provide an alternative reading on change in modern organizations that demonstrates that existence within this paradox is possible and that, in fact, organizations can accomplish change despite implied threats to the ostensibly enduring nature of their identities. The result of our analysis is a heightening of the sense that identity and image are indeed key notions but that these concepts and their interplay are much more complex and elusive than current treatments would cast them.

Organizational Identity

Organizational identity is typically taken by scholars to be an organization's members' collective understanding of the features presumed to be central and relatively permanent, and that distinguish the organization from other organizations (Albert & Whetten, 1985). Core features of identity are presumed to be resistant to ephemeral or faddish attempts at alteration because of their ties to the organization's history. Gagliardi argues that the main strategy of an organization is usually geared to maintaining its identity, perhaps especially under threatening conditions of change (although he also notes that organizations "usually change to remain what they have always been...[they] must change in order to preserve identity" [1986: 124–125]). Yet, this paradoxical statement nonetheless suggests that identity is not, and indeed cannot be, enduring in any strict sense, even though it apparently retains continuity in its essential features. There must be fluidity to the notion; otherwise, the organization stagnates in the face of an inevitably changing environment.

In examining the fluid nature of identity, it is useful to differentiate between an enduring identity and an identity having continuity. Whereas Ashforth and

Mael (1996) see the two concepts as synonymous, we believe the difference is subtle, yet theoretically important. The notion of an identity that is enduring implies that identity remains the same over time—that it has some permanency. An identity with a sense of continuity, however, is one that shifts in its interpretation and meaning while retaining labels for "core" beliefs and values that extend over time and context.

Identity is imputed from expressed values, but the *interpretation* of those values is not necessarily fixed or stable. Interpretations change, so invocations like "We stand for service!" or "We are an innovating company" mean different things to different groups at different times. There is a reassuring continuity for members (and also for interested external constituents) in saying that their mission or central values stay the same, but the representations and translations into action take different forms over time. Thus, even though the core appears stable, it is effectively in flux because of its practical ambiguity (allowing for flexible interpretations; see Gioia & Chittipeddi, 1991) and its complexity (allowing a repertoire of values to fit many instances; see Reger, Gustafson, DeMarie, & Mullane, 1994). A continuous feature of Hewlett-Packard's identity for many decades, for instance, has been based on the idea of the "H-P Way" as an expression of core values. Yet, the meaning of the specific values and actions associated with the "H-P Way" has changed many times over the years (see Collins & Porras, 1994), to arrive at its current form of elaboration (see *www.hp.com*).

It is also important to recognize that identity, even at the individual level, is a social construction (Gergen & Davis, 1985), deriving from repeated interactions with others (Cooley, 1902). This feature of identity has been at the heart of most theory and research on social and individual identity (Ashforth & Humphrey, 1995; Ashforth & Mael, 1996). For instance, James, as long ago as 1918, noted that people have markedly different identities for different roles and situations. As Weick puts it, "Identities are constituted out of the process of interaction. To shift among interactions is to shift among definitions of the self" (1995: 20). Similarly, Giddens (1991) noted that self-identity presumes reflexive awareness over time (i.e., identity must be actively created and sustained through interactions with others).

Thus, a sense of continuous formulation and preservation of the self through interaction is essential to notions of individual identity. This is an important recognition not only for individuals but also for organizations, because organizational identity is constructed via similar processes of interaction with outsiders—for instance, customers, media, rivals, and regulatory institutions (cf. Ashforth & Mael, 1996; Berg & Gagliardi, 1985; Fombrun, 1996; Gioia, 1998). As Fiol states in her anthropomorphic example of an acute care teaching hospital undergoing change in its identity, "You can no longer ask only me or look inside of me to understand my identity. You can also no longer take a single snapshot of me at one point in time and believe you have captured my identity" (1998: 68).

All of these views of organizational identity suggest that it is not only a complex phenomenon but also one that can vary with the context for which it is expressed (Fiol, Hatch, & Golden-Biddle, 1998; Wilkins, 1989). A sense of continuity in the self-interpretation of an organization in relation to its environment might prevail, but identity is nonetheless inherently dynamic. Such observations raise questions about the typically assumed durability of identity—an assumption that becomes more problematic when we consider the concept of organizational image and its relationships with identity.

Organizational Image

Organizational image has been the subject of many different conceptualizations and definitional debates. Dutton and Dukerich (1991) argued that organizational image is the way organization members believe others view the organization (although Dutton et al., 1994, appropriately relabeled this particular definition of image *construed external image*). Whetten et al. (1992) took some issue with this definition and argued instead for defining image as the way "organizational elites" would like outsiders to see the organization. This orientation highlights top management's concern with projecting an image of the organization that is based (ideally) on identity. Such a "projected image" could be a bona fide attempt to represent essential features of organizational identity to others. It could also take the form of the projection of a desired future image (Gioia & Thomas, 1996) that communicates to insiders and outsiders a vision to be achieved.

Projected image, however, might also encompass attempts to convey a socially desirable, managed impression that emphasizes selected aspects of identity; it could even conceal or misrepresent identity. In fact, Bernstein (1984) held that image should be defined as a construction of public impressions created to appeal to an audience (and not necessarily the attempt to represent some ostensible reality). All these views, however, take image to be essentially an internal conception—that is, perceptions held or communicated by insiders.

Berg (1985) took a decidedly more external approach by focusing on perceptions held by outsiders. He defined image as the public's perception or impression of an organization, usually associated with a given action or event (which we term an external *transient impression*). This definition is related to Fombrun's (1996) definition of reputation as the collective judgments (by outsiders) of an organization's actions and achievements. Reputation can be distinguished from transient impressions in that the concept of reputation implies a more lasting,

353

cumulative, and global assessment rendered over a longer time period; transient impressions concern more limited and/or ephemeral events.

To further complicate the conceptualization of image and its relationship with identity, in other disciplines scholars treat the notions of image and identity somewhat differently from those in the field of organizational study. In the fields of public relations and marketing, for instance, researchers employ the concepts of corporate identity, corporate image, and image management in their attempts to understand a corporation's relationship with its constituents (Brown & Cox, 1997; Grunig, 1993; van Riel & Balmer, 1997). Corporate identity (actually, a form of projected image, despite the label) scholars focus on how the "central idea" of a corporation is presented to its various constituents to achieve the corporation's strategic goals (Olins, 1995). Those in the corporate identity field are most concerned with visual representations of the corporation emphasized through the design and management of corporate symbols and logos (Hatch & Schultz, 1997; Olins, 1989). Although the concept of corporate identity is closely related to Bernstein's (1984) conception of a projected image, in recent work on corporate identity, van Riel and Balmer (1997) and Hatch and Schultz (1997) argue that projection of identity is equally important to both internal and external constituents. Projected images, however, might be differentiated from corporate identity in that projected images typically are associated with specific contexts, events, issues, and audiences; corporate identity usually is taken to include all verbal, graphic, and symbolic representations used by a company in its managed, corporate-level communication with various constituents.

We have summarized these multiple—sometimes overlapping and even conflicting—forms of image in Table 1. These differing notions suggest that image is a wide-ranging concept connoting perceptions that are both internal and external to the organization (see also Boorstin, 1961), as well as perceptions that are both projected and received. In fact, Grunig usefully explicates such divergent perspectives by making a distinction between image "as something that a communicator creates—constructs and projects or gives to other people . . . a message produced by the organization" (1993: 126) and an alternative notion of image wherein "receivers construct meaning—images—from their personal observations of reality or from the symbols given to them by other people . . . image as some sort of composite in the minds of publics" (1993: 126).

We next employ these various forms of image to provide a theoretical description of the processes by which identity and image are interrelated. These interrelationships (which we present in narrative form but also represent graphically as a dynamic process model) strongly suggest the fluidity of identity. Following the presentation of this process model, we bring the revisionist history and postmodern perspectives to bear on the question of how image and identity are interrelated, and we explore the consequences for the reconceptualization of identity.

Table 1. Forms of Image

Label	Definition in literature	Representative examples
Construed external image	Organization members' perceptions of how outsiders perceive the organization	Dutton & Dukerich (1991) Dutton, Dukerich, & Harquail (1994)
Projected image	Image created by an organization to be communicated to constituents; might or might not represent ostensible reality; singular image of the organization	Alvesson (1990) Bernstein (1984)
Desired future image	Visionary perception the organization would like external others and internal members to have of the organization sometime in the future	Gioia & Chittipeddi (1991) Gioia & Thomas (1996)
Corporate identity	Consistent and targeted representations of the corporation emphasized through the management of corporate symbols and logos; strategically planned and operationally applied internal and external self-representation	Olins (1989) van Riel & Balmer (1997)
Transient impression	Short-term impression constructed by a receiver either through direct observation or interpretation of symbols provided by an organization	Berg (1985) Grunig (1993)
Reputation	Relatively stable, long-term, collective judgments by outsiders of an organization's actions and achievements	Fombrun (1996) Fombrun & Shanley (1990)

Identity–Image Interrelationships

Image in its multiple guises provides a catalyst for members' reflexive examination of their organizational self-definition. Image often acts as a destabilizing force on identity, frequently requiring members to revisit and reconstruct their organizational sense of self. To examine the processes by which identity becomes interrelated with, and susceptible to, the influence of image, we begin with the assumption that organization members (especially top management members) have developed some sense of "who we are as an organization" (Albert & Whetten, 1985) and have communicated that identity to internal and external constituencies. Over time, organization members receive feedback about their organizational portrayal, or some event occurs that makes identity concerns salient (cf. Dutton & Dukerich, 1991; Elsbach & Kramer, 1996). Because organization members are simultaneously also members of external groups (e.g., as customers, as members of special-interest groups monitoring

355

the organization's actions, or simply as audiences for media portrayals of their company), and thus sensitized to outsider views of their own organization, the tendency to compare their views of their organization with others' views of the organization is heightened further (Hatch & Schultz, 1997).

Shell Oil's experience with the burgeoning controversy over its plan to dispose of the mammoth Brent Spar offshore storage and loading platform by sinking it in the Atlantic provides a good example of these processes in action. The original plan was opposed by Greenpeace, and eventually by national governments in northern Europe, as environmentally unsound. The controversy and negative feedback not only influenced Shell ultimately to reconsider and revise its plan but also to reconsider its own identity. Shell asked a series of self-reflective questions, prompted by the images it projected to the public and the images conveyed in return in revising its identity to that of a more socially responsible business practitioner (see *www.shellexpro.brentspar.com* for a detailed corporate report).

Figure 1 presents a skeletal depiction of the processes by which various forms of image are likely to destabilize and foster changes in identity. As is the case with most process frameworks, however, Figure 1 presents a distilled, somewhat sterile, and even overly rational depiction of a process that is, in actuality, a richer, more complex, more subtle, and often more tacit process. Within this simplified theoretical portrayal, we have included several representative questions as a way of highlighting and illustrating some of the key comparisons that members make between identity and image.

When information from outsiders conveys an unexpected transient impression (Berg, 1985; Grunig, 1993) or reputation (Fombrun, 1996), organization members are prompted to compare their identity and image. Who we believe ourselves to be as an organization is partly based on how others see us (cf. Cooley, 1902; Gergen & Davis, 1985), so feedback from outsiders concerning the impression we are making on them prompts us to look at our own sense of self and to assess the similarity of the two views. This assessment specifically involves an explicit or implicit comparison between identity and construed external image (Dutton et al., 1994). Rhetorically, the comparison might be framed in terms of Albert and Whetten's fundamental self-reflective question, "Who are we as an organization?" (although it is theoretically more revealing to cast the question as "Who do we think we are?" or even "Who do we think we should be?"), and the parallel other-reflective questions, "Who do *they* think we are" and "Who do *they* think we should be" (see Dutton & Dukerich, 1991, for a classic example).

If the outcome of this comparison is a sense that there is no discrepancy between the two perceptions—that the way "we see ourselves" corresponds with how "others see us"—then identity is affirmed, and no apparent need for

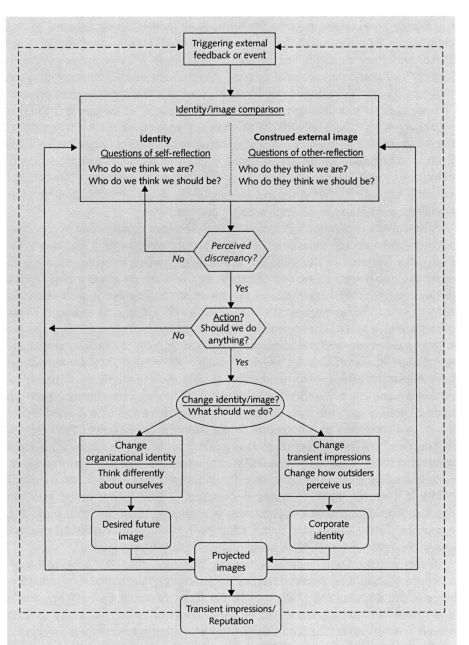

Fig. 1. Process model of identity–image interdependence.

change exists. This was Shell's initial response after receiving approval from the British government to sink the Brent Spar in the North Atlantic. If this comparison, however, results in a sense that the way "we see ourselves" is inconsistent with how we think "others see us" (i.e., there is a discrepancy between identity and construed external image), then several implicit or explicit questions arise (e.g., "Should we be concerned about this mismatch in perceptions?" "Do we need to take action to resolve the discrepancy?"). One possibility is that organization members will see the discrepancy as acceptable or not worthy of the effort needed to reconcile the differing perceptions (e.g., negative feedback from a stakeholder group not deemed important to the organization's self-definition or mission); they might therefore elect to do nothing ("We can live with it"), with no further considerations or implications for identity, which was Shell's early response to Greenpeace's objections.

Alternatively, however, the discrepancy could be seen as important by top management and a decision made to take some action to resolve it. This occurred at Shell after Greenpeace occupied the Brent Spar, leading to widespread media attention, public awareness, and objection by the German government. Such a decision suggests two major options: (1) change something about the way we see ourselves (i.e., change aspects of our identity) or (2) attempt to change the way others perceive us (i.e., change others' external impression/reputation). If the discrepancy is pronounced and consequential, it can suggest the need to reevaluate and change aspects of identity, which ultimately occurred at Shell. Because direct interventions or exhortations to members to alter their conceptions of the organization are unlikely to be effective (Reger et al., 1994), a viable alternative for top management is to project an attractive vision in the form of a desired future image as a precursor to a hoped-for future identity. For instance, Shell created websites and published a set of revised guiding principles, the *Report to Society*, portraying itself as not only technically competent but also as socially sensitive. Such desired future images can serve to "pull" identity into subsequent alignment (Gioia & Thomas, 1996). A public declaration of that future image also can signal to outsiders that the organization is changing; thus, the projection of a compelling future image can directly affect both identity and construed external image, as well as external perceptions of the organization (Figure 1).

If top management members decide, however, that the identity-image discrepancy should be resolved instead by attempting to change how outsiders perceive the organization ("We need to get them to see us the way we would like"), they can attempt several tactics. First, they can project an image to their outside constituencies that more clearly or more strongly conveys their conception of the organization's identity. Such an attempt at strategically altering images of the organization to better communicate the organization's sense of identity—a central function of an organization's corporate identity program—is aimed at influencing outsiders' perceptions to be better aligned with self-definitions. Shell's initial response to the negative publicity, for instance, involved numerous corporate identity efforts aimed at helping outsiders see who the "real Shell" was.

Second, top management members can project images aimed not at better communicating identity but at highlighting and emphasizing certain socially desirable aspects of their identity, thus attempting to manipulate outsider perceptions by engaging in organizational impression management. For example, Shell projected images aimed at highlighting its engineering identity and scientific prowess, as well as calling repeated attention to its core principles.

Last, in the extreme, the organization can project patently false images in an attempt to misrepresent the organization to its publics. In the Brent Spar case, Shell did not make a concerted effort to misrepresent itself to external audiences. In an interesting twist, however, Greenpeace—Shell's original protagonist in the conflict—did supply misinformation to the media in an attempt to misrepresent Shell's image. This misinformation concerning the alleged volume and toxicity of the Brent Spar's contents was eventually refuted, enabling Shell to regain credibility.

Regardless of the initial purpose of the projected images, however, outsiders develop their own images (transient impressions) of the organization from their idiosyncratic interpretations and from other available information obtained from media sources and other agents (Fombrun & Shanley, 1990). Thus, organizationally projected images are likely to have more indirect effects via subsequent feedback to the organization, depending on how the constituencies and other intermediaries interpret them. In some cases the external audience might indeed affirm the organization's image projection. More likely, however, is some alteration of the projected image as intermediaries transmit, distort, add to, and otherwise modify it (into a *refracted image*, in Rindova & Fombrun's, 1998, terms) so that the identity/image comparison process recurs anew in cyclical fashion. For example, Shell launched a series of conversations with public constituencies—a process that prompted repeated reflection within Shell over the life of the Brent Spar saga (1991–1999).

It is important to note that either in trying to change identity or in trying to change others' perceptions, an organization's projection of some altered image for the consumption of insiders and/or outsiders is likely to influence and alter subsequent conceptions of identity because of the close relationships between image and identity. Even the projection of an intentionally false image arguably can influence later conceptions of identity. The essence of this aspect of the process is that projected images are received, given their own interpretations by constituents and intermediaries, and fed back to the organization, often in modified form, which subsequently affects insider perceptions of their own identity (connoted by the feedback loops in Figure 1; see also Fiol & Kovoor-Misra, 1997). As Hatch and Schultz note, "Who we are is reflected in what we are doing and how others interpret who we are and what we are doing" (1997: 54).

There are some summary observations to make about this description of the process. First, organizational identity is not solely an internally determined concept. Identity involves interactions and interrelationships between insiders and outsiders and, perhaps especially, insider perceptions of outsider impressions. Construed external image, thus, is key to the process of initiating changes in identity; it represents organization members' interpretation of the feedback received from outsiders regarding the organization's fulfillment of expectations. It also represents the medium through which members determine how outsiders perceive the organization, thus affording a benchmark against which they can compare their own sense of the organization. In this way construed external image acts as the primary concept linking organizational self-definition through self-reflection with self-definition through other-reflection.

Second, the bases for asserting the interrelationships between identity and image are well established in the literature. In principle, those bases reach back at the individual level to Cooley (1902) and James (1918), and extend forward at the organizational level to Albert and Whetten (1985), Dutton and Dukerich (1991), Dutton et al. (1994), Reger et al. (1994), Elsbach and Kramer (1996), Gioia and Thomas (1996), and the insightful synopses contained in Whetten and Godfrey (1998), among others. Assembling these essential processes into a coherent framework demonstrates that the relationships between identity and image create the potential, and often the likelihood, for a mutable identity.

In addition to these processes, wherein communicated image encourages (usually) incremental shifts in identity, there are other processes that tend to exacerbate and even accelerate changes in identity. In the following sections we highlight two perspectives—revisionist history and postmodernism—which provide alternative views augmenting the argument that identity is dynamic. Each suggests provocative conclusions about the effects of image on the stability of identity. Revisionist history offers a compelling demonstration that members typically reinterpret the past in light of current insider beliefs and outsider perceptions, which has the effect of making identity appear stable to perceivers, even as it changes. The postmodern perspective offers an unsettling argument for the relentless power of market and media images, which implies an extraordinary influence of images on identity over relatively short periods of time. Consideration of these arguments leads to further reflection about the nature of organizational identity and the implications for organizational change.

Revisionist History, Identity, and Image

Just as organizational history is important to any change process, the revision of that history is equally important. Plausible change proposals by top management must be seen as somehow related to "who we have been," yet proposals for major change usually imply some inconsistency with previous identity. Whenever the question comes up about "who we are" or, especially, "who we want to be," not only do organization members revise their current perceptions of their organization (Ashforth & Mael, 1996), they also engage in a process of revising their current perceptions of the past (cf. Loftus, 1980). The "facts" of the past might not be in doubt, but their meaning always is.

All organizational history, in an important sense, thus becomes revisionist history. Both identity and image sustain only indirect inheritances from the past; other aspects of that inheritance are supplied by current orientations and (re)constructions of the meaning of past events. What organization members in earlier times took as "roots" are subjected to revised interpretations, as current needs or desired future image fuels the reinvention of the past. This process tends to foster the construction of a partially mythological history that modifies previous identity to conform to some image of a current or a desired future state. As old Hungarian folk wisdom puts it, "The future is not in doubt; it is the past we worry about." Seen in this light, revisionist history has unavoidable implications; it virtually assures some infidelity to previous conceptions of identity.

When organizations design and launch a planned change effort, they frequently employ a visionary projected future image as an impetus and a guide for achieving some desired revision in their structure, process, performance, and prestige (Gioia & Thomas, 1996). Such images, which include symbolic representations of imagined future states that compromise present and past views, demand the reexamination of current identity. If the existing identity cannot be altered in some way, the change effort is unlikely to be successful.

Biggart's (1977) study of the U.S. Postal Service's reorganization effort is illustrative of the efficacy of revising the interpretation of the past. She found that executives charged with managing the change process pointedly discredited previously valued attributes of the organization (including former management styles, systems, structures, and even logos that were considered central to the organization's self-definition) in favor of newly espoused attributes. Thus, they reevaluated organizational history and identity as out of touch with the times, and they reinterpreted it as a way of justifying and motivating the need for change (Chreim, 1998).

A related tactic for changing members' ways of understanding their organization is to inject intentional ambiguity into a complacent organization to produce the necessary interpretive instability that creates opportunities for changing aspects of identity. When top managers induce "ambiguity-by-design" (Gioia & Chittipeddi, 1991), they tend to destabilize existing interpretations and create a desire for resolution of the ambiguity (i.e., a desire for a revised way of understanding that can alter the existing interpretations now deemed to be unworkable and yet still connect with the organization's history; cf. Pondy & Huff, 1985). Top management can then fill the interpretational vacuum by offering a preferred view that lends structure to the equivocal setting (e.g., see Gioia & Chittipeddi's, 1991, example of a university's ambiguous "top 10" future image, or Barney's, 1998, example of Koch Industries' labeling itself as a "discovery" company, both of which fostered change and adaptation). Such revised images require a reconsideration of "who we have been" if members are to maintain their desire for continuity in identity, so revisions to the current interpretation of past identity occur. Ambiguity-by-design thus fosters consistency with, but departure from, the historical identity in need of current revision.

The upshot of the revisionist history perspective is the presentation of a view of identity as even more malleable than our process model suggests, simply because historical identity is susceptible to reinterpretation as organizations try to align their identities with current images. The attempts to maintain continuity with past understandings make identity appear stable to perceivers, even as it changes. The revisionist history view suggests that image strongly influences identity; the postmodern view, however, pushes that argument to the limit.

The Postmodern Lens on Identity and Image

The implications of the blurred distinctions between identity and image are taken even further in a postmodern perspective. One finds the suggestion that image not only influences, but comes to dominate, organizational sensemaking in its most radical version in postmodern portraits of contemporary organizational life (Baudrillard, 1988, 1990; Hassard & Parker, 1993). In spite of the sophisticated vocabulary, the conclusion is simple: regardless of the starting point, everything ends up as image. More dramatically, everything ends up as *illusion*.

According to postmodernists, the usual portrayal of identity within a modernist tradition is one emphasizing the influence of origin (founding) and asserting that the sense of identity is held at a deep level in the cultural surround of an organization (Schultz, 1992). In this traditional view there is a relatively fixed notion of the historical development of identity that assumes the persistence of an essential identity, despite changing events, times, and perceptions. Modernists, thus, see identity as the center anchor that endures and preserves its distinctiveness, despite the need for organizations to change. This identity is carefully projected onto the external environment, where it blends with "cultural capital" (Bourdieau, 1984) in the social construction of an image. Shifting images might, of course, influence the way organizational members perceive their identity but rarely are assumed to challenge the permanent core of the organizational identity.

This portrayal is markedly different from the dynamic, ephemeral, artificial, and even superficial portrait of organizational life in the postmodern literature, which stresses the process and predominance of image over claims of substantive bases for identity. In short, the relationship between identity and image is turned upside-down when seen through a postmodern lens; instead of emerging from organizational depth and origin, identity becomes a chameleon-like imitation of images prevailing in the postmodern marketplace. Organizational identity, thus, moves from a stable and distinct origin toward a copy of images of dominating organizations.

In their analyses, Baudrillard (1988) and Perniola (1982) have pursued this line of thought; they argue that identity is transformed into "image without identity" (Perniola, 1982: 59), because identity is replaced by simulations of external images (which Baudrillard terms *simulacra*). Identity no longer holds a distinct and persistent core of its own but becomes a reflection of the images of the present moment. These authors see these images largely as constructed and transmitted by mass media and professional communicators within a given context.

Thus, images themselves do not originate from some basic organizational reality but, rather, have been transformed through the pursuit of success in an increasingly volatile and hypercompetitive marketplace. Baudrillard (1988) particularly emphasizes this perspective, tracing the progression of image from (1) its beginnings as a reflection of some basic reality, to (2) a means of masking and perverting a basic reality, to (3) masking an absence of reality, to (4) no longer bearing a relation to reality. As radical as such a depiction is, it points to the shifting nature of image and its distancing from original character. In this sense, image not only supplants identity; image and identity both end up as illusions.

Those holding a postmodern perspective, even in its less radical forms, see identity as most likely an illusion (Rosenau, 1992), albeit a necessary illusion—one required to reassure organization members. We work diligently, if perhaps unconsciously, at constructing identity similarly from day to day to maintain the belief that we are the same person or organization that we were yesterday. Only over the long run, by retrospectively bracketing experience (Weick, 1979), do we become aware that progressive changes have occurred.

Thus, postmodernists hold that given identity's susceptibility to the vagaries of image, the presumption that organizational identity "exists" and is deeply held by its members is better construed as an illusion. In this view the alleged abiding character of identity is instead cast as a comforting falsification intended to maintain a sense of consensuality where none might actually exist, because of the inherent fluidity associated with the production of an immediate, visible, changeable image. Given the superficiality, malleability, and influenceability of image in the postmodern view (Baudrillard, 1988; Schultz, 1992), the assertion that either image or identity is "enduring" is simply dismissed.

Is It Really All Just Image?

If one considers the arguments about the interrelationships between identity and image, particularly from revisionist history and postmodern perspectives, one is confronted with increasing doubt or even skepticism about the viability of the notion of a stable organizational identity. At best, a bona fide identity appears to "exist" only in the first stages of an organization's history, but it soon becomes subject to the significant influence of image, perhaps ultimately to be transformed into an illusory image (if one accepts a radical postmodern position). This is a rather provocative portrayal of identity for scholars and practitioners. Is it accurate? Or is there some intellectual sleight-of-hand operating here? On the one hand, revisionist history and the processes articulated by postmodernists constitute conceptually viable views, so it is important to acknowledge that shifts in identity and image can occur. On the other hand, there are some limiting reasons why these shifts are not necessarily carried to their extreme conclusions.

First of all, the organizational environment itself serves to constrain extreme changes in identity. The same environment that fosters shifts in identity in the first place (by reflecting altered images of an organization's preferred projections of identity) simultaneously operates to limit the degree of those shifts. Agents and institutions in the environment work to maintain some semblance of recognition and stability in the environment in which they deal. They would like to believe that organizations with which they interact are similar to what they were yesterday, so they seek to affirm stability in their own perceptions and, consequently, communicate a desire for nonradical shifts in identity and image. Organizations cannot construct just any arbitrarily chosen identity. Changes in identity are constrained within nonspecified, but nonetheless moderating, environmental bounds. One of the main assumptions in the population ecology perspective, for instance, is that organizations face strong internal and external inertial forces that hinder their attempts at adapting to environmental changes (Hannan & Freeman, 1977, 1984). Research has shown that there are certain conditions under which organizational inertia plays an even stronger role (e.g., in times of organizational decline; Cameron, Whetten & Kim, 1987; Whetten, 1981), thus making a complete shift of identity into image unlikely for many organizations.

Second, some research on threats to organizational identity implies that elements of identity remain separate from image for organization members, even during times of focused image management (i.e., when organizations are trying to achieve some desired image, such as membership in an elite group). Elsbach and Kramer (1996) found that university faculty members felt that some key aspects of their identity were threatened even when an esteem-enhancing image of the organization was portrayed (i.e., a high ranking in the

Business Week survey). Such a ranking "implied that other central and valued dimensions of their organization were unimportant or undervalued" (1996: 468). Receiving the ranking based on the success of the MBA program, for instance, threatened aspects of identity associated with the Ph.D. program. Thus, even in situations where an organizational image positively changes from that originally associated with the organization, identity can remain a distinct and important concept.

Finally, the fact that organizations have multiple identities in multiple contexts with multiple audiences not only undermines the idea of a holistic identity but also implies that neither identity nor image changes in a uniform or unified fashion. Identities consist of constellations of features and labels appropriate for different contexts and interactions. Yet, some of the labels are shared in common across different identities, which implies that meanings for the common labels are flexible enough to accommodate the differing demands of multiple possible contexts and audiences (e.g., customers, employees, and competitors). Still, the degree of change in meaning is likely to be inhibited, because companion identities are unlikely to be shifting together. Therefore, the multiple identities common in large, complex organizations actually can work to insulate the organization from wholesale alterations in the common core features of identity. Nonetheless, this self-same multiplicity also implies incremental shifts in the many facets of identity, thus maintaining identity in a state of flux and again suggesting that a stable, common identity cannot endure in any strict sense.

Taken together, the upshot of the arguments for the progressive transformation of identity into image (and perhaps into illusion), as well as arguments noting limits on such transformations, is that organizational identity is inevitably influenced by image but does not necessarily *become* image in some insidious fashion. Nonetheless, the overarching implication is that both identity and image are dynamic. The result of this dynamism and consequent instability is not as disheartening as it might sound, however. We argue instead that it is this very instability in identity that facilitates organizational adaptation to changes in internal and external environments.

Adaptive Instability

The basic concept of adaptive instability in organizational identity is a straightforward one: as a consequence of its interrelationships with image in its various guises, organizational identity becomes dynamic and mutable. This instability in identity actually confers benefit to the organization, because it allows better adaptation to the demands of an environment that is itself undergoing continuous change. This notion builds upon the process description offered earlier, wherein organizational identity forms the basis for the development and projection of images, which are then received by outsiders, given their own interpretations, fed back to the organization in modified form, and subsequently affect insiders' perception of their own identity.

This reciprocal process of projection and modification accounts for the observations noted by both revisionist historians and postmodernists, but it is distinct in one critical way: the strong role of image does not result in the wholesale dissolution of identity over time and replacement with image or (in the extreme) illusion but, rather, in a kind of dynamism that fosters adjustment. With the notion of adaptive instability, we see the interrelationship between identity and image as mutually influencing and ultimately useful in aligning an organization's sense of self-definition with its environment. Without this recursive process, an organization would find itself trapped with an inevitably stagnant identity, unprepared to address demands that might have survival implications.

Identity change can occur either reactively or proactively. The interpretation of an organization's projected image(s) by outsiders most often results in a reactive examination of identity. An obvious, but nonetheless striking, example exists in the relationship organizations currently have with the media. Over time, an organization is subjected to multiple interpretations of its identity and image, most often transmitted through the media. This relationship results in a process of identity and image change, similar to the punctuated equilibrium processes described by Gersick (1991) and exemplified by Dutton and Dukerich's (1991) study of the New York/New Jersey Port Authority's attempts to reconcile its changing image with its strongly held identity.

Another example concerns IBM; IBM had both an identity and a reputation as a single-minded mainframe company, which hindered its ability to capitalize on the burgeoning PC market in the 1980s. Over a relatively short period of time, IBM responded to its negative public impression—that of a ponderous giant unable to take advantage of a lucrative market exploited by smaller, more adroit companies. It shifted its identity into that of a multifaceted technology organization, ready to compete with smaller PC companies through advances in PC technology and expansion into such businesses as network computing and management consulting. IBM took a substantially new way of approaching business, which, in turn, changed the way it thought of itself and how others perceived it. The interplay of identity and image worked dynamically to foster a necessary change in IBM's basic orientation toward itself and the market; image influenced identity, which, in turn, influenced image. Unexpected disruptions and their associated reactive changes constitute the most obvious examples of identity-image interaction.

Other research, however, has demonstrated that organizations can also be proactive in inducing identity change, even in the absence of obvious external pressure or crisis. As previously noted, Gioia and Chittipeddi (1991) described a case wherein top managers intentionally introduced ambiguity into a change situation to destabilize a strongly held (albeit outmoded) identity in preparation for a strategic change effort. In a later study of the same organization, Gioia and Thomas (1996) found that the top managers sustained the ongoing change effort by projecting and touting a captivating future image (becoming a "top-10 public research university") to help guide the organization toward a new, desired identity. They projected this desirable future image on the assumption that the image would channel identity into alignment.

Such a proactive tack can facilitate change in an organization that is not (or is not likely to be) ready for the changes inevitably occurring in the environment, and it is based on the belief that an organization cannot change if it is complacent about its self-definition—a self-definition held to be maladaptive. To induce change, the organization must be destabilized and convinced that there is a necessity for a different way of seeing and being. This proactive stance acts to head off an eventual crisis by self-inducing a more moderate sense of urgency for change within the organization (a manifestation of Reger et al.'s, 1994, notion of tectonic change).

These two positions on adaptive instability—reactive and proactive—represent two sides of the same coin. Identity and image are dynamically and recursively interrelated; the organization's self-definition is inherently unstable, yet this instability is adaptive for the organization. The difference is one of agency; reactive change stems from the actions of outsiders, and proactive change is self-induced. Regardless of the nature of the change, these arguments suggest a reconceptualization of identity that has both theoretical and practical implications.

Implications of a Mutable Identity for Theory and Research

In most writings on organizational identity, scholars use Albert and Whetten's (1985) definition, typically invoking the main dimensions of identity as that which is core, distinctive, and enduring. This definition has served us well as a good first approximation and point of departure for explorations into organizational identity. Yet, even as this definition has furthered investigations, it also has tended to impose limits on our ability to explore the concept's richness and dynamism. The foregoing discussion strongly suggests that because of the close relationships between identity and image, the characterization of identity as an enduring or stable notion becomes problematic, especially under conditions of change. Recognizing the socially constructed nature of organizational identity, and accounting for the implications of revisionist history processes and postmodernist considerations, imply the need for some alteration in the conceptualization of identity. The theoretical implication of acknowledging a socially constructed (and reconstructed) organizational identity is that even though we might use the same labels to describe the elements of a core identity, those elements are nonetheless subject to multiple and variable interpretations, which implies that identity changes with changing interpretations. Because we use the same labels over time to describe core elements of identity, it is deceptively easy to presume that identity is stable or enduring. The durability is in the *labels*, however—not in the interpretation of the meanings that make up the ostensible core.

We seem to have operated on an assumption that if some aspect of identity is core, it is, by definition, stable, and conversely, that if some aspect is changing, it is almost, by definition, peripheral. We need to be careful of this presumption; because of the processes described earlier, even the core can shift, not only because of altered beliefs and values but also because of changing interpretations of persistent labels. Although we maintain a belief in "core" elements of identity, that belief does not imply that the core is some tangible entity. Because identity is not a "thing" but, rather, a concept constructed and reconstructed by organization members, it is theoretically important to avoid its reification.

All these considerations tend to render the traditional definition of organizational identity as too static to capture the pace of change of modern organizations. The guiding notion of a stable identity encourages researchers to continue to frame organizational identity as enduring, even as it becomes more apparent that identity changes over relatively short periods. Ironically, researchers continue to invoke the durability criterion, even as they acknowledge and produce evidence that identity is malleable—for example, Ashforth and Mael (1996), Dutton and Dukerich (1991), and Dutton et al. (1994). We would encourage researchers to be more open to the idea of a changeable identity. For cross-sectional studies, it is possible to act *as if* identity is stable. Such an assumption makes for parsimony, simplicity, clarity, and convenience in research reporting—and it has served us well. For longitudinal studies and more complex portrayals, however, we need to have the theoretical wherewithal to account for the dynamism of identity.

Another way to make this important point is to note that theoretical conceptions need to keep up with the changing character and form of modern organizations. Unless we revise and expand our theoretical assumptions, how might we account for "virtual organizations" (i.e., those temporary networks of people or organizations that come together quickly to accomplish a task and then dissolve, such as the temporary organizations assembled to make movies)? Such organizations are ephemeral by design, but they have a distinct identity.

Similarly, how might we account for "hollow corporations" that outsource many of their operations, or organizations operating in volatile, hypercompetitive environments that seem to incorporate changeability into the definitions of themselves (e.g., Silicon Valley companies)? How do we examine the identity of an organization like the Florida Marlins baseball team, which won the 1997 World Series and then was decimated in the space of months by the trading of key players? All these examples point to new ways of organizing, in which impermanence is a hallmark, and even a source of pride. Because these kinds of organizations are burgeoning, it becomes imperative to develop theoretical concepts that might more appropriately represent them.

The defining portrayal of identity is no longer represented by the assertion "This is who we are as an organization!" nor even by the question "Who are we as an organization?" Capturing the ambiguity and mutability of identity instead revolves around such questions as "Is this who we really are as an organization?" or, more provocatively, "Is this who we are becoming as an organization?" or even "Is this who we want to be?" These latter questions more adequately capture the important features of organizational identity as a negotiated, interactive, reflexive concept that, at its essence, amounts to an organizational work-in-progress.

It should be clear that identity will be called into question with increasing frequency in the modern and postmodern environment of organizations. Consequently, we believe that it is necessary to encourage the study of identity as something other than an enduring, reified concept. We need to study how organization members adapt to frequent information that suggests reconsideration of their organization's identity. We also need to better understand the interrelationships among different projections of identity and the feedback received by organization members. In particular, we need to investigate the processes by which discrepancies between identity and different types of image are reconciled (Corley & Gioia, 1999). In addition, we need to study how organization members work to maintain continuity in the interpretation of identity in the face of the increasing influence of image in a media-dominated environment (Alvesson, 1990)—for example, Canon Camera's "Image is Everything" ad campaign. Although we are skeptical of a radical postmodern view that identity soon becomes transformed into image and, ultimately, into illusion, we nonetheless believe that identity can shift relatively quickly because of its interrelationship with image. The mutability of identity demands not only revised theoretical concepts but also revised empirical approaches.

Implications of a Mutable Identity for Managers and Consultants

These theoretical considerations also have practical manifestations. They suggest that a strategic concern for organizations might be the management of instability in identity, rather than the more frequently touted idea of trying to maintain an identity perceived as fixed. Of course, the attempt to balance stability and instability in identity is both delicate and dangerous. In its most risky form, it can lead to the unintended substitution of faddish image for key values and can unwittingly produce the postmodern picture of identity as illusion (if managers are overly attuned to popular but potentially fleeting images in the media). Yet, successful accomplishment of this balance creates a sense of adaptiveness, affording the organization increased capacity for change, while maintaining a continuing sense of connection to central values.

Do we really believe that intentionally destabilizing identity for the sake of instigating change is a viable recommendation for top managers? Yes, as long as that attempt is guided by a compelling future image that remains sensitive to the maintenance of continuity in elements of identity that provide the necessary security to accomplish change. Such a recommendation stems from the recognition that identity change is not always triggered by events in high-velocity environments (Gioia & Chittipeddi, 1991; Gustafson & Reger, 1995), by environmental jolts (Meyer, 1982), or by stigma (Fiol & Kovoor-Misra, 1997; Sutton & Callahan, 1987), but also by proactive preparation for envisioned change to maintain viability.

We find two striking examples in the transformations of a former computer peripherals manufacturing firm in Pittsburgh and of the Danish hearing-aid manufacturer, Oticon. In the case of the computer peripherals manufacturer, the vice president of operations described how, in mere months, they transformed the organization from a hardware manufacturer into an Internet publishing firm by changing not only what they offered their customers but also their self-definition: "We had to think differently of ourselves in order to change from a product oriented company to a service-oriented firm" (personal conversation with vice president of operations, The Internet Group, May 1997).

At Oticon, the CEO—Lars Kolind—undertook the task of transforming the organization from a production-focused company to a service-focused company. Under the slogan "think the unthinkable," the company communicated a new identity through the use of "The Spaghetti Organization" metaphor and through the key symbols of a paper-free organization with flexible working environments (Morsing & Eiberg, 1998). The company shared this future image with the local media, who were then invited to talk with Oticon employees about their feelings toward the company's new image. Over the next several months, the projected Oticon image made international headlines. This intense external interest served to shake loose the old identity held by the organization's members and to move the company toward achieving the CEO's vision for an altered identity (Morsing & Eiberg, 1998).

Both firms, then, accomplished their transformations by projecting a new image of themselves and then working toward that image to transform identity (see Abratt, 1989; Balmer, 1995; and Dowling, 1994, for discussions of related issues in the corporate image literature).

If we take seriously the tenet that organizations must change, and if we take seriously the idea that bona fide change requires an alteration in some core beliefs about the character of the organization, then our conceptual representations, as well as our practical recommendations, must also specifically account for the malleability of identity. As is the case with many aspects of organizational change, consultants often play key roles in an organization's attempts to deal with identity change. Recasting identity as a more dynamic concept holds several implications for identity and image consultants, who deal primarily in the realm of "corporate identity." Their main intent is to project an image that captures the "central idea" of a corporation, expressing the core values of the company mainly through visual representations that also aid the corporation in achieving its strategic goals.

Given their vanguard role in corporate identity management, consultants are now beginning to recognize that the traditional, sequential process of identity management (identifying the core beliefs, forming a visual image of the core, obtaining internal consensus for that image, launching the symbolic representation to the public, and, finally, "making it stick"; Olins, 1995: 63) becomes problematic when trying to account for the fluid and dynamic identity now characterizing many client organizations. No longer can they rely on the organization having a single, stable identity that can be identified, agreed upon, and easily projected. Instead, identity management now must involve the simultaneous formation of identity and image by linking internal preferences with internal and external projections and perceptions in a dynamic process. Here, the consultant's task is not only to figure out the corporate identity (or at least the identity that the corporation wants to project) but, concurrently, to assess what will be successful in the marketplace as a projected representation.

Thus, consultants find themselves in the often awkward position of trying to tell top managers what they would like to hear while also expressing what others would like the organization to be. Therefore, we argue that identity consultants now operate in a world that requires them to help define or even transform an identity in a way that simultaneously connotes stability and continuity with an adroit adaptiveness to the preferences and demands of multiple audiences and different situations. In other words, identity consultants find themselves at the crossroads of the paradox that organizations must execute the delicate balancing act of simultaneously changing while staying the same.

British Airways (BA) is an example of a company that has transformed its corporate identity and image with the assistance of identity consultants. As of the early 1990s, BA had become a running joke in the airline industry ("BA = Bloody Awful"). Its consulting firm confronted top management with the uncomfortable conclusion that BA harbored an identity that included

371

a misplaced pride in the traditional British disdain for customer service (and was therefore suffering in a competitive business travel world that emphasized service). BA then transformed its expression of corporate identity by adopting a dynamic logo and a new slogan ("the world's favorite airline"), aimed at both insiders and outsiders, while also touting those nonproblematic features of identity that employees held dear. Along with other substantive and symbolic changes, both audiences came to accept the projection; as of 1998, BA was the number one rated international business travel airline.[1]

The now more apparent relationships between corporate identity and image also have implications for the kinds of services offered by identity and image consultants and desired by organizations. Traditionally, identity and image management have developed as two separate types of professional services. Identity services were provided specifically by corporate identity consultants, whereas image management has been the purview of advertising and public relations (Fombrun, 1996). Consultants now are crossing the boundaries between identity and image management, however, by creating new services that necessarily integrate the concerns for both identity and image. These new services focus on integrating internal and external communication practices, while creating new forms of interactive relations between customers and organizational members. Fundamental to these changes is the recognition by consultants that shifting and multiple interpretations of identity must be reflected in the creation of the identity program itself. Taking a fluid approach to identity change implies that a "central" characteristic of identity might be its ability to shift and transform according to the context in which it is being expressed.

Conclusion

With our questioning of the alleged enduring character of organizational identity, we have attempted to advance its conceptualization in a way that better represents the essential nature of perceptual life in organizations. The concept of identity is key to understanding modern organizations. In fact, acknowledging the interrelationships among identity and image allows the recognition that it is the very fluidity of identity that helps organizations adapt to changes. Accordingly, a concern of theorists and researchers is no longer solely the study of a durable organizational identity but also a concern for the implications of a mutable identity.

The necessity to change in order to adapt, but nonetheless to retain a sense that identity stays the same, has been argued by Gagliardi (1986). In his view, to preserve the character of identity, organizations, paradoxically, must change. We argue instead that the project of management is now different, because of the influential interrelationships between identity and image, and also because of the rise to prominence of image in the current era. The strategic concern of management is no longer the preservation of a fixed identity but the ability to manage and balance a flexible identity in light of shifting external images. Maintenance of consistency becomes the maintenance of *dynamic* consistency. Instability fosters adaptability.

Notes

We thank Samia Chreim, *AMR* special issue editor Jane Dutton, Martin Kilduff, Kristian Kreiner, Dave Lepak, Mette Morsing, Gary Weaver, and three anonymous *AMR* reviewers for constructive comments on earlier versions of this article.

1. It also is interesting to note that BA more recently introduced yet another alteration in its corporate identity that can be seen as an attempt to balance stability and change. This new program symbolizes the multicultural diversity of "the world's favorite airline" in its use of a series of distinct tailfin designs, each created by leading designers from different countries and each clearly referring to a different national heritage. Stability is symbolized in a BA logo on the front of each airplane; change and multiple identities in the distinctive tailfins. The international attention devoted to the corporate identity campaign has clearly led to the increasing globalization of a formerly very British identity.

References

Abratt, R. 1989. A new approach to the corporate image management process. *Journal of Marketing Management*, 5(1): 63–76.

Albert, S., & Whetten, D. 1985. Organizational identity. In L. L. Cummings & B. M. Staw (Eds.), *Research in organizational behavior*, vol. 7: 263–95. Greenwich, CT: JAI Press.

Alvesson, M. 1990. Organization: From substance to image? *Organization Studies*, 11: 373–94.

Ashforth, B., & Humphrey, R. H. 1995. Labeling processes in the organization: Constructing the individual. In L. L. Cummings & B. M. Staw (Eds.), *Research in organizational behavior*, vol. 17: 413–61. Greenwich, CT: JAI Press.

Ashforth, B., & Mael, F. 1989. Social identity theory and the organization. *Academy of Management Review*, 14: 20–39.

Ashforth, B., & Mael, F. 1996. Organizational identity and strategy as a context for the individual. In J. A. C. Baum & J. E. Dutton (Eds.), *Advances in strategic management*, vol. 13: 19–64. Greenwich, CT: JAI Press.

Balmer, J. M. T. 1995. Corporate branding and connoisseurship. *Journal of General Management*, 21(1): 22–46.

Barney, J. 1998. Koch industries: Organizational identity as moral philosophy. In D. Whetten & P. Godfrey (Eds.), *Identity in organizations: Developing theory through conversations:* 106–9. Thousand Oaks, CA: Sage.

Baudrillard, J. 1988. Simulacra and simulations. In M. Poster (Ed.), *Jean Baudrillard: Selected writings:* 166–84. Stanford, CA: Stanford University Press.

Baudrillard, J. 1990. *Cool memories.* London: Verso.

Berg, P. O. 1985. Organization change as a symbolic transformation process. In P. Frost, L. Moore, M. R. Louis, C. Lundberg, & J. Martin (Eds.), *Reframing organizational culture:* 281–300. Beverly Hills, CA: Sage.

Berg, P. O., & Gagliardi, P. 1985. *Corporate images: A symbolic perspective of the organization-environment interface.* Paper presented at the SCOS Conference on Corporate Images, Antibes.

Bernstein, D. 1984. *Company image and reality: A critique of corporate communications.* Eastbourne, UK: Holt, Rinehart & Winston.

Biggart, N. W. 1977. The creative destructive process of organizational change: The case of the post office. *Administrative Science Quarterly,* 22: 410–25.

Boorstin, D. J. 1961. *The image.* New York: Harper & Row.

Bourdieau, P. 1984. *Distinctions: A social critique of the judgment of taste.* Cambridge: Cambridge University Press.

Brown, S. L., & Eisenhardt, K. M. 1997. The art of continuous change: Linking complexity theory and time-paced evolution in relentlessly shifting organizations. *Administrative Science Quarterly,* 42: 1–34.

Brown, T. J., & Cox, E. L. 1997. Corporate associations in marketing and consumer research: A review. *Corporate Reputation Review,* 1(1): 34–9.

Cameron, K. S., Whetten, D. A., & Kim, M. U. 1987. Organizational dysfunctions of decline. *Academy of Management Journal,* 30: 126–38.

Chreim, S. 1998. *Continuity and change in organizational identity: A process perspective.* Paper presented at the annual meeting of the Academy of Management, San Diego.

Collins, J. C., & Porras, J. I. 1994. *Built to last: Successful habits of visionary companies.* New York: HarperCollins.

Cooley, C. H. 1902. *Human nature and the social order.* New York: Scribner.

Corley, K. G., & Gioia, D. A. 1999. *Reconciling scattered images: The consequences of reputation management for insider audiences.* Paper presented at the Third International Conference on Reputation, Identity, & Competitiveness, San Juan, Puerto Rico.

D'Aveni, R. A. 1994. *Hypercompetition: Managing the dynamics of strategic maneuvering.* New York: Free Press.

Dowling, G. R. 1994. *Corporate reputations: Strategies for developing the corporate brand.* London: Kogan Page.

Dutton, J. E., & Dukerich, J. M. 1991. Keeping an eye on the mirror: Image and identity in organizational adaptation. *Academy of Management Journal,* 34: 517–54.

Dutton, J. E., Dukerich, J. M., & Harquail, C. V. 1994. Organizational images and member identification. *Administrative Science Quarterly,* 39: 239–63.

Eisenhardt, K. M. 1989. Making fast strategic decisions in high-velocity environments. *Academy of Management Journal,* 32: 543–76.

Elsbach, K. D., & Kramer, R. M. 1996. Members' responses to organizational identity threats: Encountering and countering the *Business Week* rankings. *Administrative Science Quarterly,* 41: 442–76.

Fiol, C. M. 1998. The identity of organizations. In D. Whetten & P. Godfrey (Eds.), *Identity in organizations: Developing theory through conservations*: 66–8. Thousand Oaks, CA: Sage.

Fiol, C. M., Hatch, M. J., & Golden-Biddle, K. 1998. Organizational culture and identity: What's the difference anyway? In D. Whetten & P. Godfrey (Eds.), *Identity in organizations: Developing theory through conversations*: 56–9. Thousand Oaks, CA: Sage.

Fiol, C. M., & Kovoor-Misra, S. 1997. Two-way mirroring: Identity and reputation when things go wrong. *Corporate Reputation Review*, 1(2): 147–52.

Fombrun, C. J. 1996. *Reputation: Realizing value from the corporate image*. Boston: Harvard Business School Press.

Fombrun, C. J., & Shanley, M. 1990. What's in a name? Reputation building and corporate strategy. *Academy of Management Journal*, 33: 233–58.

Gagliardi, P. 1986. The creation and change of organizational cultures: A conceptual framework. *Organization Studies*, 7: 117–34.

Gergen, K. J., & Davis, K. E. (Eds.). 1985. *The social construction of the person*. New York: Springer-Verlag.

Gersick, C. J. 1991. Revolutionary change theories: A multilevel exploration of the punctuated equilibrium paradigm. *Academy of Management Review*, 16: 10–36.

Giddens, A. 1991. *Modernity and self-identity: Self and society in the late modern age*. Cambridge: Polity Press.

Gioia, D. A. 1998. From individual to organizational identity. In D. Whetten & P. Godfrey (Eds.), *Identity in organizations: Developing theory through conversations*: 17–31. Thousand Oaks, CA: Sage.

Gioia, D. A., & Chittipeddi, K. 1991. Sensemaking and sensegiving in strategic change initiation. *Strategic Management Journal*, 12: 443–8.

Gioia, D. A., & Pitre, E. 1990. Multiparadigm perspectives on theory building. *Academy of Management Review*, 15: 584–602.

Gioia, D. A., & Thomas, J. B. 1996. Image, identity and issue interpretation: Sensemaking during strategic change in academia. *Administrative Science Quarterly*, 41: 370–403.

Grunig, J. E. 1993. Image and substance: From symbolic to behavioral relationships. *Public Relations Review*, 19(2): 121–39.

Gustafson, L. T., & Reger, R. K. 1995. Using organizational identity to achieve stability and change in high velocity environments. *Academy of Management Proceedings*: 464–8.

Hannan, M. T., & Freeman, J. 1977. The population ecology of organizations. *American Journal of Sociology*, 82: 929–64.

Hannan, M. T., & Freeman, J. 1984. Structural inertia and organizational change. *American Sociological Review*, 49: 149–64.

Hassard, J., & Parker, M. (Eds.). 1993. *Postmodernism and organizations*. London: Sage.

Hatch, M. J., & Schultz, M. 1997. Relations between organizational culture, identity and image. *European Journal of Marketing*, 31: 356–65.

James, W. 1918. *The principles of psychology*. New York: Holt.

Loftus, E. 1980. *Memory*. Reading, MA: Addison-Wesley.

Meyer, A. D. 1982. Adapting to environmental jolts. *Administrative Science Quarterly*, 27: 515–37.

Morsing, M., & Eiberg, K. (Eds.). 1998. *Managing the unmanageable for a decade: Oticon*. Working paper, Copenhagen Business School.

Olins, W. 1989. *Corporate identity: Making business strategy visible through design*. Boston: Harvard Business School Press.

Olins, W. 1995. *The new guide to identity*. London: Gower.

Perniola, M. 1982. *Dazzling images*. Aarhus, Denmark: Sjakalen.

Pondy, L. R., & Huff, A. S. 1985. Achieving routine in organization change. *Journal of Management*, 11: 103–16.

Reger, R. K., Gustafson, L. T., DeMarie, S. M., & Mullane, J. V. 1994. Reframing the organization: Why implementing total quality is easier said than done. *Academy of Management Review*, 19: 565–84.

Reger, R. K., Barney, J. B., Bunderson, J. S., Foreman, P., Gustafson, L. T., Huff, A. S., Martins, L. L., Sarason, Y., & Stimpert, J. L. 1998. A strategy conversation on the topic of organizational identity. In D. Whetten & P. Godfrey (Eds.), *Identity in organizations: Developing theory through conversations*: 99–168. Thousand Oaks, CA: Sage.

Rindova, V. P., & Fombrun, C. J. 1998. The eye of the beholder: The role of corporate reputation in defining organizational identity. In D. Whetten & P. Godfrey (Eds.), *Identity in organizations: Developing theory through conversations*: 62–6. Thousand Oaks, CA: Sage.

Rosenau, P. M. 1992. *Post-modernism and the social sciences: Insights, inroads, and intrusions*. Princeton, NJ: Princeton University Press.

Schultz, M. 1992. Postmodern pictures of culture. *International Studies of Management and Organization*, 22(2): 15–35.

Schultz, M., & Hatch, M. J. 1996. Living with multiple paradigms: The case of paradigm interplay in organization culture studies. *Academy of Management Review*, 21: 529–57.

Sutton, R. I., & Callahan, A. L. 1987. The stigma of bankruptcy: Spoiled organizational image and its management. *Academy of Management Journal*, 30: 405–36.

van Riel, C. B., & Balmer, J. M. T. 1997. Corporate identity: The concept, its measurement, and management. *European Journal of Marketing*, 31: 341–55.

Weick, K. 1979. *The social psychology of organizing* (2nd ed.). Reading, MA: Addison-Wesley.

Weick, K. 1995. *Sensemaking in organizations*. Thousand Oaks, CA: Sage.

Whetten, D. A. 1981. Organization responses to scarcity—exploring the obstacles to innovative approaches to retrenchment in education. *Educational Administration Quarterly*, 17(3): 80–97.

Whetten, D. A., & Godfrey, P. (Eds.). 1998. *Identity in organizations: Developing theory through conversations*. Thousand Oaks, CA: Sage.

Whetten, D. A., Lewis, D., & Mischel, L. J. 1992. *Towards an integrated model of organizational identity and member commitment*. Paper presented at the annual meeting of the Academy of Management, Las Vegas.

Wilkins, A. L. 1989. *Developing corporate character: How to successfully change an organization without destroying it*. San Francisco: Jossey-Bass.

www.hp.com

www.shellexpro.brentspar.com

15

The Dynamics of Organizational Identity

Mary Jo Hatch and Majken Schultz

In a world of increased exposure to critical voices, many organizations find creating and maintaining their identities problematic (Albert & Whetten, 1985; Cheney & Christensen, 2001). For example, the media is taking more and more interest in the private lives of organizations and in exposing any divergence it finds between corporate images and organizational actions. This exposure is fed by business analysts who now routinely supplement economic performance data with evaluations of internal business practices such as organizational strategy, management style, organizational processes and corporate social responsibility (Fombrun, 1996; Fombrun & Rindova, 2000). As competition among business reporters and news programs increases, along with the growth in attention to business on the Internet, this scrutiny is likely to intensify (Deephouse, 2000). In addition, when employees are also customers, investors, local community members and/or activists, as they frequently are in this increasingly networked world, they carry their knowledge of internal business practices beyond the organization's boundaries and thus add to organizational exposure.

Exposure is not the only identity-challenging issue faced by organizations today. Organizational efforts to draw their external stakeholders into a personal relationship with them allow access that expands their boundaries and thereby changes their organizational self-definitions. For instance, just-in-time inventory systems, value chain management and e-business draw suppliers into organizational processes, just as customer service programs encourage employees to make customers part of their everyday routines. This is similar to the ways in which investor- and community-relations activities make the concerns of these stakeholder groups a normal part of organizational life. However, not only are employees persuaded to draw external stakeholders into their daily thoughts and routines, but these same external stakeholders are encouraged to think of themselves and behave as members of the organization. For example, investors are encouraged to align their personal values with those of the companies to which they provide capital (e.g. ethical investment funds), whereas customers who join customer clubs are invited to consider themselves organizational members. Suppliers, unions, communities and regulators become partners with the organization via similar processes of mutual redefinition. Combined, these forces give stakeholder groups greater and more intimate access to the private face of the firm than they have ever experienced before.

One implication of increased access to organizations is that organizational culture, once hidden from view, is now more open and available for scrutiny to anyone interested in a company. By the same token, increased exposure means that organizational employees hear more opinions and judgments about their organization from stakeholders (i.e. they encounter more images of their organization with greater frequency). Our departure point for this article lies in the idea that the combined forces of access and exposure put pressure on organizational identity theorists to account for the effects of both organizational culture as the context of internal definitions of organizational identity, and organizational images as the site of external definitions of organizational identity, but most especially to describe the processes by which these two sets of definitions influence one another.

Following Hatch and Schultz (1997, 2000), we argue that organizational identity needs to be theorized in relation to both culture and image in order to understand how internal and external definitions of organizational identity interact. In this article we model four processes that link identity, culture and image (see Figure 1)—mirroring (the process by which identity is mirrored in the images of others), reflecting (the process by which identity is embedded in cultural understandings), expressing (the process by which culture makes itself known through identity claims), and impressing (the process by which expressions of identity leave impressions on others). Whereas mirroring and impressing have been presented in the literature before, our contribution lies in specifying the processes of expressing and reflecting and in articulating the interplay of all four processes that together construct organizational identity as an ongoing conversation or dance between organizational culture and organizational images.

Defining Organizational Identity

Much of the research on organizational identity builds on the idea that identity is a relational construct formed in interaction with others (e.g. Albert & Whetten, 1985; Ashforth & Mael, 1989; Dutton & Dukerich, 1991). For example,

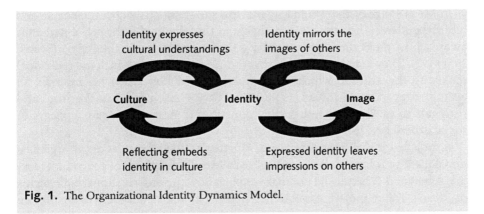

Fig. 1. The Organizational Identity Dynamics Model.

Albert and Whetten (1985: 273, citing Erickson, 1968) described the process of identity formation:

... in terms of a series of comparisons: (1) outsiders compare the target individual with themselves; (2) information regarding this evaluation is conveyed through conversations between the parties ('polite boy,' 'messy boy') and the individual takes this feedback into account by making personal comparisons with outsiders, which then; (3) affects how they define themselves.

Albert and Whetten concluded on this basis 'that organizational identity is formed by a process of ordered inter-organizational comparisons and reflections upon them over time.' Gioia (1998; Gioia et al., 2000) traced Albert and Whetten's foundational ideas to the theories of Cooley (1902/1964), Goffman (1959) and Mead (1934). While Cooley's idea of the 'looking glass self' and Goffman's impression management have been well represented in the literature that links organizational identity to image (e.g. Dutton & Dukerich, 1991; Ginzel et al., 1993), Mead's ideas about the 'I' and the 'me' have yet to find their way into organizational identity theory.

The idea of identity as a relational construct is encapsulated by Mead's (1934: 135) proposition that identity (the self):

... arises in the process of social experience and activity, that is, develops in the given individual as a result of his relations to that process as a whole and to other individuals within that process.

Here, Mead made clear that identity should be viewed as a *social* process and went on to claim that it has two 'distinguishable phases', one he called the 'I' and the other the 'me'. According to Mead (1934: 175):

The 'I' is the response of the organism to the attitudes of the others; the 'me' is the organized set of attitudes of others which one himself assumes. The attitudes of the others constitute the organized 'me', and then one reacts toward that as an 'I'.

In Mead's theory, the 'I' and the 'me' are simultaneously distinguishable and interdependent. They are distinguishable in that the 'me' is the self a person is aware of, whereas the 'I' is 'something that is not given in the "me"' (Mead, 1934: 175). They are interrelated in that the 'I' is 'the answer which the individual makes to the attitude which others take toward him when he assumes an attitude toward them' (Mead, 1934: 177). 'The "I" both calls out the "me" and responds to it. Taken together they constitute a personality as it appears in social experience' (Mead, 1934: 178).

Although it is clear that Albert and Whetten's (1985) formulation of organizational identity is based in an idea similar to Mead's definition of individual identity, Albert and Whetten did not make explicit how the organizational equivalents of Mead's 'I' and 'me' were involved in organizational identity formation. Before turning to this matter, we need to address the perennial question of whether individual-level theory can be generalized to organizational phenomena.

Generalizing from Mead

In relation to the long-standing problem of the validity of borrowing concepts and theories defined at the individual level of analysis and applying them to the organization, Jenkins (1996: 19) argued that, where identity is concerned:

...the individually unique and the collectively shared can be understood as similar (if not exactly the same) in important respects...and the processes by which they are produced, reproduced and changed are analogous.

Whereas Jenkins took on the task of describing how individual identities are entangled with collectively shared identities (see also Brewer & Gardner, 1996, on this point), in this article we focus on the development of identity at the collective level itself, which Jenkins argued can be described by processes analogous to those defined by Mead's individual-level identity theory.

Jenkins (1996) noted that the tight coupling that Mead theorized between the 'I' and the 'me' renders conceptual separation of the social context and the person analytically useful but insufficient to fully understand how identity is created, maintained and changed. Building on Mead, Jenkins (1996: 20, emphasis in original) argued that:

the 'self' [is] an ongoing and, in practice simultaneous, synthesis of (internal) self-definition and the (external) definitions of oneself offered by others. This offers a template for the basic model...of the *internal–external dialectic of identification* as the process whereby all identities—individual and collective—are constituted.

Jenkins then suggested that Mead's ideas might be taken further by articulating the processes that synthesize identity from the raw material of internal and external definitions of the organization. The challenge that we take up in this article is to find organizational analogs for Mead's 'I' and 'me' and to articulate the processes that bring them together to create, sustain and change organizational identity. We begin by searching for ideas related to organizational identity formation processes in the organizational literature.

Drawing on work in social psychology (e.g. Brewer & Gardner, 1996; Tajfel & Turner, 1979; Tedeshi, 1981) and sociology (Goffman, 1959), a few organizational researchers have given attention to the processes defining identity at the collective or organizational level. For example, as we explain in more detail later, Dutton and Dukerich (1991) pointed to the process of mirroring organizational identities in the images held by their key stakeholders, whereas Fombrun and Rindova (2000; see also Gioia & Thomas, 1996) discussed the projection of identity as a strategic means of managing corporate impressions. However, although these processes are part of identity construction, they focus primarily on the 'me' aspect of Mead's theory. Thus, they do not, on their own, provide a full account of the ways in which Mead's 'I' and 'me' (or Jenkins' internal and external self-definitions) relate to one another at the organizational level of analysis.

It is our ambition in this article to provide this fuller account using analogous reasoning to explicate Mead's 'I' and 'me' in relation to the phenomenon of organizational identity and to relate the resultant organizational 'I' and 'me' in a process-based model describing the dynamics of organizational identity. To address the question—How do the organizational analogs of Mead's 'I' and 'me' interact to form organizational identity?—requires that we first specify the organizational analogs of Mead's 'I' and 'me'. We now turn our attention to this specification and invite you to refer to Figure 2 as we explain what we mean by the organizational 'I' and 'me'.

Organizational Analogs of Mead's 'I' and 'Me'

Dutton and Dukerich (1991: 550) defined organizational image as 'what [organizational members] believe others see as distinctive about the organization'. In a later article, Dutton et al. (1994) restricted this definition of organizational image by renaming it 'construed organizational image'. Under either label, the concept comes very close to Mead's definition of the 'me' as 'an organized set of attitudes of others which one himself assumes'. However, the images formed and held by the organization's 'others' are not defined by what insiders believe about what outsiders perceive, but by the outsiders' own perceptions (their images), and it is our view that these organizational images are brought directly into identity processes by access and exposure, as explained in the introduction to this article.

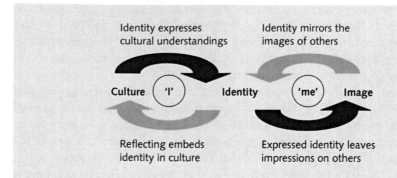

Fig. 2. How the organizational 'I' and 'me' are constructed within the processes of the Organizational Identity Dynamics Model.

It is our contention that the images offered by others (Jenkins's external definitions of the organization) are current to identity processes in ways that generally have been overlooked by organizational identity researchers who adopt Dutton and Dukerich's definition of organizational image, though not by strategy, communication or marketing researchers (e.g. Cheney & Christensen, 2001; Dowling, 2001; Fombrun & Rindova, 2000, to name only a few). Specifically, what organizational researchers have overlooked is that others' images are part of, and to some extent independent of, organizational members who construct their mirrored images from them. For this reason we define organizational image, following practices in strategy, communication and marketing, as the set of views on the organization held by those who act as the organization's 'others'. By analogy, the organizational 'me' results when organizational members assume the images that the organization's 'others' (e.g. its external stakeholders) form of the organization. What Dutton and Dukerich (1991) referred to as organizational image, and Dutton et al. (1994) as construed organizational image, we therefore subsume into our notion of the organizational 'me' as that which is generated during the process of mirroring (see the discussion of mirroring in the following section of the article).

Defining the 'me' of Mead's theory in relation to organizational identity is much easier than defining the 'I'. By application of Mead's theorizing, the organizational 'I' must be something of which the organization is unaware (otherwise it would be part of the organizational 'me') and 'something that is not given in the "me"'. In addition, the 'I' must be responsive to the attitudes of others. We believe that culture is the proper analogy to Mead's 'I' in that Mead's descriptors of the 'I' fit the organizational culture concept quite closely. First, organizational culture generally operates beneath awareness in that it is regarded by most culture researchers as being more tacit than explicit (e.g. Hatch & Schultz, 2000; Krefting & Frost, 1985). Second, culture is not given by what others think or say about it (though these artifacts can be useful indicators), but rather resides in deep layers of meaning, value, belief and assumption (e.g. Hatch, 1993; Schein, 1985, 1992; Schultz, 1994). And third, as a context for all meaning-making activities (e.g. Czarniawska, 1992; Hatch & Schultz, 2000), culture responds (and shapes responses) to the attitudes of others.

For the purposes of this article, organizational culture is defined as the tacit organizational understandings (e.g. assumptions, beliefs and values) that contextualize efforts to make meaning, including internal self-definition. Just as organizational image forms the referent for defining the organizational 'me', it is with reference to organizational culture that the organizational 'I' is defined.

The Conceptual Minefield of Culture and Identity

As can be seen from the discussion above, culture and identity are closely connected and the early literature on organizational identity often struggled to explain how the two might be conceptualized separately. For example, Albert and Whetten (1985: 265–6) reasoned:

Consider the notion of organizational culture . . . Is culture part of organizational identity? The relation of culture or any other aspect of an organization to the concept of identity is both an empirical question (does the organization include it among those things that are central, distinctive and enduring?) and a theoretical one (does the theoretical characterization of the organization in question predict that culture will be a central, distinctive, and an enduring aspect of the organization?).

Fiol et al. (1998: 56) took the relationship between culture and identity a step further in stating that: 'An organization's identity is the aspect of culturally embedded sense-making that is [organizationally] self-focused'. Hatch and Schultz (2000) in their examination of the overlapping meanings ascribed to organizational culture and identity, stated that the two concepts are inextricably interrelated by the fact that they are so often used to define one another. A good example of the conflation of these terms comes from Dutton and Dukerich (1991: 546):

. . . an organization's identity is closely tied to its culture because identity provides a set of skills and a way of using and evaluating those skills that produce characteristic ways of doing things . . . 'cognitive maps' like identity are closely aligned with organizational traditions.

The early conflation of concepts does not mean, however, that the two concepts are indistinguishable, or that it is unnecessary to make the effort to distinguish them when defining and theorizing organizational identity. Using

383

the method of relational differences that they built on Saussurean principles, Hatch and Schultz (2000: 24–6) distinguished between identity and culture using three dimensions along which the two concepts are differently placed in relation to one another: textual/contextual, explicit/tacit and instrumental/ emergent. They pointed out that although each of the endpoints of these dimensions can be used to define either concept, the two concepts are distinguishable by culture's being *relatively* more easily placed in the conceptual domains of the contextual, tacit and emergent than is identity which, *when compared with culture*, appears to be more textual, explicit and instrumental.

Defining Organizational Identity in Relation to Culture and Image

Reasoning by analogy from Mead's theory, our position is that if organizational culture is to organizational identity what the 'I' is to individual identity, it follows that, just as individuals form their identities in relation to both internal and external definitions of self, organizations form theirs in relation to culture and image. And even if internal and external self-definitions are purely analytical constructions, these constructions and their relationships are intrinsic to raising the question of identity at all. Without recognizing differences between internal and external definitions of self, or by analogy culture and image, we could not formulate the concepts of individual or organizational identity (i.e. who we are vs. how others see us). Therefore, we have taken culture and image as integral components of our theory of organizational identity dynamics.

In the remainder of the article we argue that organizational identity is neither wholly cultural nor wholly imagistic, it is instead constituted by a dynamic set of processes that interrelate the two. We now investigate these processes and explain how they operate, first articulating them separately, and then examining them as an interrelated and dynamic set.

Organizational Identity Processes and Their Dynamics

In this section we define the processes by which organizational identity is created, maintained and changed and explain the dynamics by which these processes are interrelated. In doing so we also explain how organizational identity is simultaneously linked with images held by the organization's 'others' and with cultural understandings. The processes and their relationships with culture, identity and image are illustrated in Figure 2, which presents our Organizational Identity

Dynamics Model. The model diagrams the identity-mediated relationship between stakeholder images and cultural understandings in two ways. First, the processes of mirroring organizational identity in stakeholder images and reflecting on 'who we are' describe the influence of stakeholder images on organizational culture (the lighter gray arrows in Figure 2). Second, the processes of expressing cultural understandings in identity claims and using these expressions of identity to impress others describe the influence of organizational culture on the images of the organization that others hold (the darker gray arrows in Figure 2). As organizational analogs for the 'I' and the 'me', the links between culture and image in the full model diagram the interrelated processes by which internal and external organizational self-definitions construct organizational identity.

Identity Mirrors the Images of Others

In their study of the Port Authority of New York and New Jersey, Dutton and Dukerich (1991) found that when homeless people congregated in the Port Authority's bus and train stations, the homeless problem became the Port Authority's problem in the eyes of the community and the local media. Dutton and Dukerich showed how the negative images of the organization encountered in the community and portrayed in the press encouraged the Port Authority to take action to correct public opinion. They suggested that the Port Authority's organizational identity was reflected in a mirror held up by the opinions and views of the media, community members and other external stakeholders in relation to the problem of homelessness and the Port Authority's role in it. The images the organization saw in this metaphorical mirror were contradicted by how it thought about itself (i.e. its identity). This led the Port Authority to act on behalf of the homeless in an effort to preserve its identity and to change its organizational image.

On the basis of their study, Dutton and Dukerich (1991) claimed that the opinions and reactions of others affect identity through mirroring, and further suggested that mirroring operates to motivate organizational members to get involved in issues that have the power to reduce public opinion of their organization. Thus, Dutton and Dukerich presented a discrepancy analysis, suggesting that, if organizational members see themselves more or less positively than they believe that others see them, they will be motivated by the discrepancy to change either their image (presumably through some action such as building homeless shelters) or their identity (to align with what they believe others think of them). These researchers concluded that we 'might better understand how organizations behave by asking where individuals look, what they see, and whether or not they like the reflection in the mirror' (1991: 551). In regard to defining the mirroring process in terms that link identity and image,

Dutton and Dukerich (1991: 550) stated that:

...what people see as their organization's distinctive attributes (its identity) and what they believe others see as distinctive about the organization (its image) constrain, mold, and fuel interpretations.... Because image and identity are constructs that organization members hold in their minds, they actively screen and interpret issues like the Port Authority's homelessness problem and actions like building drop-in centers using these organizational reference points.

We argue that the mirroring process has more profound implications for organizational identity dynamics than is implied by Dutton and Dukerich's discrepancy analysis. As we argued in developing our organizational analogy to Mead's 'me', we believe that external stakeholder images are not completely filtered through the perceptions of organizational members (as Dutton & Dukerich, 1991 suggested in the quote above). Instead, traces of the stakeholders' own images leak into organizational identity, particularly given the effects of access discussed in the introduction to this article by which external stakeholders cross the organizational boundary. Furthermore, in terms of the mirroring metaphor, the images others hold of the organization are the mirror, and as such are intimately connected to the mirroring process.

The notion of identity is not just about reflection in the mirroring process, it is also about self-examination. In addition to describing mirroring, the Port Authority case also showed how negative images prompted an organization to question its self-definition. In making their case that organizational identities are adaptively unstable, Gioia et al. (2000: 67) made a similar point: 'Image often acts as a destabilizing force on identity, frequently requiring members to revisit and reconstruct their organizational sense of self.' As we have argued already, matters of organizational self-definition are also matters of organizational culture.

Reflecting Embeds Identity in Organizational Culture

Organizational members not only develop their identity in relation to what others say about them, but also in relation to who they perceive they are. As Dutton and Dukerich (1991) showed, the Port Authority did not simply accept the images of themselves that they believed others held, they sought to alter these images (via the process of impressing others via identity expressions, to which we will return in a moment). We claim that they did this in service to a sense of themselves (their organizational 'I') that departed significantly from the images they believed others held. In our view, what sustained this sense of themselves as different from the images they saw in the mirror is their organizational culture.

We claim that once organizational images are mirrored in identity they will be interpreted in relation to existing organizational self-definitions that are embedded in cultural understanding. When this happens, identity is reinforced or changed through the process of reflecting on identity in relation to deep cultural values and assumptions that are activated by the reflection process. We believe that reflecting on organizational identity embeds that identity in organizational culture by triggering or tapping into the deeply held assumptions and values of its members which then become closely associated with the identity and its various manifestations (e.g. logo, name, identity statements).

Put another way, we see reflexivity in organizational identity dynamics as the process by which organizational members understand and explain themselves *as an organization*. But understanding is always dependent upon its context. As Hatch (1993: 686–7) argued, organizational culture provides context for forming identities as well as for taking action, making meaning and projecting images. Thus, when organizational members reflect on their identity, they do so with reference to their organization's culture and this embeds their reflections in tacit cultural understandings, or what Schein (1985, 1992) referred to as basic assumptions and values. This embedding, in turn, allows culture to imbue identity artifacts with meaning, as was suggested by Dewey (1934).

According to Dewey (1934), aspects of meaning reflectively attained gradually become absorbed by objects (cultural artifacts), that is, we come to perceive objects as possessing those meanings experience adds to them. It follows that when meanings are expressed in cultural artifacts, the artifacts then carry that meaning from the deep recesses of cultural understanding to the cultural surface. The meaning-laden artifacts of a culture thereby become available to self-defining, identity-forming processes.

Following Dewey, we therefore further argue that whenever organizational members make explicit claims about what the organization is, their claims carry with them some of the cultural meaning in which they are embedded. In this way culture is embodied in material artifacts (including identity claims as well as other identity artifacts such as logo, name, etc.) that can be used as symbols to express who or what the organization is, thus contributing culturally produced, symbolic material to organizational identity. So it is that cultural understandings are carried, along with reflections on identity, into the process of expressing identity.

Identity Expresses Cultural Understandings

One way an organization makes itself known is by incorporating its organizational reflections in its outgoing discourse, that is, the identity claims referred to above allow organizational members to speak about themselves *as an organization* not only to themselves, but also to others. Czarniawska's (1997) narratives of institutional identity are an example of one form such organizational self-expression could take. But institutional identity narratives are only one instance of the larger category of cultural self-expression as we define it. In more general terms, cultural self-expression includes any and all references to collective identity (Brewer & Gardner, 1996; Jenkins, 1996).

When symbolic objects are used to express an organization's identity, their meaning is closely linked to the distinctiveness that lies within any organizational culture. As Hatch (1993, following Ricoeur) explained, artifacts become symbols by virtue of the meanings that are given to them. Thus, even though its meaning will be re-interpreted by those that receive it, when a symbol moves beyond the culture that created it, some of its original meaning is still embedded in and carried by the artifact. The explanation for this given by Hatch rests in the hermeneutics of interpretation through which every text (a category that includes symbolic objects and anything else that is interpreted) is constituted by layered interpretations and thus carries (a portion of) its history of meaning within it.

Based on the reasoning presented above, it is our contention that organizational cultures have expressive powers by virtue of the grounding of the meaning of their artifacts in the symbols, values and assumptions that cultural members hold and to some extent share. This connection to deeper patterns of organizational meaning is what gives cultural explication of assumptions in artifacts their power to communicate believably about identity. Practices of expression such as corporate advertising, corporate identity and design programs (e.g. Olins, 1989), corporate architecture (e.g. Berg & Kreiner, 1990), corporate dress (e.g. Pratt & Rafaeli, 1997; Rafaeli & Pratt, 1993), and corporate rituals (Rosen, 1988; Schultz, 1991), when they make use of an organizational sense of its cultural self (its organizational 'I') as a referent, help to construct organizational identity through culturally contextualized self-expression.

Part of the explanation for the power of artifacts to communicate about organizational identity lies in the emotional and aesthetic foundations of cultural expression. Philosophers have linked expression to emotion (e.g. Croce, 1909/1995; Scruton, 1997: 140–70) and also to intuition (Collingwood, 1958; Croce, 1909/1995; Dickie, 1997). For instance, referring to Croce, Scruton (1997: 148) claimed that when a work of art 'has "expression," we mean that it invites us into its orbit'. These two ideas—of emotion, and of an attractive force inviting us into its orbit—suggest that organizational expressions draw stakeholders to them by emotional contagion or by their aesthetic appeal. As Scruton (1997: 157) put it: 'The expressive word or gesture is the one that awakens our sympathy'. We argue that when stakeholders are in sympathy with expressions of organizational identity, their sympathy connects them with the organizational culture that is carried in the traces of identity claims. That sympathy and connection with organizational culture grounds the 'we' (we regard this 'we' as equivalent to the organizational 'I') in a socially constructed sense of belonging that Brewer and Gardner (1996) defined as part of collective identity.

However, organizational identity is not only the collective's expression of organizational culture. It is also a source of identifying symbolic material that can be used to impress others in order to awaken their sympathy by stimulating their awareness, attracting their attention and interest, and encouraging their involvement and support.

Expressed Identity Leaves Impressions on Others

In their work on corporate reputations, Rindova and Fombrun (1998) proposed that organizations project images to stakeholders and institutional intermediaries, such as business analysts and members of the press. In its most deliberate form, identity is projected to others, for example, by broadcasting corporate advertising, holding press conferences, providing information to business analysts, creating and using logos, building corporate facilities, or dressing in the corporate style. Relating these projected images to organizational identity, Rindova and Fombrun (1998: 60) stated:

Projected images reflect not only a firm's strategic objectives but also its underlying identity. Images that are consistent with organizational identity are supported by multiple cues that observers receive in interacting with firms.

Whereas strategic projection, or what others have called impression management (Ginzel et al., 1993; Pfeffer, 1981), is a component of organizational identity dynamics, Rindova and Fombrun (1998) also noted that projection of organizational identity can be unintentional (e.g. communicated through everyday behavior, gestures, appearance, attitude):

Images are not projected only through official, management-endorsed communications in glossy brochures because organizational members at all levels transmit images of the organization.

Thus, expressions of organizational culture can make important contributions to impressing others that extend beyond the managed or intended impressions created by deliberate attempts to convey a corporate sense of organizational identity. This concern for the impressions the organization makes on others brings us back from considerations of culture and its expressions (on the left side of Figure 2) to concerns with image and its organizational influences (shown on the right side of Figure 2).

Of course there are other influences on image beyond the identity the organization attempts to impress on others. For example, one of the determinants of organizational images that lies beyond the organization's direct influence (and beyond the boundaries of our identity dynamics model) is the projection of others' identities onto the organization, in the Freudian sense of projection. Assessments of the organization offered by the media and business analysts, and the influence of issues that arise around events such as oil spills or plane crashes, may be defined, partly or wholly, by the projections of others' identities and emotions onto the organization ('I feel bad about the oil spill in Alaska and therefore have a negative attitude toward the organization I hold responsible for the spill'). Thus, organizational efforts to impress others are tempered by the impressions those others take from outside sources. These external impressions are multiplied by the effects of organizational exposure that were discussed in the introduction to this article because increased exposure means more outside sources producing more images to compete with those projected by the organization.

The influences of others will be counted or discounted by the organization when it chooses self-identifying responses to their images in the mirroring and reflecting processes that relate organizational image back to organizational culture. Having made these connections between organizational culture, identity and image, we are now ready to discuss the model of organizational identity dynamics shown in Figure 2 in its entirety.

The Dynamism of Organizational Identity Processes and the Role of Power

The way that we have drawn the identity dynamics model in Figure 2 is meant to indicate that organizational identity occurs as the result of a set of processes that continuously cycle within and between cultural self-understandings and images formed by organizational 'others'. As Jenkins (1994: 199) put it: 'It is in the meeting of internal and external definitions of an organizational self that identity...is created'. Our model helps to specify the processes by which the meeting of internal and external definitions of organizational identity occurs and thereby to explain how organizational identity is created, maintained and changed. Based on this model, we would say that at any moment identity is the immediate result of conversation between organizational (cultural) self-expressions and mirrored stakeholder images, recognizing, however, that whatever is claimed by members or other stakeholders about an organizational identity will soon be taken up by processes of impressing and reflecting which feed back into further mirroring and expressing processes. This is how organizational identity is continually created, sustained and changed. It is also why we insist that organizational identity is dynamic—the processes of identity do not end but keep moving in a dance between various constructions of the organizational self (both the organizational 'I' and the organizational 'me') and the uses to which they are put. This helps us to see that organizational identity is not an aggregation of perceptions of an organization resting in peoples' heads, it is a dynamic set of processes by which an organization's self is continuously socially constructed from the interchange between internal and external definitions of the organization offered by all organizational stakeholders who join in the dance.

A word on power might be beneficial at this point. Power suffuses our model in that any (or all) of the processes are open to more influence by those with greater power. For example, the choice of which cultural material to deliberately draw into expressions of organizational identity usually falls into the hands of those designated by the most powerful members of the organization, such as when top management names a creative agency to design its logo or an advertising firm to help it communicate its new symbol to key stakeholders. When the powerful insist on the right to make final decisions regarding logo or advertising, the effects of power further infiltrate the dynamics of organizational identity. Another example, drawn from the other side of Figure 2, is the power that may be exercised over conflicting views of what stakeholder images mean for the organization's sense of itself. If powerful managers are unwilling to listen to the reports presented by market researchers or other members of the organization who have less influence than they do, the processes of mirroring and reflecting will be infiltrated by the effects of power. Of course not only can the powerful disrupt organizational identity dynamics, they can just as easily use their influence to enhance the dynamics of organizational identity by encouraging continuous interplay between all the processes shown in Figure 2. In any case, although we cannot explicitly model the effects of power due to their variety and complexity, we mark the existence of these influences for those who want to apply our work. We turn now to consideration of what happens when identity dynamics are disrupted.

Dysfunctions of Organizational Identity Dynamics

Albert and Whetten (1985: 269) proposed that disassociation between the internal and external definitions of the organization or, by our analogy to Mead, disassociation of the organizational 'I' and 'me', may have severe implications for the organization's ability to survive:

The greater the discrepancy between the ways an organization views itself and the way outsiders view it..., the more the 'health' of the organization will be impaired (i.e. lowered effectiveness).

Following their lead, it is our belief that, when organizational identity dynamics are balanced between the influences of culture and image, a healthy organizational identity results from processes that integrate the interests and activities of all relevant stakeholder groups.

However, a corollary to Albert and Whetten's proposition is that it is also possible for organizational identity dynamics to become dysfunctional in the psychological sense of this term. We argue that this happens when culture and images become disassociated—a problem that amounts to ignoring or denying the links between culture and images that the pressures of access and exposure, addressed earlier, make so noticeable. In terms of the Organizational Identity Dynamics Model, the result of such disassociations is that organizational identity may be constructed primarily in relation to organizational culture or stakeholder images, but not to both (more or less) equally. When this occurs, the organization is vulnerable to one of two dysfunctions: either narcissism or hyper-adaptation (see Figure 3).

Organizational Narcissism

Within the Organizational Identity Dynamics Model the first dysfunction emerges from a construction of identity that refers exclusively or nearly exclusively to the organization's culture with the likely implication that the organization will lose interest and support from their external stakeholders. We believe that this is what happened to Royal Dutch Shell when it ignored heavy

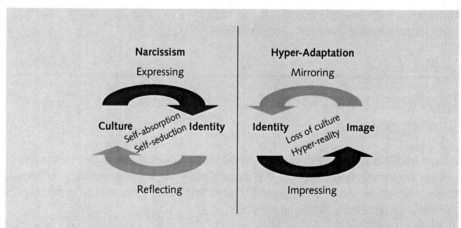

Fig. 3. Sub-dynamics of the Organizational Identity Dynamics Model and their potential dysfunctions.

criticism from environmentalists, especially Greenpeace, who were concerned with the planned dumping of the *Brent Spar* oil rig into the North Sea. Shell's early responses to Greenpeace were based in Shell's engineering-driven culture. This culture was insular and oriented toward the technical concerns of risk analysis supported by scientific data provided by the British government. Shell's framing of the *Brent Spar* issue caused them to ignore the symbolic effects of dumping the oil rig. The subsequent spread of negative images from activist groups to the general public and to Shell customers exemplifies one effect of exposure in which media generated and communicated images of activists tying themselves to the oil rig were repeatedly sent around the world. Shell's initial denials of guilt and refusals to dialog with Greenpeace clearly fit the description of a dysfunctional identity dynamic: Shell's identity in the crisis was embedded in a culture that insulated the company's management from shifting external images, in this case shifting from bad to worse in a very short time.

As explained by Fombrun and Rindova (2000) this incident, along with Shell's crisis in Nigeria, provoked considerable self-reflection within Shell (2000: 78). The reflection then led to their giving attention to two-way communication and to their innovative Tell Shell program (an interactive website designed to solicit stakeholder feedback). Shell's subsequent careful monitoring of global stakeholder images of the corporation represents one of the ways in which Shell sought to combat the limitations of its culture by giving its stakeholders increased access to the company.

In terms of the Organizational Identity Dynamics Model, we claim that dysfunctional identity dynamics, such as occurred in the case of Shell, result when identity construction processes approach total reliance on reflecting and expressing (shown in the left half of Figure 3). That is, organizational members infer their identity on the basis of how they express themselves to others and, accordingly, reflect on who they are in the shadow of their own self-expressions. What initially might appear to be attempts at impressing outsiders via projections of identity, turn out to be expressions of cultural self-understanding feeding directly into reflections on organizational identity that are mistaken for outside images. Even though organizational members may espouse concern for external stakeholders as part of their cultural self-expression processes ('Our company is dedicated to customer service!'), they ignore the mirroring process by not listening to external stakeholders and this leads to internally focused and self-contained identity dynamics. As in the case of Shell, we see that when companies ignore very articulate and media-supported stakeholders, as did Shell for a substantial period, they will not be able to accurately assess the impact of influential external images on their identity or anticipate their lasting effect on their organizational culture.

Following Brown (1997; Brown & Starkey, 2000) we diagnosed the condition of being unwilling or unable to respond to external images as organizational narcissism. Based on Freud, Brown claimed that narcissism is a psychological response to the need to manage self-esteem. Originally an individual concept, Brown (1997: 650) justified its extension to organizations on the basis of a collective need for self-esteem:

...organizations and their subgroups are social categories and, in psychological terms, exist in the participants' common awareness of their membership. In an important sense, therefore, organizations exist in the minds of their members, organizational identities are parts of their individual members' identities, and organizational needs and behaviors are the collective needs and behaviors of their members acting under the influence of their organizational self-images.

Brown then defined narcissism in organizations as a psychological complex consisting of denial, rationalization, self-aggrandizement, attributional egotism, a sense of entitlement and anxiety. While noting that a certain amount of narcissism is healthy, Brown (1997: 648) claimed that narcissism becomes dysfunctional when taken to extremes:

Excessive self esteem...implies ego instability and engagement in grandiose and impossible fantasies serving as substitutes for reality.

Or, as Brown and Starkey (2000: 105) explained:

...overprotection of self-esteem from powerful ego defenses reduces an organization's ability *and* desire to search for, interpret, evaluate, and deploy information in ways that influence its dominant routines.

As Schwartz (1987, 1990) argued on the basis of his psychodynamic analysis of the *Challenger* disaster, when taken to extremes, organizational narcissism can have dire consequences.

In terms of the model presented in Figure 3, a narcissistic organizational identity develops as the result of a solipsistic conversation between identity and culture in which feedback from the mirroring process is ignored, or never even encountered. No real effort is made to communicate with the full range of organizational stakeholders or else communication is strictly unidirectional (emanating from the organization).

A related source of dysfunctional identity dynamics occurs when organizations mistake self-referential expressions (i.e. culturally embedded reflections on identity) for impressions projected to outsiders. Christensen and Cheney (2000: 247) diagnosed this dysfunction as organizational self-absorption and self-seduction leading to an 'identity game':

In their desire to be heard and respected, organizations of today participate in an ongoing identity game in which their interest in their surroundings is often overshadowed by their interest in themselves.

They argue that organizations in their eagerness to gain visibility and recognition in the marketplace become so engaged in reflections about who they are and what they stand for that they lose sight of the images and interests of their external stakeholders. Instead, they act on tacit assumptions based in their culture, such as that their stakeholders care about the organization's identity in the same way that they do.

Large corporations and other organizations have become so preoccupied with carefully crafted, elaborate, and univocal expressions of their mission and 'essence' that they often overlook penetrating questions about stakeholder involvement.

Christensen and Askegaard (2001: 297) point out, furthermore, that organizational self-absorption is exacerbated by a

cluttered communication environment, saturated with symbols asserting distinctness and identity...[where]...most people today only have the time and capacity to relate to a small fraction of the symbols and messages produced by contemporary organizations.

These researchers claim that stakeholders only rarely care about who the organization is and what it stands for. When organizational members are absorbed within self-referential processes of expressing who they are and reflecting about themselves, external stakeholders simply turn their attention to other, more engaging organizations. Their violated expectations of involvement and of the organization's desire to adapt to their demands then cause disaffected stakeholders to withdraw attention, interest and support from companies that they perceive to be too self-absorbed.

We find such self-absorption not only at the level of organizations such as was illustrated by the Shell-Greenpeace case, but also at the industry level. For example, we believe that industry-wide self-absorption is beginning to appear in the telecommunications industry, where companies are constantly struggling to surpass each other and themselves with ever more sophisticated and orchestrated projections of their identity. While their actions seem to be based on their belief that stakeholders care about their self-proclaimed distinctiveness, it would seem prudent to test these beliefs with the judicious use of market research or some other means of connecting with the images of organizational 'others'.

We argue that organizational self-absorption parallels organizational narcissism in that both give evidence of discrepancies between culture and image. Instead of mirroring themselves in stakeholder images, organizational members reflect on who they are based only in cultural expressions and this leads to organizational (or industrial) self-absorption and/or narcissism. In the case of Shell, we believe that this explains the persistence with which Shell ignored its external stakeholders and, by the same token, explains the depth of Shell's identity crisis when the external images were finally taken into account (described by Fombrun & Rindova, 2000). The Shell example, however, illustrates that organizational narcissism is rarely a static condition for organizations. Narcissism or self-absorption might occur for periods based in temporary disassociations between image and culture, but the dynamics of organizational identity will either correct the imbalance or contribute to the organization's demise.

Hyper-adaptation

The obverse of the problem of paying too little attention to stakeholders is to give stakeholder images so much power over organizational self-definition that cultural heritage is ignored or abandoned. Just as a politician who pays too much attention to polls and focus groups may lose the ability to stand for anything profound, organizations may risk paying too much attention to market research and external images and thereby lose the sense of who they are. In such cases, cultural heritage is replaced by exaggerated market adaptations such as hyper-responsiveness to shifting consumer preferences. We argue that ignoring cultural heritage leaves organization members unable to reflect on their identity in relation to their assumptions and values and thereby renders the organization a vacuum of meaning to be filled by the steady and changing stream of images that the organization continuously exchanges with its stakeholders. This condition can be described as the restriction of organizational identity dynamics to the right side of the model shown in Figure 3. Loss of organizational culture occurs when the processes of mirroring and impressing become so all-consuming that they are disassociated from the processes of reflecting and expressing depicted in the left half of Figure 3.

Alvesson (1990: 373) argued that 'development from a strong focus on "substantive" issues to an increased emphasis on dealing with images as a critical aspect of organizational functioning and management' is a 'broad trend in modern corporate life'. Although he did not define the shift from 'substance to image' as contributing to organizational dysfunction, we find in his article evidence of the kind of self-contained identity dynamics depicted on the right side of our model. According to Alvesson (1990: 377):

An image is something we get primarily through coincidental, infrequent, superficial and/or mediated information, through mass media, public appearances, from second-hand sources, etc., not through our own direct, lasting experiences and perceptions of the 'core' of the object.

According to Alvesson, the conditions under which image replaces substance are produced by distance (geographical or psychological) from the organization

396

and its management, which in turn is created by organizational size and reach, by its use of mass communication and other new technologies, and by the abstractness of the expanding service sector of the globalizing economy. When image replaces substance, 'the core' of the organization (its culture) recedes into the distance, becoming inaccessible.

Alvesson's thesis was that when managers become concerned with the communication of images to stakeholders, their new emphasis replaces strong links they formerly maintained to their organization's cultural origins and values and this ultimately leads them to become purveyors of nonsubstantial (or simulated) images. In his view, such organizations become obsessed with producing endless streams of replaceable projections in the hope of impressing their customers. In relation to our model, Alvesson points to some of the reasons why culture and image become disassociated, arguing that image replaces culture in the minds of managers which leads to loss of culture. However, although he states this as an increasingly 'normal condition' for organizations, we conceptualize loss of culture as dysfunctional, questioning whether companies can remain reliable and engaging to their stakeholders over time without taking advantage of their culture's substance.

We acknowledge that periods of loss of organizational culture may be on the increase for many organizations as they become more and more invested in 'the culture of the consumer'. This position has been forcefully argued by Du Gay (2000: 69) who claimed that: 'the market system with its emphasis on consumer sovereignty provides the model through which all forms of organizational relations [will] be structured'. Following Du Gay we argue that, when market concerns become influential determinants of the internal structures and processes that organizations adopt, they will be vulnerable to the loss of their organizational culture.

We find a parallel to the processes by which companies lose the point of reference with their organizational culture in the stages of the evolution of images that Baudrillard (1994) described in his book *Simulacra and simulation*. In stage one, the image represents or stands in for a profound reality and can be exchanged for the depth of meaning the image (or sign) represents. In stage two, the image acts as a mask covering the profound reality that lies hidden beneath its surface. In stage three, the image works almost alone, in the sense that it masks not a profound reality, but its absence. Finally, in stage four, the image bears no relation whatsoever to reality. There is neither reference nor representation. The image becomes 'its own pure simulacrum'. In Baudrillard's (1994: 5–6) words:

Such is simulation, insofar as it is opposed to representation. Representation stems from the principle of equivalence of the sign and of the real (even if this equivalence is utopian, it is a fundamental axiom). Simulation, on the contrary, stems from the utopia of the principle of equivalence, *from the radical negation of the sign as value*, from the sign as the reversion and death sentence of every reference. Whereas representation attempts to absorb simulation by interpreting it as a false representation, simulation envelops the whole edifice of representation itself as a simulacrum.

In our terms, stage four of the evolution of images, the relationship between images and their former referents is broken—images no longer represent cultural expressions, but become self-referential attempts to impress others in order to seduce them. As an example of this development, Eco (1983: 44) offered his interpretation of Disneyland where you are assured of seeing 'alligators' every time you ride down the 'Mississippi'. Eco claimed this would never happen on the real Mississippi rendering the Disney experience a 'hyper-reality'.

Whereas Baudrillard used his argument to celebrate what Poster called 'the strange mixture of fantasy and desire that is unique to the late twentieth century culture' (Poster, 1988: 2) for us, Baudrillard's argument that reality gives way to hyper-reality is a way to understand the disassociation between culture (we claim culture is a referent) and image that transforms identity into simulacrum. In terms of our Organizational Identity Dynamics Model, identity is simulated when projections meant to impress others have no referent apart from their reflections in the mirror, that is, when the organizational culture that previously grounded organizational images disappears from view. In their attempt to manage the impressions of others, organizational members take these images to be the only or dominating source for constructing their organization's identity. This implies that images are taken by the organizational members to be the organizational culture and it no longer occurs to them to ask whether image represents culture or not.

In spite of the seductiveness of the seduction argument, we believe its proponents go too far. It is our contention that access and exposure mitigate against organizational identity as pure simulacra by re-uniting culture and images, or at least by spotlighting a lack of connection between cultural expressions and projected images. Just as stakeholders will turn away from extremely self-absorbed, narcissistic organizations, so we believe they will find they cannot trust organizations whose identities are built on image alone. On the margins, some organizations will thrive from the entertainment value of having a simulated identity (what will they think of next?), but the need to support market exchanges with trust will pull most organizations back from pure simulacra.

Thus, for example, in their eagerness to please consumers, organizations may think they can credibly project any impression they like to consumers, no matter what their past heritage holds. And, for a time, bolstered by clever marketing they may get away with being unconcerned with their past and what the company stood for a year ago to their employees or consumers. But, at other times, market research-defined consumer preferences will not overshadow the same stakeholders' desires to connect with the organization's heritage. This happened when consumers protested the introduction of New Coke in spite of the fact that the world's most careful market research had informed the company of a need to renew its brand. The research led the Coca-Cola Company to neglect the role played by cultural heritage and underestimate its importance to consumers who saw the old Coke as part of their lives. Other illustrations of organizations losing their cultural heritage only to seek to regain it at a later time come from recent developments in the fashion industry. Companies such as Gucci, Burberry and most recently Yves Saint Laurent lost their cultural heritage in the hunt for market share that led them to hyper-adaptation. But those same companies have re-discovered (and to some extent re-invented) their cultural heritage and this reconnection with their cultures has allowed them to reestablish their once strong organizational identities.

As was the case with organizational narcissism, we are not arguing that loss of culture is a permanent condition for organizations. Rather culture loss represents a stage in identity dynamics that can change, for example, either by the effects of organizational exposure or by giving stakeholders greater access to the organizational culture that lies beyond the shifting images of identity claims. Examples of such correctives are found, for example, where companies create interactive digital communities for their consumers to be used for impression management purposes, only to discover that interactivity also raises expectations of access to the organizational culture and provokes many consumers to question the company about the alignment between its projected images and its less intentional cultural expressions.

Conclusions

We began this article by pointing out how increasing levels of organizational access and exposure to stakeholders contribute to the need to theorize about organizational identity and how these current trends give theories of organizational identity dynamics enormous practical value. We then located the academic theorizing about organizational identity in the works of Cooley, Goffman and Mead, whose ideas are considered foundational to the social identity theory on which most organizational identity research is based. In this context, we developed organizational analogs to the 'I' and the 'me' proposed by Mead. On the basis of the reasoning derived from Cooley, Goffman and Mead, and from others who have used their work to develop organizational identity theory, we offered a process-based theory of organizational identity dynamics. We concluded with consideration of the practical implications of our model by examining two dysfunctions that can occur in organizational identity dynamics when the effects of access and exposure are denied or ignored. We argued that these dysfunctions either leave the organization with culturally self-referential identity dynamics (leading to organizational narcissism), or overwhelmed by concern for their image (leading to hyper-adaptation).

We believe that this article contributes to organizational identity theory in three important respects. First, finding analogs to Mead's 'I' and 'me' adds to our understanding of how social identity theory underpins our theorizing about organizational identity as a social process. By defining these analogies we claim to have made an important, and heretofore overlooked, link to the roots of organizational identity theory. Second, the article provides a strong argument for the much-contested claim that identity and culture not only can be distinguished conceptually, but must both be considered in defining organizational identity as a social process. Finally, by articulating the processes that connect organizational culture, identity and image, we believe our theory of organizational identity dynamics offers a substantial elaboration of what it means to say that identity is a social process.

In a practical vein, it is our view that knowing how organizational identity dynamics works helps organizations to avoid organizational dysfunction and thus should increase their effectiveness. Based on the implications we see in our model, organizations should strive to nurture and support the processes relating organizational culture, identity and images. An understanding of both culture and image is needed in order to encourage a balanced identity able to develop and grow along with changing conditions and the changing stream of people who associate themselves with the organization. This requires organizational awareness that the processes of mirroring, reflecting, expressing and impressing are part of an integrated dynamic in which identity is simultaneously shaped by cultural understandings formed within the organization and external images provided by stakeholders. This, in turn, requires maintaining an open conversation between top managers, organizational members and external stakeholders, and keeping this conversation in a state of continuous development in which all those involved remain willing to listen and respond. We know that this will not be easy for most organizations, however we are convinced that awareness of the interrelated processes of identity dynamics is an important first step.

Acknowledgements

We would like to express our sincere appreciation for the helpful comments and suggestions provided by Linda Putnam and three anonymous reviewers.

References

Albert, S. & Whetten, D.A. Organizational identity. In L.L. Cummings and M.M. Staw (Eds), *Research in organizational behavior.* Greenwich, CT: JAI Press, 1985, vol. 7, pp. 263–95.

Alvesson, M. Organization: From substance to image? *Organization Studies,* 1990, *11,* 373–94.

Ashforth, B.E. & Mael, F. Social identity theory and the organization. *Academy of Management Review,* 1989, *14,* 20–39.

Baudrillard, J. *Simulacra and simulation* (trans. S.F. Glaser). Ann Arbor: University of Michigan Press, 1994.

Berg, P.O. & Kreiner, K. Corporate architecture: Turning physical settings into symbolic resources. In P. Gagliardi (Ed.), *Symbols and artifacts: Views of the corporate landscape.* Berlin: Walter de Gruyter, 1990.

Brewer, M.B. & Gardner, W. Who is this 'we'?: Levels of collective identity and self-representations. *Journal of Personality and Social Psychology,* 1996, *71,* 83–93.

Brown, A.D. Narcissism, identity, and legitimacy. *Academy of Management Review,* 1997, *22,* 643–86.

Brown, A.D. & Starkey, K. Organizational identity and learning: A psychodynamic perspective. *Academy of Management Review,* 2000, *25,* 102–20.

Cheney, G. & Christensen, L.T. Organizational identity at issue: Linkages between 'internal' and 'external' organizational communication. In F.M. Jablin and L.L. Putnam (Eds), *New handbook of organizational communication.* Newbury Park, CA: Sage, 2001.

Christensen, L.T. & Askegaard, S. Corporate identity and corporate image revisited. *European Journal of Marketing,* 2001, *35,* 292–315.

Christensen, L.T. & Cheney, G. Self-absorption and self-seduction in the corporate identity game. In M. Schultz, M.J. Hatch and M.H. Larsen (Eds), *The expressive organization: Linking identity, reputation, and the corporate brand.* Oxford: Oxford University Press, 2000.

Collingwood, R.G. *The principles of art.* New York: Oxford University Press, 1958.

Cooley, C.H. *Human nature and the social order.* New York: Schocken, 1964. [Originally published 1902.]

Croce, B. *Aesthetic as science of expression and general linguistic* (trans. D. Ainslie). New Brunswick, NJ: Transaction, 1995. [Originally published 1909.]

Czarniawska, B. *Exploring complex organizations: A cultural perspective.* Newbury Park, CA: Sage, 1992.

Czarniawska, B. *Narrating the organization: Dramas of institutional identity.* Chicago, IL: University of Chicago Press, 1997.

Deephouse, D.L. Media reputation as a strategic resource: An integration of mass communication and resource-based theories. *Journal of Management,* 2000, *26,* 1091–112.

Dewey, J. *Art as experience.* New York: Capricorn Books, 1934.

Dickie, G. *Introduction to aesthetics: An analytic approach.* New York: Oxford University Press, 1997.

Dowling, G.R. *Creating corporate reputations: Identity, image, and performance.* Oxford: Oxford University Press, 2001.

Du Gay, P. Markets and meanings: Re-imagining organizational life. In M. Schultz, M.J. Hatch and M. Holten Larsen (Eds), *The expressive organization: Linking identity, reputation and the corporate brand*. Oxford: Oxford University Press, 2000.

Dutton, J. & Dukerich, J. Keeping an eye on the mirror: Image and identity in organizational adaptation. *Academy of Management Journal*, 1991, *34*, 517–54.

Dutton, J., Dukerich, J. & Harquail, C.V. Organizational images and member identification. *Administrative Science Quarterly*, 1994, *39*, 239–63.

Eco, U. *Travels in hyperreality* (trans. W. Weaver). San Diego, CA: Harcourt Brace Jovanovich, 1983.

Erickson, E.H. *Identity, youth and crisis*. New York: Norton, 1968.

Fiol, C.M., Hatch, M.J. & Golden-Biddle, K. Organizational culture and identity: What's the difference anyway? In D. Whetten and P. Godfrey (Eds), *Identity in organizations. Building theory through conversation*. Thousands Oaks, CA: Sage, 1998.

Fombrun, C. *Reputation: Realizing value from the corporate image*. Boston: Harvard Business School Press, 1996.

Fombrun, C. & Rindova, V. The road to transparency: Reputation management at Royal/Dutch Shell. In M. Schultz, M.J. Hatch and M. Holten Larsen (Eds), *The expressive organization: Linking identity, reputation and the corporate brand*. Oxford: Oxford University Press, 2000.

Ginzel, L.E., Kramer, R.M. & Sutton, R.I. Organizational impression management as a reciprocal influence process: The neglected role of the organizational audience. *Research in Organizational Behavior*, 1993, *15*, 227–66.

Gioia, D.A. From individual to organizational identity. In D. Whetten and P. Godfrey (Eds), *Identity in organizations. Building theory through conversations*. Thousands Oaks, CA: Sage, 1998.

Gioia, D.A., Schultz, M. & Corley, K. Organizational identity, image and adaptive instability. *Academy of Management Review*, 2000, *25*, 63–82.

Gioia, D.A. & Thomas, J.B. Identity, image and issue interpretation: Sensemaking during strategic change in academia. *Administrative Science Quarterly*, 1996, *41*, 370–403.

Goffman, E. *The presentation of self in everyday life*. New York: Doubleday, 1959.

Hatch, M.J. The dynamics of organizational culture. *Academy of Management Review*, 1993, *18*, 657–93.

Hatch, M.J. & Schultz, M.S. Relations between organizational culture, identity and image. *European Journal of Marketing*, 1997, *31*, 356–65.

Hatch, M.J. & Schultz, M.S. Scaling the Tower of Babel: Relational differences between identity, image and culture in organizations. In M. Schultz, M.J. Hatch and M. Holten Larsen (Eds), *The expressive organization: Linking identity, reputation and the corporate brand*. Oxford: Oxford University Press, 2000.

Jenkins, R. Rethinking ethnicity: Identity, categorization and power. *Ethnic and Racial Studies*, 1994, *17*, 197–223.

Jenkins, R. *Social identity*. London: Routledge, 1996.

Krefting, L.A. & Frost, P.J. Untangling webs, surface waves, and wildcatting. In P.J. Frost, L.F. Moore, M.R. Louis, C.C. Lundberg and J. Martin (Eds), *Organizational culture*. Beverly Hills, CA: Sage, 1985.

Mead, G.H. *Mind, self and society*. Chicago, IL: University of Chicago Press, 1934.

Olins, W. *Corporate identity*. Boston, MA: Harvard Business School Press, 1989.

Pfeffer, J. Management as symbolic action. In L.L. Cummings and B. Staw (Eds), *Research on organizational behavior* (Vol. 3). Greenwich, CT: JAI Press, 1981.

Poster, M. Introduction. In M. Poster (Ed.), *Jean Baudrillard. Selected writings.* Stanford, CA: Stanford University Press, 1988.

Pratt, M.G. & Rafaeli, A. Organizational dress as a symbol of multilayered social identities. *Academy of Management Journal*, 1997, *40*, 862–98.

Rafaeli, A. & Pratt, M.G. Tailored meanings: On the meaning and impact of organizational dress. *Academy of Management Review*, 1993, *18*, 32–55.

Rindova, V. & Fombrun, C. The eye of the beholder: The role of corporate reputation in defining organizational identity. In D. Whetten and P. Godfrey (Eds), *Identity in organizations: Developing theory through conversations.* Thousand Oaks, CA: Sage, 1998.

Rosen, M. You asked for it: Christmas at the bosses' expense. *Journal of Management Studies*, 1988, *25*, 463–80.

Schein, E.H. *Organizational culture and leadership* (1st edn). San Francisco, CA: Jossey-Bass, 1985.

Schein, E.H. *Organizational culture and leadership* (2nd edn). San Francisco, CA: Jossey-Bass, 1992.

Schultz, M. Transitions between symbolic domains in organizations. *Organizational Studies*, 1991, *12*, 489–506.

Schultz, M. *On studying organizational cultures: Diagnosis and understanding.* Berlin: Walter de Gruyter, 1994.

Schwartz, H.S. On the psychodynamics of organizational disaster: The case of the space shuttle *Challenger. Columbia Journal of World Business*, 1987, *22*(1), 59–67.

Schwartz, H.S. The symbol of the space shuttle and the degeneration of the American dream. In P. Gagliardi (Ed.), *Symbols and artifacts: Views of the corporate landscape.* New York: Aldine de Gruyter, 1990.

Scruton, R. *The aesthetics of music.* Oxford: Clarendon Press, 1997.

Tajfel, H. & Turner, J.C. An integrative theory of intergroup conflict. In W.G. Austin and S. Worchel (Eds), *The social psychology of intergroup relations.* Monterey, CA: Brooks/Cole, 1979.

Tedeshi, J.T. (Ed.). *Impression management theory and social psychological research.* New York: Academic Press, 1981.

III.iii. IDENTITY AS NARRATIVE AND DISCOURSE

16

Narratives of Individual and Organizational Identities

Barbara Czarniawska-Joerges

> In spite of the claim that machines and organisms are the most popular images of organization (Morgan, 1986), the conception of organizations as *super-persons* is another metaphor that is as popular and taken for granted. This superperson is seen as a decision maker, understood sometimes as the leader, sometimes the management group or the organization as a collective.
>
> (Czarniawska-Joerges, 1993).

Organizations as Superpersons

Conceptualizing organizations as superpersons is probably most typical for apologetic theories that present organizations as consensus based. Accordingly, they tell us how organizations learn, unlearn, produce strategies, and all the things that individuals usually do. The following quotation illustrates this image. "As an organization gets older, it learns more and more about coping with its environment and with its internal problems of communication and coordination. At least this is the normal pattern, and the normal organization tries to perpetuate the fruits of its learning by formalizing them" (Starbuck, 1983, p. 480).

The constructionist view espoused in this essay attempts to problematize this image of organizations. Organizations are not people at all (whether aggregates, collectives, or superpersons) but *sets of collective action* undertaken in an effort to shape the world and human lives (Czarniawska-Joerges, 1992a). This definition, like all others, is related to a certain understanding of human nature, namely, that "there is nothing to people except what has been socialized into them—their ability to use language, and thereby to exchange beliefs and desires with other people" (Rorty, 1989, p. 177).

By using language, people endow their action (and inaction) with meaning. Consequently, understanding organizations calls for an understanding of meanings ascribed to and produced by a given set of collective actions. Both actions and their meanings are socially constructed in exchanges taking place between people. Human beings are social *constructors* and organizations are social *constructions*.

While my definition and assumptions are arbitrary, they serve as a useful point of departure to examine the "organization-as-superperson" metaphor. If the everyday and theoretical languages insist on certain usages, it is meaningless to claim that they "miss the point" or "use a wrong definition." One has to scrutinize the context of such usages to understand their emergence. A promising route is that of conceiving of individuality as a modern institution.

Individuality as an Institution

Individual identity is a modern institution, claims Meyer (1986). But what is an institution? For current purposes, the definition adopted by Meyer, Boli, and Thomas ("institutions as cultural rules giving collective meaning and value to particular entities and activities"; 1987, p. 13) is not adequate because it begs an explanation of what the "cultural rules" are. Another kind of problem is created by Mary Douglas's definition ("institution [as] legitimized social grouping"; 1986, p. 46), whereby both institutions and organizations are groups of people, and it is hard to say how they differ. Berger and Luckmann's definition is more appropriate. They argue that "institution posits that actions of type X will be performed by actors of type X" (1966/1971, p. 72). In their work, a constructive reciprocity is assumed; that is, performing an X-type of action leads to the perception that a given actor belongs (or aspires to) type X and vice versa.

For the purposes here, *institution* can be simply considered a pattern of social action. In our case, *actors* are, in fact, "legitimized social groupings." Actors include work units, profit centers, departments, corporations and public organizations, associations of organizations, and all those whose interactions "constitute a recognized area of institutional life," anything that can be called an "organization field" (DiMaggio & Powell, 1983, p. 148). Actors leave or are being pushed out of the field whereas new actors arrive (witness the powerful entry of environmentalists into political, industrial, and academic fields). Action patterns, in spite of their stability and repetitiveness, which earn them the name "institution," change both in their form and in their meaning. Finally, the process itself is recursive. Actors perform actions; actions create actors or, rather, their identities.

One conventional school of thought claims that an identity is to be found in the individuals themselves, whether in their genotype or a "soul." To acquire an identity means therefore to find one's true "I" and exhibit it. The argument is of course much more complex than this (see Bruner's, 1990, discussion of "essential" and "conceptual" self). This perspective has been severely criticized by the social environment school, who claim that the society creates individuals as persons. This "nature or nurture" debate is bypassed in the constructivist thinking where a creation of identity is a two-way process, an idea that begins, most likely, with George H. Mead's "transactional self" (Bruner, 1990; Mead, 1934). Identity is created by individuals' interactions with the social environment where the individual comes, indeed, with his or her genotype, and the society, with all its rules, institutions, values, and, above all, language. In this process of construction, not only individual identities are created but the society is reproduced or changed.

May this reasoning be used in relation to organizations? Using it, we come to a possible answer as to why the image of organization as a superperson persists. In the first place, the notion of an individual as an institutional myth developed within rational theories of choice is core to organization theory (Meyer et al., 1987). Second, and as a result of it, organizations are personified to embody the critical notion of accountability (Douglas, 1990). This is required because individuality as an institution fits together with other modern institutions—the state and the market. The invention of a "legal person," which makes organizations accountable both as citizens and as consumers and producers is a necessary link between the three and is then reflected in the everyday language. Thus, in organizational literature, there is an equivalent of the "essential self" definition, where an organization's identity is seen as that which its members believe to be its distinctive, central, and enduring characteristics (Albert & Whetten, 1985; Alvesson & Björkman, 1992; Dutton & Dukerich, 1991).

Both in everyday language and in organization theory, this operation is mostly seen as unproblematic; organizations "make decisions," "learn," "unlearn," and "behave ethically" (or not, as the case may be). In this essay, we shall problematize the notion of organization as superperson by setting it in the context of *modernity* and, in this light, examine the fruitfulness of the analogy between the organizational and personal identities. Its promise lies in the fact that the notion of individuality as modern institution both depsychologizes the concept of "identity" (Bruner, 1990; Gergen & Davis, 1985) and frees it from a sociological determinism. It also decouples and this may be the most difficult aspect to accept, the notion of identity from subjectivity and consciousness (which are, for example, still closely connected in Berger, Berger, & Kellner, 1974). It socializes the notion through and through by eschewing the duality of the "agency" and "structure," in the way radical constructivists do (Fuller, in press; Latour, 1992).

To understand organizational life, for example, one must grasp its social character, the way it is produced by human and nonhuman actors. Identities are one product of such a construction, being produced in interactions, where people account for their actions by placing them in a relevant narrative (MacIntyre, 1981/1990). The individual identity, a typical institution of "high modernity" (Giddens, 1991), persists through an ability to narrate one's life, formulate it into a narrative composed of terms that will be accepted by the relevant audience (on the importance of rhetoric in this process, see Cheney, 1992). But questions remain. Which terms are accepted and what audience is relevant? These will change with time and place so that we have to limit our analysis to the *modern identity narrative*.

The Modern Identity Narrative

Traditionally, one speaks about a "form" and a "content" or "substance" of a narrative. This dichotomy unavoidably brings to mind an image of the form as being external, holding the contents inside ("a container"). Thus it seems perfectly possible to analyze the form irrelevant of the content, the contents irrelevant of the form. From such a point of view, surely any narrative, any text, has a content, a core, an inside? Surely any form, any shell, any vessel can be holding many different contents? To those who believe in such a separation, no other position makes much sense.

This misapprehension causes many troubles in criticism but even more when transferred to the analysis of identity as a narrative. Thus we shall replace it with a terminology borrowed from Russian formalists (Bakhtin & Medvedev, 1928/1985) and speak about *material and device* in the place of form and content. With *material* and *device*, this outer-inner dichotomy vanishes and thus it is easier to see why the one cannot be considered without the other. In addition, their metaphorical character attracts more attention to their analytical possibilities, whereas form and content are truly dead metaphors (Lakoff & Johnson, 1980). Note that discussing any material presumes a device—a formless material does not exist.

In analyzing a text, we may choose a device other than its author—indeed, we often do so, but we are simply constructing a new text with the original material for the next analysis. By the same token, whenever we set out to analyze a "device," it simply becomes material to be elaborated with the use of a meta-device, as it were. These metaphors coming from the vocabulary of culture (work) rather than nature (force) make the essence of the operation more clear.

Materials are usually denoted by uncountable nouns (*wood, wool, concrete*), which even grammatically call for a device to make them into analyzable units. Devices are, obviously, always made of some kind of material. This makes the distinction arbitrary and spurious, its usefulness judged only by the purpose at hand. In fact, the following discussion of identity's material and devices begins with a typical "device material," which combines the traits of the two.

Modern Identity: The Material

What is "an identity" in this conception? According to Vytautas Kavolis (as quoted by R. H. Brown, 1989), the concept of identity encompasses three elements:

an overall coherence between the individual's experience and the way this experience is expressed,

a memory—on the part of the individual and others—of a continuity in the course of the individual's life, and

a conscious but not excessive (artificial or manipulative) commitment to the manner in which the individual understands and deals with his or her "self."

Kavolis evokes the concepts of opinion, memory, and self-awareness, thus emphasizing that it is not a matter of identity as "essence" but an impression of identity that a self-narrative achieves or fails to achieve. Hence the peculiarity of modern identity: based on interaction, it aims to achieve an impression of individuality, that is, independence from other people's reactions. If we contrast modern identity with, for example, the one typical of so-called heroic societies, we notice that the latter was composed on the basis of *particularity* (roughly put, a social stance) and *accountability* (of an individual toward the community, not toward the abstract societal institutions; MacIntyre, 1981/1990), both related to the community and not, as with modern identity, the individual's own life history.

There are further specifications of a modern identity that distinguish it from any other historical form of identity: *self-respect, efficiency, autonomy* (internal locus of control in psychological terms) and *flexibility*, that is, the absence of a long-term commitment to one and the same object (Meyer, 1986). These can again be contrasted with, for example, traditional Roman virtues (Pitkin, 1984): *pietas* (reverence for the past), *gravitas* (bearing the sacred weight of the past), *dignitas* (a manner worthy of one's task and station), and *constantia* (faithfulness to tradition).

It is modern identity's individual and not community-based character that makes *autobiography* the most appropriate device analogy. As one of the leading specialists in the field, Philippe Lejeune (1989), put it:

Through autobiographical literature appears the conception of the person and the individualism characteristic of our societies: we would find nothing similar in ancient societies, or in so-called primitive societies, or even in other societies contemporaneous

411

with our own, like the Chinese communist society where the individual is . . . prevented from looking at his personal life like private property that is capable of having exchange value. (pp. 161–162)

Of interest (but not surprising), modern identity as described by Berger et al. (1974) tallies more with what nowadays is described as a postmodern identity and thus it is treated together with the latter topic in the final section of this essay.

Modern Identity: The Device

Treating identity as a narrative—or, more properly, identity construction as a continuous process of narration where both the narrator and the audience formulate, edit, applaud, and refuse various elements of the ever-produced narrative—leads us to the literary genre of autobiography. In fact, this is an analogy that works both ways: Elizabeth W. Bruss (1976) presents autobiographics as an institutional way of creating personal identities, thus proposing to see text as action much as I propose to see action as text:

All reading (or writing) involves us in choice: we choose to pursue a style or a subject matter, to struggle with or against a design. We also choose, as passive as it all may seem, to take part in an interaction, and it is here that generic labels have their use. The genre does not tell us the style or the construction of a text as much as how we should expect to "take" that style or mode of construction—what force it should have for us. And this force is derived from a kind of action that text is taken to be. Surrounding any text are implicit contextual conditions, participants involved in transmitting and receiving it, and the nature of these implicit conditions and the roles of the participants affects the status of the information contained in the text. (Bruss, 1976, p. 4)

Genre is a system of action that became institutionalized, and it is recognizable by repetition. Its meaning stems from its place within symbolic systems making up literature and culture (and therefore is diacritical, like that of the other signs). In the same sense that we can characterize the modern identity only by contrasting it with nonmodern identities, we may see autobiography as a genre acquiring specificity by difference from other genres. This permanence and autonomy (Lejeune, 1989), constitutive of a genre, become with time forces impeding its change and transformation. And yet, genres are never homogeneous and clearly separate. To begin with, several textual strategies are possible within one and the same genre (Harari, 1979). These can be characterized by a role that is given in the text to three personages typical of the genre: an Author, a Narrator, a Character (Eco, 1990; Lejeune, 1989). I shall illustrate these in the examples relating to construction of organizational identity.

One typical strategy is that of an omnipresent Author, who claims responsibility both for the acts reported in the text (and supposed to be taking place in "reality") and for the text itself. This strategy is often taken by the founders and the leaders of big corporations. When there is a ghostwriter involved, like in the "Iaccoca story," it is truly ghostly in that the writer is not allowed to appear in the text (Lejeune, 1989). The text and the world in the text have the same creator and, by the same token, create the author's identity. One could claim that this is the most pure form of autobiography as identity creation, where a person, an organization, and a text all become one.

An introduction of a Narrator is a common device. There is a person who tells the story, but the story could have been written by somebody else, although it might be the narrator acting within the text in the role of the author. The distance created gives more room for manipulation: The narrator can praise the author in a way the author could not do herself but also can distance herself if necessary. In terms of organizational identity, this strategy opens up many possibilities. A narrator can be, for example, a PR officer who is telling a story of a mighty author—a founder, a CEO. Or the narrator might be only a sample of a collective author—an organization.

The strategy that is most complex and therefore gives most room to a skillful writer is one that introduces a Character. Here the possibilities of distancing, identification, and self-reflection are limitless. The three can be one but they can also be separate if needed. In *A Portrait of the Artist as a Young Man*, the mature James Joyce is the narrator, the young James Joyce is the character, whereas James Joyce the writer authors both of them. These actorial shifting operations (Latour, 1988) are actually easier to perform in relation to an organizational identity because of its assumed collective character. Additionally, while the shifting of personal identity might sin against the coherence or continuity requirement or else put into doubt the reality claim, narrating organizational identities sails clear from all these dangers. There can be several and different authors (for example, top executives); the narrators can distance themselves at their will; and there are a variety of characters accessible without the danger of producing a schizophrenic impression. Here is, then, the point when organizational identity and personal identity are at their closest and at their furthest: An organization cannot be legitimately claiming autism or boast of defective "other perception" ("nobody understands us"; Bruss, 1976). Organizational identity makes sense in relation to institutions of market and state, and one of them must "understand it." The process of identity formulation is always an interactive one and there are rules to this interaction as there are rules to the material and device with which to form a modern identity.

To sum up, I am proposing a concept of organizational identity, which is based on four elements:

(a) a definition of individual identity as *modern institution* (i.e., temporal and local),

(b) an (institutionalized) metaphor of *organization as person*,

(c) a description of an individual identity as *emerging from interactions* between actors rather than existing as a form of an essence that is consequently exhibited, and

(d) an analogy between organizational narratives and autobiographies as *narratives constituting identity* ("autobiographical acts").

Let us now move from the concepts to three exemplifications in organizational practice. The first case relates a refusal of a group of organizational actors to accept an established identity of the other; the second examines the particulars of identity formulation and change; and the third illustrates a massive effort on the part of the relevant organization field. The three cases come from separate studies conducted within the Swedish public sector in the years 1985 to 1992.

The Beauty Contest

In 1976, after a long period of Social-Democratic rule in Sweden, a bourgeois government came to power inheriting a budget deficit that since then has continued to grow. It has been repeatedly stated that the prime responsibility for the poor shape of the public sector rests with the public administration (it was not until the 1990s that the politicians were added to the list of the accused). The so-called bureaucrats, control greedy and inefficient, spent taxpayers' money in an effort to control them with an ever-increasing strength. The private sector became the positive hero of the Swedish nation as the one who survived world crisis thanks to its thrift and in spite of the obnoxious state interventionism (which, to an observer, looks more like a repeated bailing out of the companies in crisis). The public sector must then follow the example and become economical and service oriented, decentralize power, and strive for efficiency. It was in this context that I conducted a study of the general directors of Swedish state agencies upon which the following description is based (Czarniawska, 1985).

When the Social Democrats came back into power in 1982, they found a budget deficit of 63 million Skr and the guilty in place: state administration (Siven, 1984). Domestic programs were searched for cutback budgets, savings, rationalization, and so on. The private sector, previously a profit-greedy villain, became a hero, a model, and a source of inspiration. In the eyes of the audience, the public administration went from being the Public Benefactor to the Public Devil.

Traditional Identity Challenged

The identity of the public sector organizations, taken for granted for more than 50 years (if the 1938 agreement between labor and industry is taken as the turning point), suddenly became problematic as it became clear to both politicians and administrators that the government can change and that no economic growth can continue forever. The context changed, and the narrative of success began to show at the seams.

The state agencies were told that even production of values, the only domain of some of them, can be seen as a process that shares many similarities with other production processes. And the most common trait of all production processes is that they can be analyzed in terms of their effectiveness (assessment of output) and in terms of efficiency (costs versus benefits). This kind of analysis, even if not completely alien to the public administration, is best developed within the private sector. Thus the private sector became the most obvious source of inspiration for the new identity formation, but not, however, without problems.

The outcome should be measured, but how? Is money a good output measure for most agencies? Furthermore, the measures are meaningful only when they can be compared with a standard. In the private sector, competitors are such a standard, but that can be applied only to some agencies like the State Rail and the like. The others were looking for such standards—could, for example, the public agencies in other Nordic countries be used?

In the terms used in this essay, the material of one type of identity (economic categories) became a metaphorical device for another. But "efficiency," "cost-benefit analysis," "profit-orientation," and such are not freefloating devices. Separated from a coherent narrative where they belonged, they lead to awkward linguistic inventions and sometimes even more awkward reality (see, e.g., Rombach, 1991).

The split between the material (public services) and the device (economic categories) was only one of the problems in construction of the new identity. Another was the problem of double identity, expressed in the uncertainty as to who the narrator is and who the audience is. It has been discovered, to the surprise of many, that public administration is a producer and, consequently, also employer, a utilizer of human labor. The state agencies considered themselves immune to problems related to this exploitation, the need for workers' protection. A challenge to traditional identity brought to light not only a realization of a new role, of a new material to be taken into account, but also the awareness that there were not many devices to elaborate it in a satisfactory way. The private sector became again the model of consistency, continuation, and self-awareness, even if the accompanying ethical judgment is somewhat ambiguous. It is expedient to be able to hire, fire, and restaff the personnel according to organizational needs, but is it moral? Or, in terms of double identity, are state organizations the master of the public or a public servant?

The ambiguity is not new; it is the arrangement that has been reversed. Within the previously legitimate identity, the administration had to become a Public Master to better fulfill its role as a Public Servant: a paradoxical sweep but with a great rhetorical value. According to the current demands, public sector organizations are to become Organization Masters to remain Public Servants. The inconsistency was moved inside: To serve citizens, the public employer must tightly control them as employees. As a result of the requirement of coherence, the narrative became fragmented.

How to Tell the Control Story

In the study conducted in 43 state agencies (Czarniawska, 1985), my inter-locutors—the general directors of the agencies—were well aware of the demand for change put on the identity of their agencies and the internal and external communication problems it created. The central issue was that of control. Is the agencies' identity basically that of the controlled or of the controllers?

Many of my interviews began by a spontaneous rendering of what the interlocutors perceived as a specificity of the Swedish system: the formal inde-pendence of agencies that, unlike those in other Western countries, were not the internal organizational units of ministries but separate bodies whose autonomy was guaranteed by the constitution. Legally, however, nothing pre-vents the ministries from steering and controlling the agencies (Tarchys, 1983). Are the agencies then autonomous or not?

Paraphrasing one of my interlocutors, I introduced a notion of the myth of independence, which is a very successful narrative strategy. In reality, the ministries have at their disposal three basic instruments of formal control: budget, appointment of executives, and special commissions (task forces). Applied fully and directly, they do indeed provide an ample opportunity for control. A shared myth of agencies' independence, however, allows for creat-ing, within the same legal framework, a range of relations varying from a strong dependence to a strong independence. Relative to a constellation of fac-tors such as the personalities of the main actors, the historical precedents, the political weight of the agency, the political weight of the ministry—a ministry can fully use existing instruments and actually if not formally make an agency into an internal unit of a ministry. In an opposite situation, general directors use the same instruments as their means of control. Budget becomes a tool for obtaining a minister's commitment, to be called upon during the final battle with the Ministry of Finance. Some general directors propose their candidates for top executive positions within the agency while the ministry only confirms the choice. Some even choose their own positions. Between these two extremes, there are a wide range of situations in which the formal instruments of control become the bargaining fields. Needless to say, the informal contacts decide on the actual contents of the formal processes, whereas the "myth of independence" puts a nice historical gloss on the narrative.

The challenge that came from the private sector can be compared to a challenge to a person to prove the consistency of words and deeds. But a narrative of identity is expected to produce an impression of coherence, continuation, and self-awareness, and not to stand a "reality test." If we look at actual actions, they often appear incoherent, disjointed, and with few signs of awareness. This is because

the individual is an institutional myth evolving out of the rationalized theories of economic, political and cultural action. This myth leads people to posture as individuals, in a loosely coupled way, and they can be fairly convincing about it.... This enactment of the institutionalized theory of rational behavior is rarely troubled by the internal inconsistencies and self-contradictions that are so typical of human action. (Meyer et al., 1987, p. 26)

The private sector seems not to be playing fair, claiming that public administration has a double face. Actually, there is no reason to expect fair play from a reader or a spectator. A typical reader of an autobiography, like a spectator of an autobiographical act, "has a tendency to reduce the ambiguity instead of analyzing it; he [or she] wants to know clearly 'which of the two is speaking'" (Lejeune, 1989, p. 56). Also, as usual, there is more to the story than meets the eye.

Whose Story Is This?

One can say that the private sector usurps the role of the narrator and even the author, relegating the public administration to a side character in its own autobiography. No wonder that the public sector organizations have trouble formulating a new identity on the competitor's terms.

This is, however, but a mirror reflection of a manoeuvre successfully accomplished by the public administration in the 1960s. As the social problems were to be solved once and for all due to the efforts coming from the public sector, the private sector seemed of no importance. Those were the times when the public sector was the narrator and the author, with the private sector lurking backstage as a shady character.

Is this seesaw between the narratives the only possibility? Do both sectors need to define their identities at the expense of each other? A possible alternative is a diacritical definition of both sectors as complementing each other and giving meaning to each other's activities. Heilbroner (1988) imagines a future historian (a narrator) who thus perceives the authorship of our times:

A single socioeconomic whole where the task of authority maintenance and of production are divided into two spheres of responsibility and competence. The economic responsibility of the private sphere can be defined as production of those services and goods which can be produced with profit, whereas its political responsibility lies in maintaining the societal discipline in the matter of work habits.... In this light, the political task of the public sphere lies in acting in accordance with the ancient privilege—that of maintaining the state's authority—whereas its economic function consists in producing all those goods and services which are needed by the socio-economic whole but impossible to produce within the private sphere as they cannot be produced with profit. (pp. 41–42)

This is a coauthorship of the socioeconomic sphere, as it were, maintained even by changing narrators. This is a matter of a future possibility rather than today's reality. As to the latter, I ended my exploration of state agencies by writing the following allegorical tale of two sisters, making use of narrative knowledge.

Once upon a time there were two sisters who, like all siblings, sometimes fought and sometimes were nice to each other. They lived together in a big country. One was called Patricia while the other's name was Ophelia (the name an allusion to *offentlig sektor*, or "public sector," in Swedish).

Ophelia was the pretty, the lively, the interesting one of the two. She had many friends and admirers. Neighbors came by just to say hello to her. Everybody loved Ophelia.

One day somebody knocked at the door. Two dark knights stood there, one's name was Oil Crisis and the other's Budget Deficit. "Welcome," said Ophelia, who opened the door. But they went past her and started talking to Patricia in confidence.

"What's wrong with me?" Ophelia asked a sympathetic neighbor. "Haven't the faintest, but recently Patricia has gone out to meet a consultant very often indeed. Maybe you should go and talk to him too." And this is what Ophelia did.

"To begin with," the consultant said, "your clothes are in bad taste." Ophelia was surprised. "What do you mean? I have comfortable clogs, well-fitting jeans, and my favorite college sweatshirt on!" "Nobody wears those anymore," said the consultant. "Worse still, you are too fat for elegant clothes."

"How can you say that! People used to say that I look healthy and relaxed!"

"This was when you were young and fresh. Besides, you look awful without any makeup!"

"I thought that water and soap were the best friends of a girl!"

"No," said consultants. "Apart from diamonds, the best is Lancôme. Soap contains alkalines and God knows what water contains nowadays."

And this is how it went. While Patricia met interesting strangers from all over the world, Ophelia went more and more often to the consultant.

Let us follow her there.

Identity as Do-it-yourself Kit

In the 1980s, Swedish public sector organizations became clients of major consulting companies and then began to form consulting companies for their own purposes. Although much of it concerned technical matters, especially EDP, the major part of it, and the focus of this section, was management consulting. The following analysis is supported by a study I conducted of management consulting in public sector organizations (Czarniawska-Joerges, 1990).

In the late 1970s, the Swedish Ministry of Industry employed the Boston Consulting Group to help them plan industrial policies. County governments, state agencies, and local authorities began to pay high fees to well-known consultants to restructure their organizations, to prepare cutback programs, or, more generally, to instill "economic thinking" in organizations (Brunsson & Olsen, 1992). Typically, for public sector operations, central permission was given:

At the end of August, 1984, the Ministry of Civil Affairs, represented by the Minister... and the State Secretary... organized a meeting with about 20 consulting companies, the majority of which were privately owned, but some of them were subsidiaries of multibranched Statskonsult AB [a state-owned consulting company]. Other participants were representatives of other Ministries and some central agencies. The aim was to propose an inventory of consulting competence which can be used in works of the Ministry of Civil Affairs on what was expected to be a large government bill concerning the public sector. (Premfors, Eklund, & Larsson, 1985, p. 6)

And large it became: At the conference organized by the National Audit Bureau in 1989, "Good Advice or Only Expensive?" a sum of 6 billion Skr (about $1 billion U.S.) was mentioned as an annual consulting cost in the public sector (Czarniawska-Joerges, Gustafsson, & Björkegren, 1990).

What was the main attraction of management consulting for the public sector organizations? To understand this, one must know more about what is called "an investigation culture," for many years a trademark of the public sector. Said one consultant:

What the public sector is good at, and what they devote a great deal of their time to, is to investigate things, establishing a basis for a decision. The report is then distributed for formal comments and there is then a long process where people sit around and change and correct the text of the document until finally it goes up for decision. This drawn-out process reduces the propensity-for-change that is implicit in the whole thing, so that finally they are left with some sort of diluted document which some board has to decide upon and then do something about it.

What do consultants offer instead? Let us take a closer look to see how management consulting can help in establishing a new identity.

419

Barbara Czarniawska-Joerges

Name-Giving and Labels

It is popular knowledge that the first, and perhaps the most important, phase of consulting is that of making a diagnosis. This is either a cause or a result of two common similes: the work of consultants as compared to that of physicians ("company doctors") or that of car mechanics ("fixing the system").

An alternative understanding can be reached via other similes. In my study, I compared consultants to traveling merchants who sell tools that produce control in the form of shared meaning, which is necessary for any collective action. During the first contact with an organization, merchants have to establish what is needed or what can be sold (these might or might not be the same things). To do that, a merchant/consultant must give names to the most important matters, must introduce a preliminary order in the existing system of meaning, must establish a *starting point identity*, as it were, for the client. And so, for instance, a consultant might say: "You used to be an 'appropriation authority' but now you are to become an 'assignment authority.' Your problem is the misfit of goals and functions. Your internal organization did not follow the change in your identity. Our main target will be the accounting system" (from an interview with a consultant).

How does one arrive at a set of successful labels? There appear to exist two schools of thought. The "doctor/mechanic" school claims that labels must be authoritatively attributed by consultants, the rationale being that the "patients" do not like to face unpleasant truths given a choice (alternatively, that it does not make much sense to talk to a car to establish the defect). Also, there are usually some labels already in place and in conflict with each other. Another school, more of the merchant type, claims that labeling must be done by the clients themselves. Labeling gives understanding, and this is what the whole process is all about.

Which labels are effective? Those that produce an "aha!" experience, a feeling that important but somehow hidden knowledge and understanding have been released with the production of the label. But labels still refer to what is or what has been. Often enough, labeling serves to establish what has to be changed, the identity that has to be rejected. The future and the hope of change lie in metaphors.

Metaphors and Change

Metaphors serve a very important function in the construction of new identities (see Czarniawska-Joerges & Joerges, 1988, for a detailed discussion of the role of linguistic artifacts—like metaphors, labels, and platitudes—in organizational control). They convene new meanings by fitting them into imagination-stimulating

420

messages. Their role consists partly in reducing the uncertainty produced by an encounter with what is new; they refer to something that is better known than the object of the metaphor. They can be seen as shortcuts in explanation as they are used to evoke a single image that encompasses the entire range of meanings of the object. They are also easily acceptable because their "decorative" characteristics answer the need for color and a touch of life in otherwise gray organizational reality. It is the metaphor's evocative, and not reflective, power that is the most important (Geertz, 1973). Metaphors are the material of which future identities are made.

Metaphors are rarely sold per unit. They usually come in systems or kits of metaphors. I encountered at least three types of kits: (a) analytic kits, (b) personal and organizational identity kits, and (c) construction kits. The kits are more or less ready-made. Again, the "doctor/mechanics" have usually complete kits, whereas the "merchants of meaning" have Lego-like elements that can be assembled for a specific purpose. A consultant so explained a presentation of the identity kits: "We give them four or five metaphors to choose from, a whole range of different roles; teacher, broker, free-lancer."

Where do metaphors come from? They come from reading the work of other consultants and from researchers, from public lectures, seminars, and fiction. In large consulting companies, the metaphors are tried on and polished or ornamented in internal seminars before being offered for sale.

How do metaphors work? If a label introduces order, certainty, by giving names to things, a metaphor has almost an opposite effect. It breaks through old labels, creating a hope for change, for something new. Labels say what things are; metaphors say what they are like and what they could be like. The positive effect of metaphorical thinking is especially visible when there is a feeling of a trap, exhaustion, and a cul-de-sac as a result of prolonged difficulties.

But the strength of the metaphor does not lie only in its aesthetic appeal. A powerful metaphor initiates and guides social processes. An organizational identity formulation is a collective process, which must be coordinated and organized like any other organizational process. Consultants take care of this too.

Translation as the Mechanism of Change

At the time of my study, consultants and clients alike agreed that the public administration was hungry for identity kits. Central questions were these: Who are we? What do we do? Who are we like? The labels from the private sector became metaphors in this specific context. This created a need for translation. Public opinion formulated a powerful demand that the public administration should become market and service oriented, profitable, and self-supporting. But what does this mean in a public sector organization?

Barbara Czarniawska-Joerges

The head of a leading consulting agency remembered the case of announcing the era of "adaptation to the market" to his public sector client:

They really do not understand any of it. "Are we really supposed to sell? Shall we do it? Are we not going to follow the budget?" and so on. There is a widespread confusion. And then I came in here and defined the assignment, which involved helping them to create an organization which we called [the delegated responsibility for results].

The "delegated responsibility for results" reads "profit centers" in the language of the private sector. One can look for equivalents of all the crucial concepts in a similar manner. An internal consultant who wanted to use the idea of "service management" had to do a thorough translating job first.

I've got it in my blood and I have remade it so that it fits into our world. We don't talk about market segments, we talk about target groups. We don't speak about service concept we deal in service-ideas. We have to go down to the language level and adapt it so that we can align with our world. It makes sense in our world and it's exciting.

The language problem does not exist on one side only. People from business companies do not understand the public sector language either, but, fortunately, they do not have to understand it very often. Imagine, then, formulating your identity in a language alien to yours and one in which your competitor is fluent!

While all this might sound like a very specific, locally limited case, I would like to suggest that, in fact, it grasps the mechanism of change much better than traditional models of it. Innovation, because this is the type of change we are speaking about here, is traditionally connected to the idea of "diffusion" (for a recent review, see Levitt & March, 1988).

Diffusion assumes that objectlike ideas move through space in accordance with the law of inertia (Latour, 1986). The movement starts with the "initial energy" ("initiative," "order," "command," "instruction"). The initial energy is usually connected to power and leadership and seen as coming from an individual source. According to the law of inertia, the objects will move uninhibited unless met with "resistance." This resistance takes the form of "resistance to change," "political resistance," and so on. Resistance produces "friction," which diminishes the initial energy. Friction, in the social world as well as in the technical world, is a negative phenomenon when movement is desired. That is, so long as the model of diffusion is accepted.

[The] model of diffusion may be contrasted with another, that of the model of translation. According to the latter, the spread in time and space of anything—claims, orders, artefacts, goods—is in the hands of people; each of these people may act in many different ways, letting the token drop, or modifying it, or deflecting it, or betraying it, or adding to it, or appropriating it. (Latour, 1986, p. 267)

Ideas do not "diffuse." It is people who pass them from one to another, each of them translating it according to his or her own frames of reference. Such

422

meeting of *traveling ideas* with a frame of reference, that is, *ideas in residence*, can be called "friction," but now it acquires a positive tone. There is no initial energy (all ideas exist all the time; Merton, 1985). Energy comes precisely from friction, that is, from the meeting of ideas and their "translators." Insofar as one can speak about inertia of social life, that is, habits, routines, and institutional behavior, it is this inertia that stops the movement of ideas. Without friction, there is no translation; at best, it is the case of *received ideas*. Friction can be seen as the energizing clash between ideas in residence and traveling ideas, which leads to transformation of both.

Thus we have the role of consultants as merchants of ideas and the initial translators. However significant their role, however ready-made their kits, they cannot provide their clients with a ready-made identity. If identity is an autobiographical narration, sooner or later the clients must try their voices themselves, and the patience of the audience. Thus we come to the final stage of identity formation. The first described the initial shock that challenges the old identity; the second showed how professional help can be used; the third demonstrates the actual attempt.

In Search of a New Identity

By the 1990s, the Swedish public sector was put into a pillory. In the political arena, there was talk of a crisis of legitimacy. At the organizational level, it would be more appropriate to speak of an identity crisis. The "Swedish Model," a child of Social Democracy, was announced dead and buried, among other places, in the report *Study of Power and Democracy in Sweden* (1990), which attempted to describe current trends that as yet lack a clear status or distinct identity.

What was demanded next was the creation of new identities that clearly demonstrate the break with the past (public authorities with a supervisory function) but that, nonetheless, avoid the mechanical imitation of models in the private sector. In the following, I shall exemplify this process with observations coming from an ethnographic study of municipalities and social insurance offices in Sweden (Czarniawska-Joerges, 1992b). Units at the local level (municipalities), county level (social insurance offices), and central level (the government and its agencies on the one hand the federative bodies on the other) will be explored.

The "municipality" is managing rather well, at least in external presentation. Local government offices are turned into limited companies, speculating in the financial markets, speaking the same language as the inhabitants, using visual presentations, and trying to depict themselves as "producers in the service sector." But things are not working so smoothly internally: The municipality's traditional identity as a miserly employer that expects sacrifices on the part of its personnel continues to be a burdensome image. The "Association of Local Authorities," on the other hand, is having considerable success, both internally and externally. The association's internal identity is easily established because it is a highly professional organization. In the outside world, gales are blowing, both from government quarters and in the major municipalities, but the association is nonetheless fighting for a new role as a "molder of public opinion" and a "guide." This also applies to the "Federation of Social Insurance Offices,"[1] but, in this case, it is more a question of tornadoes blowing in all directions. The federation itself is more political than professional, and this is a disadvantage when building up a consistent organizational identity.

The "social insurance offices" are facing considerable problems in their search for an identity because there are many external mandatory restrictions and very little autonomy. The "parent body," that is, the National Social Insurance Board, has even more serious problems of identity because it is perhaps the state agency that has been the most bitterly attacked and most heavily criticized.

It is the modern identity that organizations in the public sector are once again trying to construct because the one they acquired with the emergence of the welfare state has lost its legitimacy. Self-respect was felt to be self-righteousness; efficiency was regarded as nonexistent; autonomy was seen as arrogance; and flexibility, as political opportunism. What they try to do, then, is to find a narrative expressing a new identity through changes in legitimate rhetorics (McCloskey, 1986).

Public sector employees are well aware that their rhetoric must change—particularly when they present themselves to the outside world. But there still exists the traditional rhetoric that holds back every attempt to achieve change. Perhaps it would be appropriate to speak of several traditional rhetorics that used to be accepted as legitimate in discussion within and about the public sector.

Traditional Rhetorics

There were at least three legitimate rhetorics within the public sector—political rhetoric, "officialese," and the language of experts.

Political statements are usually poor at *logos*—that is, the logical argument—but this is counterbalanced by rich *pathos*, appealing to the audience's emotions. Hyperbole is favored. Threats are described as black and sinister, while promising developments are depicted in all the colors of the rainbow. This rhetoric is also often employed by the mass media (journalists report what politicians say and politicians learn to formulate their ideas in media terms).

Officialese—the language of bureaucracy—has three main characteristics. It is full of *congeries* (the obvious is reiterated) and its *logos* are unnecessarily complicated (it can take time and require some expenditure of energy to perceive the repetition). The third characteristic is the low aesthetic level, which is partly due to lack of skill but more often is the product of commitment to bad (clumsy) rhetoric.[2] Figures of speech such as metaphors and irony are avoided in favor of empty parallelism—that is, phrases that are built identically, therefore achieving the effect of monotony. In terms of narrative strategies, suspense is avoided, and both *ethos* and *pathos* kinds of appeals—that is, references to the speaker or to the listener—are sacrificed to logos.

It is true that officials who can write well have existed throughout the ages, but officialese has always been under constant fire. Of course, "writing well" means different things in different eras. In recent years, the language of experts has become the ideal. *Expert* rhetoric is based on the "objective truth." It is designed to give the impression that the expert in question has direct contact with reality, while the readers suffer from distortions resulting from their subjectivity. Ethos, that is, a claim to credibility based on the authority of the speaker, actually forms the basis of the argument, in spite of the claim that it is logos only, that is, the force of argument as such—that persuades. In addition, the expert would hotly deny that any rhetoric was being employed. The aim is to imitate science, thus the argumentation consisting of "proofs" and "confirmation" is achieved by employing statistics. A great many metaphors are employed (derived from the world of science and describing objects and their characteristics), resulting literally in an impression of "objectivity," that is, that the argumentation involves material objects and not symbols and ideas.

All three have problems now. Political rhetoric is attacked for its "emptiness," and this is no news. The main ally of the politician, the journalist, however, is at the same time their foe. On the other hand, the mass media shape what is accessible and popular in mass communication, therefore encouraging politicians to follow their example. On the other hand, one of their favorite pastimes is turning against the politicians and attacking them for exactly this kind of "journalistic" rhetoric without "proper weight" to it. As the aesthetic claims gain in legitimacy, officialese is perceived as litter in our literary ecology. Expert rhetoric, the most legitimate of the three in the earlier periods, suffers most under the postmodern winds that unmask the hidden authority claim and refuse to give anybody the status of the metanarrative. The utterances coming from the public sector organizations try to adjust.

Trying to Change

I chose, for scrutiny, an article in *Dagens Nyheter* (a Swedish daily) that was something of an event during the time of my study, was widely discussed by my interlocutors, and represents attempts to change the traditional rhetorics, albeit with mixed success. I should also add that the daily press has an enormous role in the formation of public opinion in Sweden—every household subscribes to at least one of the two main dailies, which are much alike. In addition, the identity discussed here is that of a state agency among the most criticized and at the same time very central.

In the article, titled "Scrap the National Insurance Board" (April 13, 1989), a principal administrative officer employed by the board wrote:

Several articles have appeared in these pages which have dealt with activities in the public sector. Amongst other things, views have been presented regarding methods for restricting the development of costs, thus benefiting the tax-payer.

Thus the article establishes its legitimacy by linking into an ongoing discussion. It is claimed, however, that something is missing in this public debate:

Evaluation of the Insurance Board's operations is not undertaken in a manner which gives the state information as to whether the resources invested in the Board have provided the yield which was intended. What specific services does the Board produce? Who demands these services? Are they necessary and, if so, do they give value for money?

The first sentence quoted above implies that the government receives "information as to whether the resources invested have provided the yield which was intended" from all other government bodies, with the exception of the National Insurance Board. The reader is confronted with a conspiratorial hypothesis, and this impression is reinforced by the rhetorical technique characteristically employed in this context: *interrogation*. Rhetorical questions, of course, mean asking questions that have an apparently given answer. In the above case, the answers will be a triple "no." This total state of negation means that argumentation once more has to start from the beginning:

There are 26 insurance offices in Sweden and each office is a separate legal entity managed by a board. . . . As a result of the board representation on these boards and committees, the general public has a good insight into the operations of the insurance offices. In addition, the offices have jointly formed an organization to promote their interests—the Federation of Social Insurance Offices—which provides the county offices with administrative services. . . . There is an established contact network with the general public, providers of social care, employers, other organizations, etc.

These are just a few sentences extracted from a full column of descriptions of the status of the county insurance offices. Unfortunately, the effect created by use of the rhetorical question technique drowns in the volume of information provided. The conspiratorial introduction is allowed to fade away and, when the author returns to his original point ("This is the perspective in which the need for the Board's supervisory function should be discussed"), the reader has forgotten the introduction and the original drama has dissipated.

Now, however, comes the dark side of the picture:

The central control of data-procession operations and the day-to-day workload of the county offices means that the offices rely on up-to-date instructions from the Board on services required with regard to the general public. If there are delays in making payments due to the malfunctioning of the computer system or because personnel are waiting for new instructions before they can explain the position to the public, county office staff have to deal with the complaints.

The description is unclear and this effect is reinforced by the complex language employed ("services required with regard to"). The reader is distracted by several hidden implications. Why doesn't the computer system work? Do the county offices always have to wait for the board's instructions? What is the connection between the two? In addition, the argumentation is weakened by the conditional use of "if," which implies that the problems described have not (yet) happened. "Central control by the Board also inhibits the creativity of the county offices, hindering initiatives to achieve more effective routines and improved service to the general public."

This arouses the reader's suspicions because "creativity"—something that is desirable per se—is not exactly what is expected of a county insurance office. The reader is pacified, however, by mention of "improved service," which is a familiar, albeit empty, concept.

The article examines at length the various departments at the National Social Insurance Board and finally presents a proposal:

There are major opportunities to achieve more efficient administration in the social insurance sphere and thus to reduce costs significantly. It is no longer justified to continue the Board's supervisory activities. County offices should be entrusted with the task of administering social insurance and the benefits system on their own responsibility. . . . This would provide greater scope for creative initiatives to reduce the risks of injuries, improve the health environment and undertake rehabilitation measures, in conjunction with employers, worker protection organizations, employment offices and local care services. . . . A review of the Board's role in the social insurance field is therefore required from an economic point of view. It is important that this review adopts an unbiased approach and has access to a broad range of expert resources, including people with experience of structural change and business know-how.

Here we have a mixture of political and bureaucratic rhetoric. On the one hand, a solution to several societal problems is promised, while, on the other, the article employs all the expressions commonly found in bureaucratic documents that are devoid of content. On the one hand, a proposal is made that is totally at variance with conventional practice (When have there ever been "unbiased" official reports?), while, on the other, a coupling is made with trendy ideas (expert resources from the business world) that the reader may find unpalatable.

The above example is, in my perception, very typical of the attempted change. The provocation achieved was extremely weak. The inconsistent logos, in combination with the officialese language, diluted the message to such an extent that I wonder if the readers from outside the board could understand how revolutionary the ideas expressed actually were. What was meant to be revolutionary ended up as a cryptic message to the insiders that to those outside looks exactly like what they know and do not like about the public administration. But is it at all possible to change a dominant rhetoric? Will not the old identity always reappear from behind the attempts to appear different?

Long Live Officialese

Most of the people I talked to were extremely dissatisfied with language like that employed in official documents. This dissatisfaction could be summarized by saying that officialese was regarded as both incomprehensible and aesthetically unsatisfying. The incomprehensibility is partly because the language of bureaucracy does not keep pace with developments in everyday Swedish.

Old-fashioned language is often linked to legal rhetoric. The local offices claimed, however, that "officialese is not the result of the fine distinctions required in a legal context, but because the written text is supposed to look as if it emanates from a public authority". As Michel Foucault might have put it: Language creates power, and incomprehensibility is one of the most significant ways of expressing the fact that the speaker is an important person.

It would be an exaggeration, however, to say that my interlocutors were the only people to perceive officialese as a problem. On the contrary, there is a campaign going on in the media ridiculing the language of the bureaucracy. And at the insurance offices, there are special brochures about how to write and speak good Swedish. The question is why officialese continues to survive.

Part of the answer is routines, but another part is power. Officialese belongs to the narrative of Authoritative Administration, not to the new one—Humble Administration. There are, in fact, many factors that impede changes in the language used. It is very difficult to deal with certain hidden linguistic habits, for example, and there are not so many positive models to turn to either. Media language contains platitudes and fashionable trendy phrases, which seem attractive at first but become increasingly repulsive, rather like a cake that one has eaten too much of.

Even the most heavily committed protagonists in the struggle for better official language think in terms of "correct," or possibly "simple," language. Hardly anyone refers to language as "interesting" or as something that can "involve the reader." Is anyone brave enough to imagine "a beautiful bureaucratic language?"

Everyone in the organizations I studied agreed that traditional communication modes fail to meet contemporary requirements. But, at the same time, both the diagnosis and the cure seemed to be trapped in the same perspective that had originally caused the disease. There is continued faith in the modernist, naive-realist perspective in which words refer directly to phenomena in the real world. There is a firm belief that, if you find the "right" word, everyone will understand. This is reinforced by a fear of rhetoric, as such. It is condemned in advance as "empty" or merely a matter of "verbal initiatives." Such views are the result of bitter experience (especially of politicians), but they are also partly due to failure to distinguish between the symbolic and the practical. Accusations that politicians "don't do what they say" are peculiar in that politicians never do anything, in a physical sense. They always talk. Sometimes there is a connection between what they say and what happens, and sometimes there is no such link. This may be due to hypocrisy, but it is at least as likely to be the result of their lack of skill (in transforming their words into someone else's deeds) or of random factors. Understanding this requires a grasp of the complex role played by rhetoric in the actions of organizations, and this attempt has hardly begun (for interesting examples, see Cheney & McMillan, 1990).

As it is now, rhetoric is an instrument of power for veterans but seems "blackboxed" to newcomers. The result is a kind of fatalism, where people consider it "normal" for official documents to be both incomprehensible and deadly boring. Attempts to improve the situation are based on a mechanical or, rather, a cybernetic view of "communication" in which a "sender" transmits a "message" to a "receiver" in the hope that the "channels are set free." Within the social constructivist perspective, the discourse and its conditions, including the participants and their identity, are created and re-created in the interaction itself. A rhetoric is never "right" or "wrong" per se. Rhetorics and identities must be tried out and accepted within the relevant organizational field.

Tentative Identities Within Blurred Organizational Fields

The search for a new identity can be seen as an attempt to change the public sector organization field (DiMaggio & Powell, 1983). Following Giddens (1984), an organizational field can be analyzed in terms of actors and structures, where structures are patterns of interactions between the actors.

A Search or a Quest?

The interesting point about the creation of a new field is that the actors are uncertain of their identity and also that the structures are not given. *Identities* and *structures* are the result of structuration processes. Actors' identity can be created with the help of models, but in practice their relevance is confirmed or rejected in concrete interactions. It is not sufficient to select an attractive model and then present it. The new identity must be accepted by the other actors involved, both those who are operating on an established stage with a clear identity (e.g., the private sector) and also by others who find themselves in a similar situation. The same applies to structures. The government's actions have created a new space, a certain amount of freedom, a vacuum, but new rules have not been established. These new rules must be created through action. You can only know what is right or wrong after you have acted (or someone else has). The difference between this process and the trial and error method is that there are no rules to be "discovered" and no "referees" who know the answers (even if the local authorities, for example, would be happy to see the government take on the referee role and while the Association of Local Authorities is trying to grab the role for itself).

The problem is exacerbated by the fact that it is not just individual identities that are disintegrating but also other institutions. In the case of persons, building up an identity is described as an interaction between an individual (who is developing) and relatively stable institutions. But, in this case, we have the reverse situation—there are "individuals" who used to have strong identities and there is an organizational environment of institutions that are in a state of radical change.

Processes of this kind obviously involve great risks. On the one hand, the risks are concrete (e.g., municipal currency speculation scandals) while, on the other hand, there is considerable risk of public ridicule. The transformation is taking place on stage. The citizens, who want good entertainment without paying too much, are sitting expectantly in the audience along with competitors who would prefer to see a real fiasco and press critics who will be writing their review of what "actually" happens.

Is there any help coming from a narrative approach as presented here? At least two insights emerge. One is that public sector organizations, like everybody else, are only partly authors of their autonarrative. This insight is twofold. First, the acknowledgment of this fact can widen the understanding of the situation without pushing toward finalism. Second, self-conscious attempts may be made to limit the role of others as authors and increase one's own role.

Within this second task, another insight is at hand encompassed in the difference between a "search" and a "quest." *Search* has been, until now, a legitimate term in organization theory, and this might be part of the problem rather than the solution. The notion of *quest*, as used in medieval ballads, was not the meaning of a search for something already adequately defined like oil or gold.

It is in the course of the quest and only through encountering and coping with the various particular harms, dangers, temptations and distractions which provide any quest with its episodes and incidents that the goal of the quest is finally to be understood.

A quest is always an education both as to the character of that which is thought and in self-knowledge. (MacIntyre, 1981/1990, p. 219)

A search for excellence, or only for a new identity, assumes that such an identity already exists and waits to be discovered. This can be correct only if this new identity is to be authored by somebody else, for example, the private sector. If the public sector wants to remain its own author, then it must embark on a quest where identity will be formed as an autobiography but in accordance with what are legitimate autobiographies of our times. This, however, must be discovered in the process of formulation itself.

A Postmodern Identity: An Oxymoron or a New Quest?

It has been claimed here that one of the major problems in searching or questing for a new organizational identity is the general turbulence in organization fields: Institutions are undergoing transformations. It has also been postulated that individual identity is a modern institution. Should it not follow that the institution of individual identity is undergoing a transformation as well?

The defenders of modernity will come up with a negative answer (e.g., the untiring defender of modernity, Marshall Berman, 1992). Another negative answer can be grounded not in the faith that modernism will "win" but in a claim that all phenomena described as "postmodern" belong, in fact, to modernity. Indeed, Berger et al.'s (1974) description of modern identity is very close to what has been considered an emergent postmodern identity, to which I shall turn later. They point out four peculiar aspects of modern identity: its *openness* (life as a project), *differentiation* (due to the individual's immersion in plural and unstable lifeworlds, reality loses substance and acquires complexity), *reflectivity* (necessarily resulting from the other two), and *individuality* (the individual as the final test of existence and reality). For Berger et al. (1974), identity is still related to subjectivity and, although strongly influenced by institutions, not an institution itself.

What are the claims of those who see institutional transformations taking place? The most radical claim problematizes the notion of identity, calling it a myth, an illusion, and claiming that "in postmodern culture, the subject has disintegrated into a flux of euphoric intensities, fragmented and disconnected" (Kellner, 1992, p. 144), thus "postmodern selves... are allegedly devoid of the expressive energies and individualities characteristic of modernism" (p. 146). Kellner himself presents a less radical version of the claim that can be of great relevance for organizations in quest for an identity.

First and foremost, Kellner emphasizes the central role played by the mass media in structuring contemporary identity. Television everywhere and newspapers specifically in Scandinavian countries (where every household subscribes to at least one daily) assume some of the traditional socializing functions of myth and ritual—integrating individuals into the social order, celebrating prevalent values, offering role models (Kellner, 1992). In the times of mourning a lack of public participation, it is important to point out that television is not only a competitor for politics in offering sports or entertainment, it also offers central politics as played before the cameras rather than a local meeting with little drama to it.

The main characters of TV genres, considered typical for postmodernity, have multiple identities and multiple pasts that might or might not have influence on the present, with the character of influence being changeable as well. "In each case, their identity is fragmented and unstable, different and distinctive in each character, yet always subject to dramatic change" (Kellner, 1992, p. 151). Looking for analogies in organizational worlds, one immediately thinks about large corporations who humbly give up their established role to engage in a quest for the good of the community, where the "ecological conversion" is the most popular type of dramatic change. In both personal and organizational identities, speed and mobility are values that replaced resistance to change and stability.

The changes and adaptations in identity also set the public's role differently. The social environment is not any more ready to accept the "adult personality" as formed once and for all; it is supposed to appreciate chameleonic changes. This is based on a shared assumption that identity is constructed and not given, that it is a matter of choice and style rather than of genotype or soul. Redefined as matter of choice and style, individual identity moves from a "serious" arena of life to "leisure." It becomes a game, a play, celebrated by organizations with even more fanfare than by individuals (even if, as in the case of Benneton, the playfulness signals, at the same time, a very serious involvement in the matters of the world).

Thus both societal arenas and organization fields are filled with players rather than *actors* in the literal sense of the world. Postmodern identities are "constituted theatrically through role-playing and image construction." There are no referees in this game, Rorty (1992) reminds us, because nobody knows the rules in advance. It is the admiration and applause from another player that demonstrates the "winners." Language and pictures are of utmost importance in the play.

In this context, it will come as no surprise to say that fashion is very important for the ways identities are constructed and changed. Fashion promotes both conformity and freedom, creativity and reification (Simmel, 1904/1973)—all these are needed for a modern identity. It is the device that changed more than the materials; multiplicity and constant change, which for the moderns was both the main discovery and the main source of anxiety (Berger et al., 1974), acquire a taken-for-granted place in the postmodern identity formation.

There is, both Kellner (1992) and Rorty (1992) point out, a continuity between modernism and postmodernism that some radical postmodernists negate. For organizations, then, there is no need to despair of plunging into unknown, frightening relativism. It is a quest where their active role gives them a possibility of influencing the rules as much as the other players. What they cannot count upon, though, is an arrival of an arbiter who will tell everybody what the new rules are (although, no doubt, many will try).

Notes

1. Social insurance covers medical care, rehabilitation in case of work accidents, and so on for all citizens. Although the resources are administered centrally by a National Social Insurance Board, the activity is carried out by county social insurance offices. The local origins of social insurance are still sedimented in its former federative organ, the Federation of Social Insurance Offices.
2. This is connected with the belief that skillful rhetoric is a sign of dishonesty. Roger Brown (1969, p. 340) speaks ironically of "tweed rhetoric," observing that "one can be quiet, modest, tweedy, and yet a villain."

References

Albert, S., & Whetten, D. (1985). Organizational identity. In L. L. Cummings & B. M. Staw (Eds.), *Research in organizational behavior* (Vol. 7, pp. 263–295). Greenwich, CT: JAI.

Alvesson, M., & Björkman, I. (1992). *Organisatorisk idenitet*. Lund, Sweden: Studentlitteratur.

Bakhtin, M. M., & Medvedev, P. N. (1985). *The formal method in literary scholarship*. Cambridge, MA: Harvard University Press. (Original work published 1928)

Berger, P. L., Berger, B., & Kellner, H. (1974). *The homeless mind*. London: Penguin.

Berger, P. L., & Luckmann, T. (1971). *The social construction of reality*. New York: Doubleday. (Original work published 1966)

Berman, M. (1992). Why modernism still matters. In S. Lash & J. Friedman (Eds.), *Modernity and identity* (pp. 33–58). Oxford: Basil Blackwell.

Brown, R. H. (1989). *Social science as civic discourse*. Chicago: University of Chicago Press.

Brown, R. W. (1969). *Words and things*. New York: Free Press.

Bruner, J. (1990). *Acts of meaning*. Cambridge, MA: Harvard University Press.

Brunsson, N., & Olsen, J. (Eds.) (1993). *The reforming organization*. London: Routledge.

Bruss, E. W. (1976). *Autobiographical acts*. Baltimore: John Hopkins University Press.

Cheney, G. (1992). The corporate person (re)presents itself. In E. Toth & R. Heath (Eds.), *Rhetorical and critical approaches to public relations* (pp. 165–183). Hillsdale, NJ: Lawrence Erlbaum.

Barbara Czarniawska-Joerges

Cheney, G., & McMillan, J. J. (1990). Organizational rhetoric and the practice of criticism. *Journal of Applied Communication Research, 18*(2), 93–114.

Czarniawska, B. (1985). The ugly sister: On relationship between the private and the public sectors in Sweden. *Scandinavian Journal of Management Studies, 2*(2), 83–103.

Czarniawska-Joerges, B. (1990). Merchants of meaning. In B. Turner (Ed.), *Organizational symbolism*. Berlin: de Gruyter.

Czarniawska-Joerges, B. (1992a). *Exploring complex organizations*. Newbury Park, CA: Sage.

Czarniawska-Joerges, B. (1992b). *Styrningens paradoxer*. Stockholm: Norstedts.

Czarniawska-Joerges, B. (1993). *The three-dimensional organization*. London: Chartwell-Bratt.

Czarniawska-Joerges, B. Gustafsson, C., & Björkegren, D. (1990). Purists vs. pragmatists: On Protagoras, economists and management consultants. *Consultation, 9*(3), 241–256.

Czarniawska-Joerges, B., & Joerges, B. (1988). How to control things with words: Organizational talk and control. *Management Communication Quarterly, 2*(2), 170–193.

DiMaggio, P. J., & Powell, W. W. (1983). The iron cage revisited. *American Sociological Review, 48*, 147–160.

Douglas, M. (1986). *How institutions think*. Syracuse, NY: Syracuse University Press.

Douglas, M. (1990). *Thought style exemplified: The idea of the self*. Unpublished manuscript.

Dutton, J. E., & Dukerich, J. M. (1991). Keeping an eye on the mirror: Image and identity in organizational adaption. *Academy of Management Journal, 34*(3), 517–554.

Eco, U. (1990). *The limits of interpretation*. Bloomington: Indiana University Press.

Fuller, S. (in press). Talking metaphysical turkey about epistemological chicken and the poop on pidgins. In D. Stump & P. Galison (Eds.), *Disunity and context: Philosophies of science studies*.

Geertz, C. (1973). *The interpretation of cultures*. New York: Basic Books.

Gergen, K. J., & Davis, K. E. (Eds.), (1985). *The social construction of the person*. New York: Springer-Verlag.

Giddens, A. (1984). *New rules of sociological method*. London: Hutchinson.

Giddens, A. (1991). *Modernity and self-identity*. Oxford: Polity.

Harari, J. V. (1979). *Textual strategies*. Ithaca, NY: Cornell University Press.

Heilbroner, R. L. (1988). Rhetoric and ideology. In A. Klamer, D. McCloskey, & R. Solow (Eds.), *The consequences of economic rhetoric*. Cambridge: Cambridge University Press.

Kellner, D. (1992). Popular culture and the construction of postmodern identities. In S. Lash & J. Friedman (Eds.), *Modernity and identity* (pp. 141–177). Oxford: Basil Blackwell.

Lakoff, G., & Johnson, M. (1980). *Metaphors we live by*. Chicago: University of Chicago Press.

Latour, B. (1986). The powers of association. In J. Law (Ed.), *Power, action and belief*. London: Routledge & Kegan Paul.

Latour, B. (1988). A relativistic account of Einstein's relativity. *Social Studies of Science, 18*, 3–44.

Latour, B. (1992). The next turn after the social turn. In E. McMullin (Ed.), *The social dimensions of science*. Paris: Notre Dame Press.

Lejeune, P. (1989). *On autobiography*. Minneapolis: University of Minnesota Press.

Levitt, G. & March, J. (1988). Organizational learning. *Annual Review of Sociology, 14*, 319–340.

MacIntyre, A. (1990). *After virtue*. London: Duckworth. (Original work published 1981)

McCloskey, D. N. (1986). *The rhetorics of economics*. Brighton, Sussex: Harvester.

Mead, G. H. (1984). *Mind, self and society from the standpoint of a social behaviorist.* Chicago: University of Chicago Press.

Merton, R. (1985). *On the shoulders of giants: A Shandean postscript.* San Diego: Harcourt Brace Jovanovich.

Meyer, J. W. (1986). Myths of socialization and of personality. In T. C. Hellner, M. Sosna, & D. E. Wellbery (Eds.), *Reconstructing individualism* (pp. 208–221). Stanford, CA: Stanford University Press.

Meyer, J. W., Boli, J., & Thomas, G. M. (1987). Ontology and rationalization in the Western cultural account. In G. M. Thomas, J. W. Meyer, F. O. Ramirez, & J. Boli (Eds.), *Institutional structure.* Newbury Park, CA: Sage.

Morgan, G. (1986). *Images of organization.* Beverly Hills, CA: Sage.

Pitkin, H. (1984). *Fortune is a woman.* Berkeley: University of California Press.

Premfors, R., Eklund, A., & Larsson, T. (1985). *Privata konsulter i offentlig förvalting* (Wp No. 9). Stockholm, Sweden: Department of Political Science.

Rombach, B. (1991). *Det går inte alt styra med mål.* Lund, Sweden: Studentlitteratur.

Rorty, R. (1989). *Contingency, irony and solidarity.* Cambridge: Cambridge University Press.

Rorty, R. (1992). Cosmopolitanism without emancipation: A response to Lyotard. In S. Lash & J. Friedman (Eds.), *Modernity and identity* (pp. 59–72). Oxford: Basil Blackwell.

Simmel, G. (1973). Fashion, In G. Wills & D. Midgley (Eds.), *Fashion marketing.* London: Allen & Unwin. (Original work published 1904)

Siven, C. (1984). Politik och ekonomi i Sverige under 1970-talet. *Ekonomisk debatt, 2,* 83–95. *Demokrati och makt i Sverige. Maktutredningens huvudrapport* [The study of power and democracy in Sweden]. (1990). SOU.

Starbuck, W. H. (1983). Organizations as action generators. *American Sociological Review, 48,* 91–102.

Tarchys, D. (1983, September 1). Regeringskansliet behöver förstärkning. *Dagens Nyheter.*

17 Identity Regulation as Organizational Control Producing the Appropriate Individual*

Mats Alvesson and Hugh Willmott

Introduction

Conceptualizations of organizational control have tended to emphasize its impersonal and behavioural features with scant regard for how meaning, culture or ideology are articulated by and implicated in structural configurations of control. Mintzberg's (1983) review of control structures, for example, identifies five means of coordination, each of which is concerned principally with such configurations. Yet, the coordinating and controlling of organizing practices is hardly restricted to the design and implementation of impersonal, generally bureaucratic, mechanisms, where issues of identity are less overtly addressed.

A couple of decades ago, Ouchi (1979, p. 840) observed how 'present organization theory . . . concentrates on the bureaucratic form to the exclusion of all else'. Since then, interest in organizational culture and symbolism has undoubtedly increased (*Administrative Science Quarterly*, 1983; Alvesson, 2001; Frost et al., 1985, 1991; Gagliardi, 1990; Martin, 1992; Parker, 2000; Pondy et al., 1983). Ouchi's observation remains salient, however, as the literature on 'structure' and 'design' remains largely de-coupled from studies of culture and symbolism; also, much work on culture itself adopts a bureaucratic-engineering approach wherein its constituent elements are treated as building blocks in organizational design (Barley and Kunda, 1992). Other, less mechanistic and technocratic perspectives on organizational culture or ideology have often interpreted corporate values principally as means of legitimating objective social control (Burris, 1989); and, finally, illuminating studies of the negotiation of identity at work (e.g. Collinson, 1992; Knights and Murray, 1994; Kondo, 1990) do not focus upon the management of identity as a medium of organizational control.

In contrast, we are here concerned primarily with how organizational control is accomplished through the self-positioning of employees within managerially inspired discourses about work and organization with which they may become more or less identified and committed. As Deetz (1995, p. 87; see also Knights and Willmott, 1989) puts it, 'the modern business of management is often managing the "insides"—the hopes, fears, and aspirations—of workers, rather than their behaviors directly' (Deetz, 1995, p. 87). Consider, for example, the now widely used terms 'leader' and 'team leader'. The commonsensically valued identities associated with such discourse, which appeal to the positive cultural valence assigned to discourses of supremacy and sport, have replaced less 'attractive' titles such as 'foreman', 'supervisor' or even 'manager'. We interpret such moves as symptomatic of efforts to secure organizational control through the use of cultural media—in this case, the positive and seductive meanings associated with leadership (and teams, see Knights and Willmott, 1987, 1992) that are more congruent with 'postmodern', postFordist times, when, arguably 'there are far fewer identity givens...and more frequent changes over the life course' (Albert et al., 2000, p. 14). As Albert et al. (p. 14) suggest:

...it is because identity is problematic—and yet so crucial to how and what one values, thinks, feels and does in all social domains, including organizations—that the dynamics of identity need to be better understood.

We seek to draw attention to identity as an important yet still insufficiently explored dimension of organizational control. Drawing upon the work of Simon (1945), Tompkins and Cheney (1985, cited in Barker, 1998, p. 262) forge an important link between the process of identification and the idea that rational decision-making, or the exercise of discretion in organizations, is bounded. 'Organizational identification', they note, effectively acts to 'reduce the range of decision' as choice is, in principle, confined to alternatives that are assessed to be compatible with affirming such identification. From a managerial viewpoint, 'member identification' presents a less obtrusive, and potentially more effective, means of organizational control than methods that rely upon 'external stimuli'.

This understanding resonates with recent interest in managing organizational culture and the 'informal' qualities of workplace organization. Notably, advocates of 'strong corporate cultures' have sought to persuade managers that 'soft is hard' and that 'all that stuff you have been dismissing for so long as intractable, irrational, intuitive, informal organization *can* be managed' (Peters and Waterman, 1982, p. 11)—for example, by shaping and influencing processes of organizational identification through the mobilization of diverse corporate cultural media (Kunda, 1992). Although we do not share the faith and enthusiasm for managing culture that has been exhibited by consultants and practitioners during the past 20 years, we concur with their understanding of its increasing significance in circumstances where established bureaucratic controls have been found insufficiently responsive and adaptable to intensifying competitive pressures (Willmott, 1992). In general, however, analysts of organization have not explored this terrain. It is notable, for example, that in Whetton and Godfrey's *Identity in Organizations*, the issue of *managing* employee identity and identification is examined directly in a single chapter by James Barker, who references few studies aside from those undertaken by Cheney and Tompkins and their co-workers (e.g. Barker and Tompkins, 1994; Cheney, 1991; Tompkins and Cheney, 1985).

When exploring processes of organizational identification, it is relevant to temper an attentiveness to the oppressive effects of 'concerted' forms of control with consideration of expressions of employee resistance and subversion of such control (Ezzamel and Willmott, 1998). We reject any suggestion that management is omnipotent in its definition of employee identity. The organizational regulation of identity, we argue, is a precarious and often contested process involving active identity work, as is evident in efforts to introduce new discursive practices of 'teamwork', 'partnership', etc. Organizational members are not reducible to passive consumers of managerially designed and designated identities. Nor do we assume or claim that the organization is necessarily the most influential institution in identity-defining and managing processes. Nonetheless, we concur with a number of other commentators (e.g. Barker, 1993; Casey, 1995; Deetz, 1992; Knights and Willmott, 1989; Kunda, 1992) who argue that identity regulation is a significant, neglected and increasingly important modality of organizational control,[1] especially perhaps in larger corporations and those that are more readily located in the New E-conomy in addition to the longer established province of the professional service sector.

A continuing preoccupation with 'formal' and 'objective' aspects of control reflects the dominance of a positivist epistemology and a widespread self-understanding of management as a neutral technology or branch of engineering—a view that is routinely articulated and legitimized in functionalist forms of organizational analysis (Burrell and Morgan, 1979). This self-understanding largely disregards or marginalizes the issue of how control mechanisms are enacted by organizational members (Barnard, 1936; Weick, 1969). It is assumed that control is achieved by designing and applying appropriate structures, procedures, measures and targets; and, relatedly, that resistance to these mechanisms is symptomatic of 'poor design' or 'poor management' that can be rectified by restructuring and / or training or staff replacement. Those working in interpretive and critical traditions of organizational analysis, in contrast, have paid attention to the negotiated and problematical status of allegedly shared meanings, values, beliefs, ideas and symbols as targets of, as well as productive elements within, normative organizational control (e.g. Barley and Kunda, 1992; Kunda, 1992; Mumby, 1988; Ray, 1986; Rosen, 1985). Such studies have shown how managers may promote, more or less self-consciously, a particular form of organizational experience for 'consumption, by employees' (e.g. Alvesson, 1993, 1996; Kunda, 1992; Smircich and Morgan, 1982; Willmott, 1993). But these studies have not focused *directly* upon the discursive and reflexive processes of identity constitution and regulation within work organizations. Our concern is to appreciate how mechanisms and practices of control—rewards, leadership, division of labour, hierarchies, management accounting, etc—do not work 'outside' the individual's quest(s) for self-definition(s), coherence(s) and meaning(s). Instead, they interact, and indeed are fused, with what we term the 'identity work' of organizational members. Identity work, we contend, is a significant medium and outcome of organizational control.

Of particular relevance for our analysis is an emergent literature that is attentive to how control is exercised through the 'manufacture' of subjectivity (Barker, 1999; Deetz, 1992, 1994; Hollway, 1984; Jacques, 1996; Knights and Willmott, 1989; Rosen, 1985; Weedon, 1987). We are, however, eager to avoid seduction by 'stronger' versions or interpretations of this literature, in which dominant discourses or practices are seen to place totalizing, unmediated constraints upon human subjects (Newton, 1998). One intended contribution of this article is to advance an understanding of identity construction as a process in which the role of discourse in targeting and moulding the human subject is balanced with other elements of life history forged by a capacity reflexively to accomplish life projects out of various sources of influence and inspiration. A second, related contribution is our specification of the different means of pursuing control in work organizations through the regulation of identity. We regard identity regulation as a pervasive and increasingly intentional modality of organizational control, but we do not suggest that this is unprecedented or that it is necessarily effective in increasing employee commitment, involvement or loyalty. Indeed, its effect may be to amplify cynicism, spark dissent or catalyse resistance (Ezzamel et al., 2000). In the absence of counter-discourses that interpret the mechanisms of regulation as intrusive, 'bullshit' or hype, however, we can anticipate not only instrumental compliance but also increased, serial identification with corporate values, albeit that such 'buy-in' is conditional upon their compatibility with other sources of identity formation and affirmation.

In the next section, we position our attentiveness to identity regulation within the context of contemporary 'post-bureaucratic' efforts to introduce greater flexibility and self-organization within workplaces. Illustrative empirical material is drawn from studies conducted by the authors, as well as from the rich accounts available in the literature.

....

Identity Regulation in Context

Discourses of quality management, service management, innovation and knowledge work have, in recent years, promoted an interest in passion, soul, and charisma. These discourses can also be read as expressions of an increased managerial interest in regulating employees 'insides'—their self-image, their feelings and identifications. An appreciation of these developments prompts the coining of a corresponding metaphor: *the employee as identity worker* who is enjoined to incorporate the new managerial discourses into narratives of self-identity. A common-place example of this process concerns the repeated invitation—through processes of induction, training and corporate education (e.g. in-house magazines, posters, etc)—to embrace the notion of 'We' (e.g. of the organization or of the team) in preference to 'The Company', 'It' or 'They'. Although courting hyperbole, the sense of a shift in the modus vivendi of advanced capitalist economies is conveyed by the understanding that:

The relatively stable aesthetic of Fordist modernism has given way to all the ferment, instability and fleeting qualities of a postmodern aesthetic that celebrates difference, ephemerality, spectacle, fashion, and *the commodification of cultural forms.* (Ezzamel et al., 2000, p. 156, emphasis added)

This 'ferment' is expressed *inter alia* in the destabilization of identity, as something comparatively given and secure, and an increasing focus upon identity as a target and medium of management's regulatory efforts. As cultural mechanisms are introduced or refined in an effort to gain or sustain employee commitment, involvement and loyalty in conditions of diminishing job security and employment durability, *the management of identity work becomes more salient and critical to the employment relationship.* In these circumstances, organizational identification—manifest in employee loyalty, for example—cannot be presumed or taken for granted but has to be actively engendered or manufactured.

Currently, there are struggles in the workplace around a number of identity-intensive issues, including the feminization of managerial roles, the shifting meaning of professionalism and the internationalization of business activity. The increased numbers of women occupying managerial and professional positions traditionally populated by men (and infused by masculine meanings) has disrupted the earlier taken for granted identification of management, men and masculinity. There are also pressures to make sense of, and re-order, the relationship between gender and managerial work, partly through a 'de-masculinization' of management (Alvesson and Billing, 1997; Fondas, 1997; Gherardi, 1995). Knowledge-intensive work, especially in the professional service sector, spawns conflicting loyalties between professional affiliation and organizational responsibility that compound difficulties in retaining bureaucratic means of control (Alvesson, 2000). International joint ventures and other kinds of complex interorganizational arrangements (e.g. partnerships) render issues of social identity associated with national, organizational and professional affiliations more salient (Child and Rodriguez, 1996; Grimshaw et al., 2001). More generally, the complexities and ambiguities of modern organizations make the struggle for securing a sense of self a continuing and more problematical as well as self-conscious activity (Casey, 1995; Jackall, 1988; Knights and Murray, 1994; Watson, 1994). As Casey (1995, pp. 123–4) reports of her study of Hephaestus Corporation (a pseudonym), a world leader in the development and manufacture of advanced technological machines and systems,

employees increasingly refer to themselves, not as physicist, engineer, computer scientist, but primarily as a Hephaestus employee with a job designation indicating team location... Without a union or a professional association, and only the official Hephaestus social or sports club, employees find that there is nowhere to go (at work) except to the team's simulated sociality and relative psychic comfort.

Identity becomes a locus and target of organizational control as the economic and cultural elements of work become de-differentiated (Willmott, 1992). The picture is not necessarily as bleak as Casey paints it, however. Employees are also being encouraged to be more creative and innovative, and are therefore being invited to question and transgress the 'iron cage' of established 'Fordist' or 'bureaucratic' control mechanisms. It is romantic or nostalgic to assume that the existence of firm anchors for identity construction is an unequivocal benefit or, relatedly, that their loss is self-evidently disadvantageous. Great fluidity can present opportunities for what has been termed 'micro emancipation' (Alvesson and Willmott, 1996) when employees have greater scope for arranging their own schedules and working practices, albeit with the parameters (e.g. quantity and quality targets) set by others. These changes invariably involve the removal of some oppressive restrictions even when or as they are accompanied by increased stress and job insecurity. At the same time, emancipatory practice based upon the politics of identity, such as the membership of a work group or team, is precarious and can result in the substitution of more totalizing, 'concertive' forms of control (Barker, 1999) for bureaucratic, supervisory methods of job regulation. As Axford (1995, p. 207) has observed, identity is 'capable of service in more suspect causes... because it is grounded in nothing more compelling than the legitimation of difference, rather than in institutional scripts which give meaning and legitimacy to certain kinds of behaviour than others'. In the context of work organizations, the language of liberation and self-actualization may be promulgated as a seductive means of engineering consent and commitment to corporate goals such that the 'feel-good' 'effect of participation and "empowerment" disguises their absence' (Casey, 1995, p. 113). Flexible activation and de-activation of a set of identity elements is increasingly on the agendas of human resource strategists and developers.[2] New forms of control may be seen to involve or solicit a *processing of subjectivity* in order to constitute employees who are not only more 'adaptable' but also more capable of moving more rapidly between activities and assignments where they may occupy quite varied subjective orientations or subject positions, especially within self-managing, multi-functional work groups or teams (Ezzamel and Willmott, 1998). In turn, increased flexibility and 'multiskilling' can be accompanied by, or stimulate keener questioning of, established hierarchies and practices, and can create pressures and opportunities for the removal of constraints upon the exercise of initiative and responsibility. In principle, such movement may foster forms of micro-emancipation. In practice, however, the fluidity and fragmentation of identity may render employees more vulnerable to the appeal of corporate identifications, and less inclined to engage in organized forms of resistance that extends their scope for exercising discretion and/or improves their material and symbolic rewards.

Having pointed to some relatively far-reaching social and organizational changes affecting constructions of self-identity, a few qualifying comments are called for. It is important to check any inclination to assume that the trends sketched above are already universally established. There is certainly space for debate and doubt regarding how significant the claimed changes are (Gray, 1999; Roibok et al., 1999; Warhurst and Thompson, 1998). There is also a danger of exaggerating the fragility and 'vulnerability' of subjects to the discourses through and within which they are allegedly constituted (Alvesson and Kärreman, 2000; Newton, 1998). We do not argue that the production of subjectivity has changed radically during recent decades. We argue, nonetheless, that contemporary developments make processes of constructing and securing identity an increasingly relevant focus for conceptual and empirical analysis.

Studies of identity that have a direct bearing upon organizational control include analyses of institutional and other macro level phenomena (e.g. Albert and Whetten, 1985; Christensen, 1995; Czarniawska-Joerges, 1994) as well as studies that concentrate upon individuals and forms of identification and subjectivity (Alvesson, 2000; Deetz, 1992). *Identity regulation* encompasses the more or less intentional effects of social practices upon processes of identity construction and reconstruction. Notably, induction, training and promotion procedures are developed in ways that have implications for the shaping and direction of identity. When an organization becomes a significant source of identification for individuals, corporate identity (the perceived core characteristics of the organization) then informs (self-)*identity work*. Analyses that focus directly upon processes of identity (re)formation and regulation have been governed by one or more of the following overlapping and interrelated ways of constructing and exploring identity: central life interest, coherence, distinctiveness, direction, positive value and self-awareness.

'Central life interest' refers to questions about a person's—or a group or a social institution's—feelings and ideas about basic identity concerns and qualities. The question 'Who am I?' or 'What are we?' calls for a response in terms of some dominant or defining identity. In the context of work organizations, this may be answered in terms of, for example, professional or occupational affiliation (e.g. engineer, electrician) or organizational position (e.g. head of the production department), but also in less formal terms, e.g. 'highly interested in ideas and experiments' or 'a people manager'. 'Coherence' describes a sense of continuity and recognizability over time and situation. A sense of identity is understood to connect different experiences and to reduce fragmentation in feelings and thinking. It counteracts or closes the possibility of responding to contingencies with limitless plasticity. 'Distinctiveness' means that somebody is definable, by herself and others, as different to someone else. Such a characteristic, sometimes deemed to be unique (e.g. a genius), is shared with others (e.g. men, employed), but still different from others (women, unemployed, retired). A fourth aspect is 'direction'. It implies what is appropriate, desirable and valued for a specific subject. The identity or self-image of a person offers guidelines for decision-making (Mitchell et al., 1986). A 'manager' manages. Implications for action may be vague, but nevertheless they make some routes appear reasonable and others less so. A fifth aspect concerns 'social values'. Identity is invariably related to self-esteem as aspired-for identity is attributed a positive social meaning. Conversely, one's enemies, but also others who serve as objects of comparison, tend to be seen and described in less positive terms (Turner, 1984). A sixth aspect is 'self-awareness'. Identity is also an 'object' of self-consciousness. An awareness of self-identity (see below) is a medium and outcome of how a person feels, as well as how she thinks and ascribes value (Hassard et al., 1999).

Giddens' concept of 'self-identity' usefully differentiates such concerns from those who study 'personal' or 'social' identity as a comparatively conscious set of self-images, traits or social attributes, although the concepts overlap and share common elements. Following Giddens, self-identity is conceptualized as a reflexively organized narrative, derived from participation in competing discourses and various experiences, that is productive of a degree of existential continuity and security. 'Self-identity is not a distinctive trait, or even a collection of traits, possessed by the individual. It is the self as reflexively understood by the person ... self-identity is continuity (across time and space) as interpreted reflexively by the agent' (Giddens, 1991, p. 53). The reflexive construction of self-identity is assembled out of cultural raw material: language, symbols, sets of meanings, values, etc. that are derived from countless numbers of interactions with others and exposure to messages produced and distributed by agencies (schools, mass media), as well as early life experiences and unconscious processes. It forms a complex mixture of conscious and unconscious elements, an interpretive and reflexive grid gradually shaped by processes of identity regulation and identity work.

In comparatively stable or routinized life situations, the narrative of self-identity runs fairly smoothly. Identity work is comparatively unselfconscious, albeit contingent upon life history and the unchallenged position of the hegemonic discourse(s) through which identity is reproduced. In conditions of late modernity, however, identities are comparatively open and achieved rather than given or closed, as we noted earlier (see also Giddens, 1991; Willmott, 1994). Roles are improvised rather than scripted. Given the accomplished and sometimes precarious nature of contemporary identity, much, if not all activity involves active *identity work:* people are continuously engaged in forming, repairing, maintaining, strengthening or revising the constructions that are productive of a precarious sense of coherence and distinctiveness. Specific events, encounters, transitions, experiences, surprises, as well as more constant strains, serve to heighten awareness of the constructed quality of self-identity and compel more concentrated identity work. Conscious identity work is thus grounded in at least a minimal amount of self-doubt and self-openness, typically contingent upon a mix of psychological-existential worry and the scepticism or inconsistencies faced in encounters with others or with our images of them. Such tensions are stopped, or at least suspended, when a receptiveness to identity-securing positions and routines is matched by corporate and managerial opportunities for investing self in organizing practice. At the same time, such suspension is itself subject to disruption. When a familiar feeling tone, associated with the sensation of 'being myself', becomes unsettled, feelings of tension, anxiety, shame or guilt arise. Occasionally a sense of contradiction, disruption and confusion may become pervasive and sustained. Intensive remedial 'identity work' is then called for, perhaps even of a therapeutic kind. When such identity work fails, tensions and the possibility of breakdown follow.

Managing continuity, including typical or familiar levels of emotional arousal, against a shifting discursive framework provided by socially established truths about what is normal, rational and sound is the basis for identity work. Such monitoring work—involving strains and identity uncertainties—is well documented in Watson's (1994) study of managers in a large UK company. One manager accounts for his work situation as follows, illuminating a situation that calls for identity work: 'I really do wonder what my bloody job is sometimes. I say to myself "I am in charge of this office and the office in Birmingham"

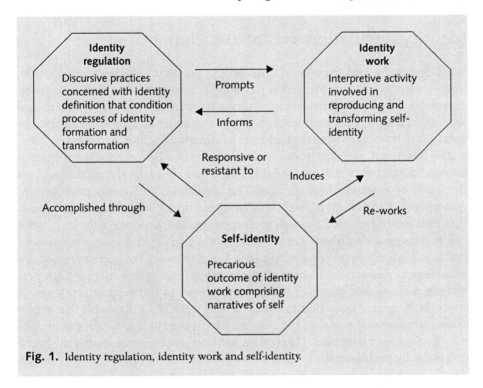

Fig. 1. Identity regulation, identity work and self-identity.

but then I ask whether I'm really in charge of even myself when it comes down to it. I get told to jump here, jump there, sort this, sort that, more than I ever did before I was even a section leader' (p. 29). In this example, the manager clearly experiences himself as a target of contradictory identity regulation as he, while institutionally positioned as a fairly senior manager, feels himself being managed much more than ever he was as a section leader. At the same time, he hints that the strains and frustrated expectations associated with his managerial position are producing an unwelcome and probably unfamiliar level of tension or emotional arousal that leads him to express doubts about 'whether I am really in charge of myself'.

Our understanding of the relationship between self-identity, identity work and identity regulation is summarized in Figure 1. There, we indicate how self-identity, as a repertoire of structured narrations, is sustained through identity work in which regulation is accomplished by selectively, but not necessarily reflectively, adopting practices and discourses that are more or less intentionally targeted at the 'insides' of employees, including managers.

The three elements in our model are equally important. It is relevant to bear this in mind as we now consider regulation.

Identity Regulation as Organizational Control

We have emphasized the role of discourse in processes of identity formation, maintenance and transformation. Through attending to, and mobilizing discourses, we identify ourselves as separate independent entities; and by engaging (other) discourses we embellish or repair our sense of identity as a coherent narrative that is attentive to the concerns summarized earlier. As Hollway (1984, p. 252) has noted, social practices 'depend on the circulation between subjectivities and discourses which are available', including those discourses that address the world of work and organization. The 'availability' of discourses is contingent upon gaining access to, and mobilizing, resources institutionalized in practices that are represented through such concepts as 'corporate cultures', 'work and professional ideologies', etc. But discourses also depend upon the interpretation and inventive powers of employees. Employees are not passive receptacles or carriers of discourses but, instead, more or less actively and critically interpret and enact them. For example, Watson (1994, pp. 114–18) reports resistance to attempts by senior managers to promote and establish a discourse that represented employees in terms of the *skills* they were deemed to possess rather than the *jobs* that they occupied. Employees, including many managers, challenged this move by problematizing the sense and the 'truth' of the 'language reform' desired by senior managers. They sought to defend a more traditional, counter-discourse, stressing the value of job security for maintaining morale, but did so by appealing to a hegemonic discourse of corporate performance, arguing that it would be adversely impacted by lowered morale.

As Watson's study illustrates, there is generally some scope for articulating discourses to construct situations in ways that render actions (or non-actions) more or less reasonable and legitimate, at least within the terms of a particular world-view. That said, in any given situation, possibilities of using language to make differentiations and to structure (social) reality are not limitless. They are constrained as well as enabled by material conditions, cultural traditions and relations of power. Management (and others) act, more or less strategically, to introduce, reproduce, influence and legitimize the presence/absence of particular discourses. The meanings of, and membership within, social categories and claims about how the world is plausibly represented are constant sites of struggle where identities are presented, resisted and fought over (Clegg, 1989). Inter alia, ideological and disciplinary forms of power operate through (a) the supply/restriction of availability of discourses, (b) the frequency or intensity of their presence, and (c) the specific linking of discourse and subjectivity (O'Doherty and Willmott, 2001).[3]

The management of discursive presence through varied and repeated exposure to ideological messages has been explored in a number of studies (e.g. Alvesson, 1995; Kunda, 1992; Rosen, 1985). It is not, however, merely the availability of discourses or even the frequency of their articulation that is important for pursuing organizational control through the regulation of identity. Of critical importance is the *linking* of discourse to processes of self-identity formation and reproduction. Regulation through the management of identity is conditional upon the strengthening of this link. Yet, to repeat, discourses may be produced and circulated without 'sticking' to their targets. The next section considers how discourses are more or less intentionally used to accomplish this control in contemporary management/organization contexts.

Targets of Identity Regulation

Despite a growing number of studies of cultural-ideological modes of control, very few have sought to explicate the specific means, targets and media of control through which the regulation of identity is accomplished. At best, broad-brush categories such as cultural, ideological, bureaucratic, clan or concertive control have been identified and supported by reference to examples or types of discourses. There is a need for something in between, showing the diverse ways in which identity regulation is enacted. To that end, we present a preliminary and certainly not exhaustive overview of how identity is influenced, regulated and changed within work organizations. It is our hope that this overview can facilitate a more focused orientation and agenda for the empirical analysis of identity regulation.

1. *Defining the person directly.* Explicit reference is made to characteristics that have some validity across time and space and that distinguish a person from others. These characteristics suggest expectations of those people who occupy the social space that is thereby defined for them. The more precise the definition, the less vague are the implications. For example, if a person is addressed as 'a middle manager', s/he may 'manage' but perhaps primarily through following imperatives from above. A '*male* middle manager' may do so with a stiffer upper lip (indicating masculinity) and may want to conceal the element of subordination for himself and others (cf. Laurent, 1978) without deviating from the imperative of being below the top. 'A male 50 year old middle plateaued manager' may manage with slightly less enthusiasm than before he was identified as 'plateaued'. This kind of control may emerge from the operation of formal procedures (e.g. appraisal) or it may be used in informal ways (Ezzamel and Willmott, 1998).

2. *Defining a person by defining others.* A person (or a group) can be identified indirectly by reference to the characteristics of specific others. In a study of advertising agencies, reference to other agencies as amateurish, insincere and sometimes duplicitous tended to be interpreted as implicitly communicating professionalism, honesty and openness as significant and desirable attributes among the members of the researched agency (Alvesson, 1994), even though these positive qualities

were not explicitly expressed. In a US insurance sales organization, populated solely by men, managers and others emphasized that the work was not suitable for women. A manager said that he would never hire a woman. This portrayal of the other as lacking the necessary psychology for the job (e.g. 'killer instinct') ensured that the job and appropriate jobholders were constructed as masculine (Leidner, 1991). Indirectly, the salesmen were constructed as 'real men'. In turn, this identification invited them to accept conditions that might otherwise have been experienced as frustrating and negative.

3. *Providing a specific vocabularly of motives.* A particular interpretive framework is commended and promoted by management through which employees are encouraged to understand the meaning of their work. Through a particular vocabulary of motives (Mills, 1940), including archetypes and stories, a set of reference points about what is important and natural for a person to do becomes established. Earlier we gave an example from Watson's (1994) study where senior managers sought to displace a 'jobs' discourse with a 'skills' discourse. In a fast-growing computer consultancy company, the management tried to develop a non-instrumental orientation on behalf of the workers by emphasizing workplace climate and corporate pride (Alvesson, 1995). Social motives—having fun, working in groups, feelings of community—were stressed. Criteria for recruitment and a multitude of social activities supported this orientation. Instrumental motives were overtly de-emphasized. The relative absence of hierarchy was stressed and the significance of pay was played down. As one senior manager said in an introductory course for recent employees: 'I do not persuade people to work here by offering high wages, nor do I retain them by out-bidding other employers. The wage should be fair, but not more than that'. This kind of signalling invited employees to construct themselves as intrinsically motivated rather than pay-oriented.[4]

4. *Explicating morals and values.* Espoused values and stories with a strong morality operate to orient identity in a specific direction or at least stimulate this process. This involves the sorting and ranking of alternative moralities and defining oneself accordingly, in a more or less coherent way. Self-managing teams may, on occasion, generate a strong consensus about values, leading to a close identification with the value system created. As Barker (1993, p. 436) concludes, 'if [workers] want to resist their team's control, they must be willing to risk their human dignity, being made to feel unworthy as a "teammate"'. A rather different example of this process is provided by Jackall (1988) when he shows how strong feelings of morality, although accepted or even celebrated in other life contexts, are understood to be misplaced in the business world.

5. *Knowledge and skills.* The construction of knowledge and skills are key resources for regulating identity in a corporate context as knowledge defines the knower: what one is capable of doing (or expected to be able to do) frames who one 'is'. Education and professional affiliation are powerful media of identity construction. The extensive use of management education programmes, for

example, presents self-images of people who have been recently appointed or promoted as managers. Watson (1994, p. 5) describes one of his key tasks as a consultant/researcher to be 'identifying ways of encouraging all their managers to see themselves as "business managers", rather than as specialist or departmental managers' (see also Knights and Willmott, 1987). Casey (1996) reports how team membership and work area displaced occupational identification as a greater emphasis was placed upon the acquisition of skills to perform multiple functions. Knights and Morgan (1991) and Sveningsson (2000) contend that 'strategic management' as a field of knowledge and practice encourages the construction of managers as 'strategists'. An important measure of a manager's competence then becomes the capacity to articulate a strategy discourse and thereby 'pass' as a strategist.

6. *Group categorization and affiliation.* One frequently powerful way of regulating identity is through developing social categories to which the individual is ascribed. The dividing up of the social world into 'us' and, by implication although more or less clearly pronounced, 'them' creates or sustains social distinctions and boundaries (Ashforth and Mael, 1989; Turner, 1982, 1984). By engendering feelings of belonging and membership, a sense of community, however contrived this may be (Alvesson, 1995; Rosen, 1985), can be developed. Casey (1996, p. 331) argues that 'the devices of workplace family and team manifest a corporate effort to provide emotional gratifications at work to counter the attractions of rampant individualism and consumption'. Being a team member and/or a member of the wider corporate family may then become a significant source of one's self-understanding, self-monitoring and presentation to others. This kind of identity regulation works through social events and the management of shared feelings more than through linguistic distinctions or cognitive operations (cf. Van Maanen and Kunda, 1989). Group categorization can occur without any references to specific values or a distinctive content.[5]

7. *Hierarchical location.* In most organizations social positioning and the relative value of different groups and persons is carved out and supported by repeated symbolism (Kunda, 1992; Martin and Siehl, 1983; Sculley, 1987, Ch. 1). Superiority/subordination in relation to significant others is central in answering the question 'who am I?'. Hierarchy in organizations is often formally based, but status distinctions between different communities and functions can also be central for the regulation of identities. Some progressive organizations avoid conspicuous hierarchy symbolism, celebrating its progressive, egalitarian character (Alvesson, 1995). Hierarchy is, however, typically still expressed, albeit in more subtle and often contradictory ways that call for complex negotiations of identity in terms of superiority/equality/subordinateship (Ezzamel and Willmott, 1998). A less explicit version of this is informal rankings. These may be intra- or extra-organizational. In progressive companies where the explicit, formal, internal hierarchy is downplayed there are frequently efforts to construct the entire company

and its members as élite, e.g. through being an organic, adhocratic, leading-edge company rather than a 'bureaucracy', implying that organizational members are ahead of rest of the competition in their orientations and capacities.

8. *Establishing and clarifying a distinct set of rules of the game.* Established ideas and norms about the 'natural' way of doing things in a particular context can have major implications for identity constructions. The naturalization of rules and standards for doing things calls for the adaptation of a particular self-understanding. There is, for example, in many companies, an established but unspoken code of proper conduct as a 'team player':

A team player is alert to the social cues that he receives from his bosses, his peers, and the intricate pattern of social networks, coteries, and cliques that crisscross the organization. . . . He is a 'role player' who plays his part without complaint. He does not threaten others by appearing brilliant, or with his personality, his ability, or his personal values. He masks his aggressiveness with blandness. He recognizes trouble and stays clear of it. He protects his boss and his associates from blunders. (Jackall, 1988, p. 56)

These rules of good corporate citizenship are not 'values' or morals in the sense of a clear statement of what is good or bad. They are rather a network of meanings and guidelines for 'getting by' in ambiguous, politically charged social settings. They offer guidance on what is natural or necessary for corporate work to function. In a study of a global retailer that pursued a disastrous strategy of diversification into a variety of brand-based strategic business units, a recovery strategy was based upon the widely disseminated slogan and recipe of 'simplify, focus, act' (Ezzamel and Willmott, 1999). By learning and acting upon such 'rules', a collective sense of identity and purpose may be forged, thereby smoothing operations in the work context.

9. *Defining the context.* Through explicating the scene and its preconditions for the people acting in it, a particular actor identity is implicitly invoked. By describing a particular version of the conditions in which an organization operates (e.g. the market situation) or the zeitgeist (the age of informational technology), identity is shaped or reinterpreted. When, for example, globalization is said to lead to massive uncertainty, harsh competition and rapid changes, then it is implied that adaptability, anti-bureaucracy and enterprising qualities are valued. In turn, this definition of the context invites employees 'to acquire capacities and dispositions that will enable them to become "enterprising" persons' (du Gay, 1996, p. 27).

To summarize, identity may be a more or less direct target for control as organizing practices address the actor, the other, motives, values, expertise, group membership, hierarchical location, rules of the game, the wider context, etc. The nine modes of regulation may grouped into those that focus respectively upon:

- *The employee*: regulations in which the employee is directly defined or implied by reference to the Other (1 and 2).

- *Action orientations*: regulations in which the field of activity is constructed with reference to appropriate work orientations (3, 4 and 5).
- *Social relations*: regulations of belongingness and differentiation (6 and 7).
- *The scene*: regulations indicating the kind of identity that fits the larger social, organizational and economic terrain in which the subject operates (8 and 9).

These nine modes of regulation offer a broad view of how organizational control may operate through the management of identity, primarily by means of discourse. We have stressed that regulation is not just targeted at individuals and groups per se, but may work indirectly and may be accomplished, in more or less focused ways, through diverse media of control. That said, it is important to appreciate how our specification of modes of identity regulation is an analytical device intended to bring a degree of order and clarity to complex and pervasive processes of organizational control. In practice, these forms of identity regulation occur simultaneously, and may contradict as well as reinforce each other. Moreover, to reiterate our earlier discussion, employees may be more or less receptive or resistant to identity-oriented or identity-consequential modes of organizational control.

Organizing practices and discourses may have implications for identity without being narrowly or exclusively dependent upon the precise self-understanding of the individual. An assembly line or a McDonald's outlet, for example, operates without presupposing a fine-tuned self-identity as an assembly-line worker. Nonetheless the work organization and its associated discourses have consequences for self-identity as the employee positions his or her sense of identity in relation to them. To be of significance for the regulation of identity, practices and discourses must have valency—whether affirming or negating—for its framing and fixing. This implies a certain intensity of meaning and some amount of emotionality (relating to anxiety, enthusiasm, involvement, etc.). Even wages as a motivator and source of meaning assume a strong value attached to money and its uses, which is then supported by an identity in which consumption or accumulation is central. The potency and influence of the media of regulation is always conditional upon organizational members' receptiveness to them. Discourses may be comparatively familiar and readily interpreted within an ongoing identity narrative and associated emotional condition; or they may be experienced as disruptive of it. Kunda (1992) gives the example of the corporate propaganda or 'bullshit' that continuously promotes the values and virtues of the organization. The influence of propaganda as a regulator of identity may increase, diminish or may even backfire. People may distance themselves from the company as a key source of identification and draw upon the occupation, subunit or non-work sources of self-definition ('I am a family man rather than a career person'). In the latter, the 'loop' to the left of Figure 1 takes precedence as responses illustrated by the arrows to and from the box labeled 'identity work' become less significant. When there is discontinuity, the identity narrative is actively explored, defended or modified—either temporarily or with longer lasting consequences. Here, the 'loops' in the upper and right parts of the figure are dominant. Of course, discourses are rarely experienced unequivocally as confirmation/continuation or disruption/discontinuation. Different discursive elements may point in different directions as ambiguity persists. In the following empirical cases, a number of the modes specified earlier are reviewed. The first case illustrates concentrated identity work in response to a threat, while the second describes a confirmation of ongoing identity constructions.

Two Illustrative Cases

Case 1. The Angry Worker: On Refusing to Say 'Business'
A young worker in an industrial company was asked to report to the marketing manager who tried to persuade him to say 'business' instead of 'product' when referring to the crowbars produced by the company (from Alvesson and Björkman, 1992). It was part of a corporate effort to make the firm more 'market oriented', to make people in production recognize that there are customers buying the 'business'/'product', and to create a common orientation across the different areas of the company. This attempt to adopt the term 'business' instead of 'product' encountered sustained resistance from some employees. According to the shopfloor worker,

Roland (the factory manager) has also been brainwashed with that term. I am convinced that the expression originates from the marketing manager. I have nothing whatever to do with the 'business' crowbar. It is the marketing side which has to do with the business. *There* it is a matter of business, but not *here*. I am not interested in getting closer to the market. I have enough to do as it is. [The marketing manager] tried to impress upon me that it is a matter of businesses, not of the product. He tried to find out what kind of person I am. I thought it was a damned thing to do. His job is to deal with the market. He should not come down here and mess with me, that's the task of my own boss. Roland also thought it was a bit unpleasant. (He was also there). One wonders what kind of people they have up there.

This example illustrates how an episode may trigger intensive identity work, in which a particular identity is defended and strengthened against experienced attack. (Other outcomes could have been an active embrace or passive acceptance of the regulative effort, or simply disregarding it without any reaction.) Inter alia, the worker expresses his basic sense of (work) identity: somebody working with physical objects ('I have nothing whatever to do with the "business" ');

coherence: the refusal to comply with a vocabulary indicating another orientation and attitude to work—he sticks to his knitting ('I am not interested in getting closer to the market'); distinctiveness: he is very different to the other person ('There it is a matter of business, but not here'); commitment: he works with production ('I have enough to do as it is'). In general, the situation is defined (or re-constituted) in terms that are defensive and protective of a sense of identity regulated by established, but now questioned, organizing practices. This is accomplished, in this case, through a pejorative construction of the other, who is allegedly responsible for brainwashing, interfering, almost bullying a worker who, in any event, is considered to be outside his jurisdiction.

In terms of the modes of regulations indicated above, this brief example exemplifies an attempt to change the rules for the game (8)—the concern to become more oriented to the market and the customer. The marketing manager tries to establish the subordinate positioning of the worker by calling him to the manager's office and instructing him about what language to use (7). Relatedly, the episode may be understood as an effort to rank different kinds of knowledge (5): production is subordinated to marketing knowledge. These aspects of hierarchy and ranking are reinforced by the fact that the factory manager was also present during the episode. However, the outcome of the intervention is, contrary to intention, a reinforced identification of the worker with production and the factory. Marketing is viewed as 'them', rather than 'us'.[6] It is the strength of identification with production work that informs the worker's emotionally charged response to pressures to embrace an upgrading of marketing and customer talk. The exchange invited a reorientation of the worker to become a market/business-oriented person, receptive to the signals/requirements from marketing. In response, his identity work takes the form of a process of defining the self (1), the other (2), a certain morality (4), group belongingness (6), illegitimate hierarchical relations (7) and the rules of the game (8).[7]

Case 2. Processing Managerial Subordinates: The Case of an Information Meeting
The situation is an information meeting in a business sector of a large industrial company. The president has gathered 100 individuals to inform them about a reorganization. He introduces the meeting with a rhetorical question 'Why are you here? It is because you are managers in this company!' (The following day the remaining personnel receive similar information, in groups of 500 people.)

The meeting continues with the president asking the audience 'what is the best way to organize ourselves?'. He does not directly address the question for the next 30 minutes. Instead, he describes various aspects of the entire company, its historical development, its size and its strategy. He then states some general principles about how to organize. 'Decentralization' and the need for personnel 'to decide for themselves' and to provide 'feedback' are mentioned several times. The president uses the word 'we' frequently. He then informs his audience about the overall structure of the new organization, in which three divisions are central. The new divisional managers talk briefly about their respective units. The staff of the business sector are then introduced: they stand up when their names are called. After a few questions, the meeting is over (from Alvesson, 1996).

At this meeting, managerial identity is explicitly and visibly confirmed. Those present were identified as 'managers', not as employees, co-workers, subordinates, engineers and marketers, etc. The identification of those present as managers accentuates certain ideas and values about the job. This is done by invoking broadly shared contextual meanings associated with the term 'manager': it is a question of responsibility, loyalty, work morale, results orientation, being positive about changes, etc. Related to these meanings are references to feedback and self-determination as important elements of the re-organization. The meeting serves to remind the audience that they should perceive the planned reorganization as 'managers', and that this has specific implications. That employees in the company had grown weary of frequent reorganizations made it even more important for the president to appeal to an identity that carries with it a responsibility to assume a positive attitude towards change.

Our commentary on this case has already incorporated reference to the focal persons, a vocabulary of motives, a set of values and social belongingness to the category of managers (see 1, 3, 5 and 6 above). There were also implicit references to 'non-managers', i.e. those employees who were absent from this meeting (see 2), thus reminding those present of their shared, exclusive identity in relationship to the rest of the personnel.

During the course of the meeting, the 'managers' were interpellated primarily as subordinates. Despite talk of 'we', and indications of a shared group identity as managers, they were treated as passive recipients of the new organizational design upon which senior management had autocratically decided. They were not encouraged to take an active role in the decision process that had preceded the meeting, nor were they encouraged to become involved during it. Four hierarchical levels were signalled and corresponding identities presented (mode 7 above). Further, the framing of the reorganization in the context of the firm's world-wide business had the effect of playing down the relevance of the audience's local knowledge of the specific situation (modes 5, 8 and 9). In interviews with members of the audience, they indicated that the president's address and the organization of the situation were familiar and to a degree reassuring, despite the hierarchical distance between themselves and the top manager being strongly felt. The meeting did not seem to trigger transgressive or innovative identity work, but instead appeared to facilitate the maintenance of established identities (that is, it fuelled ongoing identity constructions).

Discussion

Identity regulation may be pursued purposefully or it may be a by-product of other activities and arrangements typically not seen—by regulators or the targets of their efforts—as directed at self-definition. Media or regulation may be strategically employed; or they may be produced by actors in their everyday interactions as part of cultural traditions and institutionalized patterns of behaviour. Our two illustrative cases show how the two modes may coincide. More or less conscious actions by senior managers are expressed in relatively mundane contexts in which identity regulation may not be at the forefront of managers' minds.

Analyses of organizational control have tended to focus upon one or more neatly integrated and dominating types of control or continua between two or three types. Friedman (1990) counterposes 'direct control'—a detailed specification of tasks with close supervision where, in principle, employees' sense of identity is seemingly irrelevant—against 'responsible autonomy' which involves mobilizing or developing employees' capacity to exercise discretion in ways that are consistent with corporate values and priorities. The issue of identity is unexplored. The presentation and comparison of theories 'X', 'Y' (McGregor, 1960) and 'Z' (Ouchi, 1981) is also largely silent on the issue of identity regulation and identity work. It is indicated that management arrangements more or less automatically produce a certain kind of work orientation. The practical application of such types of control is rarely located in the interplay of dense networks of groups, acts, events, cultural meanings and symbols that are mobilized in processes of identity work, processes which may create a large discrepancy between intent and outcome.

To further explicate the complexities and dynamics of identity regulation, we make an analytical distinction between three patterns of identity regulation— 'managerial', 'cultural-communitarian' and 'quasi-autonomous'—that, in practice, are frequently intertwined. By focusing upon these three interacting 'sources' of inputs to identity regulation, process aspects are highlighted and uncertainties in terms of (temporary) outcomes are taken seriously.

Managerial theory and arrangements supply discourses through which self-identity is constructed and maintained. For example, 'leadership' is 'effective' when it coalesces and regulates identity, de-activating alternative constructions. Indeed, leadership has been conceptualized as the management of meaning (Smircich and Morgan, 1982). As meaning is contingent upon identity, managing meaning is integral to managing identity.[8] Managerial and corporate regulation may reduce anxiety for employees when it assists them in coping with ambiguity or when undertaking focused, productive work. Less positively, the domination of managerially orchestrated identities implies limited space for critical reflection

(Alvesson and Willmott, 1996), places constraints upon ethical judgement (Jackall, 1988) and exerts a strong corporate grip over people's lives (Deetz, 1992). It may also encourage and sanction a new inflexibility when employees become devotees of a particular set of meanings (Barker, 1993). On the other hand, standardized constructions of top managers may act to demoralize or constrain, rather than facilitate, the work and interaction of organizational members (Willmott, 1997). Managers are the 'recipients' and 'bearers' of powerful regulative efforts that may be counter-productive when transmitted to the shopfloor, as was evident in the case of the angry worker.

Cultural-communitarian patterns of identity regulation emerge from broadly shared understandings and convictions; they may be organizational in origin and effect, but are more often occupationally/societally rooted (Ezzamel and Willmott, 1998). The case of the angry worker (see earlier) illustrates how a factory-based identity (albeit one to which prior managerial practices may have contributed) frames a response to managerial regulations that are sensed to threaten it. Cultural-communitarian inputs may oppose, support or work independently of management-driven identity regulation. Organizational cultural control is generally anchored in broader, historically derived collective patterns of belief and legitimacy. Managerial action takes place within, rather than above, these patterns. For example, Whittington (1989, p. 298) notes how the managers in his study 'were able to synthesize patriotic, paternalistic, professional and religious ideals into local ideologies supporting their private purposes'—purposes that were themselves fashioned from these and other identical resources.

What may be characterized as *quasi-autonomous* patterns of identity regulation can be conceptualized as moves towards 'micro emancipation' (Alvesson and Willmott, 1996).[9] The circulation of a plurality of discourses and practices through which identities are formed makes it more likely that identities are only partly or temporarily regulated by management-driven or other group-controlled processes of regulation. Other processes are present that may discredit or impede managerial identity regulation, as in the case of our angry worker example. The struggle to forge and sustain a sense of self-identity is shaped by multiple images and ideals of ways of being. This presents both opportunities and difficulties in changing/reconstructing identities in a liberating direction. Preconditions include (1) a combination of elements of stability/integration with elements of change/plurality, (2) a space as well as resources, for critical reflection, and (3) a supportive form of social interaction (Payne, 1991; Willmott, 1998).

Poststructuralists have developed a concept of process subjectivity to point towards a way of transgressing the disciplinary effects of regulation (Deetz, 1992; Weedon, 1987). Central to this process is a willingness to acknowledge the disunity of the 'I' and the associated urge to deny discontinuity and fragmentation and/or the compulsion to restore the ideal of sovereignty. One must bear in mind that micro-emancipation is not only an intellectual project; it involves emotional labour (Fay, 1987; Willmott, 1998). Providing 'counter-discourses' to managerial regulations and socio-emotional support through groups and networks is important, but what can be accomplished by this alternative organizing should not be exaggerated nor should the problems arising from contradictory pressures and identifications in corporate settings be minimized. As 'the unity of the I is risked', Deetz comments, 'the fixed self/other/world configuration gives over to the conflictual, tension filled antagonisms out of which objects are differentiated and redifferentiated and preconceptions are given over to new conceptions' (Deetz, 1994, p. 30). The letting go of an illusory sense or ideal of integrity and autonomy creates space for enacting and exploring what has previously been suppressed, contained or 'othered'.

Some aspects of contemporary organizations can facilitate this possibility. Organizations are multi-discursive or at least settings open to the multiplicity of ideas, vocabularies and practices of the contemporary world.[10] This is so not only because of the complexity of task requirements, the multitude of centres of power and social identities, but also because increasingly complex and dynamic operations—as in social life itself—demand adaptability and employee adoption of a variety of subject positions. The case of the angry worker is illustrative. The managerial intent is, of course, not to transform the person into a businessperson but to encourage a broadening of the workers' mindset so that marketing aspects are incorporated—such as working flexibly to meet orders—into the worker's sense of his responsibilities as an employee. The use of business vocabulary is, we suggest, intended to loosen an identification with established, production-centric discourses of factory work. However, it is naïve to assume that identity can be pushed in any direction without inertia, pain, resistance and unintended consequences, as the case of the angry worker demonstrates. Such resistance may be an unreflective response contingent upon communitarian forms of control, but the interplay between managerial regulatory efforts and belongingness to several 'communities of practice' (Lave and Wenger, 1991) speaks in favour of a continuing and potentially expanding space for micro-emancipation and quasi-autonomy.

Conclusion

Our purpose in this article has been to highlight and explore the significance of identity regulation for processes of organizational control. By exploring the linkages between organizational control and identity regulation, we have developed an analysis of identity work that circles around the interplay of self-identity, identity work and the regulation of identity. To this end, we have:

- Located the regulation of identity within the contemporary, post-Fordist context of discourses and practices that are significant for identity work, arguing against tendencies to compartmentalize or neglect identity in analyses of organizational control.
- Outlined a conceptual framework for the analysis of identity regulation and different responses to it, focusing upon the interplay between regulatory interventions, identity work and self-identity.
- Specified some of the means, targets and media of identity regulation through which organizational control may be accomplished.
- Illustrated how modes of identity regulation are enacted by reference to two brief case studies and numerous other examples.
- Differentiated three common patterns of identity regulation.
- Argued for, and tried to develop, a conception of micro-emancipatory possibilities.

In conclusion, we draw out some methodological and theoretical implications of our analysis. Theoretically, our discussion invites analysts of work organization to pay greater attention to, and to contribute towards, an emergent literature that places processes of identity (re)formation at the centre of social and organizational theory. More specifically, our analysis urges students of organizational and management control to incorporate within their conceptual frameworks an appreciation of the dynamics of identity regulation. This invitation is no less relevant for many 'radical' perspectives on work organization (e.g. labour process theory) than it is for more mainstream studies of organizational functioning. In taking up this challenge to pay greater attention to processes of identity (re)formation in organizational control, we have commended theory that understands the processes to be fluid, unstable and reflexive—a condition that presents opportunities for micro-emancipation as well as openings for 'new' forms of subordination and oppression. Methodologically, our discussion suggests the relevance of in-depth and longitudinal studies based upon participant observation, or at least semi-structured interviews, for investigating processes of identity regulation rather than, say, survey-based research or closed ended interviews. To illuminate processes of identity regulation, it is important to examine their contextual product in some detail and over time. In this way, it is to be hoped to penetrate and interrogate processes of organizational identification in ways that are illuminating and empowering for those who are affected by these 'new' media of control.

Notes

* In addition to the incisive reviews of *JMS* referees we would like to thank Craig Prichard for his valuable comments.

1. Of course, it has long been noted how bureaucratic control mechanisms tend to attract and (re)produce 'the bureaucratic personality' (Merton, 1940) whose identification with the office and its procedures precludes the possibility of taking responsibility for actions that are not directly authorized by the rules. The intent, but not necessarily the effect, of new, cultural mechanisms associated with 'the postbureaucratic organization', in contrast, is to produce employees who find meaning in corporate values, and who do not simply comply with established rules and procedures to ensure better coordination and flexibility but are committed to processes of 'continuous improvement'. The role of the 'professional', 'competent' manager now extends to taking responsibility for scoping and shaping others' identities so that they are more receptive to such commitments. Managers are themselves also more or less intended targets of identity regulation, as well as 'managers' of their own identities (Jackall, 1988; Watson, 1994).

2. It should be emphasized that the term 'element' is not deployed in this paper to indicate a fixed psychological trait but to convey the presence of qualities that link together life history and everyday experiences in distinctive complexes of feeling, valuing, thinking and fantasizing. Each element stands in a dynamic relationship to other elements as they are mobilized in regulative efforts and routine identity work.

3. It is frequently argued that subjectivity is constituted within discourse, which implies that there is no 'external' relationship between discourses and subjects. While not arguing that people are (actually, or even potentially) autonomous in relationship to discourse, we prefer a less totalizing and deterministic notion of discourse. We allow for the inclusion of elements to work on or with subjectivity. Notably, there are somatic and tacit aspects of social interaction and human development and that a more totalizing or 'muscular' concept of discourse inadequately appreciates. Recognition of the significance of discourse as a way of understanding identity does not exclude consideration of other aspects.

4. It is rather common that instrumental rewards are downplayed, at least rhetorically, in knowledge-intensive companies (Alvesson and Lindkvist, 1993; Kanter, 1983). In identity terms, this means that people are constructed as committed, dedicated professionals, etc.

5. That this does not necessarily include a distinct value represents one difference compared to what we covered in point 2 above. Another difference is that there is not any direct reference to a 'them' (the Other).

6. This distinction was pervasive and strongly felt by many in the production department of the company (Alvesson and Björkman, 1992). The example could, of course, be interpreted as a case of interdepartmental rivalry, although the acceptance of the production manager of the business vocabulary tends to contradict this interpretation. It is worth noting, however, that the focus upon identity favoured here does not stand in opposition to a group-conflict view. Negative relations between units or functions invariably involve identity issues: social identities are highly salient in group conflicts.

7. This example also confirms the (late) modern condition of the worker who is less deferential, more sceptical. A non-authoritarian, questioning attitude was reported to be

common among the worker's cohort and exemplary of the spirit broadly fostered by Swedish socializing agencies during recent decades, partly related to social egalitarianism, the welfare system, low unemployment and relatively secure employment conditions. A supervisor in the factory compares younger and older workers: the younger are more mobile, more creative, perhaps too much so, he says. They sometimes lack inhibitions. They are a bit lacking in respect, they question things not only once but several times: 'Why should it be like that?' 'Why don't I get a pay rise?' Many of the older workers do not say anything: 'Thank you. May I go now?'. But, equally, our production worker is not rigidly caught in an anti-management discourse. Although clearly resistant to the demand by the marketing manager to change his orientation, he refers to his immediate manager in comparatively sympathetic terms, including the use of his first name.

8. It is relevant to note here how the research interview itself acts as an open-ended input to identity work. Research interventions such as interviews or questionnaires do not measure the 'truth' of identity but interactively provoke its articulation and may stimulate a reappraisal of identities (see Alvesson and Sköldberg, 2000).

9. We have used the rather clumsy phrase *'quasi-autonomous'* patterns of identity regulation to indicate that the sense of autonomy arises from the tension and associated zone of indecision associated with the presence of competing identity-regulating discourses. This 'autonomy' is 'quasi' in the sense that it is socially organized through an engagement with 'the other' rather than something that is essentially given and 'liberated' through resistance.

10. The attendant risk is one of being pushed around by the multitude of agencies and discourses constructing an 'open', malleable subject taking different forms according to functional demands. This may include unquestioning loyalty to the group or corporation (Barker, 1999), an enthusiastic adherence to any new management fashion concept, chameleon-like willingness to serve the whims of any client willing to pay, and, more generally, an unreserved acceptance of whatever discourse is currently in circulation, etc.

References

Albert, S. and Whetten, D. (1985). 'Organizational identity'. In Cummings, L. L. and Staw, B. M. (Eds), *Research in Organizational Behaviour*. Greenwich, CT: JAI Press, 263–95.

Albert, S., Ashforth, B. E. and Dutton, J. E. (2000). 'Organizational identity and identification: charting new waters and building new bridges'. *Academy of Management Review*, 25, 1, 13–17.

Alvesson, M. (1993). 'Cultural-ideological modes of management control'. In Deetz, S. (Ed.), *Communication Yearbook*, Vol. 16. Newbury Park, CA: Sage.

Alvesson, M. (1994). 'Talking in organizations. Managing identity and impressions in an advertising agency'. *Organization Studies*, 15, 4, 535–63.

Alvesson, M. (1995). *Management of Knowledge-Intensive Companies*. Berlin/New York: de Gruyter.

Alvesson, M. (1996). *Communication, Power and Organization*. Berlin/New York: de Gruyter.

Alvesson, M. (2000). 'Social identity and the problem of loyalty in knowledge-intensive companies'. *Journal of Management Studies*, 37, 6.

Alvesson, M. (2001). *Understanding Organizational Culture*. London: Sage.

Alvesson, M. and Billing, Y. D. (1997). *Understanding Gender and Organization*. London: Sage.

Alvesson, M. and Björkman, I. (1992). *Organisationsidentitet och organisationsbyggande*. Lund: Studentlitteratur.

Alvesson, M. and Deetz, S. (2000). *Doing Critical Management Research*. London: Sage.

Alvesson, M. and Kärreman, D. (2000). 'Varieties of discourse. On the study of organizations through discourse analysis'. *Human Relations*, 53, 1125–49.

Alvesson, M. and Lindkvist, L. (1993). 'Transaction costs, clans and corporate culture'. *Journal of Management Studies*, 30, 3, 427–52.

Alvesson, M. and Sköldberg, K. (2000). *Reflexive Methodology*. London: Sage.

Alvesson, M. and Willmott, H. (1996). *Making Sense of Management. A Critical Analysis*. London: Sage.

Ashforth, B. and Mael, E. (1989). 'Social identity theory and the organization'. *Academy of Management Review*, 14, 20–39.

Astley, G. (1985). 'Administrative science as socially constructed truth'. *Administrative Science Quarterly*, 30, 497–513.

Axford, B. (1995). *The Global System: Economics, Politics and Culture*. Cambridge: Polity.

Barker, J. (1993). 'Tightening the iron cage: concertive control in self-managing teams'. *Administrative Science Quarterly*, 38, 408–37.

Barker, J. R. (1998). 'Managing identification'. In Whetton, D. A. and Godfrey, P. C. (Eds), *Identity in Organizations: Building Theory Through Conversations*. London: Sage, 257–67.

Barker, J. (1999). *The Discipline of Teamwork*. Sage: London.

Barker, J. R. and Tompkins, P. K. (1994). 'Identification in the self-managing organization: characteristics of target and tenure'. *Human Communication Research*, 21, 223–40.

Barley, S. and Kunda, G. (1992). 'Design and devotion: surges of rational and normative ideologies of control in managerial discourse'. *Administrative Science Quarterly*, 37, 363–99.

Barnard, C. (1936). *The Functions of the Executive*.

Burrell, G. and Morgan, G. (1979). *Sociological Paradigms and Organizational Analysis*. Aldershot: Gower.

Burris, B. (1989). 'Technocratic organization and control'. *Organization Studies*, 10, 1–20.

Calhoun, C. (1992). 'Culture, history, and the problem of specificity in social theory'. In Seidman, S. and Wagner, D. (Eds), *Postmodernism & Social Theory*, Cambridge, Oxford: Blackwell.

Casey, C. (1995). *Work, Self and Society: After Industrialism*. London: Routledge.

Casey, C. (1996). 'Corporate transformations: designer culture, designer employees and 'post-occupational solidarity'. *Organization*, 3, 3, 317–39.

Cheney, G. (1991). *Rhetoric in an Organizational Society: Managing Multiple Identities*. Columbia: University of South Carolina Press.

Christensen, L. T. (1995). 'Buffering organizational identity in the marketing culture'. *Organization Studies*, 16, 4, 651–72.

Clegg, S. (1989). *Frameworks of Power*. Newbury Park: Sage.

Collinson, D. (1992). *Managing the Shopfloor*. Berlin: de Gruyter.

Collinson, D. (1994). 'Strategies of resistance: power, knowledge and subjectivity in the workplace'. In Jermier, J., Knights, D. and Nord, W. (Eds), *Resistance and Power in Organizations*. London: Routledge.

Czarniawska-Joerges, B. (1994). 'Narratives of individual and organizational identities'. In Deetz, S. (Ed.), *Communication Yearbook*, Vol. 17. Newbury Park: Sage.

Deetz, S. (1992). *Democracy in an Age of Corporate Colonization: Developments in Communication and the Politics of Everyday Life*. Albany: State University of New York Press.

Deetz, S. (1994). 'The micro-politics of identity formation: the case of a knowledge intensive firm'. *Human Studies*, 17, 23–44.

Deetz, S. (1995). *Transforming Communication, Transforming Business: Building Responsive and Responsible Workplaces*. Cresskill, NJ: Hampton Press.

Denzin, N. (1994). 'The art and politics of interpretation'. In Denzin, N. and Lincoln, Y. (Eds), *Handbook of Qualitative Research*. Thousand Oaks: Sage.

Du Gay, P. (1996). 'Making up managers: enterprise and the ethos of bureaucracy'. In Clegg, S. and Palmer, G. (Eds), *The Politics of Management Knowledge*. London: Sage.

Ezzamel, M. and Willmott, H. C. (1998). 'Accounting for teamwork'. *Administrative Science Quarterly*, 43, 2, 358–96.

Ezzamel, M. and Willmott, H. C. (1999). 'Strategy as Discourse and Discipline'. Working Paper, Manchester School of Management, UMIST.

Ezzamel, M., Willmott, H. and Worthington, F. (2000). 'Control and Resistance in "The Factory that Time Forgot"'. Working Paper, Manchester School of Management.

Fay, B. (1987). *Critical Social Science*. Cambridge: Polity Press.

Fondas, N. (1997). 'Feminization unveiled: management qualities in contemporary writings'. *Academy of Management Review*, 22, 257–82.

Friedman, A. (1990). 'Management strategies, techniques and technology: towards a complex theory of the labour process'. In Knights, D. and Willmott, H. (Eds), *Labour Process Theory*. London: Macmillan.

Frost, P. et al. (1985). *Organizational Culture*. Beverly Hills: Sage.

Frost, P. et al. (1991). *Reframing Organizational Culture*. Newbury Park: Sage.

Gherardi, S. (1995). *Gender, Symbolism and Organizational Cultures*. London: Sage.

Giddens, A. (1991). *Modernity and Self-Identity*. Cambridge: Polity Press.

Gray, C. (1999). 'Change in Organizations?'. Working Paper, Judge Institute of Management, Cambridge.

Grimshaw, D., Vincent, S. and Willmott, H. (2001). 'Going Privately: Practices of Partnership in the Outsourcing of Public Services'. Working Paper, Manchester School of Management.

Harvey, D. (1989). *The Condition of Postmodernity*. Oxford: Blackwell.

Hassard, J., Holliday, R. and Willmott, H. C. (Eds) (2000). *Body and Organization*. London: Sage.

Hollway, W. (1984). 'Gender difference and the production of subjectivity'. In Henriques, J. et al. (Eds), *Changing the Subject*. London: Methuen.

Jackall, R. (1988). *Moral Mazes. The World of Corporate Managers*. New York: Oxford University Press.

Jacques, R. (1996). *Manufacturing the Employee*. Thousand Oaks: Sage.

Kanter, R. M. (1983). *The Change Masters. Innovations for Productivity in the American Corporation*. New York: Simon and Schuster.

Knights, D. (1992). 'Changing spaces: the disruptive impact of a new epistemological location for the study of management'. *Academy of Management Review*, 17, 514–36.

Knights, D. (1996). 'Refocusing the case study: the politics of research and researching politics in IT management'. *Tech Studies*, 2/2, 230–84.

Knights, D. and Morgan, G. (1991). 'Corporate strategy, organizations, and subjectivity: a critique'. *Organization Studies*, 12, 251–73.

Knights, D. and Murray, F. (1994). *Managers Divided*. London: Wiley.

Knights, D. and Willmott, H. (1985). 'Power and identity in theory and practice'. *Sociological Review*, 33, 1, 22–46.

Knights, D. and Willmott, H. (1987). 'Organizational culture as management strategy: a critique and illustration from the financial service industries'. *International Studies of Management and Organization*, 17, 3, 40–63.

Knights, D. and Willmott, H. (1989). 'Power and subjectivity at work'. *Sociology*, 23, 4, 535–58.

Knights, D. and Willmott, H. (1992). 'Conceptualizing leadership processes: a study of senior managers in a financial services company'. *Journal of Management Studies*, 29, 761–82.

Kondo, (1990). *Crafting Selves: Power, Gender, and Discourses of Identity in a Japanese Workplace*. Chicago: Chicago University Press.

Kunda, G. (1992). *Engineering Culture. Control and Commitment in a High-Tech Corporation*. Philadelphia: Temple University Press.

Lasch, C. (1979). *The Culture of Narcissism*. New York: Norton.

Laurent, A. (1978). 'Managerial subordinancy'. *Academy of Management Review*, 3, 220–30.

Lave, J. and Wenger, E. (1991). *Situated Learning: Legitimate Peripheral Participation*. Cambridge: Cambridge University Press.

Leidner, R. (1991). 'Serving hamburgers and selling insurance: gender, work, and identity in interactive service jobs'. *Gender & Society*, 5, 2, 154–77.

Martin, J. (1992). *The Culture of Organizations. Three Perspectives*. New York: Oxford University Press.

Martin, J. and Siehl, C. (1983). 'Organizational culture and counter culture: an uneasy symbiosis'. *Organization Dynamics*, Autumn, 52–64.

McGregor, D. (1960). *The Human Side of Enterprise*. New York: Harper and Row.

Merton, R. K. (1940). 'Bureaucratic structure and personality'. *Social Focus*, 18, 560–8.

Meyer, J. W. and Rowan, B. (1977). 'Institutionalized organizations: formal structure as myth and ceremony'. *American Journal of Sociology*, 83, 2, 340–63.

Mills, C. W. (1940). 'Situated actions and vocabularies of motives'. *American Sociological Review*, 5, 904–13.

Mintzberg, H. (1983). *Structure in Fives. Designing Effective Organizations*. Englewood Cliffs, NJ: Prentice-Hall.

Mitchell, T., Rediker, K. and Beach, L. R. (1986). 'Image theory and organizational decision making'. In Sims, H. and Gioia, D. (Eds), *The Thinking Organization*. San Francisco: Jossey-Bass.

Mumby, D. (1988). *Communication and Power in Organizations: Discourse, Ideology and Domination*. Norwood, NJ: Ablex.

Newton, T. (1998). 'Theorizing subjectivity in organizations: the failure of Foucauldian studies'. *Organization Studies*, 19, 415–47.

Ortner, S. (1973). 'On key symbols'. *American Anthropologist*, 75, 1338–46.

Ouchi, W. G. (1979). 'A conceptual framework for the design of organizational control mechanisms'. *Management Science*, 25, 833–48.

Ouchi, W. G. (1981). *Theory Z*. Reading: Addison-Wesley.

Parker, M. (2000). *Organizational Culture and Identity*. London: Sage.

Payne, S. (1991). 'A proposal for corporate ethical reform: the ethical dialogue group'. *Business & Professional Ethics Journal*, 10, 1, 67–88.

Peters, T. J. and Waterman, R. H. (1982). *In Search of Excellence*. New York: Harper and Row.

Pondy, L. R., Frost, P. J., Morgan, G. and Dandridge, T. C. (Eds) (1983). *Organizational Symbolism*. Greenwich, CT: JAI Press, Inc.

Ray, C. A. (1986). 'Corporate culture: the last frontier of control'. *Journal of Management Studies*, 23, 3, 287–96.

Reskin, B. and Padavic, I. (1994). *Women and Men at Work*. Thousand Oaks: Pine Forge Press.

Rosen, M. (1985). 'Breakfirst at Spiro's: dramaturgy and dominance'. *Journal of Management*, 11, 2, 31–48.

Ruigrok, W. et al. (1999). 'Corporate restructuring and new forms of organizing: evidence from Europe'. *Management International Review*, 39, 2, 41–64.

Salancik, G. R. and Pfeffer, J. (1978). 'A social information processing approach to job attitudes and task design'. *Administrative Science Quarterly*, 23, 224–53.

Sculley, J. (1987). *Odyssey: Pepsi to Apple*. New York: Harper and Row.

Sennett, R. (1977). *The Fall of Public Man*. New York: Vintage Books.

Sennett, R. (1998). *The Corrosion of Character; The Personal Consequences of the Work in the New Capitalism*. New York: W.W. Norton and Company.

Shotter, J. and Gergen, K. (1994). 'Social construction: knowledge, self, others, and continuing the conversation'. In Deetz, S. (Ed.), *Communication Yearbook, Vol. 17*. Newbury Park: Sage.

Simon, H. A. (1945). *Administrative Behaviour: A Study of Decision-Making Processes in Administrative Organizations*. New York: Free Press.

Smircich, L. and Morgan, G. (1982). 'Leadership: the management of meaning'. *Journal of Applied Behavioural Science*, 2, 3, 257–73.

Steier, F. (Ed.) (1991). *Research and Reflexivity*. London: Sage.

Sutton, R. and Staw, B. (1995). 'What theory is not'. *Administrative Science Quarterly*, 40, 371–84.

Sveningsson, S. (2000). 'Strategy as a disciplinary technology—discursive engineering in the newspaper world'. Working paper series 2000/7. Lund Institute of Economic Research.

Tompkins, P. K. and Cheney, G. (1985). 'Communication and unobtrusive control'. In McPhee, R. and Tompkins, P. K. (Eds), *Organizational Communication: Traditional Themes and New Directions*. Beverley Hills, CA: Sage, 179–210.

Townley, B. (1993). 'Foucault, power/knowledge, and its relevance for human resource management'. *Academy of Management Review*, 18, 3, 518–45.

Turner, J. (1982). 'Towards a cognitive redefinition of the social group'. In Tajfel, H. (Ed.), *Social Identity and Intergroup Relation*. Cambridge: Cambridge University Press.

Turner, J. (1984). 'Social identification and psychological group formation'. In Tajfel, H. (Ed.), *The Social Dimension. Vol. 2*. Cambridge: Cambridge University Press.

Van Maanen, J. and Kunda, G. (1989). 'Real feelings: emotional expression and organizational culture'. In Staw, B. M. and Cummings, L. L. (Eds), *Research in Organizational Behaviour, Vol 11*. Greenwich, CT: JAI Press.

Warhurst, C. and Thompson, P. (1998). 'Hands, hearts and minds: changing work and workers at the end of the century'. In Thompson, P. and Warhurst, C. (Eds), *Workplaces of the Future*. London: Macmillan.

Watson, T. (1994). *In Search of Management*. London: Routledge.

Weedon, C. (1987). *Feminist Practice & Poststructuralist Theory*. Oxford: Basil Blackwell.

Weick, K. E. (1969). *The Social Psychology of Organizing*. Reading: Addison-Wesley.

Whetton, D. A. and Godfrey, P. C. (Eds) (1998). *Identity in Organizations: Building Theory Through Conversations*. London: Sage.

Whittington, R. (1989). *Corporate Strategies in Recession and Recovery: Social Structure and Strategic Choice*. London: Unwin Hyman.

Willmott, H. (1992). 'Postmodernism and excellence: the de-differentiation of economy and culture'. *The Journal of Organizational Change Management*, 5, 1, 58–68.

Willmott, H. (1993). 'Strength is ignorance; slavery is freedom: managing culture in modern organizations'. *Journal of Management Studies*, 30, 4, 515–52.

Willmott, H. (1994). 'Theorizing human agency: responding the crises of (post)modernity'. In Hassard, J. and Parker, M. (Eds), *Towards a New Theory of Organization*. London: Routledge.

Willmott, H. (1997). 'Rethinking management and managerial work: capitalism, control and subjectivity'. *Human Relations*, 50, 11, 1329–60.

Willmott, H. (1998). 'Making learning critical'. *Systems Practice*, 10, 6, 749–71.

Ziehe, T. and Stubenrauch, H. (1982). *Plödoyer für ungewöhnliches Lernen. Ideen zur Jugendsituation*. Hamburg: Rowholt Taschenbuch.

III.iv.   AUDIENCES FOR IDENTITY

18 Members' Responses to Organizational Identity Threats: Encountering and Countering the Business Week Rankings

Kimberly D. Elsbach and Roderick M. Kramer

Out of the four billion people on earth, everyone in our class must be in at least the most fortunate two-tenths of one percent. But we figure if this school were ranked first or second instead of ninth [by the *Business Week* survey], we'd be in the top *one*-tenth of one percent, so we're all pissed off.

Stanford MBA, responding to the 1990 *Business Week* rankings of U.S. business schools

(quoted in Robinson, 1995: 189; *emphasis in original*)

An organization's identity reflects its central and distinguishing attributes, including its core values, organizational culture, modes of performance, and products (Albert and Whetten, 1985; Dutton and Dukerich, 1991; Whetten, Lewis, and Mischel, 1992). For members, organizational identity may be conceptualized as their cognitive schema or perception of their organization's central and distinctive attributes, including its positional status and relevant comparison groups (Dutton and Penner, 1993; Kramer, 1993; Dutton, Dukerich, and Harquail, 1994). Consequently, external events that refute or call into question these defining characteristics may threaten members' perceptions of their organization's identity (Dutton and Dukerich, 1991). For example, journalists have recently criticized the socially responsible firm, the Body Shop, for exploiting the very populations it was supposedly serving. Such criticisms may threaten members' perceptions of what the organization is and what it stands for.

Kimberly D. Elsbach and Roderick M. Kramer

The purpose of this paper is to describe how organization members respond to such identity-threatening events, which represent a symbolic and sensemaking dilemma for organization members that is distinct from most previously studied organizational image threats (i.e., events that threaten members' perceptions of an organization) (cf. Weick, 1993; Elsbach, 1994; Dutton, Dukerich, and Harquail, 1994). While most existing research on organizational image management has focused on how formal spokespersons use impression management tactics to improve external perceptions of the organization following controversies arising from what an organization has done (i.e., verbal accounts following public health crises, scandals, and accidents) (Sutton and Callahan, 1987; Marcus and Goodman, 1991; Elsbach, 1994), we propose that organizational identity threats cause organization members to use cognitive tactics to maintain both personal and external perceptions of what their organization is or stands for.

Dutton, Dukerich, and Harquail (1994) recently proposed that it is important to distinguish between two types of organizational identity perceptions: (1) members' perceived organizational identity (i.e., what members themselves believe are the central, distinctive, and enduring attributes of their organization) and (2) their construed external identity (i.e., what members think outsiders believe are the central, distinctive, and enduring attributes of their organization). From the standpoint of the present analysis, it is important to note that perceived organizational identity and construed external organizational identity are both cognitive representations held by individual members, and both may be affected by external attributions of organizational identity. When we speak of members' identity perceptions, therefore, we are referring to *both* their perceived organizational identity and their construed external identity. Similarly, when we speak of tactics used to affirm identity perceptions, we are referring to tactics that affirm both perceived and construed identities.

Using this conceptual perceptive, as well as insights from social identity theory (Ashforth and Mael, 1989), self-affirmation theory (Steele, 1988), and impression management theory (Tedeschi, 1981; Tedeschi and Melburg, 1984; Elsbach, 1994), we develop a framework of members' responses to organizational identity threats that emerged from a qualitative examination we did of business school members' responses to *Business Week* magazine's rankings of U.S. business schools. As we describe below, our preliminary examination of these responses, as reported in the popular business press (Putka, 1990; Hall, 1990; Hay, 1992), in casual conversations with colleagues and students at a few top business schools, and in an initial interview with survey founder John Byrne, suggested that the *Business Week* rankings threatened many members' perceptions of their school's central and distinctive attributes, i.e., their school's identity.

470

The *Business Week* Rankings as an Organizational Identity Threat

Business Week magazine has ranked the top-20 U.S. business schools every two years since 1988. The survey evaluates business schools on two primary criteria: (1) recent Master of Business Administration (MBA) graduates' satisfaction with the school and (2) recruiters' satisfaction with recent graduates of the school. *Business Week* uses a composite score of these two dimensions to evaluate and rank the top-20 U.S. business schools. Our preliminary readings and interviews suggested that, prior to the *Business Week* rankings, the absence of a dominant standard for evaluating business schools, along with the wide variety of possibly distinct niches, enabled schools to decide which identity attributes were important and with whom they should be compared. By imposing an ostensibly objective and uniform metric for evaluating all U.S. business schools, the *Business Week* rankings dramatically disrupted the status quo that these schools had long enjoyed, creating an organizational identity threat for some institutions. Early interviews suggested that this new ranking metric posed a two-pronged threat to many members' perceptions of their business schools' identities. First, the survey often devalued central and distinctive dimensions of a school's identity. Second, in many instances, it challenged members' prior claims about the positional status of their schools.

Devaluing Core Identity Dimensions

Our pilot investigations suggested that the *Business Week* rankings threatened some members' perceptions of their organization's identity by calling into question the merit or importance of core, distinctive, and enduring organizational traits associated with their institutions. For example, in emphasizing MBAs' satisfaction with teaching as a primary evaluative criteria, *Business Week* implicitly challenged the value of many schools' longstanding research mission. Moreover, according to several business school admissions directors, as the rankings received increasing attention and achieved greater legitimacy with students, recruiters, and alumni, dimensions of a school's identity that were not included in the survey became perceived as less important and perhaps even irrelevant as indicators of a school's performance or quality. As one MBA student put it, "I don't need 'balanced excellence' [between teaching and research] in my program. I came here to benefit from research, not support it." Notwithstanding the shortsightedness of this view, by excluding certain historically important and

471

enduring institutional characteristics, the *Business Week* survey threatened the core identities of many business schools, even those ranked near the top.

Such threats to identity value may be, in some respects, a unique consequence of the particular methodology used to generate the *Business Week* rankings. Our preliminary investigation suggested that, prior to the first *Business Week* survey, many business schools took pride in touting what they perceived as valuable attributes and distinctive competencies. For example, MBA catalogs from the University of Chicago and Stanford University business schools frequently drew attention to their excellent research faculty, noting their impressive record of scholarly accomplishments. By contrast, descriptions of other prominent business schools, such as Dartmouth and Cornell, frequently alluded to their close-knit communities and "user-friendly" MBA cultures. Although other surveys of business schools have existed for some time (e.g., *Barron's Profiles of American Colleges, Peterson's Guide to American Colleges, Brecker and Merryman Inc.'s Survey of U.S. Business Schools*, and *U.S. News and World Report*), none were perceived to have clear dominance or compelling merit within the business school community. In addition, the criteria for evaluating schools differed: Some drew distinctions between private vs. public institutions; others collapsed across such distinctions (cf. Hay, 1992). As a result, schools could select which surveys and which attributes to emphasize in their own evaluation.

The *Business Week* rankings dramatically changed all of this. They implied that "top" schools had to have national stature and an elite ranking among recently graduated MBAs and their recruiters. By framing this as an objective measure (i.e., based on over 6,000 responses), the survey implied that other ranking schemes (e.g., those based purely on deans' ratings of schools' academic quality) were overly narrow and of dubious validity. Thus, members of schools with strong regional or research reputations suddenly found that these core identity dimensions had little influence in determining their school's ranking.

Challenging Claims of Positional Status

The rankings also challenged—and in some instances outrightly repudiated—members' prior claims about the relative standing or status of their school among U.S. business schools. In particular, they challenged the credibility of many schools' assertions that they were a leading, cutting-edge, or "top-tier" institution. As John Byrne, the creator and editor of the *Business Week* survey, noted, "For years and years there were probably 50 [business] schools that claimed that they were in the top 20 and probably hundreds that claimed they were in the top 40.... What the *Business Week* survey does is eliminate the ability of some schools to claim that they are in a top group."

Members who had always considered their schools to be elite institutions suddenly found them ranked out of the top five or the top ten and categorized instead as "merely" a top-20 school. Perhaps the most dramatic example of this was the Harvard Business School, which had often been characterized in the press and by chief executive officers as the leading business school in America. Suddenly, Harvard found itself only a "runner up" in what one scholar aptly called "the *Business Week* beauty contest." Such threats to positional status are important to an organization's identity because they threaten the perceived favorability of comparisons with its peers. As Frank (1985: 7) noted, many of the rewards or goods for which individuals and organizations compete are positional goods, "sought after less because of any absolute property they possess than because they compare favorably with others in their own class. A 'good' school, for example, is sought less for its absolute quality than for its high rank among schools in general."

To better understand conceptually what such organizational identity threats might mean to organizational members and how we would expect members to respond to them, we next examined organizational and individual-level research on identity threats. This research is grounded in several theoretical perspectives, including impression management theory (Tedeschi, 1981), self-affirmation theory (Steele, 1988), and social identity theory (Ashforth and Mael, 1989).

Conceptualizing Members' Responses to Organizational Identity Threats

As noted, organizational identities define members' perceptions of their organization's central, distinctive, and enduring traits (Dutton, Dukerich, and Harquail, 1994). Individuals also maintain perceptions of their own *social identity*, which is a measure of their self-concept defined by their association and affiliation with various social groups (see Tajfel, 1982; Brewer and Kramer, 1986; Turner, 1987; Hogg and Abrams, 1988, for overviews). At a cognitive level, individuals' social identities are assumed to be organized in terms of multiple, hierarchically organized categories, including social categories based on such things as age, gender, and race, as well as institutional and organizational affiliations. Thus, members' perceptions of their organization's identity may have a direct effect on their perceptions of their own social identities.

Effects of Organizational Identity Threats

Because of these psychological links between organizational and social identities, organizational scholars have increasingly argued that individuals

473

attach considerable significance to their organization's identity (Brown and Williams, 1984; Ashforth and Mael, 1989; Kramer, 1993). A person can acquire a more positive social identity through association with organizations that have positive identities (Mael and Ashforth, 1992; Dutton, Dukerich, and Harquail, 1994) because "the attributes that comprise an organization's identity, by association, are transferred to individuals who work there" (Dutton and Penner, 1993: 103). Conversely, events that threaten the organization's identity constitute a threat to members' own social identities. According to this view, organizational identity threats create a predicament for organizational members. In response, theorists have suggested that members will be motivated to protect and affirm positive perceptions of their organization's identity to restore and affirm a positive social identity (Dutton, Dukerich, and Harquail, 1994). Yet, to date, theorists have not examined how members carry out such identity affirmations.

Most existing research on the management of organizational perceptions is grounded in an impression management theory perspective (e.g., Sutton and Callahan, 1987; Marcus and Goodman, 1991; Elsbach and Sutton, 1992). This research has identified a variety of externally directed tactics used by spokespersons who are responsible for justifying organizational performance and practices to various constituents to whom the organization is accountable (Staw, McKechnie, and Puffer, 1983; Salancik and Meindl, 1984; Elsbach, 1994). Yet most of this work has focused on one-time crises (i.e., an oil spill, a plane crash, a food safety crisis) that threatened the legitimacy of important practices or procedures (i.e., the clean-up protocol for an oil spill, the meat inspection process at a meat packing plant). By contrast, no studies have examined members' responses to events that challenge members' perceptions of the value of an organization's central, distinctive, and enduring attributes. Such events may pose greater threats to members' social identities and self-concepts than to their perceptions of the organization's external legitimacy (Dutton and Penner, 1993). In turn, these events may lead members to engage in self-directed identity affirmations, rather than externally directed excuses or justifications of the event, as predicted by impression management theories. While current organizational research does not discuss members' responses to organizational identity threats, social identity research provides some hints about how members might respond to such threats.

Responses to Organizational Identity Threats

Social identity theorists suggest that people use cognitive tactics to maintain positive perceptions of their social identities. Turner's (1987) research on self-categorizations, for example, suggests that people can affect their social identities by selectively highlighting those social categories (e.g., triathlete, mother, female, professor) that most accentuate or contribute to a positive identity in a given situation. When membership in one category implies a negative social identity or is identity-threatening, a person can restore a positive sense of self by selectively increasing the salience of other unthreatened or untarnished categories (Hogg and Abrams, 1988). While organizational membership has not been studied in this context, this research suggests that, if organizational membership (i.e., Stanford professor) is viewed as an undesirable or threatening categorization, people may choose to describe themselves in terms of their professional affiliations (i.e., social psychologist) or nonwork social groups (i.e., a masters swimmer).

Another consequence of highlighting selective categorizations is that it influences the salience of interpersonal or intergroup comparisons.[1] As social identity theorists have noted, people can enhance their social identities by highlighting their membership in categories that are widely viewed as high status in comparison with other categories (Tajfel and Turner, 1979; Hogg and Abrams, 1988; Hinkle and Brown, 1990). Members of low-status groups may improve their relative status by selecting different groups with which to be compared. For example, studies have shown that, in response to threats to self-esteem, people sometimes invoke categorization schemes that highlight downward social comparisons to those who are worse off on some dimension (i.e., "I may have breast cancer, but at least I didn't have a double mastectomy") (Wood, Taylor, and Lichtman, 1985). In other cases, they may invoke categorization schemes that highlight similarities to highly performing others to improve perceptions of their status (Wheeler, 1966).

A variety of laboratory experiments provide evidence that highlighting selective categorizations and social comparisons affects people's self-perceptions (e.g., Tajfel, 1969; Kramer and Brewer, 1984; Gaertner et al., 1989, 1990). This notion also receives strong support from recent and closely related research on self-affirmation (Steele, 1988) and constructive social comparison processes (Goethals, Messick, and Allison, 1991). The portrait of the individual that emerges is that of a cognitively flexible, adaptive, and opportunistic social perceiver, one who responds to identity-threatening events by highlighting *personal* membership in select social categories to make salient his or her positive identity attributes, favorable status among peers, and favorable similarity or uniqueness relative to others. Yet this research has not discussed members' attempts to highlight selectively their *organization's* membership in favorable categories following events that threaten their *organization's* identity, nor do current models of social identity or self-affirmation describe any of the cognitive tactics members may use to affirm perceptions of their organization's identity following events that call into question or devalue their organization's central, distinctive, and enduring traits.

The above shortcomings in organizational theories of impression management and psychological theories of social identity, coupled with our preliminary findings about members' responses to the *Business Week* rankings, suggest that our understanding of the relationship between organizational identities and members' social identities may be enhanced by an investigation of members' responses to organizational identity-threatening events. We describe such an investigation in the following sections of this chapter.

Methods

We conducted a study of business school members' responses to the 1992 *Business Week* rankings of U.S. business schools. Although we reviewed data from the 1988 and 1990 *Business Week* rankings as well, we focused on the 1992 *Business Week* rankings because (1) complete records data were not available from earlier rankings, and (2) we were interested in assessing current organizational members' contemporaneous reactions to the rankings. We collected data for this study from January 1993 through December 1993.

Business Schools

We restricted our sample to schools in the top 20 because it was the major category emphasized by the *Business Week* survey and because schools falling outside the top 20 were merely grouped together as the "second twenty" schools. Thus, focusing on the top 20 allowed us to track a school's exact movement in rank and to examine how members responded to an institution's change in ranking.

We also focused our study on schools that we believed experienced a representative range of identity threats in response to the rankings. On prima facie grounds, we reasoned that the level of organizational identity threat would reflect both a school's absolute rank (e.g., being in or out of the top-ten category), as well as its change in rank (e.g., movement up or down in the top-20 rankings).

We initially chose twelve schools that represented a range of possible absolute ranks (high, medium, and low ranking), as well as a range of changes in rank (significant moves up, down, or relative stability in ranking between the 1990 and 1992 surveys). To narrow our sample to a smaller set of schools for more intensive study, we then collected evidence of initial reactions (e.g., claims that the rankings did not reflect the school's true identity, claims that a school should

Table 1. Business Schools Selected for Study

Change in Rank, 1990 to 1992	Place in Rankings				
	Top Tier	Middle Tier		Bottom Tier	
Moved up	Chicago 4→2	Indiana 15→8			
Little change	Northwestern 1→1	Stanford 9→7	Cornell 16→14	Berkeley 19→18	
Moved down				Carnegie-Mellon 9→17	Texas 18→out

have been ranked higher, etc.) from various members of these schools. We examined responses to the survey in the schools' MBA newspapers and in local newspapers.

Based on the availability and credibility of this evidence, we subsequently selected eight business schools for more intensive examination. We summarize their rankings and movement in rank in Table 1. These schools were (1) Carnegie-Mellon University's Graduate School of Industrial Administration, (2) University of Texas' Graduate School of Business, (3) Stanford University's Graduate School of Business, (4) Cornell University's Johnson Graduate School of Management, (5) University of California's Haas School of Business, (6) Northwestern University's J. L. Kellogg Graduate School of Management, (7) University of Chicago's Graduate School of Business, and (8) Indiana University's Graduate School of Business.

Respondents

We interviewed a total of 43 respondents from the eight schools. To get a representative range of reactions, and because we were interested in how organizational members throughout the organization responded to the survey, we interviewed a cross section of business school members. We selected individuals who we thought would have generally high levels of identification with their organizations (i.e., their social identities would be strongly affected by their association with their school) and, as a consequence, would be interested in and affected by the *Business Week* rankings. Thus, from each business school we interviewed (a) two faculty members from the management area of the business school, (b) an MBA student editor or publisher of the MBA newspaper, (c) a dean or assistant dean highly involved with the MBA program, and (d) a director of public relations or communications for the business school. This sample thus included, but was not limited to, those in image-management roles.

Data Sources

Interviews

We conducted semistructured interviews lasting 30–60 minutes with each respondent. All interviews were either tape-recorded or hand-transcribed. We first asked respondents a series of questions concerning their perception of their school's identity, its unique attributes, and how it compared with other top-20 business schools.

We then asked them to describe their general reactions to the rankings and others' reactions they had observed (including reactions from school administrators, faculty, and students). Because we were specifically interested in individuals' personal reactions to the rankings, we framed the questions to elicit their own opinions and candid responses. For example, we asked respondents to explain why they thought their school had achieved its current rank. We also asked them to provide their opinions of the responses given by other schools, if they knew of any. Finally, we asked respondents to give their opinions about the long-term effects of the *Business Week* rankings.

Records Data

To provide a benchmark that would help us better interpret and calibrate individuals' responses to the rankings and to get an accurate definition of each school's enduring identity dimensions, we obtained records data that were published prior to the first *Business Week* rankings in 1988 and covering the four years between that first ranking and the 1992 rankings. These sources included the 1987–88, 1989–90 and 1991–92 MBA program catalogs for each of the eight schools and *Business Week's* 1991 edition of the book, *The Best Business Schools*. We searched each of these sources for statements about a school's unique and defining characteristics.

We also used records data to obtain information about the eight schools' responses following the 1992 rankings. We searched for stories about the rankings in each school's MBA newspapers and its alumni magazines published during the six months following the rankings. Additionally, we searched for stories concerning the 1992 rankings in national and local newspapers published from cities near the eight schools (e.g., the *Chicago Sun Times*, the *Chicago Tribune*, the *New York Times*, the *Los Angeles Times*, the *San Francisco Chronicle and Examiner*, the *Philadelphia Inquirer*, and the *Dallas Morning News*). A few schools also provided internal documents and memos related to their reactions and responses to the rankings. A total of 47 different publications provided responses to the 1992 rankings.

Data Analysis

Our qualitative data analysis followed an iterative approach of traveling back and forth between the emerging theory, the existing literature, and our data (Glaser and Strauss, 1967; Eisenhardt, 1989). Based on our previous observations about business schools' intense interest in the *Business Week* rankings, our initial goal was to determine the specific ways in which these rankings affected members of business schools.

Early Iterations

In our first iterations, we coded respondents' statements about their initial reactions to the rankings and the positiveness and strength of those reactions. We collected 162 statements of initial reactions to the rankings from respondents and records data (between 15 and 27 per school). Most respondents' initial reactions reflected some degree of cognitive distress related to the rankings' attributions about a school's identity. The degree of cognitive distress appeared to be related to the strength of respondents' statements about the rankings. As a rule of thumb, we interpreted data as indicating strong distress if all respondents or records data from a category (i.e., students, administrators, or faculty) made similar statements revealing cognitive distress about the rankings. Moderate evidence was indicated if only about half of the respondents indicated cognitive distress.

We also analyzed respondents' and records data statements that offered explanations of the rankings. We collected 554 statements from interview and records data describing reasons for and responses to the rankings. This analysis produced a preliminary typology of tactics that members from the eight schools used in response to the *Business Week* rankings. These tactics primarily took the form of organizational categorizations (i.e., highlighting a school's membership in a category). These categorizations appeared to be used to affirm their perceptions of their organization's identity to make sense of the rankings. For example, in responding to a poor ranking, a member might make a statement highlighting the "product" categories that defined his or her school but may have hurt it in the rankings, such as "we're a research-oriented school" or "we're dedicated to producing technical MBAs." Through further analysis, we defined four primary cognitive tactics members used for identity affirmation and sensemaking: (1) selective categorizations to highlight alternate identity attributes, (2) selective categorizations to highlight alternate comparison groups, (3) selective categorizations to excuse a ranking, and (4) selective categorizations to justify a ranking. Four researchers analyzed the data during these iterations to define these tactics. Two researchers confirmed the classification of each identity-affirmation or sensemaking tactic. Strong evidence for a tactic was indicated if most of the respondents or records data in a category (i.e., students, administrators, or faculty) used the tactic.

479

Middle Iterations

In our next iterations, we analyzed data about the eight schools' identities during the five years prior to the 1992 *Business Week* rankings. We did this to provide a benchmark against which to examine members' identity affirmations or sensemaking responses. We searched for members' statements about their school's unique and defining characteristics from each school's 1987–88, 1989–90, and 1991–92 business school catalogs and biographies in *Business Week*'s 1988 and 1990 editions of *The Best Business Schools*. We focused on statements from members that roughly fit the prototypes: "our school is an X type of school," "our school is different from most schools on dimension X," "a central dimension of our school is X," or "we have always been a type X school." We collected a total of 844 identity statements from the eight schools (between 60 and 200 statements from each school). We grouped these statements iteratively to determine the central, distinctive, and enduring dimensions of each school prior to the 1992 rankings. We retained only those dimensions that consistently appeared in publications over the five years analyzed (i.e., were included in every publication), including the year prior to the first *Business Week* rankings.

Later Iterations

In our final iterations we looked for relationships between members' reactions to the rankings and their identity-affirmation or sensemaking responses. Extrapolating from individual-level research, we anticipated that members' perceptions of identity threats would predict the strength of their responses (Steele, 1988). We thus searched for trends in the quantity and quality of cognitive responses for schools whose members exhibited a high or low degree of threat to identity perceptions. We also searched for other predictors and trends in members' identity affirmations.

Findings

As background, we first summarize our findings on the eight business schools' preexisting and enduring identities. We then summarize our findings about members' perceptions of the *Business Week* rankings as an organizational identity threat and describe the cognitive tactics members used in responding to these threats. Finally, we attempt to explicate the relationship between the magnitude of perceived threat and use of categorization strategies to respond to that threat.

Evidence of Enduring Organizational Identities

Our analysis of preexisting identity statements revealed that each school maintained a set of core identity dimensions over the six-year period we examined (i.e., 1987–1992). Table 2 presents a summary of all eight schools' core identity

Table 2. Dimensions of Business School Identities*

School	Identity Dimension	Example
Berkeley	1. Participatory culture	"At Cal, students really get involved in everything"
	2. Diverse students	"Haas' richest asset is the diversity of its students"
	3. Creative students	"We select students who are intrinsically more creative"
	4. Global program	"Special opportunities to examine . . . managing in a global environment"
	5. Interdisciplinary program	"I don't believe any other B-school has as many programs that are a product or real joint planning with other units on campus"
	6. Entrepreneurial	"Haas differs from other top schools in . . . entrepreneurship"
	7. Public institution	"There is no other public institution of such quality"
	8. Renowned university	"part of one of the world's preeminent institutions of teaching/research."
	9. High value	"A top dollar education for a bargain basement price"
	10. Elite internationally	"Internationally recognized for our quality of faculty and programs"
Carnegie-Mellon	1. Small/friendly culture	"The thing I remember most is the size and intimacy of the place"
	2. Rigorous/technical	"There is one word to describe the school—intense"
	3. Innovative program	"Innovation and the transfer of knowledge are part of our heritage"
	4. Elite performer	"[We] rank among the most respected of business schools in the world"
Chicago	1. Quantitative program	"We're going to keep our pocket protectors"
	2. Academic values	"At Chicago we're interested in theory"
	3. Elite performer	"for decades one of the leaders in graduate business education"
	4. Innovative program	"the home of many of this century's innovations in business education"
	5. Research institution	"an integral part of a major research institution"
Cornell	1. Small/friendly culture	"Because [Cornell's] small, you actually get to know people"
	2. Teaching values	"[faculty have] made a commitment to teaching"
	3. Strong alumni	"not-so-secret weapon for graduates—an alumni network of 170,000"
	4. Renowned university	"[The business school is] . . . Part of a world-recognized institution"
	5. Top-tier school	"The respected position of the Johnson School . . . was important to me"
Indiana	1. Friendly culture	"This isn't a snake pit, and a lot of schools are. It's a nice place to be"
	2. Participatory culture	"MBA students at Indiana have a tradition of involvement"
	3. Teaching values	"Professors at Indiana are willing to teach well"
	4. Work ethic	"our graduates are willing to roll up their sleeves and do the work"
	5. Innovative	"Indiana is truly a leader embracing change"
Northwestern	1. Group culture	"[Kellogg's] driving esprit de corps is unique among business schools"
	2. Elite performer	"[in] a select group ranked outstanding by scholars and practitioners"
	3. Continuous improver	"many other top schools appear complacent by comparison"

481

Table 2. *Continued*

School	Identity Dimension	Example
Stanford	1. Friendly culture	"A spirit of cooperative is an integral part of the culture"
	2. Balanced program	"Teaching is a natural companion to research"
	3. Public management program	"A special feature of the Standard MBA is its Public Management Program"
	4. Elite students	[listed as a distinctive characteristic] "the world class students"
	5. Diverse culture	"People here come from all types of backgrounds"
	6. Research values	"The engine of the Stanford MBA is the faculty's research"
Texas	1. Diverse culture	"At Texas, there is no such thing as a typical business student"
	2. Participatory culture	"One of the best aspects is how involved students are"
	3. Academic values	"students are genuinely concerned about receiving a good education"
	4. Public institution	"[MBAs have] opportunities unique to a large university"
	5. Top-tier performer	"Having established a position of national prominence, [the b-school] continues its commitment to professional excellence in business education"
	6. High-value program	"For the price of education, there is not a finer school in the country"
	7. Regional program	"A top-20 business school located in the southwest"

* Based on identity statements from business school catalogues printed in 1987–88, 1989–90 and 1991–92, and *Business Week's The Best Business Schools*, printed in 1991.

attributes and dimensions. As this table shows, a few schools maintained fairly narrowly defined identities (e.g., Northwestern was defined by only three attributes: group culture, elite performer, and continuous improver), while others were more broadly defined (e.g., Texas was defined by ten distinct identity dimensions). Further, many of the core attributes and distinctive competencies associated with these schools are quite different from those that are implied to be important by *Business Week*. Berkeley and Texas, for example, highlighted the fact that their MBA programs were embedded in a large public institution with sound academic and research values. Similarly, Cornell and Dartmouth highlighted their programs' small, user-friendly cultures as valued dimensions. As we will show, the perceived value of these identity dimensions—which were not emphasized by the *Business Week* rankings—played an important role in members' cognitive responses to those rankings.

Evidence of Perceived Organizational Identity Threats

Our data suggest that business school members' preexisting perceptions of their schools' identities were threatened by the *Business Week* rankings. In this paper, we view cognitive distress about the rankings as evidence of identity threats, and all of the respondents in our sample expressed some level of cognitive distress over *Business Week's* characterization of their school. We found it useful to conceptualize this cognitive distress as a kind of "identity dissonance," which reflected cognitive dissonance related to the disparity or inconsistency between members' perceptions of their organization's identity (e.g., their perception that their school is "a dynamic, still growing program") and the identity attributed to it by the *Business Week* survey (the assertion that the school "is standing still"). Evidence of members' identity dissonance is summarized in Table 3.

Degree of Threat
Not surprisingly, the more severe degrees of threat, indicated by high levels of identity dissonance, were associated with disappointment with the rankings, either in terms of the absolute ranking achieved, a fall in the rankings, or an insufficient rise in the rankings (i.e., a rise to a position still far below a school's

Table 3. Evidence of Identity Dissonance Following the *Business Week* Rankings*

Ranking event	High Dissonance	Moderate Dissonance	Low Dissonance
Berkeley Stability at bottom	A/F/S "doesn't reflect true rank"		
Carnegie-Mellon Significant, unexpected move to bottom.	A/F/S "It was a travesty"		
Chicago Small but significant move at top.			a/f "I just don't see how [Northwestern] can be consistently ranked #1"
Cornell Insignificant move in middle.		A/S "unhappy out of top 10"	
Indiana Significant, unexpected move to top.			f/s "*Business Week* detailed none of the changes that have taken place*"
Northwestern Stability at top.			a/f "It made us sound like we were standing still"
Stanford Disappointing stability in middle.	A/F/S "most don't think we were ranked properly"		
Texas Significant move down to out of top-20	A/F/S "I applied to a top 20 school and this is not a top 20 school"		

* A, a = strong or moderate evidence from administrators: F,f = strong or moderate evidence from faculty; S,s = strong or moderate evidence from students. Strong evidence indicates that all of the respondents in a category made similar statements; moderate evidence indicates that about half the respondents made such statements.

expected rank). In these instances, the rankings may have refuted specific claims members made about their schools' prestige or status. Such contradictions may have been especially distressing to business school members because they not only threatened members' perceptions of their school's positional status (see below) but also suggested that they had misrepresented their school in a self-serving manner. Thus, members of Berkeley, Carnegie-Mellon, Stanford, Cornell, and Texas expressed higher levels of dissonance in response to the rankings than members of Chicago, Indiana, and Northwestern.

Type of Threat
In line with our pilot study findings, we also found that the rankings posed two types of organizational identity threats: (1) threats to the value of core attributes and (2) threats to perceived positional status of the organization. Threats to the value of a school's core identity attributes reflected respondents' reactions to the discrepancy between their beliefs about the value of their institution's core attributes and the value attributed to them by the survey (e.g., *Business Week's* assertion—or, in some instances, even implication—that a school lacked an important attribute or that it possessed "irrelevant" attributes). Threats to a school's perceived status, by contrast, reflected reactions to the discrepancy between members' beliefs about their institution's positional status and that assigned to it by the *Business Week* rankings.

Threats to the value of core-identity dimensions. Our data suggest that many respondents felt that *Business Week* either underestimated the importance of, or overlooked entirely, key attributes of their organization's core identity. A respondent from Carnegie-Mellon, for example, claimed that *Business Week* had completely overlooked the innovativeness of its program:

What other programs tend to be doing this year, we may have been doing 5 or 6 or 7 years ago. The mini-semester system that Wharton is doing, and Texas is doing, we started 8 years ago. *U.S. News and World Report* was touting Stanford for a new course in design of manufacturing and marketing new products when they were ranked #1. . . . we started that 6 years ago.

Similarly, Stanford respondents complained that the survey failed to recognize its excellence in faculty research. As one put it, "What bothers me is the need to quantify all this down to one number. They end up measuring things that aren't important. For example, we've spent time talking to *Business Week* about including faculty research in the survey." Finally, a Berkeley respondent expressed frustration over the survey's neglect of student culture by claiming, "An enormous part of what makes our school special is not susceptible to quantification. Students have risen to major roles which would be unheard of at other schools."

It is important to note that even members of highly ranked or highly improved schools seemed to perceive the survey results as threatening and displayed signs of distress over the fact that the rankings overlooked or devalued cherished dimensions of their school's identities. For example, one Indiana respondent, noting its highly innovative program, complained, "*Business Week* has detailed none of the changes that have taken place within the IU MBA program over the past two years." Similarly, rather than dwelling on positive attributes that *Business Week* had attributed to its program, a Northwestern respondent complained that the rankings failed to recognize its continuous improvement, i.e., "I was a little upset about the *Business Week* article when we went through it. *It made us sound like we were standing still" [emphasis added]*. Finally, several Chicago respondents claimed that the ranking's focus on teaching was perceived as a threat to the value of faculty research. As one respondent put it, "Some think the whole thing is ridiculous and are hostile that we pay more attention to it than things like research."

Threats to perceived organizational status. Evidence also suggested that members from lower-ranked schools experienced varying levels of dissonance regarding their beliefs about their school's position in the rankings. Many respondents reacted with statements of disbelief and denial, claiming that their school's ranking was not indicative of its true stature. For example, one Berkeley respondent asserted, "I look at some of the schools, and I have a hard time believing, from what I know of colleagues and what I know of the schools, that they really belong ahead of us. So in that sense I'm in denial." Similarly, a Carnegie-Mellon respondent noted, "The students were disappointed. Certainly the second-year MBAs took the view that we're better than that." Finally, a Texas spokesperson reported, "Students were upset; many said, 'I applied to a top 20 school, and it's not a top 20 school'."

Overall, our data indicate that members did not passively accept their *Business Week* ranking, nor, however, did they completely discount it. Because the rankings were open to multiple and conflicting interpretations and value orientations, they generated interpretive ambiguity and dissonance and motivated members to engage in sensemaking behavior. As Weick (1995: 100) argued, occasions that seem incongruous or that "violate expectational frameworks" prompt organizational sensemaking. Along these lines, we found that members used several distinct strategies to restore and affirm their positive perceptions of organizational identity following the *Business Week* rankings.

Responses to Organizational Identity Threats

Organizational members' primary response to threats posed by the *Business Week* rankings was to make salient their school's membership in selective and favorable social groups through (1) categorizations that highlighted positive identity attributes not emphasized by the rankings and (2) categorizations that highlighted favorable social comparisons not emphasized by the rankings. It is important to note that members were not attempting to place their schools in new categories but, instead, were highlighting their school's preexisting membership in categories that the rankings did not recognize.

Members appeared to use these categorization tactics for two purposes: (1) to affirm positive aspects of their school's identity that the rankings had neglected and (2) to make sense of and explain why their school achieved a specific, disappointing ranking. Responses used for the first purpose turned attention away from the rankings and focused it on favorable aspects of the school's identity that members felt should be included in an evaluation of business schools. Responses used for the second purpose directed attention toward the ranking itself and showed how it was misleading in its representation of the school and ignored aspects of the school's identity that were more important than the criteria used in the survey. Members' use of these categorization tactics for these purposes are summarized in Table 4 and described below.

Affirming Organizational Identities
Two important attributes of members' responses indicated that they were designed, at least in part, to affirm organizational identities. First, a majority of members' selective categorizations highlighted cherished attributes of the organizations' enduring identities that were neglected by the rankings, suggesting to us that members were attempting to categorize their organizations selectively along core dimensions in the same way that individuals categorize themselves to affirm positive social identities (Steele, 1988). As Steele (1988: 291) noted, following identity-threatening events, "[The perceived integrity of the self may be restored] by affirming and sustaining valued self-images. To be effective these images must be at least as important to the individual's perception of self-adequacy as are the negative images inherent in the threat."

The second indication we found that members' responses were designed as identity affirmations was that even members of schools that did well in the rankings responded by selectively categorizing their schools along central identity dimensions not recognized by the rankings. In these cases, members had no reason to manage organizational images, since the favorable rankings, in objective terms, were image-enhancing. To the extent that the survey overlooked or minimized other cherished dimensions, however, they seemed to motivate members to affirm neglected facets of their organization's identity.

Tactic 1: Selective categorizations highlighting alternate identity attributes. As noted earlier, researchers have shown that, when responding to personal identity threats, people can enhance their self-worth by highlighting positive dimensions of their identities that are unrelated to the threat (Steele, 1988).

Table 4. Selective Categorization Tactics in Response to Organizational Identity Threats*

	Alternate Identity Dimensions		Alternate Comparison Groups	Type	Group
Berkeley					
Identity	High value	A	Entrepreneur	AFS	West Coast schools
affirmations	Entrepreneur	AFS	Public	A	Public schools
	Public	A			
	Participatory	AFS			
Sensemaking	Participatory	AS	Public	A	Public schools
	Entrepreneur/ creative				
Carnegie-Mellon					
Identity	Innovative	AFS	Rigor/tech	A	Quantitatively oriented
affirmations	Rigor/tech	F			schools
	Small	AS			
	Innovative	AS			
Sensemaking	Innovative	A			
Chicago					
Identity	Academic	AFS	Academic	A	Research-oriented schools
affirmations	Innovative	F			
Cornell					
Identity	Small	AFS	Small	AFS	Small schools
affirmations					
Sensemaking			Small	FS	Small schools
Indiana					
Identity	Innovative	AFS			
affirmations					
Northwestern					
Identity	Continuous	AFS			
affirmations	improvement				
Stanford					
Identity	Public Mgmt	AFS	Elite student	AFS	Top-tier schools
affirmations	Research	AFS	Research	AFS	Research-oriented schools
	Elite students	A			
Sensemaking	Elite students	AF	Research	AF	Research-oriented schools
Texas					
Identity	Public	AF	Regional	AS	Southern schools
affirmation	Regional	F	Public	AF	Public schools
	Academic	A			
Sensemaking	Regional	AS	Public	A	Public schools
			Regional	AF	Southern schools

* A, F, S = strong evidence from administrators, students, and faculty, respectively. Strong evidence indicates that most of the respondents or records data from that category (i.e., administrators, faculty, or students) used that tactic.

As Ashforth and Mael (1989: 35) suggested, "Individuals have multiple, loosely coupled identities, and inherent conflicts between their demands are typically not resolved by cognitively integrating the identities, but by ordering, separating, or buffering them." Similarly, theorists have proposed that organizations may emphasize identity dimensions that portray them in the most favorable light (Albert and Whetten, 1985; Dutton and Dukerich, 1991). As Albert and Whetten (1985: 269) proposed, "In those cases in which a distinctive identity is prized, one might expect organizations to select uncommon dimensions of inter organizational comparison as well as uncommon locations along more widely employed dimensions."

Our data indicate similarly that when respondents felt that the rankings undervalued distinctive and central dimensions of their schools that they believed should be considered when evaluating a business school, they selectively categorized their schools along these alternate but cherished identity dimensions. Respondents from Berkeley, for example, categorized their school as a "public management" program, implying that it was distinct from other business schools. They also noted that their program was entrepreneurial and catered to the needs of West Coast students better than other schools, including those ranked higher by *Business Week*. As one Berkeley respondent noted in arguing the importance of their entrepreneurial dimension, "We really value our entrepreneurial culture. If the Haas emphasis on high-tech and entrepreneurship were to change, *the school would lose its identity and competitive advantage*" [emphasis added]. One Stanford respondent similarly noted that the Stanford Business School was uniquely oriented to the entrepreneurial needs of its students, which the respondent felt was unappreciated or underestimated by the *Business Week* survey, i.e., "More Stanford MBAs have non-Fortune 1000 interests, choosing instead, smaller and entrepreneurial ventures, as well as public management, and non-profit firms. . . . *Some of the things that improve rankings are part of what we don't want to change*" [emphasis added]. Finally, one Texas respondent categorized his school in terms of its regional standing, noting that its MBA program catered to "regional labor markets" better than other schools and that regional standing was a more important metric for evaluating its program than its standing in a survey that compared all schools across the nation.

Members of the more highly ranked schools also used this strategy. They seemed to feel that their schools' identities were threatened because the *Business Week* rankings did not recognize some positive or distinctive dimension of their school, even though it rated them highly on other dimensions. Chicago respondents, for example, emphasized that, despite their high student satisfaction ratings, they had not given up their highly valued academic values: "*the core of the place has not been altered*. It was never our intention to say our solid social science traditions are irrelevant" [emphasis added]. In all of these instances, members' selective highlighting of alternative categories made positive organizational identity attributes salient and, by implication, affirmed positive perceptions of organizational and social identities.

Tactic 2: Categorizations highlighting alternate comparison groups. As noted earlier, social identity researchers have suggested that people may accentuate intergroup differences that reflect positively on the group to which they belong (Tajfel and Turner, 1979). As Hogg and Abrams (1988: 23) noted: "By differentiating ingroup from outgroup on dimensions on which the ingroup is at the evaluatively positive pole, the ingroup acquires a *positive distinctiveness*, and thus a relatively *positive social identity* in comparison to the outgroup." Following unfavorable social comparisons, for example, people may invoke comparisons based on other, more flattering dimensions (Salovey and Rodin, 1984) or dimensions on which they appear to have an advantage (Taylor, Wood, and Lichtman, 1983). In much the same way, we found that following the *Business Week* rankings, many business school members selectively categorized their schools in ways that placed them in more favorable interorganizational comparison groups. This strategy seemed to affirm both their perceptions of core identity dimensions and their perceptions of the school's positional status.

First, we found that many business school members used categorizations that increased the salience of identity dimensions that were also held by well-respected and highly ranked schools but were neglected or undervalued by *Business Week*. By categorizing their institutions in terms of attributes of well-respected schools, these members affirmed the value of their organization's core identity dimensions and implied that their school should be compared favorably with other schools in the same way that highly ranked schools were (Tajfel, 1969; Tajfel and Wilkes, 1973). In effect, these categorizations allowed an institution and its members to "bask in the reflected glory" of another's achievement (cf. Cialdini et al., 1976). For example, in categorizing their school as a regional leader, some Texas respondents proposed that this put their school in the same category as more highly ranked Michigan. They also implied that this categorization would provide them with positive social comparisons to others in their region: "We are considered to be the best in our region. . . . like Michigan, which is a very powerful regional school, and is also of national stature with Stanford, Harvard, and Wharton. So that's how we'd like to be seen. We'd like to be a school that totally dominates a region, and yet is not known as only a regional school." Similarly, members of Stanford affirmed the value of having an elite student body by suggesting this categorization put them in the same class as #3-ranked Harvard. As one member noted, "We've got the brightest students in the country. . . . I think 1/3 of our students turned down Harvard to come here." This strategy was also used by members of schools that did well in the rankings. Even members of #2-ranked Chicago attempted to affirm the value of their school's academic identity by equating themselves with other well-respected research institutions. As one respondent claimed, "We're a top research institution. I think of us in the same academic league as Harvard and Stanford."

Organization members also used these types of categorizations to affirm their preexisting perceptions of their school's high positional status among U.S.

business schools. For example, members from Berkeley and Texas selectively categorized their organizations as public institutions to change their organization's relevant comparison group to a smaller set of highly ranked *public* institutions. From the reference point of this category, both schools compared more favorably than they had in the *Business Week* rankings. As one Berkeley respondent aptly noted, *"In its market,* Berkeley does a better job than most schools. But [*Business Week's*] throwing the Fords and the Chevys and the Porsches in the same mix" [*emphasis added*]. Carnegie-Mellon respondents suggested, similarly, that they should be assessed against other technical business schools. As one respondent noted, "It's really not fair. It's like judging apples and oranges, and *we're not the same type of school as many others*" [*emphasis added*]. In these examples, members suggested that comparison groups consisting of few schools possessing similar characteristics were more valid than the comparison groups based on *Business Week's* single performance measure (i.e., customer satisfaction); thus, selective categorizations narrowed or reduced the size of the organization's relevant comparison group. These findings are similar to previous results showing that people prefer performance comparisons with others on similar dimensions that they believe are related to or predictive of performance, rather than comparisons with similar performance outcomes directly (Wheeler and Zuckerman, 1977; Miller, 1982). Zanna, Goethals, and Hill (1975), for example, found that competitive swimmers preferred comparisons based on age, experience, and recent training, rather than solely on performance. Researchers suggest people prefer comparisons based on these related attributes because they allow them to better determine the meaning of outcomes (e.g., whether a favorable comparison is due to ability or training) and to feel more satisfied with those outcomes (Wood, 1989).

Explanations and Sensemaking

While many respondents used categorizations primarily to affirm positive organizational identities by highlighting valued identity dimensions or comparison groups that they believed should be included in business school evaluations, some went beyond identity affirmation, using these same types of categorizations to explain their ranking. In particular, members of several low or disappointingly ranked schools described their schools in terms of categories that, they suggested, prevented them from achieving a higher ranking (i.e., an excuse) or were more important than categorizations necessary to achieve a higher ranking (i.e., a justification) (Schlenker, 1980; Tedeschi, 1981). These responses directed attention toward the methodology of the survey and implied that it misrepresented a school's true stature by ignoring these important dimensions. While we recognized these explanatory responses as fitting traditional forms of impression management (i.e., they resemble excuses and justifications), in most cases organizational members appeared to use them to make sense of the rankings and improve their own, rather than others' perceptions of their school's identity. As Weick (1993: 158) suggested, justifications may serve a sensemaking role for people who are motivated by feelings of dissonance (e.g., due to the *Business Week* rankings) to reexamine their organization and its identity, i.e., "Justification is often the result of focused attention that reveals new properties of a situation that unfocused attention missed." In such sensemaking contexts, selective categorizations appeared to be used primarily to bolster the credibility and believability of organizational excuses and justifications for the rankings.

Tactic 1: Categorizations highlighting alternate identity dimensions. Some business school members used categorizations to make salient valued and core identity dimensions, not emphasized by the rankings, to suggest that "they had good reason" for their poor ranking. In this way, members justified their poor showing in the survey by claiming their school maintained identity dimensions that were more important than student or recruiter satisfaction. At Carnegie-Mellon, for example, members suggested that their school's single-minded emphasis on innovation justified its poor showing on student satisfaction. One respondent noted, "We had an ethic here that placed a very high premium on innovation and creativity, but the notion of being good listeners and gathering information from students was not a part of that culture. We didn't have time for that." In a similar example, Berkeley respondents highlighted their school's entrepreneurial, West Coast identity as a distinctive categorization that justified its lower ranking: "Certain criteria in the rankings cannot be met by all schools. Berkeley's placement statistics at East Coast or Midwest firms will never be as good as, say, Harvard's, because of our students' preferences for entrepreneurial, West Coast firms." Finally, several Stanford informants noted that their distinction of recruiting and training the brightest students in the country may have actually hurt their rankings with recruiters looking for multiple placements from schools at which they interview. These informants suggested that maintaining their "elite student" distinction justified their disappointing ranking. As one informant put it, "A lot of our problems in the rankings came from recruiters' perceptions that you can't get Stanford students. They know we have very selective students. . . . and we don't want to change that."

In using these types of explanations, members suggested that a low ranking based on one dimension (i.e., recruiter satisfaction) may have actually affirmed their schools' positive organizational identity on an alternate and potentially more important dimension (i.e., incredibly selective student body well-adapted to the independent, entrepreneurial careers its students would pursue). This finding parallels that observed in experimental research showing that people may sometimes affirm or admit to a negative but less central dimension of their personal identity if it simultaneously enhances a more positive, global dimension (Swann, 1987; Steele, 1988).

Tactic 2: Categorizations highlighting alternate comparison groups. Members also suggested that the comparison groups imposed on them by the *Business Week* survey hurt their institution's ranking. In most of these cases, members used categorizations to highlight alternate comparison groups, not emphasized by the rankings, to make the excuse that the ranking "wasn't their fault" (Tedeschi, 1981). Respondents from Berkeley and Texas, for example, used the fact that their schools were public institutions as an excuse for their poor showing. They claimed that their schools had responsibilities for funding basic research and for educating state taxpayers that prevented them from competing with higher-ranked, private schools. As one Texas respondent put it, "I personally don't think a public institution, with its multiple missions, can compete with private schools like Stanford, Harvard, or Northwestern." Similarly, a Berkeley respondent argued, "It would be much easier to be a top-10 business school if we had an agreement like at Harvard, where they're a separate professional school. There's always going to be that research aspect [because we're a state supported school]." Finally, a Texas respondent argued that the fact that they were a regional program had a negative impact on recruiters' perceptions: "There's a stereotype about us that we're only a regional school. . . . I do think the regional issue probably hurts us with recruiters."

In other cases, members used such categorizations to show that their school was similar to more highly ranked schools (i.e., they highlighted inclusion in a more prestigious comparison group) to justify their ranking. For example, Berkeley respondents noted that their students' entrepreneurial preferences put them at the same disadvantage as Stanford: "We have the same problem as Stanford, 40% of our graduates want to stay in California . . . so [East Coast] recruiters naturally get a little defensive [when we don't accept their offers]." In a similar fashion, Stanford respondents categorized their institution as a research-oriented school to highlight its similarity to other research institutions that had been poorly ranked. As one Stanford publication noted, "MIT's Sloan School, ranked twelfth in the most recent *Business Week* survey, has made a major commitment and contribution to research and education in manufacturing technology. On a 10 year time horizon, I believe these efforts, and others like them will yield important benefits to business. . . . We believe our own agenda should be set, in part, by field-based research." These categorizations and comparisons implied that an inferior ranking was not indicative of an inherently defective or poorly run program but, rather, of a program that adhered to valued ideals that were representative of other esteemed institutions. In this way they excused or justified their ranking in this particular survey. This behavior corresponds to research showing that, following poor performance, people may compare themselves to similarly performing others to highlight the commonness of their performance, especially among highly respected others, and to imply that such performance should not be attributed to them personally or viewed as unique or distinctive (Alicke, 1985).

Relationship Between Members' Responses and Level of Perceived Threat

The above findings suggest that categorization processes are useful both to help organizational members make sense of threats to organizational identity (for themselves and external audiences) and to reduce the perceived threat to their own social identities. Thus one might expect that the greater the perceived threat to organizational and social identities, the greater would be members' use of categorization processes. In line with this argument, we observed relationships between members' level of identity dissonance and their use of the selective categorization strategies we have identified.

Categorizations Highlighting Alternate Identity Attributes and Justifications
First, our data revealed that schools in which members experienced the greatest identity dissonance were also schools in which members used the greatest proportion of available categorizations to affirm the value of their core identity or to justify their poor ranking. As can be seen in Table 4, members from Berkeley, Carnegie-Mellon, Stanford, and Texas, who had the highest dissonance (as reported in Table 3), referred to an average of half of their total available bases of categorization to affirm their schools' identities. In addition, members from all of these schools highlighted valued identity dimensions as justifications for their ranking. In contrast, members from Chicago, Indiana, and Northwestern, who had the lowest dissonance, averaged only about a quarter of their available categorization schemes and did not use categorizations as excuses or justifications. Members from Cornell, who experienced moderate dissonance, also used a small portion of its available categorizations.

By affirming a positive identity on many different dimensions, members may have had a better chance of relieving the dissonance related to a single dimension (i.e., status or prestige related to rank). In this respect, Steele (1988) has proposed that people may tolerate inconsistencies in their feelings about a specific dimension of their self-concept by affirming other valued dimensions. By contrast, respondents who experienced less identity dissonance had less motivation to affirm organizational identities by highlighting alternate identity dimensions. The favorable rankings, themselves, affirmed members' perceptions of their organization's identity, especially identity perceptions related to rank or customer satisfaction. Thus members of these schools may have emphasized only those identity dimensions that were obviously congruent with their top ranking, to minimize the chance of revealing disconfirming evidence. These findings are congruent with research showing that to confirm their self-identities, people may conspicuously display self-verifying identity cues, such as titles, labels, and physical appearance (Swann, 1987), and surround themselves with others who confirm their self-views (Swann and Pelham, 1987).

Categorizations Highlighting Alternate Comparison Groups and Excuses
Our data also suggest that members experiencing moderate to high levels of identity dissonance were most likely to highlight organizational categorizations that increased the salience of alternative interorganizational comparisons to affirm their organization's identity or provide an excuse for its ranking. Thus, members from Berkeley, Carnegie-Mellon, Cornell, Stanford, and Texas categorized their schools in terms of smaller and more specialized groups and claimed that the rankings unfairly lumped them into more generalized comparison groups. This strategy may have been attractive to those experiencing higher levels of dissonance because it allowed members to improve their school's relative standing on important identity dimensions, including those emphasized by the rankings, by placing it in a comparison group in which it ranked higher than the *Business Week* survey indicated. These higher rankings appeared consonant with members' previous perceptions of their organization's identity. This behavior is consonant with research demonstrating that people will often choose comparison groups that show them as superior to others on some cherished dimensions (Campbell, 1986).

By contrast, of the three schools whose members reported low dissonance, only Chicago invoked alternative comparisons. Members experiencing low identity dissonance may have preferred not to alter their organization's comparison groups because those changes usually meant categorizing their organization into a smaller group, whose top performers were viewed as less prestigious than top performers of larger groups. Members seemed willing to categorize their organizations into more exclusive groups only if they could not achieve a high ranking in a more inclusive group. This suggests that members paid attention to the relative prestige invoked by interorganizational comparisons and that they sometimes preferred being a big fish in a big pond to being the biggest fish in a much smaller pond.

....

Discussion

Our inductive analysis of how members respond to organizational identity threats suggests several important insights. First, we found evidence that many business school members perceived the *Business Week* rankings as a threat to their organization's identity, even when their school was highly ranked, because it devalued central and cherished identity dimensions and refuted prior claims of positional status. Second, we found that organization members commonly used selective categorizations to reemphasize positive perceptions of their organization's identities, for themselves and external audiences, by highlighting identity dimensions and interorganizational comparison groups not emphasized by the rankings. These tactics functioned to deflect members' attention away from threatened dimensions of their organization's identity, rather than addressing threatened dimensions directly. Finally, we found that members' identity management tactics were related to their level of perceived threat, as indicated by variation in their expressed dissonance over the rankings.

One can use the metaphor of a microscope, as it is used to view material on a slide, to visualize the above organizational identity management tactics and the identity affirmation and sensemaking functions they serve. Using this metaphor, selective categorization can be likened to increasing or decreasing magnification to manipulate the field of view available to the perceiver and, by implication, the inclusiveness or exclusiveness of comparisons, as shown in Figure 1. Thus, the first strategy, of highlighting cherished identity attributes not recognized by the rankings, is like using a high level of magnification to focus on a single organization and moving the slide around to highlight or make salient alternate facets of that organization's identity. Moving toward positive identity attributes and away from tarnished attributes can help

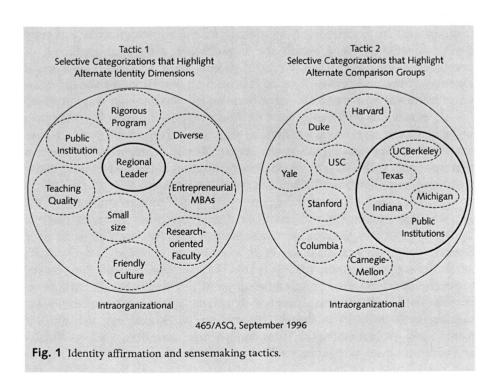

465/ASQ, September 1996

Fig. 1 Identity affirmation and sensemaking tactics.

members establish a more positive overall perception. In contrast, a lower level of magnification can focus on a set of organizations. Thus, the second strategy, of highlighting alternate comparison groups, involves moving the slide at this lower level of magnification to focus on different subsets of organizations and their interrelationships. By placing the organization in a more diffuse, broader visual field, its relationship to other organizations and its perceived similarity and distinctiveness can be manipulated. By focusing on a social comparison group in which the organization has high status, members can affirm their perceptions of their organization's relative value and prestige. In both cases, the principle of perceptual contrast influences perceived attractiveness, distinctiveness, and the commonality of objects (cf., Tajfel, 1969; Cialdini, 1984). As the microscope metaphor suggests, selective categorization is a gestalt-like process, in which elements of figure and ground come forward and recede in response to the perceiver's motives or goals. Accordingly, positive perceptions depend on their context.

The prominent use of affirmation and sensemaking processes suggested by this metaphor contrasts with previous work on organizational impression management, which suggests that people primarily employ repair tactics when responding to identity-threatening predicaments. While the present research does show evidence of excuses and justifications in response to organizational identity threats, it also suggests that members can attenuate or mitigate organizational identity threats simply by making salient other legitimate and competing dimensions along which the organization should be evaluated or construed. Thus, rather than having to defend, deny, or explain a particular external claim—and perhaps have to change their perception of the organization's identity in response to it—members can emphasize other ways in which the organization is intrinsically good or functioning well. Similarly, rather than respond directly to external attributions about an organization's status relative to other organizations, members can invoke alternate categorization schemes that make salient the ways in which the organization is different from or better than other organizations with which it is being compared.

The significance of these findings rests on several unique attributes of the *Business Week* rankings that differentiate them from other forms of external attribution that can threaten an organization's identity (such as stock price forecasts or industry expert polls). First, a distinctive feature of *Business Week's* attributions about business schools is that they are heavily dependent on the subjective interpretations of only one subset of the organization's total membership—and a subset that consisted of short-term, temporary members at that (i.e., second-year MBA students). The *Business Week* rankings also did not include any evaluation inputs from longer-term members, such as faculty and administrators, nor did they take into consideration a number of important, central traits of these institutions, such as research productivity, and contributions to other missions of the university, such as undergraduate teaching, that had been used in prior evaluations and rankings. Because of these characteristics, the *Business Week* rankings could fluctuate greatly, depending on the idiosyncratic approbations and grievances of a small and narrow sample of organizational members, all of whom were soon to become ex-members. Yet the rankings carried all the weight of a long-term measure that had important reputational and self-esteem implications for current and more permanent members. As a consequence, these members may have felt helpless to influence this important measure and may have perceived their identities to be more threatened by the rankings than by other forms of external attribution.

At the same time, compared with other kinds of external threats studied in the impression management literature, the *Business Week* rankings may have seemed less life-threatening to the specific organizations we studied because the rankings did not attack widely accepted perceptions of their legitimacy (i.e., the appropriateness of their structures, procedures, and goals). All of the schools we examined were ranked in the upper echelons of U.S. business schools, clearly enjoying high status and prestige relative to other business schools throughout the United States. In this respect, the threat posed by the rankings was substantially different from the kinds of external threats that have affected many other industries, such as the tobacco and cattle industries (Rosenblatt, 1994; Elsbach, 1994). In these industries, companies are facing intense public scrutiny about the legitimacy of their products and even their right to exist. In contrast, the *Business Week* rankings merely attacked or called into question members' perceptions of the value and distinctiveness of a school's central identity dimensions. As a result, members may have felt that the *Business Week* rankings provided somewhat misleading and incomplete characterizations of their institutions but were not completely wrong (i.e., they fairly accurately report the perceptions of a small group of students about a narrow range of student-related concerns such as teaching and recruitment). The *Business Week* rankings thus represented a strong organizational identity threat, but a rather weak organizational legitimacy threat. Consequently, members may have been more motivated to make sense of the rankings to affirm their preexisting perceptions of their organization's identity rather than to explain or justify the rankings to external audiences. Our findings about these types of responses have numerous theoretical and managerial implications.

Theoretical Implications

Organizational Identity Theory
Our findings have a number of implications for organizational identity theory. First, they provide support for recent arguments that a significant psychological

interdependence exists between individuals' social identities and their perceptions of their organizations' identities. As Dutton and Dukerich (1991: 550) proposed, "The relationship between individuals' senses of their organizational identity and image and their own sense of who they are and what they stand for suggests a very personal connection between organizational action and individual motivation." These arguments imply that because members' own social identities and self-esteem are intimately connected to the identity and reputation of their organizations, they care about how their organizations are described and also how they compare with other organizations. In accord with such arguments, our results document the cognitive distress or identity dissonance people experience when they think their organization's identity is threatened by what they perceive as inaccurate descriptions or misleading (and, by implication, unfair) comparisons with other organizations.

Second, our findings extend current theories of organizational identity by showing that in response to such cognitive distress, members may restore and affirm positive self-perceptions by affirming alternate dimensions of their organization's identity or highlighting their organization's membership in alternate comparison groups. These responses are quite distinct from results reported in research on social identity and self-affirmation. On the basis of those studies, we would expect people to attempt to restore positive self-perceptions and social identities by highlighting other personal or social categorizations (i.e., membership in other organizations) as a means of distancing themselves from the tarnished identity of their business schools. Yet we observed almost no evidence of this sort in our study. These results show that organizational identity affirmation is distinct from previously defined self-affirmation and social identity repair tactics because of its emphasis on affirming organizational traits rather than individual traits.

Third, the results of this study imply that identity affirmation is distinct from externally directed image management. The most compelling evidence for this distinction came from several instances in which clearly image-enhancing outcomes (e.g., receiving a top ranking) were construed by organizational members as identity threatening because they implied that other central and valued dimensions of their organization were unimportant or undervalued. If image-management concerns were the only factor motivating the selective categorizations we observed, then members had little reason in these instances to manage their organization's images or defend its general prestige or status. Instead, however, we found that members' responses were directed at highlighting the value of key organizational dimensions they perceived as neglected or undervalued. Such responses seemed to have had more to do with attempting to reaffirm to themselves a school's positive identity in light of the rankings than with simply enhancing their school's image to external audiences. In advancing this argument, we should emphasize that it is not possible to disentangle completely self-affirmation from self-presentational explanations for our findings. Nor, frankly, is it necessary to do so. As numerous theorists have previously argued, these two motives are not logically incompatible and, in fact, both motives are typically present in such situations (e.g., Tetlock and Manstead, 1985). Selective categorization processes, when they are used as part of members' public accounts, are probably directed simultaneously at shaping and enhancing both their own and others' perceptions of their organization's identity.

Finally, and perhaps most importantly, the present research contributes to our understanding of the specific cognitive tactics that organizational members use to maintain and affirm organizational identities. Our findings suggest that by selectively highlighting organizational categorizations, members are capable not only of affirming positive organizational identities when some dimensions are threatened, but also of influencing theirs and others' perceptions of the validity of favorable and unfavorable categorizations and social comparisons (e.g., the validity of organizational rankings).

Throughout our study, we were struck with the pervasive and creative use of selective categorization processes to maintain positive perceptions of an organization's identity. One example, brought to our attention after we completed our study, involved a school that heard it was to be ranked as one of the top 50 U.S. business schools in the next *U.S. News* and *World Report*. A memo from the dean sent to all faculty and staff proclaimed that the school was the *"youngest public* school" ever to be so ranked (*emphasis added*). The memo further read, "With the possibility of TV cameras wandering our halls, I would like to encourage you to wear business attire on that day."

Social Identity and Self-affirmation Theories
While a primary goal of our research was to contribute to organizational theory by importing insights from social identity and self-affirmation research, our findings return something to these theories as well. First, our findings suggest that one way people can protect and affirm their own social identities is by selectively categorizing their organizations. We found that most members elected to categorize their organization selectively rather than categorize themselves in a different way. As noted above, these findings run contrary to what social identity, self-affirmation, and impression management theories have usually found. They also support individual-level findings suggesting that people often tolerate inconsistencies in self-perceptions by affirming other valued dimensions of themselves (Steele, 1988). Organizational categorization thus provides another route to self-affirmation, and one not addressed in any previous research. Broadly construed, our findings thus highlight the adaptive role of organizational categorization as a route to self-esteem and social identity maintenance, especially with respect to influencing individuals' perceptions of the relative status or prestige of their organizations. As Frey and Ruble

(1990: 168) have argued, "healthy [psychological] functioning may depend on the ability to exhibit flexibility in the choice of evaluative comparisons in order to maintain a sense of competence and high self-esteem." To paraphrase Frank (1985), even though organizational members cannot always choose the best pond for themselves and their institutions, they at least have considerable cognitive flexibility in creating the perception that they are a reasonably large-sized frog in a reasonably good pond.

Impression Management Theory

Finally, our findings also have important implications for theories of organizational impression management. First, our findings explicate some of the conditions necessary to motivate impression management. Our findings suggest that, following an organizational identity threat, if alternate organizational categorizations are available and organizational legitimacy is not threatened, sensemaking motivations may be greater than impression management motivations. Thus the rather weak threat to organizational legitimacy posed by the *Business Week* rankings, coupled with the ready availability of organizational recategorization as a low-cost identity affirmation strategy, may explain why we observed so little evidence in our data of what affirmation theorists call spontaneous attributional search and generation of causal accounts (see Weiner, 1986). If people can make adequate sense of a threat and resolve dissonance surrounding it simply by affirming alternate identity dimensions that already exist and are readily available, then the need to generate detailed causal explanations for the event may be considerably attenuated. Identity affirmation processes thus may sometimes cause individuals to cut short such attributional search. As attribution theorists have frequently noted, generating complete causal attributions is an effortful process, sometimes likened to conducting a multivariate analysis of variance inside one's head. People engage in such processes only occasionally. Our results shed some light on the conditions under which people might be motivated to do so: when alternative selective categorizations are not available as a means of sensemaking and when organizational legitimacy is threatened.

Yet in those cases in which there is a motivation for impression management, our findings also suggest that organizational members may include selective organizational categorizations in their excuses and justifications to bolster the credibility of these externally directed accounts. Highlighting selective categorizations reminds both organizational members and outside audiences of long-held identity dimensions that should be considered in forming perceptions of the organization. If audiences agree that these identity dimensions are valuable, such categorizations may provide evidence of a school's favorable identity and thus make excuses and justifications more believable (Elsbach, 1994). Recognizing organizational categorizations as potential evidence or "content" for verbal accounts is a new addition to theories of organizational impression management.

A Theory of Organizational Identity Management

Theory and research on organizational identity is still in its early stages, and explicating the basic cognitive processes that constitute the underpinnings of identity is an important first step in integrative theory linking organizational and individual identity processes. Our findings can be summarized in a new framework of *organizational identity management* that integrates them with insights from social identity and impression management theories. According to this framework, when organizational members perceive that their organization's identity is threatened, they try to protect both personal and external perceptions of their organization as well as their perceptions of themselves as individuals. As Table 5 indicates, this identity management perspective builds on and integrates findings from the current study with insights from social

Table 5. Theoretical Perspectives on Perception Management

Perception Management Variable	Theoretical Perspective		
	Organizational Impression Management	Social Identity Maintenance	Organizational Identity Management*
1. Primary target of perception management	External perceptions of an organization's legitimacy (Elsbach, 1994).	Individual's perceptions of self based on their association with social groups (Ashforth and Mael, 1989).	Members' and audiences' perceptions of the organization's identity *and* members' perceptions of self based on their affiliation with the organization.
2. Primary motivation for perception management	Event that casts doubt on the organization's legitimacy (Marcus and Goodman, 1991).	Context or event that highlights a person's association with a negatively viewed social group (Hogg and Abrams, 1988).	Event that devalues or disputes cherished identity dimensions that are part of the organization's enduring identity *and* part of the member's social identity.
3. Who manages perceptions	A member spokesperson (Sutton and Callahan, 1987).	Any person who identifies with the group (Abrams and Hogg, 1990).	Any member who identifies with the organization.
4. Tactics used	Verbal accounts. Display of legitimate organizational structures and procedures.	Self-categorizations. Social comparisons.	Organizational categorizations. Verbal accounts containing organizational categorizations.

* Based on findings from the current study.

501

identity theory and impression management theory in several ways. First, it indicates that members are motivated by both self-affirmation concerns and impression-management concerns when responding to threats to their organization's identity. Second, it notes that identity management appears to follow events that devalue or refute identity dimensions members cherish both as a part of the organization's enduring identity and as a part of their own social identities. Third, it portrays organizational identity management as a pervasive activity that is carried out not only by organization members who formally occupy public relations roles but also by any member who identifies with the organization. Finally, it describes tactics used in identity management that involve both selective organizational categorizations (commonly used in self-affirmation models) and verbal accounts (commonly used in impression management models).

Managerial Implications

The results of this research have a number of practical implications. First, categorization processes can contribute to important sensemaking activities in organizations (Weick, 1995). As March (1994: 71) observed, "Organizations shape individual action both by providing the *content* of identities and rules and by providing *appropriate cues* for invoking them." Categorization processes can play a central role in this process, especially in terms of linking and helping rationalize organizational members' cognitions and actions (Weick, 1993; March, 1994). Organizational categorizations may allow leaders to focus members' attention on what they should be doing and why. The findings from this study thus suggest a rich set of tools for managers involved in the symbolic management of their organizations. As Pfeffer (1981: 26) noted, "Every organization has an interest in seeing its definition of reality accepted...for such acceptance is an integral part of the legitimization of the organization and the development of assured resources." Much of the research on this symbolic management process over the past ten years has focused on the use of verbal accounts, including excuses, explanations, and justifications (e.g., Elsbach and Sutton, 1992; Ginzel, Kramer, and Sutton, 1993; Elsbach, 1994) and the manipulation of causal attributions (e.g., Salancik and Meindl, 1984) to explain identity-threatening organizational events, but categorization processes may offer advantages over verbal accounts.

Our findings also suggest that managers may use categorization processes for symbolic management and sensemaking, both with respect to helping people inside the organization make sense of what their organization is about and in explaining it to external constituents and audiences. Many of the identity threatening predicaments that have been studied in prior organizational research were unique, organization-specific events. For example, the explosion of the space shuttle *Challenger*, the Union Carbide Bhopal crisis, and the Exxon Valdez oil spill were distinctive events that threatened the identity of a single organization. In contrast, the *Business Week* rankings of U.S. business schools simultaneously affected multiple organizations, forcing comparative appraisals along multiple dimensions. In situations having this greater complexity, selective categorizations and interorganizational comparisons can be powerful and flexible tactics for organizations and their members to maintain positive identities. By selectively directing and focusing attention, categorization processes heighten the salience of some dimensions while deflecting attention away from others. They can be used therefore to influence perceptions of positivity and negativity, similarity and dissimilarity, uniqueness and distinctiveness, or commonality and difference. In this respect, they function much like other kinds of general framing processes that have been found to influence the perceived positivity and negativity of events (Kahneman and Tversky, 1984; Brickman and Bulman, 1985).

Finally, our findings suggest that categorization processes may help organizations to change or reshape their identities. Strategic management theorists have recently proposed a theory of "strategic dissonance," suggesting that managers may purposely take advantage of distress related to incongruencies between an organization's strategic intent and managers' strategic action. In their discussion of managing strategic dissonance, these theorists imply that organizational identity management may play a role. They suggest that "Top management must use information that is generated by strategic dissonance when trying to discern the true new shape of the company. . . . It must be a realistic picture grounded in the company's distinctive competencies—existing ones or new ones that are already being developed. . . . Getting through the period of immense change requires reinventing—or perhaps rediscovering— the company's identity" (Burgelman and Grove, 1996: 20). Our findings support and extend these notions by suggesting that managers may use categorization processes following strategic dissonance to reinvent or rediscover their firm's identity.

Study Limitations

There are some limitations to our study that need to be acknowledged, in particular, issues of external validity and the generalizability of our results. First, our study focused on schools that, in absolute terms, had generally fared rather well in the *Business Week* rankings. All of the schools in our sample were relatively elite performers relative to the population of business schools throughout the U.S. For these highly ranked schools, their legitimacy was not directly threatened by the rankings. As a result, the impact of the threat on the schools we studied may have been very different from other business schools, especially those who failed even to obtain a ranking. For business schools that were ranked much lower by *Business Week* (or not ranked at all), the survey results could threaten their legitimacy and even their very existence. A small, regional business school, for example, might have claimed to be a good school comparable to other elite institutions, but if it was not even ranked by the survey, external constituencies might begin to question whether the university should continue to fund an MBA program and compete for increasingly scarce MBA students. As Meyer Feldberg, dean of Columbia's Business School, noted, as long as the survey creates a contest for status and reputation, there is the implicit long-term threat that "the strong schools will get stronger *and the weak will get wiped out*" (quoted in Fombrun, 1996: 267, *emphasis added*). Similarly, some identity threats may strike so close to the central or core identity of an institution that selective categorization tactics alone may be insufficient. For example, when the space shuttle *Challenger* exploded, NASA's identity as the "can do" organization was severely damaged. Once such core identity attributes are tarnished, categorizations may not only be inadequate, they may be dysfunctional and approach denial.

In evaluating the generalizability of our arguments about the motives underlying selective categorization, we need to emphasize that our analysis has focused almost exclusively on identity affirmation and restoration following threat. But there may be other motives for using categorization strategies, including the desire for accurate self-assessment and self-improvement. Researchers have long argued that there are many reasons for engaging in categorization processes, including the desire to obtain information that will contribute to realistic self-appraisal and to generate informative and useful social comparisons (Tajfel, 1969; Brewer, 1991). On balance, however, we were struck by how infrequently such goals or motives were expressed in our interviews. Instead, the preponderance of our data pointed toward more defensive (i.e., self-protective) uses of categorization and comparisons. Repeatedly in our interviews we observed evidence of organizational members attempting to reduce the dissonance between their perceptions of their organization's identities and the identity attributed to them by the *Business Week* survey results.

Conclusion

We have portrayed selective categorization processes primarily as useful cognitive tactics for helping organizational members both make sense of organizational identity threats and affirm positive organizational and social identities. But categorization processes are basic cognitive processes that can contribute to a number of other important organizational processes and outcomes, including shaping perceptions of emerging opportunities and future ventures. Reger and her colleagues (1994), for example, noted the important role organizational identity beliefs play in a constructive change process. As Reger et al. (1994: 33) asserted, "Organizational members interpret new management initiatives through their existing mental models. . . . A particularly powerful mental model is the set of beliefs members hold about the organization's identity." We view categorization processes as one of the fundamental building blocks of such mental models.

We have argued that using selective categorization processes creatively can help organizations decide not only where emerging opportunities lie, but also what the appropriate and useful responses to them are. Further, we have noted how these same processes help organizational members understand their organizations and their relationship to the external environment. Our framework of identity management thus provides the foundation for a more general model that emphasizes the functional role categorization processes play in attempts by organizations and their members to make sense of themselves and their environments.

Notes

We wish to thank Susan Ashford, Jim Baron, Marilynn Brewer, Michael Cohen, Jane Dutton, Janet Dukerich, Ben Hanna, Joanne Martin, Michael Morris, Jeff Pfeffer, Bob Sutton, Michelle Walker, Jim Walsh, Janet Weiss, and Dave Whetten for their comments and contributions to this paper. Thanks also go to Keith Murnighan and the three anonymous *ASQ* reviewers for their substantial and constructive comments. Earlier versions of this research were presented at the National Academy of Management annual meetings, University of Michigan's Graduate School of Business, and University's Johnson Graduate School of Management, University of Texas' Graduate School of Business, and Standford Asilomar Conference on Organizations. We are grateful for comments provided by participants at those conferences. Finally, we wish to thank the business school members who generously gave their time for this study. This study was supported by funding from Emory University's Goizueta Business School, Standford University's Graduate School of Business, and a James and Doris McNamara Faculty Fellowship.

1. Social identity theorists posit a very close relationship between categorization and comparison processes. As Turner (1987: 46) noted, "categorization and comparison depend upon each other and neither can exist without the other: the division of stimuli into classes depends upon perceived similarities and differences (comparative relations), but stimuli can only be compared in so far as they have already been categorized as identical, alike, or equivalent at some higher level of abstraction."

References

Abrams, Dominic, and Michael A. Hogg 1990 Social Identity Theory. Constructive and Critical Advances. New York: Springer-Verlag.

Albert, Stuart, and David A. Whetten 1985 "Organizational identity." In B. M. Staw and L. L. Cummings (eds.), Research in Organizational Behavior, 7: 263–95. Greenwich, CT: JAI Press.

Alicke, Mark D. 1985 "Global self-evaluation as determined by the desirability and controllability of trait adjectives." Journal of Personality and Social Psychology, 49: 1621–30.

Ashforth, Blake, and Fred Mael 1989 "Social identity and the organization." Academy of Management Review, 14: 20–39.

Brewer, Marilynn B. 1991 "The social self: On being the same and different at the same time." Personality and Social Psychology Bulletin, 15: 475–82.

Brewer, Marilynn B., and Roderick M. Kramer 1986 "The psychology of intergroup attitudes and behavior." Annual Review of Psychology, 43: 219–43.

Brickman, Philip, and Ronnie J. Bulman 1985 "Pleasure and pain in social comparison." In J. M. Suls and R. L. Miller (eds.), Social Comparison Processes: Theoretical and Empirical Perspectives: 149–86. New York: Wiley.

Brown, Rupert, and Jennifer Williams 1984 "Group identification: The same thing to all people?" Human Relations, 37: 547–64.

Burgelman, Robert A., and Andrew S. Grove 1996 "Strategic dissonance." California Management Review, 38: 8–28.

Campbell, Jennifer D. 1986 "Similarity and uniqueness: The effects of attribute type, relevance, and individual differences in self-esteem and depression." Journal of Personality and Social Psychology, 50: 281–94.

Cialdini, Robert B. 1984 Influence: The New Psychology of Modern Persuasion. New York: Quill.

Cialdini, Robert B., Richard J. Borden, Avril Thorne, Marcus Randall Walker, Stephen Freeman, and Lloyd Reynolds Sloan 1976 "Basking in reflective glory: Three (football) field studies." Journal of Personality and Social Psychology, 34: 463–76.

Dutton, Jane E., and Janet M. Dukerich 1991 "Keeping an eye on the mirror: Image and identity in organizational adaptation." Academy of Management Journal, 34: 517–54.

Dutton, Jane E., Janet M. Dukerich, and Celia V. Harquail 1994 "Organizational images and member identification." Administrative Science Quarterly, 39: 239–63.

Dutton, Jane E., and Wendy J. Penner 1993 "The importance of organizational identity for strategic agenda building." In J. Hendry and G. Johnson (eds.), Strategic Thinking: Leadership and the Management of Change: 89–113. New York: Strategic Management Society, Wiley.

Eisenhardt, Kathleen M. 1989 "Building theory from case study research." Academy of Management Review, 14: 532–50.

Elsbach, Kimberly D. 1994 "Managing organizational legitimacy in the California cattle industry: The construction and effectiveness of verbal accounts." Administrative Science Quarterly, 39: 57–88.

Elsbach, Kimberly D., and Robert I. Sutton 1992 "Acquiring organizational legitimacy through illegitimate actions: A marriage of institutional and impression management theories." Academy of Management Journal, 35: 699–738.

Fombrun, Charles J. 1996 Reputation: Realizing Value from Corporate Image. Boston: Harvard Business School Press.

Frank, Robert 1985 Choosing the Right Pond: Human Behavior and the Quest for Status. New York: Oxford.

Frey, Karin S., and Diane N. Ruble 1990 "Strategies for comparative evaluation: Maintaining a sense of competence across the life span." In R. J. Sternberg and J. Kolligan (eds.), Competence Considered: 167–89. New Haven: Yale University Press.

Gaertner, Samuel L., Jeffrey Mann, John F. Dovidio, and Audrey J. Murrell 1990 "How does cooperation reduce intergroup bias?" Journal of Personality and Social Psychology, 59: 692–704.

Gaertner, Samuel L., Jeffrey Mann, Audrey Murrell, and John F. Dovidio 1989 "Reducing intergroup bias: The benefits of recategorization." Journal of Personality and Social Psychology, 57: 239–49.

Ginzel, Linda E., Roderick M. Kramer, and Robert I. Sutton 1993 "Organizational impression management as a reciprocal influence process: The neglected role of the organizational audience." In L. L. Cummings, and B. M. Staw (eds.), Research in Organizational Behavior, 15: 227–66. Greenwich, CT: JAI Press.

Glaser, Barney, and Anselm L. Strauss 1967 The Discovery of Grounded Theory: Strategies for Qualitative Research. London: Wiedenfeld and Nicholson.

Goethals, George R., David M. Messick, and Scott T. Allison 1991 "The uniqueness bias: Studies of constructive social comparison." In J. Suls and T. A. Wills (eds.), Social Comparison: Contemporary Theory and Research: 149–76. Hillsdale, NJ: Erlbaum.

Hall, Carl T. 1990 "Why business school rating can rankle." San Francisco Chronicle, March 26: C1.

Hay, Tina M. 1992 "Education's love-hate relationship. Colleges abhor the rankings—but adore the attention." Case Currents, Sept.: 14–20.

Hinkle, Steve, and Rupert J. Brown 1990 "Intergroup comparisons and social identity: Some links and lacunae." In D. Abrams and M. A. Hogg (eds.), Social Identity Theory: Constructive and Critical Advances: 48–70. New York: Springer-Verlag.

Hogg, Michael A., and Dominic Abrams 1988 Social Identifications: A Social Psychology of Intergroup Relations and Group Processes. London: Routledge.

Kahneman, Daniel, and Amos Tversky 1984 "Choices, values, and frames." American Psychologist, 39: 341–50.

Kramer, Roderick M. 1993 "Cooperation and organizational identification." In J. K. Murnighan (ed.), Social Psychology in Organizations: 244–69. Englewood Cliffs, NJ: Prentice-Hall.

Kramer, Roderick M., and Marilynn B. Brewer 1984 "Effects of group identity on resource use in a simulated commons dilemma." Journal of Personality and Social Psychology, 46: 1044–57.

Mael, Fred, and Blake E. Ashforth 1992 "Alumni and their alma mater: A partial test of the reformulated model of organizational identification." Journal of Organizational Behavior, 13: 103–23.

March, James G. 1994 A Primer on Decision Making. New York: Free Press.

Marcus, Alfred A., and Robert S. Goodman 1991 "Victims and shareholders: The dilemmas of presenting corporate policy during a crisis." Academy of Management Journal, 34: 281–305.

Miller, Carol T. 1982 "The role of performance-related similarity in social comparison of abilities: A test of the related attributes hypothesis." Journal of Experimental Social Psychology, 18: 513–23.

Pfeffer, Jeffrey 1981 "Management as symbolic action." In L. L. Cummings and B. M. Staw (eds.), Research in Organizational Behavior, 3: 1–52. Greenwich, CT: JAI Press.

Putka, Gary 1990 "Colleges rankled by how they're ranked." Wall Street Journal, March 23: B1.

Reger, Rhonda K., John V. Mullane, Loren T. Gustafson, and Samuel M. DeMarie 1994 "Creating earthquakes to change organizational mindsets." Academy of Management Executive, 8: 31–46.

Robinson, Peter 1995 Snapshots from Hell: The Making of an MBA. New York: Time-Warner.

Rosenblatt, Roger 1994 "How tobacco executives live with themselves." Business and Society Review, Spring: 22–34.

Salancik, Gerald R., and James R. Meindl 1984 "Corporate attributions as strategic illusions of management control." Administrative Science Quarterly, 29: 238–54.

Salovey, Peter, and Judith Rodin 1984 "Some antecedents and consequences of social-comparison jealousy." Journal of Personality and Social Psychology, 47: 780–92.

Schlenker, Barry R. 1980 Impression Management: The Self-concept, Social Identity, and Interpersonal Relations. Monterey, CA: Brooks/Cole.

Staw, Barry M., Pamela I. McKechnie, and Sheila M. Puffer 1983 "The justification of organizational performance." Administrative Science Quarterly, 28: 582–600.

Steele, Claude M. 1988 "The psychology of self-affirmation: Sustaining the integrity of the self." Advances in Experimental Social Psychology, 21: 261–302. New York: Academic Press.

Sutton, Robert I., and Anita L. Callahan 1987 "The stigma of bankruptcy: Spoiled organizational image and its management." Academy of Management Journal, 30: 405–36.

Swann, William B. 1987 "Identity negotiation: Where two roads meet." Journal of Personality and Social Psychology, 53: 1038–51.

Swann, William B., Jr., and Brett W. Pelham 1987 "The social construction of identity: Self-verification through friend and intimate selection." Unpublished manuscript, Department of Psychology, University of Texas, Austin.

Tajfel, Henri 1969 "Cognitive aspects of prejudice." Journal of Social Issues, 25: 79–97.

Tajfel, Henri 1982 Social Identity and Intergroup Relations. Cambridge: Cambridge University Press.

Tajfel, Henri, and John C. Turner 1979 "An integrative theory of intergroup conflict." In W. G. Austin and S. Worchel (eds.). The Social Psychology of Intergroup Relations: 7–24. Monterey, CA: Brooks/Cole.

Tajfel, Henri, and A. L. Wilkes 1973 "Classification and quantitative judgment." British Journal of Social Psychology, 54: 101–14.

Taylor, Shelley E., Joanne V. Wood, and Rosemary R. Lichtman 1983 "It could be worse: Selective evaluation as a response to victimization." Journal of Social Issues, 39: 19–40.

Tedeschi, James T. 1981 Impression Management Theory and Social Psychological Research. New York: Academic Press.

Tedeschi, James T., and Valerie Melburg 1984 "Impression management and influence in the organization." In S. B. Bacharach, and E. J. Lawler (eds.), Research in the Sociology of Organizations, 3: 31–58. Greenwich, CT: JAI Press.

Tetlock, Philip E., and Antony S. R. Manstead 1985 "Impression management versus intrapsychic explanations in social psychology: A useful dichotomy?" Psychological Review, 92: 67–82.

Turner, John C. 1987 Rediscovering the Social Group: A Self-categorization Theory. Oxford: Basil Blackwell.

Weick, Karl 1993 "Sensemaking in organizations." In J. K. Murnighan (ed.), Social Psychology in Organizations: 10–37. Englewood Cliffs, NJ: Prentice-Hall.

Weick, Karl 1995 Sensemaking in Organizations. Thousand Oaks, CA: Sage.

Weiner, Bernard 1986 An Attributional Theory of Motivation and Emotion. New York: Springer-Verlag.

Wheeler, Ladd 1966 "Motivation as a determinant of upward comparison." Journal of Experimental Social Psychology, Supplement, 1: 27–31.

Wheeler, Ladd, and Miron Zuckerman 1977 "Commentary." In J. M. Suls and R. L. Miller (eds.), Social Comparison Processes: Theoretical and Empirical Perspectives: 335–57. Washington, DC: Hemisphere.

Whetten, David, Debra Lewis, and Leann Mischel 1992 "Towards an integrated model of organizational identity and member commitment." Paper presented at the Academy of Management Annual Meeting, Las Vegas.

Wood, Joanne V. 1989 "Theory and research concerning social comparisons of personal attributes." Psychological Bulletin, 106: 231–48.

Wood, Joanne V., Shelley E. Taylor, and Rosemary R. Lichtman 1985 "Social comparison in adjustment to breast cancer." Journal of Personality and Social Psychology, 49: 1169–83.

Zanna, Mark P., George R. Goethals, and Janice F. Hill 1975 "Evaluating a sex-related ability: Social comparison with similar others and standard setters." Journal of Experimental Social Psychology, 11: 86–93.

Organizational Identity: Linkages Between Internal and External Communication

George Cheney and Lars Thøger Christensen

As a man adjusts himself to a certain environment he becomes a different individual; but in becoming a different individual he has affected the community in which he lives. It may be a slight effect, but in so far as he has adjusted himself, the adjustments have changed the type of environments to which he can respond and the world is accordingly a different world.

George Herbert Mead (1934, p. 215)

With few exceptions, the externally directed communications of organizations have been defined by organizational communication scholars as activities outside the province of their concerns. Because the study of organizational communication traditionally has been focused on acts of communication between senders and receivers within the "container" of the organization—that is, within clearly defined organizational borders—most communication aimed at *external* audiences, and markets in particular, has been regarded as alien to the field. Such a division is neither fruitful nor justifiable any longer. The notion of organizational boundaries is becoming increasingly problematic (although, it seems, an inescapable point of reference), and "internal" and "external" communications no longer constitute separate fields in practice (Ashforth & Mael, 1996; Berg, 1986; Christensen, 1994a; see also Alvesson, 1990; Berg & Gagliardi, 1985; Cheney, 1991). Further, from an epistemological perspective, organizational communication researchers are beginning to recognize the implications and limitations of their own metaphors, seeking to reconfigure notions such as "open" versus "closed" systems, the organization-environment interface, and the idea of the organization itself (cf. Putnam, Phillips, & Chapman, 1996; Smith, 1993; Taylor, 1993).

To secure and maintain a legitimate and recognizable place in material and symbolic markets, many organizations of today pursue a variety of complex communication activities. Such activities are not neatly circumscribed and often involve both internal and external functions in ways that blur their presumed boundaries. Nowhere is this clearer than in the fields and practices of public relations and issue management where internal groups now comprise part of the general audience that the organization wishes to address and where externally directed messages, accordingly, become an integral part of the organization's operating discourse. Many organizations have begun to realize the difficulties of convincing an external audience about their deeds (e.g., their protection of the environment or defense of human rights) if the *internal* audience does not accept the message—and vice versa. Although the stated goals of public relations and issue management traditionally have had a strong external orientation—for example, building relational bonds with publics, facilitating effective policy making, developing favorable images in the media, managing strategic stakeholders, and making the organization more responsible to society—practitioners are becoming aware that the pursuit of these goals directly affects the organization itself and its own members. Public relations and issue management, therefore, should be regarded in close connection with other forms of organizational communication.

Within such a perspective, the most interesting question may not be what distinguishes the various kinds of communication practices from one another (although we do recognize that such differences are relevant in some contexts), but rather how these endeavors are integrated for the organization to communicate at least somewhat consistently to its many different audiences. Without such consistency, the organization of today will have difficulties sustaining and confirming a coherent sense of "self" necessary to maintain credibility and legitimacy in and outside the organization. As a consequence, a growing proportion of professional communication activities becomes integrated around the same overall concern: *identity* (see, e.g., Christensen & Cheney, 1994; Czarniawska-Joerges, 1994; Hatch & Schultz, 1997). While the problem of identity is not the only concern of large organizations and often not an explicitly stated objective, we observe the surprising extent to which the question of what the organization "is" or "stands for" or "wants to be" cuts across and unifies many different goals and concerns. In the corporate world of today, identity-related concerns have, in other words, become organizational preoccupations, even when organizations are ostensibly talking about other matters.

The preoccupation with *identity as an issue* indicates at least two difficulties facing contemporary organizations and their communication: (1) a persistent problem for organizations in drawing lines between themselves and the outside world—a problem that requires a thorough rethinking of our long-held notions of institutions as discrete units (such as a university's being "contained" by a campus or a multinational firm's having a "base" or a "headquarters"); and

(2) the growing problem of *being heard* in a communication environment saturated with corporate messages. Of course, both of these trends are intensified by the rise of new computer and communications technologies. In the contemporary activities of public relations, issue management, marketing, advertising, and the like—what we might, for purposes of terminological economy here call "external organizational communication"—the ongoing rhetorical struggle for organizations of most kinds is to establish a clearly distinctive identity and at the same time connect with more general concerns so as to be maximally persuasive and effective. Because organizational messages are often organized around more than one purpose and aimed at more than one audience, we need to think of internal and external organizational communication as being closely intertwined, recognizing that along with attempts to speak "for" an organization using a unitary voice there will almost inevitably be the expression (or suppression) of multiple voices, identities, cultures, images, and interests (see Cheney, 1991, 1999; cf. Bakhtin, 1991).

Purpose and Outline of the Chapter

In this essay, we discuss and illustrate the ways in which organizations attempt to manage both identifiable issues and their own identities, arguing that those efforts have become so interwoven as to make their analytical separation unproductive if not impossible except in a discussion that is largely divorced from the reality of contemporary corporate communications. To accomplish our purposes, the essay unfolds through a number of subthemes each discussed in relation to the overall question of managing issues and identities.

First, it is crucial to recognize central features of the communication environment if we are going to understand well how contemporary organizations are behaving today through their dazzling array of highly visible communication practices. One purpose of this essay, then, is to establish a clear connection between the (post)modern symbolic environment of today and the integration of so-called external (e.g., public relations, marketing, and issues management) and internal (e.g., employee relations, statements of mission and policy, and organizational development) forms of organizational communications. Following this line of thought, we will consider how the contests over identity are related to such things as a growing fuzziness of organizational boundaries and the self-referential and sometimes nearly autonomous nature of public corporate symbols.

A second purpose of this essay is to bring together trends in corporate communications in seemingly disparate areas and in areas typically seen as foreign to the rubric of organizational communication (as a subdiscipline)—for example, corporate issue management, marketing, issue advertising—by revealing and analyzing their underlying and common concerns. None of this is to say that these various domains of communication activity are identical or that the differences between them are insignificant, but rather that their common features can be productively examined from the perspectives of communication and rhetoric, especially through assessments of the powerful and puzzling ways in which persuasion takes place in the organizational world of today.

A third purpose of our essay is to extend Cheney and Vibbert's (1987) commentary on the fields of public relations and issue management (in the previous handbook). Their analysis included both a historical section and an analysis of contemporary public relations practice. Among other things, their interpretive historical survey showed how conceptions of the organization as rhetor (or persuader) vis-à-vis its audiences have shifted over a century's time from a "reactive" and sometimes accommodative stance toward external threats toward more aggressive attempts to shape the *grounds* for discussing social and political issues of the day. That is, while public relations began with attempts by the railroads and oil companies to fend off harsh criticisms in the late 1800s, today the activity is far more broadly conceived. Cheney and Vibbert's analysis of contemporary practices and related research was organized around three dimensions, arguing that the public relations activity of large organizations today is (1) *rhetorical* in its attempt to establish the general premises for later and more specific claims, (2) *identity related* in that each organization must work to establish its unique "self" while connecting its concerns to those of the "cultural crowd," and (3) *political* in that many large organizations today are trying to exert political influence while usually avoiding being labeled as political actors. Together these features imply, as Cheney and Vibbert noted, that strict divisions between "internal" and "external" aspects of the corporate discourse become problematic. This observation is even more relevant today than it was a few years ago: The communication environment has intensified in a number of significant ways (see, e.g., Baudrillard, 1981, 1988), and with that intensification comes the need to integrate more fully the communicative efforts directed to the various publics of the organization (see, e.g., Cheney & Frenette, 1993). In our discussion, we will comment on these trends while extending Cheney and Vibbert's analysis and interpreting an even wider range of organizational communication activities (including some aspects of marketing, advertising, and strategic management).

Our discussion is based on descriptions and interpretations of current trends as they are represented in the scholarly literature. Moreover, we will draw on current and illustrative examples from print media, television, and the Internet. The overall purpose is to stimulate the discussion in and outside the broad field of organizational communication by offering a nontraditional and communication-centered perspective on the numerous and diverse ways in which large organizations relate to and "see" themselves as relating to their environments today and in the future.

The remainder of this essay is therefore divided into five sections: (1) an introduction to the area of external organizational communication, including a brief overview of the field of corporate issue management; (2) a characterization of the communication environment within which contemporary organizations operate and to which they contribute; (3) a discussion of the fuzziness of organizational boundaries and its implications for organizational identity and communication; (4) a reconceptualization of issue management through a discussion of self-reference and paradox in communication management; and (5) a conclusion, including a discussion of the wider context of this essay presented as surprises, paradoxes, and ethical concerns to which future research needs to be directed.

Corporate Issue Management in the Context of External Organizational Communication

Because scholars of organizational communication traditionally have regarded external communication as being outside their purview, there is only a vague idea of the nature of such activities within the field. And most often this idea confirms the self-image of organizational communication as a contained activity, confined within formal organizational boundaries. Today, this image makes little sense and actually tends to obscure important theoretical and practical questions (cf. Smith, 1993). If we define organizational communication in general terms as a set of processes through which organizations create, negotiate, and manage meanings (including those related to their own constitution), *external* organizational communication can be thought of as a subset of those processes specifically concerned with meaning construction by way of an "external" environment (Taylor, Flanagin, Cheney, & Seibold, in press). However, since this understanding implies assumptions about boundaries that our discussion later in the essay will work against, we will talk about external organizational communication as communication directed to and from audiences considered in everyday terms to be nonmembers of the organization.

Convergence in External Organizational Communication

To conceive of internal and external communication as interrelated dimensions of organizational sensemaking means to move our focus beyond the "container" metaphor and to embrace communication activities traditionally relegated to academics and professionals in communication functions such as advertising, marketing, and public relations.

Each of these domains of activity, professions, and disciplines has its own history, tone, mythology, and reasons for announcing its importance in society. Advertising, born in the mid-19th century, used to concern itself primarily with the direct "selling" of a product or a service (Dyer, 1990). Public relations arose in the late 19th century as a defense-based means of responding to public attacks on an organization (Cheney & Vibbert, 1987). And marketing, developed as a response to the growing number of consumer movements after World War II, established itself strongly in the 1960s as a strategic perspective for anticipating, detecting, and responding to desires, needs, or preferences of target audiences of consumers (Kotler, 1991).

Today, each of these areas has a far less certain and specific orientation than previously. Advertising, for example, has expanded its focus to include "social advertising" on important sociopolitical causes, such as the preservation of tropical rain forests or the cancellation of the Third World debt. Public relations now embraces within its reach highly proactive activities such as "issues management" and "identity management." And as we shall discuss below, the marketing perspective has gradually become a prevailing norm in the reordering of many organizations as customer driven or consumer driven (see the *Journal of Market-Focused Management*). This is to say that the genres have become blurred and may, as a consequence, have more in common than has usually been acknowledged within the self-promoting discourse of each field. As each area or profession has sought to extend its influence and reassert its specific importance, sometimes in a rather imperialistic way, this blurring of disciplinary boundaries becomes even more evident. Among the major external communications functions, marketing has probably been the most expansive in recent years.

The Expansion of the Marketing Orientation

Since the consumer unrests of the 1960s made business aware of the potential power of the market, marketing has established itself as a dominant principle of organizing in institutions of many different types. Traditionally speaking, marketing has comprised organizational activities designed to detect, assess, and respond to consumers' needs, wants, and desires. In more general terms, marketing can be thought of as a managerial *orientation* concerned primarily with the *satisfaction* of target audiences. The mythos of the marketing field sees the discipline as being an important advancement over earlier mass-production and sales-oriented perspectives chiefly because marketing *respects and engages* the consumer and his or her preferences (e.g., Keith, 1960; Kotler, 1991); marketing thus asserts itself as participatory, responsive, and above all democratic.

Regarding publics as consumers or customers, the marketing orientation has gradually made its way into all sectors of society such that many organizations, public as well as private, now openly describe themselves as "customer driven" (see, e.g., Gay & Salaman, 1992). And even where such descriptions seem somewhat inappropriate (e.g., in health care), we still find marketing present as a managerial ethos committing the organization to monitor its environments to keep abreast of changes in the market.

The expansive tendencies of marketing have often been criticized by leading public relations thinkers eager to distinguish their discipline from that of marketing (e.g., Grunig & Grunig, 1991). Among the differences typically emphasized to justify such a distinction are orientations with respect to target groups and operational goals. Whereas marketing traditionally concentrates on building and maintaining mutually satisfactory relationships with *customers*, public relations often sees itself dealing with a much broader range of *publics* to attain not only satisfaction but "accord and positive behavior among social groupings" (Broom, Lauzen, & Tucker, 1991; see also Grunig, 1993).

While acknowledging the significance of such differences, we would point out that marketing and public relations today have more in common than is commonly believed. Since Kotler and Levy (1969) introduced their "broadened concept of marketing," the marketing discipline has widened its scope considerably to include activities traditionally thought of as belonging in the realm of public relations. In line with traditional public relation concerns, scholars and practitioners in marketing have gradually begun to realize the importance of creating and maintaining a hospitable environment by fostering goodwill among all relevant stakeholders. As a consequence, a growing number of marketers are broadening their notion of the "customer" to include families, friends, and sometimes even society. Moreover, marketing principles are no longer restricted to the realm of private business but are applied to an increasing extent in social change efforts, such as birth rate limitation programs, antismoking campaigns, and heart disease prevention programs (e.g., Fine, 1981; Fox & Kotler, 1980; Kotler & Andreasen, 1987; Kotler & Roberto, 1989; Lazer & Kelly, 1973; Zaltman, Kotler, & Kaufman, 1972).

Obviously, these tendencies are not without practical problems. Since marketers take their point of departure as the wish to satisfy the needs and wants of (more or less broadly defined) customers, they may typically, as Fennell (1987, p. 293) claims, "seek to participate in behavior that is underway" rather than work to change behavioral patterns as they find them. Although marketing as a principle has a democratic impulse (Bouchet, 1991; Laufer & Paradeise, 1990)—in seeking out public opinion and suitable responses—it may not be the most appropriate model for dealing with more complex social and political issues or for soliciting deeper forms of citizen participation (a problem we shall return to later in the essay).

Nevertheless, the ubiquity of the marketing orientation and its reflection in the discourse and practice of management (Christensen, 1995a; Gay & Salaman, 1992) deserve careful analysis in today's society where we commonly speak of the marketing of hospitals, churches, schools, and individuals and their careers (see, e.g., Coupland, 1996; Fairclough, 1993; McMillan & Cheney, 1996). In other words, although the specific influences from marketing are often odd or problematic we want to emphasize that marketing—as a way of seeing and responding to environmental changes and developments—has become deeply rooted in the institutions of contemporary society. In fact, so taken for granted is this orientation that in the United States the term *American consumers* has now largely replaced *American people* and *American citizens* in public discourse. The same is true in public discourse with reference to China and other nations (Cheney, 1999, in press).

Further, and even more interesting from the perspective of this essay, marketing and public relations often operate from similar perspectives concerning organizations, boundaries, and environments. Because both disciplines have historical reasons for seeing their audiences as external forces able to make potent and often expensive claims on a business corporation, they share an image of the organization as an open and externally influenced system. Moreover, confronted with challenging and sometimes hostile environments, both disciplines have realized the value of organizational flexibility and the importance of being responsive to changes in opinions and preferences of target audiences. Interestingly, the value of flexibility is often so pronounced that organizational identity—in terms of stability or essence—is ignored or downplayed as a central management issue (see Christensen, 1995a; Kaldor, 1971). Following these values and implicit prescriptions, public relations and marketing have come to conceive of their communication with the external world as an ongoing dialogue. Although PR and marketing have grown out of rather asymmetrical perspectives on the communication between organizations and their publics, they both emphasize today that communication is, or at least should be, a two-way process through which the voices of all relevant parties are heard (see, e.g., Cheney & Dionisopoulos, 1989; DeLozier, 1976; Grunig, 1992; Leitch & Neilson, in press; Nickels, 1976; Pearson, 1989; Shimp, 1990; Stidsen & Schutte, 1972). Consequently, most organizations influenced by public relations or marketing experts find themselves engaged in frequent and extensive scanning and information-gathering activities. The differences and similarities between marketing and public relations are summarized generally in Table 1.

Public relations and marketing conceive of their audiences with different global labels—as "publics" and as "consumers"—but the fields' notions of how the organization should conceive of its own role vis-à-vis these audiences have interesting points in common. While management practices often contradict

Table 1. Differences and Similarities Between Marketing and Public Relations

	Marketing	Public Relations
Traditional differences		
Target group	Markets/customers/consumers	Politics/stakeholders
Principal goal	Attracting and satisfying customers through the exchange of goods and values	Establishing and maintaining positive and beneficial relations between various groups
Shared perspectives		
General image of organization	An open and externally influenced system	
Communication ideal	Communication as an ongoing dialogue with the external world	
Prescription for management	Organizational flexibility and responsiveness vis-à-vis external wishes and demands	

these shared perspectives and ideals, these ideas are extremely relevant in terms of how organizations of today see themselves handling their relations with their environments.

Corporate Issue Management

We now turn our attention to the areas of study and practice commonly known today as "issue management" or "corporate advocacy." Issue management has become visible since the late 1970s, largely as a broader and more systematic analysis of how organizations engage the larger society through strategic communication. Although growing out of public relations, especially in its more proactive form, issue management also bears a resemblance to some contemporary marketing practices and concepts. Further, issue management (as an area of study) has come to employ a range of rhetorical principles while also drawing on the social-scientific study of persuasion. Issue management thus provides an important forum for exploring many of the ideas and concerns of this essay.

Corporate issue management grew out of a rising managerial concern with the intensified critique since the 1960s of industrial products (e.g., Nader & Green, 1973; Nader, Green, & Seligman, 1976), seductive advertising (e.g., Packard, 1969), and lack of environmental concern. Adding to this the attacks on the oil and other industries in the United States during the early to mid-1970s and the low ebb for U.S. public opinion of big business (Chase, 1984), it is hardly surprising that organizations of many types, but especially those in the embattled industries of oil, chemicals, and tobacco, began to address simultaneously in public discourse their own identities and the sociopolitical issues of the day (see the overview in Cheney & Vibbert, 1987, for a more detailed account).

Initially, corporate issue management was thought of as a "fire fighting" function centered primarily around bottom-line concerns (e.g., Ewing, 1987; Wartick & Rude, 1986). Issue management, thus, has often been described as an "early warning system" that makes it possible for organizations to minimize surprises (e.g., Wartick & Rude, 1986) and to manage more effectively in a turbulent environment (see also Arrington & Sawaya, 1984). Since the early 1980s, issue management and the related terms *crisis management, issue diagnosis*, and (corporate) *advocacy advertising* have come to refer to a range of more intensive activities on the part of the modern organization to shape and manage its environment more directly (e.g., Chase, 1984). As Hainsworth and Meng (1988) found in their survey of 25 large U.S. corporations, issue management is now seen by managers as "an action-oriented management function" that helps the organization identify potential issues relevant for its business and to organize activities to influence the development of those issues "in an effort to mitigate their consequences for the organization" (p. 28). Thus, while the development of corporate issue management as a discipline had a defensive impetus, its primary focus has gradually become the question of how to maintain and expand corporate control. In the words of Chase (1984), "History can be created, not just survived" (p. 7).

At the same time, we witness a growing interest in more *symmetrical* relations, meaning some form of real dialogue between organizations and their publics (Grunig, 1992, in press); however, issue management has typically been *asymmetrical* in terms of how the organization actually deals with its constituencies or publics. Asymmetrical tendencies are often downplayed or denied today by references to corporations' involvement and responsibility in public policy processes, but the idea that "issue management is about power [over]," as Ewing (1987, p. 1) puts it, is still quite prevalent. In this one-way view of the communication process, communication itself is seen largely as the transmission of information and the shaping of audiences' attitudes, beliefs, and perhaps actions.

Issue Management as Communication

In line with Ewing's (1987) observation—though recognizing that the exercises of power and persuasion involved are more complex and subtle (see, e.g., Cheney & Frenette, 1993)—we would like to offer a definition of issue management that highlights its rhetorical dimension. Implicit in this definition is the view that communication not only mediates the space between human beings and "reality out there" but also helps to create the reality to which we respond. In this perspective, the world becomes real to us in large part through the symbolic and rhetorical constructions that we, as social actors, employ. For example, consider the point at which the mainstream media decide to recognize a "social movement" by calling it just that. While this is not to suggest that our words or labels bring the whole world into being—like a reduction (or extension) of the argument into mere "nominalism" would imply—it helps us to remember the creative, evocative, even "magical" potency of language in use and thus be aware of the powerfully creative *and* restrictive dimensions to the terms and images by which we describe our world (cf. Burke, 1966; Douglas, 1986).

In prevailing thought, an *issue* is often thought of as an unresolved or contestable matter "ready for decision" (Chase, 1984, p. 38). Understood this way, issues represent a more advanced stage in terms of awareness than simply trends or problems. According to Crable and Vibbert (1985, p. 5), issues are created "when one or more human agents [attach] significance to a situation or perceived problem" and, we should add, decide to *articulate* this attention publicly (see also Heath, 1988). In fact, this articulation may significantly affect the way an issue is understood to the general public. Such is precisely why debates over "what to call" important events and groups—even those yet to be noticed—can have such a broad persuasive impact. Rhetorical disputes over the meaning of such hallowed terms as *democracy, freedom, efficiency*, and *progress* often take on such importance in the United States and in other industrialized nations, although any measure of control over meaning must be seen as uncertain, tentative, and often only localized. And such terms often function *simultaneously* as repositories of many meanings and as clichés almost devoid of meaning (cf. Cheney, 1999; McGee, 1980; White, 1984).

In rhetorical terms, *issue management* means that the organization attempts to both "read" the premises and attitudes of its audience and work to shape them, often *in advance* of any specific crisis or well-defined debate (Heath, 1980). Understood this way, then, the *issue* becomes a universe of discourse designed, managed, and ultimately, shaped by organizational rhetors and strategists in an attempt to shape the attitudes the audience hold toward the organization or its concerns. From this perspective, the audience or public becomes something that is "pursued" with the goals of understanding, persuasion, and control (cf. Bryant's, 1953, conception of the function of rhetoric as the adjustment of ideas to people and people to ideas; see also Crable and Vibbert's, 1986, reformulation of that famous definition in terms of organizations and their environments; see in addition Kuhn's, 1997, treatment of issue management as a genre of communication).

Clearly, the rhetorical perspective suggested here conceives of communication in much broader terms than is usually the case in prevailing theories of issue management (cf. Sproull, 1988, 1990). Rather than distinguishing between the strategic and the communication-related aspects of the issue management process (e.g., Grunig, in press; see also Chase, 1984), we see communication as a metaconcept that refers broadly to constructions and deconstructions of meaning at many different levels, including not only explicit communication campaigns but also the strategic planning process, the process of monitoring and analyzing issues, and corporate efforts to comply with changing norms and standards of social responsibility (cf. Heath & Cousino, 1990). In all such situations, corporate actors deal significantly with symbols and interpretations. To see communication merely as an identifiable campaign *tool* that supplements whatever an organization *does* (its behavior) is to fail to grasp the significance of interpretation in a wide range of organizational processes. Further, such a perspective ignores the possibility that corporate rhetorical persuasion has become more complex and subtle in the communication environment of today in which an excess of messages is the order of the day. (On the other hand, of course, we must resist the temptation to say that "everything is communication.")

Only recently have scholars in the communication discipline identified the fundamental rhetorical and communication-related aspects of corporate issue management practices. And only recently have organizational communication studies (and we perceive a similar trend in the transdisciplinary study of organizations) begun to reclaim the broad sociological and political interests that shaped the early works on organizations by Marx, Weber, Durkheim, and Simmel. Such research efforts are necessary and potentially significant for at least two reasons:

1. By continuing to refer unreflectively to a division of "internal" versus "external" organizational communication, we fail to recognize dramatically new communication practices. These practices include, for example, the intended influences on multiple audiences with a single organizational message and, conversely, adaptations made for different audiences. Also, observe the ways in which the "container" metaphor for organization has become so problematic even as it is still desired as a pragmatic and comforting point of reference (Cheney, 1992).

2. Note the ways organizational communication must be situated within the context of larger social and cultural trends, for example, in terms of the "marketing culture" and its relentless but problematic pursuit of consumers' opinions (Christensen, 1995a; Laufer & Paradeise, 1990).

In the following section, we will present and highlight a number of sociohistorical trends relevant for our understanding of external organizational communication and its specific conditions in contemporary society.

Setting the Scene: Identity and Communication in the Corporate Society

A shipwrecked woman stranded on a remote island puts a message in a bottle. As she sets out to throw the bottle into the sea, she realizes that she cannot see the water. It is covered with messages in bottles. In a nutshell, this is the problem confronting corporate communications of today. At the beginning of the 21st century, any communicator is confronted with the fact that professional communications have taken on a previously unseen scope and intensity pervading almost all aspects of human life. "The space is so saturated," as Baudrillard (1988, 24ff.) puts it, "the pressure of all which wants to be heard so strong that [we] are no longer capable of knowing what [we] want" or, perhaps more important, who we are. The "explosion" of communication that we are witnessing, in other words, goes hand in hand with the question of identity. "Standing out" with a distinct and recognizable identity in this cluttered environment is at once absolutely necessary and almost impossible. As an organizing problem, the issue of identity, however, has deeper sociohistorical roots.

The Issue of Identity

The social order instituted by modernity implied a weakening of the bonds of local community and authority through which people traditionally defined their roles and positions in society (e.g., Nisbet, 1970). With the image of traditional society as a body (corpus) that provides its members with stable identities, Mongin (1982) describes modernity as a process of "decorporation" that dissolves ancient relations of community and authority. Without these relations, the modern individual is left without "markers of certainty" (Lefort, 1988) to guide the search for meaning and identity. Although modernity has established new and quite resilient points of guidance (e.g., individuality, the nation-state, the market, rationality, and bureaucracy), its foundations are open to questioning and are thus basically fragile (Bouchet, 1991; see also Weigert, Teitge & Teitge, 1986). As a result, the question of identity has become a standing and often pressing issue for individuals and institutions in many different contexts (see Giddens, 1991; Lasch, 1978, 1984). The "extraordinary availability of identities" (Weigert et al., 1986) also signals a lack of and quest for meaning.

Today, individuals and organizations are in hot pursuit of solid, favorable identities even as such identities become harder to capture and sustain. This is especially the case in situations when issues turn into crises. For Royal Dutch Shell—today the largest corporation in Europe—identity has often been a salient issue. Well known for its controversial business interests in apartheid South Africa, the Shell name has for many years been associated, in the views of its critics, with cynicism and unethical business activities. To many observers, this negative image was confirmed by its 1995 decision, approved by the British government, to dump the oil platform Brent Spar into the North Sea. Following the announcement of the decision, the Shell corporation faced a previously unseen rash of negative reactions from organizations, consumers, and politicians, especially in northern Europe. While Greenpeace occupied Brent Spar to force Shell to scrap the platform on land, consumers and business corporations started a boycott of Shell that finally made the organization give up its dumping plans (see, e.g. Wätzold, 1996).

From the perspective of this essay, it is interesting to note that this case—behind the negotiations and strategic choices of the different actors—was *about* identity: that of Shell (that had struggled for several years with a bad image), of Greenpeace (that gradually had lost legitimacy and feared falling into oblivion), and of the involved politicians always eager to trade politically on the whims of the public. In this game, the environmental issue (how to retire an oil platform most safely) was often pushed aside to the benefit of identities and power positions of influential actors. Obviously, Shell lost this battle, but that does not necessarily imply that the consumer, or the environment, *won*. In 1996, Brent Spar was "parked" in a fjord in Norway waiting to be scrapped on land: a solution far more harmful to the environment, according to many environmental experts, than a dumping at sea. Although later findings seem to support Shell's initial position on the issue, the organization has realized that negative connotations are still related to the name of Shell. And as the recent media attention to its activities in Nigeria and Turkey indicates, identity has indeed become a standing and very complex issue for the organization.

But even in less critical and problematic situations, the question of identity is quite evident. If we accept the idea that organizational communication is essentially a process through which meaning is created, negotiated, and managed, we should expect to find identity at issue in most organizing processes, especially in those explicitly concerned with addressing external audiences.

The Communication Environment of Today

In the corporate landscape of today, the issue of identity is closely tied up with the ways organizations organize their "world" in terms of communication. To begin with, the key communication elements of source, message, and receiver are all much more complicated and less easily distinguished than in prior periods. As many organizations have come to realize, the principal management problem in today's marketplace of goods and ideas is not so much to provide commodities and services or to take stands on the salient issues of the day, but to do these things with a certain distinctiveness that allows the organization to create and legitimize itself, its particular "profile," and its advantageous position. This quest for visibility has made disciplines such as public relations, issue management, marketing, and advertising chief architects of organizational identity. To help organizations stand out and "break through the clutter," practitioners within these fields are continuously operating on the edge of established strategies and perspectives, hoping to discover the idea that will provide the organization with a momentary relief from the pressures of intensified communication. Interestingly, however, such measures are creating a situation in which established communication is continuously challenged and the *conditions* for communication are in constant change (Christensen, 1995b). Many organizations today engage in ongoing efforts to (re)shape their images, ever seeking the support of both internal and external audiences (see, e.g., Allen & Caillouet, 1994; Alvesson, 1990; Treadwell & Harrison, 1994), even though there may be in any given case little real harmony among various constituencies and the images they hold of the organization.

This problem is clearly present in advertising for consumer goods, but it is observable in the marketing of services and issues as well. As an example of the former, the strategies chosen by various computer companies in their attempts to emulate IBM comes to mind. Trading, for example, on IBM's well-known slogan "Think," another computer company, ICL, chose to suggest "Think ICL" (Olins, 1989). By *leaning on*, or exploiting, more well-known images or positions, such messages hope to *"capture* the mystery of other organizations" (Gallagher, 1990, emphasis added) while emphasizing small, but in a way still, significant differences. For less wellknown companies or products, such "positioning" strategies are often necessary to gain visibility in a crowded marketplace.

Similar principles are activated when organizations take stands on prominent social and political issues. Benetton Corporation, for example, is well known for displaying tragedies and human disasters in its ads and this way attracting attention to pressing social and political issues. One recent example is its 2000 ad campaign, which features death row inmates. However, because Benetton's ads are not explicitly taking stands on these issues—the situations are merely *exhibited*—more directly expressed positions on these issues are open for other corporations to take up. Following the launch of one of Benetton's widely disputed ads showing a man dying of AIDS surrounded by his family, Esprit, another clothing company, tried to exploit the situation by stating that it was in fact donating money to *fight* AIDS. Similar strategies have been employed by other clothing companies. Although these companies will have difficulties challenging Benetton's number-one position in terms of media attention and public interest, their positioning attempts have definitely had an impact on Benetton and its communications. In later ads showing an undressed Luciano Benetton saying, "Give me back my clothes," the corporation asks the public to donate their used clothes to Caritas, a relief organization supported by Benetton. As this example demonstrates, corporate identities are often intertwined with the issues that organizations seek to address. Further, the case indicates that the *way* issues are managed is strongly affected by the dynamics of the communication environment.

In this complex and volatile environment, crowded with symbols referencing each other, any discourse on issues tends to develop its own logic relatively independent of its referent. The symbolism surrounding an organization's identity *can*, in other words, become something of a world of its own, even though it may often rely on other symbols to express what the organization is or is not. This is precisely why many contemporary consulting firms can speak of "giving organizations identities" or "creating identity packages." Further, because positions within this environment are defined in terms of other positions, the identity aimed at by the corporate actor is potentially reduced to what Perniola (1980) and Baudrillard (1981) call a "simulacrum," that is, an "autonomized" image without reference to anything but other images.[1]

Organizations that wish to express their stances on social issues need to take these dynamics of the communication environment into serious consideration. While striving to make the position of the organization clear, the issue manager of today has to realize that the impact of symbols employed to define a situation or bolster an image is fragile and often more dependent on the significance of other corporate symbols than on the specific issue in question.

At a more global level, issue managers need to realize that communication is not an unproblematic solution to crises or queries over identity. In terms of the plethora of corporate messages and their often peculiar character, the communication environment of today is radically different in substantive respects from that of, say, 40 to 50 years ago. On the one hand, *more* communication appears as a necessary solution to the constant challenges to corporate identity and legitimacy. The fact of more communication requires more communication, from the standpoint of any organization that seeks to be heard. On the other hand, we have to realize that communication itself, even in its widest sense, is an integral part of the problem it sets out to handle. A deeper understanding of the still emergent communication environment requires that the growing access to "information" and the mountain of messages are viewed not only in terms of the meanings or effects of *specific* or isolable messages but in terms of effects of the expansion of the communication universe *as a whole*. What is, on the one hand, the intensity of modern communication seems, on the other hand, to be the dissolution of communication itself, at least as understood in any deep or understanding-oriented way (cf. Baudrillard, 1983; Dervin, 1994).

The Fuzziness of Organizational Boundaries

At the same time that organizations have become preoccupied, even obsessed, with the communication of their identities, the problem of defining organizational boundaries has become more acute than ever. As a consequence, organizations find it increasingly difficult to maintain clear distinctions between their internal and external communication.

To be sure, the problem of defining organizational boundaries was recognized in the scholarly literature two decades ago (see, e.g., Starbuck, 1976; Weick, 1979), but its present manifestations are directly related to the marketing ethos. With its ideal of organizational flexibility and responsiveness vis-à-vis external demands, the marketing ethos and its related management practices not only defy established images of the organization but also question traditional notions of the organization–environment interface (Christensen, 1996). Because such notions are central for our understanding of how issues are perceived and managed, we will sketch out below some relevant trends that today challenge the traditional reliance on the "container" metaphor for understanding organizational life. We do not have the space to examine in detail all relevant trends, but we will mention a few powerful indicators of what we mean.

Organizing Beyond the Organizational Boundary

It is well known that *service organizations* have often had difficulties in maintaining a clearly defined "sense of self," in large part because their clients or service recipients straddle the boundary of the organization (see, e.g., Adams, 1976). Long-term service recipients, in particular, are difficult to define as being fully "outside" the organization (see, e.g., Cheney, Block, & Gordon, 1986; Starbuck, 1976). Students, regular clients of advertising agencies, users of various therapies, and clients of image and identity consultants often find themselves in this category. Seemingly pedantic exercises such as determining whether an individual or group is "inside" or "outside" the organization (as depicted, e.g., with Venn diagrams) thus have tremendous practical implications.

This is especially the case today where the marketing orientation is being copied and implemented by organizations in all sectors. In many institutions of higher education in North America, Europe, and Australasia, the student is increasingly being talked about as a "consumer" or "customer," meaning not only that the organization is seeking to adapt to its primary audience (the service recipients) but also that the activities of many universities take on more and more of a self-promotional quality (see Fairclough, 1993; McMillan & Cheney, 1996), where the objective is often adding commodifiable "value" to the self and by extension to the institution (Gay, 1996). In such arrangements, students can become shapers of services to a greater degree than they have been in the past, largely through immediate responses to courses and instructors and through the registering of their desires with quick changes in curricula and student services. Such forms of "participation" or "engagement" tend to be rather shallow, however, requiring only limited exchanges of "information" and ignoring possibilities for intersubjective understanding.

Today, the spread of the marketing attitude seems to reach its apotheosis in some production arrangements where integration and flexibility have become central managerial criteria (see Christensen, 1996). In auto manufacturing, for example, the customer can be almost incorporated into the design process by way of new computer technology. As Achrol (1991) reports, some Japanese automobile companies have developed a system "by which the customer designs his or her car (from available options) in the dealer showroom on a computer linked directly to the factory production line" (p. 79). Such production arrangements are not necessarily dependent on advanced technology, although the expansion of e-commerce does facilitate this kind of consumer involvement. With relatively simple measures, the production of bicycles, for example, has in many cases become adapted considerably to individual preferences. Management practices like these seriously challenge the organization's ability to distinguish between inside and outside and, accordingly, its sense of "self." Because the specific operationalizations of the marketing ethos—as "consumer influence," "custom-made products," and so forth—are blurring the boundaries between the organization and its environment, identity is a standing issue for organizations influenced by this organizing ideal.

In principle, this is true as well for "network forms of organization," such as long-term strategic alliances and flexible manufacturing networks. These can be found in industries as diverse as construction, publishing, and film. Such organizational creatures are, as Powell (1990) observes, difficult to classify: Neither markets nor firms, they exhibit greater predictability than the former but greater flexibility than the latter (see also Arndt, 1979; Webster, 1992). Simultaneously, electronic and computerized communication systems now permit some organizations to exist without any spatially located headquarters. As a consequence, many employees now find themselves with "virtual offices" (e.g., James, 1993). As one example: In mountainous and long Norway, the health care system is experimenting with methods of electronic diagnosis where data collected from a patient in one place are received and "read" simultaneously by physicians in other locations. Such arrangements can serve to challenge traditional notions of where and what the organization *is*, especially because some service providers (in this example, physicians assistants or nurses) may rarely or never experience copresence with the doctors with whom they must coordinate efforts. These, and other, hard-to-classify organizational types, offer still more challenges to the idea of the organization as, in Richardson's (1972) apt description, "islands of planned coordination in a sea of market relations" (see Chapter 12, 2001).

Under all the circumstances mentioned here, the identity of the organization becomes more problematic and more precious (Scott & Carroll, 1999).

This observation, however, is not restricted to these examples but applies as well to the management of *issues*. As contemporary organizations face a growing demand to listen to relevant publics before they carry out their operations, systematic efforts to *integrate* these publics somehow into deliberations when taking stands on salient issues gradually becomes a more common phenomenon. While this kind of integration may sometimes be more superficial than profound, organizations that implement such efforts no doubt find it increasingly difficult to distinguish clearly between themselves and their environment. This problem has important implications for contemporary corporate communications. Thus, it is hardly surprising that many organizations are consolidating their internal and external communications in a single office or function.

Communicating Across Boundaries

To uphold a sense of "self" while being flexible or existing as part of a larger network, organizations of today seek to integrate internal and external dimensions of their activities with the overall purpose of communicating one identity, although they may indeed pursue variations on a central theme. And while changes in an organization's identity over time are necessary for the organization to be adaptable, they are also risky in potentially undermining employee or consumer identification with the organization (see, e.g., Carroll, 1995). People become accustomed to an organization's "look." Thus, changes in the Betty Crocker persona of General Mills are made incrementally and carefully in response to cultural shifts and the public's image of the "appropriate" woman for the label (now a composite, computer-generated figure). We find much corporate communication today organized around identity as the overarching concern. In the following, we shall illustrate how this concern tends to blur the differences between external and internal messages.

In advertising, the content of messages often reflects the fact that contemporary organizations feel the need to remind not only consumers but also their own employees that they are still part of the corporate landscape, that their actions are legitimate, and their business ventures sound. Besides its functions as a traditional external medium, advertising may have an important *self*-enhancing dimension. When the German corporation Bayer expresses its concern for the environment in large expensive ads, it simultaneously addresses the consumer *and* tells its employees and investors that they are part of a "competent and responsible" corporation. An advertisement from BP America has a similar dual focus. Showing a dirty worker with a pipe wrench in his hand, the ad says: "It takes energy to make energy. From our riggers and roughnecks. From our planners, our traders, our service station attendants. From 38,000 BP America employees in all. Their energy has made BP America the largest producer of American oil, producing 800,000 barrels of oil a day. To make the most of our country's energy resources, we're making the most of our human ones." By linking the issue of energy resources to the question of work and employment, BP America hopes to establish in the minds of its many audiences an image of an industrious caretaker concerned at once with its employees and the environment. Speaking even more broadly, eight oil producers (BP, Norol, Shell, Chevron, Statoil, Texaco, Q8, and Total) have issued a joint ad that almost presents their product as the life-blood of society and a Promethean gift to humanity (cf. Crable & Vibbert, 1983). Composed of a number of simple images—icons of an oil refinery, an oil tanker, and an airplane—connected by pipelines, the ad says, trading on Walt Disney's famous TV show, "To all of you from all of us."

In these and similar cases, the messages are communicating both externally and internally, hoping to influence both consumers and stakeholders and to confirm the sending organization's own merits or good intentions. This way, market-related communication seeks to link internal and external audiences around the same concern, identity. And as van Riel (1995) points out, a strong corporate identity can raise employee motivation while inspiring confidence among an organization's external target groups.

Other kinds of corporate communications may serve a similar function. Corporate identity programs (Olins, 1989), design and architecture (Berg & Kreiner, 1990), art collections (Joy, 1993), and autobiographies (Ramanantsoa & Battaglia, 1991) are all examples of communications that cut across traditional organizational boundaries and seek to unify different audiences. As Ramanantsoa and Battaglia (1991) note, organizational autobiographies, memoirs, and self-portraits are becoming increasingly important for firms that actively want to manage their identity: "At first invisible and silent, later object of a discourse and battle-field, companies have now become the subject of their own discourse in an effort to win coherent identities, legitimacy, and institutionalization" (p. 2). Autobiographies are, in other words, playing several important roles for contemporary organizations. Externally, the autobiography may supplement more traditional public relations or marketing functions. Internally, it enacts a mirror structure that makes it possible for the members of the organization to perceive themselves as part of a whole, autonomous, and anthropomorphic entity with a strong and original (yet not too eccentric) personality. This is clearly the case with Procter & Gamble's own story as it is told in *The House That Ivory Built: 50 Years of Successful Marketing* (1989). Here an effort to claim a specific and very "personal" identity internally is combined with the wish to market itself externally as a legitimate corporate actor.

Whether or not such communications convince the audience about their *specific* content is, of course, an empirical question. In fact, formal, established, and public symbols of an organization—as seen in the logo, mission statement, and so on—may well have little connection in a particular case with how individual organizational members image their organization. A full treatment of the range of influences inside the organization is certainly beyond the scope of this essay. But we emphasize that, despite the apparent "autonomy" of many of the public symbols that come to (re)present the organization, there is much that transpires between organizational members (both powerful decision makers and others) to determine the course of an organization's rhetorical enterprise. So in no way do we wish to presume a monolithic organization that speaks univocally to the world (cf. Bakhtin, 1981; Cheney, 1992; Christensen, 1997; Motion & Leitch, 2000), nor are we suggesting that corporate symbols have a complete life of their own. Still, given our intention here to bring activities such as marketing, public relations, and some kinds of advertising within the purview of organizational communication, we are necessarily stressing the creation, positioning, and transformation of those symbols that come to represent the organization to a variety of stakeholders.

When externally directed communication becomes an integral part of an organization's operating discourse, the self-enhancing dimension of communication may turn out to be more important than the substantive messages themselves. In such cases, organizations are not merely engaging in communication, in the sense of sending or receiving messages, but also *auto*-communicating, that is, communicating with themselves. Auto-communication, according to Lotman (1977, 1991), is a process of organizing through which a communicator evokes and enhances its own values or codes (see also Broms & Gahmberg, 1983). As many anthropologists (e.g., Geertz, 1973) and sociologists (e.g., Parsons, 1949) have noted, all societies communicate with themselves in a self-reinforcing manner about their most salient values or concerns (see also Lotman, 1977, 1991). In this process, the role of the external audience becomes more complex than is usually acknowledged: besides acting as receiver of the corporate message, the external audience represents an ideal reference point in terms of which the sender evaluates itself. In this "looking-glass" (Cooley, 1983), the communicator (person or group) recognizes itself, chiefly in terms of how it wants to be seen by others.

In contemporary organizations, auto-communication is stimulated by the quest for identity and a growing need among organizational members for identification and belongingness (see, e.g., Cheney, 1983a, 1983b, 1991; Cheney & Tompkins, 1987; Scott, Corman, & Cheney, 1998; Tompkins & Cheney, 1983, 1985). Rapid change in the job market makes organizational loyalty problematic, yet it is still desired by individuals and organizations. Within many organizations of varying types, members are searching for a connection with something larger than the self. This is particularly observable in value-based organizations such as religious and voluntary associations, but it applies as well to a range of organizations in all sectors. Under growing economic pressure and internal drives toward centralization, the Mondragón Cooperative Corporation, one of the largest systems of worker-owned co-ops in the world, is working to fortify its fundamental values, such as social solidarity and democracy, while reconfiguring itself as a "customer-driven" multinational corporation. However, it is clear that for this organization of 42,000 worker-owner-members, located in the Basque Country in Spain, many presumably externally driven programs and messages are serving also to maintain a need to identify with one's place of work. However, that strategy is meeting receptivity in some quarters and resistance from others, as internal constituencies struggle over the true "essence" or the defining goals and values of the corporation. Some worker-member-owners are identifying strongly with the cooperatives' new competitive posture toward the European Union and the global market (e.g., "We must grow or die"), while others are maintaining greater allegiance to what they see as the "soul" or "heart" of the cooperatives: individual unit (or co-op) autonomy, employee participation in policy making, relative equality of members, and regional grounding of cooperative groups (or sectors). As the first author has discovered through his interviews in the worker–cooperative complex, a great deal of self-persuasion (about "who we are") is going on, fueled both by individual need and by perceived economic and social necessity. Interesting, too, is the fact that the organization is consciously moving into public relations and marketing activities at the same time that it is trying to expand its market base, maintain and increase jobs, implement self-directed work teams, and foster renewed member commitment to the larger cooperative enterprise (Cheney, 1999).

As these different examples indicate, organizations often communicate with themselves when they address audiences outside the "container" of the organization. Our discussion of the linkages between internal and external organizational communication, however, would be incomplete if it did not simultaneously acknowledge the significant ways in which *internal* communication activities and campaigns can be used for external purposes. Indeed, the organizational world of today is rich with such examples, with some being more apparent than others. In the following paragraphs, we will mention briefly a number of internal–external relationships ranging from unintentional effects of internal communication on external environments to deliberate and planned efforts to communicate externally by way of the organization's own employees (see Christensen, 1997).

Today, many organizations have come to realize that so-called internal matters—their organization of production, their use of resources, their handling of waste, and their treatment of employees—potentially communicate a strong message to the external world. For example, when the largest bank in Denmark, Danske Bank, announced internally that it would henceforth depend more on younger employees than on older ones in terms of its personnel policies, this message was caught by the media and turned into a public case of corporate cynicism, a case that severely damaged the bank's image.

Realizing that affairs *inside* the organization have shaping implications for *outside* communications, a growing number of organizations have begun to think of their employees as customers who, in accordance with the marketing orientation, also need to be satisfied. The concern for employees is not only reflected in public celebrations of internal achievements such as those found in annual reports, in the well-known "employee of the month" plaques (as displayed prominently for visitors of the organization to see), and in public awards ceremonies (e.g., for the most "family-friendly" governmental or third-sector agency, as is now popular in many communities in the United States and elsewhere) but also in efforts to respond to the needs and wants of employees beyond their worklife. While some organizations build fitness and child care centers for employees and families, others offer education and psychological support to spouses and offspring. Because such efforts are often described enthusiastically by the media, they have the potential of becoming part the organization's public relations campaign. But, of course, they can undermine PR efforts if the organization is seen as not living up to its very public standards.

It is not unusual that an organization makes a policy of building its business by building relationships with clients and other constituencies and is explicit in its commentary about this. For example, at Arthur Andersen, a group of accounting and consulting firms, employees are regularly urged to get involved in community organizations as a central part of their business. By doing so, the representatives of the companies can achieve several things at once: tout the accomplishments of the firm, make part of the external environment of the organization part of the organization (by "bring the community in"), and expand their client base.

Among the more direct efforts to communicate externally by way of internal voices we find attempts to use organizational members or employees as advocates or "ambassadors" to outside constituencies. General Motors, for example, consciously developed this strategy in the early 1980s when it integrated internal employee communications and external advertising and public relations. More specifically, the corporation relied on employees—who would receive both internally distributed memos and televised commercials—to spread the word about GM's new emphasis on safety as a foremost concern (Paonessa, 1982). In the case of an enormous organization like this one, employees can, in other words, be seen as a large "PR force" in themselves. Similarly, Gulf States Utilities (an electric and gas utility of Louisiana and Texas that was bought out by Entergy in the mid-1990s) invested a great deal of time and financial resources in communicating with employees in the early 1980s about a controversial nuclear power plant project in the clear hope that they, in turn, would talk with wider audiences about the company's record of safety, efficiency, and good management. In the view of top management, the corporation had over 3,500 potential employee–ambassadors (T. Zorn, personal communication, March 1997).

Clearly, the primary concern behind such efforts is the desire for control, not only of employees but also of the organization's identity, that is, how the organization is commonly represented. And since many organizations have come to believe that the points of contact between its members and the outside world communicate much stronger than well-crafted advertisements, the interest in understanding and managing these points of contact has increased remarkably. In line with Jan Carlzon's (former CEO of Scandinavian Airlines System) notion that every contact with a potential customer represents a "moment of truth" (i.e., a point when the customer decides to continue or discontinue further business with the organization) (Carlzon, 1987), many organizations have begun to think of their employees as fragments of their overall market communication strategy (see also Olins, 1989). Although there is a big difference between the sports organization that tries to foster a sense of internal cohesion and enthusiasm (and hopes that these feelings will be contagious to outsiders and potential supporters of a team) and the organization that develops extensive rules for how its employees can conduct their lives away from work, the same concern is at issue: the organization's identity.

Of course, many efforts at communicating an organization's preferred self-image, such as enhanced "efficiency," are today contradicted by employees' reports to outside "others" of, for example, wasted resources, cases of lavish spending, or cuts in staff that do not include reduced layers of upper administration. This seems to be precisely one of the problems faced by many institutions of higher education in the United States and elsewhere. Added to this is the complication of the public visibility of a campus. If a university complains of drastically limited funding and yet proudly displays new elegant buildings, the public will be understandably skeptical.

While acknowledging such limitations to organizational control of the external communication process, we need to be aware of the many ways in which presumably internal organizational communications emerge as or come to be part of an organization's external communication. Along with the cases of auto-communication mentioned earlier, these examples demonstrate that a clear distinction between internal and external organizational communication is impossible to uphold. Moreover, since the question of identity is so prominent—cutting across different messages often in attempts to link different audiences—we should expect this question to be present in most organizing processes that relate the organization to its surroundings, to shape the organization's outlook, and to affect its way of handling upcoming issues. In the following section, we shall discuss how this self-centeredness may prevent the organization from being as open and responsive toward its surroundings as the disciplines of public relations, marketing, and issue management envision and prescribe.

....

Rethinking Corporate Issue Management: Identity, Self-reference, and Paradox

In contrast to traditional perspectives within issue management, public relations, and marketing, we offer in the next section of this essay a more detailed consideration of the possibility that internal perceptions (identities, expectations, and strategies) strongly affect what problems are "seen," what potential solutions are envisioned, and how the problems are ultimately addressed. The discussion will proceed from a rather straightforward example of how organizational identity affects the diagnosis of issues to notions of self-reference in organizational information management and then to the more complex question of how the organizational approach to the environment may define and shape the issue in question.

Identity as Point of Reference

In their interesting study of the Port Authority of New York and New Jersey, Dutton and Dukerich (1991) illustrate very well how identity is a salient issue closely related to the ways organizations define, diagnose, and respond to problems in their surroundings. Dutton and her colleagues in other studies (e.g., Dutton, 1993; Dutton & Duncan, 1987) defined the diagnosis of strategic issues as an "individual-level, cognitive process through which decision makers form interpretations about organizational events, developments, and trends" (Dutton, 1993, p. 339). However, their interpretation of the Port Authority case necessarily moved them to a larger, social level of analysis. Among other things, Dutton and Dukerich found that "the organization's identity served as an important reference point that members used for assessing the importance of the issue at hand" (p. 543). Specifically, their study showed how much the organization's response to the growing homelessness problem in the 1980s and the organization's internal communication activities at the time were tied up with how organizational members *deliberately imagined* that their organization was being seen by outsiders. Further, Dutton and Dukerich even found that organization members' treatments of homelessness to some degree reflected how they perceived outsiders to be judging their *individual* characters.

While the case analysis of the Port Authority is quite revealing of the extent to which, even over time, an organization's response to an issue may be framed by perceptions of a collective identity, it fails to specify clearly the role of the external audience in shaping and in part constituting the organization's identity. Defining organizational identity in line with Albert and Whetten (1985),

534

Dutton and Dukerich interpreted it as "what organizational members believe to be its central, enduring, and distinctive character" (p. 520). This definition focuses attention on what the organization's members think about their organization and does not address explicitly how the organization *is represented* either in its presumably univocal "corporate voice" or by outsiders (cf. Cheney & Tompkins, 1987). Although Dutton and Dukerich (1991) recognize the importance of outsiders in the construction of an organization's image, their definitions lead them to focus exclusively on the "inside" of the organization. Thus, the "mirror image" in terms of which the Port Authority, according to Dutton and Dukerich, judged and evaluated the issue of homelessness is simply seen as a passive reflection of the perception of the organization's members, not as a product related to social norms and values. In the self-referential perspective that we will introduce below the "external" audience, by contrast, assumes a more central role. Besides being an ideal reference point in terms of which the organization continuously evaluates its own actions (e.g., through opinion polls and market analyses), the "external" audience becomes a social construct, shaped by prevalent managerial discourses and proactive organizations and constantly appealed to in the rhetoric of corporate actors (cf. Black's, 1970, notion of "the second persona").

Information in the Context of Organizational Self-Reference

At the same time that organizations are preoccupied with the issue of identity, they display an almost compulsive concern about their publics: consumers, politicians, interest groups, and so on. This concern—fueled by increased environmental uncertainty and shaped by marketing-inspired management norms—implies that most organizations of today are involved in extensive information-gathering programs and in constant attempts to predict and manage their future (see also Sutcliffe, Chapter 6, 2001). For that reason, contemporary organizations appear more open and sensitive toward their environments than ever before. Ironically, this openness often coexists with organizing practices that tend to close the organization in on itself.

The continuous collection and analysis of information are regarded by both public relations and marketing experts as indispensable for organizations operating in turbulent environments; however, the attitude toward information is not unified or consistent. As Thompson and Wildavsky (1986, p. 275) argue, people and organizations often *do not want* more information (see also Fornell & Westbrook, 1984; Weick & Ashford, Chapter 18, 2001), and when they do, they tend to handle it automatically and rather reductively within established frames of knowledge (see also Manning, 1986, 1988). More specifically, Manning (1986) argues that organizations inevitably translate external data into "idiosyncratic semiotic worlds" that reduce the complexity of the environment to more or less predetermined codes. This way, internal aspects of organizational communication merge in with the dialogue that organizations carry on with their environments.

Often the culture of an organization constitutes a "terministic screen" through which the organization views and evaluates its environment (Burke, 1966; Heath, 1990). This is clearly the case for the successful and well-known toy producer LEGO. For three generations, the culture of the LEGO Corporation has been characterized by a remarkable stability—a stability reflected in explicit corporate values such as tradition, reliability, managed and steady growth, long-term planning, economic independence, and central coordination (Thygesen Poulsen, 1993). To bolster this stability, LEGO has defined itself as being outside more volatile "May-fly markets." Moreover, its product program is standardized to fit a global consumer. Rather than adapting to local differences, the LEGO Corporation is taking the position that LEGO is a product for "everybody" and that it should be available, in more or less the same form, all over the world. To back up this perspective, LEGO is involved in research into the themes of "play" and "creativity" in different cultures and is continuously conducting its own surveys and focus groups to test the universality of its own products. Still, most of these measures are organized to detect and confirm *similarities* across cultures (as found in the second author's field research). While LEGO managers *do* recognize differences between markets, their interests are primarily vested in the issue of "sameness." Information that challenges this position and points in the direction of more *adaptive* strategies in terms of segmentation and communication has often been encountered, both via external and internal sources, but has usually been rejected on the basis of LEGO's standardized global philosophy.

The interesting point here is the way organizations, such as the LEGO Corporation, establish systems of communication that tend to enhance organizational self-perceptions by grounding their own worldview and strategies in external opinions and demands. As initial assumptions are backed up by market research and strategic long-term planning, the relation with the environment tends to form a tightly closed circuit in which the organization confirms the basic elements of its own culture. Obviously, this practice can be quite detrimental to an organization. In his discussion of the asbestos industry and its earlier attempt to present its product as vital to society, Heath (1990) shows how management can be trapped by its own rhetoric and thus become insensitive to certain kinds of information. And clearly, this tendency may be one of the reasons why the LEGO Corporation was less successful for some years—a development that finally made the corporation move into new areas, such as computer technology.

Another important aspect of organizational information handling is related to the fact, explained so well by Feldman and March (1981), that often *the gathering process itself is more important than the actual information collected*. The sheer accumulation of information, in other words, is done by many organizations not so much because they use *all* those bits of data but because the gathering process and the heap assembled make organizations feel comfortable and appear rational to the outside world (see also Meyer & Rowan, 1977; Pfeffer, 1981; Pondy, Frost, Morgan, & Dandridge, 1983; Weick, 1979). Here too, the ritual *is* the message. Interestingly, formalized systems designed to help organizations perceive, analyze, and respond better to strategic issues (SIM systems) may serve similar functions. According to Dutton and Ottensmeyer (1987), "The simple presence of a formal SIM system may convey a sense of organizational potency or potential mastery over [the] environment" that helps preserve an illusion of organizational control (p. 361). In such cases, the rationalistic ritual of information pursuit becomes not only necessary but also sacred.

Through the use of systematic analyses and opinion polls, contemporary organizations demonstrate their adherence to a culture shaped by the marketing ethos. Likewise, by constantly putting out reports, organizations are able to assert their rational participation in the public discourse of the day (e.g., Feldman, 1989). However, as the following quotation suggests, the quest for information has further implications:

The image given by the opinion poll is the image of opinion. It reflects to the perception of the politician a symmetrical image of the political activity that shapes it. As a consumer seduced by the images of products in the economic world, the man whose opinion is polled is also a consumer of images in the political sphere, which he regurgitates in the form of answers to survey questions. (Laufer & Paradeise, 1990, pp. 87–8)

In line with Baudrillard's writings on the masses (e.g., 1983), Laufer and Paradeise's essay on our "marketing democracy" points out that the relentless pursuit of "public opinion" enshrined in politics, public relations, advertising, and front-page surveys—and we could easily substitute "the organization" for "the politician" in the above passage—has created a world of discourse with its own internal dynamics. The talk about opinion polls that measure everything from political preferences to fashion consciousness engages everyone today in the sense that all are now able to participate in that discursive world. Having been polled on nearly every conceivable issue or preference, "the masses," according to Laufer and Paradeise, know they should be ready to express opinions on cue. Further, since the polling institution, according to Baudrillard (1983), has become a simulation process characterized by mutual seduction, the idea of uncovering or controlling a true or deep "public opinion" becomes rather elusive (see Christensen & Cheney, in press). By "communicating" systematically with selected audiences, organizations promote the elusive ideal of "public opinion" while presuming to identify and respond to it. In this process, the message or text gives way to a metatext that communicates to

the corporate culture of today its most basic myths about democracy, communication, and identity.

As a consequence, the "dialogue" between organizations and their environments takes on ironic, new meanings. In line with developments within self-
referential systems (e.g., Luhmann, 1990; see also Maturana & Varela, 1980), it
can be argued that organizations communicate with their "environment" not
only to exchange information but also, and quite significantly, to maintain
themselves and confirm their identities. As Maturana and Varela (1980) contend, identity is the primary issue of all living systems, an issue handled
through self-referential communication, that is, communication through which
the system specifies its own environment and the information necessary to
maintain itself. As we have indicated above, organizations often seem to collect
and handle information in such a self-referential manner. Of course, in a social
system this tendency toward self-referential closure is modified by the need
for external legitimacy and accreditation (e.g., Berg & Gagliardi, 1985; see also
Meyer & Rowan, 1977). But this does not ensure the kind of openness prescribed by prevailing theories within public relations, marketing, and issue
management. Since the preoccupation with *external* data often reflects an
adherence to a certain management *discourse* rather than a sincere interest in
information, organizations may still function as self-referentially closed even
within an apparently open communication structure (cf. Luhmann, 1990).

Much organizational communication thus can be described as self-referential
communication or auto-communication. And organizations often imitate one
another in their attempts to be "cutting edge." As the management of corporate communications becomes more strategic—that is, proactive, integrative,
and oriented toward long-term goals—this tendency is accentuated further.

The Paradox of Proactivity

In the corporate world of today, issue management reaches far beyond the
practice of collecting and responding to information. As Cheney and Vibbert
(1987) explain with respect to transformations in public relations activity and
research since the mid-1970s, this practice has become more aggressive, more
forward looking, more proactive (see also Chase, 1984; Hainsworth & Meng,
1988; Heath, 1988).

In everyday managerial usage, *proactivity* has come to refer to a more or less
unspecified set of nondefensive or nonreactive practices through which organizations handle their relations with the external world. Instead of waiting for
threats and opportunities to become manifest imperatives, the proactive organization attempts to influence and shape external developments in ways considered favorable in terms of its own aspirations. Organizations are clearly

displaying proactive behavior when they seek to avoid being "caught by surprise" by demands or pressures from the environment: for example, new rules of trade within the European Union, increasing regulation of industrial waste, rising quality standards, or changing demands by labor unions. While this idea of *non-reactivity* certainly grasps an important aspect of the activities of contemporary organizations, the wide-ranging implications of proactive management actually necessitate a deeper understanding of the phenomenon.

Ironically, the proactive stance can be seen as a creative *reaction* to the increasing turbulence and the related reduction of predictability experienced in the market since the late 1950s (see Heath & Cousino, 1990). Within the fields of marketing and strategic management, these developments gave birth to a more prescriptive theory-building effort simultaneously concerned with the consumer or the public and the possibilities of extending managerial control through strategy and long-term planning. Together these considerations constitute what we have described above as the "marketing ethos." With its ambiguous norm of seeking to serve market needs and wants *before* these are expressed and objectified, the marketing orientation *is* largely proactive. As one marketing manager told the second author in a personal interview, the best strategy is "being at the forefront of the development we expect."

Being proactive means being involved in the definition and construction (albeit not necessarily control) of reality. Proactivity, thus, is implicated by Weick's (1979) notion of enactment whereby an organization's actions to a significant extent define the environments to which it is able to attend (e.g., governmental economic statistics, consultants' forecasts, the norms of competitors). By projecting internal concerns, intentions, and strategies onto its surroundings, the organization creates or simulates its own "environment" and, this way, sets the stage for its own future acts and sensemaking. But, because organizations are not always realizing just how narrowly they circumscribe their environments, this process can often be rather unintentional. In other cases, the process is largely intended through strong, controlling efforts to define the situation in self-serving and self-referential terms.

The relation between enactment and proactivity, thus, needs to be specified further. In contrast to Daft and Weick's (1984) often-cited model of organizations as interpretation systems, we need to emphasize that also apparently passive or reactive behaviors fall within the frame of enactment (cf. Weick, 1979). Interestingly, routine and largely reactive actions, such as explaining corporate performance to stockholders in annual reports, show the power of *defining* the situation. The "competitive edge" of the organization can be credited when the organization is successful, yet "fierce competition" from others can be blamed for sagging profits during the next year (Conrad, 1993). Whether the organization takes on the role of the accidental viewer, the passive detective, the active discoverer, or the experimenting doer (Daft & Weick, 1984), its ways of relating to its surroundings will always influence the definition of the situation in question. That is to say, diverse sorts of organizational "intentions" can lead to similar results. The differences among these different "enactment postures," however, are not trivial. Through *proactive* programs, the enactment dimension of organizational behavior becomes explicit and intensified to the extent of making the very enactment of the "environment" *itself* the primary goal of the management process. And clearly, organizations *have* become very self-conscious about their stances vis-à-vis the larger environment and about the "world" they are helping to bring into being. For example, as Bostdorff and Vibbert (1994) explain, large corporations and other organizations now routinely try to promote certain values (e.g., particular interpretations of "freedom") that they can then use to ground future persuasive campaigns.

What is at stake in this strategic approach is the desire for control. And often much of this activity is designed to get citizens as well as consumers to identify with some level of the organization. Whether the strategy involved can be characterized as "catalytic" or "dynamic"—that is, more or less offensive and assertive (Crable & Vibbert, 1985; cf. Jones & Chase, 1979)—its aim is to determine not only strategic outcomes but also the very *conditions* for business, including those of communication and competition themselves. Although the proactive approach claims to take its point of departure in the market or the larger environment, its preoccupation with *internal* aspirations and considerations makes proactivity in fact a rather self-centered enterprise. As Crable and Vibbert (1985) point out, an organization that wants to influence the development of issues needs continuously to "assess what it is, what it wants to be, and how the environment could be altered to the advantage of the organization" (p. 10).

This is not to suggest that various publics (e.g., activist groups, stockholders, governments, competitors, and communities) are insignificant in the process of shaping issues and images of major corporations. Such groups often make powerful claims on the corporate actor—claims that sometimes force organizations to reconsider fundamentally their activities (e.g., Heath, 1988). However, this is most often the case when organizations respond reactively to changes in their larger environments. The more proactively such changes are managed, the more the direct role of the public is circumscribed by the organization through determining, for example, which voices from the outside deserve a hearing or how different opinions should be prioritized. Further, as Sutcliffe (2001) points out, simply knowing *what* issues publics or stakeholders are concerned with does not help us understand *how* these issues are perceived, defined, and managed by the organization. Although many issues originate and unfold in environments regarded as external to the organization, the process of managing such issues strategically brings the organization and its specific outlook into the process (see also Kaldor, 1971; Smircich & Stubbart, 1985).

Issue Management as Proactive Communication

Through the pursuit of understanding and managing within a complex and turbulent environment of issues, organizations often establish the symbolic systems to which they are able to respond (Weick, 1979). This is especially the case when organizations are managed proactively.

Vibbert and Bostdorff (1993) offer an excellent example of corporate pro-activity, spanning the private and public sectors, in their analysis of the behavior of the U.S. insurance industry during the so-called lawsuit crisis of the mid-1980s. In that instance, the Insurance Information Institute (III), an industrywide lobbying organization, employed a series of visible ads to explain rising insurance costs largely in terms of a litigation-crazy society and the corporate need for protective insurance. As the authors observe, there had been only a vague sense expressed in public discourse about something like a lawsuit "crisis." Yet the III apparently succeeded in locating the problem within the institution of the legal system, thereby defining a complex situation in polarizing terms, and clearly placing blame outside its own institutional borders.

It may be argued, of course, that the organizational rhetor in the case analyzed by Vibbert and Bostdorff (1993) not only defined the problem but also *identified* the problem in the first place, a strategy that could not have worked, rhetorically speaking, had the organization not "tapped into" some sort of suspicion or resentment already held by a significant segment of the citizenry. Whether this was exactly the case or not, Vibbert and Bostdorff's (1993) study clearly points out the way in which "crises" often emerge through being declared, defined, and interpreted by proactive corporate actors. This, of course, can be seen in a variety of discursive domains: political, economic, and social (see also Bostdorff's, 1994, treatment of the rhetorical shaping of various crises by U.S. presidents). To succeed in proclaiming a situation as urgent and especially to identify blameworthy parties is to mobilize opinion and responses. Conversely, if the reaction of an organizational rhetor comes to be viewed as insufficient or as minimizing a generally acknowledged crisis, then organizational credibility is threatened. This was indeed the case for the Exxon Corporation, following the Valdez oil spill in Alaska in 1989, as the corporation tried to define the disaster as an individual rather than a policy-related problem, focusing blame on the ship's captain and diverting attention away from potential regulations for strengthening ships' hulls (cf. Benson, 1988, on the Tylenol case; Ice, 1991, on the Bhopal disaster; and Benoit, 1995, on the image-restoration strategies of Sears).

What Vibbert and Bostdorff's (1993) analysis fails to describe is the relationship between issues and identities and the growing interrelatedness of internal and external organizational communication. In the self-referential perspective laid out in this chapter, the rhetorical efforts of the III would be described not only in terms of its presumed effects on an external audience but also as an auto-communicative ritual that helps constitute the rhetor itself and its identity in an emergent environment. The self-referential view, however, would include another important dimension. While a proactive management of issues may allow organizations (large, powerful organizations in particular) to define rhetorically their own discursive domain, it makes it possible for such organizations to determine the appropriate responses to the issues in question. And clearly, the III did have its own solution ready: raising insurance premiums. When organizational responses come, as some issue management scholars recommend (e.g., Chase, 1984), *before* the opinions by key audiences are crystallized, the organization has a tendency to close itself off from the larger, extraorganizational environment and communicate mainly within its own symbolic universe.

In proactive management, organizational responses may, in other words, often precede environmental stimuli. Still, the notion of a "response" suggests that even the proactive organization is in *dialogue* with its stakeholders. This assumption, however, needs to be modified. When organizations operate within a discursive universe enacted, in large part, through proactive strategies, they are significantly talking to themselves. The fact that many issues are not controlled, or controllable, by the organization (e.g., Hainsworth & Meng, 1988) does not undermine the logic of this particular argument: that organizations, when responding to their own enactments of an issue, are often communicating basically with themselves about their own expectations and concerns. Self-referential communication should thus be seen as a compelling tendency of issue management. This is clearly the case in the following example, which illustrates all the central dimensions discussed above: proactivity, auto-communication, and accordingly, identity.

The medical corporation Novo Nordisk (based in Denmark but with offices, manufacturing facilities, and associated companies in numerous countries) has become well known for its proactive stance on the "green" issue. In the early 1990s, the corporation issued a 40-page report on this issue, including a detailed evaluation of its own contributions to pollution. To disarm possible criticism, Novo Nordisk furthermore chose to let a well-known environmentalist evaluate publicly the report and the corrective measures taken. Managers within Novo Nordisk explained the report with reference to the growing environmental consciousness among investors and customers since the 1980s. While this influence is highly significant in the corporate world of today, the step taken by Novo Nordisk was proactive and not a reaction to *specific* environmental demands. The proactive strategy of Novo Nordisk has several interesting dimensions that will be discussed below.

As long as relatively few organizations are issuing comprehensive evaluations of themselves, those that *do* appear more responsible, internally as well as externally. And indeed, Novo Nordisk is now being cited widely as a *responsible organization* concerned about its employees, the local community, and the environment in general: an image that instills a sense of pride and belongingness among its employees and attracts new qualified personnel. The fact that this image or reputation most often is reproduced by people who have *not* read the report tells us a great deal about the communication environment of today. When the social space is saturated with corporate communication asserting social righteousness, only the indirect or more unusual messages are able to stand out and attract attention. And the report issued by Novo Nordisk is indeed communication. Although the report does reflect real changes in the *behavior* of the organization, including a number of internal measures taken to reduce pollution, it is first of all an elaborate piece of communication: a meta-text that tells, by its very existence, the general public including Novo Nordisk's own members that this organization is willing to let action follow words.

And the report *did* commit Novo Nordisk to a number of specific goals. With its "eco-productivity index"—a notion that divides the amount of sold goods with the amount of raw materials, energy, water, and packing used in the production process—the report prescribed quite specifically how pollution was to be reduced: as an ongoing increase in the eco-productivity index. This self-imposed prescription is not easy to fulfill and puts a heavy burden on all departments of the organization. Interestingly, the proactive introduction of this index allows Novo Nordisk to define itself the measures necessary to reduce its pollution. This has tremendous advantages for the organization. Instead of responding *re*actively to environmental issues as they "pop up" in its surroundings, Novo Nordisk defines and shapes proactively the issues that it addresses: a strategy that allows it to operate in a more familiar universe defined, in large part, by its own actions.

Such measures cannot stand alone but require careful follow-up advocacy (see, e.g., Arrington & Sawaya, 1984) in many different fora: in the local community, the European Union, international environmental organizations, and the media. In the present case, the first steps to make environmental reporting compulsory in the chemical industry have already been taken by an industrial association of which Novo Nordisk is a prominent member. Further, Novo Nordisk carefully cultivates its relations with different publics by hosting regular meetings with neighbors, journalists, investors, insurance companies, employees, environmental groups, and politicians. In line with Grunig's (1992, in press) notion of "symmetrical public relations," these efforts seem to demonstrate a sincere interest on the part of Novo Nordisk in establishing a two-way dialogue with affected and relevant publics. Without rejecting this interpretation, it should be added that these relations also serve the very important function of making sure that the change measures imposed proactively by Novo Nordisk on itself in fact become the *future standards* of social responsibility. Since the organization's relations with these mentioned groups are very close—several powerful environmental groups publicly express their admiration of Novo Nordisk—there is a great likelihood that Novo Nordisk will be successful in its efforts to shape future discussions on and standards of social responsibility.

In such cases, it is tempting to suggest that the relations are symbiotic and that the communication involved tends to establish a relatively closed universe of mutual understanding, not easily accessible to other publics. At least, this is an interesting possibility that any critical perspective on public relations needs to consider seriously. When operating effectively within this network, the organization is able to communicate with itself and, this way, confirm its up-to-date outlook and its identity as a responsible organization ready to take substantial measures to protect the environment.

Similar communication systems are being developed these days by many different kinds of organizations. German-based Bayer Corporation, for example, has established a communication center, BayKomm, that "actively seeks frank and open dialogue with the public about problems and questions relating to the chemical industry" (brochure from Bayer AG, Leverkusen, Germany). In its promotional material, Bayer describes BayKomm as "an important interface between the company and society." In BayKomm, the brochure continues, "Bayer tries to place dialogue with the public on a broad footing. BayKomm is designed as a bridge between Bayer and the outside world, between the chemical industry and society." For most of the public, however, the "communication" with Bayer is restricted to guided tours of the impressive BayKomm center. The professional dialogues and discussion rounds that BayKomm initiates are usually organized around selected *strategic* publics. Also, the topics discussed in these communication fora are not open questions of general interest but topics delimited to issues of strategic relevance to Bayer, such as recycling and gene technology. While such issues are often important to the general public as well, their shaping by Bayer in this particular setting implies that the dialogue may not be as open and symmetrical as it first appears.

Communication scholars who study organizations and their interactions with the environment, thus, should be aware of the possible limitations to the ideals of dialogue and responsiveness advocated so strongly today within public relations, marketing, and issue management. Such awareness is crucial, especially when we note that the restrictions on dialogue and responsiveness are not always intentional on the part of the organization. While many organizations today clearly hope to control their environment better by being proactive and at the forefront of new trends, the tendencies for proactive organizations to develop closed circuits of auto-communication may well be unintended consequences.

Conclusion: Public Discourse, Ethics, and Democracy

As this essay has argued, in an unstable symbolic world issue management becomes closely tied up with the question of organizational identity. Following our description of today's communication environment, we commented on the preoccupation with "identities" in the public discourse of contemporary organizations. Specifically, we observed how identity and image have become perhaps the central issue (or set of issues) for many organizations today as they "talk" about themselves in a variety of media and communication arenas.

A central and overarching theme of this essay concerns the blurring of domains of organizational communication. We have illustrated how so-called external communication activities of contemporary organizations must be seen as closely connected to those presumably inside the container of the organization. Moreover, we have presented theoretical, historical, and practical reasons for establishing such a linkage both more strongly and more clearly in the scholarship of organizational communication. Finally, we have demonstrated how this complex communication situation is structuring the way organizations of today perceive and manage issues *as* identities, and identities as issues. In the remaining part of this chapter, we will summarize major points of the essay in the form of paradoxes, indicate a number of ethical concerns, and finally, point out some implications for research and practice.

Summary

To illustrate the complexity of managing issues in today's corporate world, it is useful to think of the communication involved as being based on a set of interrelated paradoxes. Besides summarizing and synthesizing the major points in the essay, it is our hope that these paradoxes will point the reader beyond the present text and stimulate further thinking within the field.

1. Because internal and external aspects of organizing are closely intertwined, communication that seems to be directed toward others may actually be auto-communicative, that is, directed primarily toward the self.

2. As a consequence of the "explosion" of information and communication that we are witnessing—an explosion that, ironically, seems to imply an *implosion* among receivers (see Baudrillard, 1983)—any corporate identity becomes a fragile construction whose uniqueness is entirely dependent on *other* identities and whose persistence over time requires even more communication.

545

3. Because proactive management, as we have indicated, has a *reactive* basis in the consumer unrest of the 1960s and beyond, the environments enacted through proactive corporate measures are rhetorically described as something "out there" to which the organization needs to adapt. However, within the self-referential perspective laid out in this essay, it can be argued that what is adapted (to) is in fact "the public," operating largely in a discursive universe defined by large corporate actors.

4. The kind of openness displayed by contemporary marketing-oriented organizations in their relentless pursuit of "the will of the market" may, in other words, represent a certain kind of organizational closedness. Indeed, as Luhmann (1990) has explained so well, identity—for an individual or for a group—rests on the tension between *openness* and *closedness* (cf. Morin, 1986). Too open a system has no identity at all, no possibility for being distinguished from the larger universe. Too closed a system, in contrast, has no possibility for adaptation, and in its extreme form, ceases to have any self-reference when it has no reference to the larger world. To the extent that these terms are still meaningful descriptors of organizational communication practices, openness and closedness should be seen in dialectical interdependence.

Implications for Theory and Practice

In closing, the concepts and principles discussed in this essay present enormous practical and ethical challenges for analysts and practitioners in the broad and diverse field of organizational communication. We do not mean to suggest, however, that "there's *no* way through" the ambiguities, paradoxes, and circularities characterizing communication practices today. Below we will sketch out some possible implications based on the major points of the essay.

First, it is important to realize that there is great practical value in being *aware* of the features of an expanding yet constraining universe of communication. Awareness of the set of issues described here does not liberate the organizational message maker or critic from that universe, but it does give him or her certain places to stand, however contingent or local they may be, in making sense of what's going on and in saying something meaningful and perhaps helpful about it. Within the communication context we depict, coping becomes a reasonably high-minded goal. This does not imply that there cease to be opportunities for real betterment in the organization's relations with individuals and with the larger society. Clearly, the modernist confidence in advancing the human condition must be tempered and modified by postmodern understandings of the limits of all of our rational pursuits but that does not negate our noblest goals (such as vibrant democracy) as points of reference that are occasionally approachable and that keep us from allowing society to become worse than it would be without such images of progress. We simply must remember that our very own creations, symbols, can play games with us, such that today's vision of democracy through marketing can become tomorrow's antidemocratic or pseudo-democratic institution.

Second, and more specifically, there are a number of important implications related to the observation that internal and external aspects of organizational communication are interrelated. If traditional, internal communication is relevant to external audiences—and this may often be the case in a world that expects organizations to be socially and environmentally responsible—scholars and practitioners need to understand much organizational communication as market-related communication, that is, as communication with the potential of shaping opinions and actions among consumers and other publics. If externally directed messages have the strongest impact on the organization and its members—and, as our discussion and examples suggest, this is often the case—we may need to think of marketing communications and public relations as an integral part of the organizational discourse. Whereas the former observation logically implies that organizational communications and relations should be evaluated not only as internal phenomena but also in terms of their impact on external audiences (an idea implicit in some approaches to public relations; see, e.g., Grunig, 1992, in press), the consequences of the latter observation are, as we shall indicate below, more complex.

As we have already pointed out, marketing, strategy, and issue management justify themselves primarily through their claimed sensitivity to symbols, trends, and developments in markets and other public arenas. To acknowledge fully their *internal* significance, these disciplines need to develop and widen their sensitivity to cover also an understanding of the organization and its own central symbols and values. This kind of sensitivity makes it possible to integrate external communications with such internal concerns as, for example, the need to mobilize human resources (Berg, 1986). Clearly, such integrative efforts are necessary for all kinds of organizations that wish to operate consistently with their goals. Moreover, since organizational symbols and values to a great extent determine what environments organizations are able to "see," this latter kind of sensitivity or *self-reflectivity* may sometimes be more important than collecting information about external trends. To know the environment better, organizations should, in other words, try to know themselves (cf. Weick & Ashford, 2001). This point is probably the most important practical implication of the self-referential perspective laid out in this chapter. Scholars and practitioners within the field of what traditionally is thought of as external communication need to learn to communicate consciously with themselves and their organizations about their most central meanings. These meanings include internal images and perceptions of what the organization "is," key symbols of pride and motivation, basic assumptions about relevant publics and environments, established procedures and routines involved in opinion polls and market analyses, tacit norms for interpreting data, briefing procedures and information exchange between departments, and more generally, perceptions of external information throughout the organization (see Christensen, 1994b). Being self-reflective and sensitive to such dimensions thus means trying to be aware of one's own auto-communicative predispositions. Only through such exercise can organizations hope to counter the self-referential tendencies described in this essay.

Third and finally, we are aware that our description of current communication and management practices can have negative consequences in the sense that some organizations, for strategic reasons, may choose to develop communication systems of a more closed and self-referential nature. Organizations, for example, that wish to *appear* open and responsive may find inspiration in our discussion of proactive organizing practices and the possibility of "integrating" stakeholders through the use of focused strategic dialogues. Although such *as-if dialogues* are not a new phenomenon confined to the corporate world but are part of our experience with politics, their present forms do present a real danger to our ideals of participation and democracy. Still, such worries should not keep us from describing, discussing, and critiquing significant tendencies in the corporate world—whether they conform to our ideals or not.

The tendencies discussed in this chapter indicate a great potential for changing the scope and outlook of a number of disciplines such as organizational theory, communication, marketing, management strategy, and issue management. Clearly, the greatest challenge for the organizational communication researcher is to develop new and meaningful concepts able to reflect the real complexity of contemporary organizational communication, that is, concepts that are not confined within traditional dichotomies between "open" and "closed," "internal" and "external," "formal" and "informal," and so forth. Thus, we need to ask more probing questions about the relationships between various audiences and publics with organizations that would presume to speak to them. For example: How much openness is there in corporate communications that are seemingly directed outward? How much democracy is there even in debates and discussions that appear to include divergent parties and stakeholders? And how much concern is there on the part of people for corporate identities and other messages that organizations spend so much time, energy, and money on (Cheney & Christensen, 2001; Christensen & Cheney, in press)? At the same time, of course, each researcher must make decisions about "where to stand" with respect to these phenomena. What practical–epistemological position to take, whether or not to seek social change, and what sort of ethical principles to develop represent perhaps the most crucial decisions.

Note

We wish to thank Craig Carroll, James E. Grunig, Robert L. Heath, Fredric M. Jablin, Linda L. Putnam, Juliet Roper, Phillip K. Tompkins, Sarah Tracy, and Ted Zorn for their helpful comments on earlier drafts of this chapter.

1. We would like to circumnavigate the *"This* is postmodernity?" discussion by arguing simply that the point is not to label contemporary society but rather to understand it better. While we recognize the fact that trends brought together under the rubric of postmodernism have influenced a whole range of academic disciplines from literature to physics and that debates continue to rage over what each discipline "looks like" from a postmodernist perspective, the point of this essay is not to take sides in this debate.

References

Achrol, R. S. (1991, October). Evolution of the marketing organization: New forms for turbulent environments. *Journal of Marketing, 55*, 77–93.

Adams, J. S. (1976). The structure and dynamics of behavior in organizational boundary roles. In M. D. Dunnette (Ed.), *Handbook of industrial and organizational psychology* (pp. 1175–1199). Chicago: Rand McNally.

Albert, S., & Whetten, D. A. (1985). Organizational identity. In B. M. Staw & L. L. Cummings (Eds.), *Research in organizational behavior* (Vol. 7, pp. 263–295). Greenwich, CT: JAI.

Allen, M. W., & Caillouet, R. H. (1994). Legitimation endeavours: Impression management strategies used by an organization in crisis. *Communication Monographs, 41*, 44–62.

Alvesson, M. (1990). Organization: From substance to image? *Organization Studies, 11*(3), 373–394.

Arndt, J. (1979). Toward a concept of domesticated markets. *Journal of Marketing, 43*, 69–75.

Arrington, C. B., & Sawaya, R. N. (1984). Managing public affairs: Issues management in an uncertain environment. *California Management Review, 26*(4), 148–160.

Ashforth, B. E., & Mael, F. A. (1996). Organizational identity and strategy as a context for the individual. *Advances in Strategic Management, 13*, 19–64.

Bailey, W. (1996). Corporate/commercial speech and the marketplace first amendment: Whose right was it anyway? *Southern Communication Journal, 61*, 122–138.

Bakhtin, M. (1981). *The dialogic imagination: Four essays* (C. Emerson & M. Holquist, Trans., M. Holquist, Ed.). Austin: University of Texas Press.

Baudrillard, J. (1981). *Simulacres et simulation.* Paris: Galilée.

Baudrillard, J. (1983). *In the shadow of the silent majorities.* New York City: Semiotext(e).

Baudrillard, J. (1988). *The ecstasy of communication.* New York: Semiotext(e).

Benoit, W. L. (1995). Sears' repair of its auto service image: Image restoration discourse in the corporate sector. *Communication Studies, 46*, 89–105.

Benson, J. A. (1988). Crisis revisited: An analysis of strategies used by Tylenol in the second tampering episode. *Central States Speech Journal, 39*, 28–36.

Berg, P. O. (1986). Symbolic management of human resources. *Human Resource Management,* 25, 557–579.

Berg, P. O., & Gagliardi, P. (1985). *Corporate images: A symbolic perspective of the organization-environment interface.* Paper presented at the SCOS Corporate Images conference, Antibes, France.

Berg, P. O., & Kreiner, K. (1990). Corporate architecture: Turning physical settings into symbolic resources. In P. Gagliardi (Ed.), *Symbols and artifacts: Views of the corporate landscape* (pp. 41–67). Berlin: Walter de Gruyter.

Black, E. (1970). The second persona. *Quarterly Journal of Speech,* 56, 109–119.

Bostdorff, D. M. (1994). *The presidency and rhetoric of foreign crisis.* Colombia: University of South Carolina Press.

Bostdorff, D. M., & Vibbert, S. L. (1994). Values advocacy: Enhancing organizational images, deflecting public criticism, and grounding future arguments. *Public Relations Review,* 20, 141–158.

Bouchet, D. (1991). Advertising as a specific form of communication. In H. H. Larsen, D. G. Mick, & C. Alsted (Eds.), *Marketing and semiotics* (pp. 31–51). Copenhagen, Denmark: Handelshøjskolens Forlag.

Broms, H., & Gahmberg, H. (1983). Communication to self in organizations and cultures. *Administrative Science Quarterly,* 28, 482–495.

Broom, G. M., Lauzen, M. M., & Tucker, K. (1991). Public relations and marketing: Dividing the conceptual domain and operational turf. *Public Relations Review,* 17(3), 219–225.

Bryant, D. (1953). Rhetoric: Its functions and its scope. *Quarterly Journal of Speech,* 39, 401–424.

Burke, K. (1966). *Language as symbolic action.* Berkeley: University of California Press.

Carlzon, J. (1987). *Moments of truth.* Cambridge, MA: Ballinger.

Carroll, C. (1995). Rearticulating organizational identity: Exploring corporate images and employee identification. *Management Learning,* 26, 467–486.

Chase, W. H. (1984). *Issue management: Origins of the future.* Stamford, CT: Issue Action.

Cheney, G. (1983a). On the various and changing meanings of organizational membership: A field study of organizational identification. *Communication Monographs,* 50, 343–363.

Cheney, G. (1983b). The rhetoric of identification and the study of organizational communication. *Quarterly Journal of Speech,* 69, 143–158.

Cheney, G. (1991). *Rhetoric in an organizational society: Managing multiple identities.* Columbia: University of South Carolina Press.

Cheney, G. (1992). The corporate person (re)presents itself. In E. L. Toth & R. L. Heath (Eds.), *Rhetorical and critical approaches to public relations* (pp. 165–184). Hillsdale, NJ: Lawrence Erlbaum.

Cheney, G. (1999). *Values at work: Employee participation meets market pressure at Mondragón.* Ithaca, NY: Cornell University Press.

Cheney, G. (in press). Arguing about the place of values and ethics in market-oriented discourses of today. In S. Goldzwig & P. Sullivan (Eds.), *New approaches to rhetoric for the 21st century.* East Lansing: Michigan State University Press.

Cheney, G., Block, B. L., & Gordon, B. S. (1986). Perceptions of innovativeness and communication about innovations: A study of three types of service organizations. *Communication Quarterly,* 34, 213–230.

Cheney, G., & Christensen, L. T. (2001). Public relations as contested terrain: A critical response. In R. L. Heath & G. Vazquez (Eds.), *Handbook of public relations* (pp. 167–182). Thousand Oaks, CA: Sage.

Cheney, G., & Dionisopoulos, G. (1989). Public relations? No, relations with publics: A rhetorical-organizational approach to contemporary corporate communications. In C. H. Botan & V. Hazleton, Jr. (Eds.), *Public relations theory* (pp. 135–158). Hillsdale, NJ: Lawrence Erlbaum.

Cheney, G., & Frenette, G. (1993). Persuasion and organization: Values, logics and accounts in contemporary corporate public discourse. In C. Conrad (Ed.), *The ethical nexus* (pp. 49–74). Norwood, NJ: Ablex.

Cheney, G., & Tompkins, P. K. (1987). Coming to terms with organizational identification and commitment. *Central States Speech Journal, 38*, 1–15.

Cheney, G., & Vibbert, S. L. (1987). Corporate discourse: Public relations and issue management. In F. M. Jablin, L. L. Putnam, K. H. Roberts, & L. H. Porter (Eds.), *Handbook of organizational communication: An interdisciplinary perspective* (pp. 165–194). Newbury Park, CA: Sage.

Christensen, L. T. (1994a). *Markedskommunikation som organiseringsmade. En kulturteoretisk analyse.* Copenhagen, Denmark: Akademisk Forlag.

Christensen, L. T. (1994b, November). Talking to ourselves: Management through auto-communication. *MTC Kontakten* (Jubilæumstidsskrift), pp. 32–37.

Christensen, L. T. (1995a). Buffering organizational identity in the marketing culture. *Organization Studies, 16*(4), 651–672.

Christensen, L. T. (1995b). Fra kosmetisk markedsføring til integreret strategi. Reflektioner over den "grønne" kommunikation. In J. P. Ulhøi (Ed.), *Virksomhedens miljøhåndbog* (No. 5, pp. 1–10). Copenhagen, Denmark: Børsens Forlag.

Christensen, L. T. (1996, February). *Communicating flexibility: A critical investigation of the discourse of organizational change.* Paper presented at the Organizational Communication and Change: Challenges in the Next Century conference, Austin, Texas.

Christensen, L. T. (1997, May). Marketing as auto-communication. *Consumption, Markets & Culture, 3,* 197–227.

Christensen, L. T., & Cheney, G. (1994). Articulating identity in an organizational age. In S. A. Deetz (Ed.), *Communication yearbook 17* (pp. 222–235). Thousand Oaks, CA: Sage.

Christensen, L. T., & Cheney, G. (in press). Self-absorption and self-seduction in the corporate identity game. In M. Schultz, M. J. Hatch, & M. H. Larsen (Eds.), *The expressive corporation.* Oxford, UK: Oxford University Press.

Christensen, L. T., & Jones, R. (1996). En symmestrisk dialog om miljøspørgsmålet? En kritisk analyse af nye dialogformer mellem virksomheder og forbrugere. In J. P. Ulhøi & H. Madsen (Eds.), *Miljøledelse—Tanker, erfaringer og visioner* (pp. 151–167). Copenhagen, Denmark: Børsens Forlag.

Coleman, J. S. (1974). *Power and the structure of society.* New York: Norton.

Conrad, C. (Ed.). (1993). *The ethical nexus.* Norwood, NJ: Ablex.

Cooley, C. H. (1983). *Human nature and the social order.* New Brunswick, NJ: Transaction Books.

Cooren, F. (2000). *The organizing property of communication.* Amsterdam, the Netherlands: John Benjamins.

Coupland, J. (1996). Dating advertisements: Discourse of the commodified self. *Discourse & Society, 7,* 187–208.

Crable, R. E., & Vibbert, S. L. (1983). Mobil's epideictic advocacy: "Observations" of Prometheus-bound. *Communication Monographs, 50*, 380–394.

Crable, R. E., & Vibbert, S. L. (1985). Managing issues and influencing public policy. *Public Relations Review, 11*, 3–16.

Crable, R. E., & Vibbert, S. L. (1986). *Public relations as communication management*. Edina, MN: Bellweather.

Czarniawska-Joerges, B. (1994). Narratives of individual and organizational identities. In S. A. Deetz (Ed.), *Communication yearbook 17* (pp. 193–221). Thousand Oaks, CA: Sage.

Daft, R. L., & Weick, K. E. (1984). Toward a model of organizations as interpretation systems. *Academy of Management Review, 9*, 284–295.

Davis, K., & Blomstrom, R. L. (1971). *Business, society, and environment: Social power and social response* (2nd ed.). New York: McGraw-Hill.

Deetz, S. (1995). *Transforming communication, transforming business: Building responsive and responsible workplaces*. Cresskill, NJ: Hampton.

DeLozier, M. W. (1976). *The marketing communication process*. New York: McGraw-Hill.

Dervin, B. (1994). Information ↔ democracy. *Journal of the American Society of Information Science, 45*, 369–385.

Donaldson, T. (1989). *The ethics of international business*. New York: Oxford University Press.

Douglas, M. (1986). *How institutions think*. Syracuse, NY: Syracuse University Press.

Dutton, J. E. (1993). Interpretations on automatic: A different view of strategic issue diagnosis. *Journal of Management Studies, 30*, 339–357.

Dutton, J. E., & Dukerich, J. M. (1991). Keeping an eye on the mirror: Image and identity in organizational adaptation. *Academy of Management Journal, 34*, 517–554.

Dutton, J. E., & Duncan, R. (1987). The creation of momentum for change through the process of strategic issue diagnosis. *Strategic Management Journal, 8*, 279–295.

Dutton, J. E., & Ottensmeyer, E. (1987). Strategic issue management systems: Forms, functions, and contexts. *Academy of Management Review, 12, 2*, 355–365.

Dyer, G. (1990). *Advertising as communication*. London: Routledge.

Ewing, R. P. (1987). *Managing the new bottom-line: Issues management for senior executives*. Homewood, IL: Dow Jones-Irwin.

Fairclough, N. (1993). Critical discourse analysis and the marketization of public discourse: The universities. *Discourse & Society, 4*, 133–168.

Feldman, M. (1989). *Order without design: Information production and policy making*. Stanford, CA: Stanford University Press.

Feldman, M. S., & March, J. G. (1981). Information in organizations as signal and symbol. *Administrative Science Quarterly, 26*, 171–186.

Fennell, G. (1987). A radical agenda for marketing science: Represent the marketing concept! In A. F. Firat, N. Dholakia, & R. P. Bagozzi (Eds.), *Philosophical and radical thought in marketing* (pp. 289–306). Lexington, MA: D. C. Heath.

Fine, S. H. (1981). *The marketing of ideas and social issues*. New York: Praeger.

Finet, D. (1994). Sociopolitical consequences of organizational expression. *Journal of Communication, 44*, 114–131.

Finet, D., & Bal, V. (1995, May). *The rhetoric of ethics and economics in organizational discourse*. Paper presented at the annual meeting of the International Communication Association, Albuquerque, NM.

Fornell, C., & Westbrook, R. A. (1984). The vicious cycle of consumer complaints. *Journal of Marketing, 48*, 68–78.

Fox, K., & Kotler, P. (1980). The marketing of social causes: The first 10 years. *Journal of Marketing, 44*, 24–33.

Gallagher, V. J. (1990, November). *Symbolic action, culture, permanence and change: A critical addition to organizational studies*. Paper presented at the Speech Communication Association convention, Chicago.

Gay, P. du. (1996). *Consumption and identity at work*. London: Sage.

Gay, P. du., & Salaman, G. (1992). The cult[ure] of the customer. *Journal of Management Studies, 29*(5), 615–633.

Geertz, C. (1973). *The interpretation of cultures*. New York: Basic Books.

Gerbner, G., Gross, L., Morgan, M., & Signorielli, N. (1980). The "mainstreaming" of America: Violence profile No. 10. *Journal of Communication, 30*, 10–29.

Gibson, K. (1994). Fictitious persons and real responsibilities. *Journal of Business Ethics, 13*, 1–7.

Giddens, A. (1991). *Modernity and self-identity*. Palo Alto, CA: Stanford University Press.

Grunig, J. E. (1992). *Excellence in public relations and communication management*. Hillsdale, NJ: Lawrence Erlbaum.

Grunig, J. E. (1993, September). Forholdet mellem public relations og marketing. *Mediekultur, 20*, 6–14.

Grunig, J. E. (in press). Public relations management in government and business. In J. L. Garnett (Ed.), *Handbook of administrative communication*. New York: Marcel Dekker.

Grunig, J. E., & Grunig, L. A. (1991). Conceptual differences in public relations and marketing: The case of health-care organizations. *Public Relations Review, 17*(3), 257–278.

Habermas, J. (1981). Modernity versus postmodernity. *New German Critique, 22*, 3–22.

Hainsworth, B., & Meng, M. (1988). How corporations define issue management. *Public Relations Review, 14*(4), 18–30.

Hatch, M. J., & Schultz, M. (1997). Relations between organizational culture, identity and image. *European Journal of Marketing, 31*, 356–365.

Heath, R. L. (1980). Corporate advocacy: An application of speech communication perspectives and skills—and more. *Communication Education, 29*, 370–377.

Heath, R. L. (Ed.). (1988). *Strategic issues management: How organizations influence and respond to public interests and policies*. San Francisco: Jossey-Bass.

Heath, R. L. (1990). Effects of internal rhetoric on management response to external issues: How corporate culture failed the asbestos industry. *Journal of Applied Communication Research, 18*, 153–167.

Heath, R. L., & Cousino, K. R. (1990). Issues management: End of first decade progress report. *Public Relations Review, 16*(1), 5–18.

Held, D. (1996). *Models of democracy* (2nd ed.). Stanford, CA: Stanford University Press.

Hirschman, E. C. (1983). Aesthetics, ideologies and the limits of the marketing concept. *Journal of Marketing, 47*, 45–55.

Ice, R. (1991). Corporate publics and rhetorical strategies: The case of Union Carbide's Bhopal crisis. *Management Communication Quarterly, 4*, 341–362.

Jablin, F. M., & Putnam, L. L. (Eds) (2001). *The new handbook of organizational communication*. Thousand Oaks: Sage Publications.

James, B. (1993, November 8). If only work could be virtual, too. *International Herald Tribune*, p. 1.

Joy, A. (1993). The modern Medicis: Corporations as consumers of art. *Research in Consumer Behavior, 6*, 29–54.

Jones, B. L., & Chase, W. H. (1979). Managing public policy issues. *Public Relations Review, 2*, 3–23.

Kaldor, A. G. (1971). Imbricative marketing. *Journal of Marketing, 35*, 19–25.

Keith, R. J. (1960). The marketing revolution. *Journal of Marketing, 24*, 35–8.

Kingo, L. (1996, March). *Stakeholder interaction—A future challenge*. Keynote paper presented at the 3rd Conference of the Nordic Business Environmental Management Network, Aarhus, Denmark.

Kotler, P. (1991). *Marketing management: Analysis, planning, implementation, and control* (7th ed.). Englewood Cliffs, NJ: Prentice Hall.

Kotler, P., & Andreasen, A. R. (1987). *Strategic marketing for non-profit organizations* (Vol. 1). Englewood Cliffs, NJ: Prentice Hall.

Kotler, P., & Levy, S. J. (1969). Broadening the concept of marketing. *Journal of Marketing, 33*, 10–15.

Kotler, P., & Roberto, E. L. (1989). *Social marketing: Strategies for changing public behavior.* New York: Free Press.

Kuhn, T. (1997). The discourse of issues management: A genre of organizational communication. *Communication Quarterly, 45*, 188–210.

Lasch, C. (1978). *The culture of narcissism.* New York: Norton.

Lasch, C. (1984). *The minimal self: Psychic survival in troubled times.* London: Picador.

Laufer, R., & Paradeise, C. (1990). *Marketing democracy: Public opinion and media formation in democratic societies.* New Brunswick, NJ: Transaction.

Lazer, W., & Kelly, E. J. (Eds.). (1973). *Social marketing: Perspectives and viewpoints.* Homewood, IL: Irwin.

Lefort, C. (1988). *Democracy and political theory.* Cambridge, UK: Polity.

Leitch, S., & Neilson, D. (in press). Public relations and a theory of publics. In R. L. Heath & G. Vazquez (Eds.), *Handbook of public relations.* Thousand Oaks, CA: Sage.

Livesey, S. (1999). McDonald's and the Environmental Defense Fund: A case study of a green alliance. *Journal of Business Communication, 36*, 5–39.

Lotman, J. M. (1977). Two models of communication. In D. P. Lucid (Ed.), *Soviet semiotics: An anthology* (pp. 99–101). London: Johns Hopkins.

Lotman, J. M. (1991). *Universe of the mind: A semiotic theory of culture.* London: I. B. Tauris.

Luhmann, N. (1990). *Essays on self-reference.* New York: Colombia University Press.

Lukes, S. (1974). *Power: A radical view.* New York: Macmillan.

Manning, P. K. (1986). Signwork. *Human Relations, 39*(4), 283–308.

Manning, P. K. (1988). *Symbolic communication: Signifying calls and the police response.* Cambridge, MA: MIT Press.

Maturana, H. R., & Varela, F. J. (1980). *Autopoiesis and cognition: The realization of the living.* Dordrecht, Holland: D. Reidel.

McDonald, P., & Gandz, J. (1992). Getting value from shared values. *Organizational Dynamics, 20*(3), 64–77.

McGee, M. C. (1980). The "ideograph": A link between rhetoric and ideology. *Quarterly Journal of Speech, 66*, 1–16.

McMillan, J., & Cheney, G. (1996). The student as consumer: Implications and limitations of a metaphor. *Communication Education, 45*, 1–15.

Mead, G. H. (1934). *Mind, self, & society* (Vol. 1). Chicago: University of Chicago Press.

Meyer, J. W., & Rowan, B. (1977). Institutionalized organizations: Formal structure as myth and ceremony. *American Journal of Sociology, 83,* 340–363.

Monge, R. P., & Contractor, N. S. (2001). Emergence of communication networks. In F. M. Jablin, & L. L. Putnam (Eds.), *The new handbook of organizational communication.* Thousand Oaks: Sage Publications.

Mongin, O. (1982, February). La democratie a corps perdu. *Esprit, 2,* 206–212.

Morin, E. (1986). *La méthode 3: La connaissance de la connaissance. Livre premier: Antropo logie de la connaissance.* Paris: Seuil.

Motion, J., & Leitch, S. (2000, March). *The technologies of corporate identity.* Working paper, University of Auckland and University of Waikato, Hamilton, New Zealand.

Nader, R., & Green, M. J. (1973). *Corporate power in America: Ralph Nader's conference on corporate accountability.* New York: Grossman.

Nader, R., Green, M. J., & Seligman, J. (1976). *Taming the giant corporation.* New York: Norton.

Nickels, W. G. (1976). *Marketing communication and promotion.* Columbus, OH: Grid.

Nisbet, R. (1970). *The sociological tradition.* London: Heinemann.

Olins, W. (1989). *Corporate identity: Making business strategy visible through design.* New York: Thames & Hudson.

Packard, V. (1969). *The hidden persuaders* (21st printing). New York: McKay.

Paonessa, K. A. (1982). *Corporate advocacy in General Motors Corporation.* Unpublished master's thesis, Purdue University, IN.

Parsons, T. (1949). *The structure of social action.* New York: Free Press.

Pearson, R. (1989). Business ethics as communication ethics: Public relations practice and the idea of dialogue. In C. H. Botan & V. Hazleton, Jr. (Eds.), *Public relations theory* (pp. 111–131). Hillsdale, NJ: Lawrence Erlbaum.

Perniola, M. (1980). *La societá dei simulacri.* Bologna, Italy: Capelli.

Pfeffer, J. (1981). Management as symbolic action: The creation and maintenance of organizational paradigms. In L. L. Cummings & B. M. Staw (Eds.), *Research in organizational behavior* (Vol. 3, pp. 1–52). Greenwich, CT: JAI.

Pondy, L. R., Frost, P. J., Morgan, G., & Dandridge, T. C. (Eds.). (1983). *Organizational symbolism.* Greenwich, CT: JAI.

Powell, W. M. (1990). Neither market nor hierarchy: Network forms of organization. In B. M. Staw & L. L. Cummings (Eds.), *Research in organizational behavior* (Vol. 12, pp. 295–336). Greenwich, CT: JAI Press.

Procter & Gamble. (1989). *The house that Ivory built: 150 years of successful marketing.* Lincolnwood, IL: NTC Business Books.

Putnam, L. L., Phillips, N., & Chapman, P. (1996). Metaphors of communication and organization. In S. R. Clegg, C. Hardy, & W. R. Nord (Eds.), *Handbook of organization studies* (pp. 375–408). London: Sage.

Ramanantsoa, B., & Battaglia, V. (1991, June). *The autobiography of the firm: A means of deconstruction of the traditional images.* Paper presented at the eighth International SCOS Conference, Copenhagen, Denmark.

Richardson, G. B. (1972). The organization of industry. *Economic Journal, 82,* 883–896.

Scott, C. R., & Carroll, C. E. (1999, November). *If not now, then when? Exploring situated identifications among members of a dispersed organization.* Paper presented at the annual conference of the National Communication Association, Chicago.

Scott, C. R., Corman, S. A., & Cheney, G. (1998). The development of a structurational theory of identification in the organization. *Communication Theory, 8,* 298–336.

Sennett, R. (1978). *The fall of public man: On the social psychology of capitalism.* New York: Vintage.

Shimp, T. A. (1990). *Promotion management and marketing communications* (2nd ed.). Chicago: Dryden.

Smircich, L., & Stubbart, C. (1985). Strategic management in an enacted world. *Academy of Management Review, 10,* 724–736.

Smith, R. (1993, May). *Images of organizational communication: Root-metaphors of the organization-communication relation.* Paper presented at the annual meeting of the International Communication Association, Washington, DC.

Sproull, J. M. (1988). The new managerial rhetoric and the old criticism. *Quarterly Journal of Speech, 74,* 468–486.

Sproull, J. M. (1990). Organizational rhetoric and the rational-democratic society. *Journal of Applied Communication Research, 74,* 192–240.

Starbuck, W. H. (1976). Organizations and their environments. In M. D. Dunnette (Ed.), *Handbook of industrial and organizational psychology* (pp. 1069–1123). Chicago: Rand McNally.

Stidsen, B., & Schutte, T. F. (1972). Marketing as a communication system: The marketing concept revisited. *Journal of Marketing, 36,* 22–27.

Sutcliffe, K. M. (2001). Organizational environments and organizational information processing. In F. M. Jablin, & L. L. Putnam (Eds.), *The new handbook of organizational communication.* Thousand Oaks: Sage Publications.

Taylor, J. R. (1993). *Rethinking the theory of organizational communication: How to read an organization.* Norwood, NJ: Ablex.

Taylor, J. R., Flanagin, A. J., Cheney, G., & Seibold, D. R. (in press). Organizational communication research: Key moments, central concerns, and future challenges. In W. B. Gudykunst (Ed.), *Communication yearbook 24.* Thousand Oaks, CA: Sage.

Thompson, M., & Wildavsky, A. (1986). A cultural theory of information bias in organizations. *Journal of Management Studies, 23*(3), 273–286.

Thygesen Poulsen, P. (1993). *LEGO—En virksomhed og dens sjæl.* Albertslund, Denmark: Schultz.

Tompkins, P. K., & Cheney, G. (1983). Account analysis of organizations: Decision making and identification. In L. L. Putnam & M. E. Pacanowsky (Eds.), *Communication and organizations: An interpretive approach* (pp. 123–147). Beverly Hills, CA: Sage.

Tompkins, P. K., & Cheney, G. (1985). Communication and unobtrusive control in contemporary organizations. In R. D. McPhee & P. K. Tompkins (Eds.), *Organizational communication: Traditional themes and new directions* (pp. 179–210). Beverly Hills, CA: Sage.

Tracy, S. (1995). *Can public relations about social responsibility be socially responsible?* Unpublished paper, University of Colorado at Boulder.

Treadwell, D. F., & Harrison, T. M. (1994). Conceptualizing and assessing organizational image: Model images, commitment, and communication. *Communication Monographs, 61,* 63–85.

van Riel, C. B. M. (1995). *Principles of corporate communication.* London: Prentice Hall.

Vibbert, S. L., & Bostdorff, D. M. (1993). Issue management in the "lawsuit crisis." In C. Conrad (Ed.), *The ethical nexus* (pp. 103–120). Norwood, NJ: Ablex.

Wartick, S. L., & Rude, R. E. (1986). Issues management: Corporate fad or corporate function. *California Management Review, 29*(1), 124–140.

Wätzold, F. (1996). When environmentalists have power: A case study of the Brent Spar. In J. P. Ulhøi & H. Madsen (Eds.), *Industry and the environment: Practical applications of environmental management approaches in business.* Aarhus, Denmark: Aarhus Business School.

Webster, F. E., Jr. (1992). The changing role of marketing in the corporation. *Journal of Marketing, 56,* 1–17.

Weick, K. E. (1979). *The social psychology of organizing* (2nd ed.). Reading, MA: Addison-Wesley.

Weick, K. E., & Ashford, S. J. (2001). Learning in organizations. In F. M. Jablin, & L. L. Putnam (Eds.), *The new handbook of organizational communication.* Thousand Oaks: Sage Publications.

Weigert, A. J., Teitge, J. S., & Teitge, D. W. (1986). *Society and identity: Toward a sociological psychology.* Cambridge, UK: Cambridge University Press.

White, J. B. (1984). *When words lose their meaning: Constitutions and reconstitutions of language, character, and community.* Chicago: University of Chicago Press.

Zaltman, G., Kotler, P., & Kaufman, I. (Eds.). (1972). *Creating social change.* New York: Holt, Rinehart & Winston.

Index

Notes: **Bold** page numbers indicate chapters. Sub-entries are arranged alphabetically, except where chronological order is more significant.

Index

Index

Index

Index

Index

Index

Index

Index

Index

Index

Index

Index

Index

Index

Lightning Source UK Ltd.
Milton Keynes UK

178645UK00001B/1/P